SERVICES AND FREE MOVEMENT IN EU LAW

Services and Free Movement in EU Law

Edited by

MADS ANDENAS and WULF-HENNING ROTH

BIICL
THE BRITISH INSTITUTE OF
INTERNATIONAL AND
COMPARATIVE LAW

OXFORD
UNIVERSITY PRESS

OXFORD
UNIVERSITY PRESS

Great Clarendon Street, Oxford OX2 6DP

Oxford University Press is a department of the University of Oxford.
It furthers the University's objective of excellence in research, scholarship,
and education by publishing worldwide in

Oxford New York

Auckland Bangkok Buenos Aires Cape Town Chennai
Dar es Salaam Delhi Hong Kong Istanbul Karachi Kolkata
Kuala Lumpur Madrid Melbourne Mexico City Mumbai Nairobi
São Paulo Shanghai Taipei Tokyo Toronto

Oxford is a registered trade mark of Oxford University Press
in the UK and in certain other countries

Published in the United States
by Oxford University Press Inc., New York

First published 2002

British Library Cataloguing in Publication Data
Data available

Library of Congress Cataloging in Publication Data
Services and free movement in EU law.
p. cm.
1. Service industries—Law and legislation—European Union countries. 2. Financial
services industry—Law and legislation—European Union countries. 3. Free
trade—European Union countries. 4. Freedom of movement—European Union countries.
KJE5174 .S47 2001
341.7'543'094—dc21 2001033954

ISBN 0-19-829938-9

1 3 5 7 9 10 8 6 4 2

Typeset in Sabon
by Cambrian Typesetters, Frimley, Surrey
Printed in Great Britain
on acid-free paper by
Biddles Ltd., Guildford and King's Lynn

Contents

Introduction

THE HON JUDGE DAVID EDWARD

Services is a field of Community law that deserves more attention than it has had. Achieving a genuinely open market for the cross-frontier provision of services presents technical problems far more complex than those that beset the market for goods.

Perhaps I am biased because services was the field in which I first had to grapple with the mysteries of Community law, though not as a judge, practitioner or academic, but as representative of the Scots Bar in the negotiations that led in 1977 to the Directive on the Provision of Services by Lawyers. At that time very little had been written to help us to understand what it was all about.

Even today, services and (to a lesser extent) establishment are poor relations in the literature of the four freedoms. For every hundred references to *Cassis de Dijon* and the 'mandatory requirements', there can hardly be more than five to *Van Binsbergen* and its acceptance of 'requirements justified by the general good'. Yet *Van Binsbergen,* decided six years before *Cassis,* pointed the way the Court was to follow in resolving the underlying conflict, which both judgments set out to solve, between the imperatives of the internal market, the right of free movement and other imperatives of public interest not specifically mentioned in the Treaty.

In the case of goods, this conflict did not really become apparent until the late 1970s. During the early years of the EEC, the need to dismantle barriers to free trade in goods was seen as a self-evident precondition of economic recovery and Article 36 (now Article 30) was assumed to provide all the derogations that were needed in the public interest. In the mid-1970s, the economic downturn led to new pressures for protection, while the rise of consumerism and a new concern for the environment, hardly dreamed of in 1957, created new political imperatives for the Member States. The Community could not ignore these pressures, but political acceptance of the Luxembourg Compromise meant that its legislative machinery was effectively stalled. So the task of resolving the conflict between the Treaty rules and new political imperatives fell in the first instance on the Court of Justice. Hence *Cassis* and, eventually, the Single Act and Article 100A(3) and (4) (now Article 95A(3) and (4) EC).

By contrast, in the field of establishment and services the same conflict had become apparent almost from the start, and it is not accidental that it did so in connection with access to the courts and the legal profession (*Reyners, Van Binsbergen* and *Thieffry*). Regulation of lawyers in the interests of the administration of justice, going back to the Middle Ages (if not before), is the archetype of regulation of the freedom to provide services.

The Member States regulated the legal profession in different ways, not simply because the professions had developed differently but also because their legal systems started from different assumptions about what lawyers did and how they should do it. So, achieving a more open market in legal services was not simply a matter of dismantling 'protectionist' barriers. The most substantial barriers consisted in differences of structure, organization and method going back hundreds of years which could not simply be ignored.

It was argued that the legal profession as a whole should be excluded from the purview of the Treaty on the basis of Articles 55 and 66 (now Articles 45 and 55 EC). This argument failed in *Reyners* and the conflict between treaty prescriptions and professional structures and rules had then to be faced in *Van Binsbergen* and *Thieffry*. *Reyners* unblocked progress on the Directive on Provision of Services by Lawyers, passed in 1977, but it took a further 20 years to achieve a Directive on Establishment.

The experience of the legal profession illustrates in an acute form how difficult it is to achieve the reality of an 'internal market in which free movement of goods, persons, services and capital is ensured'. It is not simply a matter of dismantling protectionist barriers to cross-frontier trade. Many technical barriers to cross-frontier movement exist simply because Member States do things differently, make different assumptions about how society ought to be organized and regulate people's activities in different ways.

In the early days, it was thought that harmonizing sectoral directives would provide the solution. Such directives were adopted in the 1960s for wholesale trade, commercial agents and retail trade, but it took a further decade to achieve directives for the medical and allied professions for which special provision had been made in Article 57 (3) (now Article 47 (3) EC). In spite of the care and detail with which those directives were drafted, the Court is still faced today with problems whose source lies in differences of approach to the teaching of medicine and the structure of the medical profession.

In other fields, with greater specialization has come a corresponding increase in the number and range of professional activities that are subject to state regulation, self-regulation or a combination of both. New professions and para-professions have grown up in the Member States with different structures and lines of demarcation which it would be impossible to harmonize even if the political will existed to do so.

Following the Single Act, the search for a solution through sectoral directives was abandoned and replaced by the directives on mutual recognition of diplomas. This solution was, once again, foreshadowed in *Reyners* and *Thieffry*.

During the same period, pressure has increased for regulation of banking, insurance and other financial services. This has been generated, on the one hand, by concern for consumer protection and fiscal supervision and, on the other, by new problems of terrorism, drugs and money-laundering. Again, the solutions adopted by the Member States differ. The need for a coordinated approach is obvious: the means of achieving it are less so, not least because the Treaty provisions are based on an assumption that is no longer valid. In 1957 it was reasonable to assume that cross-frontier services would be provided by physical movement across a frontier of the person providing the service, the person receiving it, or both. Nowadays the most complex services can be provided without any physical movement at all. Who, then, is to regulate what? Meanwhile, differences of regulatory methods and criteria, as well as conflicts of regulatory jurisdiction, are technical barriers to cross-frontier provision of financial services.

Again, different approaches to the taxation of earnings and pensions make cross-frontier activity more difficult, or at least less attractive. And differences in social legislation (on the minimum wage, the length of the working week, paid holidays, parental leave, etc.) raise problems, on the one hand, for the authorities charged with enforcing the legislation and, on the other, for the employer who sends his own staff to work on a contract in another country.

All these problems are illustrated by recent case law of the Court of Justice and, for me, their interest lies in finding a proper balance between the desire to ensure that the impetus of the internal market (still far from complete) is maintained and the claims of subsidiarity in relation to fiscal, social and environmental policy, to mention only three. Potentially, the scope for conflict is wide, and its divisive nature is deep.

This book fills a gap in the literature and will, I hope, stimulate further debate about a fascinating subject that spills over from law into the choice between differing political, economic and social objectives. In some respects, however, the problems of services are the same as those of goods, and the early chapters explore the extent to which the case law on goods, especially *Keck*, can or should be transposed to services. Later chapters explore the relationship between establishment and services and the overlap between them. Then there are chapters devoted to the problems of cross-frontier finance and financial regulation. Finally, we are reminded that, for the legal profession, in spite of all the differences and difficulties, the Community has already achieved a degree of liberalization and, with it, a sense of common purpose that has still not been achieved in the United States. The editors are to be congratulated on drawing together so much valuable material.

European Court of Justice
Luxembourg
28 February 2001

Editors' Introduction

This book offers a critical analysis of the present state of EU services law. It provides a contribution to the development of the right to provide services which is increasingly important. The role for scholarship is well demonstrated in the contributions of this book. The book also—and we do not mean this in any derogatory sense!—demonstrates the need for further scholarship.

The book is an extension of the research activities the editors are involved with in Bonn and in London. One event was a broader seminar which we jointly organized in 1999 in the Senate House of the University of London. The seminar was chaired by Lord Slynn, the former Advocate General and Judge of the European Court and now a Law Lord (or Supreme Court Judge) in the UK, and by David Edward, the Judge of the European Court. Both have, through their writing and their judgments, contributed to the development of EC services law. A number of people not represented in this book also contributed to this seminar, either by presenting papers or in the preparation, including Francis Jacobs, Walter Van Gerven, Stephen Weatherill, Jan Wouters, and Derrick Wyatt. The 1999 seminar is only one of many research orientated events. Miguel Poiares Maduro, whose article is included in this book, took a seminar at the British Institute in 2000 with Damian Chalmers and Jukka Snell: the latter is represented by two articles. At Bonn University, Wulf-Henning Roth directs a broad programme in the financial services field including a Graduiertenkolleg with a number of doctoral candidates and associated research events. At the British Institute of International and Comparative Law, London, and the Institute of European and Comparative Law, University of Oxford, Mads Andenas continues a research programme that he started up at the Centre of European Law, King's College, University of London.

The legal and regulatory foundations of the European services economy are in the process of being reformed. Many issues are unresolved. Some can only be resolved by the European Court or by Community legislation. But a more fundamental analysis of several of these issues is still lacking and here legal scholarship has a role to play.

One issue is the reconciliation of the case law on goods and services. The conventional view was that the freedoms should follow different routes: the free movement of goods went further than the right to provide services. Have we now got a universal law of free movement making these distinctions redundant? Or have services law gone further than goods law?

Another unresolved issue is the division between the regulatory powers of home and host countries in the principle of home country control: does it work? The broad exceptions, relying on concepts such as the general good, do not leave a high degree of certainty.

This book makes use of the financial services sector to analyse the practical implementation of home country control and its exceptions. The recent EC legislative initiatives on e-commerce show the limitations of the traditional concepts. The relationship between the country of origin concept and home country control is not clear. And the technological developments may prove to render the whole regulatory framework ineffective. E-commerce is not a primary topic of this book but we pursue these issues in other research projects.

In this book, we have assembled a group of EU scholars from different jurisdictions and with different views on these matters of such fundamental and practical importance for EU law. We hope the book will contribute to further debate on EC law.

Bonn and London, January 2001 *Wulf-Henning Roth* and *Mads Andenas*

List of Contributors

Mads Andenas
Director of the British Institute of International and Comparative Law, London; Fellow, Harris Manchester College, Oxford.

José Luís da Cruz Vilaça
Partner, PLMJ (AM Pereira, Sáragga Leal, O Martins, Júdice & Associados) Lisbon; Director of the Institute of European Studies, Lusíada University; former President of the European Court of First Instance and former Advocate General, European Court of Justice.

J H Dalhuisen
Professor, King's College, University of London.

Marc Dassesse
Professor, Institute for European Studies, Université Libre de Bruxelles; Partner, McKenna & Cuneo, LLP.

José M Fernández-Martín
Lawyer, European Central Bank, Frankfurt, on secondment from the European Investment Bank.

Roger J Goebel
Professor and Director of the Center on European Union Law, Fordham University School of Law.

Jesper Lau Hansen
Lecturer in Law, Department of Legal Science A, University of Copenhagen. Dr. juris (Copenhagen); LLM (Cantab).

Hans D Jarass
Professor of German and European Public Law, University of Münster.

Anders Kjellgren
Research Fellow, University of Stockholm.

Eva Lomnicka
Professor, King's College, University of London.

Síofra O'Leary
Visiting Fellow, Law Faculty, University College, Dublin.

Miguel Poiares Maduro
Faculdade de Direito da Universidade Nova de Lisbon.

Wulf-Henning Roth
Professor and Director, Centre of European Economic Law, University of Bonn.

Jukka Snell
Lecturer in Law, University of Swansea. Formerly Lord Slynn Foundation Fellow, King's College, London; Ph.D. (London).

Michel Tison
Professor, Financial Law Institute, Ghent University, Belgium.

John A Usher
Salvesen Professor of European Institutions and Director of the European Institute, University of Edinburgh.

Tables of Cases

EUROPEAN COURT OF JUSTICE

Numerical

Alphabetical

COURT OF FIRST INSTANCE OF THE EUROPEAN COMMUNITIES

Numerical

Alpabetical

1

The European Court of Justice's Case Law on Freedom to Provide Services: Is Keck *Relevant?*

WULF-HENNING ROTH

I. LOOKING BACK: THE CASE LAW OF THE ECJ IN A NUTSHELL

1. Prohibition of Restrictions Approach Versus Discrimination Test

For a long time the conventional view had it that the interpretation of the basic freedoms should follow different lines:[1] whereas Article 28 (ex 30) EC—the free movement of goods—was to be considered as a far-reaching prohibition of any measures restricting the import of goods, whether indistinctly applicable or not, the provisions on the free movement of persons—workers, establishment and services—were regarded as a mere expression of the general principle of non-discrimination on grounds of nationality as set forth in Article 12 (ex 6) EC.[2] Recent case law of the ECJ—the *Bosman* judgment[3] with regard to the free movement of workers (Article 39, ex 48 EC) and the *Gebhard* judgment[4] concerning the right of establishment (Article 43, ex 52 EC)—seems to indicate a move towards a convergence of the freedoms,[5] replacing the discrimination test by a broader concept of

[1] eg Wyatt and Dashwood, *The Substantive Law of the EEC* (2nd edn., 1987) 134 (goods), 173 (workers), 203 (establishment), 219 (services); Grabitz and Hilf (-*Randelshofer*), *Das Recht der Europäischen Union* (1992), Art. 48 ECT paras 26–28 (only discrimination), Art. 52 ECT para 36–42 (discrimination), para 43–43c (indicating that the Court may move beyond this narrow view).

[2] De Burca, 'The Role of Equality in European Community Law', in Dashwood and O'Leary (eds), *The Principle of Equal Treatment in EC Law* (1997) 13, 20–21 (No 2.09–2.10); Roth in Dauses (ed), *Handbuch des EU-Wirtschaftsrechts* (1993), EI para 61.

[3] ECJ 15 December 1995, Case C-415/93 *Bosman* [1995] ECR I-4921.

[4] ECJ 30 November 1995, Case C-55/94 *Gebhard* [1995] ECR I-4165.

[5] Such a convergence in the interpretation of the freedoms has been foreseen, demanded, and analysed by doctrine; eg Behrens, 'Die Konvergenz der wirtschaftlichen Freiheiten im europäischen Gemeinschaftsrecht', EuR 1992, 145; Classen, 'Auf dem Weg zu einer einheitlichen Dogmatik der Grundfreiheiten?', EWS 1995, 97; Eberhartinger, 'Konvergenz und Neustrukturierung der Grundfreiheiten', EWS 1997, 43; Tesauro, *The Internal Market of the EC in the Light of the Recent Case-Law of the Court of Justice* (Zentrum für Europäisches Wirtschaftsrecht, Vorträge und Berichte, No 65, 1996) 18; Weatherill, 'After *Keck*: Some Thoughts on How to Clarify the Clarification' (1997) 33 CMLRev 885; in-depth analysis presented by Eilmansberger, 'Zur Reichweite der Grundfreiheiten des Binnenmarktes', Juristische Blätter 1999, 345, who (rightly) advocates a differentiated view; see also

restrictions to be abolished ('restriction prohibition' approach). Nearly at the same time, the case law of the Court has undergone a change (or, at least, a clarification) in the interpretation of Article 28 EC by the *Keck* judgment with its differentiation between product-related regulations and the so-called selling arrangements: whereas *product-related* measures are to be governed by the *Cassis* approach,[6] extending the prohibition of Article 28 EC also to indistinctly applicable regulations that impede the free movement of goods, the regulation of *selling arrangements* are to undergo a discrimination test.[7]

Some commentators—also in the United Kingdom[8]—have found it surprising that the Court has moved from a discrimination test to a prohibition-of-restrictions approach with regard to freedom of establishment, whereas with regard to the free movement of goods the Court seems to have taken the opposite way to a more lenient approach to indistinctly applicable measures. One commentator has attempted to explain these moves of the Court in strategic terms: 'less activism on the free movement of goods may correspond to more activism with regard to other movement rules.'[9]

2. Freedom to Provide Services

Where do we find freedom to provide services (Article 49, ex 59 EC) in this development? In its first judgment, handed down more than 25 years ago (*van Binsbergen*),[10] the Court seemed to conceive this freedom in terms of a discrimination (equality of treatment) test. The Court, dealing with the notion of 'restrictions to be abolished' in ex Article 59 ECT, referred to 'all requirements imposed on the person providing the service by reason in particular of his nationality or of the fact that he does not habitually reside in the State where the service is provided, which do not apply to persons established within the national territory or which may prevent or otherwise obstruct the activities of the person providing the service'.[11]

In *Koestler*, the Court held that freedom to provide services 'prohibits discrimination', but it 'does not impose any obligation to treat a foreigner

Hatzopoulos, 'Recent Developments of the Case Law of the ECJ in the Field of Services' (2000) 37 CMLRev 43, 70: despite verbal convergence different impact on the States' power to regulate; Daniele, 'Non Discriminatory Restrictions to the Free Movement of Persons' [1997] ELRev 191.

[6] ECJ 20 February 1979, Case 120/78, *Rewe-Zentral-AG* [1979] ECR 649.

[7] ECJ 24 November 1993, Cases C-267/91 and C-268/91 *Keck & Mithouard* [1993] ECR I-6097.

[8] eg Steiner and Woods, *EC Law* (5th edn, 1996) 293.

[9] Maduro, *We the Court* (1998), 99.

[10] ECJ 3 December 1974, Case 33/74 *van Binsbergen* [1974] ECR 1299.

[11] ECJ (n 10 above) 1309 cons. 10.

providing services more favourably, with reference to his domestic law, than a person providing services established in the Member State where the services have been provided'.[12]

The case law of the Court in the 1980s can be described as moving step-by-step away from this position: three years after *Koestler*, the Court—in *Webb*—held that national legislation applicable to nationals of the Member State established therein could not be applied in its entirety to temporary activities of undertakings that are established in other Member States.[13] In *Commission v Germany* (1986), the Court treated an indistinctly applicable authorization requirement of the host State as a restriction under ex Article 59 ECT.[14] And, finally, in *Säger v Dennemeyer*, the Court outspokenly turned to language reminding us of the *Cassis* approach: 'Article 59 requires not only the elimination of all discrimination against a person providing services on the ground of his nationality but also the abolition of any restriction, even if it applies without distinction to national providers of services and to those of other Member States, when it is liable to prohibit or otherwise impede the activities of a provider of services established in another Member State where he lawfully provides similar services',[15] a formula that has more than once been repeated in recent judgments.[16]

With regard to the issue of *justification* of those restrictive measures, the Court has—in substance, though with varying terminology—adopted the *Cassis* approach: restrictions on the provision of services by the host State can be justified beyond the reasons listed in Article 46 para 1, Article 55 EC by 'imperative reasons relating to the public interest'.[17] The measures will have to be tested on the basis of the standards of appropriateness, necessity and proportionality,[18] whereby the rules of the State of origin will have to

[12] ECJ 24 October 1978, Case 15/78 *Koestler* [1978] ECR 1971, 1981 cons. 5.

[13] ECJ 17 December 1981, Case 279/80 *Webb* [1981] ECR 3305, 3324 cons. 16; ECJ 4 December 1986, Case 205/84 *Commission v Germany* [1986] ECR 3755, 3802 cons. 26; ECJ 25 July 1991, Case C-76/90 *Säger* [1991] ECR I-4421, 4243 cons. 13. These judgments may be taken for the proposition that, indeed, the evenhanded application of regulations to *temporary* activities may be regarded as discriminatory because temporary activities are *inherently different* from permanent ones.

[14] Also ECJ 9 July 1997, Case C-222/95 *Parodi* [1997] ECR I-3899, 3922 cons. 19.

[15] *Säger* (n 13 above) [1991] ECR I-4243 cons. 12; ECJ 23 November 1999, Case C-369/96 and C-376/96 *Jean-Claude Arblade* (not yet published) cons. 33: 'or make it less attractive'.

[16] eg *Parodi* (n 14 above) [1997] ECR I-3921 cons. 18; ECJ 28 March 1996, Case C-272/94, *Guiot* [1996] ECR I-1905, 1920 cons. 10; ECJ 12 December 1996, Case C-3/95 *Reisebüro Broede* [1996] ECR I-6511, 6537 cons. 25; ECJ 5 June 1997, Case C-398/95 *SETTG* [1997] ECR I-3091, 3119 cons. 16.

[17] *Parodi* (n 14 above) [1997] ECR) I-3922 cons. 21; the 'imperative reasons' (or 'overriding reasons'; see e.g. *Guiot* (n 16 above) [1996] ECR I-1920 cons. 11; 'imperative requirements'; see e.g. *Reisebüro Broede* I-6537 cons. 28) are identical with the 'mandatory requirements' of the *Cassis* case law (n 16 above) [1996] ECR.

[18] *Parodi* (n 14 above) [1997] ECR I-3922 cons. 21, 3925 cons. 31.

be taken into account[19]—an approach that has been evolved in many judgments relating to the free movement of goods.

One word of explanation may be in order as to why the Court nevertheless started out with the discrimination test. In *van Binsbergen*, the Court was confronted with the issue whether and to what extent freedom to provide services should be regarded as *directly applicable*, thereby creating individual rights. One should keep in mind that in the early 1970s the notion of 'direct effect' as applied to freedom to provide services (and freedom of establishment) was very much in dispute because of the very vagueness of the term 'restriction': we have to remember the wording of ex Article 59 ECT that 'all' restrictions were to be abolished and of ex Article 62 ECT that 'no' new restrictions were to be introduced—with no justifications beyond ex Article 56 para 1, 66 ECT at hand.[20] It is suggested that the somewhat restrictive interpretation of freedom to provide services as being limited to the principle of non-discrimination (equal treatment) reflects an attitude of *judicial restraint* with regard to the application of the notion of *direct effect*.

A close reading of the *van Binsbergen* judgment may provide some backing for this contention. With respect to direct applicability the Court held that 'as regards at least the specific requirement of nationality or of residence, Articles 59 and 60 ECT impose a well-defined obligation',[21] adding an important 'at least', and thereby leaving the way open to broaden the scope of direct applicability to encompass other types of discriminatory and, perhaps, non-discriminatory measures.

Given the explicit reference to the principle of equal treatment in ex Article 60 para 3 ECT, dealing with the case of a person pursuing his/her activities in the State where the service is provided, and given the fact that ex Article 62 ECT prohibited any new restrictions to be introduced, the cautious approach taken by the Court at the outset seems to be highly sensible and convincing, leaving it to the other Community institutions to abolish actual and potential restrictions of and burdens on the interstate provision of services.

In the 1980s the Court for quite some time pretended to apply a discrimination test even in cases where indistinctly applicable measures were involved. The German insurance case—*Commission v Germany*[22]—may serve as an example.

[19] Cf. *Säger* (n 13 above) [1991] ECR I-4244 cons. 15; *Reisebüro Broede* (n 16 above) [1996] ECR I-6538 cons. 28; *Jean-Claude Arblade* (n 15 above) cons. 34.

[20] The prohibitions contained in ex Articles 30, 31 ECT were, of course, as far-reaching: the present author has therefore suggested giving the public order justification in ex Article 36 ECT a broad reading if the notion of measures with equivalent effect were to be extended beyond a prohibition of discriminatory measures; see Roth, *Freier Warenverkehr und staatliche Regelungsgewalt in einem Gemeinsamen Markt* (1977) 16, 44, 54.

[21] *van Binsbergen* (n 10 above) [1974] ECR 1311 cons. 26.

[22] See n 13 above [1986] ECR 3755.

The Court repeats the formula used in *van Binsbergen* that ex Articles 59 and 60 ECT require 'the removal not only of all discriminations against a provider of a service on the grounds of his nationality but also all restrictions on his freedom to provide services imposed by reason of the fact that he is established in a Member State other than that in which the service is provided'.[23]

This formula is clearly directed not only against discrimination based on nationality, but also those based on the location of the seat of the undertaking. However, the Court in its application of the formula goes *beyond* a discrimination test based on these criteria, when it applies ex Articles 59 and 60 ECT not only to an establishment requirement for out-of-state undertakings, but also to the requirement to obtain an *authorization* from the supervisory authority of the host state, such an authorization requirement being *indistinctly applicable* to out-of-state undertakings and undertakings established within the State alike. Indeed, the Court does not regard the authorization requirement as a regulation that is imposed 'by reason of the fact' that the undertaking 'is established in a Member State other than that in which the service is to be provided'.[24] It rather regards the authorization requirement that is indistinctly imposed on domestic undertakings as a *restriction* on the freedom to provide services 'inasmuch as' it 'increase(s) the cost of such services in the State in which they are provided'. It is the effect of a *double regulation* by the State of origin and the State of destination that is being addressed.

The approach taken by the Court reflects the insight that an indistinctly applied measure such as an authorization requirement may have a *different effect* on the interstate provision of services, especially when the business is transacted only occasionally, compared to the activities of an undertaking that is established within the State. The Court did not, however, approach the issue by expanding the notion of discrimination, but rather by turning to the notion of 'restriction', as used in ex Article 59 ECT, without giving an explanation for this shift in perspective. One explanation could be that the concept of discrimination may turn out to be too slippery when applied to indistinctly applicable measures.[25]

Already six years before handing down *Commission v Germany*, the Court had been confronted with an indistinctly applicable prohibition of TV advertising in *Debauve*. The judgment certainly may not be regarded as an outstanding example of lucid reasoning, but its message seems to be clear: indistinctly applicable prohibitions to provide advertising services are caught by ex Article 59 ECT,[26] even if no 'in effect' discrimination is appar-

[23] ibid 3802 cons. 25.
[24] ibid 3802 cons. 25.
[25] Cf Steiner and Woods (n 8 above) 291.
[26] ECJ 18 March 1980, Case 52/79 *Debauve* [1980] ECR 833, 856–857 cons. 13–15: the Court starts out (in cons. 13) with the contention that the indistinctly applicable rule cannot

ent. The Court spelled out this approach to indistinctly applicable rules in *Säger v Dennemeyer*, replacing the notion of 'restrictions . . . imposed by reason of the fact that he is established in a Member State other than that in which the service is provided' by the formula 'restriction' by an indistinctly applicable measure 'when it is liable to prohibit or otherwise impede the activities of a provider of services established in another Member State where he lawfully provides similar services'.[27]

3. Summary

Summing up this rather short glance at the history of the services case law, three points should be stressed.

(1) Whereas with regard to the free movement of goods the Court, in *Dassonville,* had started out with *sweeping language* to define the scope of ex Article 30 ECT ('All trading rules . . . which are capable of hindering, directly or indirectly, actually or potentially, intra-Community trade'),[28] a language that needed some corrections by *Keck*, the 'services' case law started *at the other end*, using the discrimination test, and then gradually and cautiously expanding the scope of the freedom towards a restriction test, however, without relying on the broad *Dassonville* formula.

(2) The Court, moreover, has *never replaced* the discrimination test by the restriction test. Rather, the Court has constantly used a formula that seems to indicate that it is the *discrimination test* that is *generally* available, whereas the *restriction test* becomes applicable *only in specific cases*.[29] Note the language in *Säger*: 'Article 59 of the Treaty requires not only the elimination of all discrimination against a person providing services on the ground of his nationality but also the abolition of any restriction, . . . when it is liable to prohibit or otherwise impede the activities of a provider of services established in another Member State where he lawfully provides similar services.'[30]

Thereby it is up to the Court to determine *what kind* of indistinctly

be regarded as a 'restriction', but goes on with a close analysis of the Belgian legislation (cons. 14). The Court refers to the 'residual power' of each Member State to regulate television advertising (cons. 15) and links this power to 'grounds of general interest' (cf also cons. 12).

[27] See n 13 above [1991] ECR I–4243 cons. 12. Note that the reference to the establishment of the provider in another Member State is not any longer relevant to the criterion of discrimination, but to the *personal scope* of the freedom to provide services.

[28] ECJ 11 July 1974, Case 8/74 *Procureur du Roi v Dassonville* [1974] ECR 837, 852 cons. 5.

[29] The same approach is now taken with regard to the free movement of workers in ECJ 27 January 2000, Case C-190/98 *Graf v Fitzmoser* (nyp) cons. 14 (dealing with the discrimination test) and cons. 21–23 (dealing with restrictions on the freedom to move from or to a Member State).

[30] See n 13 above [1991] ECR I-4243 cons. 12; *SETTG* (n 16 above) [1997] ECR I-3119 cons. 16.

applicable measures should be regarded as a 'restriction', leaving all other measures and regulations to the discrimination test. In short: with regard to 'services' there is *no need* for a *Keck* judgment because the Court has never attributed the 'restriction prohibition' approach such a wide scope as in the free movement of goods area.

(3) In one respect, however, the case law on services has gone *beyond* the standards applicable in the free movement of goods area. Whereas regulations with regard to the *export* of goods have been—up till today—controlled by a discrimination test only,[31] the Court has gone beyond that, applying the 'restriction prohibition' standard in an export of services setting in *Alpine Investments*.[32]

In summary: when we compare the case law of the Court with regard to the relevant freedoms, we may indeed recognize a convergence of the freedoms in more than one way. It is only with regard to export regulations where the Court can be characterized as being more active in the field of services than in the field of goods.

II. LOOKING BACK: A CONCEPT BEHIND THE CASE LAW?

Before analysing the case law of the Court in more detail, we should speculate for a moment on the question of whether this case law is based on a certain *concept* of the single market and on a certain perception of the relevant institutions responsible for making the necessary decisions.

1. General Considerations

It should be stressed from the outset that any discussion of the *scope* of the EC Treaty freedoms does not merely deal with legal niceties and technical details, but with *fundamental choices of policy* for a single market which is characterized by a system of (still) decentralized decision-making on the level of the Member States. The question to be posed is under what conditions and to what extent the determination of social and economic policies by the Member States, as agents of the system of decentralized decision-making, should remain unrestrained, and to what extent and under what

[31] ECJ 8 November 1979, Case 15/79 *Groenveld* [1979] ECR 3409, 3415 cons. 7; for further references and a critical assessment of this case law, see Roth, 'Wettbewerb der Mitgliedstaaten oder Wettbewerb der Hersteller?' ZHR 159 (1995) 78; von Wilmowsky, 'Ausnahmebereiche gegenüber den EG-Grundfreiheiten?' EuR 1996, 362, 363–367; Oliver, 'Some Further Reflections on the Scope of Articles 28–30 (ex 30–36) EC' (1999) 36 CML.Rev 783, 799–803. As for the latest judgments see ECJ 23 May 2000, Case C-209/98 *Sydhavnens Sten* (nyr); 16 May 2000, Case C-388/95 *Belgium v Spain* (nyr).

[32] ECJ 10 May 1995, Case C-384/93 *Alpine Investments* [1995] ECR I-1141, 1177 cons. 35.

conditions, the decisions taken by the Member States should be controlled or even replaced by a Community institution like the Court—or as an alternative: by Council and Parliament.

One *caveat* is, however, in order: as far as the freedoms are interpreted to cover not only *direct*, but also *indirect* discrimination, there seems to be a consensus that *judicial scrutiny* is legitimate and should be exercised by the Court. Accordingly, in such a case the Court should enter into an analysis of the justification at hand ('general good'; 'public interest'), and should control the relevant measures by the standards of appropriateness and necessity. The discussion of the scope of the freedoms does not put into question the given competence of the Court to closely look for a justification for certain measures of the Member State, but it rather relates to the issue of *under what circumstances* such control should legitimately be exercised.

2. Representative Malfunction Versus Rights of Traders and Consumers

Control of Member State measures by the ECJ involves a replacement of a decision reached in the national political process through the Community judiciary.

Some authors have recently argued that such a replacement calls for a specific basis of *legitimacy* vis-à-vis the respect for national diversity and autonomous policy making of the level of the Member States. Indeed, the United States Supreme Court, in its commerce clause case law regarding interstate transportation, has referred to an institutional malfunction or deficiency that is likely to arise when decentralized decision-making takes place in the setting of a single market.[33] Decisions at the national level, even taken by a parliament, may tend to be biased insofar as the interests of people *residing outside* the State are not represented adequately in the national political process and are therefore not reflected in the adoption of those measures that adversely affect them. On the basis of this analysis it is argued that the ECJ should apply the freedoms and control the national political process *only* in those cases where there is a basis for a suspicion that such a malfunction exists in the national political process, working to the disadvantage of the nationals and undertakings of the other Member States.[34]

Leaving aside the question of whether the US Supreme Court has evolved a consistent case law concerning 'representative malfunctions' and developed criteria that could be applied in a convincing manner, it should be pointed out that the ECJ has never alluded to such an argument in order to

[33] Cf Roth (n 20 above) 212, 320, 327 with references to the case law.
[34] *Maduro* (n 9 above) 174.

legitimize its own case law, and, as I would like to submit, rightly so. This is for two reasons:

(1) The diagnosis of a malfunction of the national political process requires an in-depth study of the decision-making process at the national level, the relevant alternatives in decision-making procedures and results, etc. To carry out such an analysis with respect to a specific piece of legislation would meet with practical difficulties and might easily lead to arbitrary results. If, however, such analysis were to be replaced by the mere suspicion or assumption that the decision-making process at the national level *might be* tainted by representative malfunctions, we would be confronted with the question of whether such a suspicion should really be sufficient to replace the national political process by a judicial decision at Community level.

(2) Moreover, the representative malfunction argument is based on the assumption that if the under-representation of interests of people from other Member States were corrected in the national political process, the outcome of the decision-making process would be different, protecting the interests of people residing out-of-state.[35] It is submitted that this kind of analysis begs the question: if people residing out-of-state were indeed represented in the national political process, it is by no means clear whether their voice would be heard if they held just a minority view. Protection of their—legitimate—interests would perhaps still be needed as some sort of *minority protection*. And such protection would, of course, still necessitate the control of the national political decision, and, perhaps, its replacement by judicial *fiat*.

In contrast, it may well be argued that the *function of the freedoms* is not to correct the representative malfunctions in the national political process, but to serve and protect the interests of traders and consumers in realizing the advantages of the single market: the right of undertakings to provide services everywhere in the Community, and the right of consumers to receive services everywhere and from everywhere.[36] It is suggested that it is this notion of fundamental *rights* of individuals[37] that the ECJ has developed in its case law relating to the freedoms. In *Säger v Dennemeyer*, the Court classifies professional qualifications as preventing an undertaking from providing services in a national territory, and as preventing potential

[35] *Maduro* (n 9 above) 174.

[36] See *Roth* (n 31 above) 78.

[37] For the notion of the freedoms as *rights* ('subjektiv-öffentliche Rechte') see Kingreen and Störmer, 'Die subjektiv-öffentlichen Rechte des primären Gemeinschaftsrechts', EuR 1998, 263, 274; Kingreen, *Die Struktur der Grundfreiheiten des Europäischen Gemeinschaftsrechts* (1999) 23, 190; see generally Schubert, *Der Gemeinsame Markt als Rechtsbegriff—Die allgemeine Wirtschaftsfreiheit des EG-Vertrages* (1999).

recipients from 'freely choosing' the service they need.[38] And the *Alpine Investments* judgment, dealing with the prohibition of interstate 'cold calling', recognizes a right to export services to other Member States by qualifying such a prohibition as a 'restriction', even if it is indistinctly applicable.[39]

The right of traders and consumers to provide and receive cross-border services everywhere in the Community should, however, not be misconceived as enforcing some concept of 'economic due process'. Freedom to provide services is not an instrument for deregulation, but should be regarded as an instrument to secure *access to the market* of other Member States, and, once access is provided, to guarantee *competition on equal terms*.[40] The principle of 'undistorted competition' and the standard of 'market access' are nicely reflected in the formula of the Court which refers to the 'elimination of all discriminations' and to the abolition of those restrictions that 'prohibit or impede' the activities of a service provider established in another Member State.[41]

III. THE DISCRIMINATION STANDARD: HOW FAR DOES IT REACH?

Some authors in the United Kingdom[42] as well as on the Continent[43] have argued that the discrimination test—as opposed to a 'prohibition of restrictions' approach—should be regarded as the adequate standard for the freedoms. The claim is that such a standard would constitute a more satisfactory approach than the road the Court is presently taking.

1. The Notion of Discrimination

Let us start with direct and indirect discriminations based on nationality. It is undisputed that freedom to provide services encompasses a prohibition of both these types of discriminatory measure. The basic principles of the single market—market access and undistorted competition—are both implemented by the discrimination test. The prohibition of discrimination

[38] See n 13 above [1991] ECR I-4244 cons. 14.

[39] See n 32 above [1995] ECR I-1176 cons. 28, I-1177 cons. 35.

[40] For such a concept with regard to the right of establishment, see Roth, 'Die Niederlassungsfreiheit zwischen Beschränkungs- und Diskriminierungsverbot', in *Gedächtnisschrift für Brigitte Knobbe-Keuk* (1997) 729, 737.

[41] *SETTG* (n 16 above) [1997] ECR I-3119 cons. 16.

[42] e.g. Bernard, 'Discrimination and Free Movement in EC Law' [1996] ICLQ 82.

[43] Marenco, 'Pour une interprétation traditionelle de la notion de mesure d'effet équivalent à une restriction quantitatitve', 1984 Cah. dr. europ. 291; Defalque, 'Le concept de discrimination en matière de libre circulation des marchandises', 1987 Cah. dr. europ. 471; Jarass, 'Elemente einer Dogmatik der Grundfreiheiten', EuR 1995, 202.

should not only extend to overt discrimination based on nationality, but also to covert, indirect discrimination by indistinctly applicable rules that produce the same effect.

The test of covert and indirect discrimination implies two questions.

(1) First, the question of discriminatory *effect*: where a regulation substitutes the nationality criterion by some other, ostensibly neutral, criterion, we may nevertheless encounter at least to some degree the same effect as the nationality criterion would produce.
(2) Whereas formal (direct) discrimination can, according to the case law of the ECJ only be justified by the reasons listed in Articles 30 and 46 EC,[44] indirect (covert) discriminatory measures can also be justified by considerations of the 'general good'.[45] In this respect, the approach to justifying national regulations is not different from the 'restriction prohibition' approach:[46] the discriminatory measure can only be justified if a 'general good' consideration is available and the measure meets the proportionality test.[47]

Two points need to be stressed. It is not the discriminatory *intent* of the legislature that should count, but only the discriminatory *effect*. Though the Court, in cases concerning the free movement of goods, has more than once referred to the purpose of national legislation,[48] the Court has never ventured into analysing the legislative process, and, it is submitted, it should never do so. Legislative intent is too slippery a notion and is, indeed, more fiction than reality. What should count is the *effect* of the measure on the functioning of the single market, the effect on imports and exports of goods and services, and not whether such effects are intended.

A more critical remark relates to the issue of justification. The Court, more than once, has held that discriminatory measures based on nationality—and with regard to undertakings: place of establishment—can only be justified by the reasons listed in ex Article 56 (1) ECT (public policy, public security, public health) and *not* by other 'public interest' considerations,[49]

[44] As for Article 28 EC: e.g. ECJ 17 June 1981, Case 113/80 *Commission v Ireland* [1981] ECR 1625, 1639 cons. 10–11; as for Article 49 EC: e.g. ECJ 26 April 1988, Case 352/85 *Bond van Adverteerders* [1988] ECR 2085, 2134–2135 cons. 32–33.

[45] eg ECJ 20 May 1992, Case C-106/91 *Ramrath* [1992] ECR I-3351, 3384 cons. 27, 29.

[46] For an analysis of the case law, see Roth, 'Diskriminierende Regelungen des Warenverkehrs und Rechtfertigung durch die "zwingenden Erfordernisse" des Allgemeininteresses', WRP 2000, 979; *contra* Martin, ' "Discriminations", "entraves" et "raisons impérieuses" dans le Traité CE: Trois concepts en quête d'identité', 1998 Cah. dr. europ. 261, 300.

[47] In this respect, the need to control the decision reached in the national political process seems to be undisputed.

[48] eg with regard to Article 28 EC: ECJ 24 November 1993 *Keck* (n 7 above) [1993] ECR I-6130 cons. 12; in its case law concerning Article 29 EC (n 31 above), the Court consistently refers to legislative purpose.

[49] See n 44 above.

as eg consumer protection. Such a justification by 'imperative reasons relating to the public interest' are to be available only for measures that *indistinctly* apply to all persons or undertakings pursuing economic activity in the state of destination.[50] It is hard to find a convincing reason for this differentiated approach.

In a number of judgments the Court has classified a provision requiring a person or an undertaking to be *established* within the Member State where the services are to be provided as a restriction on the freedom to provide services that amounts to the 'very negation' of that freedom,[51] depriving Article 49 EC of all its effectiveness, but has nevertheless opened the way to a justification by *imperative reasons* of the public interest. It is submitted that it is just a *matter of legislative technique* to forego an overtly discriminatory rule: a regulation may require that (as a prerequisite to conduct intrastate business) out-of-state undertakings have to set up an establishment within the State; such a regulation would constitute an *overt discrimination* against undertakings established in another Member State. The regulation may, in contrast, merely require that any undertaking intending to do intrastate business has to have an establishment within the State.[52] Such a regulation may be considered as being *indistinctly applicable* to undertakings established intrastate and out-of-state. Whatever the technique of 'creative drafting', an establishment requirement should be judged by common standards. Accordingly, the Court should modify its approach to overtly discriminatory regulations, opening the way towards a potential justification by 'imperative reasons relating to the public interest'.[53]

Perhaps, the *Svensson*[54] judgment may be considered as a step in the right direction:[55] The Court refers to its case law that an overtly discriminating regulation, based on the criterion of establishment, can only be justified by the reasons listed in ex Article 56(1) ECT, but then goes on to consider whether the discriminating regulation can also be justified by the need to 'ensure the cohesion and integrity of the tax system'—a consideration that had been accepted in the *Bachmann* judgment as a mandatory requirement relating to the public interest.[56]

[50] ECJ 25 July 1991 *Säger* (n 13 above [1991] ECR I-4244 cons. 15.

[51] eg *Parodi* (n 14 above) [1997] ECR I-3925 cons. 31 with further references.

[52] cf ECJ 13 January 2000, Case C-254/98 *TK Heimdienst* (nyr).

[53] See for a more in-depth argument Roth (n 46 above).

[54] ECJ 14 November 1995, Case C-484/93 *Svensson* [1995] ECR I-3955, 3976, paras. 15–16.

[55] See also ECJ 28 April 1998, Case C-118/96 *Safir* [1998] ECR I-1897, 1926 cons. 24, and, most notably, ECJ 13 March 2001, Case C-379/98 *Preüssen Electra AG* (nyr) with regard to Art. 28 EC.

[56] ECJ 28 January 1992, C-204/90 *Bachmann* [1992] ECR I-249, 284–285, paras. 32–33.

2. Double Regulation as Discrimination?

A second question to be discussed relates to the issue whether *double regulation* by the home state of the service provider and the host state can be (and should be) adequately considered as a matter of discrimination by the host State[57] or whether the Court's 'restriction prohibition' approach should be preferred.

The argument for a *discrimination test* could be advanced on the following lines: a provider of a service who is established in another Member State may be regarded to be in a different situation compared to his competitors who are established within the regulating State, insofar as he lives under a different régime of regulations, concerning organizational requirements as to professional qualifications, or as to the service to be provided. *Discrimination* may not only arise from the application of *different* rules to comparable situations, but also from the application of the *same* rule to different situations.[58] Accordingly, a regulation by the host state concerning an issue that is also covered by a regulation of the home state may be regarded as treating *different* situations—double regulation in the interstate setting versus regulation by the host state only in the intrastate situation—alike, and therefore be classified as discriminatory[59] and thus in need of a justification.

Such an approach has to be viewed with serious reservations. To classify double regulation as discriminatory requires a strict analysis with regard to the question of how the host Member State could *evade* the blame of discriminating against an out-of-state provider of a service by formulating a non-discriminatory regulation: we would need standards as to how different the rules for transnational settings have to be as compared to rules for intrastate settings. Where a Member State modifies its regulations for transnational services to escape the accusations of discrimination, the analysis of whether there are still discriminatory *effects* may prove to be difficult and distracting from the decisive issue whether and to what extent a *justification* is available. In summary: the issue of double regulation could be approached as a matter of discrimination. But the concept of discrimination will be hard to apply;[60] it is submitted that the Court's 'restriction prohibition' approach is to be preferred as being straightforward and directed towards the decisive issues of justification.

The discrimination criterion seems to be even less convincing when it

[57] In favour of such an analysis are eg Marenco (n 43 above); Kingreen and Störmer (n 37 above) 120; Jarass (n 43 above) 214.

[58] ECJ 7 May 1998, C-390/96 *Lease Plan Luxembourg* [1998] ECR I-2553, 2582, para 34.

[59] In other words, the State of destination may not treat intrastate situations and transnational situations alike; cf Kingreen and Störmer (n 37 above) 120 ff.

[60] Steiner and Woods (n 8 above) 291–292.

comes to an evenhandedly applied *prohibition* to provide a service, set forth by the *host* Member State.

The *Debauve* judgment[61] may serve as an example, dealing with a Belgium regulation prohibiting all TV advertising. Such a prohibition had the effect of impeding out-of-state programmes to be televised in Belgium. If one takes advertising as the service to be regulated (prohibited), we would have to accept that the host State (Belgium) is not discriminating against out-of-state providers in so far as the prohibition is applied evenhandedly. If the discrimination analysis were to be extended to the issue of double regulation, we would have to ask whether the host State is discriminating against out-of-state providers, because it treats *different* factual settings—the transnational and the intrastate setting—in the same way. The simple prohibition of the host State does not take into account that the out-of-state provider is providing a *lawful* service in the State of origin. If double regulation creates a 'different situation' for the purposes of discrimination analysis (lawfulness of a service in the *home* State being also a kind of regulation), the decisive question to be posed would have to be what kind of regulation the *host* State may apply to 'imported' services without being subjected to the charge of discrimination? The application of the discrimination test cannot be addressed without getting involved in the issue of *justification* at this stage of analysis.

3. Conclusions

The discrimination criterion corresponds to the *principle of undistorted competition* which is fundamental to the single market. As such the prohibition of discrimination based on nationality (or establishment) is encompassed by Articles 49 and 50 EC. However, it is not a sufficient standard to guarantee *access* to the market for out-of-state providers of services.

The extension of the discrimination analysis to the principle that different situations have to be treated in a different manner, will run into problems when it comes to define the *scope* of this analysis. The Court, therefore, seems to be well advised when it combines the discrimination standard with the 'prohibition of restrictions' test.

IV. REGULATIONS OF THE HOST STATE

The analysis of the case law has shown:

(1) first, that with regard to freedom to provide services, the Court has refrained from taking a sweeping approach comparable to *Dassonville*,

[61] See n 26 above.

but has rather opted for a more restrained approach, *combining* the *discrimination* standard with the *restriction* approach;
(2) secondly, that this approach cannot and should not be overcome by applying just *one* standard, either the discrimination or the restriction standard.

The Court's approach is based both on the principle of undistorted competition and on market access for providers (and recipients) of services. These principles correspond to the discrimination and restriction test. This by necessity leads to the question of how to define the scope of each test and how to delineate one from the other.

1. Discrimination

It is suggested that the prohibition of direct and indirect discrimination on the basis of nationality (or establishment) should be regarded as the *general principle* encompassed by Articles 49 and 50 EC.[62] More than once, the Court has stressed that the freedoms should be considered as *leges speciales* to the prohibition of discrimination contained in Article 12 EC.[63] It should be submitted at this point that the discrimination standard appears to be the *adequate standard of control* for all regulations and measures except for those *related to the market access* of the provider of the service. This contention is reflected in the case law of the Court concerning, eg, issues of public procurement,[64] subsidies,[65] and housing regulations[66] where just the standard of discrimination has been applied.

Application of the discrimination standard as a *general standard* under Articles 49 and 50 EC takes care of two issues that have been controversially discussed recently.

First, as already indicated, there will be *no need* for a *Keck*-like judgment in the field of freedom to provide services if the discrimination standard is adopted as the general rule, with the 'restriction' approach being applied in addition but *restricted to issues of market access*. Viewed in this perspective, *Keck* may be considered as a judgment *re-establishing* the discrimination standard as the *basic* standard in the free movement of goods area, thereby converging the case law concerning the free movement of goods and the relevant standards applicable to the provision of services.

[62] This seems to be the approach taken by the Court to Article 39 EC in ECR 27 January 2000 *Graf v Fitzmoser* (n 29 above) cons. 14–17.

[63] cf ECJ 28 October 1999, Case C-55/98 *Vestergaard* (nyr) cons. 16–17; 13 April 2000, Case C-176/96, *Jyri Lehtonen* (nyp) cons. 37–38.

[64] ECJ 5 December, C-3/88, *Commission v Italy* [1989] ECR 4035, 4059 cons. 8; 3 June 1992, Case C-360/89 *Commission v Italy* [1992] ECR, I-3401, 3418 cons. 11.

[65] ECJ 14 January 1988, Case 63/86 *Commission v Italy* [1988] ECR 29, 52–53 cons. 12–20.

[66] ECJ 30 May 1989, Case 305/87 *Commission v Greece* [1989] ECR 1461, 1478 cons. 21.

Secondly accepting the discrimination test as the *basic* standard offers another laudable side effect. The sometimes troubling demarcation line between Article 49 and Article 12 EC[67] becomes irrelevant—at least if it becomes accepted that the standards of justification under Articles 49 and 12 EC with regard to direct and indirect discriminations are the same as well.[68]

2. Prohibition of Restrictions

A need to supplement the discrimination test with a 'prohibition of restrictions' approach arises out of cases in which *market access* for the provider (and the recipient) of the services is impeded by a regulation (though indistinctly applied to intrastate and out-of-state providers). For the purpose of analysis, four different kinds of regulation may be distinguished:

(1) regulations which impose certain *conditions* that have to be fulfilled before the provision of services may be taken up;
(2) regulations as to the *organizational structure* of the provider of the service;
(3) regulations concerning the *service as a product*, and
(4) regulations concerning the *distribution* of the service.

Regulations that impose certain *conditions* to be fulfilled before the service may be provided directly impinge on market access. A classic example is the authorization requirement as a *precondition* for the provision of services.[69] The need for a *strict control* of such a (indistinctly applicable) requirement is twofold. If the service is to be provided only on an occasional basis, any form of authorization requirement tends to discourage the provision of services because of the relative costs involved. Moreover, if the provider of the service is authorized to do business in its *home* State, the authorization requirement of the *host* State amounts to a double regulation (double burden), likely to impede access to the market, and to make access less attractive.

Regulations of the *host* State that concern the *organizational structure* of the provider of the service are likely to impede access to the market as well. Take a regulation that certain (medical, legal) services may only be offered

[67] eg ECJ 2 February 1989, Case 186/87 *Cowan* [1989] ECR 195, 220–222 cons. 14–20; ECJ 15 March 1994, Case C-45/93 *Commission v Spain* [1994] ECR I-911, 918–920 cons. 5–10; ECJ 20 March 1997, Case C-323/95 *Hayes* [1997] ECR I-1711, 1723–1724 cons. 16; cf also the Opinion of Advocate General la Pergola [1996] ECR I-4663, 4668, paras 13–15.

[68] See eg *Hayes* (n 67 above) [1997] ECR I-1725–1726 cons. 23–24.

[69] *Commission v Germany* (n 13 above) [1986] ECR 3807–3808 cons. 42–51; *Parodi* (n 14 above) [1997] ECR I-3922.

by natural persons.[70] Such a regulation by necessity excludes the right to provide interstate services for undertakings that are established in another Member State. Another example may be a regulation requiring the fulfilment of certain standards as to the financial structure of the undertaking: such a regulation tends to shut out providers established in another State from access to the national market.

A third type of regulation that should be encompassed by the 'restriction prohibition' approach relates to the service as a 'product'.[71]

One group of regulations concerns the 'quality' of the service, generally regarded as a consequence of the professional qualification of the provider. As regulations concerning professional qualifications diverge among the Member States, they tend to create barriers for the interstate provision of services similar to the ones created by those dealing with the organizational structure. Again, such regulations imposed by the host State directly impede on the *access* to a national market for providers from other Member States. *Säger*[72] is a case in point: patent renewal services could be offered in Germany only by *patent attorneys* whereas in the United Kingdom a comparable qualification was not required.

Another aspect of 'product' regulation by the host State has recently been discussed in the *Greek Tourist Guide* judgment of 1997 (*SETTG*).[73] Greek labour regulations provided for a mandatory *classification* of the employment relationship between tourist guides carrying on their activities in Greece and their employer as a contract subject to Greek *labour law*. The Court, rightly, applied the 'restriction prohibition' approach as the Greek regulation deprived all tourist guides established in other Member States from *access* to the market *as a self-employed* person.

The *Greek Tourist Guide* judgment points also to another dimension of the problem. As far as the service as a *product* is shaped by mandatory provisions of *contract law*, such regulations may be considered to impede market access for services that are provided on the basis and according to the standards of the contract law of some other Member State. The *Greek Tourist Guide* case gives an indication that the doctrinal discussion on the influence of freedom to provide services on the law of insurance and banking contracts[74] may not have been a purely 'academic' discussion after all.

[70] This issue has been mentioned but not discussed by Advocate General Jacobs in *Säger* [1991] ECR I-4229, at 4233, para 18.

[71] As to analysing a service as a 'product' see Advocate General Jacobs in *Säger* (n 13 above) [1991] ECR I-4229, 4235, para 26.

[72] ibid at I-4244 cons. 14.

[73] See n 16 above.

[74] See Franzen, *Privatrechtsangleichung durch die Europäische Gemeinschaft* (1999) 118–216; Klauer, *Die Europäisierung des Privatrechts* (1998) 62–101; Roth, 'Das Allgemeininteresse im europäischen Versicherungsvertragsrecht', VersR 1993, 129; Roth, 'Freiheiten des EG-Vertrages und nationales Privatrecht', ZEuP 1994, 5; Steindorff, *EG-Vertrag und Privatrecht* (1996) 78, 266; Wernicke, *Privates Bankvertragsrecht im EG-*

With regard to 'product' regulations of the *host* Member State, a somewhat delicate problem arises in case the product has to be adapted, if not constructed, with regard to local factual and legal conditions. Are the indistinctly applicable regulations of the host State concerning construction safety to be qualified as 'restrictions' that have to be justified by the 'general good', or does the discrimination test apply as the general standard? The answer will probably depend on whether the services offered are standardized products or not. With regard to construction services, those regulations will not specifically impede the market access for the provider: construction work has by its nature always to adapt to the factual conditions and surroundings of the location of the construction. As such it is not a standardized, prefabricated product that may be 'sold' on another market, but it has to be provided on the basis and with regard to the relevant legal order of the host State. To that extent, the provider of the service is *not* confronted with problems that derive from the existence of diverging regulations in the host and the home State.

A fourth type of regulation concerns the *distribution* of services. With regard to this type of regulation it should be admitted that drawing a convincing line of demarcation for the 'restriction prohibition' approach may prove to be a difficult task, because—as we have learned from the discussion following *Keck*—regulations concerning the distribution of goods may have a *varying impact* on access to the market. Sunday trading laws do not impede out-of-state producers for gaining access to the market, whereas the prohibition of door-to-door selling may. One aspect calls for special attention: the *Keck* case law concerns for the most part regulations dealing with the *resale* of goods at the retail level. Services are different insofar as there is no comparable retail level for their distribution.[75] However, there is no need to think in analogies to the *Keck* judgment (regulations concerning agents as comparable to selling modalities etc): the discrimination test being the *general* standard to be applied, it is merely our task to sort out those regulations that impose a specific burden on the access to the market and should therefore be governed by the 'restriction prohibition' approach.

Freedom to provide services requires that the service provider has access to potential recipients. Article 49 EC actually defines the scope of the freedom by referring to the place of establishment of the intended recipient. Cross-border provision of services presupposes that the avenues of communication with the intended recipient are open. Given this person-to-person

Binnenmarkt (1996); von Wilmowsky, 'Der internationale Verbrauchervertrag im EG-Binnenmarkt', ZEuP 1995, 735; von Wilmowsky, 'EG-Freiheiten und Privatrecht', JZ 1996, 590. A monograph by Remien will be published soon.

[75] For a similar argument see Hatzopoulos (n 5 above) at 68.

relationship as a precondition for the provision of services,[76] it may be argued that all regulations that impede the provider's *access to potential customers* deserve judicial scrutiny to the same extent as 'product', or organizational regulations, and must therefore be judged as 'restrictions'. In this analysis, a prohibition of 'cold calling' by telephone or fax, enacted by the *host* State has to be classified as a restriction under Article 49 EC.

Advertising of services is not different from advertising of goods. Accordingly, the same principles as have been laid down in the *de Agostini* decision,[77] should be applied:

(1) in as far as the regulation (or prohibition) of advertising amounts to a burden on the service to be provided, advertising regulations of the host State will be governed by the discrimination test;[78]
(2) advertising itself has to be regarded as a service and may come within the scope of Article 49 EC where the advertising service is provided on a transnational basis. In such a case any regulation or prohibition of advertising will amount to a product regulation and will have to pass the restriction test.[79]

3. Some Consequences

Let me close the discussion of the *double standard* test—'restriction prohibition' approach and discrimination test[80]—with two observations.

The Court has developed its case law concerning the 'restriction prohibition' approach on the basis that the provider of the service is established in another Member State where he *lawfully* provides similar services.[81] It can be argued that this reference to the legal environment of the *home* State is essential for the demarcation of the discrimination test and the 'restriction prohibition' approach. We apply the restriction approach to indistinctly applicable regulations of the *host* State deviating from those of the *home* State in order to ensure market access. It is the double burden that is imposed on the service which legitimizes the application of the restriction standard. In contrast, we have no such reason to apply the restriction test in a setting where the provider does not offer the service in conformity with

[76] cf *Alpine Investments* (n 32 above) [1995] ECR I-1174 cons. 18–22.

[77] ECJ 9 July 1997, Cases C-34/95 and 36/95, *de Agostini* [1997] ECR I-3843, 3890–3891 cons. 39–47 (with regard to Article 28 EC), I-3892–3993 cons. 48–54 (concerning Article 49 EC).

[78] ibid at I-3891 cons. 44.

[79] ibid at I-3892 cons. 50–51.

[80] This double standard has again been alluded to in *Jean-Claude Arblade* (n 15 above) at para 33.

[81] *Säger* (n 13 above) [1991] ECR I-4243 cons. 12; *SETTG* (n 16 above) [1997] ECR I-3119 cons. 16; *Parodi* (n 14 above) [1997] ECR I-3921 cons. 18; *Jean-Claude Arblade* (n 15 above) cons. 33.

the standards set by the *home* State. The special burden resulting from potentially diverging or conflicting legal régimes is not present in such a setting. Accordingly, the application of the discrimination test seems to be appropriate.

The double standard test—discrimination test and 'restriction prohibition' approach—is also the key to an adequate treatment of those cases in which a service provider is established in one State, but directing its activities entirely or principally towards the territory of another State. I refer to the case law of the Court, especially the *van Binsbergen*[82] and *Commission v Germany*[83] judgments. In these judgments the Court held that in a case where the provider of the service intentionally attempts to evade rules of conduct of the host State, the chapter on freedom to provide services should be replaced by application of the chapter relating to the right of establishment.[84] The Court obviously took that approach in order to be able to resort to the discrimination test which the Court had traditionally applied to freedom of establishment, thereby evading the 'restriction prohibition' test applicable under ex Article 59 ECT to the provision of transnational services. Under the *double standard* approach, it is easy to explain why the application of the rules of the *host* State should be controlled only by the *discrimination test* in such a setting. It is the *host* and not the *home* State that is most affected by the activities of the service provider. And there is no legitimization to switch from the discrimination test to the 'restriction prohibition' approach. In a case where the service provider does not offer the services in its *home* State, there is no double burden (and no potential conflict of rules) and therefore no *specific* impediment for the access to the market of the *host* State. Such an approach may be found in the recent case law of the Court. In its *Veronica*[85] and *TV 10*[86] judgments the Court has departed from its earlier approach to replace the chapter of freedom to provide services by the application of the chapter on freedom of establishment: the services chapter was expressly held applicable,[87] however only the *discrimination test* was (implicitly) applied.

82 See n 10 above [1974] ECR 1309 cons. 13.

83 See n 13 above [1986] ECR 3801 cons. 22.

84 In these judgments the Court obviously proceeded on the assumption that *different* standards are applicable with regard to freedom to provide services and freedom of establishment.

85 ECJ 3 February 1993, Case 148/91, *Vereniging Veronica Omroep Organisatie v Commissariaat voor de Media* [1993] ECR I-487, 519, paras 12–15.

86 ECJ 5 October 1994, Case 23/93, *TV 10 SA v Commissariaat voor de Media* [1994] ECR I-4795, 4831, paras 15–16.

87 cf also ECJ 5 June 1997, Case C-56/96, *VT4* [1997] ECR I-3143, 3168 cons. 22, where the Court stressed that the Treaty does not prohibit an undertaking from exercising the freedom to provide services if it does not offer services in the Member State in which it is established.

V. REGULATIONS OF THE PROVIDER'S HOME STATE

1. Freedom to Export Services

Regulations of the State where the provider of the service is established may be caught by Article 49 EC. The freedom to provide services is not only directed towards the *host* State, but towards the *home* State as well. With regard to the free movement of goods, Article 29 EC ensures a right to export. The Court has interpreted the right of establishment (in *Daily Mail*)[88] and the free movement of workers (in *Bosman*)[89] as a right to move out. In *Corsica Ferries*,[90] *Peralta*,[91] and *Alpine Investments*,[92] the Court has transposed this approach to freedom to provide services.

2. 'Restriction Prohibition' Approach

The *basic standard* to be applied under Article 49 EC is, again, the *discrimination* test, encompassing direct and indirect discrimination as well. The home Member State may not discriminate against recipients of services on the basis of their nationality,[93] or their establishment in another Member State. The only issue of interest is, of course, whether and, if at all, under what conditions a 'restriction prohibition' approach should be applied to indistinctly applicable measures impeding the export of services.

We should be aware that the Court continues to interpret Article 29 (ex 34) EC as a freedom which only prescribes discriminatory measures.[94] In striking contrast, the Court has gone beyond such a standard in its *Alpine Investments* judgment concerning an indistinctly applicable prohibition of 'cold calling' by the *home* State. This approach of the Court is based on a concept of the single market which attributes to the individual trader (and consumer) a right to do business everywhere in the Community.

The Court thereby implicitly rejects other conceptions (discussed above under section II.2) that have been proposed with regard to the interpretation of the freedoms.

[88] ECJ 27 September 1988, Case 81/87, *Daily Mail* [1988] ECR 5483, 5510 cons. 16.
[89] See n 3 above [1995] ECR I-5069 cons. 96.
[90] ECJ 17 May 1994, Case C-18/93, *Corsica Ferries* [1994] ECR I-1783, 1822 cons. 30.
[91] ECJ 14 July 1994, Case C-379/92 *Peralta* [1994] ECR I-3453, 3501 cons. 40; see also ECJ 5 October 1994, Case C-381/93 *Commission v France* [1994] ECR I-5145, 5168 cons. 14.
[92] See n 32 above [1995] ECR I-1176 cons. 29–31.
[93] *Commission v Spain* (n 67 above), however, decided under Article 12 EC.
[94] *Groenveld* (n 31 above); further references to the case law of the Court in Grabitz and Hilf (-Leible), *Das Recht der Europäischen Union*, vol 1 (2000) Article 29 EGV, paras 3, 7; cf also references to the doctrinal discussion in n 31 above.

(1) As far as it is argued that judicial scrutiny beyond discrimination is meant to correct deficiencies with regard to the national political process,[95] such deficiencies (concerning the interests of traders *outside* the relevant Member State) are non-existent in this setting: the 'exporting' service providers may raise their voice in the national discussion. In contrast, it may be argued that it is the function of the freedoms to protect the interests of traders—who may perhaps be only a small voiceless minority—vis-à-vis national regulations impeding the export of services to other Member States.[96]

(2) Proponents of a concept of 'competition between legal orders'[97] would leave the control of such export regulations to the *competitive process* among the Member States. Such a concept allows for judicial restraint. But it is submitted that it is not 'competition among the States', but rather *competition among the traders*—the service providers etc—that is at the basis of the freedoms.[98]

Given this concept for the interpretation of Article 49 EC, we still have to answer the question, which measures should be left to the discrimination test, and which measures need judicial scrutiny under the 'restriction prohibition' approach.

Regulations that relate to the *conditions* under which the provider of the service may establish himself in his home State—authorization requirements, professional standards etc—should be governed by the *discrimination test*. The same holds true for all regulations that relate to the organizational set-up of the undertaking (eg company law)[99] and the legal environmental for its functioning (labour law, social law etc).[100] As far as these regulations impede exports, because other States apply less burdensome rules, such a competitive disadvantage is inherent in the decentralized structure of decision-making at the level of the Member States and should

[95] See text at n 34 above.

[96] In this respect it is argued that the freedoms contain a human rights element; cf Callies and Ruffert (Kluth), *EUV/EGV* (1999) Article 50, para 41. The relationship of the freedoms to a general (human) right of free trading ('allgemeine Wirtschaftsfreiheit') is explored in Schubert, *Der Gemeinsame Markt als Rechtsbegriff—Die allgemeine Wirtschaftsfreiheit des EG-Vertrages* (1999).

[97] cf generally Reich, 'Competition between Legal Orders: A New Paradigm of EC law?' (1992) 29 CMLRev 861; Gerken (ed), *Europa zwischen Ordnungswettbewerb und Harmonisierung* (1995); Gerken, *Der Wettbewerb der Staaten* (1999); Woolcock, *The Single European Market—Centralization or Competition among National Rules?* (1994); Sun and Pelkmans, 'Regulatory Competition in the Single Market' (1995) 33 JCMSt 67; Koenig and Capito, 'Europäischer Systemwettbewerb durch Wahl der Rechtsregeln in einem Binnenmarkt für mitgliedstaatliche Regulierungen?' EWS, 1999, 401.

[98] See Roth, 'Wettbewerb der Mitgliedstaaten oder Wettbewerb der Unternehmen', ZHR 159 (1995) 78.

[99] cf also Article 43 section 2 EC.

[100] For a similar view (concerning Article 29 EC) see Grabitz and Hilf (-Leible) (n 94 above) Article 29 EGV, para 4; *Oliver* (1996) 36 CMLRev 783, 799.

therefore not be considered as a restriction of freedom to provide services. The relevant disadvantage can only be corrected by harmonization measures, or by the trader moving his establishment to some other Member State.

In contrast, the 'restriction prohibition' approach should be applied to all regulations that relate to the access to the markets of other Member States: examples are regulations that prevent or burden the communication with potential recipients in other Member States and/or the development of products that are adapted to the legal environment of the other Member States.

Alpine Investments[101] deals with a Dutch prohibition of 'cold calling' that applied also to calls across the border to other Member States. Such a regulation by the *home* State impedes access to potential customers in other Member States. The argument that other avenues of access may still be open does not displace the fact that *access* to the market of other Member States is concerned. An interstate provision of services presupposes a legal relationship between the provider and the (potential) recipient—a relationship that has to be established by cross-border communication. The Court discusses the potential application of the *Keck* principles, but dismisses their application on the facts. Dealing with the argument that the Dutch regulation would only affect 'the way in which services are offered' and should therefore be considered as analogous to the non-discriminatory measures (selling arrangements) dealt with in *Keck*, the Court points out that a prohibition of cold calling would affect the 'offers made to potential recipients in the other Member States';[102] regulating the *modalities* of access to the recipient of a service in another Member State always amounts to regulating *access* to another market.

The implications of this approach for *product regulations* concerning services may be briefly indicated: mandatory requirements of the home State that shape the content or structure of the service as a product (eg a credit contract) may be regarded as a 'restriction' insofar as they require the service provider to adapt his product to the legal environment and the competitive forces in the host Member State. Mandatory contract rules may therefore need a justification if they are applied[103] to services provided in another Member State.

It could be argued that extending the 'restriction prohibition' approach to product regulations of the *home* State might contravene the *Säger* (and *Cassis*) philosophy with its reliance on the criterion of 'lawfully provided services' in the home State of the provider. A closer look reveals, however, that there is no such conflict: product regulations by the *host* State should

[101] See n 32 above. [102] ibid at I-1178 cons. 38.
[103] By a mandatory conflicts rule.

be checked by the 'restriction prohibition' approach only if the service *complies* with the regulations of the *home* State of the provider. If the service does not conform to the legal regime of the home State, the *host* State may apply its regulations in a non-discriminatory fashion.[104] Accordingly, no regulatory lacuna will arise if, as proposed, the regulations of the home State were checked by the 'restriction prohibition' approach. Rather, the provider of the service would be offered a choice: either to adapt his product to the legal regime of the *host* State (with the *home* State regulations under judicial scrutiny of the restriction test), or to offer the service adapted to the legal system of the *home* State, with the host State regulations to be controlled by the 'restriction prohibition' approach.

[104] See discussion in the text at nn 81–86 above.

2

On the Application of Keck *in the Field of Free Provision of Services*

JOSÉ LUÍS DA CRUZ VILAÇA*

I. INTRODUCTION

The judgments of the European Court of Justice (ECJ) in *Alpine Investments*[1] and *de Agostini*[2] raised the controversial issue of the applicability of the principles laid down in *Keck* and *Mithouard*[3] to the field of the free provision of services. A number of articles and commentaries have been devoted by the doctrine to those judgments. Some of them are marked by the acceptance of the idea that the judgments in question are to be interpreted as meaning that the ECJ refused, once and for all, to transpose the *Keck* doctrine to the field of application of Article 49 (ex 59) of the EC Treaty.

In this context, the purpose of this chapter is twofold. First, to put this line of case law in perspective and try to ascertain what might be its real scope. Secondly, to explore possible ways of clarification in this field which, without hampering the functioning of the internal market and the ability of the Treaty provisions to ensure the realization of the freedom to provide intra-Community services, would allow the maintenance of parallelism and the coherent approach in the interpretation of the provisions of the Treaty concerning the free movement of goods and the free provision of services.

II. ALPINE INVESTMENTS

In this case, the Court was called upon to scrutinize Dutch legislation prohibiting undertakings established in the Netherlands from contacting individuals by telephone without their prior consent in writing in order to offer them various financial services (a practice known as 'cold calling').

* A first version of this chapter was published in *Mélanges en Hommage à Michel Waelbroeck*, Bruylant, Brussels (1999). The author acknowledges the assistance of Mr Ricardo Oliveira, of *PLMJ*, and Mr Christian Kohler, head of the Library Division of the ECJ, in the preparation of the first version which was updated for the purpose of this publication.

1 Case C-384/93 *Alpine Investments BV v Minister van Financiën* [1995] ECR I-1141.

2 Joined Cases C-34, 35, and 36/95 *Konsumentombudsmannen (KO) v de Agostini (Svenska) Förlag AB*, and *KO v TV-Shop i Sverige AB* [1997] ECR I-3843.

3 Joined Cases C-267 and 268/91 *Keck and Mithouard* [1993] ECR I-6047.

Alpine Investments BV, the applicant in the main proceedings, was a company incorporated under Dutch law and established in the Netherlands, specialized in commodities futures.[4] Alpine Investments offered three types of service in relation to commodities futures contracts: portfolio management, investment advice and the transmission of clients' offers to brokers operating on commodities futures markets both within and outside the Community. It had clients not only in the Netherlands but also in Belgium, France, and the United Kingdom. It was, however, only established in the Netherlands.[5]

The Dutch Government and the United Kingdom, intervening in the proceedings, submitted that, since the prohibition in question was a generally applicable measure, was not discriminatory and had neither as its object nor as its effect to put the national market at an advantage over providers of services from other Member States, and since it affected only the way in which the services were offered, it was analogous to the non-discriminatory measures governing 'selling arrangements' which, according to *Keck*, fell outside the scope of Article 28 (ex 30). In their view, ex Article 59 ECT was thus not applicable to the case under analysis.

The Court did not accept those arguments and held that, since the prohibition in question deprived the operators concerned of a rapid and direct technique for marketing and for contacting potential clients in other Member States, it could therefore constitute a restriction on the freedom to provide cross-border services.[6]

Some authors question the meaning of this ruling in the light of the *Keck* doctrine; some believe that it expresses the rejection by the Court of any transposition of that doctrine to the field of the free provision of services.

Laurence Idot[7] took the view that '[d]ans la mesure où l'application de l'article 59 CE suppose en toute hypothèse une prestation intracommunautaire, toute tentative d'extension de la jurisprudence *Keck* paraît condamnée'.

Hatzopoulos[8] considered that the judgment of the Court, in this respect, could give rise to (at least) three different interpretations, which he stated as 'distinguishing *Keck*', 'limiting the scope of *Keck*' and 'ignoring *Keck*'. Actually the opinion of the author was that the Court 'completely ignored'

[4] As the Court explained, 'the parties to a commodities futures contract undertake to buy or sell a specified quantity of a commodity of a given quality at a price and date fixed at the time the contract is concluded. They do not, however, intend actually to take delivery of or to deliver the commodity, but contract solely in the hope of profiting from price fluctuations between the time the contract is concluded and the month of delivery. This can be done by entering into a mirror-image transaction on the futures market before the beginning of the month of delivery' (para 4 of the judgment).

[5] See para 5 of the judgment.

[6] See para 28 of the judgment.

[7] Europe 1995 July, Comm no 264, 11.

[8] Vassilis Hatzopoulos, 'Annotation to Case C-384/93, *Alpine Investments v Minister van Financiën*' (1995) 35 CML Rev 1427–1445.

the *Keck* judgment and that throughout its *Alpine Investments* judgment, the Court 'reflects the traditional pre-*Keck* approach to such an extent, that *Keck* seems to be a remote nightmare'.[9]

In another commentary on the Court's case law, J-G Huglo[10] was of the opinion that the Court has explicitly excluded in its judgment in Alpine Investments 'toute pollution de la matière de la libre prestation des services par la jurisprudence *Keck et Mithouard* inaugurée récemment pour les marchandises'. The author went on to state that 'on discerne mal comment, en effet, transposer cette jurisprudence en matière de libre prestation des services où la notion d'entrave est plus étroite, et en tout cas, moins détachée du comportement de l'opérateur économique que la formule de l'arrêt Dassonville'.

Some commentators pointed to the Court's lack of reasoning in the *Alpine Investments* judgment when refusing to apply by analogy the *Keck* case law and to the fact that the Court did not clearly state whether this refusal of transposition represented a 'total ban' or simply a decision relating to the concrete case under consideration.[11] In contrast, another commentator[12] took the view that even if the Court did not uphold the submissions of the two intervening governments as regards the concept of 'selling arrangements' developed by *Keck*, it nevertheless did not set aside the latter case law. Miguel Maduro[13] is of the opinion that the Court accepted in *Alpine Investments* 'the potential application of *Keck* to the freedom to provide services'.

For my part, I would not draw from the Court's ruling in *Alpine* any definitive or decisive inference as to our question concerning the transposition of *Keck* into the field of free provision of services. Like in principle any other judgment of the Court, this one has to be read in the light of the precise circumstances of the case.

Actually, as the Court acknowledged in paragraph 36 of the judgment, the prohibition of 'cold calling' laid down in the Dutch legislation is not analogous to the legislation concerning selling arrangements held in *Keck* to fall outside the scope of Article 30 ECT. The Court there takes on its own account the point made by Advocate General Jacobs in his Opinion.[14]

[9] See ibid at 1438.

[10] Comm. RTDE, 1995, 827–834.

[11] See Carlos Gimeno Verdejo, 'La noción de servicios y la eventual traslación de la jurisprudencia *Keck* al ámbito de la libre prestación de servicios en la sentencia *Alpine Investments*', Cuadernos Europeos de Deusto, no 14, 1996, 186–190. See also F Berrod, *Revue du marché unique européen*, 1995, no 3, 305–308. The doubts raised by the Court's ruling are underlined by the latter author when he states cautiously: 'il semble que la Cour refuse l'application de la jurisprudence *Keck et Mithouard* aux services.'

[12] Monique Luby, Journal du droit international, 2–1997, 564–566.

[13] Miguel Poiares Maduro, 'The Saga of Article 30 EC Treaty: To Be Continued' (1998) 5 Maastricht Journal of European and Comparative Law 298–316.

[14] See para 60.

According to him, 'there is a significant difference between *Keck* and the present case. In *Keck*, the Court was concerned with rules of the importing State relating to selling arrangements for the sale of goods in the territory of that State. In the present case, the exporting State requires compliance with its own rules of marketing not only for the provision of services in its territory but also in the territory of other Member States.'

Should both cases have been in fact analogous, would the Court have accepted the application of the *Keck* solution? We cannot be sure. But what, in my view, the judgment itself does not permit to infer is the opposite conclusion, ie that the Court ruled out the possibility of extending *Keck* to intra-Community provision of services.

The fact is that the Court's ruling in *Alpine Investments* corresponds to the nature, subject matter and effects of the national rules in question in that case as well as to the scope of Article 49 (ex 59) of the Treaty as compared with Articles 28 and 29 (ex 30 and 34) EC.

First of all, the nature and effects of the national provisions are at issue. As Advocate General Jacobs rightly pointed out,[15] those rules constituted a restriction on the freedom to provide intra-Community services as they directly and substantially restricted the ability of operators established in the Netherlands to market their services in the territory of other Member States.[16] The Court upheld this understanding in paragraph 38 of the judgment. Of course, a Member State is free to regulate the marketing in its territory of services provided by persons established in that State. However, it does not have unlimited freedom to regulate the marketing of such services in the territory of other Member States.[17] Being a restriction on marketing services in another Member State, the rules under analysis in *Alpine Investments* constituted thus a restriction on the provision of intra-Community services which fell within the scope of ex Article 59 ECT.

Indeed, in the first place, we have to bear in mind that as follows from

[15] See paras 47, 48, 51–56 of the Opinion.

[16] This is why the judgment of the Court in Case C-379/92 *Peralta* [1994] ECR I-3453, is irrelevant as regards a situation like the one at issue in *Alpine Investments*. Not only did the rules at issue in *Peralta* not regulate either the provision or the market of services, but also their effect on the freedom to provide services 'was so remote, tenuous and indirect as hardly to constitute a restriction within the meaning of Article 59' (Opinion of Advocate General Jacobs in *Alpine Investment*, para 58). A discussion of *Peralta* and its relations with *Alpine Investments* can be found in Ole-Andreas Torgensen, 'The Limitations of the Free Movement of Goods and the Freedom to Provide Services: B in Search of a Common Approach' [1999] European Business Law Review 371–387. The author submits that 'the judgment in Peralta confirmed a common approach to the Treaty provisions governing goods and services' and therefore 'provides a striking contrast to that in *Alpine Investments*'. As regards this latter judgment, Torgensen takes the view that it 'was inconsistent with the Court's previous case law concerning the free movement of services and that it marked a deviation from the case law concerning the free movement of goods' (381). As stated above this does not coincide with my view.

[17] Opinion of the Advocate General, para 51.

the well-established case law of the Court,[18] Article 59 ECT covers non-discriminatory restrictions as well as the discriminatory ones. The Court has always interpreted Article 59 as a means of eliminating the restrictions on the freedom to provide intra-Community services and not as a means of merely ensuring equal treatment of operators established in different Member States.[19]

In the second place, as the ECJ stated at paragraph 30 of the *Alpine Investments* judgment: 'The first paragraph of Article 59 of the Treaty prohibits restrictions on freedom to provide services within the Community in general. Consequently that provision covers not only restrictions laid down by the State of destination but also those laid down by the State of origin.'[20] Then the Court concluded (para 31): 'It follows that the prohibition of cold calling does not fall outside the scope of article 59 of the Treaty simply because it is imposed by the State in which the provider of services is established.' In this context, the relevant feature for the purpose of our analysis is that as regards free provision of services in the Common Market, the Treaty makes no formal distinction between 'export trade' and 'import trade' in services. In this field, a single provision of the Treaty, Article 49 EC, plays the role of both Articles 28 and 29 EC with regard to free movement of goods. Therefore, if an analogy were to be made between the application of ex Article 59 ECT to rules such as the prohibition of cold calling which was at issue in *Alpine Investments* and the case law of the Court on the free movement of goods, it should naturally be with the case law on ex Article 34 ECT (restrictions on *exports* of goods) and not with the one on ex Article 30 ECT (restrictions on *imports* of goods).

In such circumstances, the *Keck* case law was of no assistance to solve the case under scrutiny in *Alpine Investments*, since that case law does not concern the interpretation of Article 34 ECT but of Article 30 ECT.

Should the case pending before the national judge concern the application

[18] See eg Case C-76/90 *Säger v Dennemeyer* [1991] ECR I-4221; Case C-275/92 *Schindler* [1994] ECR I-1039; Case C-288/89 *Collectieve Antennevorziening Gouda* [1991] ECR I-4007.

[19] See in this respect Case 279/80 *Criminal proceedings against Alfred John Webb* [1981] ECR 3305. See also Case 427/85 *Commission v Germany* [1988] ECR 1123 and Case C-398/85 *SETTG v Ypourgos Engasias* (*Greek Tourist Guides*) [1997] ECR I-3091, para 16. As follows from that case law, the Court has consistently adopted the broader interpretation of Article 59 ECT in order to give the principle of free provision of services full useful effect even where it implied granting more favourable treatment to service providers from other Member States.

[20] The Court goes on to remind that, as it has frequently held, the right freely to provide services may be relied on by an undertaking as against the State in which it is established if the services are provided for persons established in another Member State. The Court cites in this context Case C-18/93 *Corsica Ferries Italia v Corpo dei Piloti del Porto di Genova* [1994] ECR I-1783, para 30; *Peralta* (n 16 above) para 40; and C-381/93 *Commission v France* [1994] ECR I-5145, para 14.

of the prohibition of 'cold calling' to providers of services coming from another Member State, it is correct to assume that the question would then arise whether the *Keck* doctrine applies to services in the same circumstances as it was applied to the interpretation of Article 30 ECT.

A final point must be made in relation to the parallel interpretation of the Treaty provisions on free movement of goods and free provision of services. We know that the Court has given the notion of restrictions on exports of goods under ex Article 34 ECT an interpretation which is narrower than its interpretation of the notion of restrictions on imports of goods under ex Article 30 ECT. As a matter of fact, whereas Article 28 (ex Article 30) EC also covers non-discriminatory rules, the application of Article 29 (ex 34) EC requires the existence of a discrimination (a 'difference in treatment') between the domestic trade of the Member State in question and its export trade, in such a way as to provide a particular advantage for national production or for the domestic market of the State in question at the expense of the production or of the trade of other Member States.[21] In such conditions, it is obvious that there was no need for a *Keck*-type judgment in the domain of application of Article 34 ECT. Nevertheless, it does not follow from the foregoing that the above-mentioned parallelism has been entangled by the *Alpine Investments* ruling. Indeed, as Advocate General Jacobs pointed out,[22] it may be doubted whether the case law of the Court under Article 34 ECT applies to rules of the exporting Member State concerning the marketing of goods. As underlined by the Advocate General, 'a trader cannot be required by the exporting Member State to abstain from using in another Member State a form of advertising which is prohibited in the exporting State but is permitted in the other Member State in order to market his products in the latter, unless there is a good reason for the prohibition'.

III. *DE AGOSTINI*

The situation in *de Agostini* was different from the one examined in *Alpine Investments*. In *de Agostini*, the ECJ was called upon to give a ruling on two questions referred by a Swedish court on the interpretation of ex Articles 30 ECT and 59 ECT of the Treaty and of Council Directive 89/552/EEC of 3 October 1989 on the coordination of certain provisions laid down by law, regulation or administrative action in Member States

[21] See, in this respect, the ECJ's judgments in Case 15/79 *Groenveld v Produktschap voor Vee en Vlees* [1979] ECR 3049, para 7; Case 155/80 *Oebel* [1981] ECR 1993, para 15; Case 172/82 *Fabricants Raffineurs d'Huile de Graissage v Inter-Huiles* [1983] ECR 555, para 12; and Case 47/90 *Delhaize et le Lion* [1992] ECR I-3669, para 12.

[22] See para 55 of the Opinion.

concerning the pursuit of television broadcasting activities ('Television without Frontiers Directive' or 'TwF Directive').[23]

Questions had been raised in connection with three applications made by the Swedish Consumer Ombudsman—the *Konsumentombudsman* (*KO*)—for injunctions to restrain de Agostini and TV-Shop from using certain marketing practices in television advertising concerning a children's magazine, skin-care products and a detergent. De Agostini was a Swedish publisher belonging to an Italian group who advertised on TV3 (broadcasting by satellite from the UK to Denmark, Sweden and Norway) and TV4 (a Swedish channel) for its children's magazine, *Everything about Dinosaurs*. The KO applied to the competent national court, the *Marknadsdomstol* (the Market Court), for an order primarily prohibiting de Agostini from marketing the magazine by attracting children below 12, in contravention of the Swedish Marketing Practices Act. TV-Shop was the Swedish subsidiary of TV-Shop Europe whose activity consisted in presenting products in television spots and subsequently arranging the telephone ordering and the postal delivery of the relevant goods. TV-Shop broadcast 'infomercials' on TV3 (the above-mentioned United Kingdom-based company) and on the Swedish station Homeshopping Channel for skin-care products and detergents. The KO took the view that such advertisements contravened the prohibition of misleading statements laid down in the national legislation. The respondents in the national proceedings argued that the Swedish legislation in question contravened the TwF Directive as well as ex Articles 30 and 59 ECT.

As regards Article 30 ECT, the ECJ recalled that it is settled case law since *Leclerc-Siplec*[24] that legislation which prohibits television advertising in a particular sector concerns selling arrangements within the meaning of *Keck*, inasmuch as it prohibits a particular form of promotion of a particular method of marketing products.

It then went on to hold, in accordance with *Keck*, that Article 30 ECT will not oppose the Swedish legislation as long as said legislation affects in the same way, in law and in fact, the marketing of domestic and imported products, and, if that condition is not met, insofar as the rules in question are necessary for meeting overriding requirements of general public importance or one of the aims laid down in ex Article 36 ECT, are proportionate for that purpose, and those aims or overriding requirements cannot be met by measures less restrictive of intra-Community trade.[25]

With respect to Article 59 ECT, the Court, after recalling its judgment in

[23] OJ 1989 L298 23.

[24] Case C-412/93 *Société d'Importation Édouard Leclerc-Siplec v TF1 Publicité SA and M6 Publicité SA* [1995] ECR I-179.

[25] See paras 40–47 of the judgment.

Bond van Adverteerders[26] in which it held that advertising broadcast for payment by a television broadcaster established in one Member State for an advertiser established in another Member State constitutes provision of a service within the meaning of Article 59,[27] proceeded to examine whether domestic rules such as those in question in the cases before the national court constituted restrictions, prohibited by Article 59 ECT, on freedom to provide services.[28]

The answer of the Court was affirmative[29] since, as stated in *Gouda*,[30] where the rules applicable to services have not been harmonized, such restrictions may result from non-discriminatory application of national rules to persons providing services established in the territory of another Member State who already have to satisfy the requirements of that State's legislation.[31]

In such circumstances, the Court considered that those restrictions on cross-border television advertising could only be justified by the reasons set out in Article 56 or by way of application of the rule of reason and the test of proportionality, as admitted by the *Cassis* case law for restrictions on free movement of goods. No reference whatsoever was made by the Court to the application of the *Keck* doctrine to the case under analysis.

This led some authors to the conclusion that in *de Agostini*, even if *Keck* was confirmed and refined with regard to Article 30 ECT, it was not applied with regard to Article 59 ECT and, moreover, it was apparently rejected.[32]

Such an assertion, even when formulated in a hypothetical way, deserves further reflection.

As Professor Stuyck remarked in his commentary on *de Agostini*,[33] the approach taken by the Court in this case may be explained by the fact, in interpreting Article 59 ECT, it did 'not examine the application of the Swedish advertising rules to the advertiser, as it did with respect to Article 30 ECT, but rather the application of those rules to the broadcaster, as a provider of services to the benefit of the advertiser'.

In doing that, the Court took, as regards the advertiser, the same approach it has consistently taken when assessing the restrictive effects of advertising for goods, ie considering them in the light of Article 30 ECT.

Having carried out this test, the Court then applied Article 59 ECT to a service provision (by the broadcaster to the advertiser) whose link with trade in goods is more indirect.

This does not necessarily mean that, in making the legality of the

[26] Case 352/85 *Bond van Adverteerders v The Netherlands State* [1988] ECR 2085.
[27] See para 48 of *de Agostini* (n 2 above).
[28] See para 49.
[29] See para 50.
[30] See n 18 above at para. 12.
[31] ibid para 51.
[32] Jules Stuyck in (1997) 34 CML Rev 1446.
[33] ibid at 1467.

application of the national provisions to those services subject to the 'Cassis test',[34] the Court intended to rule out the relevance of the *Keck* doctrine in the field of services.

Indeed, had the Court made explicit reference to the application of *Keck* in this case, the result would have been the same, as will be further elaborated in the section below. We can thus assume that the Court simply did not (yet) need, in the present instance, to deal with such a delicate issue.

Nevertheless, the Court failed to explain why the service provided by the broadcaster to the advertiser should not be considered among the 'selling arrangements' involved in the marketing of goods at issue.

Neither had the Court to address the question whether any different consideration should be given to a situation where other intermediaries intervene as providers of services between the broadcaster and the advertiser or to a situation where the broadcaster is requested to advertise a service, not a good.

IV. IS *KECK* TRANSPOSABLE INTO THE FIELD OF SERVICES?

The fundamental change introduced in the Court's case law by *Keck* is based on the distinction between, on the one hand, obstacles to the free movement of goods which are the consequence of applying, to goods coming from other Member States where they are lawfully manufactured and marketed according to the legal requirements of those Member States, rules that lay down different requirements to be met by such goods (such as those relating to designation, form, size, weight, composition, presentation, labelling, packaging)—rules on the 'intrinsic characteristics' of goods—and, on the other hand, national provisions restricting or prohibiting certain 'selling arrangements'—measures regulating the 'manner in which trading activity is pursued'.[35]

In the case of rules of the first kind, the test of proportionality, as laid down in *Cassis* is applied. In fact, the obstacles created by those rules constitute measures of equivalent effect to quantitative restrictions on imports[36] prohibited by Article 28 EC, even if those rules apply without

[34] Which the Court did not perform itself, rather referred to the national court.

[35] To use the terminology proposed by Advocate General Tesauro in his Opinion in Case C-292/92 *Hünermund v Landesapothekerkammer Baden-Württemberg* [1993] ECR I-6800, paras 20, 25 ('modalités d'exercice de l'activité commerciale', in the French version). This notion would apply, as the Advocate General put it, to the questions relating to 'who sells what, and when, where and how sales can be effected').

[36] Defined in *Dassonville* (Case 8/74 [1974] ECR 837, para 5) as being '*all trading rules enacted by Member States which are capable of hindering, directly or indirectly, actually or potentially, intra-Community trade*'.

distinction to all products,[37] unless their application can be justified by a public interest objective taking precedence over the free movement of goods.[38]

Concerning the second set of measures relating to 'selling arrangements', the Court takes the view, since *Keck,* that they fall outside the scope of Article 30 EC,[39] as long as those provisions apply to all relevant traders operating within the national territory and as long as they affect in the same manner, in law and in fact, the marketing of domestic products and of those from the other Member States.

According to Judge Joliet,[40] the Court intended in *Keck* to make it clear that it is not sufficient that a national regulation concerns intra-Community trade in whatever way for Article 28 EC to apply. For that to be the case, the marketing of imported goods must be affected more intensely than the marketing of national goods. To be caught by Article 28 EC the national measures must therefore be of a protective nature and create an advantage for the national products.

The 'raison d'être' of the distinction operated by *Keck* lies, according to Joliet,[41] on the distinction between rules that affect the inherent characteristics of the goods admitted to the market and thus condition the access to the latter—such rules cannot overburden the imported goods that already have to comply with the rules laid down by the State of origin (the *double hurdle* test)—and provisions that regulate the trading conditions of any product already in market.

Article 28 EC is therefore a means of eliminating obstacles to intra-Community trade in order to establish a single integrated market, not a means of 'deregulation' of the economy intended to ensure the unhindered pursuit of commerce in individual Member States.[42]

The judgment in *Keck* gave rise to an enormous flow of articles of doctrine and commentaries in favour or against the solution adopted by the Court in that ruling.[43]

[37] Prohibitions of or discriminatory restrictions on imports can only be justified by the reasons set out in Article 30 EC, insofar as they do not constitute a means of arbitrary discrimination or a disguised restriction on trade between Member States.

[38] The test of proportionality under *Cassis* has to be carried out in three stages: first, the objective pursued by the national legislation has to be legitimate; secondly, the rules under scrutiny must be necessary and suitable for the attainment of that objective; thirdly, there must be no other measures less restrictive to attain those objectives with an equivalent degree of effectiveness.

[39] Therefore, there is no ground to apply the proportionality test.

[40] R Joliet, *La libre circulation des marchandises: l'arrêt Keck et Mithouard et les nouvelles orientations de la jurisprudence*, Exposé présenté lors de la visite des Cours suprêmes à la Cour de justice le 6 juin 1994.

[41] ibid.

[42] ibid. See also the Opinion of Advocate General Tesauro in *Hünermund* (n 35 above) at paras 1, 28.

[43] The reader can find a list of articles falling within each of those categories in Peter Oliver, *Free Movement of Goods in the European Community* (3rd edn, Sweet & Maxwell, London, 1997) 100–113.

It is out of the scope of this chapter to discuss all that literature. I would only recall that criticism was directed, on the one hand, to the reasonableness or the necessity of the *Keck* solution and, on the other hand, to the lack of a clear definition in the judgment of the concepts used to identify the different categories of rules.

Some authors would give their preference to the test set out in Article 3 of Directive 70/50[44] or would follow the opinion of Advocate General Jacobs in the *Leclerc-Siplec* case where he proposed an alternative test based on the existence or not of a substantial restriction on access to the market of the Member State concerned, in other words on a *de minimis* test.[45]

Some authors criticized the ambiguities arising from the emphasis put on and the treatment given by the Court to the issue of discrimination ('in law and in fact');[46] some pointed to the lack of precision of notions such as 'selling arrangements', as a source of legal uncertainty.

At all events, the fact is that *Keck* constitutes the actual state of the case law as it stands regarding free movement of goods. My question, at this juncture, is, as already indicated, whether the same rationale is suitable for application in the field of intra-Community provision of services.

I submit that the issue of transposition of *Keck* into the field of services will inevitably arise at one time or another in such way that it may not be avoided by the Court without striking down the parallel interpretation of Articles 28 EC and 49 EC which has always been present in the Court's

[44] Directive 70/50 EEC on the abolition of measures which have an effect equivalent to the quantitative restrictions on imports and are not covered by other provisions adopted in pursuance of the EEC Treaty OJ Special Edition 1970 (I) 17. See A Mattera, 'De l'arrêt Dassonville à l'arrêt Keck', Revue du marché unique européen, 1994, 117.

[45] A *de minimis* rule was considered by Advocate General Tesauro (Opinion in *Hünermund* (n 35 above) at paras 21, 22) as being inconsistent with the current Court's case law as well as very difficult, if not downright impossible to apply in practice. Instead, Advocate General Tesauro underlined the importance of the disparity between national laws in that (because it constrains the operators concerned to alter a sales plan lawfully put into practice in the Member State of origin) it makes access to a certain national market more costly or less profitable for the operators in question and thus are liable to constitute an indirect obstacle to the movement of goods within the Community (paras 22, 25). The fact is that mere 'selling arrangements' within the meaning of *Keck* do not fall in principle within Article 28 EC because in general they do not have a substantial impact on intra-Community trade. If they have, then Article 28 EC applies and that is what the Court acknowledged under the heading of discrimination ('in law and in fact'). Nevertheless, some problems of interpretation arise, as examined by D Waelbroeck, 'L'arrêt *Keck and Mithouard*: les conséquences pratiques', Journal des Tribunaux—Droit européen, no 1, 13, November 1994, 165. Anyway, the Court itself used the formula of restrictive effects which are 'too uncertain and indirect' to be regarded as being of a nature to hinder trade between Member States in *Peralta* (n 16 above) at para 24 as well as in further cases (C-96/94 *Centro Servizi Spediporto* [1995] ECR I-2883, para 41, and C-266/96 *Corsica Ferries* [1998] ECR I-3949, para 31).

[46] See, in this respect, D Waelbroeck (n 45 above) 164–165.

jurisprudence and thus the coherent approach to the definition of the internal market.[47]

It is not contested that the concept of 'selling arrangement' as laid down by the Court applies to measures concerning advertising or sales promotion, which relate to the most obvious conditions under which goods may be marketed.

Advertising is admittedly an excellent means of illustrating the point I would like to make with respect to the application of the *Keck* formula in the field of services, since advertising may be used to promote either goods or services or even entities of another kind, such as persons,[48] images, names or places. Moreover, as admitted by the Court,[49] advertising is also a service in itself.[50] As was held in *Bond van Adverteerders*,[51] advertising broadcast for payment by a television broadcaster established in one Member State for an advertiser established in another Member State constitutes provision of a service within the meaning of Article 49 EC.

Like *de Agostini* some years later,[52] this ruling emphasized the need for a clear identification of the services involved when assessing the application of different Treaty provisions (Article 28 or Article 49 EC) in each concrete case.

Bond van Adverteerders concerned the distribution, by operators of cable networks established in a Member State, of television programmes supplied by broadcasters established in another Member State and containing advertisements especially intended for the public in the recipient Member State. In that case, the Court identified at least two separate services within the meaning of Articles 49 and 50 EC: the first was provided by cable network operators to broadcasters; the second by broadcasters to advertisers.

More generally speaking, if, as was held by the Commission in its 'Green Paper' on *Commercial Communications in the Internal Market*,[53] we define 'commercial communications' as 'all forms of communication seeking to promote either products, services or the image of a company or organisation[54] to final consumers and and/or distributors', this will include all forms of advertising, direct marketing, sponsorship, sales promotions and public

[47] See J. Stuyck (n 32 above) at 1468. See also the Opinion of Advocate General Gulmann in *Schindler* (n 18 above) [1994] ECR I-1059, para 56, and the Opinion of Advocate General Jacobs in *Alpine Investments* (n 1 above) [1995] ECR I-1159, para. 60.

[48] Such as politicians, film stars, singers or top models.

[49] See, eg, Case 155/73 *Sacchi* [1974] ECR 409 and Case 52/79 *Procureur du Roi v Marc Debauve and Others* [1980] ECR 833.

[50] See also EC Commision, Green Paper on *Commercial Communications in the Internal Market*, COM(96) 192 final, Brussels, 8 May 1996, 5.

[51] Case 352/85 *Bond van Adverteerders* [1988] ECR 2085. See also the reference made to this ruling in *de Agostini* (n 2 above) at para 48.

[52] See above.

[53] Cited in n 49 above.

[54] Or any other entities, as I stressed above.

relations. It will also cover the use of such commercial communication services by all goods and service industries as well as public and semi-public bodies, charities and political organizations.

Also according to the Commission's Green Paper, within this service sector, two general types of service may be identified.

(1) The range of services offered by the commercial communications industry ('suppliers')—including advertising agencies, direct marketing companies, sales promotion designers, media buyers, sponsorship agents, public relations companies—or by 'specialised suppliers'—such as market research companies, advertising film producers, mailing list brokers. The services of both kinds of supplier are provided to clients ('users') interested in making such communications to the public or to a part thereof.
(2) The range of delivery services offered by carriers of commercial communications, which covers a wide range of organisations including the media (TV, radio and printed world), organisers of sports and cultural events, postal and telecommunication services providers, billboard site operators etc, and may work for both suppliers and users.

The economic importance of this sector in terms of both output and employment and the role it plays for the information and the persuasion of the consumers or the public in general make it an increasingly powerful factor of competition, economic and technical progress and a more complete integration of national markets.[55]

Advertising cannot therefore be relegated to the ancillary role of mere 'selling arrangement', helping to boost the marketing of goods or other services. If necessary, it has to be appraised as a service in itself in the light of Article 49 EC.[56]

Of course, whenever a measure restricting or prohibiting a form of advertising or of sales promotion is liable to affect the trans-frontier sales of goods, Article 29 EC and the corresponding case law[57] must be called upon to assess the legality of national legislation as regards EC law.

[55] For an appraisal of the role of advertising, see also the Opinion of Advocate General Jacobs in *Leclerc-Siplec* (n 24 above) paras 19–21.

[56] If, of course, all the necessary conditions are met, namely that advertising is provided as a transfrontier service and for remuneration within the meaning of Article 50 EC (see *Bond van Adverteerders* (n 26 above) para 12).

[57] Including the *Keck* test in order to determine whether the measure in question falls within Article 29 EC or not. Indeed, the notion of 'selling arrangement' delimits the scope of Article 29 and thus makes part of its case law. This consideration paves the way for an interesting discussion concerning the legal basis for harmonization measures in the field of advertising. The case may be illustrated by the controversy about the legal basis of European Parliament and Council Directive 98/43/EC of 6 July 1998 on the approximation of the laws, regulations and administrative provisions of the Member States relating to the advertising and sponsorship of tobacco products (OJ 1998 L213, 9). The validity of this Directive was challenged

That is what the Court did in Cases *Clinique*,[58] *Mars*,[59] *Familiapress*[60] and *de Agostini*.[61]

before the Court of First Instance in Cases T-172/98, T-175/98 and T-177/98 *Salamander AG and others v European Parliament and Council*. By judgment of 27 June 2000 (not yet published), the Court dismissed the applications as inadmissible. In the meantime, Germany had also brought an action for annulment of the directive before the ECJ (Case C-376/98 *Germany v European Parliament and Council*) and a number of companies initiated proceedings before a UK court that referred a question for preliminary ruling to the ECJ (Case C-74/99 *Imperial Tobacco*). As Advocate General Fennelly stated in his Opinion, delivered on 15 June 2000 (para 3), 'The issue of competence or legal basis is the most important issue in these cases'. As we know, national rules on advertising have been considered by the ECJ as being in principle mere 'selling arrangements' since they are not designed to regulate trade in goods (see judgments in *Hünermund* (n 35 above) and *Leclerc-Siplec* (n 24 above), and provided that they comply with the conditions laid down in *Keck*. One could then argue that, in a strict application of the *Keck* doctrine, insofar as such measures do not apply to the 'intrinsic characteristics' of the product and do not affect its content as was the case in *Familiapress* (see n 60 below), they do not constitute a 'measure of equivalent effect' caught by Article 28 EC and therefore are not liable to affect the functioning of the internal market. In such conditions, it could be argued that the existence of different national rules on advertising for tobacco products were not of such nature as to lawfully give rise to Community harmonization measures based on Article 95 (ex Article 100a) at least insofar as they are of a general nature like a total or partial ban on advertising. It must be said that Advocate General Fennelly did not choose to include this approach in his Opinion. But the ECJ echoed these considerations in paragraphs 113 and 114 of its judgment of 14 December 2000 (not yet published), although with regard to the possible existence of distortions of competition.

[58] Case C-315/92 *Verband Sozialer Wettbewerb v Clinique Laboratories SNC and Estée Lauder Cosmetics GmbH* [1994] ECR I-317. The Court applied the *Cassis* test of proportionality to a German measure prohibiting the use of the name *Clinique* for a cosmetic product as being liable to mislead consumers and oblige the undertaking in question 'to bear additional packaging and advertising costs'.

[59] Case C-470/93 *Verein gegen Unwesen im Handel v Mars* [1995] ECR I-1936. The Court held a German measure prohibiting the importation and marketing of ice-cream bars presented—as part of a short publicity campaign covering the whole of Europe—in wrappers marked '+10%' as being in contravention of the Treaty (Article 30) on grounds that it 'may compel the importer to adjust the presentation of his products according to the place where they are to be marketed and consequently to incur additional packaging and advertising costs' and that the measure in question was neither proportionate to nor justified by the objective of consumer protection that it sought to attain.

[60] Case C-368/95 *Vereinigte Familiapress Zeitungsverlags-und vertriebs GmbH and Heinrich Bauer Verlag* [1997] ECR I-3689. The judgment concerned the application to German magazines of an Austrian measure prohibiting periodicals from including games with prizes. The ECJ ruled that, although the national legislation in question referred to a method of sales promotion, it applied to the actual content of the product (a review) and did therefore not concern a mere selling arrangement. It further considered that, since the prohibition in question required publishers established in other Member States to alter the content of their papers, it jeopardized access of the product to the market of the importing Member State and, consequently, hindered the free movement of goods, thus constituting a measure of equivalent effect prohibited in principle by Article 30 EC. On *Familiapress* and other post-*Keck* judgments see the article by Miguel Maduro (n 13 above).

[61] As we know, the Court found that the Swedish legislation in question in this case concerned selling arrangements, inasmuch as it prohibited a particular form of promotion of products. However, it further held that an outright ban on a type of promotion for a product which is lawfully sold in the importing Member State might have a greater impact on imported products than on national ones and that, in such conditions, Article 30 EC might apply.

However, where the advertising is not linked with the sales promotion of goods but is used to promote services or persons, Article 28 EC is not applicable. The question arises then whether, in a parallel application of Articles 28 and 49 EC, advertising can be considered as a selling arrangement for services. And, furthermore, what consideration is to be given, in this context, to the transfrontier activity of operators such as advertising agencies which consists in itself a provision of services within the meaning of Articles 49 and 50 EC?

Let us suppose that the receiving Member State, not the Member State of origin, now imposes the prohibition on cold calling examined by the Court in *Alpine Investments*.

Let us suppose also that cold calling services are not effected by the provider of the services to be promoted (eg financial services, as in *Alpine Investments*) but by a company specialized in cold calling which has among its clients both producers of goods and providers of services. Is it meaningful to give a different treatment to a national ban or a restriction on cold calling according to the object—goods or services—of that form of sales promotion? Is it to be considered as selling arrangement and examined in the light of paragraph 16 of *Keck* when regarding goods and, by contrast, captured by the prohibition laid down in Article 49 EC when regarding services?[62] Is there a reason for such difference of treatment?

In this context, one possibility is, as suggested by D. Waelbroeck,[63] to draw a distinction between rules on advertising which affect directly, as in *Clinique*, the designation of the products and rules of a more general nature not connected with the product itself (eg a general ban on advertising of alcohol).

This line of reasoning seems to me to deserve further elaboration and to be suitable for the possible transposition of the *Keck* case law into the field of intra-Community provision of services. Still taking the domain of advertising services as an example, I submit that such transposition might rely on the distinction between two groups of measures:[64]

[62] According to the 'classic' case law of the Court the assessment to be made in order to examine whether a national regulation restricts or not, in an unlawful manner, the freedom to provide services, within the meaning of Article 49 EC, implies that *discriminatory measures* can only be justified by reasons of public policy, public security or public health (Article 46 EC), provided that they can be considered as proportionate, and *non-discriminatory measures* can only be justified by overriding reasons of public interest (protection of workers or of consumers, protection of intellectual property, of fair trading or of pluralism, conservation of national and cultural heritage, linguistic policy, etc), if they are not already satisfied by the rules in the Member State of origin (principle of the country of origin legislation or of mutual recognition) and if they are not disproportionate (see *de Agostini* (n 2 above) para 52).

[63] See n 45 above at 163.

[64] Of course, this concerns only indistinctly applicable and non-discriminatory measures.

(1) rules concerning the 'intrinsic characteristics' of the service (advertising), such as the content or the nature of the images used (eg prohibition of nudity or of violence in advertisements), the method or technique of advertising or the way of presentation, which ought to be submitted to the proportionality test;
(2) rules relating to the general or 'extrinsic' conditions in which advertising services can be provided (including a total or partial ban) which ought to be considered as selling arrangements within the meaning of *Keck*.

It is submitted that the application of this test to cases such as *Alpine Investments* (if 'reconstructed' as a case concerning measures taken by the receiving Member State) and *de Agostini* would probably lead to the same answers actually given by the Court without recourse to the proposed distinction.

Indeed, even if the prohibition of cold calling may be considered as relating to a selling arrangement as regards either trade of goods or of services, it could in fact more severely affect the marketing of services from other Member States as compared with domestic services and thus particularly impede the access of the former to the market.

In *de Agostini*, it is clear that the prohibitions in question concerned the content of the advertisements and not general and extrinsic conditions by which they could or could not be effected.

The practical effects of such change of perspective will thus probably be negligible; but at some point it will be imposed for the sake of clarity and coherence of the case law.

Much will probably depend on the strain litigants may put on the Court as a result of any new saga in favour of the liberalization of market access for services. Advertising might well be the privileged battlefield.

3

Harmony and Dissonance in Free Movement

MIGUEL POIARES MADURO[1]

There is a generalized perception that the European Court of Justice has adopted different approaches to the different free movement rules included in the Treaties. In particular, the free movement of goods has 'benefited', until recently, from a wider scope of application. Contrary, to what has for long constituted the standard approach to the free movement of persons, the free movement of goods was constructed as requiring more than national treatment and non-discrimination in regard to goods from other Member States. Even non-discriminatory restrictions on trade on goods could constitute a violation of Community rules if not justified as necessary and proportional to the pursuit of a legitimate public interest. The freedom to provide services has somewhat occupied a middle ground between the interpretation given to the goods and persons provisions.[2] Recently, following the Court's decision in *Keck and Mithouard*,[3] a reversal of fortune appears to have taken place regarding the Court's approach to the different free movement provisions, with the free movement of persons and the freedom to provide services now benefiting from a more 'aggressive' interpretation in comparison with the free movement of goods. This chapter reviews, in a comparative and historical perspective, the Court's approach to the different free movement provisions,[4] arriving at some new and even paradoxical conclusions and proposals: first, the chapter reviews the most recent developments of the Court´s case law and contends that a uniform approach to the different free movement rules may be emerging in the ECJ jurisprudence; secondly, it is argued that this uniform approach is based on the application of a twofold test reviewing the impact of national measures on free movement either through the imposition of a double burden or the prevention of market access; thirdly, the chapter ends by contending that, contrary to the common assumption, a totally uniform test may not be a good thing and the

[1] I am indebted to Jukka Johannes Snell, Damian Chalmers and Bruno de Witte for discussions on the main topic of this chapter.

[2] For the purposes of this chapter, the freedom to provide services will generally be considered as distinct from the free movement of persons (which in turn will include free movement of workers and the right of establishment). Although the freedom to provide services may require a movement of persons (which leads some authors to include it in the context of the free movement of persons) that is increasingly not the case.

[3] Joined Cases C-267/ and C-268/91 *Keck and Mithouard* [1993] ECR I-6097.

[4] Excluding the free movement of capital.

Court would do better in continuing to follow its post-*Keck* approach of primarily allocating its judicial resources to the free movement of persons. The starting point of the chapter is precisely that judicial resources are limited and that the explanation for the fluctuations in the Court's case law lies precisely in that judicial constraint, which prevents courts from doing all they want to do and requires them to do what they can do best. It is argued throughout the chapter that the definition of where the Court ought primarily to devote its judicial resources depends on the institutional alternatives to the Court in different areas of the law and that this requires the Court to assume fully the institutional character of its judicial choices.

The first part of the chapter compares the case law of the ECJ with regard to the different free movement rules in the pre-*Keck* period. In other words, it reviews the more traditional approach of the Court steadily developed from the late 1960s to the early 1990s. The second part reviews and assesses the changes in that case law following the *Kec*k decision. The third part attempts to describe the current status quo and the emerging uniform approach. The last part of the chapter is devoted to a critical assessment of this emerging uniform approach.

I. HARMONY AND DISSONANCE: *PRESTO, ASSAI MENO PRESTO*

1. *Presto*: The Activist Approach to Free Movement of Goods—From *Dassonville* to Sunday Trading

The broad scope granted to the free movement of goods until 1993 was a result of successive developments in the Court's case law in which its interpretation of Articles 28 and 30 (ex 30 and 36) EC interacted with the legal community in such a way as to make possible the review of any national regulation restricting trade under the tests of necessity and proportionality vis-à-vis a Community recognized public interest. The first step in the development of a balance test in the application of the rules on the free movement of goods was taken in *Dassonville*.[5] The fact that it was sufficient for a measure to be 'captured' by Article 28 EC for it to be 'capable of hindering directly or indirectly, actually or potentially, intra-community trade',[6] in effect subjected all market regulations to a balance test review under Article 28, since they all have by their very nature an impact on trade. In other words, such test did not require a national measure to be protectionist or to discriminate against foreign products to be subject to review under Article 28 EC.

However, if *Dassonville* adopted a rule covering non-discriminatory

[5] Case 8/74 *Dassonville* [1974] ECR 837. [6] At para 5.

measures, the case law that followed it—until *Cassis de Dijon*—brought together the *Dassonville* doctrine and the Commission Directive on measures having an equivalent effect to quantitative restrictions[7] under a broad concept of discrimination: a comparison between the situation in which national and imported products are placed is always present.[8] In spite of the broad character of the Dassonville *ratio decidendi*, especially after the abandonment of the 'trading rules' words, subsequent decisions kept a close link with a discrimination test.

It was *Cassis de Dijon* that awoke the 'sleeping beauty' and gave new life to the *Dassonville* doctrine. Article 28 EC began its progressive extension which ultimately led to the inclusion in its scope of any State measure capable of interfering with the market. In itself *Cassis de Dijon* was not particularly 'revolutionary'. It could even be seen as restricting *Dassonville* once it broadened the scope of public exceptions capable of justifying restrictions on trade.[9] Moreover, it could also be constructed as re-proposing a discrimination test based on the double burden imposed on imports by having to comply with a new set of rules (the legislative disparity between the French and German rules required Cassis de Dijon producers to adapt to the German national requirements, therefore imposing on their products a double cost to which, arguably, the German domestic products would not be subject).[10]

What made *Cassis de Dijon* revolutionary, is the change in the expectations of legal and economic actors it promoted and the reversal of the burden of proof on the legitimacy of national measures restricting trade. The Court stated:

> Obstacles to movement within the Community resulting from disparities between the national laws relating to the marketing of the products in question must be accepted in so far as those provisions may be recognized as being necessary in order to satisfy mandatory requirements relating in particular to the effectiveness of fiscal supervision, the protection of public health, the fairness of commercial transactions and the defence of the consumer.[11]

In *Dassonville* the ECJ made no distinction between discriminatory and non-discriminatory measures with an impact on intra-Community trade,

[7] Commission Directive 70/50/EEC, OJ 1970 L13/29.

[8] See, for example, Case 65/75 *Ricardo Tasca* [1976] ECR 291, para 13; Joined Cases 88 to 90/75 *Societa Sadam* [1976] ECR 323; Case 74/76 *Iannelli v Meroni* [1977] ECR 557; Case 13/77 *GB-INNO v ATAB* [1977] ECR 2115, see paras 47, 48, 52–56; Case 82/77 *Van Tiggele* [1978] ECR 25 (on material discrimination or protectionist effects, though in this case, they are already considerably flexible and extensive—see paras 14, 16 and 18, mainly the reference in para 16 to 'effects detrimental to the marketing of imported products alone'), Case 13/78 *Eggers Sohn* [1978] ECR 1935, see para 23.

[9] See Case 120/78 *Cassis de Dijon* [1979] ECR 649, para 8.

[10] On the problems of such understanding see below.

[11] Case 120/78 *Cassis de Dijon* [1979] ECR 649, para 8.

but in *Cassis de Dijon* it made it clear that all such measures were to be assessed in the light of objectives recognized as legitimate by the Community, such as those already set out in Article 30 (ex 36) EC. Moreover, *Cassis de Dijon* introduced what came to be known as the 'principle of mutual recognition' of national regulations. According to this principle, a State has to accept the marketing in its own territory of products lawfully produced and marketed in other Member States. In the words of the Court:

> There is therefore no valid reason why, provided that they have been lawfully produced and marketed in one of the Member States, alcoholic beverages should not be introduced to another Member State.[12]

This constituted an invitation to litigate and explore the limits of the *Dassonville* concept of measures having an equivalent effect to a quantitative restriction. In other words, the Court was signalling to the legal and economic communities its willingness to review all national legislative disparities, becoming, in effect, the Community market regulator.

The process by which the scope of action of Article 28 EC was extended to include virtually any national regulatory measure had its paradigmatic cases in *Oosthoek's* and *Cinethéque*.

In *Oosthoek's*,[13] the Court interpreted the scope of the *Dassonville* doctrine to include indistinctly applicable measures that do not even require any changes to be made to imported products (in the form of different production methods or labelling for example) but simply a change in their marketing methods, thereby affecting their marketing opportunities.[14] The Court argued that 'to compel a producer either to adopt advertising or sales promotion schemes which differ from one Member State to another or to discontinue a scheme he considers particularly effective may constitute an obstacle to imports even if the legislation in question applies to domestic and imported products without distinction'.[15] This decision can be argued to constitute the most important step in using Article 28 EC to review the generality of national measures regulating the market. It can be seen as going beyond *Cassis de Dijon* in broadening the scope of application of Article 28 to include even national measures, of the type referred to in *Oosthoek's*, that do not appear to impose a double burden on imported goods but simply require the abandoning of particularly effective marketing or sales methods. However, it can also be argued that the reason to include such type of rules under the concept of measures having equivalent effect to a quantitative restriction is identical to that commanding the inclusion of rules requiring changes to be made to imported products (rules on

[12] At para 14. [13] Case 286/81 *Oosthoek's* [1982] ECR 4575.
[14] At para 15. [15] *Oosthoek's* (n 13 above).

product-requirements such as those at stake in *Cassis de Dijon*): there is a double burden imposed on foreign producers when they are forced to change the strategies and methods of marketing their products (as when they have to change the characteristics of these products).[16]

That a measure does not need to be discriminatory to come under Article 28 EC was clearly stated by the Court in *Cinéthèque*,[17] a case concerning French legislation which prohibited the commercial exploitation of cinematographic works in recorded form, mainly video-cassettes, before the end of a set time limit:

> it must be observed that such a system, if it applies without distinction to both video-cassettes manufactured in the national territory and to imported video-cassettes, does not have the purpose of regulating trade patterns; *its effect is not to favour national production as against the production of other Member States*, but to encourage cinematographic production as such.
>
> *Nevertheless, the application of such a system may create barriers to intra-Community trade* . . . In those circumstances a prohibition of exploitation laid down by such system is not compatible with the principle of free movement of goods provided for in the Treaty unless any obstacle to intra-community trade thereby created does not exceed that which is necessary in order to ensure the attainment of the objective in view and unless that objective is justified with regard to Community law.[18]

The outcome of these developments in the Court's case law was that almost any national regulatory measure became susceptible to review under Article 28 EC. The proportionality test meant that a balance had to be struck between their costs and their benefits. What is normally at stake in these cases is the general restriction imposed on access to the market and competition therein. Under the balance test developed by the Court following *Dassonville* and *Cassis de Dijon*, many measures of this kind have been subjected to the balance test, even where they did not discriminate against foreign products. Examples of legislation of this kind being submitted to cost/benefit analysis include: rules on advertising and sales methods;[19] national health system rules on subsidies on medical products and on pharmaceutical monopolies;[20] price regulations;[21] national recycling systems;[22]

[16] See, for example, *Oosthoek's* (n 13 above) para 15.
[17] Cases 60 and 61/84 *Cinéthèque* [1985] ECR 2605.
[18] At paras 21 and 22, emphasis added.
[19] See *Oosthoek's* (n 13 above) Case C-362/88 *GB-INNO* [1990] ECR I-667; Case 382/87 *Buet* (*Canvassing*) [1989] ECR 1235; Joined Cases C-1/90 and C-176/90 *Aragonesa* [1991] ECR I-4151; and Case C-126/91 *Yves Rocher* [1993] ECR I-2361.
[20] See Case 238/82 Duphar, [1984] ECR 523 and Case C-369/88 *Delattre* [1991] ECR I-1487.
[21] See, for example, Case 29/83 *Leclerc* (*Prix du Libre*) [1985] ECR 1.
[22] See Case 302/86 *Commission v Denmark* [1988] ECR 4607.

prohibition on Sunday trading or on employing workers on Sundays;[23] public law monopolies on the approval of equipment;[24] and the organization of dock work.[25] This gave the Court a leading role in defining the adequate regulatory level of the Common Market and transformed Article 28 EC into a potential 'economic due process' clause. Whether or not the Court intended to include in the scope of Article 28 all national regulatory measures became quite irrelevant once even a double burden test would lead to the review of any national measure whose content was not consistent with another State's regulatory policy regarding either the characteristics or marketing of a product.

The way that the Court applied its necessity and proportionality tests to the review of national regulatory measures under Article 28 EC tell us that the final objective of the Court was to address legislative disparities and not to control the level of public regulation of the market. As I have argued elsewhere the case law of the Court in this area of the law could be characterized as a form of majoritarian activism:[26] such case law is more understandable as the product of a 'legislateur de substituition',[27] which does not intend to impose a constitutional conception of the market and of economic organization, but which aims to transfer economic decisions affecting the internal market from State level to the Community level, in the pursuance of the judicial harmonization of State rules the diversity of which is capable of restricting free trade and the optimal gains offered by the Common Market. I have argued that the criterion guiding the Court in balancing the costs and benefits of national regulations has not been a specific (de)regulatory ideology but an attempt to identify the majoritarian view on that issue, taking the Community as the relevant polity.

For the Court, the Common Market could not support the costs of non-harmonized national rules. This means that State regulations can no longer diverge on the basis of different national traditions and policy choices. The Court distrusted the national political process to regulate the Common Market but, at the same time, it also distrusted the ability of the Community political process to bring about the necessary harmonization between the different national regulatory traditions. The consequence was the Court signalling to the legal and economic community its willingness to review national regulations and bring about harmonization through the

[23] See Case C-145/88 *Torfaen Borough Council* [1989] ECR 3851, Case C-312/89 *Conforama* [1991] ECR I-991; Case C-332/89 *Marchandise* [1991] ECR I-1027; Case C-169/91 *Stoke-on-Trent* [1992] ECR I-6635.

[24] Case C-18/8 *RTT* (*Telephone Equipment*) [1991] ECR I-5941.

[25] Case C-179/90 *Merci Convenzionali Porto di Genova* [1991] ECR I-5889.

[26] See Maduro, *We The Court* (1998) ch 3.

[27] This expression is taken from M Bettati, 'Le "Law-Making Power" de la Cour', 48 Pouvoirs 1989, 57, at 62.

judicial process. This was done through the broad interpretative scope given to Article 28 EC.

However, those signs were understood more broadly than the Court probably wanted them to be understood. Rules are not simply the property of courts and depend on their use by a larger legal community. Where a court chooses to apply a broad standard or balance test it will increase the amount of judicial activity, since any decision on the correct balance of the interests at stake will be subject to review by courts. In this case, the court is signalling to the legal community its willingness to second-guess the other decision-making institutions in judging the conflicting interests in that area of the law. But if their decisions transmit to the legal community the willingness or otherwise of courts to intervene in certain areas of the law, the language used by courts may sometimes lead them to say more than they wanted to say or to be interpreted more broadly than they expected to be interpreted. Language disguises thought, as Wittgenstein would say. Judicial decisions are not the property of courts but of the legal community, and this includes other legal actors whose preferences for judicial activity may vary from those of courts.

The participation of a plurality of actors in the definition of what the law is and the allocation of judicial resources, and the importance of institutional factors in determining the forms and content of judicial intervention, are particularly evident in the debate on Article 28 EC and the other free movement rules. The broad scope traditionally given to Article 28 by the ECJ was not intended to promote the review of all market regulation. The aim was not to construct Article 28 judicially as an economic due process clause controlling the degree of public intervention in the market.[28] The broad scope granted to Article 28 is more understandable when viewed in the light of the Court's suspicion that State regulation of the market may either impose a greater burden on products from other Member States or not take into account the Community interest in harmonized rules to prevent restrictions on free trade arising from differing national rules. It was this wariness of intervention by the national political process in a Common Market that explained the broad scope given by the Court to Article 28 and the degree of control which, as a consequence, was exercised by the Court over national regulatory powers.

The problem was that, once the Court had formulated a criterion which was so broad as to subject to a proportionality test any State regulation of the Common Market, the other participants in the legal community were also able to use that criterion to challenge any market regulation which opposed their economic freedom.[29] The broad scope given to Article 28 EC, designed to push for the Europeanization of regulatory law and so to reduce

[28] See n 26 above, ch 3. [29] ibid.

the costs of non-harmonized regulations, caught in its net any national regulatory measures even those where those concerns are irrelevant or do not exist at all. In reality it would be difficult for the Court to sustain a broad interpretation of Article 28 without ending up by having to review all State intervention in the market even where there was no particular burden arising from the existence of different national rules. Since the ECJ's distrust of national political processes found expression in a criterion submitting all national regulation to judicial review, economic operators were able to second-guess national regulatory policies through courts even when the original judicial concerns underlying such a criterion were not at stake. What occurred was a shift of the regulatory role from national political processes to courts. The ECJ (and, through it, national courts) became the institution responsible for deciding the adequate level of market regulation. Therefore, it was possible for domestic economic actors to challenge national regulatory policies through Community law and subject them to a second process of decision-making outside the national political process. Community law became a terrain of national internal disputes over regulatory policies.

The primary example of this were the Sunday trading cases where the Court was called in to assess on the proportionality of a national measure whose impact on free movement was merely a neutral by-product of its general impact on the market and the object of a purely internal national dispute. In these cases, the Court was called in to review the validity of national measures prohibiting trade on Sunday upon the pretext that such prohibition restricted the free movement of goods. The Sunday trading cases were also representative of the type of legal challenges that were increasingly over-burdening the workload of the Court frequently called in to assess the legitimacy of any market regulation.

2. *Assai Meno Presto*: Services and Persons

While, from *Dassonville* to *Sunday Trading*, the Court extended the scope of application of the free movement of goods, the same was not the case to the same extent with the other free movement rules. Following upon the literal content of some of these free movement rules the Court elaborated the principle of national treatment, which requires that a State should treat nationals of other Member States in the same way that it treats its own. The controlling rationale in the application of the other free movement provisions has been non-discrimination and not an extended concept of restrictions on trade. However, the principle of national treatment contains more than an obligation for states to apply the same legislation to its own nationals and to nationals of other Member States. The principle of national treatment's dependence upon the principle of non-discrimination determines that nationals of other Member States should be treated the same as home nationals, which does not mean that they should be subject to the same rules. In reality, equal treatment may mean different treatment. It is well known that the principle of equality implies a criterion for ascertaining what are identical situations deserving similar treatment and what are different situations deserving different treatment. The principle of national treatment also requires such a criterion. In other words, the application of the principle of national treatment had to be developed in accordance with a material notion of non-discrimination.

To determine what equal treatment in the field of the free movement of persons and services should consist of, the Court has elaborated what has been called the 'principle of equivalence'.[30] The first application of this principle was given in *Thieffry*.[31] Here the Court started by saying that the right of establishment is not necessarily dependent upon the adoption of the directives provided for by Article 47 of the Treaty (ex 57). In certain cases, it can be ensured 'either under the provisions of the laws and regulations in force, or by virtue of the practices of the public service or of professional bodies'.[32] The Court went on to state:

> In particular there is an unjustified restriction on that freedom where, in a Member State, admission to a particular profession is refused to a person covered by the Treaty who holds a diploma which has been recognized as an equivalent qualification by the competent authority of the country of establishment and who furthermore has fulfilled the specific conditions regarding professional training in force in that country, solely by reason of the fact that the person concerned does not possess the national diploma corresponding to the diploma which he holds and which has been recognized as an equivalent qualification.[33]

In this way, the Court considered that States are obliged to do more than merely apply the same rules to nationals of other Member States as they apply to their nationals. In the case itself, non-discrimination obliged the State in question to take into consideration the specific qualifications of foreign nationals. Moreover, where those qualifications have already been recognized as similar to national qualifications by a competent authority in the State of establishment, this fact must be taken in consideration when deciding on the request of establishment. In *Webb*,[34] a case on the provision

[30] See P Watson, 'Freedom of Establishment and Freedom to Provide Services: Some Recent Developments' (1983) 20 CMLRev 767–824. The interpretation given by this author, however, goes beyond the statements of the Court in its decisions. In fact Watson says that 'the principle of equivalence imposes on Member States an obligation to accept conditions imposed upon the provision of services in another Member State as being equivalent to those required by it' (at 823), drawing a parallel with *Cassis de Dijon*. In my opinion that does not correspond with the Court's intention as expressed in this decision.

[31] Case 71/76 *Thieffry v Conseil de l'Ordre des Avocats à la Cour de Paris* [1977] ECR 765.

[32] At para 17.

[33] At para 19.

[34] Case 279/80 *Webb* [1981] ECR 3305.

of services, the Court went even further and made it clear that this previous recognition is not a necessary condition to the application of the principle of equivalence. Instead, it imposes on States the obligation to:[35] 'take into account the evidence and guarantees already furnished by the provider of the services for the pursuit of his activities in the Member State of his establishment.'[36]

In this way, it would seem that the principle of equivalence is the basis for a substantive and material principle of non-discrimination, which imposes on States the obligation to take into consideration the specific elements of each situation (and qualifications of each person) in order to determine which are identical situations deserving similar treatment and which are different situations deserving different treatment. A Member State must take into account the position of a national of another Member State in his country of origin since, although the requirements made in both Member States can be formally distinct, they may in substance be identical.

Such principle of equivalence could, however, easily amount to proportionality. Proportionality becomes an issue in assessing the equivalence of the conditions imposed on and the requirements fulfilled by the different nationals.[37] This was particularly obvious in services cases once the Court considered, for example, that the temporary nature of the provision of services would justify less stricter rules than those applicable to those established in the home state. In *Van Weseamel* and *Webb* the cross-over between material non-discrimination and the proportionality of the national measures was already evident. In *Van Wesemael*, the Court held that the requirements imposed by a Member State on the provider of a service must be 'objectively justified by the need to ensure observance of the professional rules of conduct', and in order to protect the interests that such rules intend to safeguard.[38] In *Webb* the Court stated:

> freedom to provide services is one of the fundamental principles of the Treaty and may be restricted only by provisions which are justified by the general good and which are imposed on all persons or undertakings operating in the said State in so far as that interest is not safeguarded by the provisions to which the provider of the service is subject in the Member State of his establishment.[39]

[35] At para. 20.

[36] See also Joined Cases 110 and 111/78 *Van Weseamael* [1979] ECR 35: 'Such a requirement is not objectively justified when the service is provided by an employment agency which comes under the public administration of a Member State or when the person providing the service is established in another Member State and in that State holds a licence issued *under conditions comparable to those required by the State in which the service is provided* and his activities are subject in the first State to proper supervision covering all employment agency activity whatever may be the State in which the service is provided': para 30, emphasis added.

[37] This confirms that the important question on the free movement of goods is not whether the Court should or should not use a balance test but when this test should be used.

[38] Joined Cases 110 and 111/78 *Van Weseamael* [1979] ECR 35, para 29.

[39] At para 17.

A further step in introducing proportionality within this non-discrimination case law can be seen in a case concerning the insurance sector, where the Court ruled that:

> requirements may be regarded as compatible with Articles 59 and 60 of the EEC Treaty only if it is established that in the field of activity concerned there are imperative reasons relating to the public interest which justify restrictions on the freedom to provide services, that the public interest is not already protected by the rules of the State of establishment and that *the same result cannot be obtained by less restrictive rules*.[40]

However, in spite of these developments, the case law of the Court was never characterized, even in the area of services, as requiring more than non-discrimination from national regulations. The reason for the different understandings of the Court's approaches to goods, persons and services lies in the different institutional and litigation dynamics related to these different branches of case law. As we have seen, the broad understanding of non-discrimination in the area of services and persons could well include an application of proportionality in assessing the legitimacy of national measures restricting those freedoms. But this has never amounted to an 'invitation' to litigate by the Court in these areas. Instead, in goods, the reversal of the burden of proof inherent in the principle of mutual recognition had a clear institutional message which was supported by the majoritarian approach of the Court: the willingness of the Court to review non-harmonized national rules capable of restricting trade in goods; in this area of the law, the Court was ready to second-guess national political processes and therefore created a new forum where economic actors could attempt to reverse policy choices. Due to its limited judicial resources and the higher political sensitivity of free movement of persons, the Court was more restrictive with regard to services and persons (mainly the latter). But this limited application was not so much a consequence of the substantive criteria used in interpreting the different free movement rules (we have seen that proportionality was also involved in judgments on services and persons) as it was a consequence of the institutional elements inherent in the different case laws of the Court and its interplay with the litigation dynamics of economic actors.

II. HARMONY AND DISSONANCE: *ANDANTE, POCO SOSTENUTO*

1. The Sunday Trading Saga and the *Keck* Outcome

The Court's approach to free movement of goods was capable of generating a great degree of market integration and, to a great extent, the ECJ

[40] Case 205/84 *Commission v Germany* [1986] ECR 3755, para 29, emphasis added.

promoted or supplied the legislative harmonization which the Community political process had difficulties in delivering due to its institutional problems (such as its dependence upon unanimity until the Single European Act). This role was, however, placing a heavy burden on the resources and legitimacy of the Court. The problems arising from the traditional approach were twofold: first, the workload of the Court was becoming increasingly burdened by the growing number of cases challenging any national regulation affecting the economic freedom of economic actors; secondly, the legitimacy of the Court was being eroded by its degree of involvement in judging the reasonableness of any market regulation, something that always involves a sizeable margin of discretionary powers and complex economic and social policy analyses. These problems were expressly mentioned by the Advocate-General Van Gerven in his Opinion in the first *Sunday Trading* case. Referring to the traditional approach of the Court, the Advocate-General stated:

> the Court will inevitably have to decide in an increasing number of cases on the reasonableness of policy decisions of Member States taken in the innumerable spheres where there is no question of direct or indirect, factual or legal discrimination against, or detriment to, imported products. The question may arise whether excessive demands would not then be put on the Court, which would be confronted with countless new mandatory requirements and grounds of justification.[41]

The Sunday Trading saga, through which many national economic operators challenged under Article 28 EC national regulatory policies whose impact on trade was only marginal,[42] worked as a wake-up call to the Court, stressing both the limits of its judicial resources and the problems of legitimacy involved in such policy judgments. At the same time, the Community political process was able, from the Single European Act, to intervene much more effectively in harmonizing national measures and promoting the emergence of an internal market.[43]

The decision in *Keck and Mithouard*[44] can be seen as a natural consequence of these developments. In part, it answered to calls from legal commentators, to increase certainty and to reduce the overload of cases in the Court. But it can also be seen in the context of a broader change in the philosophy behind the Court's case law with regard to the different free movement rules.[45] In *Keck,* the Court renewed its approach to Article 28 EC. Its main concern was to discourage 'the increasing tendency of traders to invoke Article 30 of the Treaty as a means of challenging any rules whose effect is to limit their commercial freedom even where such rules are not

[41] See para 25 of the Advocate General's Opinion. [42] See above.
[43] Mainly in the area of goods and services. See Article 95 (ex 100A) EC.
[44] Joined Cases C-267/91 and C-268/91 *Keck and Mithouard* [1993] ECR I-6097.
[45] See below.

aimed at products from other Member States'.[46] To this end the Court starts by reinterpreting *Cassis de Dijon* in a way that restricts its application to product-requirements:

In *Cassis de Dijon* it was held that, in the absence of harmonisation of legislation, measures of equivalent effect prohibited by *Article 30 include obstacles to the free movement of goods where they are the consequence of applying rules that lay down requirements to be met by such goods* (such as requirements as to designation, form, size, weight, composition, presentation, labelling, packaging) *to goods from other Member States where they are lawfully manufactured and marketed*, even if those rules apply without distinction to all products unless their application can be justified by a public-interest objective taking precedence over the free movement of goods.[47]

Thus, measures laying down product requirements are submitted to a balance test: the benefits to the public interest objective must be superior to the costs that flow from the restriction imposed on free movement of goods. However, the same is not the case with regard to 'national provisions restricting or prohibiting certain selling arrangements'.[48] In the case of such measures the Court decided to reverse the interpretation given to *Dassonville* in subsequent decisions concerning national measures governing 'selling arrangements'. It held:

contrary to what has previously been decided, the application to products from other Member States of national provisions restricting or prohibiting certain selling arrangements is not such as to hinder directly or indirectly, actually or potentially, trade between Member States within the meaning of the *Dassonville* judgement, provided that those provisions apply to all affected traders operating within the national territory and *provided that they affect in the same manner, in law and in fact*, the marketing of domestic products and of those from other Member States.[49]

In the case of measures prohibiting or restricting certain selling arrangements it is therefore not sufficient that they may constitute an obstacle to free movement of goods to fall under Article 28 (ex 30) EC. Such measures must discriminate 'in law or in fact' against imported products.

Keck has, however, left us with three open questions:

(1) How does the distinction between product characteristics and selling arrangements operate in practice? To borrow an expression from Stephen Weatherill, does the clarification need clarifying?[50] And has the Court done so in its recent case law?

46 *Keck* (n 44 above) at para 14.

47 ibid at para 15, citation omitted and emphasis added.

48 ibid at para 16.

49 ibid at para 16, citation omitted and emphasis added.

50 Weatherhill, 'After *Keck*: Some Thoughts on How to Clarify the Clarification' (1996) 33 CMLRev 885.

(2) What justifies the different approaches to national rules on product requirements or selling arrangements arising from *Keck* and subsequent case law? In other words, what is the normative criterion legitimating the different degrees of judicial activism in free movement of goods and how does that criterion impact on the distribution of competencies between courts, the Community political process and the national political processes?
(3) How does the present judicial approach to the free movement of goods relate to the other free movement rules and how should it relate?

2. The Present Criteria: The Double Burden Test

Keck was bound to raise much criticism since it symbolized a paradigmatic turn in the Court's constitutional approach to free movement.[51] But even among those who accepted the change in perspective adopted by the Court the decision raised many requests for clarification and fine tuning in some of its more debatable aspects.[52] Case law subsequent to *Keck* has helped to clarify some of these points while also raising important new questions. A first question regarded the concept of 'selling arrangements'. Was this concept to be understood literally or was the Court ready to include in that concept other rules regulating market circumstances and not product requirements. As I have argued in previous writings, my understanding was that the Court was adopting a broad notion of 'selling arrangements' which corresponded to the distinction between product requirements and market circumstances advanced by Eric White at the time of the *Sunday Trading* cases.[53] Recently, Joseph Weiler has also argued that there are no reasons

[51] See, notably: Gormley, 'Two Years After *Keck*' (1996) 19 Fordham International Law Journal 866; Mattera, 'De l'arrêt "Dassonville" a l'arrêt Keck: l'obscure clarté d'une jurisprudence riche en principes novateurs et en contradictions', Revue du Marché Unique Européen 1994, 117.

[52] The literature on *Keck* is infinite. The following are some of my suggested reading, representing a wide range of different views: Reich, ' "The November Revolution" of the European Court of Justice: Keck, Meng and Audi Revisited' (1994) 31 CMLRev 459; Weatherhill, 'After *Keck*: Some Thoughts on How to Clarify the Clarification' (1996) 33 CMLRev 885; Gormley, 'Two Years After Keck' (1996) 19 Fordham International Law Journal; Mattera, 'De l'arrêt "Dassonville" a l'arrêt Keck: l'obscure clarté d'une jurisprudence riche en principes novateurs et en contradictions', Revue du Marché Unique Européen 1994 117; D Chalmers, 'Repackaging the Internal Market—The Ramifications of the *Keck* Judgement', ELR 1994, 385; N Bernard, 'Discrimination and Free Movement in EC Law' (1996) International and Comparative Law Quarterly 82; and Weiler, 'The Constitution of the Market Place: Text and Context in the Evolution of the Free Movement of Goods', in Craig and de Burca, *The Evolution of EU Law* (Oxford University Press, Oxford, 1999) 349.

[53] White, 'In Search of the Limits to Article 30 of the EEC Treaty' (1989) CMLRev 235. The distinction can also be related to a previous proposal by Marenco in 'Pour une interprétation traditionelle de la mesure d'effet equivalent a une restriction quantitative', CDE 1984, 291. According to this author indistinctly applicable national measures could be classified as one of two types: measures that require products to be manipulated and those that do not

to interpret the concept of 'selling arrangements' as excluding other 'market regulation rules—whether selling arrangements or otherwise—that do not bar access'.[54] I will submit that, in effect, the notion of 'selling arrangements' does include other types of market regulation rules which do not regulate the characteristics of a product but simply govern the conditions and methods of sale or other marketing circumstances. The best evidence for this are the two cases regarding rules restricting television advertising.[55] These rules do not directly relate to 'selling arrangements' and are capable of restricting the importation of goods. Nevertheless, the Court did include them in the notion of selling arrangements and was satisfied with the fact that they did not discriminate against imports.[56]

A different and more complex question regards the extent to which non-discriminatory rules governing selling arrangements or market circumstances are in effect totally excluded from the concept of measures having an equivalent effect to quantitative restrictions. Recent cases have stretched the border of the clear-cut distinction between selling arrangements and product requirements. A first line of cases considers selling arrangements which have a side effect on product requirements. These are easier to make compatible with the *Keck* criteria. The key element in determining whether a measure *prima facie* falls under the scope of application of Article 28 EC is whether it affects the characteristics or contents of the product (product requirements). It has become clear in the case law of the Court that the other facet of this definition is that national rules governing 'selling arrangements' or marketing circumstances but which have an impact on the characteristics of the product will also be caught under Article 28. In *Familiapress*[57] the non-discriminatory Austrian rules prohibiting offering consumers free gifts linked to the sale of goods was a regulation of a selling arrangement and not a product requirement. But this did not prevent the Court from considering it a measure having an equivalent effect to a quantitative restriction once it applied to promotions of free gifts advertised in the product itself. For the Court, the 'national legislation in question as applied to the facts of the case is not concerned with a selling arrangement

require such manipulation. Briefly restated, the argument was that measures that require changes to products such as labelling, packaging, composition or controls normally impose costs on imported products (in the form of double controls, re-labelling etc) which are not imposed on similar national products (see 308–309, 312, 320).

[54] See n 50 above at 372.

[55] Case C-412/93 *Leclerc v TF 1 Publicité* [1995] ECR I-179 and Case C-6/98 *PRO Sieben Media*, judgment of the Court of 28 October 1999, not yet published.

[56] 'legislation which prohibits televised advertising within a certain sector concerns selling arrangements since it prohibits a particular form of promotion of a particular method of marketing products' (*PRO Sieben Media* (n 55 above) para 45 and *Leclerc* (n 55 above) para 22).

[57] Case C-368/95 *Vereinigte Familiapress v Heirich Bauer Verlag* [1997] ECR I-3689.

within the meaning of the judgment in *Keck* and Mithouard' because 'even though the relevant national legislation is directed against a method of sales promotion, in these cases it bears on the actual content of the products' (newspapers).[58] This was a confirmation of the previous *Mars* decision[59] where the Court classified as rules on product requirements, national legislation which prohibited an advertising campaign that involved the promotion of the campaign in the labelling of the product. There is an important conclusion to be taken from these decisions: rules on selling arrangements or other market circumstances which indirectly lead to product requirements also fall within the scope of Article 30 EC. In other words, the impact on any characteristic of the product takes precedence over the regulation of selling arrangements. The reason is simple: in these cases there is also a double burden imposed on the imported products by having to change their characteristics even if by reason of rules on selling arrangements.

But there is a second line of cases which is more difficult to reconcile with the *Keck* test and which raises the suspicion that the distinction between product requirements and selling arrangements is being progressively blurred by the Court. I will summarily describe the four best examples of this dubious trend in which the Court arguably considered as measures having an equivalent effect to a quantitative restrictions, non-discriminatory national rules governing selling arrangements or other market circumstances:

- In *Franzén*,[60] the Court struck down the Swedish rules which subjected the sale, production and importation of alcoholic drinks to a licensing system (to which both home nationals and nationals of other Member States could apply) which the Court considered as restricting the free movement of goods (under the broad criterion of *Dassonville*) and not proportional to the public health aim pursued.[61]
- In *Aher-Waggon*,[62] the Court subjected the German prohibition of a first national registration for aircraft exceeding certain noise limits to a test of proportionality.[63]
- In *Monsees*,[64] the Austrian rules which restricted the transport by road of animals for slaughter by requiring such transport to be carried out only as far as the nearest suitable abattoir and without exceeding a total journey time of six hours and a distance of 130 km were considered a violation of Article 28 EC.[65]

[58] At para 11.
[59] Case C-470/93 *Mars* [1995] ECR I-1923.
[60] Case C-189/95 *Harry Franzén* [1997] ECR I-6783.
[61] ibid paras 69–76.
[62] Case C-389/96 *Aher-Waggon* [1998] ECR I-4473.
[63] ibid paras 18–25.
[64] Case C-350/97 *Monsees*, judgment of the Court of 11 May 1999.
[65] ibid paras 23–31.

- In *Schutzverband*,[66] the Court considered a measure having an equivalent effect to a quantative restriction, a geographic restriction prohibiting bakers, butchers and grocers making sales on rounds in a given territory (administrative district) unless they had an establishment in that territory where they offer for sale the same products as that in the rounds.

The easiest path to reconcile these cases with the *Keck* ruling would be by considering that these were all discriminatory rules regulating selling arrangements since they would *de facto* not affect in the same manner the marketing of domestic products and of those from other Member States. This justification was actually advanced by the Court in *Schutzverband* but not in any of the other decisions. In the other cases, the Court only required the measures to have a restrictive effect on trade appearing to return to the pure *Dassonville* criterion. Even in *Schutzervand*, if it is true that the measure imposes additional costs on traders from other Member States, the same costs are also imposed on Austrian traders established in other administrative districts of Austria and therefore such requirement does not discriminate on the basis of nationality. However, it is true that the notion of 'additional costs' and 'double burden' appears to play an important role in explaining the Court's inclusion of all these measures regulating 'selling arrangements' in the scope of Article 30 EC. Albeit not referring to *Keck* or to a discriminatory impact the Court stated in *Franzén* that 'the licensing system constitutes an obstacle to the importation of alcoholic beverages from other Member States in that it imposes additional costs'.[67]

These cases could therefore be related to the other circumstances, in *Mars* and *Familiapress*, where the Court has *prima facie* prohibited measures regulating 'selling arrangements' or 'marketing circumstances'. They all impose on traders from other Member States a double cost similar to that imposed by product requirements legislation. If a trader has to change its product to enter into another national market it incurs an additional cost to which home producers usually (but not always) are not subject.[68] It appears that some of the decisions mentioned could extend the rationale of product requirements to other measures which can also give rise to additional costs. But this can constitute a return to *Oosthoek's*:[69] the recognition by the

[66] Case C-254/98 *Schutzverband gegen unlauteren Wettbewerb*, judgment of the Court of 13 January 2000, not yet published.

[67] Franzén (n 60 above) para 71.

[68] According to Advocate-General Tesauro, nothing has changed in the Court's approach to measures affecting product requirements: 'Those measures made marketing subject to certain requirements that, if applied to imported products, compelled the producer to incur additional costs in order to gain access to the market of another Member State': 'The Community's Internal Market in the Light of the Recent Case-law of the Court of Justice' (1995) 15 Yearbook of European Law 1, at 4.

[69] Case 286/81, *Oosthoek's* [1982] ECR 4575.

Court that the regulation of some selling arrangements may fall within the concept of product requirements may be partly aimed at reviving the concept of measures which, albeit regulating marketing methods or selling arrangements, also impose a double burden. This would entail a distinction between two types of restrictions on trade arising from selling arrangements which was already present in *Oosthoek's*. In this decision the Court gave two reasons to justify the review of non-discriminatory national measures on marketing methods (selling arrangements). The first reason consisted of the double burden imposed on foreign producers in compelling them to 'adopt advertising or sales promotion schemes which differ from one Member State to another'.[70] The second reason did not require a double burden to be imposed on foreign producers to bring the national measure under review. It would be sufficient that the producer will be forced 'to discontinue a scheme he considers particularly effective'.[71] It would appear from the recent decisions of the Court that it would be ready partly to revive *Oosthoek's* with the additional burden test now restated as a discriminatory test.[72] But this will erode much of the certainty associated with the *Keck* distinction: will other types of double costs, such as those arising from having to change a commercial or marketing strategy according to the State in which the product is sold also be considered as giving rise to *prima facie* violations of Community free movement law?[73]

3. The Present Criteria: The Prevention of Market Access Test

The recent decisions of the Court also reflect a concern with measures which bar market access even if non-discriminatory or not regulating product requirements. That is the case even where, arguably, the best interpretation is that there is no double burden present. In *Monsees*, the Court states that the effect of the Austrian rule 'is, in fact, to make all international transit by road of animals for slaughter almost impossible in Austria'.[74] As a consequence such rule could be considered as barring market access even if not imposing a double burden on imported products.[75] That the Court may be moving to a test based on market access has been been suggested by Weatherill[76] and Snell and Andenas.[77] More

[70] Case 286/81, *Oosthoek's* [1982] ECR 4575, para 15. [71] ibid.

[72] Something which was proposed some years ago by Defalque ('Le concept de discrimination en matiere de libre circulation des marchandises', CDE, 23 année, 1987, 471, mainly at 481) in what constituted a broader dressing of Marenco's theory.

[73] One just has to recall the television advertising cases mentioned above.

[74] *Monsees* (n 64 above) para 29.

[75] However, this rule can also be considered as regarding a product requirement.

[76] After *Keck* (n 44 above).

[77] 'Exploring the Outer Limits—Restrictions on the Free Movement of Goods and Services' (1999) 10 European Business Law Review 252, notably at 272 but with doubts.

recently, Weiler has argued for a test of this type to be adopted by the Court. Weiler envisions a reading of *Keck* restricting the scope of Article 28 EC but maintaining two types of *prima facie* prohibitions. The first will be the general rule of free movement prohibiting discrimination, *de iure* or *de facto*, against imported products.[78] The second, which he calls the special rule of free movement, prohibits 'national measures which prevent access to the market of imported goods'.[79] The latter would mean that practically all national measures regarding product-characteristics, to which the Court refers in *Keck*, would have to be justified according to a legitimate and proportional public interest. In this regard, Weiler's criterion would be quite similar to that of the Court in *Keck*. But Weiler would also *prima facie* prohibit market regulations barring access to the national market such as an absolute prohibition on the sale of a certain product.[80] The key to understanding Weiler's criterion is the notion of a bar to market access. Hindering market access is not sufficient for a measure to be caught by the *prima facie* prohibition of Article 28 EC, it is necessary that such measure bars market access for public interest justification to be required. By focusing on the prevention of market access, Weiler is *prima facie* prohibiting either absolute bans on the sales of a product or national measures which do not authorize the entry into a national market of a product exactly as it is produced in its market of origin (for example, if it has to change its label or composition).

In my view, the Court is expanding the *Keck* criterion in two ways: first, by also considering as measures having an equivalent effect to a quantitative restriction national rules which govern selling arrangements or marketing circumstances but also impose an additional cost on products from other Member States by having to comply with a different set of rules from those of their State of origin; secondly, the Court is also ready to review national measures which directly affect access to the market. Interestingly, such developments in the free movement of goods can lead to a uniform interpretation of the different free movement rules.

[78] ibid at 372.

[79] ibid at 373.

[80] ibid at 372–373. Weiler departs from a parallelism with Article XI of the GATT as recently interpreted by a panel and the Appellate Body in the *Beef Hormones* Case (EC Measures Concerning Meat and Meat Products (Hormones) WT/D526/AB/R and WT/D528/AB/R, 16 January 1998). As Weiler describes, the recent developments of the WTO trade law appear to highlight a twofold strategy regarding trade restrictions: one path, corresponding to the more traditional interpretation of GATT, focusing on discrimination oriented restrictions on trade; another path, derived from Article XI, focusing on obstacles-oriented prohibition on points of entry and/or market access denial (at 358).

4. The Other Free Movement Rules: From Dissonance to an Emerging Uniform Approach

Soon after *Keck* was decided the Court appeared to extend its judicial activism to the other free movement rules. In the freedom to provide services the enhanced activism of the Court could be said to pre-date *Keck* since, as we have seen above, there was a progressive tendency for uniformity with the free movement of goods prior to *Keck*. The Court has since *Säger* adopted a test similar to the wide interpretation of *Cassis de Dijon*. It stated:

Article 59 of the Treaty requires not only the elimination of all discrimination against a person providing services on the ground of his nationality but also the abolition of any restriction, even if it applies without distinction to national providers of services and to those of other Member States, when it is liable to prohibit or otherwise impede the activities of a provider of services established in another Member State where he lawfully provides similar services. [Moreover . . .] as a fundamental principle of the Treaty, the freedom to provide services may be limited only by rules which are justified by imperative reasons relating to the public interest and which apply to all persons or undertakings pursuing an activity in the State of destination, in so far as that interest is not protected by the rules to which the person providing the services is subject in the Member State in which he is established. In particular, those requirements must be objectively necessary in order to ensure compliance with professional rules and to guarantee the protection of the recipient of services and they must not exceed what is necessary to attain those objectives.[81]

More striking than the developments in the freedom to provide services is the shift operated in the case law on the free movement of persons (establishment and workers). Two decisions signalled the shift in approach in areas where the Court had long remained closely attached to the principle of non-discrimination or national treatment. In *Gebhard*, the Court interpreted the right of establishment as a fundamental freedom guaranteed by the Treaty and proceeded to state:

that national measures liable to hinder or make less attractive the exercise of fundamental freedoms guaranteed by the Treaty must fulfil four conditions: they must be applied in a non-discriminatory manner; they must be justified by imperative requirements in the general interest; they must be suitable for securing the attainment of the objective which they pursue; and they must not go beyond what is necessary in order to attain it.[82]

[81] Case C-76/90 *Säger* [1991] ECR I-4221, paras 12 and 15. See, confirming this decision: Case C-275/92 *Schindler* [1994] ECR I-1039; Case C-3/95 *Reisebüro Broede* [1996] ECR I-6511, and Case C-398/95 *Syndesmos ton en Elladi Touristikon kai Taxidiotikon Grafeion*, judgment of the Court of 5 June 1997, not yet published.

[82] Case C-55/94 *Gebhard* [1995] ECR I-4165, para 37.

In the famous *Bosman* case, the Court extended such criteria to the field of free movement of workers.[83] This could indicate that to less activism on the free movement of goods was going to correspond more activism with regard to the other free movement rules. However, I currently believe that that would not be the case and that the Court is merging its approaches to the different free movement rules. The revival of Article 28 EC which I have noted before together with recent cases on the free movement of persons which restricted the potential of *Bosman et al*[84] lead me to conclude that the Court is preparing a single approach to free movement rules.

In the free movement of services such harmonization was already expected and should be welcomed.[85] First, the free movement of services has, in economic terms, many similarities to the free movement of goods. Secondly, as with goods, most of the legislative areas impacting on marketing integration on services are subject to majority voting in the Community legislative process and therefore this is an equal condition for goods and services to provide for legislative harmonization. Thirdly, it would frequently be extremely difficult for the Court to distinguish the effects on the free movement of goods from the effects on the freedom to provide services. Cases which presently are not accepted for review if one makes a strict application of the *Keck* test to Article 28 EC may be brought back in into the Court through the free movement of services: challenges on pharmaceutical or liquor retail sales monopolies can be challenged as a restriction on the freedom to provide services (imagine such products are sold through the Internet or by catalogue from another Member State), for example. And the same can be said of restrictions on advertising which can be seen as restrictions on the provision of advertising services by foreign companies.[86] Recent decisions of the Court have stressed once again how

[83] Case C-415/93 *Bosman* [1995] ECR I-4921, paras 102–104. This decision, however, comes in a sequence of progressive activism of the Court in this area of the law. According to Johnson and O'Keefe, writing in 1994, also in the area of free movement of workers, the Court has, 'over the past five years, begun to demonstrate a more open hostility towards national measures which although not discriminatory, are capable of hindering the free movement of workers': E Johnson and D O'Keefe, 'From Discrimination to Obstacles to Free Movement: Recent Developments Concerning the Free Movement of Workers 1989–1994' (1994) 31 CMLR 1313, at 1314.

[84] Weatherhill makes an excellent attempt to make a global and common reading of the recent case law on the four freedoms. However, even this author appears to recognize, at that time, that his reading was more a proposal to the Court (offering the possibility to construct a future single approach to the different freedoms) than an actual faithful interpretation of the decisions of the Court. See Weatherhill (n 52 above).

[85] See Jukka Snell and Mads Andenas, Chapter 4 below, Jukka Snell, Chapter 8 below and José Luís da Cruz Vilaça, Chapter 2 above.

[86] See Joined Cases C-34, 35 and 36/95 *Konsumentombudsmannen (KO) v De Agostini* [1997] ECR I-1141, and the comment by Cruz Vilaça, 'An Exercise on the Application of Keck and Mihouard in the Field of Free Provision of Services', in *Mélanges en Hommage à Michel Waelbroek* (Bruxelles, Bruylant, 1999), which argues, however, that it would have been possible for the Court to apply *Keck* in this case and arrive at the same final outcome (see 806–807).

difficult it is for the Court to prevent challenges to national rules under the free movement of services which it no longer accepted to review under Article 28 EC.[87] This explains why the Court appears, with some hesitation,[88] to move towards a uniform approach in the free movement of goods and the freedom to provide services. The *Alpine Investments* distinction from *Keck* could be seen as reflected in the more recent decisions on the free movement of goods which focus on the prevention of market access and/or market ban. In *Alpine Investments*, the Court argued that the measure was *prima facie* prohibited under the freedom to provide services because, albeit related to selling arrangements or services, it directly prevented market access.[89] We have seen that recent free movement of goods cases appear to share that rationale.

But the Court also appears to move to a coordination and symmetry of its approach on the free movement of persons with that highlighted for the free movement of goods. First, both in *Bosman* and *Gebhard* the Court also argued that the provisions at stake prevented market access to the individuals in question. They are therefore similar to the decisions barring market access to imported products which, as I have argued, the recent case law includes under the scope of measures having equivalent effect to quantitative restrictions. Similarly, the same ban occurs with regard to all those national measures which require nationals of other Member States to comply with specific qualifications or requirements. These rules both prevent market access and impose a double burden on products, services or nationals of other Member States. Previously, those types of measures were only subject to a principle of equivalence but now those requirements can no longer be imposed, even in the absence of equivalent requirements in the country of origin, if they are not proportional and necessary to the pursuit of a legitimate public interest.[90] The same occurs with regard to other restrictions on the free movement of persons which directly affect market access even if non-discriminatory against nationals of other Member States.[91] This movement towards harmony would also explain recent decisions regarding the free movement of persons which did not accept a *prima facie* challenge to measures which nevertheless restricted the free movement

[87] See Case C-67/98 *Questore di Verona*, judgment of the Court of 21 October 1999, not yet published; Case C-124/97 *Markku Juhani*, judgment of the Court of 21 September 1999, not yet published. See also the Commission decision to start an infringement proceeding against Germany over restrictions on the marketing of CDs (for violation of the freedom to provide services).

[88] See the cases in n 87 above.

[89] Case C-384/93 *Alpine Investments* [1995] ECR I-1141. Whether that was actually the case is a different question. See Maduro, 'The Saga of Article 30 EC Treaty' (1998) 5 MJECL 298, at 315.

[90] Case C-234/97 *Bobadilha* [1999] ECR I-4773.

[91] See Case C-378/97 *Wijsenbeek* [1999] ECR I-6207.

of persons. In *Futura Participations*,[92] regarding the impact of certain tax benefits on the right of establishment, the measure challenged was not discriminatory, nor a ban on market access, nor did it impose an additional burden on companies of other Member States. As a consequence the Court did not even apply a proportionality test and dismissed the case on its face.

In this way it would be possible to reconcile the case law of the different free movement rules relating to non-discriminatory provisions under the following tests:

(1) all national measures which impose an additional burden on products, services or nationals of other Member States by reason of having to comply with a set of rules different from that which they have had to comply with in their country of origin are *prima facie* prohibited and need to be justified as necessary and proportional to the pursuit of a legitimate public interest;

(2) all measures which, as a matter of law or of fact, bar access to the market to products, services or nationals of other Member States are also to be considered as *prima facie* prohibited and need to be justified as necessary and proportional to the pursuit of a legitimate public interest.

It appears that with some hesitations the Court is defining a harmonized approach to free movement rules. Whether this approach is based on the best normative criteria and whether it should be harmonized at all will be discussed next.

5. Problems with the Emerging Harmonized Approach

The double burden test arises from a concern with the additional costs imposed on imported products by having to comply with a new set of rules. This is particularly clear in the case of measures affecting product requirements. Those measures that require changes to be made to products in the form of requirements on labelling, packaging, shape, composition or controls will normally impose costs on imported products that are not imposed on national products. This is so because imported products will have to conform to two sets of rules: those of their own market and those of the market into which they are imported. Thus, they will be submitted to two sets of requirements over inspection, labelling, packaging, etc. It could even be said that all measures requiring changes to be made to imported products discriminate against imports as they impose on them an extra cost to which national products are not submitted. Therefore, it is common to associate the double burden test with a broad rationale of non-discrimination and anti-protectionism. Its extension to measures not related to product

92 Case C-250/95 *Futura Participations* [1997] ECR I-2471.

requirements would simply reflect the fact that frequently there are also additional costs involved in changing aspects of the marketing or sales strategies of a product to conform with a new set of national rules.

There are strong normative problems involved in the justification of a double burden test which, as stated, is frequently based on a broad concept of discrimination. Under the double burden test, discrimination becomes any sort of burden incurred by foreign nationals, including the cost involved in adapting to a different national legislation. The difference between discrimination and lack of harmonization is thus trivial or, even, non-existent. It is certainly possible to argue that whenever there is a double burden imposed on imports from the lack of harmonization of national regulations there is discrimination against those imports. The relevant questions are: what does this tell us and why should the Court be involved in reviewing all non-harmonized national measures? Shouldn't that harmonizing role be performed by the Community political process? A discrimination test is of little value without a normative theory of anti-protectionism or other constitutional construction supporting it.

The second element of the emerging harmonized construction of the free movement rules by the Court is the prevention of market access or, as recently argued by Joseph Weiler, the notion of a bar to market access. Hindering market access is not sufficient for a measure to be caught by the *prima facie* prohibition of Article 30 EC, it is necessary that such measure bars market access for it to require a legitimate and proportional public interest justification. By focusing on prevention of market access, Weiler is *prima facie* prohibiting either absolute bans on the sales of a product or national measures which do not authorize the entry into a national market of a product exactly as it is produced in its market of origin (this second case corresponds to the double burden test). Such criterion is very practical but it has a fundamental normative problem: prevention of market access as defined by Weiler is founded on a formal definition. If, for example, a product is required to include a label in the language of the importing country, that will bar its entry into that market (because, without the label, it cannot be imported). On the other hand, if a company sells products via catalogue from another State and is required to change the language used in that catalogue that does not bar access to the market by those products (they can still be sold, though not through those catalogues).[93] However, the latter national regulation may constitute a higher burden for imported products than the former. In the first case, the costs of adding a new label will be marginal for the company and it could easily continue to sell its

[93] Of course, it is still possible to complement the first test with a second one designed to capture measures whose economic impact on the products would amount to a prevention of market access. But, if that is done, the legal certainty and judicial restriction brought by the original test will be lost.

products on the importing State after complying with that minimum requirement. In the second case, though the product is not physically barred, the economic costs involved in changing the entire catalogue or altering a market strategy may strongly restrict the imports of those products. A strong normative criterion based on market access prevention would have to focus on the economic costs involved in changing either product characteristics, selling arrangements or other marketing conditions. But such criterion would immediately require complex economic and social judgments by courts, which both the Court and Joseph Weiler wish to prevent. The concept of prevention of market access also shares with the notion of double burden the risk of being too broad by including all legislative disparities regarding products characteristics in the *prima facie* prohibition net of Article 28 EC (all those disparities amount to a prevention of market access).

Of course, these tests attempt to make a delicate balance between the use of judicial resources and the normative aims embraced by the authors as inserted in the free movement rules. One of the conclusions from *Keck* is that what the Court gains in certainty and freeing of resources, it loses in normative coherence. But this is not, in itself, a bad choice. As I have repeatedly stated in this chapter, judicial resources (both physical and in legitimacy) are limited and this means that there are important choices regarding the allocation of judicial activity to be made. Constant trade-offs take place between what the Court should do and what it can do. The only valid question regarding the present trends in the jurisprudence of the Court is whether there is a better alternative in addressing the normative questions of free movement while efficiently allocating the resources of the Court.

III. HARMONY AND DISSONANCE: *ALLEGRO ASSAI, SOSTENUTO*

The question regarding the interpretation of the different free movement rules in the post-*Keck* period should not be whether the Court's present criteria are effective in reviewing all national measures restricting trade but whether the Court's choice to review some measures and not others is the right choice taking into account the other sources of demand for judicial activism. In a world of scarce judicial resources where should they be primarily allocated? The answer to this question depends on the institutional alternatives to the Court in promoting free trade with regard to the different free movement rules. It depends on the degree of trust we can have in national political processes to regulate those areas of the law while taking into account the broader interests of the EU and other Member States in free trade. It also depends on the capacity of the EU political process to bring about harmonized legislation in those different areas of the law.

Finally, it depends on the market structures in the economic areas corresponding to the different free movement rules and the way those structures may hinder or facilitate economic integration. Only by looking at these different institutional alternatives can one appropriately allocate the available judicial resources and decide on the different degrees of judicial activism that may be required with regard to the different free movement rules.

In the area of the free movement of goods, the Court has chosen to restrict the scope of Article 28 EC and increase the certainty of its application. The Court's case law will not mean that, as feared by Gromley, we are in 'an open season for all sorts of restrictions'.[94] It may be true that some or many national measures restricting trade will no longer be reviewed by the Court but that tell us nothing about whether the Court should review those measures. First, there are restrictions on trade arising from legislative disparities that can be better dealt with by the legislative process of the EU. Secondly, even where there may be good arguments in favour of the judicial review of national measures restricting free movement, there may be better arguments for the Court not to do it. The Court has to allocate its resources among different functions and areas of the law. As we have seen, the strong activism followed by the Court in the area of free movement of goods was possible because of the lower litigation generated in other areas of Community law and the more restricted scope given to other Treaty provisions such as the free movement of persons. There may now be good reasons for the Court to extend its activism and resources to promote the free movement of persons and the review of Community legislation.

However, it now appears that the Court is promoting a uniform approach to the different free movement rules. After *Keck*, it appeared that, at the same time that it was restricting the scope of the free movement of goods, the Court was expanding the scope of application of the free movement of services and persons.[95] But the more recent developments in the different areas of the Court's case law discussed above indicate that the Court may be moving towards a uniform approach based on the formal concepts of double burden and prevention of market access. Such a uniform approach may be praised for finally attempting to generate a higher degree of legal certainty and coherence in the interpretation of the different free movement provisions. On the other hand, a uniform approach based on the formal legal concepts currently affirmed by the Court will ignore the different claims for judicial activism arising from the different institutional contexts of the different free movement provisions.

94 'Two Years After Keck' (1996) 19 Fordham International Law Journal 866, at 885.

95 As stated above the most emblematic decisions of this expansion were the rulings in *Säger*, *Gebhart* and *Bosman*. See my analysis of this trend in *We The Court* (n 26 above) and 'The Saga of Article 30' (n 89 above).

The institutional contexts of services and goods may justify an identical degree of judicial activism to these free movement rules, since the capacity for intervention of the EU political process tends to be similar in these areas of the law and the market structures of services and goods also tend to be similar. But the same is not the case with the free movement of persons. The areas of free movement of persons tend, at this stage of the Common Market, to be those which are still more strongly dominated by national interest groups since they tend to regulate access to professional activities, work and services whose conditions are normally set up on the basis of the conditions of the national market and national education and qualifications. Moreover, these type of requirements associated with the free movement of persons (eg professional qualifications) normally imply a higher burden imposed on out-of-state nationals which further contributes to the lower mobility of people as compared to goods. Furthermore, this is an area where, unlike goods and services, the EU decision-making process is still (to some extent) dominated by a unanimity rule[96] and by high transaction and information costs that make the EU political process a less viable alternative to promote market integration through legislative harmonization (contrary to what is now the case in goods and services). The free movement of persons is the area which has deserved less legislative attention.[97] To this, one should also add the higher information and transaction costs associated with the litigants to be benefited from free movement of persons (mainly, in the case of independent professionals and workers) which requires the Court to provide higher incentives for litigation in these areas.

The problems highlighted in the institutional alternatives to the Court in integrating the market in free movement of persons justify a reversal of priorities in the Court's case law on the different free movement rules. A higher priority for judicial activity should be given to the previously more 'neglected' area of free movement of persons. This means that the Court should concentrate its judicial resources in those areas where market integration is less developed. In a world of limited judicial resources, in reviewing national measures which restrict free movement it makes more sense to give judicial priority to those restrictions which are less likely to be overcome by the other institutional alternatives.

Still, it may be argued that there is no basis in the Treaty to adopt a more active approach with regard to the free movement of persons and that it will also be difficult to keep the two trends of case law separated. The problems

[96] See the exceptions imposing unanimity voting in the specific empowering clauses of the free movement of persons (Articles 42 and 47 EC) and, for the other legislative areas affecting the free movement of persons, the requirement of unanimity of Article 95 EC.

[97] According to Johnson and O'Keefe, free movement of workers is 'an area of law which, in recent years at least, has received scant legislative attention from the Council': 'From Discrimination to Obstacles to Free Movement' (1994) 31 CMLRev 1313.

arising from the lack of a uniform legal criterion presented above in the context of the relation between goods and services may also, albeit to a lesser extent, resurface in the relation between goods and services and persons. For example, cases which presently are not accepted for review under Article 28 EC could be brought through the 'back door' via the free movement of persons: Sunday trading has already been challenged under Article 52 EC;[98] even the prohibition of a resale at a loss such as that in *Keck* can be seen as a restriction on the right of establishment of supermarket companies. This would again raise the issue of legal coherence.

The solution to this problem lies in the abandoning of formal legal concepts and the clear assumption of the institutional aspects involved in the legal options faced by the Court. A criterion which will recognize the institutional choices made by the Court and would determine the degree of judicial intervention on the basis of the available institutional alternatives to the Court in promoting market regulation and integration will safeguard legal coherence while authorizing the Court to exert different degrees of judicial activism on the basis of those different institutional alternatives. I have already designed such a test in the context of Article 28 EC, arguing that the ECJ should only second-guess national political processes where these are suspected of under-representing the interests of nationals of other Member States. I have made a distinction between rules affecting cross-national interests and national interests, the latter being suspected of suffering from an institutional malfunction in the representation of the interests of nationals of other Member States.[99] In this chapter, I cannot develop the application of such criterion to the other free movement rules but I would suggest that the extension of its rationale to the different free movement rules will maintain legal coherence while authorizing the Court to be more activist in the area of the free movement of persons. This is so, because, as argued before, the regulation of the free movement of persons tends to be subject to a higher degree of capture by national interest groups and, furthermore, the institutional alternatives to the Court in promoting market integration are less developed than in the area of services and goods. A criterion based on institutional alternatives would therefore authorize the Court to have different degrees of judicial activism with regard to the different free movement rules on the basis of their different levels of market integration and on the basis of the different conditions for intervention of the EU and national political processes.

[98] See Case C-78/93 Semeraro Casa [1996] ECR I-2975.
[99] See, for example, *We The Court* (n 26 above) at 166 ff.

4

Exploring the Outer Limits: Restrictions on the Free Movement of Goods and Services

JUKKA SNELL AND MADS ANDENAS[1]

I. INTRODUCTION

The approach of the European Court of Justice was initially more cautious to the free movement of services than to the free movement of goods.[2] However, by the early 1990s the case law in both fields showed marked similarities. The Court was clearly influenced by the strong arguments[3] in favour of a parallel approach in both areas.

Meanwhile doubts began to arise about the Court's view on the scope of Article 28 (ex 30) EC. These doubts culminated in 1993 in its decision in *Keck*[4] when the Court overruled some of its previous case law. The new approach of the Court to the free movement of goods gives new relevance to the question whether the EC Treaty provisions relating to services should be interpreted in the same way.

This chapter will explore, first of all, the economics of goods and services and the reasons for treating the four freedoms, especially the free movement of goods and services, in the same way. Second, it will examine the vertical division of power between the Community and the Member States. Arguments for decentralization will be presented. The connection between this issue and the scope given to the freedoms will be analysed. Third, the background to *Keck* and the judgment itself will be discussed. This will be followed, fourth, by an investigation of *Alpine Investments*.[5]

[1] We are grateful to Kelyn Bacon, Alison Burton, Damien Chalmers, Piet Eeckhout and Miguel Poiares Maduro for their comments.

[2] This is certainly true in relation to the general scope of the freedoms. However, some private parties are bound by Article 49 (ex 59) EC, see Case 36/74 *Walrave and Koch v UCI* [1974] ECR 1405, while the free movement of goods has a more limited personal scope, see Case 311/85 *VZW Vereniging van Vlaamse Reisbureaus v VZW Sociale Dienst van de Plaatselijke en Gewestlijke Overheidsdiensten* [1987] ECR 3801. See generally Jukka Snell, Chapter 8 below. See also Case C-384/93 *Alpine Investments BV v Minister van Financiën* [1995] ECR I-1141, analysed below in section V.

[3] See especially Advocate General Jacobs in his Opinion in Case C-76/90 *Manfred Säger v Dennemeyer & Co. Ltd* [1991] ECR I-4221.

[4] Cases C-267/91 and C-268/91 *Criminal Proceedings against Keck and Mithouard* [1993] ECR I-6097.

[5] Case C-384/93 *Alpine Investments BV v Minister van Financiën* [1995] ECR I-1141.

This is doctrinally speaking, the Court's most important post-*Keck* decision concerning the free movement of services. Fifth, some recent cases on Article 28 (ex 30) EC will be examined. Finally, some conclusions will be drawn.

We will make four propositions. The first one is normative or prescriptive: goods and services ought to be governed by the same legal principles. The second one is also normative: decentralization provides a suitable model for the Community, which implies a fairly narrow interpretation of the scope of the freedoms. The third one is positive or descriptive: in *Keck* the Court adopted such a narrow interpretation, based on the prohibition of double burden and other forms of discrimination. The fourth one is also descriptive: in *Alpine Investments*, when read together with *Bosman*, the Court constructed the scope of the freedom to provide services widely, an approach that is not in line with the judgment in *Keck*. We argue that the Court should have applied the principles that were behind its judgment in *Keck* limiting the scope of Article 49 (ex 59) EC and adopting a uniform approach to the free movement of goods and services.

II. THE UNIFORM INTERPRETATION OF THE FREEDOMS

In this section, we will examine the economics of goods and services.[6] We will argue for a parallel approach to the four freedoms, especially to the free movement of goods and the freedom to provide services. Economically speaking, goods are material and services non-material products. From the economic point of view, there are no good reasons for treating them differently. From the legal point of view, the basic concept of justice requires us to treat two similar things in the same way. To contribute to the building of a transparent European legal system, it is necessary to adopt a common approach that is based on generally accepted principles, not on dubious distinctions.

The international trade in services is not as great as the trade in goods. Transaction costs can prohibit such trade and in general economies of scale tend to be less important in the field of services than in the field of goods. Furthermore, a service provider must often perform activities in close proximity to the buyer, and this may make it necessary for the supplier to establish itself in the same country as the customer by using foreign direct investment.[7]

[6] It is important to note that some activities classified as services from the economic point of view fall under the right of establishment.

[7] See W Molle, *The Economics of European Integration Theory, Practice, Policy* (2nd edn, Aldershot, 1994) 140 and ME Porter, *The Competitive Advantage of Nations* (London 1990) 248. Permanent establishment brings the situation outside the scope of the Treaty provisions on the freedom to provide services.

The importance of international trade in services is rising, however. Inside the Community, service trade is taking an increased share of GDP[8] and in recent years intra-Community trade in services has grown particularly quickly. When compared with trade in goods, however, the significance of trade in services is still rather limited.[9]

Several factors contribute to the internationalization of services. Services are playing a growing role in domestic economic activity. Service needs are becoming more similar in many countries. Buyers are more mobile and better informed. Economies of scale are rising and service providers can differentiate themselves as European or global firms. Personnel are more mobile. New technologies are greatly increasing the capacity of service providers to supply services without the need for people to travel, and enabling competition in previously sheltered sectors. Furthermore, differences still persist as regards cost, quality and range of services available in different countries.[10]

At a general level, the economics of trade in goods and trade in services are similar. The classical theory of comparative advantage applies with equal force regardless of whether it is goods or services that are sold or bought.[11] The trade policy goals, principles, procedures and techniques that have been used to deal with goods can also be applied to services, especially when it comes to tools suitable for abolishing non-tariff barriers.[12]

In fact, markets in goods and services are generally characterized as product markets while labour, capital and entrepreneurship are considered to be parts of production factor markets.[13] Correspondingly, the former are dealt with under customs union theory and the latter under Common Market theory.

However, there are a number of points that have been raised to argue that goods and services are dissimilar and need to be treated differently. In our view, none of these arguments justifies a divergent approach.

Thus, the modes of supply of services can differ from goods and often involve the movement of factors of production. Services can move in four different ways:[14]

[8] In 1996 the service sector produced 66.4 per cent of gross value added in the European Union, *Facts Through Figures: Eurostat Yearbook at a Glance* (1998) 14.

[9] See Molle (n 7 above) 146–147. For recent figures, see *The Economist* (1 April 2000) 118.

[10] See Molle (n 7 above) 139–140 and Porter (n 7 above) 250–252.

[11] See G Feketekuty, *International Trade in Services: An Overview and Blueprint for Negotiations* (Cambridge, Mass, 1988) 123–124 and B Hindley and A Smith, 'Comparative Advantage and Trade in Services' (1984) 7 *The World Economy* 369, 386 and 388–389.

[12] See Feketekuty (n 11 above) 160 and 174.

[13] See Molle (n 7 above) 10.

[14] See P Eeckhout, *The European Internal Market and International Trade: A Legal Analysis* (Oxford, 1994) 10. Slightly different classification can be found, eg, in GP Sampson

(1) the recipient moves towards the provider, for example a patient travels to another country to receive hospital treatment;
(2) the provider moves towards the recipient, for example a construction firm sends personnel to another state to build something;
(3) the provider and the recipient both move, for example in the course of providing a transport service;
(4) the service itself travels, for example via telecommunications.

Some services may only employ one mode of supply, but often different methods are substitutable.[15] For example, a doctor giving medical advice can do so in person by moving himself or through the movement of the patient. Alternatively, the advice can perhaps be given via telecommunications. The method chosen depends on the state of technology and on the market conditions.[16] The improvements in telecommunications have enabled the service itself to move in many cases where in the past the movement of persons was required.

The existence of the different modes of supply does not change the basic economic calculus. The rationale for trade is the same even if it involves the movement of production factors. The welfare effects are similar regardless of the mode of supply.[17] From the point of view of economic efficiency, liberalization of all modes of supply is desirable in order to avoid distortions, but this does not mean that partial liberalization could not be beneficial.[18]

In the context of interpreting the Community rules on the free movement of services, the difference in modes of supply is not very significant. First, the establishment of commercial presence, and often also the movement of labour, fall under the Treaty rules on the free movement of persons. Any differences caused by these considerations affect directly the interpretation of Articles 39 (ex 48) and 43 (ex 52) EC, not the construction of Article 49 (ex 59).

Secondly, the movement of the factors of production is also a funda-

and RH Snape, 'Identifying the Issues in Trade in Services' (1985) 8 *The World Economy* 171, 172–175. See also GATS Article I:2 and F. Weiss, 'The General Agreement on Trade in Services' (1995) 32 CMLRev 1177, 1190–1193. P Oliver, 'Goods and Services: Two Freedoms Compared' in M Doris and A Walsche (eds), *Mélanges en Hommage à Michel Waelbroeck* (Bruxelles, 1999) 1384–1386 contains an interesting comparison of these modes of supply with import and export of goods.

[15] See Müller, 'An Economic Analysis of Different Regulatory Regimes of Transborder Services' in D Friedmann and EJ Mestmäcker (eds), *Rules for Free International Trade in Services* (Baden-Baden, 1990) 345–348, who examines the 'degree of separation' in locational, intermediate, and knowledge or skill-based services.

[16] See P Nicolaides, 'Economic Aspects of Services: Implications for a GATT Agreement' (1989) 23 JWT 125, 126–127 and Sampson and Snape (n 14 above) 173–174.

[17] See Feketekuty (n 11 above) 102–105 and Hindley and Smith (n 11 above) 375.

[18] See Feketekuty (n 11 above) 166–167 and Sampson and Snape (n 14 above) 177–178.

mental part of the Community system, which is not merely a simple customs union. The migration and investment issues that cause such problems in the global context do not create the same difficulties in the sphere of European integration.[19]

Another difference between goods and services is that the latter tend to be much more heavily regulated than the former. Government intervention is significantly more prevalent in the service sector.[20]

The form of regulation tends to differ as well. With goods, the regulation usually applies to the product. With services, the producer is most often the target. The content of the service itself is only seldom stipulated.[21] Instead, the legislation sets rules relating to the qualities of the service provider.[22] How a doctor should perform an operation is not stipulated, but the qualifications required of a doctor are regulated.

Legitimate concerns of consumer protection are partly behind the heavy regulation of many services. Consumers may be unable to assess the quality of the service. This may occur more often in the case of intangible services than tangible goods. Especially in the case of certain professional services, the consumers cannot determine the quality even *post facto*. The market structure may be even such that low-quality producers are able to drive out high-quality providers, with detrimental consequences for the whole market. Hence, public regulation is needed to correct the information asymmetries.[23]

It has also been claimed that the service sector is more important for the society than the goods sector and therefore needs to be regulated more intensively. This is too general.[24] Telecommunications and postal services are crucial for the functioning of a country but so are petrol and cars.

However, the existence of regulation does not make services fundamentally different from goods. Regulation is hardly unknown in the goods sector. A consumer has often less knowledge of the qualities of a good than

[19] See further below.

[20] See J Bhagwati, 'Services' in Finger and Olechowski (eds), *The Uruguay Rounds: A Handbook on the Multilateral Trade Negotiations* (Washington, 1987) 209 and Hindley and Smith (n 11 above) 377–378.

[21] In some sectors, such as insurance, the 'service product' may also be subject to regulation.

[22] Bhagwati (n 20 above) 209 and P Nicolaides, *Liberalizing Service Trade: Strategies for Success* (London, 1989) 44–45.

[23] See Nicolaides (n 16 above) 126–127, J-M Sun and J Pelkmans, 'Regulatory Competition in the Single Market' (1995) 33 JCMS 67, 85, and M van Empel, 'The Visible Hand in Invisible Trade' [1990] LIEI 23, 30–31. A different question is whether the government should intervene merely by providing information on the quality, or should it go further and regulate the entry to the industry. See on this Hindley and Smith (n 11 above) 379.

[24] See G Feketekuty, 'Trade in Professional Services: an Overview' in Jackson *et al*, *Legal Problems of International Economic Relations: Cases, Materials and Text on the National and International Regulation of Transnational Economic Relations* (3rd edn, St Paul, 1995) 894.

the vendor, especially in the case of highly technical products.[25] In addition, much service trade, especially in business services, is conducted between professionals. They are better informed and able to protect their interests than private consumers.[26] For these reasons the regulatory difference is one of degree, not one of kind.[27]

National regulation creates most barriers to trade in services. Unlike in the case of goods, it is very difficult to erect barriers to service trade at the border.[28] Tariffs and quotas are therefore not significant in the service sector.

The danger with regulatory measures is that they may create protectionist obstacles to imports.[29] In practice this may even be the real reason for regulation. The aim is sometimes the protection of domestic firms from foreign competition.[30] For practical reasons, it may have been necessary to involve service providers in regulating the industry. This is the case for example when professional bodies, due to their superior knowledge, are involved in regulating and policing the entry into the profession. The industry's main concern may naturally enough be the protection of its own interest, which usually means limiting competition, especially from abroad.[31] Service sector undertakings may also wield political power which enables them to engage in rent-seeking by lobbying.[32]

There may also be a tendency to abstain from deregulation on equity grounds. Existing service providers in regulated industries have often paid some form of entry fee in compensation for being able to reap supra-competitive profits. Deregulation which would cut the resale value of a taxi-licence would seem inequitable to somebody who has previously purchased a licence expecting it to give a permanent right to operate in a protected market. There may be a systematic tendency to resist deregulation even when the reasons for the original regulation have vanished, for example as a result of technical change.[33]

In fact, the intensive regulation of services can provide arguments both

[25] V Hatzopoulos, 'Exigences essentielles, impérativés ou impérieuses: une théorie, des théories ou pas de théorie du tout?' (1998) 34 RTD 191, 223 has emphasized that consumers need more information about services and especially about service providers than about goods and producers. He accepts, however, that there is a similar need in case of some goods. In addition, it may be argued that the origin of goods is also often of paramount importance to the consumer, as evidenced by the increasing reliance on brands.

[26] Van Empel (n 23 above) 28.

[27] See D Chalmers and E Szyszczak, *European Union Law, Vol II: Towards a European Polity?* (Aldershot, 1998) 362, Feketekuty (n 11 above) 161–162, and van Empel (n 23 above) 31.

[28] See Eeckhout (n 14 above) 11 and Feketekuty (n 11 above) 135 and 162.

[29] cf capital, where the problem might be import enticement.

[30] See Molle (n 7 above) 143, Nicolaides, *Liberalizing Service Trade* 56, and Porter 250.

[31] See Hindley and Smith (n 11 above) 380.

[32] See Porter (n 7 above) 263.

[33] See Hindley and Smith (n 11 above) 380.

against and for free trade in services. As far as regulation is necessary to protect legitimate interests, a purely free trade orientated approach could result in sub-optimal results. However, the heavy regulatory burden and the danger of protectionism, as a result of regulatory capture, mean that free trade may bring about great efficiency gains.[34]

The differences between goods and services in the intensity and methods of regulation are undoubtably real. They do not seem to necessitate a fundamentally different approach, however. The differences can be contained within the harmonization and justification mechanisms found in the Treaty and created by the case law. Some regulation of some services will be justified, just as some regulation of some goods. It may be that the Court will find more measures regulating services to be justified on the grounds of consumer protection than is the case with goods, and thus the harmonization process becomes more important in the service sector. This does not mean that a whole new approach has to be created for services, however. As stated before, the differences are of degree, not of kind.

A further difference between goods and services is the intangible, invisible character of many services. Services have been described as non-storable, requiring the simultaneity of provision and use, and as a process.[35]

This factor is important in the global context.[36] Traditionally in GATT, concessions are granted on specified and defined goods. However, due to the process-nature of services, definitions of services themselves could amount to restrictions. If the steps in a certain process were defined as a particular service, which, and only which, could be traded freely, a foreign service provider could not adjust to changing market conditions. If the service provider wanted to benefit from the concession, he would have to provide the service exactly in the manner prescribed. Any changes in the process would remove the service from the scope of the concession. Thus, the definition itself could become a protectionist straitjacket.[37] In the Community this difficulty does not create the same problems as the system is not based on carefully defined concessions.[38]

34 See Feketekuty (n 11 above) 161.

35 See Nicolaides (n 22 above) 6–12 for an excellent discussion. See also J Bhagwati, 'Splintering and Disembodiment of Services and Developing Nations' (1984) 7 *The World Economy* 133, 135–136.

36 In the Community context this means that services are not able to enter into free circulation in the same manner as goods. See Eeckhout (n 14 above) 11.

37 See Nicolaides (n 16 above) 127.

38 See, however, Chalmers and Szyszczak (n 27 above) 423, according to whom the fact that a service is a form of transaction which does not crystallize until the moment of commercialization means that the concept of double regulatory burden is inappropriate in the case of many services. In this context it is sufficient to say that most regulation of the service industry relates to the service provider rather than the service itself and the issue of double burden is just as applicable as in the field of goods. This issue will be discussed in more detail below in section V.

The non-material character of services may also increase the importance of intellectual property rules. A non-material service may be particularly susceptible to unlawful copying and retransmission.[39] This problem is hardly unique to the services sector, however. The pirating of branded goods, videotapes, CD-disks and so on is all too common.

Yet another important point is that some service sectors may be inherently imperfectly competitive. This may be due to information asymmetries about the characteristics of services.[40] In addition, in some services high costs of building and maintaining networks and large economies of scale may create (natural) monopolies or tight oligopolies. There may also be a universal service obligation, which requires the (monopolist) provider to supply the same service at the same price for all recipients at all times, regardless of cost differences. Examples of such sectors are segments of transportation and telecommunications markets.[41]

This difference may increase the importance of the rules on public undertakings, and on competition in general, in the field of services, although it has to be recognized that new technologies and growth have in recent years opened up many segments in traditionally non-competitive markets.[42] The importance of competition rules to the service sector is demonstrated, by Part II of GATS which includes rules on monopolies and exclusive services suppliers and on business practices.[43] A further discussion of the role of competition rules falls outside the scope of this chapter.[44]

Finally, it has been said that services constitute social, as well as economic, activities. Based on this it has been argued that the free movement of services could amount to economization of the social sphere and have disruptive consequences. It has been claimed that this can take place in two different ways. First of all, the free movement of services may disrupt regimes based on social consensus and accommodation but lacking any clear external objective. Secondly, it may reward the haves but not the have-nots.[45]

In our view, the social aspects of services should not lead to a divergence with goods. First, the 'social consensus and accommodation' may well be the result of rent-seeking by powerful private interest groups aimed at limit-

[39] See Hatzopoulos (n 25 above) 225.

[40] See A Sapir, 'The General Agreement on Trade in Services: From 1994 to 2000' (1999) 33 JWT 51, 52.

[41] See Feketekuty (n 11 above) 108–110 and 163–165.

[42] See Feketekuty (n 11 above) 108–109 and 164. An example of such a development are non-voice segments in telecommunications market.

[43] See generally Sapir (n 40 above) 54–55.

[44] See in general on developments in this field D Geradin, 'L'overture à la concurrence des entreprises de réseau. Analyse des principaux enjeux du processus de libéralisation' (1999) 35 CDE 13–48.

[45] Chalmers and Szyszczak (n 27 above) 363.

ing competition, especially from foreigners. The fact that a system is well entrenched (and even seemingly broadly supported) does not make it any less suspicious from a trade point of view. Take as an example a situation where one form of gambling is prohibited but another form is allowed. This may well reflect the power of the local gambling industry which has concentrated its efforts on the second market segment and does not want competition from the first segment, especially if foreign firms are well placed to enter the first segment. If the citizens really prefer the traditional domestic service providers and their methods, they can continue to purchase from them. Trade does not force consumers to change their habits, it just widens the choice available to them.

Secondly, it is somewhat difficult to complain that only rich consumers benefit from free trade in services. The trade does not in any way worsen the position of poor consumers. A system where a service not available to everybody is not available to anybody would be detrimental to the general welfare—not to mention unreasonable. In a situation where two persons would need expensive private medical treatment abroad, it is surely better to allow the one who is capable of paying to obtain it than to disallow it to both.[46]

It seems that the differences between goods and services have significant implications in the global context but not in the European one.[47] In an influential article in 1988, Professor Jackson listed reasons against incorporating services into GATT and argued for drafting a different agreement for them. His main arguments were the following. GATT was difficult to amend. It had inadequate institutional provisions. It would have been threatening and probably politically unacceptable to apply many of the GATT obligations, especially the national treatment requirement, in an indefinite and ambiguous way to all service industries. And finally, there were advantages in experimenting with rules for a few selected service industries.[48] None of these arguments seems to apply in the Community where the founding Treaty has made an unambiguous commitment to the general liberalization of services.

Altogether it may be said that all four freedoms found in the Treaty—the free movement of goods, persons, services and capital—form part of what

[46] An additional difference mentioned in Hatzopoulos (n 25 above) 224–225 is that the moment of the conclusion and execution of a contract may be more difficult to determine in the services sector. The regulator may also be able to intervene during the whole process of service provision, while in the goods sector intervention is restricted to production or commercialization stages. The importance of this difference from the point of view of the free movement of goods and services is unclear, however.

[47] See also van Empel (n 23 above) 38–42, who is much more optimistic about the prospects of the free trade in services in the Community context than in the global context.

[48] JH Jackson, 'Constructing a Constitution for Trade in Services' (1988) 11 *The World Economy* 187, 189–191.

economists call a common market.[49] For the realization of the full benefits of economic integration, both products and factors of production must be able to move freely so that economies of scale can be achieved and increased competition becomes possible. Free movement can also lead to competition between legal orders with all ensuing regulatory efficiencies. Thus, the different freedoms form a part of an economic unity. This is especially true in relation to goods and services, as both form a part of the product market. Economically, it makes little sense to have a different approach towards these two categories.

From the legal point of view, it is true that the four freedoms do appear in different provisions of the Treaty. The wording of these provisions differs from each other. Some seem to place the emphasis purely on the discriminatory nature of national measures while others can more easily be interpreted as requiring the abolition of all obstacles. Therefore, from a legal point of view, it would seem that each freedom should be interpreted separately according to the principles valid in that field.

The are two main reasons for having four separate freedoms instead of just one freedom of transfrontier economic activity. It was technically easier to write four sets of provisions instead of just one. More importantly, the Member States originally wanted to be able to control capital movements more strictly than the movement of goods, persons or services. This desire made a single set of rules impossible.[50]

However, it is clear that all four freedoms are based on the same more general provisions of the Treaty. Article 3(c) EC establishes as an activity of the Community 'an internal market characterised by the abolition, as between the Member States, of obstacles to the free movement of goods, persons, services and capital'. Article 14 (ex 7a) EC, which defines the concept of the internal market, refers to all four freedoms as well. These provisions indicate that the general approach to all freedoms must be similar.

The unity of the four freedoms is also suggested by the provisions granting regulatory competencies to the Community. For example, Article 94 (ex 100) EC does not distinguish between goods, persons, services and capital. Article 95 (ex 100a) EC grants the Community the regulatory competence *inter alia* to establish the internal market. Thus, the authority to remove obstacles is given by a single provision.[51]

[49] See Molle (n 7 above) 11.

[50] See P Behrens 'Die Konvergenz der wirtschafjtlichen Freiheiten in europäischen Gemeinschaftsrecht' (1992) EUR 145, 146–147. On reasons for controlling capital movements see Andenas, 'The Interplay of the Commission and the Court of Justice in Giving Effect to the Right to Provide Financial Services' in Craig and Harlow, *Law-making in the European Union* (London, 1998) 333–334.

[51] Article 95 (ex 100a) EC does not apply to the free movement of persons, however, and there are also harmonization provisions which only relate to certain freedom(s).

Furthermore, Article 50 (ex 60) EC defines 'services' as a residual category. This means that the chapter on the free movement of services applies only if no other freedoms are relevant. It would be peculiar if the interpretations of the free movement of goods, persons and capital diverged widely, as they share a common residual category.[52]

Moreover, and most importantly, a common approach to different freedoms would help Community law to develop into a legal *system* where the law is not just a group of particular rules but rather a coherent whole. Such a system makes the rules easier to understand and contributes to the respect for the law, as cases are decided on basis of generally approved principles, not on obscure technicalities.[53] After all, one of the basic notions of justice is that similar things are treated in the same way.

The free movements of goods and services are especially closely related when services are provided, for example, by post or by telecommunications and the movement of persons is not involved. In both cases transfrontier economic activity is at issue. The only difference is between the material and non-material nature of the product. In these situations the application of different rules to goods and services seems especially unjustified.[54] This has also been recognized in Opinion 1/94 (WTO)[55] of the European Court of Justice where it was held that the Common Commercial Policy covers the cross-frontier provision of services as well as trade in goods.

In purely practical terms it is often difficult to distinguish between goods and services. For example, a service can be provided in the form of transmission of goods. An example given by Advocate General Jacobs in his opinion in *Säger*[56] is illustrative in this respect. An educational service might be provided by sending a series of books or video-cassettes to a recipient in another Member State. This case might be dealt with either under Article 28 (ex 30) or Article 49 (ex 59) EC. It would be anomalous if the results were different depending on which provision was deemed to be applicable.[57]

The free movement of services clearly covers a wide range of circumstances. In many cases movement of persons is involved, and the closest

[52] Opinion of Advocate General Lenz in Case C-415/93 *Union Royale Belge des Sociétés de Football Association ASBL and others v Jean-Marc Bosman* [1995] ECR I-4921, para 200.

[53] See HD Jarass, 'Elemente einer Dogmatik der Grundfreiheiten' (1995) EUR 202 on the importance of dogmatic clarity.

[54] Case C-76/90 *Manfred Säger v Dennemeyer & Co. Ltd* [1991] ECR I-4221 para 24 of the opinion of Advocate General Jacobs. See also PJG Kapteyn and P VerLoren van Themaat, *Introduction to the Law of the European Communities, From Maastricht to Amsterdam* (3rd edn, London, 1998) 748.

[55] Opinion 1/94 [1994] ECR I-5276, para 44.

[56] See n 54 above at para 26.

[57] In the USA both the free movement of goods and services are regulated by the same provision: the commerce clause of the Constitution art I, § 8, which gives Congress the power to 'regulate Commerce . . . among the several states'. Similarly in Australia, s 92 of the Constitution regulates both goods and services.

connection is to the right of establishment. The distinguishing criterion is the temporary versus permanent nature of activities,[58] which is a matter of degree. Economic operators may in some instances even be able to select which set of rules applies to them. When they decide whether to provide services across borders or to form an agency, a branch or a subsidiary, they would have to consider regulatory consequences. If the approaches to the free movement of services and the right of establishment varied greatly, decisions on the form of economic activity would be affected by legal technicalities. They would not be made on purely commercial grounds as they should be. For these reasons the interpretation of Articles 43 (ex 52) and 49 (ex 59) should be roughly similar.[59]

However, the permanent nature of establishment makes it natural that all laws of the Member State in question are applied as long as they are not discriminatory. The application of every rule cannot be easily justified in the case of temporary provision of services.[60] Therefore, the Member States can justifiably impose stricter rules and the Court can afford to be more lenient over establishment than over services.[61]

It may be asked whether the Member States should be allowed to control more strictly instances where persons move than other situations. Both Articles 43(2) (ex 52(2)) and 50(3) (ex 60(3)) EC seem only to require that a person establishing himself or providing services is treated in the same way as the nationals of the host State. Moreover, free movement of persons is a sensitive area to the Member States as illustrated by decision-making rules in Articles 18 (ex 8a(2)) and 95 (ex 100a(2)). These provisions require unanimity while most other measures affecting the internal market can be adopted with a qualified majority. It could also be argued that economically the movement of natural persons is not as critical for the internal market as the other freedoms. The purpose of the Community is not to create large-scale migration. Most of the benefits of economic integration are achieved when capital and undertakings are allowed to move to take advantage of

[58] See Case C-55/94 *Reinhard Gebhard v Consiglio dell'Ordine degli Avvocati e Procuratori di Milano* [1995] ECR I-4165.

[59] See S Weatherill and P Beaumont, *EULaw* (3rd edn, London, 1999) 671. The Court has declared that Articles 43 (ex 52) and 49 (ex 59) (and 39 (ex 48)) are based on the same principles and has sometimes even declined to decide which provision is applicable. See Case 48/75 *Royer* [1976] ECR 497 and Case 36/74 *Walrave and Koch v UCI* [1974] ECR 1405.

[60] See n 54 above at para 23; Daniele, 'Non-discriminatory Restrictions to the Free Movement of Persons' (1997) 22 ELRev 1991, 196–197, and Weatherill and Beaumont (n 59 above) 671.

[61] See further the opinion of Advocate General Slynn in Case 279/80 *Criminal proceedings against Alfred John Webb* [1981] ECR 3305 at 3332, A. Arnull, *The European Union and its Court of Justice* (Oxford, 1999) 332–333, 353, Hatzopoulos (n 25 above) 225–226 and 233–234, and the Commission Interpretative Communication, *Freedom to Provide Services and the Interest of the General Good in the Second Banking Directive*, SEC(97) 1193 final, 22. See also C Hilson, 'Discrimination in Community Free Movement Law' (1999) 24 ELRev 445, 457.

abundant and correspondingly cheap human resources and when the products can then circulate freely. The movement of products and capital act as substitutes to the movement of persons.[62]

On the other hand, the wording of Articles 39 (ex 48), 43(1) (ex 52(1)) and 49 (ex 59) would seem to indicate that the provisions are not only concerned with (narrowly interpreted) discrimination.[63] In addition, the free movement of goods may also require that persons cross frontiers, for example to promote the products in question. Furthermore, the free movement of services applies also to situations where persons do not move. It would be somewhat difficult to have a split approach to a single freedom.

In a Community no longer restricted to economic issues it might be argued that the free movement of citizens is a fundamental human right which should never be restricted without weighty justification.[64] The fact that the decision-making rules require unanimity may also be seen as a reason for the Court to interfere more actively. Without the contribution of the Court, the more cumbersome nature of the decision making process might leave the Community paralysed in this field.[65]

Another reason for defending the free movement of natural persons is that a narrow interpretation would endanger the movement of undertakings. After all, according to Article 48 (ex 58) EC, companies and firms fulfilling certain criteria are treated in the same way as natural persons. The movement of undertakings is crucial to achieve the economic benefits of the internal market and for the creation of convergence between different regions of the Community.

Economic and monetary union would seem to require a greater mobility of natural persons inside the Community as exchange rate flexibility disappears. In the case of an asymmetric shock the declining area may have to 'export' persons. Take as an example a Member State whose economy depends on forestry, paper production etc. If there is a shock that hits this sector, but not the other sectors of the euro-zone economy, the unemployment in that Member State will rise relative to other Member States. As the Member State cannot use devaluation or lower interest rates to stimulate its

62 See Molle (n 7 above) 209.

63 See the Opinion of Advocate General Lenz in Case C-415/93 *Union Royale Belge des Sociétés de Football Association ASBL and others v Jean-Marc Bosman* [1995] ECR I-4921 paras 194–195 on the interpretation of Article 39 (ex 48).

64 See the Opinion of Advocate General Lenz in ibid para 203 and E Johnson and D O'Keeffe, 'From Discrimination to Obstacles to Free Movement: Recent Developments Concerning the Free Movement of Workers 1989–1994' (1994) 31 CML Rev 1313, 1330. In the USA the persons' right to move freely has sometimes been interpreted as fundamental right inherent in citizenship and given greater protection than the mere commerce clause can offer. See JE Nowak and RD Rotunda, *Constitutional Law* (5th edn, St Paul, 1995) 310. It is possible that a similar development will take place in the future also in the EU.

65 See Poiares Maduro, *We the Court* (Oxford, 1998) 101–102 and Weatherill, 'After *Keck*: Some Thoughts on How to Clarify the Clarification' (1996) 33 CML Rev 885, 906.

economy,[66] it may be that some of its citizens will have to migrate to find work. Fiscal transfers from the small Community budget cannot deal with the situation. Free movement of natural persons becomes more important.

In general it would seem that the approach of Community law to all four freedoms should be parallel. The free movement of goods and the free movement of services in particular should be dealt with in a uniform manner.

The Court has recognized the need for uniform interpretation, at least in the level of language. In *Gebhard*[67] it stated:

> national measures liable to hinder or make less attractive the exercise of fundamental freedoms guaranteed by the Treaty must fulfil four conditions: they must be applied in a non-discriminatory manner; they must be justified by imperative requirements in the general interest; they must be suitable for securing the attainment of the objective which they pursue; and they must not go beyond what is necessary in order to attain it.

III. VERTICAL DIVISION OF POWER IN THE COMMUNITY AND THE SCOPE GIVEN TO THE FREEDOMS

In this chapter we will examine the implications of different interpretations given to the freedoms for the vertical division of power between the Community and the Member States. We will also compare the merits of centralization and decentralization.

The scope given to the free movement rules is a constitutional question. At issue is the vertical division of powers in the Community. In all states, the vertical division of power between higher and lower levels of government has to be decided. The issue is especially relevant in federal states like Germany and the USA, where the correct allocation of competencies has been debated for decades and centuries.

Vertical division of powers is about centralization and decentralization. In the Community context, centralization means a system where the Community regulates economic activity intensively and the competence of the Member States is mostly pre-empted. Thus, the system of central government is replicated at the Community level. Decentralization means a system where most aspects of economic regulation are left to the Member States. However, the competence of the Member States is somewhat restricted by the Community rules on the free movement of goods, services, persons and capital.

66 Expansive fiscal policy and wage reductions remain available, however. It is also possible to build other domestic stabilisers.

67 See n 58 above at para 37.

This 'constitutional' tension underlies the case law of the Court on the scope of the four freedoms.[68] When the Court decides that a Member State measure constitutes a *prima facie* restriction on the freedom, it allocates the competence to regulate to the Community and, thus, supports the centralization argument.[69] If a national measure is held to be within the scope of the free movement provisions, its abolition or harmonization becomes necessary for the establishment of the internal market and the Community gains the competence to act.

Furthermore, the measure is seen as a restriction and thus harmonization becomes a natural, not merely a possible, policy option given the commitment of the Community to the internal market.[70] The logical reaction to a restriction is either to abolish or to harmonize it in order to remove the obstacles as required by Article 3(c) EC.[71] Thus, national regulation is seen only as a temporary stopgap solution pending Community action.[72]

If the Court, a central organ, goes further and finds a national measure unjustified or disproportionate, it dictates policy choices to the Member States. Its activities are not politically neutral: it contributes, especially if the review of national rules is intense, to a centrally determined 'arch-liberal laissez-faire policy'.[73]

Thus, the wider the scope given to the free movement provisions, the more centralized the Community system becomes. However, if the Court decides that the measure does not fall within the scope of the freedoms, it sides with decentralization, allocating the competence to the Member State.

A mechanical application of the *Dassonville*-formula according to which '[a]ll trading rules enacted by Member States which are capable of hindering, actually or potentially, directly or indirectly, intra-Community trade are to be considered as measures having an effect equivalent to quantitative restrictions'[74] leads to a great widening in the scope of the free movement

[68] Similarly, Poiares Maduro (n 65 above) 1, 59 and 67–68.

[69] This is not to say that Community regulation is only possible if a restriction has been found. The existence of a restriction is a sufficient but not a necessary condition for harmonization. See N Bernard, 'The Future of European Economic Law in the Light of the Principle of Subsidiarity' (1996) 33 CML Rev 633, 647–650 and JHH Weiler, 'The Constitution of the Common Market Place: Text and Context in the Evolution of the Free Movement of Goods' in Craig and de Búrca (eds), *The Evolution of EU Law* (Oxford, 1999) 362.

[70] See e.g. amended Proposal for a Directive concerning the distance marketing of consumer financial services (COM (1999) final, 23 July 1999). The proposal was made after the ECJ found in Case C-384/93 *Alpine Investments BV v Minister van Financiën* [1995] ECR I-1141 that a Dutch ban on cold calling was a justified restriction on the freedom to provide services.

[71] This remains true whether mandatory requirements are seen as justifying restrictions or as a part of the definition of Article 28 (ex 30) EC itself. Even in the latter case the effects of the national measure will bring it *prima facie* within the scope of the Article, and the fact that the intentions of the Member State were legitimate will not remove those adverse effects.

[72] See N Bernard, 'Discrimination and Free Movement in EC Law' (1996) 45 ICQL 82, 103.

[73] See Bernard (n 69 above) 637.

[74] Case 8/74 *Procureur du Roi v Dassonville* [1974] ECR 837, para 5.

provisions. If Article 28 (ex 30), or 49 (ex 59) EC, is thought to apply to all national regulations restricting the volume of trade and thus the volume of imports, almost any national measure can be caught by it, as nearly all rules are capable of having an adverse effect on the demand of some goods or services.[75]

A reading of the free movement provisions based on market access may be narrower, but may still lead to a control of a large number of Member State measures. Everything depends on the exact formulation and meaning given to the concept of market access.[76]

A narrower reading, based on the absence of discrimination, leads to greater decentralization. Member State regulations are respected as long as they do not place imported goods or services at a disadvantage. Again the exact definition of the concept of discrimination becomes important.

Throughout this chapter we advocate a reading based on a very wide concept of discrimination. It encompasses situations where a Member State applies its rules to circumstances which have already been subject to the regulatory system of another Member State. Thus, a double regulatory burden is considered discriminatory. In our view there is no significant difference between a national measure that treats similar situations differently, such as an imaginary French statute restricting advertising of whisky but not of cognac, and a national measure that treats different situations in a similar manner, such as the application of national composition requirements, even though foreign products have already complied with the rules of the exporting Member State. In both situations there is discrimination. The national decision-making machinery has failed, in the second scenario by omitting to take into account the legal system of the other Member States and, therefore, the objectively different situations of domestic and imported goods and services. From the point of view of foreign interests both scenarios are similar: the disadvantage they suffer is no less in the second situation.[77]

Centralization has both advantages and disadvantages. A centralized system can be politically stable, which also brings benefits of economic stability and predictability. Centralization reduces transaction costs of private operators, who only have to familiarize themselves with one set of regulations. A centrally run system can also cope with distortions caused by market failures, such as negative externalities.

[75] See Weatherill and Beaumont (n 59 above) 608–609. E White, 'In Search of the Limits to Article 30 of the EEC Treaty' (1989) 26 CML Rev 235, 253–254 shows, as an example of the absurdly wide reach of Article 28 (ex 30) so interpreted, how even national laws against violent crime could fall under the concept of a measure having equivalent effect to quantitative restriction, as they reduce the volume of sale of weapons.

[76] For criticism of this concept see below section V.

[77] On the reasons for this approach see further Snell (n 2 above) 226.

However, the economics of federalism teaches us that it is better to have multiple legislators than just a single one. The best approach is to allocate regulatory competence to the lowest appropriate level, which of course corresponds to the principle of subsidiarity. Most importantly, the existence of different jurisdictions may allow competition between legal orders with all ensuing static and dynamic efficiencies.[78]

In the absence of centrally drafted uniform rules, free movement enables regulatory competition between the legal orders of the Member States. This competition does not take place only between States but also between regional and local units. Free flow of goods, services and factors of production gives consumers and producers possibilities to engage in arbitrage.[79]

Consumers can show their preferences by purchasing products and services that have been produced under foreign regulatory systems if they correspond to their needs as regards price and quality. If domestic producers have to comply with inefficient regulations, their products will not be able to compete with those manufactured under a more favourable regulatory environment. Thus the consumers send a signal to business by 'voting with their purses'.[80]

Firms can engage in arbitrage by relocating to another jurisdiction. Further investment, in particular, can be directed towards a state with a more favourable regulatory climate. This may be a response to signals received from consumers. Thus the business demonstrates to the public authorities that regulation is not optimal for the firms in question. The business 'votes with its feet'.[81]

Similarly, individual investors may invest their capital in a state where the regulatory system produces a balance between risks and rewards that suits their preferences. Workers may relocate themselves to a country with a system corresponding to their preferences.

[78] See FH Easterbrook, 'Federalism and European Business Law' (1994) 14 Int Rev of Law and Economics 125, DW Leebron, 'Lying Down with Procrustes: An Analysis of Harmonization Claims' in Bhagwati and Hudec (eds), *Fair Trade and Harmonization, Prerequisites for Free Trade? Vol I: Economic Analysis* (London, 1996) especially at 88, Molle (n 7 above) 18–20, and van den Bergh, 'The Subsidiarity Principle and the EC Competition Rules: The Costs and Benefits of Decentralisation' in Schmidtchen and Cooter (eds), *Constitutional Law and Economics of the European Union* (Cheltenham, 1997) 149. See generally on regulatory competition, eg, Bratton *et al*, *International Regulatory Competition and Coordination* (Oxford, 1996) and N Reich, 'Competition between Legal Orders: A New Paradigm of EC Law' (1992) 29 CML Rev 861.

[79] Mobility is a precondition to regulatory competition. See Easterbrook (n 78 above) 127 and H Siebert and MJ Koop, 'Institutional Competition versus Centralization: Quo Vadis Europe?' (1993) 9 *Oxford Review of Economic Policy* 15, 17. Alternatively, firms may be able to select the jurisdiction whose principles apply to a transaction or business if the private international law of their home jurisdiction allows it. See A Ogus, 'Competition between National Legal Systems: A Contribution of Economic Analysis to Comparative Law' (1999) 48 ICLQ 405, 408.

[80] See H Siebert, 'The Harmonization Issue in Europe: Prior Agreement or a Competitive Process?' in Siebert (ed), *The Completion of the Internal Market* (Tübingen, 1990) 56 and Sun and Pelkmans (n 23 above) 76–77.

[81] ibid.

Alternatively, private agents may react by using their 'voice' to vote or to lobby the public authorities to make changes to the regulatory system. They react in the political market.[82]

The public authorities receive signals from private agents using the 'exit' or the 'voice' option. Flight of firms, capital and skilled workers can result in unemployment and lower productivity which threaten the welfare of the citizens. This gives an incentive to adapt the regulatory system in order to avoid the erosion of tax base and to ensure re-election.

Due to low transaction costs, capital tends to be the factor reacting most quickly to unfavourable regulatory environment by relocating. High transaction costs limit the movement of natural persons.[83]

Different regulators can take into account the differences in objective circumstances, namely endowments and technology, between jurisdictions.[84] In the field of environmental law, for example, one jurisdiction may have short fast-moving rivers and can therefore tolerate higher emissions to them than a jurisdiction with long slow-moving ones. It would not be efficient to have a single rule stipulating emission levels applying to both jurisdictions.

Thus, centralization would produce problems in an enlarging, increasingly heterogeneous Community, especially as the industries in less developed Member States would not be able to cope with a growing regulatory burden. If, for example, social policy legislation were harmonized close to German or Nordic levels, companies in the Mediterranean countries would lose their competitive advantage and the result would be an increase in unemployment in those states.[85]

The citizens of different jurisdictions may have different preferences, which makes uniform rules inefficient.[86] For example, the citizens of one jurisdiction may value clean environment relatively more than the citizens of another jurisdiction. Two different rules would satisfy the preferences better than a single one.

Thus, centralization can result in excessive uniformity in a heterogeneous Community where national preferences differ. Centrally produced regulation leads to 'euro-products'. Traditional manufacturing methods are prohibited, which results in loss of diversity and diminished consumer choice.[87]

[82] See Sun and Pelkmans (n 23 above) 77.

[83] See Siebert and Koop (n 85 below) 444–445 and S Woolcock, *The Single European Market: Centralization or Competition Among National Rules?* (London, 1994) 28.

[84] See Leebron (n 78 above) 67.

[85] See Siebert (n 80 above) 60 and Siebert and Koop, 'Institutional Compeition: A Concept for Europe?' (1990) 45 Aussenwirtschaft 439, 443–444.

[86] See Leebron (n 78 above) 68–69.

[87] See Weatherill and Beaumont (n 59 above) 596.

Regulatory competition, as opposed to centralization, does not only guarantee that the rules in force in a state correspond to the preferences of the majority of its subjects, but it also enables the minority to seek a more suitable regulatory climate. Workers and more generally citizens[88] of the Community can seek to settle in an area where the regulatory system suits them.[89] Investors can benefit from a diverse Community by having a wider choice of investment opportunities.

Altogether, centralization runs counter to the philosophy of international specialization. The existence of different regulatory systems enables companies to establish their facilities in locations which are most favourable to the type of business carried out. The same regulatory environment does not suit every industry and every strategy, so a diverse Community can support more types of economic activities than a homogeneous one. Centralization would reduce efficiency.[90]

Perhaps most importantly, competition between legal orders offers a discovery mechanism. Individual Member States receive signals from private agents engaged in arbitrage and are thus able to determine more easily whether the regulatory system fits their preferences. This is especially important given the imperfect information possessed by public authorities.[91] Furthermore, voting is a relatively inefficient way of revealing preferences due to the infrequency of elections.

The learning process is enhanced by competition between legal orders. Public authorities in different Member States can observe a preference for a certain regulatory system among private agents and adapt the domestic system accordingly. Thus, the Member States can emulate efficient foreign regulatory systems and benefit from experimentation. In a centralized system there is no comparable learning process.[92] A decentralized system can therefore lead to different jurisdictions adopting similar regulation. This is entirely desirable as it is a natural development arising out of the preferences of litigators of individual jurisdictions and the competitive process.

[88] The EC Treaty does not recognize a universal right to free movement of persons. This is to be deplored as it deprives individuals of the possiblity to choose a regulatory system that corresponds to their preferences and distorts competition between legal orders by increasing the influence of capital. See M Poiares Maduro, 'Striking the Elusive Balance Between Economic Freedom and Social Rights in the EU' in P Alston (ed), *The EU and Human Rights* (Oxford, 1999) 462, 470. It has to be recognized, however, that there might be free-rider problems. For example, the unemployed would have an incentive to migrate to countries with high benefits.

[89] See R Van den Bergh, 'Subsidiarity as an Economic Demarcation Principle and the Emergence of European Private Law' (1998) 5 MJ 129.

[90] See Siebert and Koop (n 85 above) 445–446 and Porter (n 7 above) 623–624.

[91] See Sun and Pelkmans (n 23 above) 83.

[92] See H Schmidt, 'Economic Analysis of the Allocation of Regulatory Competence in the European Communities' in Buxbaum *et al* (eds), *European Business Law* (Berlin 1991) 57 and Woolcock (n 83 above) 17–18.

Public authorities may try to adopt efficient regulatory solutions as early as possible since this may give their firms decisive early mover advantages.[93] This increases the dynamism of the system.

Harmonized legislation, once in place, can be difficult to change. Central systems can suffer from gigantism, and the decision-makers may be reluctant to open and renegotiate compromises that have been achieved only with great difficulty.[94]

Regulatory competition can curb the expansionist tendencies of the public sector. The public authorities might not pursue the common good, but rather try to maximize their own utility, if subject only to the weak constraints of re-election or reappointment. The possibility of the erosion of the tax base caused by private agents fleeing an oppressive system is an additional constraint and thus instils discipline on the public sector.[95]

In a centrally controlled system, the legislature can be subjected to effective lobbying by rent-seeking groups. Protectionist producers will be able to set up effective organizations at the European level and may influence centrally adopted regulation to the detriment of consumers. Regulation produced by the market mechanism cannot be influenced by interest group politics to the same extent.[96]

A further problem with centrally drafted legislation is the distance between the regulators and the regulated. This diminishes the opportunities of the citizens to participate meaningfully in the political process. It also exacerbates information problems facing the public authorities. A remote central organ may not be able to form a true picture of the situation.[97]

Finally, the costs created by centralization are reduced by competition between legal orders. A harmonization process with lengthy and costly negotiations and inefficient compromises is avoided.[98]

Regulatory competition has a potential for enhancing both static and

[93] See Porter (n 7 above) 648, Schmidt (n 92 above) 55–57, and Siebert and Koop (n 85 above) 443.

[94] See Schmidt (n 92 above) 57–58 and M Willgerodt, 'Comment on Jacques Pekmans, 'Regulation and the Single Market: An Economic Perspective' in Siebert (ed), *The Completion of the Internal Market* (Tübingen, 1990) 122.

[95] See H Hauser and M Hösli, 'Harmonization or Regulatory Competition in the EC (and the EEA)?' (1991) 46 Aussenwirtschaft 497, 501–502 and Siebert and Koop (n 79 above) 18.

[96] See Hauser and Hösli (n 95 above) and Siebert and Koop (n 79 above) 18. On the power of different interest groups in the Community see A McGee and S Weatherill, 'The Evolution of the Single Market—Harmonisation or Liberalisation' (1990) 53 MLR 578, 585 and 595.

[97] See Van den Bergh, 'Economic Criteria for Applying the Subsidiarity Principle in the European Community: The Case of Competition Policy' (1996) 16 Int Rev of Law and Economics 363, 365–366.

[98] See J Pelkmans, 'Regulation and the Single Market: An Economic Perspective' in Siebert (ed), *The Completion of the Internal Market* (Tübingen, 1990) 92 and Woolcock (n 83 above) 16.

dynamic efficiency in the economy. It is a particularly attractive concept in the context of a relatively heterogeneous Community. Some historians have concluded that the global dominance of Europe during the recent centuries was a result of the intense competition in the continent. Centralized empires stagnated while competing European states were pushed to ever greater advances.[99]

Altogether, the advantages of a decentralized system have been neatly encapsulated by Justice O'Connor of the US Supreme Court:

> The federalist structure of joint sovereigns preserves to the people numerous advantages. It assures a decentralised government that will be more sensitive to the diverse needs of a heterogenous society; it increases opportunity for citizen involvement in democratic processes; it allows for more innovation and experimentation in government, and it makes government more responsive by putting the states in competition for a mobile citizenry. Perhaps the principal benefit of a federalist system is a check on the abuses of government power.[100]

It has been feared that competition between regulators would lead to a 'race to the bottom'. Different Member States would lower the level of their regulation to attract companies from other countries. Companies might relocate to minimize the cost of complying with the regulations and would then serve the whole Community from this new base. This would encourage other countries to lower their level of regulation even further. Thus, the level of regulation in the Community would become sub-optimal.[101]

There are checking factors, however. Firms can benefit from regulation as it can enhance *inter alia* their productivity; thus, they may not wish to relocate.[102] For example, strict environmental rules that create a cleaner environment may contribute to the health and accordingly the productivity of the employees. The state of the environment may also be important when attracting high-quality labour. Clean water, quality of agricultural products, the rate of growth of forests etc can be important for the industry if they are inputs to production or if there is goodwill among consumers associated with products from a clean environment. Stringent requirements create opportunities for new industries as the demand for new clean technologies increase. Furthermore, if the country is the first to adopt strict standards

[99] See BS Frey and R Eichenberger, 'FOCJ: Creating a Single European Market for Governments' in Schmidtchen and Cooter (eds), *Constitutional Law and Economics of the European Union* (Cheltenham 1997) 209 and P Kennedy, *The Rise and Fall of Great Powers: Economic Advantage and Military Conflict from 1500 to 2000* (London, 1988) xvi–xvii and 20–28. However, the competition sometimes escalated to armed conflict, the costs of which became excessive with the development of modern weaponry and logistics. Thus, the competition had to be contained in peaceful structures like the European Union.

[100] *Gregory v Ashcroft* 501 US 452 (1991) at 458.

[101] See Siebert and Koop (n 85 above) 446–447 and Weatherill and Beaumont (n 59 above) 700–701.

[102] See Siebert (n 80 above) 63–67 and Siebert and Koop (n 85 above) 447–449.

and other countries later follow, its industries will gain early mover advantages as they are the first to adjust. Naturally the effects vary from one industry to another so while some industries are better off some may experience difficulties.[103]

A sub-optimal level of regulation makes citizens worse off. The welfare gains caused by, for example, an inflow of capital do not necessarily offset welfare losses caused by, for example, environmental degradation, especially since marginal damage increases progressively as the level of pollution rises.[104] Citizens can respond by relocating to other countries. This is a potent threat especially in the case of skilled labour. Industries that are dependent on a high level of regulation may either relocate or wither. A further response can be made in the political arena. Voters may not re-elect a government engaged in excessive deregulation and industries may lobby for higher standards.[105]

It can be argued that instead of a race to the bottom, regulatory competition produces a race towards efficient regulation.[106] However, the area remains hotly disputed.[107]

Competition between legal orders does not remove the transaction costs arising from different legal environments. For example, a company establishing a subsidiary in another Member State may need to get special legal advice, which would be unnecessary if the company laws of both countries were similar. These transaction costs can create a substantial obstacle, especially to the European expansion of smaller firms.[108]

The argument for harmonization to avoid transaction costs is not unproblematic, however. Almost any Community measure could be defended on these grounds, thus widening the scope of Community competence and threatening the principle of enumerated powers established in Article 5 (ex 3b) EC. Furthermore, a harmonization programme would be difficult to manage in practice if the agenda were this wide.[109] In fields

[103] See Porter (n 7 above) 651–652.

[104] See Siebert (n 80 above) 63–67 and 70 and Siebert and Koop (n 85 above) 447–449.

[105] From the game theory point of view, the situation facing a state is generally similar to that facing an oligopolist. The state knows its competitive deregulation may be matched by others before it gains any benefits. In the same way, an oligopolist is discouraged from lowering prices by the fact that competitors would match any price cuts.

[106] It has also been argued that competition between legal orders can lead to excessive regulation. See Sun and Pelkmans (n 23 above) 85.

[107] eg Prosi states that '[t]he notion that institutional competition will lead to zero regulation and taxation is nonsense' ('Comments on Horst Siebert, "The Harmonization Issue in Europe: Prior Agreement or a Competitive Process?" ' in Siebert (ed), *The Completion of the Internal Market* (Tübingen, 1990) G Prosi 77), while Meier-Schatz remarks that '[t]he only thing which is fairly well established is the fact that regulatory competition probably leads to a race to the bottom' (C Meier-Schatz in Buxbaum *et al*, *European Business Law, Legal and Economic Analyses on Integration and Harmonization* (Berlin, 1991) 125).

[108] See Bernard (n 69 above) 647 and Schmidt (n 92 above) 54.

[109] See Bernard (n 69 above) 647–648.

where transaction costs pose substantial obstacles to integration, harmonization would be desirable. For example, voluntary product standards are capable of greatly facilitating free movement by reducing transaction costs without endangering innovation.[110]

The market for regulation is subject to market failures that can create a need for public intervention to remedy the problem. In the context of regulatory competition, externalities is the most common market failure and usually the strongest argument for centralization. Externalities occur when activity regulated in one jurisdiction affects the well-being of people in other jurisdictions.[111] Externalities can result in a sub-optimal level of regulation. For example, if air pollution created in one country mainly causes damage in another country, the former does not have an incentive to curb emissions since it reaps the benefits but does not have to bear the costs. In the case of externalities central regulation may be desirable.[112] Appropriate regulatory level internalizes all major effects of the activity regulated. This corresponds to one aspect of the principle of subsidiarity.[113]

Information asymmetries may create a need for regulation. In some situations consumers cannot properly assess the quality of a good or a service. An example is professional services. This may lead to a predominance of cheap poor quality products. To counter this trend authorities have passed consumer protection rules which guarantee a certain minimum quality to the consumers. If goods and services from other countries with differing standards are now allowed a free access to the market, the consumers may not be able to identify the quality of these foreign products due to insufficient knowledge of foreign regulations.[114] Therefore, it may be necessary to draft common minimum standards when it comes to goods and services whose qualities consumers cannot assess.[115]

On the other hand, stringent national regulation can become a guarantee of high quality. A Member State may set high requirements for its products and if producers have to comply with these rules whether the goods or services are for domestic or foreign consumption, the consumers in other

[110] See Bernard (n 69 above) 648 and Siebert and Koop (n 79 above) 27.

[111] See Hauser and Hösli (n 95 above) 507–508 and Siebert and Koop (n 85 above) 450–451.

[112] See Van den Bergh (n 89 above) 140–145. Central regulation is not necessarily the only way to deal with externalities. In theory proper allocation of property rights can serve to correct this failure. See Willgerodt (n 94 above) 123 and Woolcock (n 83 above) 18. In practice such a solution seems hardly feasible, though.

[113] See Easterbrook (n 78 above) 129 and WPJ Wils, 'Subsidiarity and the EC Environmental Policy: Taking People's Concerns Seriously' (1994) 6 JEL 85.

[114] Thus, this problem is most prevalent in the case of private individuals.

[115] See generally Hauser and Hösli (n 95 above) 509 and P Nicolaides, 'Competition among Rules' (1992) 16 *World Competition* 113, 119–120.

countries have an assurance of quality.[116] Public regulation can fulfil a trademark-like function. Different Member States may thus specialize in goods of different quality and consumer choice will increase.[117] Altogether, competition between legal orders may be beneficial despite asymmetric information.

It may be seen from the foregoing discussion that neither regulatory competition nor centralization is alone a feasible method of regulating the Internal Market.[118] Especially where there are major transaction costs or externalities harmonization remains necessary.[119] The peculiarities of each area of law have to be taken into account. In some fields, these factors have a strong impact, while in others they hardly feature at all.[120] Nevertheless, competition between legal orders seems in many situations to be a superior instrument for managing the internal market.[121]

This has implications for both positive and negative integration, for both the Community legislature and judicature.[122] In the context of the scope of the free movement provisions, the Court should be careful not to extend their reach too far and should not embark on a project of wholesale negative harmonization.[123] Instead, it should concentrate on national measures that prevent competition between legal orders by either sheltering the domestic industry from competitive pressures thus removing the reason for

[116] In Case C-212/97 *Centros Ltd v Erhvervs of Selskabsstyrelsen*, judgment of 9 March 1999, para 36 the Court emphasized that creditors knew that a UK company did not necessarily fulfil the Danish requirements on share capital. The UK company law acted as a trademark indicating, in this instance, a potentially inferior quality.

[117] Hauser and Hösli (n 95 above) 509–510. The Court has disallowed rules requiring mandatory origin-marking in Case 207/83 *Commission v United Kingdom* [1985] ECR 1202 but producers are able to state the origin of the products if they choose to.

[118] See also R Baldwin and M Cave, *Understanding Regulation: Theory, Strategy and Practice* (Oxford, 1999) 185 according to whom 'regulatory competition and harmonizing measures should not be seen as direct alternatives but as modes of influence that can be used in harness so as to limit their individual weaknesses'.

[119] On other problems with regulatory competition see eg Sun and Pelkmans (n 23 above) 83–86 and Woolcock (n 83 above) 18–21.

[120] See, eg, D Charny, 'Competition among Jurisdictions in Formulating Corporate Law Rules: An American Perspective on the "Race to the Bottom" in the EC' (1991) 32 Harvard Int LJ 423, 435–455 on company law, Van den Bergh (n 89 above) 132–151 on private law, and Van den Bergh (n 78 above) 149–174 on competition law. See also an interesting distinction between 'facilitative' and 'interventionist' law made by Ogus (n 79 above) 410–418.

[121] This may be especially true when taking into account the risks of institutional malfunctions inherent in the Community political process. See Poiares Maduro (n 65 above) 113–126, who speaks of 'horizontal minoritarian bias' and 'vertical majoritarian bias', ie capture by supra-national interest groups and over-representation of the majority or most powerful states. It has to be noted, however, that the Community political system is not static. The increasing power of the European Parliament will alter the picture, perhaps reducing the risk of malfunction by representing diverse interests and by being independent of Member States.

[122] The Community legislator ought to concentrate on major transnational externalities and transaction costs.

[123] It should also be noted that the Court should not change its approach to reverse discrimination. It is a crucial part of the decentralized system.

arbitrage, or by preventing factors of production from relocating thus removing the possibility of arbitrage. In the case of the free movement of goods and services, the Court should thus guarantee that products from other Member States are able to compete on truly equal terms with domestic products and to maintain their competitive advantage. It should go no further as it may contribute to inefficient centralization and diminish the possibilities of beneficial competition between regulators.[124]

This aim is best achieved through a test based on the wide concept of discrimination, advocated above. A narrow concept of discrimination is not sufficient. A mere national treatment does not always create truly equal terms for competition, and allow the maintenance of competitive advantage. A wider test goes too far. National measures not compromising regulatory competition itself should be respected and left to compete with each other.

The Court will also have to be aware that regulatory competition takes place in different ways for different rules. As regards *product requirements*, the competition[125] takes place through buying decisions of consumers. The competition between rules regulating *market circumstances* happens mainly through the movement of consumers. If they do not like the rules, they select another jurisdiction.[126] The competition in *production rules* (eg, labour law and environmental law) is effected mostly through the movement of producers. If the rules are inefficient, products will be expensive or of poor quality and the consumers will not buy them. To survive, the producers will have to migrate by investing in facilities in other jurisdictions with more favourable regulation. For the competition to take place, the freedom of these movements must be guaranteed *and* all national rules not genuinely endangering them must be respected.

In general, for the regulatory competition to be maintained, the importing host country should not be required to mutually recognize the exporting home country's rules on market circumstances and the exporting home country should not be forced to mutually recognize the importing host country's production rules. Mutual recognition would lead to the destruction of

[124] This consideration is of paramount importance in assessing the case law of the Court on the free movement of goods prior to Cases C-267/91 and C-268/91 *Criminal Proceedings against Keck and Mithouard* [1993] ECR I-6097 and the case law on services after it. See below sections IV and V. See J. Snell, 'True Proportionality and the Movement of Goods and Services' (2000) 11 EBLR 50 at 52 on the implications of the economics of federalism for the proportionality test.

[125] Or rather, the competition in the economic market, since competition is also happening in the political market. In the interest of clarity, only the economic market is covered here. See further Poiares Maduro (n 65 above) 140.

[126] This competition usually takes place when a person is moving to an area and opts, according to his preferences, for a locality which is 'lively and exciting', 'family-friendly' or 'peaceful and idyllic'. The character of a locality is strongly influenced by decisions on zoning, licensing, opening hours etc.

beneficial diversity, rules on market circumstances and production could not normally be applied only to domestic situations, and mere mutual recognition might not be enough to remove the 'barrier', especially if understood in the wide *Dassonville*[127] sense as anything potentially diminishing the volume of trade.

An example will clarify the situation. A consumer can select whether to buy a good conforming to domestic product rules, or a good conforming to the product rules of another Member State. He votes with his purse.

A consumer can select whether to be the target of roadside billboard advertising by moving to a jurisdiction whose rules correspond to his preferences.[128] He can vote with his feet. However, if rules concerning market circumstances were subject to mutual recognition, this would not be an option.[129] If local rules prohibiting certain sales methods could not be applied to products from other Member States, there would be no jurisdictions where, for example, roadside billboard advertising would be absolutely prohibited.[130] The competition would not take place.

Moreover, it would often be technically impossible to restrict rules regulating selling arrangements to domestic situations; and in some situations the 'obstacle' diminishing the volume of imports could only be removed by rendering national rules regulating market circumstances totally inapplicable. For example, allowing Sunday trading in products of other Member States would not be enough even if it was technically feasible. Shops could argue that their turnover from those products alone would not be sufficient to justify opening on Sundays and therefore the volume of imports would still be diminished. Thus, mutual recognition of home country rules concerning market circumstances by the host country would not lead to a proper competition between regulations.

Similarly, a consumer can move to a jurisdiction which guarantees clean environment through stringent production regulations. The same is true for a producer who uses the clean environment as an input, as a method of attracting high quality work force, or as an element of a sales promotion strategy. If undertakings producing export goods were exempt from these production rules, there would be no jurisdiction where for example clean air could be guaranteed.

Furthermore, again it might be impossible in practice to apply domestic production rules only to export goods; and the producers would still be

[127] Case 8/74, *Procureur du Roi v Dassonville* [1974] ECR 837.

[128] Unfortunately, Community law does not (yet) guarantee the right of free movement to all citizens of the Union.

[129] Unless of course the Court has decided that the failure to mutually recognize is justified.

[130] Not only the Member States but also smaller units such as regions and municipalities would be unable to ban such activities. See eg Case C-67/97 *Criminal Proceedings against Ditlev Bluhme* [1998] ECR I-8033, para 20.

unable to achieve full economies of scale as they would have to divide their production lines. In most cases mutual recognition of host country production rules by the home country would not lead to a proper competition between regulations.[131]

The argument in this section has run as follows: different interpretations of the free movement rules result in different vertical divisions of power between the Community and Member States. A wide reading produces a centralized unitary system, while a narrower one contributes to a decentralized federal system. For the Community, a fairly decentralized approach enabling regulatory competition is preferable. Therefore, the Court ought to adopt a relatively narrow reading of Articles 28 and 49 (ex 30 and 59) EC. The approach based on a wide concept of discrimination is best capable of dealing with obstacles while at the same time respecting Member States competences.

IV. *KECK*

1. Background to the Judgment

(a) The previous case law

In the years following the ground-breaking judgments in *Dassonville*[132] and *Cassis de Dijon*[133] the ECJ slowly widened the reach of Article 28 (ex 30) EC. By applying the *Dassonville*-formula mechanically to all domestic measures restricting the volume of trade and, therefore, the volume of imports, the Court made it clear in judgments such as *Cinéthèque*[134] and *Torfaen*[135] that even truly non-discriminatory national rules could infringe the provisions on the free movement of goods.

[131] The analysis presented above corresponds to Professor Koenig's recent call for a new research agenda. He writes: 'Interjurisdictional competition between Member States must in future be incorporated in the formulation of European integration rules and principles. Even axiomatic rules and principles of the single market which have never been questioned must be fundamentally re-examined. The objective of research is to develop "model rules" which create coherence between the dual-level competition between Member States' jurisdictions and the competition between companies': see C Koenig, 'Some Brief Remarks on Interjurisdictional Competition Between EU Member States' (1999) 10 EBLR 437.

[132] Case 8/74 *Procureur du Roi v Dassonville* [1974] ECR 837.

[133] Case 120/78 *Rewe Zentrale AG v Bundesmonopolverwaltung für Branntwein* [1979] ECR 649.

[134] Cases 60 and 61/84 *Cinéthèque v Fédération Nationale de Cinemas Francaises* [1985] ECR 2605. The Court did not follow Advocate General Slynn who argued, in an Opinion that was almost ten years ahead of its time, that genuinely non-discriminatory measures do not fall within Article 28 (ex 30).

[135] Case 145/88 *Torfaen BC v B&Q* [1989] ECR 3851. Cf the opinion of Advocate General van Gerven.

The Court's case law was not entirely coherent. It seems that the Court was feeling slightly uneasy about the reach of the mechanically applied *Dassonville* test. For example, in *Oebel,*[136] *Blesgen,*[137] *Krantz*[138] and *Quietlynn*[139] the Court employed a method diverging from its normal approach and held the national measures to fall outside the scope of Article 28 (ex 30) altogether without investigating their justification at all. In all of these cases the measures were capable of reducing the volume of trade and fulfilled the *Dassonville* criterion, as normally interpreted. The impact on inter-State trade was very remote, however. Unfortunately the poor reasoning of the judgments only created confusion.[140] The Court was increasingly put under pressure to re-examine and clarify its case law.

(b) The role of the ECJ

The wide reach of the free movement of goods created problems relating to the role of the European Court of Justice in the system.[141]

A wide scope of Article 28 (ex 30) EC reduces the risk of protectionist national rules escaping judicial scrutiny. The Court can examine all measures reducing the volume of trade. It has been claimed that if a certain category of national rules were held to fall outside Article 28 (ex 30) altogether, the misuse of these rules could not be prevented.[142]

Article 28 (ex 30) can in this respect be compared with Article 81 (ex 85) EC. The wide scope of Article 81(1) (ex 85(1)), especially as interpreted by the Commission, has been motivated by and defended with reference to the need to enable the Commission to control anti-competitive and anti-integrationist agreements effectively.[143] However, the system has also been forcefully criticized for subjecting *harmless* agreements to the Commission's scrutiny under Article 81(3) (ex 85(3)).[144] The trend[145] in

[136] Case 155/80 *Oebel* [1981] ECR 1993.

[137] Case 75/81 *Belgium v Blesgen* [1982] ECR 1211.

[138] Case C-69/88 *H. Krantz GmbH & Co v Ontvanger der Directe Belastingen et al* [1990] ECR I-583.

[139] Case C-23/89 *Quietlynn & Richards v Southend BC* [1990] ECR I-3059.

[140] See critical analysis of this strand of the Court's case law in Advocate General Tesauro's opinion in the Case C-292/92 *Hünermund v Landesapothekerkammer Baden-Württemberg* [1993] ECR I-6787, paras 11–24 and in Gormley, 'Actually or Potentially, Directly or Indirectly? Obstacles to the Free Movement of Goods' (1989) 9 YEL 197, 198–200.

[141] See Poiares Maduro (n 65 above) 59. He develops an interesting theory of Article 28 (ex 30) EC based on the institutional choice between an individual Member State and the ECJ as the arbiter of the balance between the free movement and other values.

[142] See Gormley (n 140 above) 205–206.

[143] See Whish and Sufrin, 'Article 85 and the Rule of Reason' (1987) 7 YEL 1, 14–20.

[144] See B Hawk, 'System Failure: Vertical Restraints and EC Competition Law' (1995) 32 CML Rev 973, 974–984 and V Korah, *An Introductory Guide to EC Competition Law and Practice* (6th edn, London, 1997) 303–306.

[145] Another interesting development is that goods and services are increasingly being treated

competition law seems to be towards a reduction in the area of Community supervision.[146]

It is possible to question the legitimacy of the role of the Court under a wide interpretation of the scope of Article 28 (ex 30).[147] When deciding on the acceptability of the aims of a national measure and on the proportionality of the means, the Court is ruling on issues that are usually considered to be highly political. The aim pursued by the Member State may be controversial and opinions may vary greatly between the different Member States. For example, views on how to balance the right to life of an unborn child and the right of self-determination of a woman diverge inside the Community (and inside the Member States).[148] Even if the Court can decide on the legitimacy of the aim of the measure, it has to be balanced against any anti-integrationist effects. In these situations the non-representative nature of the Court becomes obvious and its considerable discretionary power a matter of concern. Democratically elected and accountable legislatures are generally assumed to be better suited to resolve such issues.

Furthermore, the Court's limited capacity to conduct an inquiry renders it difficult to investigate whether other equally effective means are available. This is an essential part of the proportionality test. The evidentiary and procedural limits inherent in any judicial review surface in these situations.[149]

The difficulties created by a wide test have been recognized by the judges themselves. Koen Lenaerts, Judge of the Court of First Instance has written,

in the same manner. See Communication from the Commission, *Application of the Community Competition Rules to Vertical Restraints: Follow-up to the Green Paper on Vertical Restraints*, OJ 1998 C365/03, and Article 2(1) of Commission Regulation (EC) 2790/1999 of 22 November 1999 on the application of Article 81(3) of the EC Treaty to categories of vertical agreements and concerted practices OJ 1999 L336/21.

[146] See R Whish, *Competition Law* (3rd edn, London, 1993) 208–209 and the judgments of the Court cited therein, Commission's *Green Paper on Vertical Restraints in E.C. Competition Policy* COM(96)721 final [1997] 4 CMLR 519, and Communication from the Commission, *Application of the Community Competition Rules to Vertical Restraints: Follow-up to the Green Paper on Vertical Restraints* OJ 1998 C365/03. See also the extension of whitelisted clauses (Article 2) in the Technology Transfer Block Exemption 240/96 as compared with whitelist (Article 2) in Patent Licensing Block Exemption 2349/84 and Commission's decision *Elopak/Metal Box-Odin* (EC Commission Decision 90/410) OJ 1990 L209/15, [1991] 4 CMLR 832. See generally R Wesseling, 'Subsidiarity in the Community Antitrust Law: Setting the Right Agenda' (1997) 22 EL Rev 35. In the Commission *White Paper on Modernisation of the Rules Implementing Articles 85 [now 81] and 86 [now 82] of the EC Treaty*, OJ 1999 C132/01 the emphasis is put on decentralized application of Community competition law.

[147] See also TJ Friedbacher, 'Motive Unmasked: The European Court of Justice, the Free Movement of Goods and the Search for Legitimacy' (1996) 2 ELJ 226, 238–240.

[148] See Case C-159/90 *Society for the Protection of the Unborn Child v Grogan* [1991] ECR I-4685. In practice the Court has shown deference towards national legislators in these circumstances.

[149] See de Búrca, 'The Principle of Proportionality and its Application in EC Law' (1993) 13 YEL 105, 108 and 127 and Poiares Maduro (n 65 above) 59.

'Even the judge questions, at times, the legitimacy and the feasibility of making policy choices, of weighing the Community interest of having an internal market, and the Member States' interest in protecting what they see as fundamental local values'.[150] Similarly, President of the ECJ, Ole Due, has stated that 'such cases often present the Court with an unnecessary and almost impossible task: to evaluate national policy choices in areas which have very little to do with intra-Community trade or with Community law in general'.[151] On the same topic, Judge René Joliet has said that, 'Können wir, die wir dreizehn sind, behaupten, über mehr Weisheit und Intelligenz als alle Regierungen und nationale Parlamente der Gemeinschaft zu verfügen?'[152]

The concerns over the legitimacy of the scrutiny by the Court and the difficulties inherent in the task may lead to problems in the application of the *Cassis* test. The Court might be forced to widen the list of mandatory requirements, as more and more questions relating to the justification of different national measures are to be submitted to it.[153] It is also necessary to determine exactly which ground of justification are applicable in a specific case, as this may influence the outcome of the proportionality test. This may prove to be difficult as the ground of justification depends on the aims pursued by the national measure. These may not be clear or the measure may have many different purposes.[154]

Furthermore, as a part of the examination of justification, the proportionality of the measures has to be established. This difficult task often falls to the national courts, as it involves questions of fact which the ECJ is not equipped to investigate and resolve. This inevitably leads to different results, especially as the answer to the question depends on the evidence presented to the national court.[155]

Traders, national courts and the ECJ itself suffer detrimental consequences from a wide scope of Article 28 (ex 30) EC. Traders are encouraged

[150] K Lenaerts, 'Some Thoughts About the Interaction Between Judges and Politicians in the European Community' (1992) 12 YEL 1, 12 (footnotes omitted).

[151] O Due, 'Dassonville Revisited or No Cause for Alarm' in Campbell and Voyatzi (eds), *Legal Reasoning and Judicial Interpretation of European Law* (Gosport, 1996), 27.

[152] R Joliet, 'Der freie Warenverkehr: Das Urfeil Keck und M; 984. 'Can we, we who are thirteen, assert that we have more wisdom and intelligence at our disposal than all the governments and national parliaments of the Community?'

[153] The opinion of Advocate General van Gerven in Case 145/88 *Torfaen BC v B&Q* [1989] ECR 3851, para 26 and C Barnard, 'Sunday Trading: A Drama in Five Acts' (1994) 57 MLR 449, 459.

[154] See J Steiner, 'Drawing the Line: Uses and Abuses of Article 30 EEC' (1992) 29 CML Rev 749, 759. In Sunday Trading cases English judges came to different conclusions about the proportionality of the legislation as they perceived the purpose of the law differently. See Barnard (n 145 above) 454.

[155] See Steiner (n 154 above) 759–760. Hoffmann J expressed the doubts felt by a national judge faced with a task of deciding on proportionality of national legislation in *Stoke-on-Trent and Norwich City Councils v B&Q* [1990] 3 CMLR 31, paras 46–52.

to bring cases that have an ever more tenuous connection with intra-Community trade.[156] This results in fruitless and disappointing litigation, as in many cases national rules will be saved by mandatory requirements or Article 30 (ex 36) EC.

National courts[157] are faced with many more cases involving Article 28 (ex 30). Because of the complexity of the tests, national courts are obliged to make references to the ECJ. This increases the cost and the length of litigation, and causes problems for judges loyal to national legislatures. National courts also need to apply the proportionality test in a great number of cases. This is a task they are not necessarily suited for or feel comfortable with.[158] The national courts might be tempted to resist the obligations imposed upon them by Community law.[159] This would create a strain on the relationship between national courts and the ECJ; a relationship that has been crucially important for the development of Community law itself.[160]

An increase in the number of references is also detrimental to the ECJ itself. One of the worst problems facing the Court is an ever-increasing case load.[161] This leads to delays that are harmful especially in the context of the Article 234 (ex 177) EC procedure, as they undermine the effective protection of individuals in practice.[162] Secondly, it may lead to a lower quality of judgments, as the Court is forced to deal with cases as quickly as possible. Such a development would be particularly worrying since the ECJ functions as the supreme court of the Community and its rulings should contribute towards the general development of Community law.[163] Thirdly, it may

[156] See White (n 75 above) 238.

[157] See MA Jarvis, *The Application of EC Law by National Courts: The Free Movement of Goods* (Oxford, 1998) 129–132 on the problems the wide reading on Article 28 (ex 30) EC created for national courts.

[158] See generally on the proportionality test and national courts Jarvis (n 157 above) 204–230, especially 228–230, and 293–294.

[159] See Steiner (n 154 above) 750.

[160] See F Mancini and D Keeling, 'From *CILFIT* to *ERT*: The Constitutional Challenge Facing the European Court' (1991) 11 YEL 1, 1–3 and JHH Weiler, 'The Transformation of Europe' (1991) 100 Yale LJ 2403, 2425.

[161] See Additional Commission contribution to the Intergovernmental Conference on Institutional Reform of 1 March 2000, 1–2 (http://europe.eu.int/comm/ifc2000/offdoc/index–en.htm). JP Jacqué and JHH Weiler, 'On the Road to European Union—a New Judicial Architecture: An Agenda for the Intergovernmental Conference' (1990) 27 CML Rev 185, 187, PJG Kapteyn, 'The Court of Justice of the European Communities after the Year 2000' in Curtin and Heukels (eds), *Institutional Dynamics of European Integration*, vol II (Dordrecht, 1994) 137, and T Koopmans, 'The Future of the Court of Justice of the European Communities' (1991) 11 YEL 15, 16. From mid-1980s to early 1990s the Court made approximately 20 decisions a year that were concerned with Articles 28–30 (ex 30–36) EC. This amounts to 8 per cent of all rulings. Wils, 'The Search for the Rule in Article 30 EEC: Much Ado About Nothing?' (1993) 18 EL Rev 475.

[162] See Jacqué and Weiler (n 161 above) 188, Kapteyn (n 161 above) 137, and Koopmans (n 161 above) 17–18.

[163] See Jacqué and Weiler (n 161 above) 188 and Kapteyn (n 161 above) 137.

become difficult for citizens and the legal community to follow the development of the case law, which would diminish the value of the Court's decisions as precedents.[164]

In other fields the Court's approach seems to have been influenced by the desire to limit its work load. In Article 230 (ex 173) cases, the Court has developed very restrictive tests of standing for private plaintiffs.[165] It has been argued that this has been done partly to avoid the Court being swamped by challenges to Community action.[166] Similarly, it has been suggested that the Court's recent stricter investigation of its jurisdiction under Article 234 (ex 177)[167] has been influenced by the need to reduce its case load.[168]

Ultimately all these problems might force the Court to adopt a more lenient approach to mandatory requirements and proportionality under Article 28 (ex 30). This would endanger the effectiveness of the provision in dealing with national measures that create real problems for the European integration.[169]

Clearly, the centralized scrutiny of nearly all Member State measures does not sit well with the decentralized structure of the Community judicature, where national courts take care of most Community law problems.[170] Centralized control forces national courts to deal with situations they are not equipped to handle and strains the resources of the ECJ. It undermines the legitimacy of the whole system. It imposes a strain on the relations between national courts and the ECJ. It also endangers the effectiveness of Article 28 (ex 30) EC. Against this background the advantages of a clear rule-like test[171] limiting the scope of Article 28 (ex 30) seem obvious.

A wide test based on, for example, a mechanical application of the *Dassonville*-formula also acts as a limitation on the discretion of the

[164] See Jacqué and Weiler (n 161 above) 139.

[165] See especially Case 25/62 *Plaumann v Commission* [1963] ECR 95 and Cases 789/79 and 790/79 *Calpak v Commission* [1980] ECR 1949. The latter test may have been liberalized in Case C-309/89 *Codorniu SA v Council* [1994] ECR I-1853. Possible liberalization will mainly serve to increase the work load of the Court of First Instance, as the ECJ functions as an appeals court in these cases.

[166] See P Craig and G de Búrca, *EU Law: Text, Cases and Materials* (2nd edn, Oxford, 1998), 484.

[167] Case C-83/91 *Meilicke v ADV/ORGA F.A. Meyer AG* [1992] ECR I-4871 and Case C-343/90 *Dias v Director da Alfandega do Porto* [1992] ECR I-4673.

[168] See T Kennedy, 'First Steps towards a European Certiorari?' (1993) 18 EL Rev 121, 129 and D O'Keeffe, 'Is the Spirit of Article 177 under Attack? Preliminary References and Admissibility' (1998) 23 EL Rev 509, 528–529.

[169] See White (n 75 above) 239.

[170] On the role of the national courts in the Community judicial system, see Jarvis (n 157 above) 1–2.

[171] On the difference between a rule-like and a standard-like test see Wils (n 161 above) 481. A test based on discrimination is rule-like. No weighing is needed to determine whether there is discrimination or not.

Community legislator. All Community organs are naturally bound by the Treaty, including the rules on free movement.[172] If those rules were only breached by discriminatory measures, the discretion of the Community legislator would be relatively unimpeded. The harmonization of the Member State rules creating obstacles to trade would be unhindered. Community measures which affect traders from all Member States uniformly could not be challenged. A wider approach, such as one based purely on *Dassonville*, however, would logically enable the Court to examine the justification of all Community measures reducing the number of imports when compared with an unregulated situation. It can be asked whether this would be a proper role for the Court.[173]

(c) General trends

The wide scope of Article 28 (ex 30) was not consistent with several general trends in the Community.

First of all, increased importance is being given to the principle of subsidiarity. The principle has arguably influenced the development of Community law for quite some time.[174] It was not given general expression until the Maastricht Treaty on European Union,[175] in the Preamble and Articles A (now 1), B (now 2) and K.3.(2)(b), and in Article 3b(2) (now 5(2)) of the EC Treaty. In Amsterdam the Member States signalled the importance they give to subsidiarity by annexing the Protocol on the application of the principles of subsidiarity and proportionality to the Treaty.

One aspect of the principle implies that priority should generally be given to Member State action, and that the Community should only get involved if the Member States cannot deal with the problem adequately.[176] The principle lends weight to an argument for a restrictive construction of Article 28 (ex 30) EC in order to protect the Member State competence against intervention by the Community.[177]

172 See for example on Article 28 (ex 30) L Gormley, *Prohibiting Restrictions on Trade within the EEC* (Amsterdam, 1985) 255 and the judgments referred to therein.

173 In Australia the High Court recently ruled in the landmark case *Cole v Whitfield (Crayfish Case)* (1988) 165 CLR 360 that s 92 of the Constitution, which provides for freedom of trade and commerce among the States, only prevents discriminatory burdens of a protectionist kind. One of the reasons for this new narrow test was the desire to let the Commonwealth exercise its powers freely. See Lane, *A Manual of Australian Constitutional Law* (6th edn, Sydney, 1995) 333–349.

174 See J Steiner, 'Subsidiarity under the Maastricht Treaty' in O'Keeffe and Twomey (eds), *Legal Issues of the Masstricht Treaty* (Chichester, 1994) 50–51.

175 The Single European Act incorporated the principle to Article 130r(4) ECT, but the provision dealt only with action relating to the environment.

176 See Bernard (n 69 above) 653–654 and N Emiliou, 'Subsidiarity: An Effective Barrier Against "the Enterprises of Ambition"?' (1992) 17 EL Rev 383, 401.

177 See Bernard (n 69 above) 638, Hilson (n 61 above) 457, and Weatherill and Beaumont (n 59 above) 608.

Secondly, in recent years the expanding scope of Community law has created both political controversy and constitutional problems in various Member States.[178] Increased attention is being paid to the competencies of the Community, as evidenced by the careful drafting of the rules on public health and culture in Maastricht. This is logical, as under majority voting jurisdictional limits are much more important than under unanimous decision-making.[179]

Thirdly, the Court has not interpreted Article 81 (ex 85) EC, read together with Article 10 (ex 5) EC, as forming a basis for Community economic constitution.[180] Instead it has sharply limited the reach of the Articles.[181] Also in this context the Court has proved unwilling to control local regulatory choices.[182]

Fourthly, the Court has recently seemed less inclined to engage in judicial activism than in the past. The Single European Act with its rules on majority voting revitalized the political process of the Community and thus enabled the Court to adopt a more conservative stance.[183] After the deadline for the achievement of the internal market, 31 December 1992, and even more so after the introduction of the euro, 1 January 1999, one might perhaps talk of a more mature market,[184] in need of market maintenance, not market building.[185]

[178] See Dashwood, 'The Limits of European Community Powers' (1996) 21 EL Rev 113, Poiares Maduro (n 65 above) 34, JHH Weiler (n 160 above) 2450–2453, and JHH Weiler, 'The Reformation of European Constitutionalism' (1997) 35 JCMS 97, 123–127. See also the decision of the German Constitutional Court concerning the ratification of the Maastricht Treaty *Brunner v European Union Treaty* [1994] 1 CMLR 57 and the 'Danish Maastricht Judgment', Højesteret, judgment of 6 April 1998, *Carlsen and others v Prime Minister*, annotated by K Høegh 'The Danish Maastricht Judgment' (1999) 24 EL Rev 80.

[179] See Weiler (n 69 above) 371–372 and Weiler (n 178 above) 122–127.

[180] Case C-2/91 *Meng* [1993] ECR I-5751. See in general K Bacon, 'State Regulation of the Market and EC Competition Rules: Articles 85 and 86 Compared' (1997) 5 ECLR 283.

[181] See also above on the more restrictive approach to the scope of Article 81 (ex 85) EC.

[182] See Reich, 'The "November Revolution" of the European Court of Justice: *Keck, Meng* and *Audi* Revisited' (1994) 31 CML Rev 459, 479–482 (n 59 above) and Weatherill and Beaumont 619.

[183] See TC Hartley, 'The European Court, Judicial Objectivity and the Constitution of the European Union' (1996) 21 EL Rev 95, 102 and Lenaerts (n 150 above) 34. For instance, Case C-91/92 *Faccini Dori v Recreb Srl* [1994] ECR I-3325 and Case C-338/91 *Steenhorst-Neerings v Bestuur van de Bedrijfsvereiniging voor Detailhandel, Ambachten en Huisvrouwen* [1993] ECR I-5475 can be seen as examples of judicial restraint. On the other hand, there are judgments pointing the other way such as Case C-312/93 *Peterbroeck v Belgium* [1995] ECR I-4599 and Joined Cases C-46 and C-48/93 *Brasserie du Pêcheur SA v Germany* and *R v Secretary of State for Transport, ex parte Factortame* [1996] ECR I-1029. The whole dichotomy between activism and self-restraint has been challenged by Tridimas, 'The Court of Justice and Judicial Activism' (1996) 21 EL Rev 199, 210.

[184] The Commission White Paper on *Modernisation of the Rules Implementing Articles 85 [now 81] and 86 [now 82] of the EC Treaty*, OJ 1999 C132/01 suggest far-reaching decentralization of the current 'centralised authorisation system' of competition law. One of the reasons given is that 'national markets are already extensively integrated'. See eg para 136.

[185] See Poiares Maduro (n 65 above) 88–99, who uses this terminology, and Weiler (n 69 above) 371.

Finally, it can be argued that the internal market is losing its premier position in the Community.[186] The Maastricht Treaty on European Union redefined the methods for achieving the tasks of the Community found in Article 2. The methods now include the implementation of a wide variety of policies, not just the establishment of a common market and the harmonization of the economic policies of the Member States.

Generally speaking, the Court has moved away from a wide, all encompassing view of the internal market. In *Titanium Dioxide*[187] it had established Article 95 (ex 100a) EC as the appropriate legal basis in a situation where the Community measure was designed both to eliminate distortions of competition and to protect the environment. However, in the *Waste Directive*[188] case Article 175 (ex 130s) EC prevailed even though the measure had an ancillary effect on the internal market. Limited scope of the free movement provisions corresponds to these developments.

2. The *Keck* Judgment

The Court's decision in *Keck*[189] should be understood against this background. In the case, the European Court of Justice, influenced by the views presented by Eric L White[190] and following Advocate General Tesauro's opinion in *Hünermund*,[191] 'reexamined and clarified' its previous case law, overruling some of its earlier decisions.[192]

The Court removed from the ambit of Article 28 (ex 30) EC national measures restricting or prohibiting certain selling arrangements even if they reduce the volume of sales. According to the Court, such rules do not by nature either prevent other Member States' products from gaining access to the market or impede their access more than the access of domestic products.[193]

[186] See D Chalmers, 'Repackaging the Internal Market—The Ramifications of the *Keck* Judgment' (1994) 19 EL Rev 385, 402–403 and D Chalmers, 'The Single Market: From Prima Donna to Journeyman' in Shaw and More (eds), *New Legal Dynamics of European Union* (Oxford, 1995) 68–71.

[187] Case C-300/89 *Commission v Council* [1991] ECR I-2867.

[188] Case C-155/91 *Commission v Council* (*Waste Directive*) [1993] ECR I-939 confirmed in Case C-187/93 *Parliament v Council* (*Shipments of Waste*) [1994] ECR I-2857. See D Geradin, 'Trade and Environmental Protection: Community Harmonization and National Environmental Standards' (1993) 13 YEL 151, 170–171 who is of the opinion that the case is difficult or even impossible to reconcile with *Titanium Dioxide*.

[189] Cases C-267/91 and C-268/91 *Criminal Proceedings against Keck and Mithouard* [1993] ECR I-6097.

[190] See White (n 75 above) 246–247. White was a member of the Commission's legal service and represented the Commission in Case 145/88 *Torfaen BC v B&Q* [1989] ECR 3851.

[191] Case C-292/92 *Hünermund v Landesapothekerkammer Baden-Württemberg* [1993] ECR I-6787.

[192] See n 189 above, paras 14 and 16.

[193] ibid paras 13, 16 and 17. Also Due (n 151 above) 20 and P Oliver, *The Free Movement of Goods in the European Community* (3rd edn, London, 1996) 103 see para 17 as explaining the reasoning behind para 16.

Rules regulating selling arrangements must fulfil certain criteria to fall outside the scope of Article 28 (ex 30). First of all, they must 'apply to all affected traders operating within the national territory'.[194] The meaning of this requirement is not clear.[195] It has been interpreted by Advocate General van Gerven as preventing national rules from impeding the market access of traders from another Member State more than the access of domestic traders, whilst leaving the Member States free to distinguish between categories of domestic economic operators.[196]

Secondly, and most crucially, national rules must 'affect in the same manner, in law and in fact, the marketing of domestic products and of those from other Member States'.[197] National measures discriminating on their face against imports are unequally applicable 'in law'. Provisions affording protection to similar or competing national products discriminate against other Member States' products 'in fact'.[198]

Thirdly, the purpose of the national rules must not be the regulation of trade in goods between the Member States.[199] If this is their aim, Article 28 (ex 30) EC becomes applicable.[200]

Accordingly, the Court held that the French legislation imposing a general prohibition of resale at a loss fell outside Article 28 (ex 30) EC altogether.[201]

[194] See n 189 above para 16.

[195] See I Higgins, 'The Free and Not so Free Movement of Goods since *Keck*' (1997) 6 IJEL 166, 172–173. See also Kapteyn and VerLoren van Themaat (n 54 above) 635, where it is wondered what the added value of the criterion is.

[196] Opinion of Advocate General van Gerven in Cases C-401/92 and 402/92 *Criminal Proceedings against Tankstation 't Heukske vof and J.B.E. Boermans* [1994] ECR I-2199 para 21.

[197] See n 189 above para 16.

[198] P Oliver, *The Free Movement of Goods in the European Community* (3rd edn, London 1996) 105–106 and Case C-391/92 *Commission v Greece* (*Processed Milk for Infants*) [1995] ECR I-1621 para 18. See generally on the application of this criterion Higgins (n 195 above) 173–176 and 179–180, who correctly deplores the paucity of the Court's factual discrimination analysis. However, in Joined Cases C-34/95, C-35/95 and C-36/95 *Konsument-ombudsmannen v De Agostini (Svenska) Förlag AB and TV-Shop i Sverige AB* I-3843, following Advocate General Jacobs, the Court took a realistic view of material discrimination, although it was left to the national court to determine whether the national measures actually discriminated against imports. This was in turn criticized by Oliver, 'Some Further Reflections on the Scope of Articles 28–30 (ex 30–36) EC' (1999) 36 CML Rev 783, 795–797.

[199] See n 189 above para 12.

[200] See O Due (n 151 above) 28 and W-H Roth, 'Joined Cases C-267 and C-268/91, Bernard Keck and Daniel Mithouard; Case C-292/92, Ruth Hünermund et al v Landesaptheker-kammer Baden-Württemberg' (1994) 31 CML Rev 845, 848. Gormley criticizes the Court's reference to purpose of the measure as incompatible with an effects doctrine test in L Gormley, 'Reasoning Renounced? The Remarkable Judgement in *Keck & Mithouard*' (1994) 5 Eur BusL Rev 63, 66. Cf Chief Justice Marshall's view of the US commerce clause. According to him the commerce clause prohibited the states from regulating commerce for its own sake, but allowed them to pursue other goals even if the rules did somewhat obstruct the trade among the states. See LH Tribe, *American Constitutional Law* (2nd edn, Minneola, 1988) 404–405.

[201] See n 189 above para 18.

The *Keck* judgment can be seen as a general move towards a more decentralized system: only national regulation partitioning the markets is open to scrutiny. The Court will not engage in general economic review. The competence of the Member States is preserved, and the quest for regulatory uniformity is abandoned.[202]

The judgment establishes a multiple burden and an effects-based concept of discrimination as the determinant factors in drawing the limits of the concept of a measure having equivalent effect to quantitative restrictions. *Product rules* have an unequal impact on imports as the imported products must comply with two regulatory systems. Goods legally produced in one country may have to be modified to correspond to the requirements of the other country. There is a multiple regulatory burden. Therefore, it can be presumed that rules relating to the products themselves fall within Article 28 (ex 30). On the contrary, a similar presumption is not valid as regards rules concerning *selling arrangements*, as they do not normally impose a heavier burden on imports. Therefore, it is only necessary to examine whether such rules apply equally 'in law and fact' to domestic and imported products to determine whether they fall inside the scope of Article 28 (ex 30). Thus, Article 28 (ex 30) applies only when the impact on imports is heavier than the impact on domestic goods.[203]

At the same time the Court took a step towards greater legal formalism. A rule-like test partially replaced the standard-based one. This approach has the capacity to provide legal certainty and thus reduce the administrative costs of applying Article 28 (ex 30).[204]

However, one aspect of the judgment is clearly open to criticism. The Court did not specify which judgments it was overruling,[205] nor did it define the elusive concept of 'certain selling arrangements'.[206] This has left traders and national courts in a state of uncertainty and has resulted in a few new references to the ECJ.[207] Yet, by applying the criteria consistently and formalistically in its case law building on *Keck*, the Court has

[202] See R Joliet, 'Der freie Warenverkehr: Das Urteil Keck und Mithouard und die Neuorientierung der Rechtsprechung' (1994) GRUR Int 979, 987, Roth (n 200 above) 851, and Weatherill and Beaumont (n 59 above) 608 and 619.

[203] See Joliet (n 202 above) 983–985 and Bernard (n 72 above) 91–93. See also Weatherill and Beaumont (n 59 above) 612–613, and Hilson (n 61 above) 446. Marenco had advocated a similar approach already in 1984 in Marenco, 'Pour une interpretation traditionelle de la notion de mesure d'effet équivalant à une restriction quantitative' (1984) Cahiers de Droit Européen 291. The approach is fully in line with the Court's case law on Article 29 (ex 34) EC, which is also based on the absence of dual burden. See below section V.

[204] See Craig and de Búrca (n 164 above) 627, Jarvis (n 157 above) 119–120 and 131, and Oliver (n 198 above) 793–799.

[205] For attempts to do this, see Joliet (n 202 above) 986–987, L Gormley, 'Two Years after Keck' (1996) 19 Fordham Int LJ 866, 877–880, and Higgins (n 195 above) 176–179.

[206] See Due (n 151 above) 21, Reich (n 182 above) 470–472, and Roth (n 200 above) 852. See Joliet (n 202 above) 985–987 for an answer to this critique.

[207] This was predicted by Chalmers (n 186 above) 386 and Reich (n 182 above) 471–472.

succeeded in achieving a degree of predictability in the application of Article 28 (ex 30).[208]

In the light of the Court's recent case law, it seems that the categories 'product rules' and 'rules concerning selling arrangements' are mutually exclusive and that all measures regulating selling arrangements fall within the latter category unless they constitute product rules by relating to the product itself.[209] Rules concerning selling arrangements include, for example, measures that regulate when, how, by whom and where goods may be sold.[210]

Recently, the most interesting critical analysis of the Court's judgment in *Keck* has come from Miguel Poiares Maduro.[211] Poiares Maduro proposes an alternative test for applying Article 28 (ex 30). According to him, the Court should review, in addition to discrimination, measures suspected of a national bias due to representative malfunctioning of the national political process.[212] He writes, '[w]henever there are no affected national interests equivalent to the interests of the nationals of other Member States affected by the legislation, the national political process will be suspected of institutional malfunction since the affected foreign interests were not represented'.[213]

We have misgivings about the usefulness of the test. First of all, the foreign interests are almost always represented in one way or another.[214] Especially foreign producers' and domestic consumers' interests may coincide. Take an example, discussed by Poiares Maduro,[215] where the sale of a product is regulated, but there are no equivalent or competing national products. Even if there were no national producers, the national consumers' interests in wider choice would correspond to the foreign producers' interests for free trade. There would be some representation. Secondly, even if

[208] See Oliver (n 198 above) 794–795 and T Tridimas, *The General Principles of EC Law* (Oxford, 1999) 129.

[209] As in Case C-470/93 *Verein gegen Unwesen in Handel und Gewerbe Köln e. V. v Mars GmbH* [1995] ECR I-1923 and Case C-368/95 *Vereinigte Familiapress Zeitungsverlags-und vertriebs GmbH v Heinrich Bauer Verlag* [1997] ECR I-3689. See Oliver (n 198 above) 794. It might be better to use a wider term such as 'market circumstances' instead of 'selling arrangements'.

[210] See Joliet (n 202 above) 985–986 and Higgins (n 195 above) 168–172. See also, generally, F Picod, 'La nouvelle approche de la cour de justice en matière d'entraver aux échanger' (1998) 34 RTCE 169.

[211] See Poiares Maduro (n 65 above), especially 83–87.

[212] See Poiares Maduro (n 65 above) 173–174.

[213] Poiares Maduro, 'The Saga of Article 30 EC Treaty: To Be Continued' (1998) SMJ 298, 310. Ensuring the virtual representation of out-of-state interests has been one of the main themes in modern commerce clause analysis in the USA. See Tribe (n 200 above) 408–413. For criticism, see DH Regan 'The Supreme Court and State Protectionism: Making Sense of the Dormant Commerce Clause' (1985–86) Michigan LR 1091, 1160–1167.

[214] See CR Sunstein 'Protectionism, the American Supreme Court and Integrated Markets' in Bieber *et al* (eds), *1992: One European Market?* (Baden-Baden, 1988) 142.

[215] Poiares Maduro (n 213 above) 309–310. He discussed this in the context of Case C-391/92 *Commission v Greece* (*Processed Milk for Infants*) [1995] ECR I-1621.

there is some representation, it is never given sufficient weight. Take the example given by Poiares Maduro[216] of a situation with no malfunction: a national regulation prohibiting the sale of sex articles in non-licensed establishments. In this situation the moral interests of citizens for regulation are pitted against the interests of the sex industry for commercial freedom and the interests of the consumers for cheaper prices. The second set of interests is not given enough weight, however, as only the domestic producers are taken into account by the national political process. To sum up: it always remains possible to argue that there is some but not sufficient representation.[217]

V. *ALPINE INVESTMENTS*

1. General

The Court's ruling in *Alpine Investments*[218] could be reconciled with *Keck* and the principles behind it. This would create a sensible doctrine, allocating regulatory competences between Member States. However, when read together with the judgment in *Bosman*,[219] it seems probable that these two decisions create a new doctrine in the internal market law of the Community. It is possible that the cases imply that the Court's approach to the free movement of workers and services is diverging from its approach to the free movement of goods. Another possibility is that the Court will use the doctrine also in connection with Article 28 (ex 30) EC and thus refine *Keck*. The desirability of the entire development is questionable.[220]

The factual situation in *Alpine Investments* was unusual. A ministerial ban prevented Dutch undertakings providing financial services from cold-calling potential customers. The ban applied also to customers in the other Member States. Thus, the Netherlands created a restraint on the export of services and disadvantaged its own firms as compared with undertakings operating domestically in the host Member States.

The Dutch measure was a general one, it did not discriminate and neither its purpose nor its effect was to put the national market at an advantage

216 Poiares Maduro (n 65 above) 174.

217 For other criticism, see D Chalmers, 'Book Review of *We the Court*' (1999) 115 LQR 148, 150. See also UB Neergaard, 'Free Movement of Goods from a Contextual Perspective, A Review Essay (1999) 6 MJ 151, 164–167, who considers the proposal as a still preliminary sketch.

218 Case C-384/93 *Alpine Investments BV v Minister van Financiën* [1995] ECR I-1141.

219 Case C-415/93 *Union Royale Belge des Sociétés de Football Association ASBL and others v Jean-Marc Bosman* [1995] ECR I-4921.

220 It seems that all the other post-*Keck* decisions on the freedom to provide services can be reconciled with *Keck* one way or another.

over providers of services from the other Member States. Therefore, the Dutch and British Governments, drawing an analogy from the Court's decision in *Keck*, argued that the measure fell outside Article 49 (ex 59) EC altogether.

The Court, following Advocate General Jacobs, held that the Dutch ban amounted to a *prima facie* restriction of the free movement of services but was justified on grounds of the general good. It distinguished the situation from *Keck* and rejected the arguments of the Dutch and British Governments.[221] By distinguishing *Keck* on the facts without referring to any differences between Articles 28 (ex 30) and 49 (ex 59), the Court seemed to implicitly accept that a similar approach could be used to deal with both the free movement of goods and services.

2. Dividing Regulatory Competences?

Alpine Investments can indeed be distinguished from *Keck*. Both cases concerned marketing rules, but in the former case the measure was imposed by the exporting home state, while in the latter case the measure originated from the importing host state. In the former case there was a dual burden. The service provider had to also comply with rules regulating selling arrangements in the host country. In the latter one only one set of rules applied. The home country rules affecting selling arrangements were of no relevance whatsoever. The situations were fundamentally different.

The dangers inherent in allowing the application of two sets of rules, whether they concerned product requirements or selling arrangements,[222] were fully recognized by Advocate General Jacobs.[223] In the worst-case scenario the rules could be contradictory, and thus negate the whole freedom. An example might be the following. The home country rule requires disclosure of the identity of the broker the orders are placed with. The host country rule prohibits such disclosure in the interest of preventing customer confusion. The combined effect of these rules would be to prevent cross-border trade completely.

Alpine Investments can also be reconciled with the Court's case law on Article 29 (ex 34). The Court has consistently refused to apply the *Cassis* test on export restrictions. It has held that Article 29 (ex 34) applies only to

[221] See n 218 above para 36.

[222] The situations where two sets of regulations apply to selling arrangements are rare. If a service provider moves to another Member State, the rules of his home state are seldom relevant. The home state loses control of goods once they cross the border. In the case of services not requiring physical movement, the service provider may stay within the jurisdiction of its home state, however, while the host state imposes requirements as well. See V Hatzopoulos, 'Case C-384/93, Alpine Investments BV v Minister van Financiën' (1995) 32 CML Rev 1427, 1436–1437.

[223] See n 218 above para 61 of his Opinion.

discriminatory measures.[224] As Advocate General Jacobs noted in his Opinion, the applicability of this case law to marketing rules was doubtful. Product rules are the exporting home country's responsibility. The importing country is not able to apply its regulations without subjecting them to the scrutiny of the Court. A dual burden does not normally arise. Therefore the Court does not need to be concerned unless the rules of the exporting home country are discriminatory.

Marketing rules, such as the one at issue in *Alpine Investments*, are different from product rules.[225] The importing host country is responsible for regulating selling arrangements and, according to *Keck*, does not infringe the Treaty unless it discriminates. If the exporting home country also tries to apply its rules to selling arrangements, a double burden is created. The justification for the measures has to be examined.

To avoid a double burden, the Court's case law has divided the regulatory capacities between Member States. The home country controls the product rules while the host country deals with selling arrangements.[226] These measures do not fall under the Treaty provisions on free movement unless the rules discriminate against interests from other Member States. The exception to this scheme is the power of a State to impose justified restrictions if its legitimate non-economic policies would otherwise be frustrated. In these situations co-ordination between Member States is not enough; harmonization by the centre becomes necessary.

The division of competencies established by the case law is similar to the one prevailing in the financial services directives. Authorization and prudential supervision are requirements relating to characteristics of the producer. They are the responsibility of the home country. Rules of conduct are a matter for the host Member State.[227]

This view of the free movement rules is fully in accordance with the philosophy of competition between legal orders. Products are allowed to enter markets freely and maintain all competitive advantages. At the same time Member States are given the greatest possible freedom to discover efficient rules suited to the preferences of their citizens.

[224] Case 15/79 *Groenveld v Produktschap voor Vee en Vlees* [1979] ECR 3409, Case 155/80 *Oebel* [1981] ECR 1993, and Case C-339/89 *Alsthom Atlantique SA v Sulzer SA* [1991] ECR I-107.

[225] This was also recognized by Advocate General Jacobs in his Opinion in n 218 above para 55.

[226] See Bernard, 'La libre circulation des marchandises, des personnes et des services dans le traité CE sous l'angle de la compétence' (1998) 34 CDE 11, 33–35 and Chalmers and Szyszczak (n 27 above) 304. The importing country may experience difficulties in enforcing its rules as regards services moving, for example, by telecommunications or by post. This is an argument for increased cooperation in the field of justice and home affairs.

[227] See eg the Investment Services Directive 93/22/EEC, Arts 3, 10 and 11. See also G Hertig, 'Imperfect Mutual Recognition for EC Financial Services' (1994) 14 Int Rev of Law and Economics 177, 179.

The language of the Court emphasizing that provisions on free movement apply also to non-discriminatory measures does not rule out this interpretation. The Court uses the term 'discrimination' in a strict, narrow sense: it only applies to situations where the unequal treatment can be *imputed* to a Member State (or in some situations to a private party).[228] It does not cover situations of multiple burden. It might be argued that when, for example, a Member State of importation is applying its product rules to foreign goods, it is treating different situations similarly.[229] After all, it applies its rules equally to domestic and imported products even though the goods coming from another Member State have already conformed with one set of regulations. Be that as it may, the Court's insistence on a narrow definition of discrimination means that its statements on equally applicable rules being caught by the Treaty do not rule out the possibility that a multiple burden is required for the free movement provisions to enter into play.

Viewed from this perspective, the Dutch measure at issue in *Alpine Investments* was caught by Article 49 (ex 59) EC precisely because it was imposed by the exporting state, causing a double burden. If the measure had been imposed by the importing host state, it would have fallen outside Article 49 (ex 59) EC altogether (assuming no discrimination in law or in fact). The same would have been true even if products marketed by cold-calling had been goods, not services.

This view of *Alpine Investments* and internal market law has its weaknesses. The viability of a distinction between product rules and rules affecting selling arrangements can be questioned. Sometimes the marketing of products combines presentation and appearance of the product with advertising; the product and its marketing cannot always be separated. The application of different rules to these interrelated aspects of distribution can create anomalous results.[230]

To resolve this problem, it has been proposed that a distinction should be made between rules regulating static and dynamic selling arrangements. The former category would include measures regulating questions such as when products may be sold while the latter category would contain rules not relating to activities situated in a fixed location. According to this view, the rules concerning dynamic selling arrangements can have a strong link to the product itself, form a threat to the free circulation and should

[228] See Kapteyn and VerLoren van Themaat (n 54 above) 171 and Marenco (n 203 above) 320.

[229] This was found to be prohibited form of discrimination in Case 13/63 *Commission v Italy* [1963] ECR 165.

[230] See Higgins (n 195 above) 170, Roth (n 200 above) 852, and Weatherill (n 65 above) 896.

therefore be treated in the same way as measures regulating characteristics of products.[231]

It may also well be that the distinction between rules affecting selling arrangements and product rules cannot really be applied 'as is' in the field of services. The distinction would be more difficult to use in practice. In addition, the Court would have to find another formula that clearly encompassed rules setting qualifications required of service providers. This is the most common form of regulating services. The application of these rules by the importing host state typically creates a double burden in the same manner as product rules do in the field of goods. Even if a new formulation could not be easily found, regulatory competences could still be divided in the field of services by applying the principles that underpin the judgment in *Keck*. The wide concept of discrimination is equally relevant in both fields.[232]

The argument about the artificiality of the distinction is valid, but the problem may not be insurmountable. A sensible demarcation of selling arrangements and product presentation is possible in most cases. For example, in the *Clinique*,[233] *Mars*[234] and *Familiapress*[235] judgments the

[231] See K Mortelmans, 'Article 30 of the EEC Treaty and Legislation Relating to Market Circumstances: Time to Consider a New Definition' (1991) 28 CML Rev 115, 130. See also Craig and de Búrca (n 165 above) 620–621. In my view this distinction is very unclear and problematic.

[232] José Luís Da Cruz Vilaça, 'An Exercise on the Application of Keck and Mithouard in the Field of Free Provision of Services' in M Dony and A de Walsche (eds), *Mélanges en hommage à Michel Walbroeck* (Bruxelles 1999) 815 suggests that *Keck* be transposed into the field of services, and that a distinction be made between '[r]ules concerning the "intrinsic" characteristics of the service . . . [and] . . . [r]ules relating to the general or "extrinsic" conditions in which . . . services can be provided'. Oliver (n 14 above) at 1395 argues that 'to distinguish between "product-bound" restrictions on services and those which concern "selling arrangements" will frequently be no easy matter . . . Nevertheless, in some cases such a distinction can usefully be made'. Finally, A Türk, 'Recent Case Law in Services and Establishment' (1998) EBLR 193, 201 suggests that in the field of services 'the Court may instead apply a modified *Keck* test, which would exclude national measures from scrutiny when they apply indistinctly in law and in fact'. Cf, however, Chalmers and Szysczcak (n 27 above) 406 and 423.

[233] Case C-315/92 *Verband Sozialer Wettbewerb v Estée Lauder* [1994] ECR I-317. The case concerned German prohibition to use the name 'Clinique' for a cosmetic product as it might mislead consumers into believing that the product had medicinal properties. This forced the producer to relabel. The Court held that the German measure constituted a product rule and, therefore, a restriction, and was unjustified.

[234] Case C-470/93 *Verein gegen Unwesen in Handel und Gewerbe Köln e. V. v Mars GmbH* [1995] ECR I-1923. The case concerned German law on unfair competition and law on restraints of competition. The plaintiffs argued that marking of '+10%' in wrappers of ice-cream bars was against German law as it was misleading to consumers and/or involved prohibited price fixing. The Court held that rules prohibiting certain publicity markings on the packaging of goods were product rules and, therefore, by nature hindered intra-Community trade. The German measures were not justified.

[235] Case C-368/95 *Vereinigte Familiapress Zeitungsverlags-und vertriebs GmbH v Heinrich Bauer Verlag* [1997] ECR I-3689. At issue was an Austrian law containing a prohibition on offering consumers gifts linked to the sale of goods. This rule was used against a German

Court rightly found that the national measures fell under the category of product rules, not rules affecting selling arrangements. The concept of 'product rules' can often be construed in a wide manner so that rules genuinely threatening the internal market fall automatically under the relevant Treaty article.

Furthermore, even if such a measure is considered to affect only selling arrangements, it can quite often be found to discriminate in fact. This might be the case if the rules force the producer to adopt a different sales promotion strategy or to discontinue an especially effective scheme in one Member State.[236]

Most, if not all, Member State measures endangering the single market would be caught under this doctrine. Take the example of obstacles to direct television marketing.[237] A system where a distributor advertises goods on television, displaying a contact number for each country in which the channel is received, is becoming increasingly common. If a Member State prohibits this scheme, an obstacle to trade is without doubt created, as distributors are deprived of an international marketing strategy. This kind of restriction would fall foul of the Treaty even under the *Keck* doctrine. First of all, it could be challenged under Article 28 (ex 30) EC. Although the rule regulates selling arrangements, it has an unequal impact on importers as they are required to modify their marketing system, which creates additional costs.[238] Secondly, the rule could be seen as a restriction on the free movement of services. Advertising and broadcasting of television signals are services. Here the national rule affects the content of the advertisements. It is a product rule. It creates a dual burden as the commercial complying with the rules of the broadcasting state also has to comply with the rules of the receiving state. Thus, the national measure would be caught by Article 49 (ex 59).[239]

magazine containing puzzles. The readers could send in their solutions and participate in a draw for prizes. The Court held, following Advocate General Tesauro, that the legislation bore on the content of the products and was, therefore, not concerned with a selling arrangement. It was for the national court to determine whether the law was justified by the objective of maintaining press diversity.

[236] Case 286/81 *Oosthoek Uitgeversmaatschapij BV* [1982] ECR 4575. See Craig and de Búrca (n 166 above) 620.

[237] Example given by Advocate General Jacobs in his Opinion in Case C-412/93 *Société d'Importation Édouard Leclerc-Siplec v TF1 Publicité SA and M6 Publicité SA* [1995] ECR I-179 para 54. Weatherill sees this situation as especially problematic. He is of the opinion that the issue could not be adequately dealt with under the *Keck* formula. Weatherill (n 65 above) 890–891 and 894.

[238] This is recognized by Advocate General Jacobs in his Opinion ibid para 37.

[239] National procedural rules might create difficulties for a challenge based on Article 49 (ex 59). However, Member States are under an obligation to grant access to the courts. See Case 222/84 *Johnston v Chief Constable of the Royal Ulster Constabulary* [1986] ECR 1651 paras 13–21, Case 222/86 *UNECTEF v Heylens* [1987] ECR 4097 para 14, M Brealy and M Hoskins, *Remedies in EC Law: Law and Practice in English and EC Courts* (London, 1994) 54–55, and J Temple Lang, 'The Duties of National Courts under Community Constitutional Law' (1997) 22 EL Rev 3, 7.

A real example is provided by the *De Agostini* case.[240] Swedish rules prohibiting certain forms of advertising on television, which were used against advertisements broadcast from the United Kingdom, were examined under both Articles 28 (ex 30) and 49 (ex 59) EC. Following Advocate General Jacobs, the Court stated that the prohibition of one method of promotion, which affected selling arrangements, could have a greater impact on goods from other Member States, as a certain form of advertising may be the only way to penetrate the market. It was left to the national court to examine, however, whether the rules were actually discriminatory in fact in this manner. The rules also fell within the scope of Article 49 (ex 59) as they established a second set of controls, thus creating a dual burden.[241]

It is true that the division between product rules and rules affecting selling arrangements is formalistic. This is not necessarily a bad thing. Formalism may make legal certainty possible, and this is a matter of great importance for national courts. It is only if formalism enables many national measures harmful to the internal market to escape scrutiny that there is a problem. This does not seem to be the case. And most importantly, even if the formalism can be criticized, this does not yet invalidate the principles behind *Keck* establishing a wide concept of discrimination as the basis of the free movement law.

It has sometimes been claimed that the double burden theory is not appropriate for many services. They only crystallize on commercialization. This will often happen in the importing host state.[242] An example is a rock concert. If an English band goes to Sweden to perform, that service is provided in Sweden, even though the band may have held similar concerts in the United Kingdom.

It is of course correct to say that the service is not subject to two rules at the same time. However, in our view the wide discrimination or double burden theory works in this context as well. The service has been shaped by the home country rules. The application of the host country rules would prevent the service provider from benefiting from his competitive advantage and would force him to make changes to the service product itself.

Take again the example of the rock band. Assume that the United Kingdom has liberal rules on noise levels in concerts while Sweden is more restrictive. The application of the Swedish rules would deprive the band from reaping the full benefits from its investments in loudspeakers etc. The band may have even advertised itself as 'the loudest band in the Universe'.

240 Joined Cases C-34/95, C-35/95 and C-36/95 *Konsumentombudsmannen v De Agostini (Svenska) Förlag AB and TV-Shop i Sverige AB* [1997] ECR I-3843.

241 See in more detail J Snell, 'De Agostini and the Regulation of Television Broadcasting' (1997) 8 Eur Bus L Rev 222–227.

242 Chalmers and Szyszczak (n 27 above) 405 and 423.

If strict noise level rules were applied, its competitive advantage would be jeopardized. The band would have to alter the show. This might be as simple as turning the knobs down but might also bring some costs with extra sound checks etc. The application of the Swedish rules would certainly amount to a *prima facie* restriction, because of the double burden they create, although the rules might well be justified on health grounds.

Naturally there still remains the problem of enforcement. The home country authorities cannot go to the host country to ensure that their rules are respected. In our example, there will be no British noise inspectors at the concert in Sweden.

This problem is not unique to services. It may also occur in the goods sector, for example, if the exporting Member State's product rules are enforced in the retail level. An example might be found in the sex industry. A Member State may have no pre-publication control of printed material, for constitutional reasons. However, the police of the Member State might do random checks in sex shops to find indecent publications. This will create a problem for the importing Member State. If a product is lawfully produced and marketed in the exporting state, it has to be mutually recognized. However, the importing state cannot really be certain that the publications comply with the exporting state's product rules. The exporting state's authorities have not controlled them in any way.

In our view, the host state authorities are entitled to check that the imported goods and services comply with at least one set of rules.[243] Of course, similar checks would have to be carried out on domestic goods and services. This is implicit in the formulas 'lawfully produced and marketed in one of the Member States' and 'established in another Member State where he lawfully provides similar services' which form the precondition to mutual recognition.[244] The idea is not that no rules apply but that one set of rules applies.

In our example this means that the Swedish authorities are automatically entitled to inspect that the performance of the UK band complies with at least the UK noise level standards, assuming of course that they do similar checks at the concerts of domestic bands. Compliance with Swedish rules can only be checked if those rules are justified.

The problem with this approach is that the host state authorities are

[243] This does not give the host state a *carte blanche* to apply home state rules. For example, the host state could check that a service provider holds an appropriate licence, but it could not second-guess the granting of the licence, or this would again constitute discrimination. See Commision interpretative communication, *Freedom to provide services and the general good in the insurance sector*, OJ 2000 C43/5 at 12.

[244] Case 120/78 *Rewe Zentrale AG v Bundesmonopolverwaltung für Branntwein* [1979] ECR 649, para 14 and Case C-76/90 *Manfred Säger v Dennemeyer & Co. Ltd* [1991] ECR I-4221, para 12.

forced to apply foreign rules. In our view this does not invalidate the theory. Foreign law is being applied all the time by national courts under private international law. The authorities in different Member States can, and should, cooperate. Article 10 (ex 5) EC imposes on the home state authorities a duty of sincere cooperation[245] so the host state authorities can seek help in determining the content of their rules.[246] If the application of the home state rules proves impossible in a particular situation, this can be easily taken into account when the justification of the host state rules is examined.

The whole problem may not be very significant in the end. The most common way to regulate services is to impose requirements on the service providers, not on the services themselves. These rules clearly create a double burden if they are applied by the host state to a service provider who has already complied with the home country requirements.

To sum up: when *Keck* and *Alpine Investments* are read together, it is possible to argue that the Court has divided regulatory competences so that the importing host state is responsible for regulating market circumstances while the exporting home state deals with product and production rules. The importing host state does not have to justify the application of its non-discriminatory rules concerning selling arrangements, only its product and production rules. Conversely, the exporting home state does not need to justify the application of its non-discriminatory product and production rules, only its rules concerning market circumstances. This coordination of national regulatory competences corresponds to a wide notion of discrimination, is very desirable from the point of view of vertical division of power in the Community and regulatory competition, and also creates a rule-like test sitting well with the role of the Court. Unfortunately, recent developments in the case law indicate that the Court's approach cannot really be explained by allocation of regulatory competences but is based on a concept of market access.

3. The Problem of *Bosman*

The judgment of the Court in *Bosman*[247] seems to invalidate the *Keck* doctrine based purely on multiple burden and discrimination. The ruling cannot be fully reconciled with *Keck* but must be seen as a refinement, indicating that the Court's view of free movements is based on market access

[245] See, eg, Case C-251/89 *Nikolaos Athanasopoulos and others v Bundesanstalt für Arbeit* [1991] ECR I-2797, para 57.

[246] The fact that non-cooperation would impede the export potential of 'their' companies might also be helpful.

[247] Case C-415/93 *Union Royale Belge des Sociétés de Football Association ASBL and others v Jean-Marc Bosman* [1995] ECR I-4921.

and that *Alpine Investments* has to be read in that light as well,[248] in contradiction to the previous analysis.

Bosman is an Article 39 (ex 48) EC case. Mr Bosman was a Belgian football player who wanted to move from his Belgian club to a French club. Rules originating from international sporting associations required the receiving club to pay a transfer fee even though Mr Bosman's contract with the Belgian club had expired. Similar fee applied also to transfers within Belgium. The question arose whether the fee was a restriction to the free movement of workers.

The defendants argued that the ruling in *Keck* should be applied by analogy, and that therefore the equally applicable transfer system should fall outside Article 39 (ex 48) EC altogether. The Court, following Advocate General Lenz, rejected that argument and held that the transfer system violated Article 39 (ex 48) and was not justified by reasons of public interest.

The judgment cannot be explained on the grounds of multiple burden or discrimination.[249] The transfer rules themselves may have indeed been discriminatory in practice,[250] but the Court's ruling did not address the issue, instead it revolved around the concept of market access.

The wording used by the Court to distinguish *Keck* in *Alpine Investments* and *Bosman* is very similar. In both judgments it stated that the

248 See Bernard (n 226 above) 23–25 and Poiares Maduro (n 65 above) 100–102 See also R Greaves, 'Advertising Restrictions and the Free Movement of Goods and Services' (1998) 23 EL Rev 305, 314–315 and D Martin, ' "Discriminations", "entraves" et "raisons impérieuses" dans le traité CE: Trois concepts en quête d'identité' (1998) 34 CDE 261, 624–625.

249 A tempting way to explain *Bosman* away would be by concentrating on the fact that the case concerned the movement of natural persons. Advocate General Lenz argued in para 203 of his Opinion that free movement of citizens is a fundamental human right which should never be restricted without a weighty justification, and in the USA, a person's right to move freely has been given greater protection than interstate commerce. However, nothing in the reasoning indicates that this was a decisive factor, and in general citizenship has been of limited value in integrating free movement rules.

250 Advocate General Lenz examined the potentially discriminatory nature of the rules in his Opinion in n 247 above paras 151–164. Bosman has been confirmed in Case C-190/98 *Volker Graf v Fitzmoser Maschienenban GmbH*, judgment of 27 January 2000. On the facts of the case, however, the Court held that Austrian legislation granting compensation payment to a worker in the case of a contract of employment being terminated, except if the termination was attributable to the worker, was in accordance with Article 39 (ex 48) EC, 'because the entitlement to compensation on termination of employment is not dependent on the worker's choosing whether or not to stay with his current employer but on a further and hypothetical event, namely the subsequent termination of his contract, without such termination being at his own initiative or attributable to him . . . Such an event is too uncertain and indirect.' The reasoning attracts the question whether, *e contrario*, an entitlement that is dependent on the worker's choosing to stay, such as a loyalty bonus or even a pay rise based on the duration of service, falls within the scope of Article 39. If so, the reach of the provisions would be great indeed, especially as it is capable of covering private measures, such as collective agreements. It is also worth noting that it might not be easy to fit such a measure into the framework of *non-economic* general interests.

rules at issue directly affect the plaintiffs' access to the market in the other Member States.[251]

Market access played an important, though indirect, part also in the Court's reasoning in *Keck*. The Court used this concept to explain its decision that non-discriminatory rules affecting certain selling arrangements do not fall within the scope of Article 28 (ex 30). It stated that the application of these rules 'is not by nature such as to prevent [other Member States' products] access to the market or impede that access any more than it impedes the access of domestic products'.[252]

In the light of this it seems that the currently used test of whether a measure falls within the free movement provisions is one centring on market access, at least in the field of workers and services. If the measure creates a direct impediment to market access, it has to be justified. This applies even if it does not create a multiple burden or discriminate otherwise against foreign interests.[253]

The requirement that an impediment to market access has to be *direct* can be interpreted in two ways. It could be argued that the impact of the national measure on market access has to be sufficiently great to trigger the application of the Treaty.[254] Alternatively, it may be argued that the cross-border nature of the restriction determines whether the impediment is direct.[255]

The first reading, based on the sufficient impact of the measure, accords with other parts of the Court's judgment in *Alpine Investments*. The Court found that the Dutch ban on cold-calling was a *prima facie* violation of Article 49 (ex 59). The 'prohibition deprives the operators concerned of a rapid and direct technique for marketing and for contacting potential clients in other Member States'.[256] The Court examined the *impact* of the measure on market access.

This is an approach that Advocate General Jacobs argued for in his Opinions in *Leclerc-Siplec*[257] and in *Alpine Investments*. According to him, the guiding principle is that all undertakings should have an unimpeded access to the whole internal market. National measures creating substantial

[251] Case C-384/93 *Alpine Investments BV v Minister van Financiën* [1995] ECR I-1141, para 38 and n 247 above, para 103. The similar wording makes *Bosman* impossible to ignore, even though it was a case dealing with the free movement of workers.

[252] Cases C-267/91 and C-268/91 *Criminal Proceedings against Keck and Mithouard* [1993] ECR I-6097 para 17.

[253] See Weatherill (n 65 above) 896–897. See also Hatzopoulos (n 222 above) 1437–1438.

[254] This view of the scope of the free movements is advocated by Weatherill (n 65 above) 896–901.

[255] See M Ross, 'Article 59 and the Marketing of Financial Services' (1995) 20 EL Rev 507, 513.

[256] See n 251 above para 28.

[257] Case C-412/93 *Société d'Importation Édouard Leclerc-Siplec v TF1 Publicité SA and M6 Publicité SA* [1995] ECR I-179.

restrictions to that access must be open to scrutiny by the Court. The test is based on the impact of the measure on market access. It is a *de minimis* test. The test would not have to be applied to overtly discriminatory measures, which are *per se* prohibited by Article 28 (ex 30) EC, and rules creating a multiple burden could be presumed to have a substantial impact on market access. Thus, only rules regulating selling arrangements would have to be tested. The result of the test would depend on a number of factors such as the scope of application of the national measure, the availability of other selling arrangements, and the nature of the effect.[258]

However, the *de minimis* test suffers from a fundamental weakness. Although the test is conceptually clear, it is very difficult to use. The point where impact to market access becomes substantial cannot be easily determined.[259] It cannot depend on the nature of the national measures. From the point of view of the producer, there is no difference between rules prohibiting certain advertising methods and rules which limit shopping hours if the reduction in sales is the same. Sunday trading rules might become fair game again.[260]

Furthermore, similar measures may substantially impede market access in one Member State or in one sector but not in another.[261] For example the importance of television advertising may vary depending on the availability and the penetration of other media and on the nature of the products. In addition, thresholds can fluctuate in time as circumstances change. For example, a ban on television advertising may become more problematic if the circulation of newspapers diminishes. Thus, the decisions of the Court would not have general applicability but each case would have to be decided individually on its merits. This would create legal uncertainty,[262] especially in national courts, and might give rise to similar problems as did the Court's pre-*Keck* case law.

In the field of competition law a *de minimis* test is not as problematic as in the field of trade law. In the former area the Commission is strongly

[258] ibid paras 41–45 of the Opinion of Advocate General Jacobs. A somewhat similar test was proposed by Advocate General van Gerven in Case 145/88 *Torfaen BC v B&Q* [1989] ECR 3851. The underlying principle would have been market access, and national measures screening off markets would have been caught. The partitioning effect would have been inspected in the light of the legal and economic context of the measure. The Court did not follow his suggestion. A *de minimis* test has also been supported by, eg, Arnull (n 61 above) 296, and Weatherill (n 65 above) 896–901.

[259] See Gormley (n 205 above) 882.

[260] See Craig and de Búrca (n 166 above) 624–626.

[261] Similarly Bernard (n 226 above) 18.

[262] See the Opinion of Advocate General Tesauro in Case C-292/92 *Hünermund v Landesapothekerkammer Baden-Württemberg* [1993] ECR I-6787, para 21, Bernard (n 226 above) 19–20, Hilson (n 61 above) 456, L Idot, 'Case C-412/93, Société d'Importation Édouard Leclerc-Siplec v TFI Publicité SA and M6 Publicité SA' (1996) 33 CML Rev 113, 120, Oliver (n 198 above) 792, and Weatherill (n 65 above) 898–901. On the other hand, it could be argued that the test is flexible and can respond to changing circumstances.

involved[263] while in the latter national courts bear the primary responsibility for applying Community law. In addition, the former field lends itself better to the application of numerical criteria than the latter.[264]

If this reading of the judgments in *Alpine Investments* and *Bosman* is correct, the Court can be criticized for increasing legal uncertainty. If the Court wanted to introduce a *de minimis* test, it would have to define very carefully the circumstances and criteria relevant for its application.[265] Now the Court has merely talked about the directness of the impediment to market access, hardly a very helpful statement.[266]

It is submitted, however, that the Court's reasoning cannot be explained with reference to a *de minimis* doctrine.[267] The decisive element was not the impact of the measure but rather its cross-border nature.

In *Alpine Investments* the Court stated in a key paragraph:

> A prohibition such as that at issue is imposed by the Member State in which the provider of service is established and affects not only offers made by him to addressees who are established in that State or move there in order to receive services but also offers made to potential recipients in another Member State. It therefore directly affects access to the market in services in the other Member States and is thus capable of hindering intra-Community trade in Services.[268]

Similar reasoning can be found in *Bosman*.[269] Furthermore, in this case the Court did not examine how substantial the hindrance to free movement was. This examination would have been essential under the *de minimis* doctrine.

263 Even if the matter is in the hands of a national court, it can consult the Commission. See *Notice on Cooperation between National Courts and the Commission*, OJ 1993 C39/5, in applying Articles 85 [now 81] and 86 [now 82] of the Treaty, in particular para 38.

264 See Bernard (n 226 above) 17–18, Craig and de Búrca (n 166 above) 626, and Idot (n 262 above) 120. Mortelmans criticized Advocate General van Gerven's proposal for being excessively demanding for the national courts. He feared that the approach would lead to conflicting decisions.

265 Opinion of Advocate General Jacobs in n 257 above para 42. The Opinion has been criticized for failing to clearly set out the criteria for applying *de minimis* test, a very difficult task indeed. See Oliver (n 198 above) 109–110.

266 Until mid-1930s the US Supreme Court's case law on the commerce clause focused on direct or indirect nature of the burden created by state law. The approach created difficulties in practice and the reasoning was criticized as conclusionary, mechanical, uncertain and removed from actualities. See Nowak and Rotunda (n 64 above) 289–290 and Tribe (n 200 above) 408.

267 The Court did not adopt the doctrine in Case C-67/97 *Criminal Proceedings against Ditler Bluhme* [1998] ECR I-8033 either. However, the case concerned national legislation regulating product characteristics, a type of rule not capable of benefiting from the *de minimis* exception as defined by Advocate General Jacobs, and does not therefore offer any conclusive proof.

268 Case C-384/93 *Alpine Investments BV v Minister van Financiën* [1995] ECR I-1141, para 38.

269 Case C-415/93 *Union Royale Belge des Sociétés de Football Association ASBL and others v Jean-Marc Bosman* [1995] ECR I-4921, para 103.

According to the Court, the decisive difference between these cases and *Keck* is that, in the latter case, the restriction directly affected only the relationship between economic operators in France. It took effect within only one Member State. Its influence on products from the other States was incidental. Thus, the measure had only an indirect effect on any decrease in the volume of imports through diminished demand in the country of importation. The rule did not directly affect the market access of imported products.

By contrast, in *Alpine Investments* and *Bosman* the rules had an immediate effect on the relationships between economic operators in different countries. The measures were not confined within one Member State. The obstacles directly affected cross-border activities. The restrictions immediately hindered the provision of services and the movement of workers from one Member State to another. The effect on market access was direct.

Advocate General Tesauro understood *Alpine Investments* and *Bosman* in this way in his opinion in *Familiapress*.[270] On basis of these judgments and the jurisprudence of the Court on selling arrangements, he adopted a restrictive reading of *Keck*. He stated that:

> the only measures excluded from the scope of Article 30 [now 28] are those which are absolutely general in nature, which apply—needless to say—without distinction, which do not impede imports and which might lead at most to a (hypothetical) reduction in the volume of imports only as a consequence of an equally hypothetical reduction in the overall volume of sales.[271]

He continued by emphasizing that a general contraction in the volume of sales leading to a reduction in the volume of imports—the *Keck* scenario—is not enough to bring a measure under Article 28 (ex 30).[272] He seems to make a distinction between general measures which affect trade only indirectly, through a reduction in the volume of sales, and measures which have a more direct impact on imports.[273]

The rules at issue in *Alpine Investments* and *Bosman* can in one sense be compared with border measures, such as charges having equivalent effect to customs duties. They also affect cross-border activities directly. Because of their close links to the crossing of borders, it is claimed that they create problems *per se*. Thus, the Community law has adopted a restrictive approach towards these measures.[274]

[270] Case C-368/95 *Vereinigte Familiapress Zeitungsverlags-und vertriebs GmbH v Heinrich Bauer Verlag* [1997] ECR I-3689.

[271] ibid para 10 of his Opinion.

[272] ibid paras 10–11 of his Opinion.

[273] For a somewhat similar, concrete, personal, rights-based interpretation on the fundamental freedoms see P Eeckhout (n 14 above) 270–271. He notes that from this perspective *Keck* will be difficult to transpose to services. See also Reich, 'Europe's Economic Constitution, or: A New Look at Keck' (1991) 19 OJLS 337, 341–344.

[274] See generally Craig and de Búrca (n 166 above) 551–560 and Weatherill and Beaumont (n 59 above) 454–465.

It seems that the Court may have adopted in *Bosman* a distinction between rules restricting access to employment and rules regulating exercise of occupation advocated by Advocate General Lenz. Naturally the former rules directly affect the hiring of workers from the other Member States and thus their access to the employment market, while the effect of the latter rules is more indirect.[275] The Advocate General sees an analogy between this distinction and the case law on Article 28 (ex 30).[276]

The approach adopted by the Court can be criticized. First of all, *Alpine Investments* and *Bosman* cannot be reconciled with *Keck*. In *Keck* the decisive aspect was the absence of an unequal burden. This is illustrated by the Court's language. The decisive factor according to the Court is that market access of other Member States' products is not prevented[277] or impeded *more* than the access of domestic products.[278] In *Alpine Investments* and *Bosman*, by contrast, the crucial factor was the *directness* of the effect to market access. Discrimination was not an issue.

By distinguishing *Keck* in *Alpine Investments* and *Bosman*, the Court did try to maintain the illusion of uniform interpretation of the freedoms. However, the principles behind the cases are truly different, and the distinction was highly dubious. In all these cases market access was subjected to certain conditions but not absolutely prevented. Furthermore, some post-*Keck* decisions, such as *Commission v Greece* (*Processed Milk for Infants*),[279] had a very strong cross-border element, and in that sense the national measures' impact on market access was direct, and yet the Court held that the domestic rules fell outside of Article 28 (ex 30) altogether.[280] Thus, either the case law on different freedoms are diverging, or the judgments in *Alpine Investments* and *Bosman* refine *Keck*.[281]

Secondly, one may wonder whether the *directness* of the effect to market

[275] Similar distinction is made in the Treaty where Article 39(3)(a) (ex 48(3)(a)) gives a right to accept offers of employment, subject only to justified limitations, while Article 39(3)(c) (ex 48(3)(c)) gives only the right to stay in a Member State for the purposes of employment *in accordance with the provisions governing the nationals* of that State (emphasis added). See also Regulation 1612/68 on Freedom of Movement for Workers, whose first title covers mainly access to employment, while the second title governs conditions of employment. The same distinction was made in relation to the free movement of services by Advocate General Gulmann in his opinion in Case C-275/92 *Her Majesty's Customs and Excise v Gerhart Schindler and Jörg Schindler* [1994] ECR I-1039, para 56.

[276] Opinion of Advocate General Lenz in n 258 above paras 205 and 210. The Court refers to para 210 of the Opinion in para 99 of the judgment.

[277] Total ban on some foreign products would prevent market access and amount to a quantitative restriction.

[278] Cases C-267/91 and C-268/91 *Criminal Proceedings against Keck and Mithouard* [1993] ECR I-6097 para 17.

[279] Case C-391/92 *Commission v Greece* (*Processed Milk for Infants*) [1995] ECR I-1621.

[280] See Bernard (n 226 above) 22–25. See also Poiares Maduro (n 65 above) 101, Poiares Maduro (n 213 above) 315–316, and Hilson (n 61 above) 456.

[281] See Weatherill (n 65 above) 896–901, who supports the refinement theory.

access is really a fully relevant criterion. Existence of a multiple burden is obviously a danger to the single market as it prevents economies of scale and the maintenance of competitive advantage, and thus also an effective competition between legal orders. In addition, some views of the internal market logically lead to the conclusion that measures having a substantial impact on market access have to be open to scrutiny by the Court. However, directness of the effect on access to the market may not be important in itself. Why focus on the question whether the measure regulates formally internal relationships and thus has only an indirect effect on market access or directly controls cross-border situations?

The fact that the rules may in some ways be comparable to border measures is not decisive. Duties and charges having an equivalent effect are repugnant to the internal market not only because they take place at the border but also, and more importantly, because they only apply to products which cross the border. Thus, they are inherently detrimental to products from other Member States. The same consideration does not apply to the rules under discussion.

Thirdly, the concept of 'a rule which directly affects market access' is not exactly a clear one. It has a conclusionary ring to it.[282] The employment of such a criterion is likely to lead to similar problems of legal uncertainty as did the pre-*Keck* case law under Article 28 (ex 30) EC.[283] Admittedly, the tiger of *Cassis*[284] is unlikely to run free in the field of free movement of services and workers as a result of these judgments. After all they correspond to a relatively narrow view of the internal market by stressing the cross-border nature of the activities.[285] However, the Court might be facing a long line of cases where it has to define the concept more clearly.[286] Due to the conclusionary nature of the concept and variety of factual situations that may arise, this may prove to be a very difficult task indeed.

Fourthly, the doctrine based on a direct impediment on market access is in conflict with the Court's well-established case law on Article 29 (ex 34) EC.[287] In *Groenveld*[288] and in subsequent cases such as *Spain v*

[282] See n 266 above on American criticism of the directness test.

[283] See above section IV.

[284] Dashwood used the expression of 'the Court riding a tiger' to describe the potential for over-extension in *Cassis* line of cases. See Dashwood, 'The Cassis de Dijon Line of Authority' in Bates, *In Memoriam JDB Mitchell* (London, 1983) 158.

[285] On *Alpine Investments* see Ross (n 255 above) 513.

[286] See JMF Martin, 'Re-defining Obstacles to the Free Movement of Workers' (1996) 21 EL Rev 313, 323.

[287] Advocate General Lenz Case C-415/93 *Union Royale Belge des Sociétés de Football Association ASBL and others v Jean-Marc Bosman* [1995] ECR I-4921, para 207 and Weatherill (n 65 above) 901–904. See also Daniele (n 60 above) 195 and 198–200, who criticizes the judgments in *Alpine Investments* and *Bosman* for not applying the Article 29 (ex 34) EC type approach.

[288] Case 15/79 *Groenveld v Produktschap voor Vee en Vlees* [1979] ECR 3409.

Council[289] and *Alsthom Atlantique*,[290] the Court has held that Article 29 (ex 34) is only concerned with measures 'which have as their specific object or effect the restriction on patterns of exports and thereby the establishment of a difference in treatment between the domestic trade of the Member State and its export trade in such a way as to provide a particular advantage for national production or for the domestic market of the State in question at the expense of the production or of the trade of other Member States'.[291] Thus the Treaty catches measures affecting exports only if they are discriminatory. The *Cassis* doctrine does not apply.

The approach of the Court is easily explained by the fact that national rules affecting exports do not create a multiple burden for the exporter. He has to comply with only one set of rules. The same measures apply both to goods for domestic and export markets.[292]

It has been suggested that a more intensive control of the exporting home states product rules would be desirable in special situations. This is the case in circumstances where the importing host state is exceptionally able to apply its product rules to imports, be they goods or services. If the application of host state rules is allowed, the application of home state regulations creates a double burden and thus discriminates factually against exports. This situation can materialize either when host state measures are justified by the general good or when the goods or services are not legally sold in the home state at all.[293] It has to be noted, however, that the more intensive control would undermine the trademark function of national legislation. Consumers could no longer fully trust products from a country known for its high regulatory standards.[294]

Alpine Investments and *Bosman* were concerned with obstacles making the 'export' of services and workers more difficult. The Court applied the test of impediment to direct market access, not a test based on multiple burdens and discrimination. The case laws on Article 49 (ex 59) and 39 (ex 48) and Article 29 (ex 34) EC are either diverging or *Groenveld* has to be

[289] Case C-9/89 *Kingdom of Spain v Council of the European Communities* [1990] ECR I-1383, para 21.

[290] Case C-339/89 *Alsthom Atlantique SA v Sulzer SA* [1991] ECR I-107.

[291] See n 288 above para 7.

[292] See R Barents, 'New Developments in MEEs' (1981) 18 CML Rev 271, 302–303 and Weatherill and Beaumont (n 59 above) 605–606. If the exporting state tries to extend its rules affecting selling arrangements to the other Member States' territory, it does create a multiple burden, however. See above.

[293] See W-H Roth, 'Wettbewerb der Mitgliedstaaten oder der Hersteller?' (1995) 159 ZHR 78, 92–93.

[294] The Court has recently emphasized the importance of the 'trademark function' in Case C-388/95 *Belgium v Spain*, judgment of 16 May 2000. See also discussion in section III above. Producers complying with national standards could of course indicate this in their advertisments etc. Many German beers, for example, already state in their labels that they have been produced in accordance with the German Beer Purity Law.

reconsidered.[295] In its recent judgments in *Dusseldorp* and in *ED Srl v Italo Fenocchio* the Court stated that according to the settled case law, Article 29 (ex 34) applies to discriminatory national measures.[296] Based on this, it seems that the case laws are diverging.

It is true that the free movement of services is only governed by one provision, Article 49 (ex 59), and the free movement of workers by only Article 39 (ex 48), while in the field of free movement of goods imports are regulated by Article 28 (ex 30) and exports by Article 29 (ex 34). It might be argued that this division makes it easier for the Court to apply different standards to the import and export of goods. The one and only provision cannot be split in its application and therefore a similar distinction cannot be made with respect to services and workers. Therefore it could be thought that while Articles 28 and 49 and 39 are construed similarly, the interpretation of Article 29 can diverge. Thus, the *Groenveld* case law could survive despite *Alpine Investments* and *Bosman*.[297]

This formalistic structural argument is not convincing, however. The wording of Articles 28 and 29 is similar, so they would *prima facie* have to be applied in the same way. So far the interpretation of the two provisions has been based on the same principles of avoidance of a multiple burden and discrimination. Furthermore, the arguments for parallel construction of Articles 28 and 49 and 39 also apply to Articles 29 and 49 and 39.[298]

Moreover, the Court seems to have established the parallel interpretation of Articles 29 and 49 in *Peralta*.[299] In the judgment the Court based its finding that the Italian measures at issue did not infringe the freedom to export services on the fact that the rules applied equally to vessels providing services internally and to vessels transporting products to the other Member States. The policy behind the ruling seems to be the same as the one behind Article 29, and the language of the Court in these two fields is quite similar.

It is doubtful whether the direct market access doctrine makes good sense as regards export restrictions. Non-discriminatory obstacles to exports are generally not problematic from the viewpoint of competition between legal orders. Such rules, applying equally to products for domestic and foreign markets, may be perfectly legitimate expressions of national preferences. If such rules are burdensome on a business, it can relocate or

[295] See G Tesauro, 'The Community Internal Market in the Light of the Recent Case Law of the Court of Justice' (1995) 15 YEL 1, 16.

[296] Case C-203/96 *Chemische Afvalstoffen Dusseldorp BV and others v Minister van Volkshuisvesting, Ruimtelijke Ordening en Milieubeheer* [1998] ECR I-4075, para 40 and Case C-412/97 *ED Srl v Italo Fenocchio*, judgment of 22 June 1999, para 10.

[297] This possibility was brought up by Hatzopoulos (n 222 above) 1442.

[298] See section II above.

[299] Case C-379/92 *Matteo Peralta* [1994] ECR I-3453. See Hatzopoulos (n 222 above) 1441.

start lobbying for a change in legislation. The plight of exporters should be taken seriously by politicians if only for balance of payments reasons. Normally the market should be allowed to find out the efficient rules and national preferences should be respected. Usually there is no need for the Court to get involved.

Control of export restrictions based on market access, not on discrimination, does not sit well with the philosophy of mutual recognition. The idea is that one set of rules apply and is then mutually recognized, not that no rules apply.

Paradoxically, the inapplicability of the rules of the exporting country makes the rules of the importing country applicable. Since *Cassis de Dijon* the Court has declared that products lawfully produced and marketed in one Member State have to be allowed into the market of the importing Member State.[300] If the rules of the exporting Member State are found to be contrary to the free movement provisions of the Treaty, the product can be exported out of that State but it does not gain the right to be marketed in the exporting State. The Treaty does not apply to fully internal situations.[301] Thus the product in question is not 'lawfully produced and marketed' in the sense of *Cassis*, and the importing State's rules may apply.[302]

Moreover, export restrictions are generally less prevalent than obstacles to imports. The Member States have traditionally in a mercantilistic spirit been eager to encourage exports, not to hinder them.[303] This does not mean that a discrimination analysis can be superficial, however. A Member State may very well want to limit the exports of valuable factors of production as this might reduce the productivity of the economy. Similarly, a Member State may try to require that raw materials be processed within its territory

[300] Case 120/78 *Rewe Zentrale AG v Bundesmonopolverwaltung für Branntwein* [1979] ECR 649, para 14. See also eg Cases C-267/91 and C-268/91 *Criminal Proceedings against Keck and Mithouard* [1993] ECR I-6097, para 15 as regards product rules under Article 28 (ex 30) EC, and Case C-76/90 *Manfred Säger v Dennemeyer & Co. Ltd* [1991] ECR I-4221, para 12 as regards services.

[301] See, however, Cases C-321/94, C-322/94, C-323/94 and C-324/94 *Criminal Proceedings against Jacques Pistre* [1997] ECR I-2343.

[302] See Roth, 'Case C-76/90 Manfred Säger v Dennemeyer & Co Ltd' (1993) 30 CML Rev 145, 152–153. Similar philosophy is partly behind *van Binsbergen*. If the service is directed purely towards a Member State where the provider is not established, the host State is allowed to apply its own rules as the home State does not exercise control. See Case 33/74 *Van Binsbergen v Bestuur van de Bedrijfsvereniging voor de Metaalnijverheid* [1974] ECR 1299, para 13. Advocate General Jacobs interpreted *van Binsbergen* in a more narrow fashion in paras 40–54 of his Opinion in Joined Cases C-34/95, C-35/95 and C-36/95 *Konsumentombudsmannen v De Agostini (Svenska) Förlag AB and TV-Shop i Sverige AB* [1997] ECR I-3843 as did the Court in Case C-212/97 *Centros Ltd v Erhvervs-og Selskabsstyrelsen* [1999] ECR I-1459, paras 24–30. See in general on this line of case law V Hatzopoulos, 'Recent Developments of the Case Law of the ECJ in the Field of Services' (2000) 37 MLR 43 at 62–64.

[303] See Marenco (n 203 above) 326–327.

before exportation and thus force foreign producers to invest in the country and improve its employment situation.[304]

The use of the doctrine based on an impediment to market access to export restrictions might also lead to over-extension.[305] A wide variety of national *production rules* ranging from environmental legislation to labour law can be said to impede the competitiveness of the undertakings of the exporting country and therefore affect the market access of their products. The control of these rules would extend the free movement provisions of the Treaty even further than the Court's pre-*Keck* case law did.

Here the directness criterion is actually helpful, for unless the Court consistently places the emphasis on the cross-border nature of the restrictions, this over-extension cannot be avoided. Non-discriminatory national production rules do not create a dual burden. Their justification should not be examined.[306] A test focusing on the directness of the impediment to the market access could exempt them from the Court's control, as it can be argued that they hinder market access only indirectly by making the production of goods or services more costly in the home country. The directness criterion might be used in this way to keep the regulatory competence for production rules firmly with the exporting home State, where it belongs.

It has been argued that the Court should treat the export of goods differently from the export of services. It has been claimed that exported goods are a legitimate concern for the home state, unlike exported services, as the production of goods can cause pollution and exported goods can infiltrate the home market, and that therefore the market access doctrine ought to be applied to the export of services but not to goods.[307] In our view this is misconceived. First, the production of services can give rise to equally legitimate concerns, such as worker protection. Secondly, according to *Säger*, services have to be present also in the home market to benefit fully from the free movement rules.[308] Thirdly, if exported services are not a matter for the home state, they must be a matter for the host state, as otherwise a lacunae would form. The allocation of regulatory competence to the host state would seriously compromise the achievement of a single market in services, however, as it contravenes the principle of mutual recognition upon which the market is built. Thus, the export of goods and services ought to be treated in a uniform manner.

Altogether, the Court seems to have taken a step towards centralization

[304] On the American experience see Tribe (n 200 above) 426–427.

[305] See D O'Keeffe and P Osborne, 'L'affaire Bosman: un arrêt important pour le bon fonctionnement du Marché unique européen (1996) RMUE 17, 36 who state, in reference to *Bosman*, that absolute freedom of access may be going just a little too far.

[306] See Roth (n 293 above) 95.

[307] Hilson (n 61 above) 454 and 459.

[308] Case C-76/90 *Manfred Säger v Dennemeyer & Co. Ltd* [1991] ECR I-4221, para 12 and Roth (n 302 above) 152–153.

with its decisions in *Alpine Investments* and *Bosman*. This reverses the trend towards a more decentralized Community observable in *Keck*. It is a curious move as the general atmosphere in the Community seems to place more emphasis on subsidiarity and limitation of Community competences.[309] It is made even more remarkable by the fact that the Court was not required to develop a new doctrine to decide the cases in the way it did. In *Alpine Investments* it could have just argued that, in line with *Keck*, the competence for regulating selling arrangements rested with the host state and therefore the home state rule was in need of justification. It could have decided *Bosman* on competition law grounds. It is also surprising that the Court's case law on services and workers seems to have overtaken its case law on goods. In the past the decisions on Article 28 (ex 30) EC have led the way.[310]

4. *PRO Sieben Media*: *Alpine Investments* Confirmed?

The recent decision of the Court in *PRO Sieben Media*[311] has confirmed that the case law on national measures restricting the export of goods and services is diverging. The case concerned German television advertising rules limiting the number of advertisements that could be shown with certain broadcasts. The relevant provision stated that, 'works such as feature films and television films . . . where they last longer than 45 minutes, may be interrupted once for each complete period of 45 minutes. A further interruption is allowed if those programmes last for at least 20 minutes longer than two or more complete periods of 45 minutes'. When calculating the duration of programmes, the length of advertisements was not taken into account, as Germany used the so-called 'net principle'. The referring national court asked, *inter alia*,[312] whether the rules infringed the provisions on free movement of goods or services.

[309] It can be hoped that the approach has not yet been set in stone. There is certainly still uncertainty about the scope of Article 49 (ex 59) EC. In Case C-266/96 *Corsica Ferries France SA v Gruppo Antichi Ormeggiatori del Porto di Genova Coop arl* [1998] ECR I-3949, in issue was Italian legislation requiring shipping companies to use in Italian ports the services of local mooring groups. These groups held exclusive concessions and provided mooring services for a charge. The mooring groups argued that *Keck* should be applied to the freedom to provide services and that, therefore, the Italian law fell outside the scope of Article 49 EC and did not restrict the freedom to provide maritime transport services. The Commision was in general agreement with this view as the increased costs affected all undertakings equally. In contrast, Advocate General Jennelly was of the opinion that the effects of the law were too remote and indirect to amount to a restriction. The Court did not decide the issue of restriction at all but simply stated that in any event the law was justified by reasons of public security.

[310] See also G de Búrca, 'The Role of Equality in European Community Law' in Dashwood and O'Leary (eds), *The Principle of Equal Treatment in EC Law* (London, 1997) 20–23, who however sees the move away from discrimination-based approach as a positive development.

[311] Case C-6/98 *Arbeitsgemeinschaft Deutscher Rundfunk-anstalten (ARD) v PRO Sieben Media AG*, judgment of 28 October 1999.

[312] The case revolved mostly around Council Directive 89/552/EEC of 3 October 1989 on

The Court decided that the 'Television without frontiers' Directive precluded Germany from using the net principle to broadcasters not under its jurisdiction.[313] It then turned to the application of the principle to broadcasters under German jurisdiction. Referring to *Keck*,[314] the Court held that the measure did not fall within the scope of Article 28 (ex 30) EC.[315] It then stated that 'since such rules limit the possibility for television broadcasters established in the State of transmission to broadcast advertisements for the benefit of advertisers established in other Member States, they involve a restriction on the freedom to provide services'.[316] It proceeded to find that the rules were justified and proportionate.[317]

The case confirmed that truly non-discriminatory export restrictions fall within Article 49 (ex 59) EC. The rules limited the possibilities of home state television broadcasters to provide services for advertisers from other Member States, and, therefore, restricted the volume of exports. The measure was truly non-discriminatory, as the reduction in the number of advertising slots affected all advertisers in the same manner. Therefore, the approach was in conflict with the *Groenveld*[318] case law on Article 29 (ex 34) and is subject to the same criticism[319] as *Alpine Investments*.[320]

It is interesting to note that in this judgment the Court did not mention the concept of market access. It could well be argued that the impact of the measure on market access was neither substantial nor direct. It limited only one form of sales promotion, television advertising, and only with feature and television films. Even with these works, it did not impose a total prohibition but only restricted the number of interruptions for advertisements. Its impact was only felt through the reduction of desirable slots and, therefore, the increase in their price. It may be predicted that if the Court persists in finding that these kinds of rules fall within the scope of the free movement of services, it may soon be faced with an increasing tendency of traders to invoke Article 49 (ex 59) EC as a means of challenging any rules whose effect is to limit their commercial freedoms.

Another interesting omission was that the Court did not mention a possible import 'restriction' of services. As noted by Advocate General Jacobs,

the Coordination of Certain Provisions laid down by Law, Regulation or Administrative Action in Member States concerning the Pursuit of Television Broadcasting Activities, OJ 1989 L298/23, as amended by Directive 97/36/EC of the European Parliament and of the Council of 30 June 1997, OJ 1997 L202/60.

[313] ibid para 33.

[314] Cases C-267/91 and C-268/91 *Criminal Proceedings against Keck and Mithouard* [1993] ECR I-6097.

[315] See n 299 above paras 45–48.

[316] ibid para 49.

[317] ibid paras 50–52.

[318] Case 15/79 *Groenveld v Produktschap voor Vee en Vlees* [1979] ECR 3409.

[319] See section V. 3 above.

[320] Case C-384/93 *Alpine Investments BV v Minister van Financiën* [1995] ECR I-1141.

the measure affected the ability of foreign service providers to advertise in Germany.[321] In the case of goods this obviously amounted to a non-discriminatory rule on selling arrangements. However, in the case of services the Court has not shown itself willing to exclude these measures from the scope of Article 49 (ex 59). Therefore, it might have been expected to find an import restriction, as well. The fact that it did not even mention this effect of the German rule might suggest that it is willing to apply *Keck* in the field of services, at least in some circumstances.

The judgment should not be given too much weight. It was delivered by a three judge chamber. The Court was mostly concerned with the Television Broadcasting Directive, and Article 49 (ex 59) was merely a side issue. The analysis of restriction was very short as the measure was obviously justified and proportionate. The ruling confirms two things, however. It shows that truly non-discriminatory measures restricting the export of services do fall within Article 49 (ex 59), and it shows that the approach of the Court is not nearly as coherent as it could be.

5. *Deliège*: The Latest Development

The recent judgment of the Court in *Deliège*[322] was concerned with an unusual factual situation and may best be limited to the area of sports. In issue were rules of sporting associations, according to which professional or semi-professional judokas could only participate in certain high-level international competitions if they had been selected or authorized by their national judo federation. In general, only one male and one female judoka could be authorized for a given weight category. The nationality of the judoka was irrelevant, as long as he or she was a member of a club belonging to the federation. The Belgian federation had not selected Ms Deliège, a distinguished judoka in the under-52kg category, for many important international competitions, including the Olympics, World Championships, European Championships and Category A international tournaments. The referring national court asked whether the selection rules were in accordance, *inter alia*, with Article 49 (ex 59) EC.

The ECJ begun its ruling by holding that the selection rules did not 'determine the conditions governing the access to the labour market by professional sportsmen' and that Ms Deliège's exclusion from the competitions was not based on her nationality.[323] It continued by stating that:

[321] See n 311 above para 75 of his Opinion.

[322] Joined Cases C-51/96 and C-191/97 *Christelle Deliège v Asbl Ligue Francophone de judo et disciplines associées and others*, judgment of 11 April 2000.

[323] ibid paras 61 and 62.

although selection rules . . . inevitably have the effect of limiting the number of participants in a tournament, such a limitation is inherent in the conduct of an international high-level sports event, which necessarily involves certain selection rules or criteria being adopted. Such rules may not in themselves be regarded as constituting a restriction . . .

Moreover, the adoption, for the purposes of an international sports tournament, of one system for selecting participants rather than another must be based on a large number of considerations unconnected with the personal situation of an athlete, such as the nature, the organisation and the financing of the sport concerned.

Although a selection system may prove more favourable to one category of athletes than another, it cannot be inferred from that fact alone that the adoption of that system constitutes a restriction on the freedom to provide services.

Accordingly, it falls to the bodies concerned . . . to lay down appropriate rules . . .

[T]he delegation of such a task to the national federations, which normally have the necessary knowledge and experience, is the arrangement adopted in most sporting disciplines . . . [T]he selection rules . . . apply both to competitions organised within the Community and to those taking place outside it and involve both nationals of Member States and those of non-member countries.[324]

Accordingly, the Court answered the national court's question by holding that the selection rules did not in themselves, as long as they derived from needs inherent in the organization of competitions, constitute a restriction on the freedom to provide services.

The judgment gives rise to some questions. The first is whether the notion of market access forms the basis of a test capable of principled and coherent application or is merely a convenient label the Court uses to condemn measures it does not like. The selection rules themselves governed participation in high-level international sport competitions. Their application had certainly affected Ms Deliège, *directly* limiting her opportunities to provide services to the organizers of competitions and probably *substantially* diminishing her ability to provide publicity for her existing sponsors and to attract new ones, as she could not participate in many of the most important international events. Advocate General Cosmas was of the opinion that the rules regulated directly the market access of high-ranking judokas, such as Ms Deliège.[325] Yet in the judgment the Court simply asserted that the rules did not determine the conditions governing market access, without giving any reasons for this statement. The lack of reasoning does not make it easy to predict what measures the Court will condemn on market access grounds.

Secondly, the Court's discussion of the need for the selection rules and their normality is slightly puzzling. This kind of analysis is common when

[324] Joined Cases C-51/96 and C-191/97, paras 64–68.
[325] ibid the Opinion of Advocate General Cosmas at para 66.

the Court is examining the justification of a *prima facie* restriction, not when it is investigating whether a measure amounts to a restriction in the first place. In addition, the Court had already held that the rules did not govern market access and that Ms Deliège had not been a victim of discrimination. Was this insufficient to keep the measures outside the scope of Article 49 EC? The Court did refer to the fact that the rules limited the number of participants in a tournament, which brings to mind the criterion of 'limiting the volume of imports' from the mechanical application of the *Dassonville* formula, and in the ruling proper it did accept selection rules as long as they derived from the needs inherent in the organization of competitions. Does this mean, *e contrario*, that a measure may constitute a restriction even if it neither discriminates nor governs market access but does contain limitations that the Court considers needless? This would be an extremely wide economic freedom reading of the EC Treaty.

It may be argued that the Court was not aiming to extend the reach of Article 49, however. First, it may have been motivated by the desire to emphasize that sporting bodies retain some of their independence. Secondly, and more importantly, the system of national federations selecting service providers is highly suspicious from the Community law point of view even if there is no nationality condition.[326] In effect, the system imposes a quota for service providers from each Member State, as judokas belonging to the clubs of a certain Member State are likely to be nationals of the same country. In most cases, the Court would surely condemn this kind of arrangement. For example, an attempt by national banking associations to select which of their members are entitled to provide banking services in other Member States would hardly be accepted by the Court. Therefore, the discussion of the need for and the normality of the selection system must have been aimed at explaining why the Court accepted the rules despite the 'quantitative restriction' they created. In effect, the Court was saying that the measure did not fall within the scope of Article 49 because it was justified by needs inherent in the organization of competitions.

It is submitted that *Deliège* is best seen as a case limited to the sports sector. The system under consideration is peculiar to sports, and the ruling of the Court seems to be of limited relevance for other economic activities.

VI. THE FREE MOVEMENT OF GOODS AND A TEST BASED ON MARKET ACCESS

The most recent case law of the European Court of Justice on the free movement of goods has only increased the lack of clarity surrounding the

[326] The fact that the same rules apply in every Member State is not decisive. For example, rules providing that only nationals may engage in certain economic activities are not acceptable even if other Member States use similar rules.

issue. In *De Agostini*[327] judgment of 9 July 1997 the Court applied the *Keck*[328] test finding that a measure only fell within Article 28 (ex 30) if it discriminated in fact. On the facts of the case, the market access test devised in *Alpine Investments*[329] could very well have resulted in finding that the measure was *prima facie* within the scope of Article 28, had that test been applied in the field of the free movement of goods. In *Franzén*[330] on 23 October 1997 the Court did not even mention *Keck* but seems to have based its judgment on the impediment to market access. The same happened in *Evora*[331] on 4 November 1997.[332]

The interesting part of *De Agostini*[333] for these purposes is the Court's approach to the question whether Article 28 applied to the Swedish laws prohibiting misleading advertising and banning television advertisements designed to attract the attention of children under the age of 12. These rules were applied to advertisements of De Agostini, a Swedish company belonging to an Italian group. De Agostini had advertised a children's magazine *Allt om dinosaurier!* ('Everything about Dinosaurs!'), which was printed in Italy. The advertisements had been broadcasted from the United Kingdom by satellite.

The Court held that the Swedish measures concerned selling arrangements and thus fell outside Article 28 (ex 30) EC unless it was shown that they discriminated, in fact or in law, against products from other Member States. This was for the national court to determine.[334] Advocate General Jacobs had stated in his Opinion that the prohibition of all television advertising directed at children might have a greater impact on other Member States' products.[335] If the national court decided that the Swedish legislation did not affect the marketing of foreign and domestic products in the same way, it would have to determine whether it could be justified.[336]

The Court could have easily selected another approach, however. It

[327] Joined Cases C-34/95, C-35/95 and C-36/95 *Konsumentombudsmannen v De Agostini (Svenska) Förlag AB and TV-Shop i Sverige AB* [1997] ECR I-3843.

[328] Cases C-267/91 and C-268/91 *Criminal Proceedings against Keck and Mithouard* [1993] ECR I-6097.

[329] Case C-384/93 *Alpine Investments BV v Minister van Financiën* [1995] ECR I-1141.

[330] Case C-189/95 *Criminal proceedings against Harry Franzén* [1997] ECR I-5909.

[331] Case C-337/95 *Parfums Christian Dior SA and Parfums Christian Dior BV v Evora BV* [1997] ECR I-6013.

[332] Similarly, P Eeckhout, 'Recent Case-law on Free Movement of Goods: Refining Keck and Mithouard' (1998) 9 EBLR 267, 270.

[333] See n 327 above.

[334] ibid paras 39–44.

[335] ibid the Opinion of Advocate General Jacobs para 99.

[336] ibid paras 45–46 of the judgment. The Court's answer in para 47 to the question referred by the national court was in conflict with the reasoning. The operative part indicates that the national rules must both affect in the same way the marketing of domestic and other Member States' products *and* be justified. The reasoning, and a comparison with the French version, makes it clear that the conditions are not cumulative. See Snell (n 241 above) 226.

could have used the market access test it invented in *Alpine Investments*.[337] The rule at issue directly affected cross-border activities.[338] It was not confined to situations within one Member State. If the product was not able to gain entry into the market without television advertising, as De Agostini claimed, the measure had an immediate effect on market access of the magazine. Its impact was not only felt through a general decrease in the volume of sales.

Furthermore, as Advocate General Jacobs stated, in practice a total ban on television advertising directed at children 'will almost certainly have a perceptible effect on imports'.[339] The prohibition deprived operators an effective way of marketing their products thereby substantially restricting their access to the market.

Thus, whether one prefers the test based on the directness of the impediment to market access or the test based on the substantiality of the obstacle, the Swedish rule could have well been caught by either one of the tests. The fact that the Court, rightly in our view, stuck to *Keck* orthodoxy seemed to indicate that it was not prepared to import a market access test into the field of the free movement of goods.

The Court muddied the waters three and a half months later in another case from Sweden, *Franzén*.[340] The case was concerned with Swedish rules dealing with production, importation and distribution of alcohol and a national commercial monopoly. For our purposes the most important part of the judgment was the Court's examination of the production and wholesale licensing system. The Swedish Law on Alcohol required that wholesalers and importers of strong beer, wine and spirits held either a production licence covering the relevant product or a wholesale licence. Licences were subject to payment of charges and annual supervision fees and fulfilment of other conditions.

The Court began the examination of the licensing system by quoting the *Dassonville* formula.[341] It continued by listing all the conditions for obtaining a licence and thus for importation and by commenting on the high level of the charges and fees.[342] It then stated that

> [t]he licensing system constitutes an obstacle to the importation of alcoholic beverages from other Member States in that it imposes additional costs on such beverages, such

[337] See n 329 above.

[338] See J Stuyck, 'Joined Cases C-34/95, C-35/95 and C-36/95, Konsumertombudsmannen (KO) v de Agostini (Svenska) Förlag AB and Konsumertombudsmannen (KO) v Tv-Shop i Sverige AB' (1997) 34 CML Rev 1445, 1464–1465, who had earlier suggested that cross-border advertising was not within selling arrangements covered by *Keck* and now had to review his opinion.

[339] See n 327 above.

[340] See n 330 above.

[341] ibid para 69. Case 8/74 *Procureur du Roi v Dassonville* [1974] ECR 837.

[342] *Franzén* (n 330 above) para 70.

as intermediary costs, payment of charges and fees for the grant of a licence, and costs arising from the obligation to maintain storage capacity in Sweden.

According to the Swedish Government's own evidence, the number of licences issued is low (223 in October 1996) and almost all of these licences have been issued to traders established in Sweden.

Domestic legislation such as that in question in the main proceedings is therefore contrary to Article 30 [now 28] of the Treaty.[343]

The Court then went on to examine whether the system could be justified on the basis of Article 30 (ex 36) EC on grounds of the protection of human health. It found that the Swedish Government had not shown that the measures were proportionate or that this aim could not have been attained by less restrictive means, and thus condemned this part of the Swedish legislation.[344]

The Court's reasoning was extremely terse. For that reason what the Court *did not* say is as interesting as what it did say. First, the Court did not refer to *Keck*[345] or to selling arrangements. Nevertheless, it might be argued that the system was concerned with the question who may sell certain alcoholic beverages in Sweden. Rules regulating this issue have always been considered to affect selling arrangements.[346] Furthermore, the Swedish, Finnish, French and Norwegian Governments and the Commission had defended the rules applicable to the Swedish alcohol monopoly as only concerning selling arrangements.[347]

Secondly, the Court made just a fleeting reference to the possibility that the rules might be discriminatory. It only mentioned the fact that most of the licences are in Swedish hands.

Finally, the Court did not mention whether the system directly affected access to the Swedish market. Yet this consideration had been decisive in both *Alpine Investments*[348] and *Bosman*.[349]

In fact it seems that the Court was looking at how substantially the Swedish rules impeded market access of goods from other Member States. It listed the conditions for obtaining a licence, commented on how high the charges and fees were and noted how few licences had been issued, especially to traders not established in Sweden. From all this it deduced that Swedish legislation was not in accordance with Article 28 (ex 30). Thus, it would seem that the Court has adopted the doctrine suggested by Advocate

343 *Franzén* (n 330 above), 71–73.

344 ibid paras 74–77.

345 Cases C-267/91 and C-268/91 *Criminal Proceedings against Keck and Mithouard* [1993] ECR I-6097.

346 See Higgins (n 195 above) 168–169 and Oliver (n 198 above) 104.

347 See n 330 above para 33.

348 Case C-384/93 *Alpine Investments BV v Minister van Financiën* [1995] ECR I-1141.

349 Case C-415/93 *Union Royale Belge des Sociétés de Football Association ASBL and others v Jean-Marc Bosman* [1995] ECR I-4921.

General Jacobs in *Leclerc-Siplec*[350] prohibiting measures which are liable to restrict market access substantially.[351]

This judgment should not be given too much weight, however. The result achieved can be explained in other ways as well. First, it might be argued that one of the purposes of the Swedish licensing system was to regulate trade in goods between Member States. After all a licence was required for importation. The judgment in *Keck* made it clear that the aim of regulating inter-State trade caused a measure to fall within Article 28 (ex 30).[352]

Secondly, the system was clearly discriminatory. It discriminated against goods coming from other parts of the Community by placing traders from other Member States at a disadvantage. An economic operator lawfully engaged in sales of alcoholic beverages in his home country was not allowed to pursue the same activity in Sweden without a licence. The trader had to fulfil the requirements of both home and host country. Clearly a dual burden was placed on the trader. If the products had been services instead of goods, there would have been no difficulty in finding that the measures fell within the scope of Article 49 (ex 59) EC as defined in *Säger*[353] and even earlier cases. However, as the Court was dealing with material products, the chapter on the free movement of goods applied, since Article 50(1) (ex 60(1)) EC defines services as a residual category. Nevertheless, the result should not depend on material or non-material nature of the products. It is also clear that discrimination against foreign traders in practice readily translates to factual discrimination against foreign goods. Advocate General Elmer was also of the opinion that the licensing system was discriminatory[354] and the Court itself referred to the fact that almost all licences were issued to traders established in Sweden.[355]

Thirdly, the system most certainly affected the access to the Swedish market directly. It did not simply restrict the volume of alcohol sales in Sweden thereby indirectly affecting also imports. It did not regulate solely internal relationships between Swedish parties but touched the very relationship between economic operators in different Member States thus directly hindering cross-border activities.

Very far-reaching conclusions should not be drawn from the judgment in *Franzen*. The factual situation was unusual due to the existence of a national commercial monopoly, and the case was primarily concerned with the application of Article 31 (ex 37) EC. The Court's terse reasoning seems

350 Opinion of Advocate General Jacobs in Case C-412/93 *Société d'Importation Édouard Leclerc-Siplec v TF1 Publicité SA and M6 Publicité SA* [1995] ECR I-179, paras 38–49.

351 Chalmers and Szyszczak (n 27 above) 309–310 come to the same conclusion.

352 See n 345 above para 12.

353 Case C-76/90 *Manfred Säger v Dennemeyer & Co. Ltd* [1991] ECR I-4221.

354 Case C-189/95 *Criminal proceedings against Harry Franzén* [1997] ECR I-5909, paras 101–103 of his Opinion.

355 ibid para 72 of the judgment.

to indicate that it is looking for substantial hindrance to market access[356] but the result can be explained in more traditional ways.

Another case where the Court's reasoning was based on the significant impact a national measure had to market access of goods from other Member States was *Evora*.[357] At issue were trademark and copyright rules in force in the Netherlands. Evora had obtained Dior products by parallel imports and had advertised them for sale. Dior objected to this claiming that Evora had infringed its trademark and copyright to the bottles and packaging. The referring court, the Hoge Raad, asked *inter alia* whether Articles 28 (ex 30) and 30 (ex 36) of the Treaty precluded Dior's claims. The question was based on the premise that national law permitted the trademark owner or the copyright holder to prohibit a reseller from advertising the commercialization of the goods.[358]

Dior contested whether the rules in force in the Netherlands constituted a measure having an equivalent effect to quantitative restrictions. The Court answered this by stating that:

> it is enough that . . . the main proceedings concern goods which the reseller has procured through parallel imports and that a prohibition of advertising such as that sought in the main proceedings would render commercialization, and consequently access to the market for those goods, appreciably more difficult.[359]

It continued by looking at the justification of the measures and, following Advocate General Jacobs, found them permissible only in certain circumstances.[360]

Once again the Court referred neither to *Keck*[361] nor to discrimination nor to direct impediment to market access. By basing its judgment on the fact that market access was made *appreciably* more difficult, the Court seems to have adopted the *de minimis* test suggested by Advocate General Jacobs in *Leclerc-Siplec*.[362]

It is true that the measures did significantly impede access to the market for the goods at issue. Parallel imports are hardly worthwhile if it is not possible to advertise them. However, some caution may still be necessary before the birth of a new doctrine is pronounced.

[356] cf, however, Hilson (n 61 above) 455 who sees this judgment as a confirmation that the Court is not willing to extend the market access doctrine to the field of goods.

[357] Case C-337/95 *Parfums Christian Dior SA and Parfums Christian Dior BV v Evora BV* [1997] ECR I-6013. See also S O'Leary, 'The Free Movement of Persons and Services' in Craig and de Búrca (eds), *The Evolution of EU Law* (Oxford, 1999) 405.

[358] See *Parfums Christian Dior* (n 357 above at para 50). See also on the Uniform Benelux Law on Trade Marks the opinion of Advocate General Jacobs para 9.

[359] ibid para 51.

[360] ibid para 59.

[361] Cases C-267/91 and C-268/91 *Criminal Proceedings against Keck and Mithouard* [1993] ECR I-6097.

[362] Case C-412/93 *Société d'Importation Édouard Leclerc-Siplec v TF1 Publicité SA and M6 Publicité SA* [1995] ECR I-179.

First of all, the Court's case law on intellectual property rights has formed 'an apparently separate and somewhat opaque chapter'[363] of its general case law on Article 28 (ex 30). The approach of the Court in the judgments dealing with intellectual property has been rather different from its usual method.[364] Therefore, very far-reaching conclusions on the general scope of the free movement of goods should not be drawn from a trademark and copyright case.

Secondly, *Evora* is an extension of a long line of case law based on combating discrimination. The exhaustion of rights cases[365] dealt with situations where domestic intellectual property right laws stipulated that the first sale in national territory exhausted the copyright, patent or trademark holder's right to control the selling of the product, but allowed him to oppose imports even when the product had been sold in another Member State with his consent. The Court dealt with these discriminatory rules by developing a system of Community exhaustion: the right was exhausted if the product had been distributed somewhere in the Community with the consent of the rightholder.[366] If Community law now allowed the prevention of advertising, the right to sell the products would not amount to much. Commercialization would not be easy if the reseller could not tell his customers about the product in an efficient manner.[367] Similarly in the repackaging cases[368] the Court has curtailed the use of rights which could be used to circumvent the Community exhaustion doctrine.[369]

Finally, the rules in force in the Netherlands had in practice the greatest impact on parallel imports. They were not general measures affecting imports only indirectly. It is very unlikely that anybody would be able to resell commercially the products first distributed in the Netherlands. Within one country it may be fairly easy to ensure that the selective distributors do not sell to unauthorized retailers. Such control may become more difficult when the goods cross borders. In addition, the price differences within one country may be non-existent or so small that reselling would not be worthwhile. The prices tend to vary much more between different Member

[363] Marenco and Banks, 'Intellectual Property and the Community Rules on Free Movement: Discrimination Unearthed' (1990) 15 EL Rev 224, 238.

[364] See on the Court's traditional approach to national laws on intellectual property Marenco and Banks (n 363 above) 224–238.

[365] Case 78/70 *Deutsche Grammophon GmbH v Metro-SB Grossmärkte GmbH & Co KG* [1971] ECR 487, Case 15/74 *Centrafarm BV v Sterling Drug Inc* [1974] ECR 1147 and Case 16/74 *Centrafarm BV v Winthrop BV* [1974] ECR 1183.

[366] See generally Craig and de Búrca (n 166 above) 1029–1041 and Weatherill and Beaumont (n 59 above) 977–993.

[367] See n 357 above the Opinion of Advocate General Jacobs para 31.

[368] Case 102/77 *Hoffmann-La Roche & Co AG v Centrafarm Vertriebsgesellschaft Pharmazeutischer Erzeugnisse mbH* [1978] ECR 1139 and Case 1/81 *Pfizer Inc v Eurim-Pharm GmbH* [1981] ECR 2913.

[369] Marenco and Banks (n 363 above) 245.

States.[370] Thus, it might be said that the rules directly hindered the access of these goods to the Dutch market.

Taken together, *Franzén* and *Evora* may indicate that the Court has at least refined *Keck* and adopted the *de minimis* doctrine to limit the reach of the free movement of goods. If this is so, market access has become the key concept for both Articles 28 (ex 30) and 49 (ex 59) EC, and this time the case law on the free movement of services has shown the way. However, the emphasis has been on different aspects of the concept. In the field of services the Court has so far talked about the 'directness' of the impediment to market access while in the field of goods the appreciability of the obstacle to market access may have been decisive. Due to the frequent cross-fertilization between the freedoms and the still small number of cases, too much weight should not be put on the differences, however.

The Court's approach is open to criticism. First, it may be asked whether a centralizing test based on market access is correct in principle[371] or workable in practice.[372] Secondly, the case law lacks coherence and clarity. The Court seems to be altering the test it uses with alarming frequency. Furthermore, its reasoning is minimal. This would be more acceptable if the Court was just applying familiar rules, but if the Court wants to develop a new test,[373] surely it should clearly say so. It does not take long to lose the clarity achieved in *Keck* and the subsequent case law.

VII. CONCLUSION

For the most part the Court's judgment in *Keck* and its subsequent decisions on Article 49 (ex 59) EC follow the philosophy of mutual recognition. At the core of this thinking is the principle that a product lawfully put on the market in one Member State must be allowed to enter the markets of the other Member States.

Prohibitions and product rules are inimical to the doctrine as they create a multiple burden. A product complying with the rules of the home state is not allowed to enter the market of the host state. Only one regulatory system, that of the home country, should apply.

The rules regulating selling arrangements fall under the competence of the host state. As long as the national measures do not discriminate against imports, the host country is free to legislate as it sees fit.

The doctrine allows the formation of economies of scale and provides for

[370] See on price differences among EU countries Molle (n 7 above) 131–134.
[371] See the discussion in section III above.
[372] See the discussion in section V above.
[373] Market access was mentioned in *Keck* but did not form part of the test proper.

the preservation of competitive edge, as an undertaking can take advantage of the most favourable business environment by producing goods and services according to the methods of one Member State and selling them inside the whole Community. This creates a framework for a European-wide competition between undertakings and also enables the competition between legal orders, especially as factors of production can relocate. The free movement provisions of the Treaty create the best preconditions for regulatory competition when they guarantee free movement but leave as much room for regulation by the Member States as possible. The doctrine based on mutual recognition achieves this aim well.

The doctrine contributes to a decentralized, federal Community, where the Member States' regulatory competence is preserved. It allays fears of a centralized super-state insensitive to national preferences and traditions and the sheer diversity of the Community. Thus, it contributes to the campaign for the hearts and minds of the Community citizens, whose primary attachment is still to the nation state.

The market forces are given the principal responsibility for bringing about the integration of national markets. Regulation only creates a framework for the operation of the market. The multitude of private decisions by economic operators is given a decisive role. Public intervention by the centre is minimized. The desired result is not imposed but comes about through the operation of the invisible hand of the market.

Alpine Investments, when read alone, could be reconciled with this system. An equally applicable marketing rule can be considered a *prima facie* restriction when it is adopted by the exporting home state. The idea is that the importing host state regulates market circumstances and the exporting home state deals with product and production. Therefore a non-discriminatory host state rule on selling arrangements does not constitute a restriction, but the application of a similar rule by the home state must be justified. Conversely, the application of the host state product and production rules amounts to a restriction, while the home state is free to regulate in a non-discriminatory manner. Regulatory competence is divided between Member States to ensure that one, and only one, rule always applies. However, when *Alpine Investments* is read together with *Bosman*, it brings a new element into play. National rules creating a direct impediment to market access are scrutinized by the Court. Cross-border measures are attacked. A step is taken towards a more centralized Community where the Court determines the optimal regulation of the internal market. The desirability of this development can be questioned, and its extent is still uncertain.

over providers of services from the other Member States. Therefore, the Dutch and British Governments, drawing an analogy from the Court's decision in *Keck*, argued that the measure fell outside Article 49 (ex 59) EC altogether.

The Court, following Advocate General Jacobs, held that the Dutch ban amounted to a *prima facie* restriction of the free movement of services but was justified on grounds of the general good. It distinguished the situation from *Keck* and rejected the arguments of the Dutch and British Governments.[221] By distinguishing *Keck* on the facts without referring to any differences between Articles 28 (ex 30) and 49 (ex 59), the Court seemed to implicitly accept that a similar approach could be used to deal with both the free movement of goods and services.

2. Dividing Regulatory Competences?

Alpine Investments can indeed be distinguished from *Keck*. Both cases concerned marketing rules, but in the former case the measure was imposed by the exporting home state, while in the latter case the measure originated from the importing host state. In the former case there was a dual burden. The service provider had to also comply with rules regulating selling arrangements in the host country. In the latter one only one set of rules applied. The home country rules affecting selling arrangements were of no relevance whatsoever. The situations were fundamentally different.

The dangers inherent in allowing the application of two sets of rules, whether they concerned product requirements or selling arrangements,[222] were fully recognized by Advocate General Jacobs.[223] In the worst-case scenario the rules could be contradictory, and thus negate the whole freedom. An example might be the following. The home country rule requires disclosure of the identity of the broker the orders are placed with. The host country rule prohibits such disclosure in the interest of preventing customer confusion. The combined effect of these rules would be to prevent cross-border trade completely.

Alpine Investments can also be reconciled with the Court's case law on Article 29 (ex 34). The Court has consistently refused to apply the *Cassis* test to export restrictions. It has held that Article 29 (ex 34) applies only to

[221] See [illegible]

[222] [illegible]

[223] [illegible]

5

A Unified Approach to the Fundamental Freedoms

HANS D JARASS*

I. INTRODUCTION[1]

The four fundamental freedoms of the EC Treaty have developed an importance far beyond what would have been expected. They encompass the free movement of goods in Article 28 EC, the free movement of workers in Article 39 EC, the freedom of establishment in Article 43 EC and free movement of services in Article 49 EC.[2] This chapter outlines the theory and basic structure of the fundamental freedoms focusing on what they have in common.[3]

The problem will be approached from a practical perspective, the aim being to structure the confusing multitude of considerations associated with the fundamental freedoms, reducing their complexity and facilitating their application. This necessitates generalizations, but only to an extent which must be justifiable. The latter is helped by the convergence in the case law of the European Court of Justice concerning the fundamental freedoms.[4] For ease of reference the structure of this presentation will mirror the order in which one should approach determining the incidence of the fundamental freedoms in an individual case. Three steps must be distinguished. First, it has to be decided whether the case falls within the scope[5] of the fundamental

* The author is deeply indebted to Mads Andenas. He took care of the translation of the chapter which was a nearly impossible task. Aside from that he contributed in many ways to the substance of the chapter.

[1] cf 'Elemente einer Dogmatik der Grundfreiheiten' [1995] EuR 202 by the same author where the case was made for a single and uniform doctrine of fundamental freedoms. This need is still there. The discussion must reflect the continuing development of the case law of the European Court of Justice, and this chapter is one contribution to it.

[2] The German expression is '*Grundfreiheiten*' which is widely used, see eg Streinz, *Europarecht* (4th edn, 1999) para 656. There is no comparable single term in the English languages apart from 'fundamental freedoms'.

[3] Other fundamental freedoms or similar institutions (cf Article 18, Article 25, Article 56, Article 90 EC) lie beyond the scope of this chapter though the same considerations may apply to them.

[4] See Eberhartinger, 'Konvergenz und Neustrukturierung der Grundfreiheiten' [1997] EWS 43; Hakenberg, *Grundzüge des Europäischen Gemeinschaftsrechts* (2nd edn, 2000) 111 and 112.

[5] This is a translation of the German term '*Anwendungsbereich*'.

freedom (section II below). Then, the question of restriction[6] arises (section III below). Where these requirements are fulfilled, the possibility of a justification[7] falls to be considered in a third step (section IV below). Taken together, the first and second steps constitute the positive requirements for the incidence of the fundamental freedom, which differ from the question of justification in a number of ways.

II. SCOPE

The first step in the test—the scope—concerns the object of the measure in question, the protected activity affected by the restrictive measure. This step includes substantive and personal elements. Thus a sub-division can be made between substantive and personal scope. Article 299 EC adds a physical or spatial scope, which is of less practical relevance and will not be considered in the following.

1. Substantive Scope

The fundamental freedoms protect specific *activities* or objects with a *cross-border connection*. These two elements—activity and cross-border connection—circumscribe the substantive scope.[8]

(a) As far as the specific activity or object is concerned, the free movement of goods in Articles 28, 29 EC applies to the trade with or sale of goods as defined in Article 23(2) EC. In the context of free movement of workers in Article 39 EC, the taking up or pursuit of an employment has to be in issue. The substantive scope of the freedom of establishment pertains to the taking up or pursuit of a self-employed activity. The substantive scope of the freedom of services extends to self-employed persons providing a service against remuneration; the service provider must not, however, be resident in the state where the service is received, as otherwise it is the freedom of establishment that is applicable instead.

(b) The fundamental freedoms are not applicable to activities which are confined in all respects within a single Member State[9] or have no factor linking them with any of the situations[10] governed by Community

[6] This is a translation of the German term '*Beschränkung*'.

[7] This is a translation of the German term '*Rechtfertigung*'.

[8] This is a translation of the German term '*sachlicher Anwendungsbereich*'.

[9] Case C-41/90 *Höfner & Elser v Macroton GmbH* [1991] ECR I-1979, para 37; Case C-134/95 USSL *v* INAIL [1997] ECR I-195, para 19; Oliver, 'Some Further Reflections on the Scope of Articles 28–30 (ex 30–36) EC' [1999] CMLRev 783.

[10] Joined Cases C-64, C-65/96 *Land Nordrhein-Westfalen v Uecker* [1997] ECR I-3171, para 16; Joined Cases C-225 to 227/95, *Kapasakalis v Greece* [1998] ECR I-4239, para 22.

law.[11] In that sense a *cross-border* element is necessary. In the context of free movement of workers and services and of the freedom of establishment, this cross-border element depends on the person benefiting from the freedom. It is provided by, for example a worker, a person establishing themselves or a provider of a service crossing intra-community borders. This is not to be interpreted restrictively. A cross-border element still exists where a national is discriminated against in his home Member State but where the discrimination is linked to a former activity pursued in another Member State or a previous receipt of a cross-border service.[12] As far as free movement of goods is concerned, the cross-border element results from the fact that the goods in question have crossed or will cross an intra-community border. In the same way, the freedom of movement of services applies also where the service alone crosses a border. This underlines the fact that the freedom of movement of services combines free movement of both goods and persons.[13]

(c) The separation of substantive competence between the Community and its Member States does not provide any hint with regard to the applicability of the fundamental freedoms. There is thus no overriding competence on the part of the Member States concerning for example cultural policy, energy policy or social policy; in all of these, the fundamental freedoms have to be complied with once the above-mentioned requirements in relation to the substantive scope are met.[14]

2. Personal Scope

In addition, the applicability of the fundamental freedoms further requires that the individuals involved fall within their scope. In this respect one can speak of a personal scope.[15] This raises two questions.[16]

(a) On the one hand, it has to be clarified what role a person has to play in order to be able to avail himself of the fundamental freedom. This is relatively

[11] Where provisions of national law are concerned, not much is required to create the necessary link, it is sufficient that they are applicable in very few situations with a cross-border element.

[12] See Case C-246/80 *Broekmeulen (C.) v Huisarts Registratie Comissie* [1981] ECR 2311 para 27; Case C-419/92, *Scholz v Opera Universitaria di Cagliari* [1994] ECR I-505, para 9; Case C-18/95 *F.C. Terhoeve v Inspecteur van de Belastingdienst Particulieren/Ondernemingen Buitenland* [1999] ECR I-345, para 27.

[13] See Jarass, 'Elemente einer Dogmatik der Grundfreiheiten' [1995] 30 EuR 205; Streinz, *Europarecht* (4th edn, 1999) para 656.

[14] Case C-158/96 *Kohll v Union des Caisses de Maladie* [1998] ECR I-1931, para 17; Hirsch, 'Die aktuelle Rechtsprechung des EuGH zur Warenverkehrsfreiheit' [1999] 2 ZEuS 505 and 506.

[15] This is a translation of the German term '*persönlicher Anwendungsbereich*'.

[16] eg Hirsch, 'Die aktuelle Rechtsprechung des EuGH zur Warenverkehrsfreiheit' [1999] 2 ZEuS 508.

straightforwardly the person intending to export or import goods, the worker or self-employed person wanting to settle or to provide services. But it extends also to the contractual counterparties of such persons. Thus an employer benefits from the free movement of his employee[17] and the recipient of a service benefits from the freedom of the provider.[18]

(b) On the other hand, the fundamental freedoms protect mainly nationals of Member States only. As a prerequisite for relying on the freedom of establishment, the person establishing himself in another Member State must, pursuant to Article 43(1) EC, be a citizen of a Member State. In the context of the secondary freedom of establishment, provided for in the second sentence of Article 43(1), the person in addition has to be resident, ie established, in a Member State. For legal persons, Article 48 EC lays down an equivalent rule.[19] The same applies to the freedom to provide services under Article 49(1) and Article 55 EC in connection with Article 48. Even though Article 39 EC lacks an explicit declaration to that effect, the free movement of workers is in fact limited to Member State nationals.[20] No equivalent restriction of the personal scope exists concerning the free movement of goods: whether the person carrying out the transaction is a Member State national or resident, or established within the Community would not appear to matter.[21]

III. RESTRICTION

Where a measure falls within the substantive and personal scope of a fundamental freedom, its reconcilability with the fundamental freedom depends on whether or not it possesses certain characteristics which enable it to be classified as a restriction or limitation.[22] One might in this context be tempted to speak of detriment, but the wording of the freedoms generally uses the terminology of restriction or limitation.[23] Of specific concern are the nature of the restricting act (section 1 below) and the characteristics of the person who instigates the restriction (section 2 below).

[17] Case C-350/96 *Clean Car Autoservice GmbH v Landeshauptmann von Wien* [1998] ECR I-2521, para 20.

[18] Case C-45/93 *Commission v Spain* [1994] ECR I-911, paras 6 and 7.

[19] See C-81/87 *R v HM Treasury & Commissioners of Inland Revenue, ex parte Daily Mail & General Trust PLC* [1988] ECR 5483, para 21; Roth, 'Niederlassungs- und Dienstleistungsfreiheit', in: Dauses (ed), *Handbuch des EG-Wirtschaftsrechts* (1993), EI para 54.

[20] Wölker, in v d Groeben *et al* (eds), *Kommentar zum EWG-Vertrag* (5th edn, 1997), preliminary remark 41 before Article 48; Hailbronner, 'Freizügigkeit', in Dauses (ed), *Handbuch des EG-Wirtschaftsrechts* (1993), DI para 18.

[21] Third country goods must have entered the internal market. Then there is no problem with the nationality of the importer.

[22] This is a translation of the German term '*Beschränkung*'.

[23] See Article 28, Article 39(3), Article 43(1), Article 49(1), Article 56 EC.

1. Nature of the Restriction

(a) Types of restriction

(i) Discrimination as the principle type of restriction

As far as the type and modalities of the restriction are concerned, a restriction of fundamental freedoms can first and foremost be identified in the case of discrimination, ie an unequal treatment based on certain criteria, details of which will be further considered below. Although there are other forms of restriction, a more precise description of 'discrimination' is important for the understanding of all other forms of restriction—other considerations apart, the wording of the fundamental freedoms explicitly mentions discriminatory restrictions and they thus constitute the basic type of restriction.[24]

A restriction of the freedom of establishment contrary to Article 43(2) exists where nationals of other Member States are not permitted to take up or pursue self-employment in another Member State 'under the conditions laid down for its own nationals'. The freedom to provide services is restricted in the sense of Article 50(3) where services cannot be provided by Member State nationals in another state 'under the same conditions as are imposed by that State on its own nationals'. The freedom of movement of workers is interfered with contrary to Article 39(2) by 'any discrimination based on nationality between workers of the Member States', thus by any distinct treatment of foreign workers. All the afore-mentioned freedoms have in common that they protect against unequal treatment based on nationality. Equivalent to this is unequal treatment based on residence, as can clearly be seen from the provisions on the freedom to provide services,[25] but also applies to the freedom of movement of workers and the freedom of establishment.[26] The wording of the provisions governing the free movement of goods is less explicit in its reference to discrimination. It would seem that this fundamental freedom covers, as a starting point, all

[24] Hirsch, 'Die aktuelle Rechtsprechung des EuGH zur Warenverkehrsfreiheit' [1999] 2 ZEuS 509. The distinction is also of importance in the step of defining a justification; see section IV.1(b), 2(b) below.

[25] Compare Oliver, 'Some Further Reflections on the Scope of Articles 28–30 (ex 30–36) EC' [1999] CMLRev 800; see Article 49 (1) and Case C-224/97 *Erich Ciola v Land Vorarlberg* [1999] ECR I-2517, para 11.

[26] See as far as freedom of movement of workers is concerned: Case C-246/80 *C. Broekmeulen v Huisarts Registratie Commissie* [1981] ECR I-2311, para 18. Freedom of establishment: Case C-115/78 *J. Knorrs v Staatssekretär für Wirtschaft* [1979] ECR 399, para 24. Compare Oliver, 'Some Further Reflections on the Scope of Articles 28–30 (ex 30–36) EC' [1999] CMLRev 801; Roth, 'Niederlassungs- und Dienstleistungsfreiheit', in Dauses (ed), *Handbuch des EG-Wirtschaftsrechts* (1993) E I paras 52 and 53; Roth, 'Wettbewerb der Mitgliedstaaten oder Wettbewerb der Hersteller?' [1995] 159 ZHR 78.

measures regulating goods crossing intra-Community borders more strictly than goods circulating within a Member State.[27]

In summary, a discrimination exists where a regulation concerning the free movement of workers, the freedom of establishment or the freedom to provide services takes account of nationality or (foreign) residence.[28] Restrictions based on former residence are also covered.[29] In the context of the free movement of goods, discrimination is characterized by a measure applying only to goods which cross an intra-Community border.

(i) Factual or material disadvantage

As the European Court of Justice has pointed out in a number of decisions, discrimination is not the only form of restriction. This is based on the understanding that a number of other forms of interference can impinge on the aim of the fundamental freedoms to the same extent as outright discrimination.[30] The aim of the fundamental freedoms, the complete abolition of economic boundaries between Member States and the consequent opening of the individual national markets (*internal market without frontiers*), is not obstructed by discrimination only. Hindrance is also caused by regulations which are not based on foreign origin, nationality or residence, but which, due to requirements which differ from Member State to Member State, lead to *de facto* disadvantages.[31] A double burden imposed by regulations of the country of origin on the one hand and of the country of destination on the other often leads to such a disadvantage. Measures of Member States which treat domestic and foreign products, nationals and foreigners, residents and non-residents legally in the exact same way—and are thus 'indistinctly applicable' measures—nevertheless constitute a restriction of fundamental freedoms where they lead to a (purely) factual disadvantage for border-crossing products, foreigners or non-residents.

(ii) Interference with the core of the freedoms (core restriction)

Both discrimination and the factual or material disadvantage are characterized by a disadvantage being suffered by cross-border activities. Is this

[27] See Jarass, 'Elemente einer Dogmatik der Grundfreiheiten' [1995] 30 EuR 212.

[28] This includes hidden discrimination (see also Jarass, 'Elemente einer Dogmatik der Grundfreiheiten' [1995] 30 EuR 213). The distinction between hidden discrimination and indistinctly applicable measures has not been applied.

[29] This is of importance for their abilities acquired in another Member State; Case C-115/78 *J. Knorrs v Staatssekretär für Wirtschaft* [1979] ECR 399; Case C-246/80 *C. Broekmeulen v Huisarts Registratie Commissie* [1981] ECR I-2311.

[30] See Behrens, 'Die Konvergenz der wirtschaftlichen Freiheiten im europäischen Gemeinschaftsrecht' [1992] 27 EuR 148.

[31] This is of importance to ability they have gained in another Member State; Case C-120/78 *Rewe-Zentrale AG v Bundesmonopolverwaltung für Branntwein* (*Cassis de Dijon*) [1979] ECR 649, para 8 on restrictions arising from the differences of the national regulation.

therefore a common feature of all restrictions of fundamental freedoms?[32] In opposition, one might point to the fact that the Court has in several decisions found a restriction without considering the issue of (relative) disadvantage. As the reasons given by the Court often are meagre, care should be taken with such interpretations.

The first observation on this matter must be that the extreme view, according to which every hindrance of an activity falling within the scope of the fundamental freedoms constitutes a restriction, is unconvincing.[33] Due to the extraordinarily wide scope of the fundamental freedoms, this would lead to the review of every single impediment of the free market, even though the freedoms merely aim to eliminate impediments connected with the existence of borders within the Community.[34] Moreover, this view is not reconcilable with the jurisprudence of the Court concerning selling arrangements in the domain of free movement, which excludes certain impediments to cross-border activities from the scope of this fundamental freedom as long as they are non-discriminatory.[35] Finally, this view is not compatible with the exclusion of discrimination against nationals.[36]

On the other hand, it is becoming increasingly difficult to recognize a (legal or factual) disadvantage being caused to cross-border activities in all the cases in which the European Court of Justice infers a restriction of fundamental rights. Thus, where requirements to be met by goods are concerned in the field of Article 28 EC, it is irrelevant whether or not a disadvantage for cross-border goods can be identified.[37] In the context of the free movement of workers, the freedom to provide services and the freedom of establishment, this observation mainly concerns cases where spatial movement is being directly hindered, as was the case in *Bosman*.[38] Despite the existence of similar domestic barriers, an interference with the fundamental freedoms is assumed in these cases. The same applies to judgments concerning secondary establishment.[39]

[32] Supported by Streinz, *Europarecht* (4th edn, 1999) para 679.

[33] As recently proposed by Lackhoff, *Die Niederlassungsfreiheit des EGV* (2000) 443 and 444.

[34] Thus rightly Roth, 'Niederlassungs- und Dienstleistungsfreiheit', in Dauses (ed), *Handbuch des EG-Wirtschaftsrechts* (1993), E I para 22; Eilmansberger, 'Zur Reichweite der Grundfreiheiten des Binnenmarktes', [1999] 121 JB 356 and 357.

[35] Eilmansberger, 'Zur Reichweite der Grundfreiheiten des Binnenmarktes', [1999] 121 JB 438 and Joined Cases C-267, 268/91, *Keck and Mithouard* [1993] ECR I-6097, para 16; Joined Cases C-401, 402/92, *Tankstation 't Heustke vof and J.B.E. Boermans* [1994] ECR I-2199/2233, para 12.

[36] See section III.2(b) below.

[37] *Keck and Mithouard* (n 35 above) [1993] ECR I-6097, para 15.

[38] Case C-415/93 *Union Royal Belge des Sociétés des Football Association ASBL v Jean-Marc Bosman* [1995] ECR I-4921.

[39] See Case C-107/83 *Ordre des Advocats v Klopp* [1984] ECR 2971, paras 19 and 20; Case C-96/85 *Commission v France* [1986] ECR 1475, para 12; Case C-212/97 *Centros Ltd v Erhvervs- og Selskabsstyrelsen* [1999] ECR I-1459, para 39; Bröhmer, in Calliess and Ruffert (eds), *Kommentar zum EU-Vertrag* (1999) Article 43, para 22.

This supports the view that a third category of restrictions exists. These would appear to consist in a direct hindrance of cross-border activities which involve preventing access to the market of another Member State. Such a core restriction[40] of the fundamental freedoms must generally be classified as a restriction, without regard being had of any detriment being caused in the specific case.[41] Within the scope of Article 28, measures concerning the product itself fall within this class of restriction. Where the other fundamental freedoms are concerned, it is in particular measures which totally exclude or seriously hinder the leaving of the country of origin which are implicated.[42] Within the domain of Article 29, no restrictions have thus far been identified by the ECJ which do not involve a disadvantage being caused; this possibly because in this area no line of cases has so far arisen in which a restriction of the free movement of goods can typically be presumed.[43] Some commentators have, however, already reached more far-reaching conclusions.[44] Quite apart from these details, core restrictions are restrictions which endanger the aims of the fundamental freedoms by their very nature and must therefore be tackled even where no specific detriment is being caused to cross-border transactions because purely domestic transactions are burdened in the same way.

Core restriction cases and those in the category of factual or material disadvantage have in common that they concern 'indistinctly applicable' measures, which is of importance as far as the availability of justifications is concerned.[45] The distinction drawn by the Court between product requirements and selling arrangements in the context of the free movement of goods can be explained by the fact that product requirements which differ between the country of origin and the country of destination *typically* put cross-border trade at a disadvantage. For this reason, a restriction is presumed and an inquiry into possible justifications becomes generally necessary. Where selling arrangements are concerned, on the other hand, such a presumption is not appropriate. The same distinction can be drawn

[40] This is a translation of the German term '*Eingriff in den Kernbereich*'.

[41] See Eilmansberger, 'Zur Reichweite der Grundfreiheiten des Binnenmarktes', [1999] 121 JBI 347 and 348; on the freedom of establishment contrary view Bröhmer, in Calliess and Ruffert (eds), *Kommentar zum EU-Vertrag und EG-Vertrag* (1999), Article 43, para 31.

[42] See Case C-415/93 *Union Royal Belge des Sociétés des Football Association ASBL v Jean-Marc Bosman* [1995] ECR I-4921, paras 96 and 97; Case C-18/95 *F.C. Terhoeve v Inspecteur van de Belastingdienst Particulieren/Ondernemingen Buitenland* [1999] ECR I-345, para 39; Hirsch, 'Die aktuelle Rechtsprechung des EuGH zur Warenverkehrsfreiheit', [1999] 2 ZEuS 511.

[43] See Oliver, 'Some Further Reflections on the Scope of Articles 28–30 (ex 30–36) EC', [1999] CMLRev 800.

[44] See ibid 801; 'Roth, Wettbewerb der Mitgliedstaaten oder Wettbewerb der Hersteller?', [1995] 159 ZHR 78.

[45] See sections IV.1(b) and IV.2(b) below.

in the domain of the free movement of persons between restrictions on access to the market of another Member State and regulations governing the exercise of a profession.[46] Thus analysed, core restrictions (as a category) have their root in a detriment being caused to cross-border activities. In their actual application they have, however, cast off this requirement. In individual cases, it is irrelevant whether or not a detriment is being caused. The fundamental freedoms thus go beyond a mere guarantee of equality.

(b) Further aspects of the characteristics of restrictions

(i) Types of measure and burden

Over and above the considerations advanced thus far, the question arises whether the concept of a 'restriction' can be further narrowed down. As far as the type of measure in question is concerned, no further qualifications can be made. The fundamental freedoms can be affected by any activity causing disadvantage to cross-border activities. This comprises legal and administrative regulations as well as individual decisions.[47] Furthermore, *de facto* actions,[48] ie measures which do not give rise to legal effects but consist in concrete actions, may constitute a restriction.[49] One such example would be the advertising of national products.[50] Even though the Court regularly refers to regulations, this is merely because these are the most important situation in practice.

It is further of no importance whether a state measure is directly aimed at an economic activity or has a merely *indirect* effect on it.[51] The European Court of Justice thus considered a less favourable treatment of non-nationals with regards to dispensation from contributions to the social security scheme, a restriction of the free movement of workers and the freedom of establishment.[52] The same applies with regard to the support of housing[53] and the acquisition and usage of real estate[54] as well as to the characteristics

[46] Case C-415/93 *Union Royal Belge des Sociétés des Football Association ASBL v Jean-Marc Bosman* [1995] ECR I-4921, para 95 focuses on access. As far as regulations like those in *Bosman* are concerned one should not forget that they permit taking up an activity at one national sports club, while changing to a club of another Member State is generally excluded.

[47] Case C-224/97 *Erich Ciola v Land Vorarlberg* [1999] ECR I-2517, para 32.

[48] *Realakte.*

[49] See Roth, 'Niederlassungs- und Dienstleistungsfreiheit', in Dauses (ed), *Handbuch des EG-Wirtschaftsrechts* (1993), E I para 19.

[50] Case C-249/81 *Commission v Ireland* [1982] ECR 4005, 4022.

[51] Supported by Roth, 'Niederlassungs- und Dienstleistungsfreiheit', in Dauses (ed), *Handbuch des EG-Wirtschaftsrechts* (1993), E I para 62 in the case of freedom of establishment.

[52] Case C-143/87 *Stanton v INASTI* [1988] ECR 3877, 3894 and 3895; Case C-18/95 *F.C. Terhoeve v Inspecteur van de Belastingdienst Particulieren/Ondernemingen Buitenland* [1999] ECR I-345 para 40.

[53] Case C-63/86 *Commission v Italy* [1988] ECR 29, 53.

[54] Case C-305/87 *Commission v Greece* [1989] ECR 1461, 1478 and 1479.

of the system of direct taxation.[55] Work-permit requirements for employees can interfere with the employer's freedom to provide services.[56] Furthermore, not only the actual but also the potential effects are to be considered,[57] as long as they are not too remote (from the point of view of causation).[58] Where to draw the limit has thus far not been discussed in detail, even though it is of significant practical importance. Finally, the *extent* of the restriction is of no importance,[59] in particular, no *substantial* restriction of the internal market is required.[60] The extent falls to be considered in the context of justification only, where it is of considerable importance.

(ii) Protective duty and omissions

As has recently become clear, the fundamental freedoms, when read together with the duty of loyal cooperation contained in Article 10 EC, impose a duty on the Community and its Member States to ensure compliance with the fundamental freedoms in relations between private individuals. Thus an inadequate protection against relevant activities of private individuals can constitute an infringement of the fundamental freedoms by the state by way of *omission*.[61] This also explains why the Treaty allows regulations adopted to flesh out the fundamental freedoms to be made binding directly on the citizen.[62]

[55] Case C-264/96 *Imperial Chemical Industries plc (ICI) v Kenneth Hall Colmer (HM Inspector of Taxes)* [1998] ECR I-4695, para 19; Case C-307/97 *Compagnie de Saint-Gobain v Finanzamt Aachen-Innenstadt* [1999] ECR I-6161, para 43; Case C-391/97 *Farmitalia Carlo Erba Srl* [1999] ECR I-5451, para 20.

[56] Case C-43/93 *Vander Elst (Raymond) v Office des Migrations Internationales* [1994] ECR I-3803, paras 21 and 22.

[57] Case C-184/96 *Commission v France* [1998] ECR I-6197, para 17 is concerned with free movement of goods.

[58] Case C-379/92 *Peralta* [1994] ECR I-3453, para 24; Case C-96/94 *Centro Servizi Spediporto v Spedizioni Marittima del Golfo* [1995] ECR I-2883, para 41; [1998] ECR I-3949, para 31; Oliver, 'Some Further Reflections on the Scope of Articles 28–30 (ex 30–36) EC', [1999] CML Rev 788 and 789.

[59] Case C-16/83 *Prantl (Karl)* [1984] ECR 1299, para 20; Becker, 'Von "Dassonville" über "Cassis" zu "Keck"—der Begriff der Maßnahmen gleicher Wirkung in Art 30 EGV', [1994] 29 EuR 170 and 171.

[60] Oliver, 'Some Further Reflections on the Scope of Articles 28–30 (ex 30–36) EC', [1999] CML Rev 790.

[61] In the context of free movement of goods see Case C-265/95 *Commission v France* [1997] ECR I-7006, paras 30–32; Epiney, in Calliess and Ruffert (eds), *Kommentar zum EU-Vertrag* (1999) Article 28, paras 48 and 49; Streinz, *Europarecht* (4th edn, 1999) para 709; Hirsch, 'Die aktuelle Rechtsprechung des EuGH zur Warenverkehrsfreiheit', [1999] 2 ZEuS 508.

[62] These provisions do not specify duties of private individuals; such duties are not included in the fundamental freedoms. Moreover, they result from the mandate to protect the fundamental freedoms.

(iii) Unilateral protection (discrimination against nationals)

The fundamental freedoms protect cross-border activities from being put in a less favourable position vis-à-vis purely domestic activities; they do not protect domestic activities vis-à-vis cross-border ones. There is thus no infringement of the free movement of goods where non-exported goods are treated less favourably than those crossing intra-Community borders.[63] Likewise, the other fundamental freedoms do not prohibit any discrimination of nationals or residents, as long as no other cross-border elements are in issue.[64] The fundamental freedoms thus throughout include a merely *unilateral* protection serving cross-border activities.[65]

2. The Acting Person and the Obliged Person (Addressee)

(a) Member States and their organs as well as institutions of the Community

For an effect to be classified as a restriction it has to be brought about by a certain protagonist. This person must be an addressee[66] of the fundamental freedom. The fundamental freedoms, according to their wording, are binding on the Member States, which includes all organs of the state.[67] This embraces institutions which do not formally belong to the national administration, but whose members are appointed by the state and whose activities are financed from public resources.[68] The same would appear to apply to institutions which are subject to supervision by the state or which are equipped with 'special powers beyond those which result from the normal rules applicable between individuals'.[69]

But it is not only the Member State (and its institutions) in which the recipient of the relevant performance is resident or in which residence is required that is bound. The state of origin (and its institutions) is also bound. For the free movement of goods this follows directly from Article 29, but the same applies for the other fundamental freedoms as has been clarified by the European Court of Justice in relation to the freedom of establishment and the free movement of workers.[70]

[63] Dauses, 'Warenverkehr', in Dauses (ed), *Handbuch des EG-Wirtschaftsrechts* (1993), CI para 96.

[64] See section II.1(b) above.

[65] See Streinz, *Europarecht* (4th edn, 1999) para 685.

[66] This is a translation of the German term '*Adressat*'.

[67] Case C-197/84 *Steinhauser v City of Biarritz* [1985] ECR 1819, para 16.

[68] Case C-302/88 *Hennen Olie v ICOVA and Netherlands State* [1990] ECR I-4625, paras 15 and 16.

[69] With respect to directives, Case C-188/89 *Foster and others v British Gas* [1990] ECR-I 3313, para 18.

[70] See as far as freedom of establishment is concerned: Case C-81/87 *R v HM Treasury &*

The question arises whether the Community itself as well as its organs are bound by the fundamental freedoms. The European Court of Justice has answered this question in the affirmative a number of times with regard to the free movement of goods.[71] In the case of the other fundamental freedoms, the situation should be similar. This position is supported by the fundamental character shared by all the fundamental freedoms which should therefore apply at least by analogy to the Community and its organs. Secondary legislation thus has to be in line with the fundamental freedoms. Nonetheless, the Community does dispose of the same potential justifications as are available to the Member States.[72] The ambit of possible justifications available to the Community are, incidentally, most likely wider than those on which Member States can rely as it is unlikely that the Community would support the economy of one Member State at the cost of another, an aim that might not be too far off where a measure of a single Member State is concerned.

(b) Private individuals and State omission

It is uncertain whether and to what extent private individuals are bound by the fundamental freedoms. In the domain of free movement of goods, the binding effect is restricted to public bodies, even though no single explanation is given.[73] Where the freedom of establishment and the freedom of services are concerned there are hardly any differing views;[74] this applies with even greater certainty to the free movement of workers. It is worth noting that collective bargaining agreements are subject to the fundamental freedoms,[75] and only recently,[76] the European Court of Justice assumed a

Commissioners of Inland Revenue, ex parte Daily Mail & General Trust PLC [1988] ECR 5483, para 16; Case C-264/96 *Imperial Chemical Industries plc (ICI) v Kenneth Hall Colmer (HM Inspector of Taxes)* [1998] ECR I-4695, para 21; Free movement of workers: Case C-415/93 *Union Royal Belge des Sociétés des Football Association ASBL v Jean-Marc Bosman* [1995] ECR I-4921, para 97.

[71] Case C-15/83 *Denkavit Nederland* [1984] ECR 2171, para 15; Case C-51/93 *Meyhui v Schott Zwiesel Glaserke* [1994] ECR I-3879, para 11.

[72] See Case C-51/93 *Meyhui v Schott Zwiesel Glaserke* [1994] ECR I-3879, paras 11, 14. To the justification in detail see also section IV below.

[73] eg Lux, in Lenz (ed), *EG-Vertrag* (2nd edn 1999, Article 28 para 16: Epiney, in Calliess and Ruffert (eds), *Kommentar zu EU-Vertrag und EG-Vertrag* (1999), Article 28 para 46; see also Case C-249/81 *Commission v Ireland* [1982] ECR 4005, para 6.

[74] Erhard, in Lenz (ed), *EG-Vertrag* (2nd edn 1999), Article 43 para 6; Hakenberg, in Lenz (ed), *EG-Vertrag* (2nd edn, 1999), Articles 49, 50 para 28; the contrary view eg Kluth, in Calliess and Ruffert (eds), *Kommentar zu EU-Vertrag und EG-Vertrag* (1999), Article 50 paras 48 and 49; Lackhoff, *Die Niederlassungsfreiheit des EGV* (2000) 205.

[75] Joined Cases C-51/96 and C-191/97, judgment of 11 April 2000 [2000] EuZW 371, para 47; Jarass, 'Die Niederlassungsfreiheit in der Europäischen Gemeinschaft – Ein Kernelement der Freiheit selbständiger wirtschaftlicher Betätigung', [1993] 39 RIW.

[76] Case C-36/74 *Walrave and Koch v Association Union Cycliste Internationale and others* [1974] ECR 1405, paras 16–24; Case C-13/76 *Dona v Mantero* [1976] ECR 1333, para 17;

more sweeping generally binding effect on private individuals.[77] On the other hand, private individuals cannot be bound to the same extent as Member States without unduly limiting civic autonomy.[78] It must thus be possible for a private individual to restrict his choice of doctor to those practising in his own country, even though there might be no adequate factual reason. Equally an individual can hardly be said to interfere with the free movement of workers where he prevents his spouse from taking up employment in another Member State.

An analysis of how these problems are to be approached from a dogmatic point of view lies beyond the scope of this chapter. What can be said with some certainty, however, is that the application of the fundamental freedoms is unproblematic where the activities of a private individual can be attributed to the State, or where a private individual exercises certain privileges and thereby acts in a State-like manner.[79] It is also possible to invoke the duty of protection incumbent on Member States, as already mentioned above.[80] Further, private individuals can rely on the invalidity of a State regulation in relations with other private individuals, insofar as the regulation violates a fundamental freedom.[81] Finally, in litigation between private individuals, provisions of Member State law have to be interpreted in conformity with the fundamental freedoms.[82]

IV. THE JUSTIFICATION OF RESTRICTIONS

Even though a measure may constitute a restriction falling within the scope of a fundamental freedom, it does not automatically represent a violation

Case C-415/93 *Union Royal Belge des Sociétés des Football Association ASBL v Jean-Marc Bosman* [1995] ECR I-4921, para 82; Case C-281/98 *Roman Angonese v Cassedi Risparnio* [2000] EuZW 468 para 36; similar in respect to the employer Case C-350/96 *Clean Car Autoservice GmbH v Landeshauptmann von Wien* [1998] ECR I-2521 paras 24 and 25.

[77] Similarly, Roth, 'Niederlassungs- und Dienstleistungsfreiheit', in Dauses (ed), *Handbuch des EG-Wirtschaftsrechts* (1993) EI para 17; Jarass, 'Die Niederfassungsfreiheit in des Europäischen Geneinschaft' [1993] RIW 7; see also the wording in Case C-415/93 *Union Royal Belge des Sociétés des Football Association ASBL v Jean-Marc Bosman* [1995] ECR I-4921 para 82.

[78] See Hirsch, 'Die aktuelle Rechtsprechung des EuGH zur Warenverkehrsfreiheit', [1999] 2 ZEuS 508.

[79] See Hailbronner, in Hailbronner *et al* (eds), *Handkommentar zum EUV/EGV* (1997) Article 52 para 15; even a step further goes Kluth, in Calliess and Ruffert (eds), *Kommentar zu EU-Vertrag und EG-Vertrag* (1999), Article 50 paras 48 and 49. This might possibly be expanded to employees as far as the free movement of workers is concerned.

[80] See B I 2 b, and Szczekalla, 'Grundfreiheitliche Schutzpflichten—eine 'neue' Funktion der Grundfreiheiten des Gemeinschaftsrechts', [1998] 113 DVBl 219; Burgi, 'Mitgliedstaatliche Garantenpflicht statt unmittelbare Drittwirkung der Grundfreiheiten', [1999] 10 EWS 327.

[81] Case C-47/90 *Delhaize Fréres v Promalvin and others* [1992] ECR I-3669 para 29.

[82] Beutler *et al*, *Die Europäische Union* (4th edn, 1993) 298; Jarass, 'Richtlinienkonforme bzw. EG-rechtskonforme Auslegung nationalen Rechts', [1991] 26 EuR 222.

of the fundamental freedom. It may nevertheless be permissible under certain conditions. This aspect of the fundamental freedoms is here referred to as justification.[83] A justification presupposes firstly an adequate basis (section I below), and secondly that the requirement of proportionality is met (section 2 below).

1. Possible bases for a justification

(a) Textual exceptions and their attributes

(i) The textual exceptions

A justification of a restriction can first be based on certain reservations in favour of restrictions contained in the relevant Treaty provisions.[84] These can conveniently be referred to as textual exceptions.[85] With regard to measures having equivalent effect under Articles 28 and 29, Article 30 EC is to be mentioned, which can be relied upon for the protection of a number of public goods.[86] For the free movement of workers, possible justifications can be found in Article 39(3) EC (public policy, public security and public health) as well as in Article 39(4) (public service). For restrictions of the freedom of establishment and, by virtue of Article 55, the free movement of services, justifications are contained in Article 45 EC (official authority) and in Article 46 EC (public policy, public security and public health).[87] As far as undertakings which have been entrusted with the operation of services of general economic interest or which have the character of a revenue-producing monopoly are concerned, a justification contained in Article 86(2) EC can be relied upon.[88] All these justifications only apply, however, where the pursued aim is entirely non-economic in character.[89]

[83] This is a translation of the German term '*Rechtfertigung*'.

[84] Justification on the basis of general interest is dealt with below. There possibly exists a justification through colliding Treaty provisions (see Jarass, 'Elemente einer Dogmatik der Grundfreiheiten', [1995] 226). Whether the European Court of Justice might take such a position seems rather doubtable (see Craig and de Búrca, *EC Law* (2nd edn, 1997) 604).

[85] This is a translation of the German term '*benannte Ausnahmen*'.

[86] This is a translation of the German term '*Rechtsgüter*'.

[87] Article 46 must not be restricted to the authority of the police in relation to foreigners; see Case C-352/85 *Bond van Adverteerders v Netherland* [1988] ECR 2085, paras 33 and 34; Case C-158/96 *Kohll v Union des caisses de maladie* [1998] ECR I-1931, para 50; Jarass, 'Die Niederlassungsfreiheit in der Europäischen Gemeinschaft—Ein Kernelement der Freiheit selbständiger wirtschaftlicher Betätigung', [1993] 39 RIW 6.

[88] Case C-179/90 *Merci Conzionali Porto di Genova v Siderugia Gabrielli* [1991] ECR I-5889, 5930 and 5931; Jarass, 'Die Niederlassungsfreiheit in der Europäischen Gemeinschaft—Ein Kernelement der Freiheit selbständiger wirtschaftlicher Betätigung', [1993] 39 RIW; cf different opinion Matthies and v Morries, in Grabitz and Hilf (eds), *Kommentar zur Europäischen Union* (1994) Article 30 para 54.

[89] Case C-324/93 *R v Secretary of State for the Home Department, ex parte Evans Medical and Macfarlan Smith* [1995] ECR I-563 para 36; Case C-224/97 *Erich Ciola v Land vorarlberg* [1999] ECR I-2517 para 16.

The textual exceptions apply to all types of restrictions, including non-discriminatory ones. The Court therefore also applies Article 30 where indistinctly applicable restrictions pursue aims covered by this provision.[90] The same is true for Article 46(1).[91]

(ii) The characteristics of the exceptions

The provisions which in certain circumstances justify a restriction of the fundamental freedoms are usually not classified as limitations of the scope of the fundamental freedoms, but are dealt with under a separate heading. The question thus arises where the line is to be drawn between the boundaries of the scope of the fundamental freedoms, in particular of the substantive scope, and the subsequent step of justification. Why should, for example, the protection of health, which is a relevant consideration in connection with all the fundamental freedoms, be examined under a separate heading rather than flowing into the definition of the substantive scope? The answer to this question is of essential importance for the understanding of justification as a separate step.

The special character of the justification step as opposed to the definition of the scope of a fundamental freedom results from the fact that the boundaries of the scope are laid down in an abstract way and that they are not concerned with the weighing up of colliding public goods. In contrast, it is a typical feature of the justification step that the restriction must be proportionate: the restriction of the fundamental freedom must be necessary in the interests of the conflicting public good.

Another important aspect is likely to be connected with this finding. Where a restriction exists within the scope of a fundamental freedom, there is a presumption that it is unlawful. Consequently, whereas the burden of proof to establish that a restriction falls within the scope of a fundamental freedom rests on the party alleging a breach, where justification is concerned, the burden of proof is reversed and lies with the party denying a breach.[92]

Not all of the above-mentioned textual exceptions can easily be classified as pertaining to the area of justification (rather than limiting the scope of the freedoms). The situation is comparatively clear for those exemptions

[90] See Case C-178/84 *Szemerey v Commission* [1987] ECR 1227, para 44; Joined Cases C-1, 176/90 *Aragonesa de Publicidad Exterior and Publivia v Departamento de Sanidad y Seguridad Social de Cataluna* [1991] ECR I-4151 para 13; Joined Cases C-13, 113/91 *Debus* [1992] ECR I-3617, para 14.

[91] Case C-279/80 *Webb* [1981] ECR 3305, para 19.

[92] Oliver, 'Some Further Reflections on the Scope of Articles 28–30 (ex 30–36) EC', [1999] CML Rev 804 and 805. Additionally there can be further distinctions: the justification of a restriction might require a legal or administrative measure (see Article 46(1)). This does not apply as far as the limits of scope are concerned; see Jarass, 'Elemente einer Dogmatik der Grundfreiheiten', [1995] 30 EuR 222.

which require restrictions to be 'justified' having regard to certain public goods or circumstances, as is the case in the context of Article 30 EC and Article 46(1) EC. It is right to say that the requirement of justification implies a need for proportionality.[93] The same must apply to the exception in Article 39(3) EC by analogy with Article 46(1).[94] As far as the other exceptions are concerned, the situation remains undecided. The ECJ does, however, generally tend to apply the other exceptions only in cases where the restrictions are necessary. This also applies to Article 39(4),[95] Article 45(1)[96] and to Article 86(2).[97] If this application is accepted, which it should be for a number of reasons, these provisions contain justifications and not limitations of the scope of the freedoms.[98]

(b) Justification by reference to the general good in cases of indistinctly applicable restrictions

(i) Scope and possible bases of general good

As has been demonstrated, the fundamental freedoms can be interfered with by measures which cannot be classified as discriminatory, ie where a factual disadvantage is caused or a core element of the guarantee is infringed. These situations can conveniently be referred to as 'indistinctly applicable restrictions'.[99] According to the jurisprudence developed by the ECJ first in the domain of the free movement of goods and later with regard to other fundamental freedoms, such restrictions are lawful as long as they are justifiable for mandatory reasons of the general good. Any considerations of general good of sufficient gravity can be pursued in this way. The limitations which apply to the possible justifications of discriminatory measures explicitly referred to in the Treaty do not find any application in this area. Excluded are, however, reasons of a purely economic character.[100]

[93] Case C-114/97 *Commission v Spain* [1998] ECR I-6717, para 34; Roth, 'Niederlassungs- und Dienstleistungsfreiheit' in Dauses (ed), *Handbuch des EG-Wirtschaftsrechts* (1993), EI para 125.

[94] Case C-249/86 *Commission v Germany* [1989] ECR 1263, para 20; Streinz, *Europarecht* (4th edn, 1999) para 694.

[95] See Brechmann, in Calliess and Ruffert (eds), *Kommentar zu EU-Vertrag und EG-Vertrag* (1999) Article 39 para 99.

[96] Case C-147/86 *Commission v Greece* [1988] ECR 1637, 1654, para 7; Case C-114/97 *Commission v Spain* [1998] ECR I-6717, para 34.

[97] Case C-393/92 *Houtwipper* [1994] ECR I-1477/1520, para 49; see also Jung, in Calliess and Ruffert (eds), *Kommentar zu EU-Vertrag und EG-Vertrag* (1999) Article 86 para 47; Lackhoff, *Die Niederlassungsfreiheit des EGV* (2000) 472 and 473.

[98] As far as Article 45 is concerned see Case C-67/98 on 21 October 1999, paras 28 and 29; the opposite opinion is taken by Streinz, *Europarecht* (4th edn, 1999), para 697.

[99] This is a translation of the German term '*unterschiedslos anwendbare Beschränkungen*'.

[100] Case C-120/95 *Decker v Caisse de maladie des employés privés* [1998] ECR I-1831, para 39; Case C-203/96 *Chemische Afvalstoffen Dusseldorp and others v Minister van Volkshuisvesting, Ruimtelijke Ordeneing en Milieubeheer* [1998] ECR I-4075, para 44.

This type of justification has been developed for indistinctly applicable restrictions and certainly used to be limited to them.[101] More recently, the Court has, albeit without further exploring the associated issues, extended the application of these justifications to cases of discriminatory regulations.[102] This is the case in both the areas of free movement of goods and of services.[103] The explicit enumeration of certain possible justifications in the Treaty would thus appear to be without significance for any of the types of restrictions. In the context of the proportionality test, the type of restriction may, however, still be relevant.

(ii) Dogmatic classification

The dogmatic classification of justification by reference to the general good is the object of some controversy. Some regard it, following on from the former enunciations of the ECJ, as a limitation of the concept of restriction. In more recent judgments, on the other hand, the Court has underlined the parallelism with the textual exemptions,[104] going so far as to talk of justification.[105] An argument for its classification as justification is the fact that the principle of proportionality is (in the same way as in the context of the textual exceptions) fundamental to the application of the general good. And it is precisely this principle which, as was developed above, lies at the heart of the step of justification.[106] Justification by reference to the general good therefore belongs under this heading.[107]

[101] Its application in the context of hidden discrimination is often rejected: see Hirsch, 'Die aktuelle Rechtsprechung des EuGH zur Warenverkehrsfreiheit', [1999] ZEuS 510; contrary view Gundel, 'Bootsliegeplatz-Privilegien für Einheimische: Verstoß gegen die Dienstleistungsfreiheit und Durchbrechung der nationalen Bestandskraft-Regeln?', [1999] EuR 782 and 783.

[102] Considered by Hakenberg, *Grundzüge des Europäischen Gemeinschaftsrechts* (2nd edn, 2000) 98, 99, 113, 119.

[103] Free movement of goods: see Case C-389/96 *Aher-Waggon v Germany* [1998] ECR I-4473, para 18; Free movement of services: Case C-158/96 *Kohll v Union des caisses de maladie* [1998] ECR I-1931, paras 37–42.

[104] See Case C-216/84 *Commission v France* [1988] ECR 793, para 7; Case C-34–36/95 *TV-Shop* [1997] ECR I-3875, para 45.

[105] Case C-415/93 *Union Royal Belge des Sociétés des Football Association ASBL v Jean-Marc Bosman* [1995] ECR I-4921, para 105, 121; Case C-368/95 *Vereinigte Familiapress Zeitungsverlags- und vertriebs GmbH v Bauer Verlag* [1997] ECR I-3689, para 18; Case C-34–36/95 *TV-Shop* [1997] ECR I-3875.

[106] See section IV.1(a) above. This is also applicable under the step of restriction, as the existence of a restriction does not depend on a test of proportionality.

[107] Hirsch, 'Die aktuelle Rechtsprechung des EuGH zur Warenverkehrsfreiheit', [1999] 2 ZEuS 511; Jarass, 'Elemente einer Dogmatik der Grundfreiheiten', [1995] 30 EuR 224 and 225.

(c) Influence of secondary legislation and fundamental rights

(i) Influence of secondary legislation

Finally, possible justifications of restrictions of fundamental freedoms are influenced by any applicable secondary legislation. In a number of cases concerning the free movement of goods, the Court has stated that Member States cannot rely on any justifications where harmonization through secondary legislation has taken place and the secondary legislation is either intended to be conclusive or on its own sufficiently protects the public good in question. This is the case not only under Article 30[108] but also for justifications by reference to the general good.[109] In the domain of the other fundamental freedoms, the Court appears so far to have stopped short of employing this analysis. It would probably be appropriate there in the same way.[110]

The dogmatic classification of this jurisprudence is not straightforward. On the one hand, it is clear that national law must comply with the requirements of both the fundamental freedoms and secondary legislation. These are two independent yardsticks which must be applied concurrently. The Court has accordingly held that the compatibility of a national provision with relevant secondary legislation does not render the examination of the primary legislation unnecessary.[111] The conclusive regulation by secondary legislation does, on the other hand, have an effect on the fundamental freedoms: any justification is precluded. The reason for this is that the Member States lack the competence of introducing regulations restricting the fundamental freedoms where existing secondary legislation (lawfully) contains conclusive provisions. An alternative analysis might be to deny the necessity for any national regulations due to the existence of the secondary legislation, but there is no hint of such reasoning in the central decisions of the Court on the matter; their wording points more in the direction of competency-based rationalization. The matter would thus appear to be a problem not of fundamental freedoms, but of competency or even of compatibility

[108] Case C-215/78 *Jubilé v Commission* [1989] ECR I-617, para 15; Case C-317/92 *Commission v Germany* [1994] ECR I-2039, para 14; Case C-320/93 *Ferguson v Council and Commission* [1994] ECR I-5243, para 14; Case C-5/94 *R v Ministry of Agriculture, Fisheries and Food, ex parte Hedley Lomas (Ireland)* [1996] ECR I-2553, paras 18 and 19.

[109] Case C-120/78 *Rewe-Zentrale AG v Bundesmonopolverwaltung für Branntwein* [1979] ECR 649, paras 8 and 9; Case C-261/81 *Cogis* [1982] ECR 3961, para 12; Case C-298/87 *Smanor* [1988] ECR 4489, para 15.

[110] As far as Article 39 is concerned see Brechmann, in Calliess and Ruffert (eds), *Kommentar zu EU-Vertrag und EG-Vertrag* (1999) Article 39 para 95; Bröhmer, in Calliess and Ruffert (eds), ibid, Article 46 para 4. Generally see Lackhoff, *Die Niederlassungsfreiheit des EGV* (2000) 460.

[111] Case C-158/96 *Raymond Kohll v Union des caisses de maladie* [1998] ECR I-1931, para 25. Thus it is rather misleading to talk of a 'priority' of secondary legislation; see Emmert, *Europarecht* (1996) § 37 para 13.

with secondary legislation. A violation of fundamental freedoms can be identified at best on a secondary level.

(ii) Fundamental rights

The above considerations apply equally to the fundamental rights recognized by Community law. There is no possibility of justification of a national measure concerning fundamental freedoms which violates fundamental rights.[112] Once again this would appear to be primarily a question of violation of fundamental rights rather than of fundamental freedoms. At least this concerns legal provision of the same rank, as both fundamental freedoms and fundamental rights are derived from primary legislation. This renders a linking even less problematic.

2. Proportionality as the Limitation of the Exceptions

(a) Requirement and significance of proportionality

Restrictions of fundamental freedoms can be saved by the exceptions provided for in the Treaty only if they are proportionate.[113] This can be gleaned from the wording of some of the relevant sections which provide that any exception must be 'justified' in relation to the pursued aims.[114] The same is true for the justification of non-discriminatory restrictions based on the general good. The principle of proportionality is relevant in these cases as well. The examination of proportionality usually represents the central part of the European Court of Justice's scrutiny of the justification of restrictions.

In detail, the Court requires that the restriction be *suitable* to meet the pursued aim; this applies to justifications based on textual exceptions[115] as well as those based on the general good.[116] Further, the restriction must be *necessary* to achieve the desired objective; this again applies

[112] Case C-260/89 *ERT v DEP* [1991] ECR I-2925 para 41; Case C-23/93 *TV10 v Commissariaat voor de Media* [1994] ECR I-4795, para 24; Case C-368/95 *Vereinigte Familiapress Zeitungsverlags- und -vertriebs GmbH v Bauer Verlag* [1997] ECR I-3689, para 24; Hirsch, 'Die aktuelle Rechtsprechung des EuGH zur Warenverkehrsfreiheit', [1999] 2 ZEuS 506 and 507.

[113] This is a translation of the German term '*verhältnismäßig*'.

[114] See section IV.1(a) above.

[115] In the context of free movement of services see Case C-260/89 *ERT v DEP* [1991] ECR I-2925, para 25.

[116] In the context of free movements of services see Case C-205/84 *Commission v Germany* [1986] ECR 3755, para 27; Case C-353/89 *Commission v Netherlands* [1991] ECR I-4069, para 19; in the context of freedom of establishment Case C-55/94 *Gebhard v Consiglio dell'Ordine degli Avvocati e Procuratori di Milano* [1995] ECR I-4165, para 37; Case C-212/97 *Centros Ltd v Erhvervs- og Selskabsstyrelsen* [1999] ECR I-1459, paras 34 and 35.

equally to justifications based on textual exceptions[117] as well as those based on the general good.[118] Finally, the reasonableness of the measure would seem to be of importance.[119] Even though the Court often only addresses the first two elements,[120] three elements can easily be distinguished.

(1) The principle of proportionality first requires the suitability[121] of the national measure. The restriction must be 'such as to guarantee the achievement of the intended aim'.[122] This criterion should not be set too high. On the one hand, the national measure does not have to be the best way of achieving the aim in question, and, on the other hand, mere promotion of the aim may be sufficient.[123]

(2) Secondly, the principle of *necessity*[124] has to be adhered to. This means there should not be an (equally effective) alternative which is less restrictive, or which does not interfere with the fundamental freedom at all. Generally, the measure must not go beyond what is necessary to achieve the pursued objective.[125] Particular scrutiny is necessary of the extent to which the regulations of the country of origin already adequately address the aim pursued by the country of destination.[126] In the case of discrimination it has

[117] In the context of free movement of goods see Case C-400/96 *Harpegnies* [1998] ECR I-5121, para 34. In the context of free movement of services see Case C-352/85 *Bond van Adverteerders v Netherlands State* [1988] ECR 2085, para 36; Case C-3/88 *Commission v Italy* [1989] ECR 4035, paras 15 and 16.

[118] In the context of free movement of goods see Case C-298/87 *Smanor* [1988] ECR 4489, para 15; Becker [1994] EuR 165 and 166. Freedom of establishment: see Case C-106/91 *Ramrath v Ministre de la Justice* [1992] ECR I-3351, paras 30–32. Free movement of services: see Case C-33/74 *Van Binsbergen v Bedrijfsvereniging voor de Metaalnijverheid* [1974] ECR 1299, para 16; Case C-288/89 *Stichting Collectieve Antennevoorziening Gouda v Commissariaat voor de Media* [1991] ECR I-4007, para 15.

[119] As far as textual exemptions are concerned see Case C-249/86 *Commission v Germany* [1989] ECR 1263, para 20; Epiney, in Calliess and Ruffert (eds), *Kommentar zu EU-Vertrag und EG-Vertrag* (1999) Article 30, para 49. In the context of justification based on general interest see Case C-76/90 *Säger v Dennemeyer* [1991] ECR I-4221, para 20 for freedom of services; Case C-184/96 *Commission v France* [1998] ECR I-6197, para 26 for free movement of goods.

[120] See Case C-19/92 *Kraus v Land Baden Württemberg* [1993] ECR I-1663, para 32; Case C-55/94 *Gebhard v Consiglio dell'Ordine degli Avvocati e Procuratori di Milano* [1995] ECR I-4165, para 37; Case C-216/97 *Gregg* [1999] ECR I-4947, para 34; all three elements are mentioned in Case C-265/87 *R v Royal Pharmaceutical Society of Great Britain, ex parte Association of Pharmaceutical Importers* [1989] ECR 2237, para 21; Case C-389/96 *Aher-Waggon v Germany* [1998] ECR I-4473, para 20.

[121] This is a translation of the German term '*Geeignetheit*'.

[122] See Case C-124/97 *Läärä and others* (21 September 1999), para 31.

[123] See Case C-152/78 *Commission v France* [1980] ECR 2299, 2316.

[124] This is a translation of the German term '*Erforderlichkeit*'.

[125] See Case C-205/84 *Commission v Germany* [1986] ECR 3755, para 33; Case C-389/96 *Aher-Waggon v Germany* [1998] ECR I-4473, para 20.

[126] As far as free movement of goods are concerned: see Case C-293/93 *Houtwipper* [1994] ECR I-4249, para 15. Free movement of services: see Case C-76/90 *Säger v Dennemeyer* [1991] ECR I-4221, para 15; Case C-106/91 *Ramth v Ministre de la Justice* [1992] ECR I-

to be examined whether a different restriction would be less restrictive of the fundamental freedom than the discriminatory one.[127]

(3) Finally, the requirement of reasonableness[128] has to be met. One might also speak of tolerability.[129] The pursued objective has to be 'sufficiently serious' in relation to the interference with the fundamental freedom.[130] In so far there should not be a severe disparity.[131]

The severity of penalties and sanctions frequently falls foul of this requirement.[132] The requirement is further of importance where the reduction of the administrative or financial burden on public authorities is in issue.[133] Another factor to be taken into account in reviewing reasonableness is whether the Member State applies equally 'severe' measures in similar cases.[134] This is unless one splits off this element and considers the principle of equivalence[135] a separate limitation of the possibility of justification.[136]

The requirement of reasonableness has a stronger effect in the context of the free movement of services than on the freedom of establishment. Where the freedom of establishment is in issue, affected persons can more reasonably (than in the area of the freedom to provide services) be expected to accept the national law of the country where they settle.[137] The freedom of establishment is thus (in practical effect) not as far-reaching as the free movement of services or even the free movement of goods.

3351, para 29. Freedom of establishment: see Case C-55/94 *Gebhard v Consiglio dell'Ordine degli Avvocati e Procuratori di Milano* [1995] ECR I-4186, para 38.

[127] Generally a discrimination is not admissible where the aim could also be pursued by an indistinctly applicable measure; see Jarass, 'Die Niederlassungsfreiheit in der Europäischen Gemeinschaft—Ein Kernelement der Freiheit selbständiger wirtschaftlicher Betätigung' [1993] 39 RIW. This is not valid in the case where the discrimination imposes a much smaller burden.

[128] This is a translation of the German term '*Angemessenheit*'.

[129] This is a translation of the German term '*Zumutbarkeit*'.

[130] See Case C-121/85 *Conegate v HM Customs & Excise* [1986] ECR 1007, para 15; Case C-389/96 *Aher-Waggon v Germany* [1998] ECR I-4473, para 20 as far as free movement of goods are concerned.

[131] Lackhoff, *Die Niederlassungsfreiheit des EGV* (2000) 465.

[132] Craig and de Búrca, *EC Law* (2nd edn, 1997) 353, 354, 693 and 694 with further annotations.

[133] See, on the one hand, Case C-104/75 *De Peijper* [1976] ECR 613, para 18; Case C-128/89 *Commission v Italy* [1990] ECR I-3239, para 22; Case C-18/95 *F.C. Terhoeve v Inspecteur van de Belastingdienst Particulieren/Ondernemingen Buitenland* [1999] ECR I-345, para 45. On the other hand, Case C-273/94 *Commission v Netherlands* [1996] ECR I-2617 para 29.

[134] See Case C-121/85 *Conegate v HM Customs & Excise* [1986] ECR 1007, para 18; Craig and de Búrca, *EC Law* (2nd edn, 1997) 597.

[135] This is a translation of the German term '*Grundsatz der Gleichwertigkeit*'.

[136] Streinz, *Europarecht* (4th edn, 1999) para 703 does so under the misleading term of prohibition of discrimination (*Diskriminierungsverbot*). The ECJ uses (while applying EC law) the term of equivalence in Case C-326/96 *Levez v Jennings Ltd* [1998] ECR I-7835, para 18.

[137] Roth, 'Niederlassungs- und Dienstleistungsfreiheit', in Dauses (ed), *Handbuch des EG-Wirtschaftsrechts* (1993) EI para 71; Jarass, 'Die Niederlassungsfreiheit in der Europäischen Gemeinschaft—Ein Kernelement der Freiheit selbständiger wirtschaftlicher Betätigung' [1993] RIW 7.

(b) Intensity of the test

The practical importance of the test of proportionality mainly depends on the density of judicial control, on the intensity of the judicial examination.[138] In particular, the examination of proportionality commonly necessitates predictions and assessments concerning the application of the national measure. Such predictions and assessments are inevitably beset with substantial uncertainty. Thus the questions arises whether Member States have a certain freedom of appreciation in making these appraisals which cannot be judicially reviewed.[139] In the context of all the other steps in the examination of the fundamental freedoms, this question properly has to be answered in the negative.

With respect to proportionality the Court proceeds differently from case to case. At times it refers to the assessment by the Member States or the review by national courts.[140] Often, however, it itself carries out a detailed and strict assessment of proportionality.[141] In principle, such a differentiated procedure is justified. The difficult question, which has (in general) thus far gone unanswered is, however, which factors influence the intensity of the examination. It is obvious that the Court is much stricter in its assessment of proportionality in the context of the fundamental freedoms, and thus where measures of Member States are concerned, than (outside the domain of the fundamental freedoms) where it deals with the proportionality of Community measures.[142] The questions whether this distinction is justifiable and which factors in any event affect the intensity of the examination lie beyond the scope of this chapter. It should be noted, however, that the density of control should be greater in the context of suitability and necessity than in the context of reasonableness. An additional factor is how uncertain the necessary predictions are.[143] Finally, the density of control should typically be higher in relation to discriminatory restrictions than in relation to indistinctly applicable restrictions.[144]

[138] Craig and de Búrca, *EC Law* (2nd edn, 1997) 352.

[139] Supported by Epiney, in Calliess and Ruffert (eds), *Kommentar zu EU-Vertrag und EG-Vertrag* (1999) Article 30 paras 46, 48; Lackhoff, *Die Niederlassungsfreiheit des EGV* (2000) 462 and 463.

[140] As far as leaving it up to the national courts see Craig and de Búrca, *EC Law* (2nd edn, 1997) 357. In so far the question is more about a procedural approach and less about the limits of substantial law.

[141] Craig and de Búrca, *EC Law* (2nd edn, 1997) 355 and 356.

[142] ibid 355.

[143] ibid 356 and 357.

[144] Lackhoff, *Die Niederlassungsfreiheit des EGV* (2000) 463.

6

Judicially-Created Exceptions to the Free Provision of Services

SÍOFRA O'LEARY AND JOSÉ M FERNÁNDEZ-MARTÍN*

I. INTRODUCTION

Articles 45, 46 and 55 EC permit exceptions from the freedom to provide services in so far as the activity in question is related to the exercise of official authority, or on grounds of public policy, public security and public health. This chapter focuses on further exceptions to the prohibition on restrictions of the free provision of services which have been fashioned by the European Court of Justice. It first reviews developments in the Court's case law which have led it, beyond direct and indirect discrimination, to prohibit, in addition, non-discriminatory national restrictions which are liable to impede the free provision of services. These indistinctly applicable restrictions are permissible if they can be justified with reference to imperative requirements of public interest. This open-ended category of justifications, created by the ECJ itself, is meant to reflect the social, moral and cultural diversity which still exists between the Member States and which, at least in the absence of further harmonization, may come into conflict with fundamental freedoms guaranteed by the EC Treaty. In order for indistinctly applicable national measures which restrict free movement to be justifiable, they must, in addition, comply with the principle of proportionality.

The purpose of this chapter is to clarify and update the law as it stands with respect to these judicial exceptions from the free provisions of services and the use made by the Court of the proportionality principle. Although the Court has actively and willingly identified imperative requirements capable of justifying restrictions to the Community's fundamental freedoms, it has frequently resorted to the principle of proportionality to reject, at least on the facts of the case, reliance on such public interest justifications, because it regards the national measure as unnecessary, inadequate or disproportionate to the legitimate aim pursued. Nevertheless, the principle of proportionality has not always been allowed to play the essential role

* The views expressed in this chapter are purely personal to the authors. This is an updated an extended version of an article previously published in (1995) *European Law Journal* 308–329.

attributed to it by the Court itself. In cases involving national measures designed to counteract the prejudicial effects of lotteries and other games of chance, for example, the Court has avoided any reference to the requirements of proportionality. This chapter reflects on this singular approach, evident in some recent case law, to the assessment of moral and ethical public interest justifications put forward by Member States and the effect which such an approach may have on the exercise of the fundamental freedoms guaranteed by Community law.[1]

II. THE PRINCIPLE OF NON-DISCRIMINATION, THE FREE PROVISION OF SERVICES AND EXPRESS EC TREATY EXCEPTIONS

Article 49 EC is a specific expression of the principle of non-discrimination in Article 12 EC. Its purpose is to secure equal access for nationals of Member States to the market for the provision of services in a Member State other than that where the provider of services is established. In *Van Binsbergen* the Court regarded Article 49 EC as a means of abolishing 'any discrimination against a person providing a service by reason of his nationality or of the fact that he resides in a Member State other than that in which the service is to be provided'.[2] However, the principle of non-discrimination is not restricted in the area of services to clear incidences of discrimination founded on nationality or establishment. It also prohibits all forms of disguised discrimination which, although applying other criteria of distinction, lead, in fact, to the same result. This is known as indirect or covert discrimination.[3]

The orthodox approach followed by the Court for many years, and indeed the theory imbibed by students of EC law since the latter part of the 1980s, dictated that national measures which were formally or directly discriminatory could only be exempt from Article 49 EC with reference to one of the express derogations from the principle of free movement contained in Articles 45, 46 and 55 EC.[4] The exceptions in Article 46 EC

[1] For a discussion of morality in the case law of the Court see P Hetsch, 'Emergence des valeurs morales dans la jurisprudence de la C.J.C.E.' (1982) RTDE 511–555.

[2] Case 33/74 [1974] ECR 1299, para 10. See also Case 63/86 *Commission v Italy* [1988] ECR 29, paras 12 and 13; Case 39/75 *Coenen v Sociaal-Economische Road* [1975] ECR 1547, para 6; Case 52/79 *Procureur du Roi v Debauve* [1980] ECR 833, para 11; and Case 279/80 *Criminal Proceedings against Alfred John Webb* [1981] ECR 3305, para 14.

[3] See Case 221/85 *Commission v Belgium* [1987] ECR 719; Case 352/85 *Bond van Adverteerders v Netherlands* [1988] ECR 2085; Case C-3/88 *Commission* v *Italy* [1989] ECR 4035, para 8; Joined Cases 62 and 63/81 *SECO v EVI* [1982] ECR 223, para 8; and Case 205/84 *Commission v Germany* [1986] ECR 3755, para 25. For a definition of overt and covert discrimination see Advocate General Jacobs in Case C-76/90 *Manfred Säger v Dennemeyer and Co. Ltd* [1991] ECR I-4221, para 19.

[4] See, for example, Case 352/85 *Bond van Adverteerders* (n 3 above) paras 32 and 33; Case

are similar in appearance and operate in a similar manner to those applicable to the free movement of workers pursuant to Article 39(3) EC. The public policy proviso is thus applicable to 'genuine and sufficiently serious threat[s] to the requirements of public policy affecting one of the fundamental interests of society'.[5] Reliance on the public policy exception cannot be determined unilaterally by each Member State, although they are afforded a margin of discretion in this respect. Furthermore, public policy considerations cannot be invoked to justify restrictions of free movement for economic reasons.[6] Article 45 EC, on the other hand, excludes activities connected, even occasionally, with the exercise of official authority from the principle of free movement in establishment and services. The Court has limited this derogation to activities within the scope of Articles 43 and 49 EC which involve direct and specific participation in the exercise of official authority.[7] Finally, exceptions from the free provision of services pursuant to Articles 45, 46 and 55 EC constitute exceptions to the fundamental Treaty principle of free movement and must therefore be limited to what is

C-288/89 *Stichtung Collectieve Antennevoorziening Gouda and others v Commissariaat voor de Media* (hereafter '*Gouda*') [1991] ECR I-4007, para 10; or, more recently, Case C-224/97 *Erich Ciola v Land Vorarlberg* [1999] ECR I-2517, para 16. See also the references in the doctrine to this 'orthodoxy' in, *inter alia*, R Giesen, annotation of Case C-120/95 *Nicolas Decker v Caisse de maladie des employés privés* and Case C-158/96 *Raymond Kohll v Union des caisses de maladie* (1999) 36 CML Rev 841–850, at 845; P Cabral, annotation of *Decker* and *Kohll* (1999) 24 EL Rev 387–395, at 394; D Martin, ' "Discriminations", "entraves" et "raisons impérieuses" dans le traité CE: trois concepts en quête d'identité' (1998) CDE 261–318 and (1998) CDE 261–318 and 561–637; V Hatzopoulos, annotation of Case C-275/92 *Her Majesty's Customs and Excise v Schindler* (1995) 32 CML Rev 841–855, at 848; A Whelan and A Schouten, annotation of *Decker* and *Kohll* (1999) 9 *Revue des Affaires Européennes* 90–105, at 97; and, in the parallel context of Article 28 EC, M Poiares Maduro, 'The Saga of Article 30 EC Treaty: To Be Continued' (1998) *Maastricht Journal of European and Comparative Law* 298–316, at 310.

[5] See Case 30/77 *R v Bouchereau* [1977] ECR 1999, para 35; or Case C-348/96 *Criminal Proceedings against Donatella Calfa* [1998] ECR I-11, para 21.

[6] See, for example, the rejection of economic policy considerations in Case 352/85 *Bond van Adverteerders* (n 3 above) para 30; Case C-353/89 *Commission v Netherlands* [1991] ECR I-4069; or Case C-398/95 *SETTG* [1997] ECR I-3091, para 23. See, however, the reasoning of the Court in Case C-158/96 *Raymond Kohll v Union des caisses de maladie* [1998] ECR I-1931, para 50, where it held that maintenance of a balanced medical and hospital service, which was 'intrinsically linked to the method of financing of the social security system', could fall within the grounds of public health under Article 46 EC. In *Kohll* the Court found that the reimbursement of medical expenses incurred abroad in accordance with the tariff of the State of insurance had no significant effect on the financing of the social security system. Nevertheless, its reasoning did signal a change in the orthodox position whereby aims of an economic nature are unable to justify restrictions on trade. See also the 'games of chance' cases discussed below.

[7] Case 2/74 *Reyners v Belgium State* [1974] ECR 631. It has been argued that the ECJ has been more restrictive in its interpretation of official authority in Article 45 EC than with respect to employment in the public service in Article 39(4) EC, which excludes employment with an indirect link with the public service from the scope of the free movement provisions: see the Opinion of Advocate General Mischo in Case C-3/88 *Commission v Italy* (n 3 above) para 30.

necessary to protect the interests which the Member States purport to guarantee thereunder.[8]

III. INDISTINCTLY APPLICABLE MEASURES AND THE FREE PROVISION OF SERVICES

Besides prohibiting direct and indirect discrimination with regard to the free provision of services the Court has also devised a line of case law on indistinctly applicable national measures which do not differentiate with respect to nationality or establishment, but which nevertheless restrict free movement.

1. Justifying Unlawful Member State Restrictions with Reference to the General Interest

In its 1991 decisions in *Säger* and *Gouda*, the Court expressly embraced the idea that indistinctly applicable national rules which restrict the freedom guaranteed by the Treaty in the field of services come within the scope of the prohibition in Article 49 EC if the application of such rules to foreign persons providing services is not justified by overriding reasons relating to the public interest or if the requirements embodied in those rules are already satisfied by the rules imposed on those persons in the Member State in which they are established.[9] The Court added that the application of national rules to providers of services established in other Member States must be such as to guarantee the achievement of the intended aim and must not go beyond that which is necessary in order to achieve that objective.[10] Despite the reference in *Gouda* to what 'the Court has consistently held', that decision has been interpreted both as an explicit departure from its previous largely discrimination-based approach to restrictive national measures and a general statement of principle for future reference.

Nevertheless, if one refers to some of the Court's earlier case law on the freedom to provide services, there is perhaps something to be said for the Court's claim that this new approach was not so new after all.[11] The Dutch legislation impugned in *Van Binsbergen*, for example, provided that only persons established in the Netherlands could appear as legal representatives or advisers before certain courts. The plaintiff's adviser was declared ineligible when, in the course of proceedings, he moved to Belgium. The question

[8] See Case 352/85 *Bond van Adverteerders* (n 3 above) para 36.

[9] Case C-288/89 *Gouda* (n 4 above) paras 12–13; Case C-76/90 *Säger* (n 3 above) para 15.

[10] Case C-288/89 *Gouda*, para 15.

[11] Indeed, the list of imperative requirements provided in Case C-288/89 *Gouda* (n 4 above) came of course, from cases decided previously.

arose whether the requirement that the provider of services be permanently established in the Member State where the service is provided is compatible with the prohibition of restrictions in Articles 49 and 50 EC. Although the requirement applied equally to nationals and non-nationals, the Court held that it was capable of depriving Article 49 EC of all effect, since the very object of the latter was to eliminate restrictions to the free provision of services by persons not established in the territory of the Member State where the service is provided.

The Court in *Van Binsbergen* accepted that the particular nature of certain services and the fact that many national technical and administrative rules regulating services have not yet been harmonized meant that specific requirements imposed on the provider of services are not automatically incompatible with the Treaty when their purpose is the application of professional rules governing such activities. Member States should be able to ensure that providers of services cannot, simply by establishing themselves in another Member State, avoid professional rules which would otherwise have applied to them had they remained in the Member State where the services are destined. Thus, the ECJ did not regard a requirement that legal representatives and advisers establish themselves as incompatible with the Treaty as such. However, such a condition had to be objectively necessary to ensure observance of the professional rules regulating the organization of the profession, the grant of qualifications and respect for the professional rules of conduct. Furthermore, such a requirement could only be justified with reference to the general interest if the objectives in question could not be guaranteed by means less restrictive of the free provision of services. The Court thus introduced, at this early stage, the principle of proportionality into its analysis of the justifications proposed by Member States of their restrictions of free movement. The facts in *Van Binsbergen* indicated that a less restrictive means, namely, a requirement of domicile for the purposes of receiving judicial communications, did exist, so that the requirement of establishment was unnecessary to achieve the objectives in question and was disproportionate.[12] The establishment requirement was also considered unlawful since the provision of the service in question was not subject to any qualification or professional regulation.[13]

[12] See also Case 39/75 *Coenen* (n 2 above) where an insurance broker who had an office in the Member State where the service was provided could not, in addition, be required to establish himself.

[13] The Court has repeatedly held since that the requirement of establishment is suspect and in need of justification. See, for example, the insurance cases: Case 220/83 *Commission v France* [1991] ECR 3663; Case 252/83 *Commission v Denmark* [1986] ECR 3713; Case 205/84 *Commission v Germany* (n 3 above); and Case 206/84 *Commission v Ireland* [1986] ECR 3817.

2. The Requirements of the Principle of Proportionality

The restriction of free movement in *Van Binsbergen* was, however, due to an indirectly discriminatory national rule. Although the conditions imposed appeared neutral, they were more likely to prejudice the provision of services by persons established outside the territory of the Member State where the services were destined. However, as we have seen, the Court subsequently developed a series of principles with respect to indistinctly applicable rules which do not differentiate on the basis of nationality or establishment. Restrictions of free movement in such circumstances may be justifiable if they are designed to protect imperative requirements of public interest. However, to remain compatible with Community law these restrictions must be necessary to achieve the objectives in question and less restrictive means to achieve that objective must not be available.[14] The existence of less restrictive means to protect the public interest was fatal to the establishment requirement in *Van Binsbergen.*

Another aspect of the principle of proportionality arose in the *Webb* case, namely, the existence of home control. This requirement is in line with the Court's case law following *Rewe-Zentrale v Bundesmonopolverwaltung fur Branntwein,*[15] better known as *Cassis de Dijon*. In *Webb*, an employment agency established in the United Kingdom was engaged in the supply of temporary staff in the Netherlands. The staff supplied were employed by the agency, which was remunerated directly by the company for which the staff worked. Although the agency held a licence under British law, it was additionally required under Dutch law to possess a licence. The Court was quick to recognize the sensitive economic and social nature of the services in question. The activities of employment agencies can directly affect relations in the employment market and the legitimate interests of the workers involved.[16] Member State legislation tended to reflect attempts to avoid any possible abuse in the provision of such services by limiting the scope of such activities, or in one case, forbidding their exercise.[17] Given the sensitive

[14] On the different elements of the Court's proportionality test and their application in practice see further E Ellis (ed), *The Principle of Proportionality in the Laws of Europe* (Oxford, Hart Publishing, 1999), and, in particular, T Tridimas, 'Proportionality in Community Law: Searching for the Appropriate Standard of Scrutiny', 65–84, at 68, who believes that the test applied by the Court is tripartite. First it must be established whether the measure is suitable to achieve a legitimate aim, secondly whether it is necessary to achieve that aim and, finally, that the measure does not have an excessive effect on the applicant's interests.

[15] Case 120/79 [1979] ECR 649.

[16] In *Webb* (n 2 above), Advocate General Slynn also emphasized the important effects which the activities of employment agencies could have on employment policy problems at national, regional and sectoral levels, and their potential effect on the role and functioning of national employment agencies and on employment relations.

[17] Case 279/80 *Webb* (n 2 above) is a good example of the Court, even prior to the development of its case law on imperative requirements in the public interest, adopting a compara-

nature of the service and the manner in which it was regulated at Member State level, the Court held that Member States could subject the supply of labour in their territory to a licence regime. Such a system constituted a legitimate political choice by Member States taken in the public interest. However, the Court emphasized in *Webb* that such justifications must be limited to what is necessary to achieve the public interest objectives in question. They can only be justified, in addition, to the extent that those interests are not already protected by the rules to which the provider of services is subject in the Member State in which he or she is established. In *Webb* the licensing system was incompatible with Article 49 EC because it duplicated the guarantees required by the provider of services in his or her state of establishment.[18]

3. What is the Overall Position of the ECJ?

At the end of the 1980s and in the early 1990s, in a number of decisions dealing with the insurance sector, the free provision of the services of tourist guides[19] and national (in particular Dutch) legislation on broadcasting,[20] the Court enunciated the orthodox approach referred to earlier. Article 49 EC required the suppression of any discrimination against the provider of services by virtue of his or her nationality, or the fact that he or she is established in a Member State other than that where the services are provided. Such discriminatory measures could only be justified with reference to an express Treaty exception such as Article 46 EC. Economic policy considerations could not qualify as justifications within the context of public policy in Article 46 EC. Given the lack of harmonization in the area of services, the Court accepted that obstacles to free movement could arise from the application of diverse national rules which affect both persons established in the territory and providers of services established elsewhere. However, unless these indistinctly applicable measures which restrict free movement could be justified with reference to imperative requirements relating to the public interest, they were also incompatible with Article 49 EC.[21]

tive analysis of Member State roles generally in order to assess whether the impugned national measure was necessary and justified.

[18] See also Joined Cases 110–111/78 *Van Wesemael* [1979] ECR 35, paras 29–30.

[19] Case C-154/89 *Commission v France* [1991] ECR I-659; Case C-180/89 *Commission v Italy* [1991] ECR I-709; and Case C-198/89 *Commission v Greece* [1991] ECR I-729.

[20] See Case 352/85 *Bond van Adverteerders* (n 4 above); Case C-288/89 *Gouda* (n 4 above); and Case C-353/89 *Commission v Netherlands* (n 6 above).

[21] It is unfortunate that the Court has not adopted one fixed term for this category of exception and stuck to it consistently. In Case C-288/89 (n 4 above) *Gouda* it referred to *overriding reasons relating to the public interest*, while elsewhere it has spoken of *imperative reasons relating to the public interest* (Case C-76/90 *Säger* (n 3 above), of *matters of overriding general interest* (Case C-264/96 *ICI* [1998] ECR I-4695) or even of *objective considerations* (Case C-

Furthermore, to keep within the justifiable restrictions permitted by that Treaty provision, the general interest objectives in question must not already be protected by rules imposed on the provider in the Member State in which he or she is established and they must not be disproportionate to the objective or interest sought to be protected and must not go beyond what is necessary to achieve it.

In *Gouda* and *Commission v Netherlands* the Court listed the imperative requirements already identified in its previous case law. These included professional rules designed to protect the recipients of services,[22] protection of intellectual property,[23] protection of workers,[24] consumer protection,[25] conservation of national artistic and historical heritage,[26] evaluation of archaeological, artistic and historical richness and the widest possible dissemination of knowledge of the artistic and cultural heritage of a country.[27] The protection of cultural policies in broadcasting and protecting TV and radio audiences from excessive advertising can now be added to this list, as can, *inter alia*, the need to ensure the cohesion of the tax system,[28] the effectiveness of fiscal supervision,[29] the need to respect professional and ethical rules,[30] the protection of a Member State's social order,[31] and the protection of the reputation and integrity of a particular economic sector.[32] Parallels clearly exist between the Court's case law on imperative requirements in the area of services and in the area of the free movement of goods.

237/94 *John O'Flynn v Adjudication Officer* [1996] ECR I-2617, albeit in the context of Article 39 EC and Regulation 1612/68). In the context of Article 28 EC, the term used since the landmark decision in *Cassis de Dijon* is *mandatory requirements*, although even this 'holy cow' has sometimes been changed to *overriding requirements* (Case C-368/95 *Vereinigte Familiapress Zeitungs Verlags und Vertriebs GmbH v Heinrich Bauer Verlag* [1997] ECR I-3689). On the difficulties caused by this lack of uniformity in the terminology used see C Hilson, 'Discrimination in Community Free Movement Law' (1999) 24 EL Rev 445–462.

22 Joined Cases 110/78 and 111/78 *Van Wesemael* (n 18 above) para 28.

23 Case 62/79 *Coditel* [1980] ECR 881.

24 Case 279/80 *Webb* (n 2 above); Joined Cases 62 and 63/81 *SECO v EVI* (n 3 above); and Case C-113/89 *Rush Portuguesa Ltd. v Office national d'immigration* [1990] ECR I-1417.

25 Case 205/84 *Commission* v *Germany* (n 3 above); Case 220/83 *Commission v France* (n 13 above); Case 252/83 *Commission v Denmark* (n 13 above); Case 206/84 *Commission v Ireland* (n 13 above); Case C-180/89 *Commission v Italy* (n 19 above); and Case C-198/89 *Commission v Greece* (n 19 above).

26 Case C-180/89 *Commission v Italy* (n 19 above).

27 Case C-154/89 *Commission v France* (n 19 above) paras 16–17; Case C-198/89 *Commission v Greece* (n 19 above).

28 Case C-204/90 *Bachmann* [1992] ECR I-249.

29 Case C-250/95 *Futura Participations SA and Singer v Administration des contributions* [1997] ECR I-2471, para 19.

30 Case C-106/91 *Claus Ramrath v Ministre de la Justice* [1992] ECR I-3351.

31 Case C-275/92 *H.M. Customs and Excise v Gerhart and Jörg Schindler* [1994] ECR I-1039; Case C-124/97 *Markku Juhani Läärä, Cotswold Microsystems Ltd, Oy Transatlantic Software Ltd v Kihlakunnansyyttäjä (Jyväskylä), Finnish State* [1999] ECR I-6067; and Case C-67/98 *Questore di Verona v Diego Zenatti* [1999] ECR I-7289.

32 Case C-384/93 *Alpine Investments BV v Minïster van Finacïen* [1995] ECR I-1141.

It has been said that the Court's jurisprudence with respect to the latter has developed a limited set of unvarying reasons while it has been less precise in the area of services. The grounds in question are generally similar, however.

To take one example of these early 1990s cases, *Commission v Netherlands*, at issue was whether Dutch legislation which imposed an obligation on national broadcasting organizations to order all or part of the services necessary for making programmes from a public body, and restricted the re-transmission in the Netherlands of programmes from other Member States which included advertisements specifically aimed at the Dutch public, was incompatible with Community law. The Dutch government relied on the public interest which it claimed lay behind the legislation—safeguarding the freedom of expression of the different social, cultural, religious and philosophical groups in the Netherlands and the protection of pluralism in Dutch broadcasting—to exclude the legislation from the prohibition in Article 49 EC. In order to guarantee the Dutch public absolute protection from commercial interests, Dutch legislation required the advertisements of foreign companies broadcasting in the Netherlands to be subject to the same conditions which applied to Dutch companies. No profit could be derived from advertisements and the company organizing advertisements was to be totally immune to commercial considerations. The Court accepted that a national cultural policy could constitute an imperative requirement of public interest. However, obliging national broadcasting bodies to procure all or part of the services they required (recording studios, technicians, orchestras, design studios) from a national company went beyond what was necessary to protect pluralism and freedom of expression. Pluralism in the audio-visual sector would not have been adversely affected if broadcasting bodies had been allowed to procure these services from other companies established in other Member States.[33] With respect to the restrictions on advertising, it held that it was disproportionate to oblige foreign companies to comply with conditions equivalent to the Dutch advertising model to ensure pluralism. It was enough, in the Court's view, to regulate the advertising of national broadcasters. The Court was also willing to accept that the protection of consumers from excess advertisements or the maintenance of the quality of programmes might justify restrictions on advertisements in certain circumstances. However, like the legislation impugned in *Bond van Adverteerders,* although to a lesser extent, the Mediawet effectively protected the income of the Dutch national advertising body and objectives of an economic nature could not, emphasized the Court, be used to justify restrictions of the free provision of services.

[33] Case C-353/89 (n 6 above) para 31.

Although not central to the main theme of this chapter, it should nevertheless be mentioned that this orthodox position broke down somewhat as the 1990s progressed.[34] Present-day students of Community law are in an unenviable position when it comes to determining how the law on the classification and possible means of justification of national measures which restrict the provision of services actually stands. Traditionally, as we have seen, in order to determine what type of justification (ie Treaty exceptions/derogations or imperative requirements) was admissible, the Court first established whether the impugned national measures should be qualified as formally discriminatory or indistinctly applicable.[35] However, in some recent cases the Court has ignored the need to classify impugned national rules as discriminatory or indistinctly applicable and has instead directly moved to the analysis of possible justifications, be they express Treaty exceptions or unenumerated judicially-created ones, or both.[36] In other cases the Court has classified national measures as discriminatory but has nevertheless analysed whether those measures could be justified by imperative requirements relating to the general interest.[37] In other cases still the Court seems to have abandoned the two-step approach previously used (with the qualification or classification of a measure followed by analysis of a suitable justification) and instead reverses the reasoning: imperative requirements can justify what might seem like formal discriminatory measures because the latter are not in fact discriminatory due to the imperative requirements which they pursue.[38] To make matters worse, the Court is still not adverse to restating its orthodox position clearly and without a semblance of doubt[39] or to including within the notions of public health or public policy, interests and justifications which it might otherwise have regarded as imperative requirements.[40]

[34] See the discussion in Hatzopoulos' annotation of Case C-250/95 *Futura Participations* (1998) CML Rev 493–518.

[35] See further the discussion of this approach and its importance in the Opinion of Advocate General Tesauro in Cases C-120/95 *Decker* and C-158/96 *Kohll* [1998] ECR I-1831 and I-1931.

[36] See, for example, Cases C-120/95 *Decker* and C-158/96 *Kohll* (n 36 above), although only the latter concerns Article 49 EC; or Case C-118/96 *Safir v Skattemyndigheten I Dalarnas Lön* [1998] ECR I-1987.

[37] See Case C-204/90 *Bachmann* (n 28 above), although the case has sometimes been restricted to its facts by commentators who emphasize that national fiscal legislation was at issue. See also Case C-302/97 *Klaus Konle v Republik Österreich* [1999] ECR I-3099.

[38] See Case C-237/94 *O'Flynn* (n 21 above); Case C-350/96 *Clean Car Autoservice* [1998] ECR I-2521; Case C-15/96 *Kalliope Schöning-Kougebetopoulou v Freie und Hansestadt Hamburg* [1998] ECR I-47; and Case C-264/94 *ICI* (n 21 above); and, in the context of Article 28 EC, see Poaires Maduro (n 4 above) 310–311.

[39] See Case C-224/97 *Ciola* (n 4 above) paras 15–17: 'National rules which are not applicable to services without distinction whatever the place of residence of the recipient, and which are therefore discriminatory, are compatible with Community law only if they can be brought within the scope of an express derogation, such as Article 56 [now Article 46] of the EC Treaty.'

[40] See, for example, Case C-158/96 *Kohll* (n 35 above) paras 50 and 51 where it was

IV. DIVERGENT APPROACHES TO NATIONAL DISCRETION WITH REGARD TO GENERAL INTEREST EXCEPTIONS

This section questions whether the ECJ is still prepared to follow an active role with respect to the evaluation of imperative requirements on which Member States seek to rely and regarding the policing of the permissible limits of such exceptions. Some recent cases suggest that the nature of the general interest justification in question may influence the extent of the margin of appreciation permitted Member States and, moreover, the extent to which the ECJ is prepared to subject the proposed justification to the requirements of proportionality. On occasions the Court has seemed loathe to get involved in what it perceives as delicate moral and ethical choices.

1. Justifying Restrictions on Economic Services

In *Säger v Dennemeyer* the defendant company, established in the United Kingdom, provided patent renewal services to titleholders of patent rights established elsewhere in the Community. The services offered by the company consisted in guaranteeing, using a computerized system, that the patents were still in force, that the titleholders were warned about the lapsing of their annuity for renewal of the patent and that those annuities were paid in their name once they had sent back the forms sent to them by the defendants. In order to provide this service, however, Mr Dennemeyer was required by German law to possess specified professional qualifications.

Since the providers of services were required to possess certain professional qualifications, it was argued that the Member State to which the services were destined was impeding firms established abroad from providing services in its territory and impeding patent titleholders established in its territory from freely choosing how to control their patents. The national legislation in question, however, was designed to protect the recipients of services from the damage they would suffer if given legal advice by persons who did not enjoy the necessary moral or professional qualifications. The Court accepted that this was a legitimate interest which could justify restrictions of the free provision of services. However, the Court's inquiry did not end here. Legislation designed to protect such an interest went beyond what was necessary if it subjected the exercise of an activity such as that in question to the possession of a particular qualification and if it was disproportionate to the needs of the recipients of services. To establish whether that was the case, the Court examined the nature of the services actually provided by Mr Dennemeyer. He did not advise clients on technical aspects

admitted that the aim of maintaining a balanced medical and hospital service open to all could fall within the derogations on grounds of public health under Article 46 EC.

of patents, or on the possibility of applying for and renewing patents. The Court regarded his activities as straightforward and held that they did not require any specific professional qualification. There was thus no valid reason for reserving the exercise of this activity to lawyers and patent agents. Furthermore, the risk run by titleholders when the company charged with controlling the patents failed to fulfil its obligations was very limited, since the German patent authorities in the event of non-payment would independently notify them. Finally, the majority of the clients of the provider of services were themselves patent agents or firms. As a result, neither the activities of the provider of services, nor the effect on clients of a failure to fulfil those activities justified reserving the provision of this service to persons holding professional titles.

This decision showed that the Court was determined to apply a strict interpretation of what the general interest required and to limit national discretion in this respect when the restrictions resulting from the national measure affected the provision of economic services which are regarded as uncontroversial and when the general interest refers to market regulatory objectives, such as consumer protection.[41] The Court in *Säger* applied a strict test of proportionality, but it also actually regulated the service itself and could be said to have judicially created a European standard for the service concerned.[42] Since German legislation required professional qualifications it could be argued that Germany wished to ensure a higher standard of protection, which is a legitimate national choice, or in the Court's words, a legitimate general interest. The Court found, however, that the higher standards chosen were incompatible with Community law, given the obstacles to the free provision of services which they created. As a result, the Court substituted Community standards for the national standards which it held to be incompatible with Community law.[43] The Court has often showed its willingness to construe strictly the requirements of the general interest and proportionality, with the result that Member State measures which restrict free movement unjustifiably, or which go beyond what is necessary to achieve the aim sought, have been found to be incompatible with EC law.[44]

[41] For a definition of market regulatory policies as distinct from redistributory policies, see G Majone, 'The European Community Between Social Policy and Social Regulation' (1993) 31 JCMS 153–170.

[42] Case C-76/90 (n 3 above) paras 17–19.

[43] See, however, the Opinion of the Advocate General in Case C-384/93 *Alpine Investments* (n 32 above) para 90, where he argued that Member States retain a discretion to establish their own standards as regards investor protection in the absence of Community harmonization.

[44] See, for example, Joined Cases C-369/96 and C-376/96 *Criminal proceedings against Arblade and Leloup* [1999] ECR I-8453.

2. Ethical and Moral Aspects of the Free Provision of Services

The details of *Society for the Protection of the Unborn Child Ireland (SPUC) v Grogan*[45] are generally well known. Various students' associations in Ireland issued welfare guides to their members which included information as to the identity, location of and method of communication with abortion clinics in the United Kingdom. SPUC sought a declaration in the High Court that any publication of the aforementioned information was contrary to the guarantee of the protection of the unborn child in the Irish Constitution. A number of questions were referred to the ECJ to establish whether the activities of abortion clinics constitute services within the meaning of Article 50 EC and, if so, whether the Treaty provisions on the freedom to supply services precluded a national rule prohibiting the provision of information concerning abortion services legally carried on in another Member State.

The Court insisted in *Grogan* (as it would subsequently do in *Schindler*) that it was not for it 'to substitute its assessment for that of the legislature in those Member States where the activities in question are practised legally'. Medical termination of pregnancy covers a number of services which are normally provided for remuneration and was thus said to fall within the scope of Article 50 EC. However, the Court held that the link between the students' associations and the clinics operating in another Member State was too tenuous for the prohibition on the distribution of information to be regarded as a restriction within the meaning of Article 49 EC.[46] Given the position adopted in *Säger*, the Court might have been expected to examine whether the prohibition on information could be justified with reference to the public policy exception in Article 46 EC or with reference to imperative requirements, depending on whether the Court regarded the prohibition as discriminatory or not. Abortion was a service legally provided in the United Kingdom and a prohibition on information regarding that service was clearly capable of restricting its provision. However, by excluding the provision of information in the instant case from the scope of Article 49 EC the Court avoided the weighing of different values which an analysis of the general interest would probably have entailed.

The Opinion of Advocate General Van Gerven in *Grogan* differed significantly from the decision of the Court. In particular, he argued that the Irish

[45] Case C-159/90 [1991] ECR 1–4685.

[46] The sole economic operators were the medical clinics operating in the United Kingdom. The information distributed by the Irish students' associations was not distributed on their behalf and was independent of the economic activity or service which the clinics performed. In such circumstances the prohibition could not be regarded as a restriction within the scope of Article 49 EC.

prohibition on information, though not discriminatory, could overtly or covertly, actually or potentially, impede intra-Community trade in services and as such it fell within the scope of Articles 49 and 50 EC. He then addressed the imperative requirements of public interest at issue in the instant case. He accepted that the objective behind the prohibition of information in *Grogan*—the protection of the unborn—was justified in Community law. It related to a moral and philosophical policy choice which Member States are entitled to make. The constitutional protection of the life of the unborn enshrined in the Irish Constitution reflected 'the fundamental values to which a nation solemnly declares that it adheres' and which they are entitled to defend and promote in Community law by invoking the ground of public policy referred to in Articles 46 and 55 EC.[47] The Advocate General then examined in detail whether the prohibition on information complied with the principle of proportionality. He came to the conclusion that the national measures were not disproportionate and, in doing so, he placed considerable emphasis on the fact that the aim of the prohibition 'is intended to effectuate a value-judgment' enshrined in the Constitution.

Having successfully avoided the key issue in *Grogan*, namely whether the Irish prohibition of information on abortion services was proportionate to the imperative requirements sought to be protected by that prohibition, a clearer statement of the role of proportionality when moral or ethical issues are at stake was left to a subsequent formation of the Court to determine in the *Schindler* case.

The Schindler brothers operated as independent agents for a public body (the Suddeutsche Klassenlotterie (SKL)) which was responsible for the organization of lotteries. Mailshot sent to the United Kingdom by the Schindlers promoting SKL's lotteries was intercepted and confiscated by British customs officials. British legislation prohibited lotteries in the United Kingdom which did not constitute gaming, subject to a few limited exceptions, and further prohibited the importation of material publicizing lotteries which might contravene such legislation.[48] The Schindlers contested the

[47] The Advocate General seemed happy to refer to the public policy proviso in Article 46 and the judicially created catalogue of imperative requirements either cumulatively or in the alternative. His Opinion was perhaps an early indication that the exceptions to free movement permitted by Article 46 EC might become subsumed into a general comprehensive category of imperative requirements of public interest in much the same way that Article 30 EC has been used after *Cassis de Dijon* as a basis for non-discriminatory measures. See, for example, Joined Cases C-l/90 and C-176/90 *Aragonesa de Publicidad Exterior SA and Publivía SA v Departamento de Sanidad y Seguridad Social de la Generalitat de Catalunya* [1991] ECR 4151, para 13.

[48] Pursuant to s 2 of the Lotteries and Amusements Act 1976, as amended by the National Lottery Act 1993 and s 1 of the Revenue Act 1893. For details of the exceptions to this prohibition see L Gormley, 'Pay Your Money and Take Your Chance?' (1994) 19 EL Rev 644. The exceptions essentially referred to small lotteries organized for no commercial gain.

seizure on the grounds that the British legislation, as a restriction on goods imported into the United Kingdom, was incompatible with Article 28 EC or, in the alternative, Article 49 EC, since the goods in question were for a lottery legally organized in another Member State. A number of questions were referred to the ECJ, *inter alia,* whether the UK legislation could be justified in accordance with Community law.

The Court found that lotteries constitute activities of an economic nature.[49] It then reiterated its decision in *Säger* to the effect that indistinctly applicable national legislation could come within the scope of Article 49 EC when it is liable to prohibit, or otherwise impede, the activities of a provider of services established in another Member State, where he or she lawfully provides services. This was the case for national legislation which prevented lottery organizers from other Member States from promoting and selling lottery tickets in its territory. Although small-scale lotteries could be organized in the United Kingdom, the Court felt that the object of such lotteries and the rules and method of organization were not comparable with the type of lotteries prohibited by the British legislation at issue.

The legislation in *Schindler* was indistinctly applicable and the Member States which had intervened in the case argued that it was justified by imperative requirements of public interest, namely, protection of consumers, prevention of delinquency, protection of public morality, limitation of the demand for gaming and financing of activities in the general interest. They also claimed that the legislation was proportionate to the aim sought to be achieved. The Court accepted that the objectives behind the British legislation, as proposed by the intervening Member States were related to the protection of the recipients of the services, of consumers in general and of social order. These objectives had already been recognized by the Court in previous cases as permissible restrictions of the free provision of services.[50]

The Court then analysed the specific nature of lotteries, as it had previously done with respect to patent renewal services in *Säger.* However, in the instant case it recalled the moral, religious and cultural considerations which surrounded lotteries and gaming at Member State level.[51] Such

[49] The Court pointed out that lotteries were not totally prohibited in Member States where restrictions operated, but that, on the contrary, they were rather commonplace. In these circumstances it was impossible to treat lotteries as activities prohibited in all Member States due to their harmful nature. In addition, reminiscent of its judgment in *Grogan,* the Court held that although the morality of lotteries may be questionable, it was not up to the ECJ to substitute its assessment for that of the Member States in which such activities were legally practised, see Case C-275/92 (n 31 above) para 32.

[50] See Joined Cases 110 and 111/78 *Van Wesemael* (n 18 above) 52; Case 220/83 *Commission v France* (n 13 above) 3709; and Case 15/78 *Société générale alsacienne de banque SA v Walter Koestler* [1978] ECR 1971, 1981.

[51] The fact that the Court dwelled in para 60 of the ruling on the moral, religious and cultural considerations surrounding gambling sits somewhat uneasily with its refusal to do so earlier on at para 32 of the decision.

considerations led Member States to limit and even prohibit gaming and to avoid it becoming a source of personal enrichment. Furthermore, given the amount of money which they generate, lotteries involve high risks of crime and fraud. They also invite people to spend, an incitement which has its own harmful social and individual consequences. Finally, although not an objective reason in itself, they are an important source of funding for charitable and social work and for sport and culture. These factors meant that national authorities should enjoy a sufficiently wide margin of appreciation to determine how to protect lottery participants and, given the socio-cultural characteristics of each Member State, to determine how lotteries are operated, the size of the stakes and the allocation of profits. As long as the restrictions imposed by Member States were not discriminatory,[52] it was up to them to decide whether it was necessary, not only to restrict lottery activities, but also to ban them. If Member States choose to prohibit large-scale lotteries, a prohibition on the importation of material to facilitate its residents participating in lotteries in other Member States does not unjustifiably restrict free movement, since it is a necessary element of the protection which that Member State seeks to secure in its own territory with respect to lotteries. The justifiable social policy and fraud considerations behind the British legislation meant that the ban in the United Kingdom did not unlawfully restrict free movement.

Schindler could have been recorded in the jurisprudential history book of the Court as a hard case whose reasoning could be restricted to the particular circumstances surrounding the case and, in particular, to the fact that when the case had been introduced, the United Kingdom was the only Member State which had an outright ban on large-scale lotteries. However, the Court was asked some years later, in the context of a preliminary ruling in the *Läärä* case, how a national court faced with restrictions on the operation of games of chance was to interpret *Schindler*.

At issue in *Läärä* was a Finnish law that granted a single national public body exclusive rights to exploit the operation of games of chance,[53] in return for remuneration, with a view to the collection of funds for charity or for other non-profit-making purposes provided for by law.[54] A licence

[52] One of the most curious aspects of the *Schindler* case was that by the time the Court delivered its decision, the restriction in question had become discriminatory since the United Kingdom had by then instituted a national lottery on its territory.

[53] The games of chance in question included casino activities, slot machines and other gaming machines or games in which, in exchange for a sum of money, the player may receive a cash prize, goods or other benefits of money's worth, or tokens to be exchanged for money, goods or benefits.

[54] See Articles 1(1) and 3 of the Arpajaislaki (Law no 491 of 1 September 1965 on gaming). The public interest aims in question included, *inter alia*, the promotion of public health, the protection of children, aid for handicapped, old or sick persons, education of young people and the treatment of alcoholism and drug addiction, see the Opinion of Advocate General La Pergola of 4 March 1999 and Article 3, paras 3 and 4 of the Law on gaming.

was issued to the Raha-automaattiyhdistys (Public Law Association for the Management of Slot Machines, hereafter 'RAY') entitling it, in return for remuneration, to operate slot machines, carry on casino activities and also to manufacture and sell slot machines and amusement machines. A regulation on slot machines specified the conditions under which the net proceeds of RAY's activities were to be paid over to the Ministry of Social Affairs and Health and then distributed amongst the organizations and foundations established to meet the charitable and non-profit-making needs specified by the Law on gaming.

Cotswold Microsystems Ltd (hereafter 'CMS'), a company incorporated under English law, entrusted Oy Transatlantic Software Ltd (hereafter 'OTS'), a company incorporated under Finnish law of which Mr Läärä was chairman, with the running in Finland of slot or fruit machines. Criminal proceedings were brought against Mr Läärä on a charge of having operated these machines in Finland without a licence. Mr Läärä denied the charge on the grounds, *inter alia*, that the Finnish legislation was contrary to EC rules governing the free movement of goods and services. According to the ECJ, the questions referred by the national court essentially sought to establish whether, in the light of the judgment in *Schindler*, Articles 28, 49 and 50 EC are to be interpreted as not precluding national legislation such as that in force in Finland, which grants to a single public body exclusive rights to exploit the operation of slot machines, in view of the public interest grounds relied on in order to justify it.[55]

In *Läärä*, the Court first reiterated the substance of paragraphs 60 and 61 of its ruling in *Schindler*: lotteries like other forms of gambling involve a number of moral, religious and cultural considerations; the general tendency in national law is to restrict or even prohibit gambling; lotteries involve a high risk of fraud and crime, particularly when they are operated on a large scale; and lotteries are an incitement which may have damaging individual and social consequences. In addition, although not itself an objective justification, lotteries may make a significant contribution to the financing of benevolent or public interest activities. As a result of these considerations and in order to enable them to determine what is required to protect the players and to maintain order in society, the Court had

[55] Case C-124/97 *Läärä* (n 31 above) para 10. The national court specifically asked: (1) whether the judgment of the Court in the *Schindler* case was applicable to circumstances such as those in *Läärä*; (2) whether Articles 28, 49 and 50 EC applied to gaming machines of the type at issue in *Läärä*; (3) (a) whether those provisions of the Treaty preclude Finland from restricting the right to manage slot machines to a monopoly operated by a public-law body, irrespective of whether the restriction applies under the applicable national legislation to domestic and foreign organizers of gaming alike; and (b) whether such a restriction could be justified, having regard to the reasons set out in the Finnish law on gaming, or on any other grounds, by the principles contained in Articles 30 and 46 EC or any other Article of the Treaty.

concluded in *Schindler* that national authorities must have a significant degree of latitude as regards the manner in which lotteries are operated, the size of the stakes and the allocation of the profits they yield. It is for Member States to assess 'not only whether it is necessary to restrict the activities of lotteries but also whether they should be prohibited, provided that those restrictions are not discriminatory'.[56] In *Läärä* the Court stated that these considerations, although relating in *Schindler* to the organization of lotteries, are equally applicable to other comparable forms of gambling such as the use, in return for a money payment, of slot machines.[57]

The impugned Finnish legislation, according to the Court, prohibited any person other than the licensed public body from running the operation of the slot machines and, as such, it involved no discrimination on grounds of nationality and applied without distinction to operators who might be interested in that activity, whether they were established in Finland or in another Member State.[58] The Court recognized, however, that the legislation constituted an impediment to freedom to provide services in that it directly or indirectly prevented operators in other Member States from themselves making slot machines available to the public and it thus sought to establish whether this obstacle to free movement could be permitted pursuant to express Treaty derogations or whether it may be justified by overriding reasons relating to the public interest.[59] The aim of the Finnish legislation was to limit the exploitation of the human passion for gambling, to avoid the risk of crime and fraud to which the activities concerned give rise and to authorize those activities only with a view to the collection of funds for charity or for other benevolent purposes. As in *Schindler*, the Court stated that these considerations, which must be taken together, amounted to concern for the protection of consumers as well as the main-

[56] Case C-275/92 *Schindler* (n 31 above) para 61; Case C-124/97 *Läärä* (n 31 above) para 14.

[57] Case C-124/97 (n 31 above) paras 15 and 18. Admittedly, the Court recognized a number of distinctions between the different forms of gambling at issue in the two cases. Although the lotteries at issue in *Schindler* could not be classified as goods within the meaning of Article 28 EC, the slot machines in *Läärä* constitute goods in themselves. In the absence of adequate detailed information on the effect which the impugned legislation had on the importation of slot machines, the Court was unwilling, however, to rule on the applicability of Article 28 EC. In addition, although the British legislation at issue in *Schindler* prohibited the holding of lotteries on the national territory, the Finnish legislation did not prohibit the use of slot machines but simply reserved their running to a public body issued with a licence. Finally, the Court felt that other provisions of the Treaty, specifically those on establishment and competition, might be applicable to the Finnish legislation.

[58] Case C-124/97 (n 31 above) para 28.

[59] In this respect the Court seemed to reiterate, at para 31, its standard approach on the scope of Articles 45, 46 and 55 EC and the Court's case law on overriding reasons relating to the public interest, citing Case C-288/89 *Gouda* (n 4 above) in this respect. However, it is interesting to note that it did not specify, as it usually had, that discriminatory restrictions could only be justified with reference to the express derogations contained in the Treaty. Perhaps it felt that in the circumstances of the case this distinction was irrelevant.

tenance of order in society, both of which may be regarded as overriding reasons relating to the public interest.

However, the Court stated that 'it is still necessary . . . that measures based on such grounds guarantee the achievement of the intended aims and do not go beyond that which is necessary in order to achieve them'. The Finnish legislation, unlike the legislation at issue in *Schindler* did not prohibit the use of slot machines but simply reserved the running of them to a licensed public body. However, despite having specifically recalled the need to respect the principle of proportionality and although there was no outright ban in Finland on the operation of the games of chance at issue in *Läärä*, the Court simply did what it had already done in *Schindler*: it held that it is for the national authorities to assess whether it is necessary, in the context of the aim pursued, totally or partially to prohibit gambling or merely to restrict it and, to that end, to establish control mechanisms, which may be more or less strict.

In other words, given the aim pursued (the maintenance of social order and the protection of consumers) and the activity in question (gambling) the Court was willing to renege on the inquiries it usually carries out (or more precisely, in the context of Article 234 EC, directs national courts to carry out)[60] concerning the proportionality of the impugned restrictive measures. National authorities should be allowed to determine in such cases the need for the measures in question and the extent to which they should go to safeguard the imperative requirements at issue. It does not matter, from the point of view of proportionality, if one Member State adopts one system of protection and another adopts a different one.[61] The impugned national provisions need only be assessed with reference to the objectives pursued by the national authorities and the level of protection which they are intended to provide. The Court then added, lest an observer be tempted to dwell on the factual differences between *Schindler* and *Läärä*:

[60] See in this respect FG Jacobs, 'Recent Developments in the Principle of Proportionality in EC Law' in Ellis (n 14 above) 1–21, at 8, who questions how far the Court itself should decide whether a measure is proportionate and how far it should merely give guidance on the appropriate criteria, their application in the concrete case being left to the national court. He notes that this issue raises some central questions about the function of the Court and its relations with national courts. The ECJ has either decided the issue of proportionality itself (Case C-67/97 *Criminal proceedings against Dieter Bluhme* [1998] ECR I-8033 (Article 28 EC), Case 16/78 *Criminal proceedings against Mîchel Choquet* [1978] ECR 2293) or left the issue to the national courts subject to some (Case C-67/98 *Zenatti* (n 31 above)) or no guidance (Sunday trading cases) or by-passed the principle altogether (Case C-275/92 *Schindler* (n 31 above) and Case C-124/97 *Läärä* (n 31 above)).

[61] Although in Case 279/80 *Webb* (n 2 above) and elsewhere such comparative inquiries seemed to form part of the analysis of whether the restrictive measure was (a) justified and (b) proportionate. On the issue of comparison see further G Kelly, 'Public Policy and General Interest Exceptions in the jurisprudence of the European Court of Justice' (1996) 4 *European Review of Private Law* 17–40, at 31.

the fact that the games in issue are not totally prohibited is not enough to show that the national legislation is not in reality intended to achieve the public interest objectives at which it is purportedly aimed, which must be considered as a whole. Limited authorisation of such games *on an exclusive basis*, which has the advantage of confining the desire to gamble and the exploitation of gambling within controlled channels, of preventing the risk of fraud or crime in the context of such exploitation, and of using the resulting profits for public interest purposes, likewise falls within the ambit of those objectives.[62]

Curiously the Court then states:

The question whether, in order to achieve those objectives, it would be preferable, rather than granting an exclusive operating right to the licensed public body, to adopt regulations imposing the necessary code of conduct on the operators concerned is a matter to be assessed by the Member States, subject however to the proviso that the choice made in that regard must not be disproportionate to the aim pursued.[63]

So, in other words, the proportionality of the measures chosen to achieve the legitimate objective pursued is a matter for the Member States, who must themselves ensure that their choices are not disproportionate.

Without reference to its long-standing position on justifications of an economic nature being impermissible,[64] the Court noted that the RAY is required to pay over to the Finnish State the amount of the net distributable proceeds received from the operation of the slot machines. This 'public interest' money could be collected by other means, such as taxation of the activities of operators of the offending machines who could be authorized to run them within the framework of a non-exclusive agreement. However, given the risk of crime and fraud associated with gambling, the obligation imposed on a licensed public body to pay over the proceeds of its operations is a more effective means of ensuring that strict limits are set to the lucrative nature of such activities. As a result, the Court concluded, in conferring exclusive rights on a single public body, the provisions of the Finnish legislation on the operation of slot machines do not appear to be disproportionate, in so far as they affect freedom to provide services, to the objectives they pursue.[65]

One could argue that the outcome in *Läärä* was dictated by the unfortunate position which the Court had already taken in *Schindler*. Yet, the Court has not been shy in other cases to distance itself from reasoning which it no longer found convincing, which perhaps it feared went too far,

[62] C-124/97 *Läärä* (n 31 above), para 37 (authors' own emphasis).
[63] ibid para 39.
[64] See Case C-353/89 *Bond van Adverteerders* (n 4 above) para 30.
[65] ibid paras 41 and 42.

or which it considered plain wrong.[66] Furthermore, grounds existed which could have allowed the Court plausibly to distinguish the two cases. There was no outright ban in Finland of slot machines. Yet, the Court had seemed to pin at least part of its reasoning in *Schindler* to the existence of such a complete ban in the United Kingdom. Thus, at paragraph 66, it stated:

[W]hen a Member State *prohibits in its territory the operation of large-scale lotteries* and in particular the advertising and distribution of tickets for that type of lottery, the prohibition on the importation of materials intended to enable nationals of that Member State to participate in such lotteries organized in another Member State cannot be regarded as a measure involving an unjustified interference with the freedom to provide services.[67]

Finally, even if one is to accept a wider margin of latitude for Member States when they seek to protect legitimate interests of particular concern to them, it is difficult to understand why the Court in *Schindler* and *Läärä* was willing to accept that judicial review of such Member State discretion, either at Community or national level, be almost non-existent.

Explaining the decision of the Court in *Läärä* becomes even more interesting, however, when one reflects on the Opinion of the Advocate General and the arguments he used to come to the opposite conclusion to the Court. Advocate General La Pergola felt that the jurisprudence of the Court required him to treat the legislation at issue in *Läärä* as indistinctly applicable.[68] He continued that, in accordance with the case law of the Court,[69] indistinctly applicable measures such as that at issue in *Läärä* could be justified, in the absence of harmonization at Community level, by imperative reasons relating to the general interest, on condition that the aim which they seek has not already been achieved by rules to which the provider of services is subject in his Member State of establishment and that the restriction which results for the freedom guaranteed by Article 49 EC is both necessary and proportionate. Advocate General La Pergola seemed unwilling to accept Finland's attempts to justify its legislation. In the first place, the fact that the system lessened the burden on the State budget since revenue from the machines was used to finance activities for which the State

66 In the past few years such U-turns have been more common than one might think. See, for example, Case C-13/94 *P v S and Cornwall County Council* [1996] ECR I-2143 and C249/96 *Lisa Grant v South West Trains Ltd.* [1998] ECR I-621; Case C-450/93 *Eckhard Kalanke v Freie Hansestadt Bremen* [1995] ECR I-3051 and Case C-409/95 *Helmut Marschall v Land Nordrhein-Westfalen* [1997] ECR I-6363; Case C-400/95 *Larsson v Dansk Handel and Service*[1977] ECR I-2757 and Case C-394/96 *Mary Brown v Rentokil Ltd.* [1998] ECR I-4185.

67 Authors' emphasis.

68 C-124/97 *Läärä* (n 31 above) para 28, especially n. 52 and the discussion of monopolies and the freedom of establishment.

69 ibid para 31 where he outlines the aforementioned orthodox approach to exceptions and restrictions.

is responsible could in no way be regarded as an imperative requirement capable of limiting the scope of the principle enshrined in Article 49 EC.[70] Secondly, even though he accepted that the Court's reasoning in *Schindler* regarding Member States' needs to protect players and their social order generally could be applied to the instant case, he felt that there were differences between the two cases, between the games of chance involved and between the revenue generated by both for players.[71]

In the Advocate General's view, Member States should not be allowed to rely on imperative requirements in an abstract manner: the restrictions adopted should correspond to the imperative requirements said to have inspired them, they should be amenable to judicial review and the judge required to apply such rules should ensure that they are justified and correspond to the principle of proportionality as defined by the ECJ's case law. Examining whether the Finnish law is necessary to achieve the aims ascribed to it, the Advocate General pointed out that the RAY itself decided how many machines there would be in Finland (there were about 16,000 at the time), that to promote these machines it had engaged in a massive and aggressive advertising campaign and that the controls imposed by the RAY on the commercial establishments which housed the machines and which were intended to ensure that minors did not use the slot machines were largely unenforced. It was clearly in the interests of those commercial establishments to install as many machines as possible and to seek to raise the volume of play as much as possible. Not only might they then attract more clients to their principal business but they would also receive greater revenue from the machines themselves, since their share was calculated as a percentage of the overall take. In the Advocate General's view, this arrangement was clearly at odds with the objective presented by the Finnish authorities as one of the principal sources of inspiration for the legislation, namely to avoid exploitation of people's passion for gambling being used as a source of private economic gain.[72] It seemed to the Advocate General that, far from exercising strict control of 'gambling fever', the RAY was in fact stimulating gambling in order to increase the financial resources which it could then pass on to the charitable and non-profit recipients mentioned in the Law on gaming.

One could of course argue that the RAY was simply stimulating the demand for games of chance in order to raise more money for worthy causes. But in this respect the Advocate General correctly pointed out the clear stance which the Court had adopted in *Schindler*: the possibility for Member States to ensure that the revenue from gaming be spent on objectives of general

[70] ibid para 33.

[71] ibid para 33.

[72] ibid para 35. For a discussion of the economic value of the betting and gaming industry in the EU see Hatzopoulos' annotation of *Schindler* (n 4 above) 841, and the Commission Report cited therein.

interest does not constitute an imperative requirement capable of justifying eventual restrictions of the free provision of services. Given the organization and operation of the Finnish monopoly, the prohibition on the installation and exploitation of gaming machines in Finland could not be regarded as a suitable means to limit efficiently the demand for gambling.

The Advocate General did concede that the monopoly was a suitable means to achieve the other objective claimed by the Finnish legislation, namely, protecting players and society in general from the risk that the activity in question be carried on with fraudulent or criminal purposes in mind. However, even in this context it was necessary to apply a *Webb*-type 'home rule' reasoning—was this objective already adequately safeguarded in the provider's Member State of establishment? It was for the national court to compare the level of protection of players and the social order which Finland wished to protect on its national territory with the controls in place in the Member State where the service originated. He noted that in the United Kingdom where CMS was established, the sale, delivery and maintenance of slot machines was already the object of controls intended to guarantee that the machines could not be fixed or used for criminal purposes.

As regards the question of the proportionality of the Finnish law and the applicability of the *Schindler* hands-off approach to that question, the Advocate General pointed out that a total ban on lotteries, such as that at issue in the *Schindler* case, does not raise the suspicion of a protectionist motive but rather reflects the authorities' opinion that such a game of chance, given its particular nature, is undesirable. A selective ban of gaming machines, such as that in Finland, which grants an exclusive right to operate them to a national operator, is a different matter. By allowing exceptions the Member State itself demonstrates that the gravity and urgency of the imperative requirements on which they rely are relative and are to be treated flexibly and such an approach has repercussions when it comes to examining whether alternative means, less restrictive of free movement, are available to achieve the objective in question. According to Advocate General La Pergola, national restrictive measures should be examined first to establish whether they apply indistinctly. The effects of such a measure should then be examined to see whether it is adequate, necessary and proportionate to the imperative requirements which it seeks to satisfy. Such a double control is important, in the view of the Advocate General, because the scope of the possible justifications of national restrictions should not be unnecessarily extended. This would be precisely the result if a Member State could regulate or rather ban access to a particular economic activity simply by basing itself on the particular nature of the activity in question.[73]

[73] C-124/97 *Läärä* (n 31 above) Opinion of Advocate General La Pergola, para 38.

In the instant case, where the provision of a particular service was reserved to a national operator, the reasoning of the Court in *Schindler* could not be used to shield the Finnish legislation from any criticism. Once it is clear that gambling is an unavoidable fact of life, it is open to Member States to introduce rules to limit and control the offers on the market. However, the controls and verifications necessary to ensure that the imperative requirements in question are protected could be introduced in a less restrictive regulatory context than that in operation in Finland. A system of non-exclusive author-ization could be introduced, for example, to which private operators could be admitted. Advocate General La Pergola pointed out that a similar type of system is in operation in other Member States, specifically the Netherlands, Germany and Portugal. Even though the burden on the administrative authorities would be greater, since they would have to deal with a large number of operators, it would not be an unreasonable burden and such a system would certainly be more proportionate to the interests which the Finnish Government seeks to protect than the monopoly actually in force. In the view of the Advocate General, it was clear that a non-exclusive authorization system would have a far less restrictive effect on free movement.[74] He therefore concluded that Article 49 EC should be interpreted in the sense that a ban on the operation and installation of gaming machines such as that provided by the Finnish law on gaming did not satisfy the principle of proportionality.

Perhaps the Court itself realized the error of its ways when, one month after *Läärä*, in a case involving the provision of betting services, it reintroduced proportionality into the equation. The legislation challenged in *Zenatti* prohibited bookmaking, subject to exceptions,[75] and reserved to certain bodies the right to organize those which were authorized. Mr Zenatti, who ran an information exchange for the Italian customers of a licensed bookmaker established in the United Kingdom in relation to bets on foreign sports events, was prohibited from acting as an intermediary in Italy for the British bookmaker. Italian public order laws forbade the taking of bets on sporting events except for bets placed on the outcome of sporting events taking place under the supervision of the national Olympic Committee or on the results of horse races organized through the National Union for the Betterment of Horse Breeds. The right was reserved to these bodies to organize the taking of bets on events arranged by them and the funds so collected had to serve to promote their sporting events, infrastructure and livestock.

The Court held, as it had done in *Läärä*, that the *Schindler* judgment is

[74] For further details of how he envisaged such a system operating see para 40 of his Opinion.

[75] See Article 88 of Royal Decree no 773 of 18 June 1931.

applicable, not only to lotteries, but also to other comparable forms of gambling. The betting at issue in *Zenatti* was to be regarded as gambling of a comparable kind. However, the Court then underlined, as it had done in *Läärä*, that the Italian legislation, unlike that in *Schindler*, did not totally prohibit the taking of bets but reserves to certain bodies the right to organize betting in certain circumstances. The Court accepted that the aim of the impugned Italian legislation was to prevent gaming from being a source of private profit, to avoid risks of crime and fraud and the damaging individual and social consequences of the incitement to spend which it represents and to allow gaming only to the extent to which it may be socially useful. These objectives, which essentially concerned the protection of consumers and the maintenance of social order, ranked among those which may be regarded as constituting overriding reasons relating to the public interest.[76] The Court then repeated the relevant paragraphs of its *Schindler* and *Läärä* judgments as regards the margin of appreciation open to Member States to determine how to achieve these legitimate aims and the suitability, in particular, of a limited authorization system of gambling on the basis of special or exclusive rights granted to assigned bodies.[77] However, the Court then stated that a system such as that established by the Italian public order legislation 'is acceptable [from the point of view of the free provisions of services] only if, from the outset, it reflects a concern to bring about a genuine diminution in gambling opportunities and if the financing of social activities through a levy the proceeds of authorised games constitutes an incidental beneficial consequence and not the real justification for the restrictive policy adopted'.[78] The Court therefore handed the duty of supervising the proportionality of the Italian measures squarely back to the national court, albeit with little guidance on how to proceed and with the shadow of *Schindler*-style *laissez-faire* still looming in the background: 'It is for the national court to verify whether the restrictions which it imposes do not appear disproportionate in the light of those objectives.'[79] Essentially, while citing *Schindler* and *Läärä*, the Court resurrected the principle of proportionality and indicated to the national court the kind of inquiry which it should undertake in applying that principle.

What the gambling cases demonstrate is that the Court ignores the principle of proportionality at its peril. By setting aside the need to respect the various elements of this principle, the Court undermines the role which it and national courts must play in policing respect for EC fundamental freedoms and risks undermining those very freedoms itself. One of the essential objectives of the freedoms established in the EC Treaty is to avoid protectionist

[76] Case C-17/98 (n 31 above) para 31. [77] ibid paras 32–35.

[78] ibid para 36. In other words, the Court remembered its long-standing case law on economic aims not being of a nature to constitute legitimate objective justifications.

[79] ibid para 37.

national trading rules and a compartmentalization of the market between Member States. The grant to a national body of an exclusive right to operate slot machines is clearly suspect from this perspective,[80] but to leave to the Member States themselves the task of verifying the proportionality of their own protectionist and restrictive measures is simply not good enough. Where, one must ask, is the spirit and body of *Les Verts*[81] whereby 'the Community is a Community based on the rule of law, inasmuch as neither its Member States nor its institutions can avoid a review of the question whether the measures adopted by them are in conformity with the basic constitutional charter, the Treaty'? As one commentator has pointed out, in Article 49 EC cases, regulations of the host Member State often lead to a potential double regulation (besides the State of origin), with a heavy burden resulting in the interstate provision of services. This effect justifies a particularly intense control of the relevant public good and the instruments to serve it.[82] The Advocate General seemed conscious of this in *Läärä*; if the Court was, it made every effort not to show it.

As far as the internal market is concerned, the upshot of the Court's recent case law is not positive. On the one hand, there seems to be a widening of the range of possible justifications of distinctly applicable restrictions on the exercise of market freedoms and the effect of such a widening is that 'a potentially greater number of lawful obstacles may be raised to market integration'.[83] On the other hand, where a service is of a sensitive nature and regulation of it involves moral, ethical or social policy considerations, the obligation of determining the proportionality of national restrictive measures has either been left to national courts with little or no guidance, or left to the Member States themselves.

V. THE DIVERGENT APPROACH OF THE ECJ AND ITS CONSEQUENCES

What are the consequences of the jurisprudence of the Court which has just been examined? Are *Grogan*, *Schindler* and *Läärä* in conformity with the methods used by the Court in previous cases such as *Säger,* namely, recognition of an extensive category of national public interest justifications and rigorous use of the principle of proportionality to assess whether the means suit the ends, or do these cases indicate a different approach? If so, what are the reasons for the Court's departure?

[80] Although of late the Court has shown itself to be not unsympathetic to national monopolies. See, for example, Case C-189/95 *Criminal Proceedings against Harry Franzén* [1997] ECR I-5909, where the Swedish alcohol monopoly passed muster almost in its entirety.

[81] Case 294/83 *Partie écologiste Les Verts v European Parliament* [1986] ECR I-1339, para 23.

[82] See W-H Roth, annotation of Case C-19/92 *Dieter Kraus v Land Baden Württemberg* (1993) 30 CML Rev 1251–1258, at 1257.

[83] See Whelan and Schouten (n 4 above) 102.

Grogan, Schindler and *Läärä* involved social and moral issues that were considered highly sensitive by the Member States whose restrictions of free movement were being challenged. In the *Grogan* case the Court avoided the difficult issue of access to abortion information by simply holding that the facts of the case did not bring the prohibition on information about abortion within the scope of Article 49 EC. There was consequently no need to subject the public interest objective—protection of the unborn—to the competing Community interest in guaranteeing free movement, or to subject the prohibition to the requirements of proportionality.[84] The Opinion of the Advocate General in *Grogan,* on the other hand, was reminiscent of the Court's previous case law and its subsequent decision in *Säger.*

In contrast to the *Grogan* decision, the Court in *Schindler* and *Läärä* did analyse the outright ban in the United Kingdom and the selective ban in Finland with reference to public interest justifications. Moreover, it analysed the interests in question in considerable detail. This contrasts with its rather terse discussion of the political and economic choices and sociocultural characteristics at issue, for example, in the Sunday trading cases[85] and with the avoidance of such discussion in *Grogan,* but ties in with the Court's active assessment in cases like Säger or *Alpine Investments.* However, in *Schindler* and *Läärä* the Court did not assess the public interest at stake in the light of the Community's established principle of proportionality. Having held that the interest in question was justifiable, the Court, first in *Schindler*, then in *Läärä*, went on to hold that the particular nature of games of chance justified national authorities enjoying a wide margin of appreciation to determine what was necessary to protect persons involved in gaming and to protect the social order generally. National authorities had to be allowed to decide whether or not it was necessary not only to restrict gaming activities, but also to ban them.

However, just as expulsion is the very negation of the free movement of persons,[86] banning a particular activity, as the United Kingdom did in

[84] A similar approach was adopted in the area of goods in Case 238/82 *Duphar BV v Netherlands* [1984] ECR 523, where the Court held that Dutch rules on the funding of the national sickness insurance system did not come within the scope of Article 28 EC, despite their undeniably serious restrictive effect on imports. It was thus not necessary to apply the proportionality test to the public health justification alleged by the Dutch Government. The Court was clearly not prepared to interfere with the organization by a Member State of its social security systems, so that even though the Dutch system restricted imports and its objectives were primarily economic, the fact that the measures were said to lie outside the scope of Community law on the free movement of goods cancelled any need for justification and consequently proportionality.

[85] See, for example, Case C-145/88 *Torfaen Borough Council v B and Q plc* [1989] ECR 3851; and Case C-169/91 *Council of the City of Stoke on Trent and Norwich City Council v B and Q plc* [1992] ECR I-6635.

[86] See Case 118/75 *Lynne Watson and Alessandro Belmann* [1976] ECR 1185, para 21.

Schindler, is the very negation of free provision of services. No mention was made of the need to assess the proportionality of such a ban, or the home control imposed in Germany. The only condition imposed was that the restrictions must not be discriminatory. Even more surprising was the Court's willingness in *Läärä* to accept, without reference to the principle of proportionality, the conferral by Member State legislation on a public body of the exclusive right to operate slot machines; machines which, as the Advocate General's Opinion revealed, are in abundance in Finland. In *Säger,* however, where an uncontroversial service was at stake, little, if any, discretion was left to national authorities and the Court went as far as redefining the measures necessary to protect the general interest in question.

Schindler and *Läärä* may represent the Court's approach in future cases where indistinctly applicable barriers to trade entail sensitive moral and ethical issues. This approach contrasts with cases such as *Säger, Commission v Netherlands* or *Webb*, where the restrictions imposed by national measures were justifiable on the grounds of the general interest, but which were subject to fairly strict scrutiny on grounds of proportionality. Most restrictions have fallen by the wayside, not because they were unjustifiable, but because they were disproportionate. It was unlikely in *Schindler,* given the unanimous support of all the intervening Member States, that the Court would reject the public interest considerations alleged by the United Kingdom. However, acceptance of an outright ban on lotteries without reference to the principle of proportionality is a significant departure from previous balancing of home and host state control, of whether the restriction was necessary to achieve the objective in question and whether less restrictive means existed to achieve that objective.

Gormley suggests, rightly in our view, that previous applications of proportionality had been 'in relation to the equivalence of tangible socio-economic concepts . . . The rather wider public interest justifications advanced by the Court [in *Schindler]* are not of such a nature as to permit an adequate assessment of equivalence.'[87] De Búrca also suggests that the ECJ does not always examine justifiability with the same degree of rigour in all cases.[88] She lists a number of factors which can usefully be kept in mind when examining the extent to which the ECJ subjects a national measure to review, *inter alia,* whether the measure relates to a nationally sensitive or ideologically contentious matter; whether it involves a complex

[87] See Gormley (n 48 above) 651–652.

[88] See G De Búrca, 'The Principle of Proportionality and its Application in EC Law' (1993) 13 YEL 105–150, 111: 'the Court of Justice is influenced not only by what it considers to be the nature and importance of the interest or right claimed by the applicant, and the nature and importance of the objective alleged to be served by the measure, but by the relative expertise, position and overall competence of the Court against the decision-making authority in assessing these factors.'

political objective; whether there is no European-wide or internationally agreed standard; or whether, if a measure were found disproportionate, it would impose a considerable financial burden on the Member State. The decisions of the Court in *Grogan, Campus Oil,*[89] *Schindler, Läärä* and *Duphar* closely correspond to these four reasons for not subjecting national measures to strict scrutiny.

If *Schindler* and *Läärä* suggest a disregard of equivalence in cases involving sensitive social and moral issues, they also resolve the difficulties which the Court might face were it confronted with a *Grogan*-like case in future. There would now be no need, given the wide margin of appreciation open to Member States with respect to such social and moral general interest issues and the means to protect them, to subject a national restriction on access to information about a service such as abortion to proportionality considerations. If one examines the Opinion of the Advocate General in *Grogan,* the really difficult issue he faced was precisely that of the proportionality of the prohibition. Once again, a parallel can be drawn with the *Duphar* case. The Advocate General there admitted that an examination of the proportionality of the Dutch legislation would be very difficult given the delicate balance of the Dutch scheme and the fact that it pursued numerous objectives.[90] As a result, he defined the public health justification very widely and left the question of proportionality to the national court.[91]

However, even if proportionality were redundant, the reasoning of the Court in *ERT*[92] and *Familiapress* would still apply. The Court there held that when a Member State invokes the derogations provided in the Treaty (be it pursuant to Articles 30, 39(3) and (4), 45, 46 and 55 EC) to justify a measure restricting free movement the measure in question must be interpreted in the light of, and be in conformity with, the Community's general principles, especially fundamental rights. Presumably, the margin of appreciation approved first in *Schindler* and subsequently in *Läärä* would not allow Member States to disregard the Community's fundamental rights principles, although the terms of the Court's judgment do not automatically point to such a conclusion. If a *Grogan*-type case were revisited following the *Schindler* and *Läärä* decisions, the Court could address the substance of the case this time and examine the regulation of information about

[89] Case 72/83 *Campus Oil v Ministry for Industry and Energy* [1984] ECR 2727, where Irish legislation requiring oil importers to purchase a certain amount of their needs from a refinery was successfully justified on grounds of national security.

[90] Case 238/82 (n 84 above) 549–552.

[91] Nevertheless, even though the requirements of proportionality may only have been loosely defined or the appreciation of compliance with this principle left to the national court in *Duphar* or the Sunday trading cases, the fact remains that the Member States' restriction of free movement was subject to some sort of judicial review.

[92] Case C-260/89 *Elliniki Radiophonia Tiléorassi AE v Dimotiki Etariapliroforissis* [1991] ECR I-2925.

abortion in other Member States. However, it would still be able to avoid the sensitive social and moral issue involved, since it is no longer obliged to examine such a prohibition with reference to proportionality. In *Grogan*, however, the Advocate General seemed to argue that if fundamental rights are at stake, an assessment of the proportionality of national measures will and should emerge anyway.

The wide margin of appreciation permitted Member States in *Schindler* and *Läärä* may be commendable from a broad perspective of subsidiarity, but it is problematic in other respects. A distinction between social and ethical public interests *(Schindler, Grogan)* and socio-economic and cultural interests *(Webb, Säger)* is not one explicitly drawn by the Court. However, its previous case law on consumer, employment or social policy issues seems to support the argument that a division is in fact developing, since these cases demonstrated the Court's readiness to subject restrictive national measures in these fields to considerable scrutiny on grounds of proportionality. However, what guidelines is the Court going to follow to determine when a public interest touches sufficiently sensitive moral and ethical issues for proportionality not to apply? The Court in *Webb* regarded the activities of employment agencies as sensitive because of their potential effect on labour relations and workers. Are these issues not reflections of the ethical choices of Member States in the area of employment which are equally worthy of the highest possible respect at Community level? The *Alpine Investments* case also illustrates that it is not always easy to distinguish between economic and ethical issues. The Court and Advocate General in that case pointed to the highly speculative nature of the financial services at issue. The Advocate General, in particular, argued that investments in the securities and commodities markets involve a high element of risk, are susceptible to abuse, are highly speculative and that the value of the investment depends on a series of extraneous factors which the ordinary investor may neither determine nor influence. In contrast, in *Schindler,* the Court discussed the nature of lottery services and betting. Participation in a lottery does not always guarantee financial gain and, as a result, it is a highly speculative practice. Nevertheless, like investors in financial markets, lottery competitors have a chance and some hope of winning. Given the similarities between these two highly speculative activities, what is the difference from the point of view of Community law between betting or participating in a lottery or, say, currency speculation in the Community's financial markets? Neither brings definite financial rewards, both presents the possibility of abuse and fraud and both can result in negative individual and social consequences. Is it so easy, after all, to differentiate between services which entail sensitive ethical issues and those which entail purely economic considerations?

The approach adopted by the Court in *Grogan* and *Schindler* could also be recognition of the fact that the Community must respect the limits to its competence in certain fields. Thus, although the Community is competent to prohibit restrictions of services such as abortion, it has no competence to regulate abortion itself or to require Member States to legalize it. Nationally sensitive or ideologically contentious issues which lie on the borders of Community competence are likely to be subject to less strict scrutiny on grounds of proportionality. However, the Court may still actively assess the nature of the public interest justification itself, which seems contradictory.

Another issue which arises in the light of *Schindler* is to whom the Court is willing to permit such a wide margin of appreciation. What, for example, if national legislation regulating a particular service was the same or similar in all Member States, bar one. Would the Court permit the remaining Member State to impose an outright ban on the performance of that service, or ancillary activities such as the provision of information, without even subjecting the ban to the requirements of proportionality? *Schindler* suggests that that is the case. Furthermore, would a decentralized Member State be answerable for restrictions to the free provision of services imposed by one of its regions which wished to protect social and moral values peculiar to it?[93] It will be interesting to see whether the Court will be willing to reject the social and ethical values peculiar to one Member State, or region, if an examination of legislation at national level reveals a similarity amongst the remaining regions in a state, or the remaining Member States.

VI. CONCLUSIONS

When it comes to the adoption of national legislation, moral, political or ethical choices are clearly within the scope of Member State competence. Nevertheless, as the Court has often reminded Member States, many policy areas may remain within their competence but Community law imposes limits to that competence. For example, measures within Member State fields of competence must not interfere with or restrict the fundamental freedoms guaranteed by Community law.[94] In some recent cases, when it would usually have examined, with reference to the principle of proportionality, the compatibility with EC law of national legislation restricting

[93] Differences in the social and ethical choices influencing Land legislation are not unknown in Germany, where, for example, one region permitted the sale of soft drugs in pharmacies, to the consternation of the Federal government and where policy regarding the famously restrictive shop opening hours can vary from one Land to the next.

[94] See Case 9/74 *Donato Casagrande v Landeshauptstadt München* [1974] ECR 773, para 12 (education policy); Case C-274/96 *Criminal proceedings against Horst Otto Bickel and Ulrich Franz* [1998] ECR I-7637, para 17 (criminal law); Case C-250/95 *Futura Participations* (n 29 above) (taxation); or Case C-302/97 *Konle* (n 37 above) (property ownership).

free movement, the Court has seemed reluctant to be seen to substitute its own judgment for that of the Member States. In contrast, where economically related issues are at stake, it has been willing to treat them as a Community law matter, even to the extent, in *Säger,* of analysing the conditions in which a service may be provided efficiently at Community level.

There are a number of problems with this approach. The distinction between economic and social, ethical and moral issues is a fine one, since it is arguable that economic choices also reflect definite ethical and political choices. The situation in the *Webb* case is surely a fine example of a service where economic, social and ethical issues converge. The same may be said about the Dutch broadcasting cases, where the political and social principles underlying the legislation had undeniable and inseparable economic consequences. It will be a difficult task indeed to define on which side of the line a specific national restriction may fall and the completion of this task will also, inevitably, lead the Court to take an ethical stance of its own. As Mishan has pointed out, the efficient allocation of resources cannot itself be justified on purely economic grounds: an ethical consensus concerning allocative issues within which notions of efficiency can be introduced must exist.[95]

The position of the Court is understandable in terms of the absence of common ethical or moral standards in the Community. Assuming that such a consensus existed in certain areas, there seems to be no effective means at Community level, at present, to translate these choices democratically into Community policies. In the absence of such consensus, or the means to express whatever consensus does exist, Member States must be accorded a large margin of discretion to give effect to their communities' ethical or political aspirations and choices without the interference of Community law. However, these limitations on Community law and the role of the ECJ reflect the pre-eminence of economic aspects of integration over aspirations for political integration. At the present stage of development of the Community or Union, this could hardly be otherwise. Only through the construction or gradual development of a European polity that shares similar values and enjoys the means to translate those common values into law may increased interference by the Court in these spheres be legitimized. Until that happens, however, the Community will either lack European democratic, moral and ethical standards, or will have to derive them from another source. It is suggested that the European Convention for Human Rights, as interpreted by the ECJ, might provide such an appropriate standard. However, this would mean that if the European Court of Human Rights handed down a decision which also affected ethical and moral

[95] See Mishan, *Economic Efficiency and Social Welfare: Selected Essays on Fundamental Aspects of Economic Theory on Social Welfare* (London, 1981).

issues, the ECJ in a similar subsequent case should be bound by the substance of the Court of Human Right's decision, whether or not, in the process, it would have to assess the proportionality of ethical or moral general interests. In cases involving fundamental rights therefore, the ECJ would have a yardstick with which to assess controversial issues which arose in the context of services at Community level. There is no doubt, however, that the Court is in an unenviable position, since the delimitation of the various moral, ethical and economic aspects of social regulation, in this case in the field of services, is bound to create controversy and to highlight the fact that, though the Community has come far, differences and tensions still persist.

7

Full Circle: Is there a Difference between the Freedom of Establishment and the Freedom to Provide Services?

JESPER LAU HANSEN*

I. INTRODUCTION

The answer to the above question was until recently without doubt in the affirmative and had been for years. The difference was thought to be that the freedom of establishment only protected against discriminating measures, whereas the freedom to provide services reached further. But in later years this proposition has been criticized[1] and with the decision of the ECJ in Gebhard[2] some would argue that the answer should be the opposite.[3] It is now obvious that there are common characteristics of the two freedoms, nevertheless, the purpose of this chapter is to bring the argument full circle, back to the proposition that there is indeed a difference. To do so, a new understanding of the rights involved is offered, which, it is argued, provides a better framework for an analysis of the Court's practice.

In order to simplify the following observations, host state is used to designate the Member State to which territory access is sought by a national of another Member State either to establish himself there or to provide services there. Conversely, the Member State left by that person is called the home state.[4] The ECJ is referred to as the Court, and by the same mode reference is made to the Commission and to the Treaty.[5]

* This chapter is a revised version of a Danish paper that appeared in (1997) 110 Tidsskrift for Rettsvitenskap 609.

1 See *inter alia*, GA Jacobs in *Konstantinidis* with reference to opinions by his fellow Advocate Generals, cf [1993] ECR I-1212, and Roth's comment on *Kraus* in (1993) 30 CML Rev 1251 at 1257.

2 Decision of 30 November 1995 in case C 55/94 *Gebhard* [1995] ECR I-4165.

3 Lombay observes in his comment on *Gebhard* in (1996) 33 CML Rev 1073 at 1083, 'It is open season on indistinctly applicable national measures, which are now caught by Article 52'.

4 *Home state* is thus not an exact phrase, as it does not attach importance to the connection between the individual and that state. It is, however, unnecessary to refine this concept, since what is at issue here is primarily the regulation of the host state. Only to the extent where reverse discrimination may be of importance, the dichotomy of host *contra* home state becomes moot in which case one may dispense with it and simply refer to the Member State in question. The dichotomy of *national* and *foreigner* is equally vague.

5 The Treaty being of course the EC Treaty, Rome 1957, with later amendments, the latest

II. THE PERCEIVED DIFFERENCE

The general perception of the difference between the freedom of establishment and the freedom to provide services was (1) that the scope of protection offered by the former was against discrimination on grounds of nationality, whereas the protection offered by the latter was against any interference with or obstruction of the provision of services; and (2) that the Court in case of an alleged infringement of the latter would apply a test similar to the *Cassis de Dijon* formula to test whether the national measure was contrary to the Treaty's provisions, whereas a similar test would not be applied with respect to the former. Discrimination was considered as a narrow concept, ie national measures that would have different provisions for nationals and foreigners or provisions that would either benefit nationals or exclude foreigners. To expand this narrow concept of discrimination, the concept of indirect discrimination was introduced in *Sotgiu*.[6] According to this notion, discrimination would also cover national measures that did not make a direct reference to nationality, if an—equally direct—reference was made to other criteria that would have the same effect, eg a reference to the place of birth, language, etc. If a national measure did not include any such reference, it was considered non-discriminating. G A Mayras stressed the intent of the Member State similar to the concept of abuse of power.[7] The concept was later applied in *Boussac* with respect to Article 12 of the Treaty (ex Article 6 and before that Article 7).[8]

This was, generally speaking, the gist of the perceived difference. When the Commission tried to blur the difference in the *Belgian Laboratories* Case by claiming that the freedom of establishment should provide protection even to non-discriminating national measures, the Court flatly refused.[9]

The perception of a clear-cut difference was disturbed by the ruling in *Klopp*.[10] The national measure in question, an obligation on lawyers only to be established within the jurisdiction of one French appeal court, did not distinguish between French *advocats* and foreign lawyers. In fact, the Court expressly refrained to rule on whether the national measure treated French lawyers better than foreigners by allowing them to have a secondary estab-

being the 1997 Treaty of Amsterdam. Of special relevance is Article 43 (ex Article 52) EC on the freedom of establishment and Article 49 (ex Article 59) EC on the freedom to provide services.

[6] Decision of 30 April 1974 in Case 153/73 *Sotgiu* [1974] ECR 153. The decision was made in reference to Article 39 (ex Article 48) EC.

[7] On the concept of abuse of power in Community law, see Schockweiler, 'La notion de détournement de pouvoir en droit communautaire', Actualité Juridique Droit Administratif 1995, 435.

[8] cf the decision of 29 October 1980 in Case 22/80 *Boussac* [1980] ECR 3427.

[9] Decision of 12 February 1987 in Case 221/85 *Commission v Belgium* [1985] ECR 734.

[10] Decision of 12 July 1984 in Case 107/83, *Klopp* [1984] ECR 2971.

lishment outside France.[11] According to the general concept of discrimination, the national measure was non-discriminating and as such it should not be subject to review by the Court according to the freedom of establishment. And yet the Court did review it and furthermore found the national measure contrary to the said freedom.

The perception was dealt an additional blow by the subsequent ruling in *Kraus*.[12] Here, the Court apparently applied the *Cassis de Dijon* formula to test a national measure according to the Treaty provisions on the freedom of establishment.[13]

And finally, with the ruling in *Gebhard*, the perception was ultimately shattered. In a clear wording the Court in one and the same paragraph made clear that it found the freedom of establishment to be violated if a national measure made the enjoyment of that freedom less attractive, irrespective of any reference directly or indirectly in the measure to nationality, and spelt out what was clearly a four-point *Cassis de Dijon* formula. It follows, however, from the Court's case law that national measures liable to hinder or make less attractive the exercise of fundamental freedoms guaranteed by the treaty must fulfil four conditions: they must be applied in a non-discriminatory manner; they must be justified by imperative requirements in the general interest; they must be suitable for securing the attainment of the objective which they pursue; and they must not go beyond what is necessary in order to attain it.[14]

Apparently, the perceived difference between the two freedoms was erroneous, which led to the conclusion mentioned in the beginning of this chapter that there was no difference at all. This is, however, an unnecessary conclusion. Let us for a beginning just assume that the perceived difference was mistaken and in its place use a new approach; we may then find that there is indeed a difference.

III. A NEW APPROACH

To clear the way for a new approach to the understanding of the Treaty's provisions on establishment and services, it is useful to divide our analysis into three independent topics:

(1) What is the nature of the rights involved?
(2) When is a national measure a restriction on these rights?
(3) How will the Court respond to a restriction?

[11] cf para 14 of the decision.
[12] Decision of 31 March 1993 in Case C 19/92 *Kraus* [1993] ECR I-1663.
[13] cf para 32 of the decision.
[14] See para 37 of the decision, emphasis added.

This hierarchy of topics will be the path to follow in the remaining part of this chapter.

1. The Rights

The Treaty limits the sovereignty of its Member States as it contains provisions that prevent the individual Member State from regulating its affairs in the way it finds fit. An apt example is Article 12 EC, according to which a Member State may not discriminate against nationals of other Member States. As such, the Treaty is kin to another result of the post-war idealism, the 1950 European Human Rights Convention. Where the Treaty prevents discrimination based on nationalism, the Convention prevents discrimination based on, *inter alia*, race, gender and religion.[15] Where a state's sovereignty is restricted towards a person, that person is said to enjoy a freedom, eg a freedom of speech, etc. The freedom in this respect could also be described as a right of that individual, eg a right of free speech. This parlance of what is usually national constitutional law can equally well describe the position of an individual of the European Union. According to Article 12 EC, it could be said that an individual enjoys a freedom from discrimination based on his nationality or a right to enjoy equal treatment irrespectively of his nationality. This is a right of the individual[16] and since the landmark decisions of 1974 in *Reyners*[17] and *van Binsbergen*,[18] it has been known that the rights associated with establishment and services are directly applicable and can be defended before national courts by the individual.

From these initial observations we have learned that a right granted by the Treaty to individuals, eg a right of establishment or a right to provide services, can best be described in the negative as a restriction upon the Member States in their choice of regulation.[19]

[15] On the inherent conflict between the rights of individuals, euphemistically referred to as *human rights*, and the sovereignty of states, see Henkin, *Human Rights and State 'Sovereignty'*, (1996) 25 Ga J Int'l & Comp L 31.

[16] These rights are bestowed on the individual irrespective of his nationality and consequently are to be respected by all Member States, including his own, cf the decision of 7 February 1979 in Case 115/78 *Knoors* [1997] ECR 399. Reverse discrimination, ie the discrimination of a national by his own state, is thus contrary to the rights granted by the Treaty. However, some rights only concern the relationship between a national and *other* Member States in which case the right does not exclude reverse discrimination simply because that relationship falls outside the scope of the right. This is the case of Article 12 EC. It is not, however, the case of the rights associated with establishment and the provision of services.

[17] Decision of 21 June 1974 in Case 2/74 *Reyners* [1974] ECR 631.

[18] Decision of 3 December 1974 in Case 33/74 *van Binsbergen* [1974] ECR 1299.

[19] This is the character of the rights of the Treaty, the so-called *primary* community law. Regulation with a positive content, ie obliging the Member States to regulate in a certain way, may be found in the *secondary* community law, eg regulations and directives. This body of law is not a restriction of the Member States' sovereignty, but the result of the Member States' joint exercise of their sovereignty in the EU Council.

To proceed with the analysis, we may contemplate the factual difference between establishment and the provision of services. Establishment is an intrastate activity, whereas the provision of services per definition according to Article 49 EC is an interstate activity. A closer look at the relevant provisions reveals that the scope of the freedom of establishment is a protection against differential treatment due to the individual's nationality, cf Article 43(2) EC. The scope of the freedom to provide services, on the other hand, is a protection against any interference with the provision of services due to the cross-border character of that activity, cf Article 49(1).

To sum up, an intrastate activity is protected against differential treatment due to nationality, whereas an interstate activity is protected against any interference with the activity due to the interstate character of that activity. This is a protection that goes beyond the protection afforded to intrastate activities. It is tempting to end the analysis here, as my point about the difference between the freedom of establishment and the freedom to provide services is seemingly vindicated. However, in order not just to explain the case law of the Court but also to provide a framework for a better understanding of these freedoms, it is useful to carry on with the analysis.

First of all, we must recognize that the Treaty's provisions on establishment and services does not follow this dichotomy of intra- and interstate activity, rather they overlap.

Establishment in the host state according to Article 43 EC is of course an intrastate activity. However, the setting up of a secondary establishment is in fact an interstate activity, nevertheless, it is found under the heading of establishment, cf Article 43(1) in fine. This explains why *Klopp* was difficult to fit in. It was to be heard according to the provisions on establishment, but it concerned an interstate activity and as such was entitled to a different scope of protection from that of the typical intrastate activity of establishment; instead it was to be afforded a protection against any interference with the activity due to the interstate character of the activity.

Equally, the provision of services according to Article 49 EC covers not only interstate activities but also intrastate activities. This was first expressed, somewhat enigmatically, by the Court in *van Binsbergen*. Here, the Court declared that if a provider of services was found to direct his services entirely or for the most part to a host state and his presence in the home state was chosen to evade the regulation of the host state, the matter should be dealt with not by the provisions on services but the provisions on establishment.[20] It was later made clear in the *TV10* Case that this situation was after all to be heard under the provisions on services, however, the

[20] cf para 13 of the decision.

protection usually afforded by these provisions to interstate activity was not to be applied as the activity was to be considered an intrastate activity.[21]

2. The Restrictions

The protection afforded to intrastate activity is different from that offered to interstate activity. Intrastate activity enjoys a freedom from differential treatment, or, in other words, a right to equal treatment. Interstate activity enjoys a freedom from interference with the pursuit of that activity, respectively, a right to carry on with the activity without interference. However, this does not tell us when a national measure is considered a restriction of the freedoms in question.

According to the above quote from *Gebhard*, a national measure is a restriction, whenever it prevents or make less attractive the exercise of a freedom. It has been argued that this is a considerable expansion of the concept of restriction. It is not so. On the contrary, the Court's practice is seldom a consistent one. In *van Binsbergen*, a decision more than 20 years senior to *Gebhard*, the Court echoes this wording:

> The restrictions to be abolished pursuant to Articles 59 and 60 include all requirements imposed on the person providing the service by reason in particular of his nationality or of the fact that he does not habitually reside in the state where the service is provided, which do not apply to persons established within the territory or which may prevent or otherwise obstruct the activities of the person providing the service. [22]

One may argue that *van Binsbergen* concerned services, ie an interstate activity, and that the usage of this wording in *Gebhard*, if not new, then at least is an expansion within the field of establishment or intrastate activities. I respectfully disagree. Plenty of decisions in the area of establishment have found a national measure to be a restriction, not because it prevented the exercise of the right of establishment, but because it was a nuisance.[23]

Thus, the concept of restrictions is a wide one leaving room for dividing them into three groups according to their form. As we shall see in 3 below, the grouping corresponds with a difference in the response of the Court to the various forms of restrictions.

The first form of restriction is that of discrimination, ie differential treatment of any sort. That may in turn be sub-divided into two separate groups. Differential treatment of an insurmountable nature may be called genuine discrimination, whereas other forms of differential treatment can be called,

[21] Decision of 5 October 1994 in Case C 23/93 *TV10* [1974] ECR 4795. Cf para 15.
[22] cf para 10 of the decision, emphasis added.
[23] cf the decision in *Thieffry* (n 42 below) regarding personal qualifications.

somewhat uninspiringly, other discrimination. The dichotomy is apparent in the cases of *Reyners* and *Thieffry*. In *Reyners*, the national requirement called for Belgian nationality in order to become a lawyer in Belgium. This was an insurmountable restriction, ie the restriction had the form of genuine discrimination.[24] In *Thieffry*, the national requirement was for a French exam and since that exam was available also for foreigners, the restriction was not insurmountable, albeit it was still an impediment for Mr Thieffry's enjoyment of his right of establishment. Thus, the restriction can be described as taking the form of other discrimination.

The distinction between genuine and other discrimination do not take into account the scope of protection available to interstate activities, eg the Treaty's provisions on service. Here, a national measure may prevent or otherwise obstruct the exercise of this freedom and thus be a restriction without being discriminating in any way. It may be that a certain activity is forbidden in a Member State not just to foreigners, but to all. This was the case in Schindler,[25] where the then British regulation on lotteries prevented the Schindler brothers from acting on behalf of a German lottery. We may call this form of restriction a subjection, as it is an attempt by the Member State to subject the individual's right to the code of that state.

Within the area of the free movement of goods (Article 28 EC), the Court's decision in *Keck* has shown a willingness on behalf of the Court to disregard national requirements that may affect the free movement of goods but does not amount to differential treatment nor is aimed at the selling modalities applied.[26] In *Alpine Investments*, the Court has ruled out the application of *Keck* within the area of services.[27] However, this may be nothing more than a rebuttal of the contention that *Keck* was based on a concept of discrimination that would render every national requirement that fell short of a clear discriminatory content inaccessible to review.[28] It could be argued that there is no need to apply the approach of *Keck* to the area of services as it is already established that a mere effect on interstate activity is not sufficient in the absence of an intent to cause such an effect.[29]

24 It may be argued that the restriction was not really unsurmountable as Mr Reyners could simply apply for Belgian nationality. However, this argument is inadmissible if the entire purpose of the Treaty is not to be set aside.

25 Decision of 24 March 1994 in Case C 275/92 *Schindler* [1994] ECR I-1039.

26 cf decision of 24 November 1993 in joined Cases C-267/268/91 *Keck and Mithouard* [1993] ECR I-6097.

27 cf the decision of 10 May 1995 in case C 384/93, *Alpine Investments* [1995] ECR I-1141.

28 cf Advocate General Jacobs Opinion in *Alpine Investments* and his earlier Opinion in Case C-412/93 *Leclerc-Siplec* [1995] ECR I-179, para 34.

29 cf *inter alia* the decision of 13 December 1984 in Case 251/83 *Haug-Adrion* [1984] ECR 4277. Cf also *Sotgiu* and the concept of indirect discrimination, where the intent to discriminate is emphasized. The idea of an intent behind national provisions is apt to confuse any analysis and should be construed as a mere indication that the discriminating effect cannot be said to be merely coincidental.

Nonetheless, it is probable that the post-*Keck* Court will be even more sceptical with respect to the threshold required before a national provision is considered to impede an intrastate activity.[30]

Although the rights may differ, and differ they do, the Court evidently applies the same notion of restriction irrespectively of the rights involved.

3. The Response

The Treaty itself envisaged only one procedure to test the justification of a restriction on the freedom of establishment and the freedom to provide services. According to Article 46 EC, a restriction is acceptable if justified in the interest of public order, security or health. This exemption is the traditional exemption of *ordre public* found in many other treaties in international law. It is joined by Article 45 EC regarding the exercise of public government. The Court has consistently applied a narrow interpretation to these exemptions.[31]

It was a far-reaching step, when the Court decided in *van Binsbergen* that the Treaty's provisions on service were directly applicable. Contrary to the provisions on establishment found directly applicable earlier that year in *Reyners*, which only provide a protection against differential treatment leaving the national regulation of commercial activity largely unrestrained, the provisions on service protect against any interference with the interstate activity of providing these services. Thus, the spectrum of possible restrictions became extremely wide and taking into account the narrow construing of the Treaty's exemptions for *ordre public*, it would render any kind of national commercial regulation by the Member States virtually impossible. It is arguable that the Court's resort to the doctrine of direct effect was a much needed response to the failure of the Member States to live up to their Treaty obligations and harmonize their national law. But the doctrine of direct effect was clearly not intended to force upon the Member States a total harmonization.[32] Consequently, it was necessary for the Court to

[30] In his Opinion in *Schindler*, Advocate General Gulmann suggested that not all impediments to intrastate activity should be considered contrary to the freedom to provide services, cf [1994] ECR I-1039, para 61.

[31] With respect to Article 45: cf *Reyners* and the decision of 15 March 1988 in Case 147/86 *Commission v Greece* [1988] ECR 1637 and the decisions of 2 July 1996 in the Joined Cases C-473/93, C-173/94, and C-290/94 *Commission v Luxembourg, Belgium and Greece* [1996] ECR I-3207. With respect to Article 46: cf decisions of 27 October 1977 in Case 30/77 *Bouchereau* [1977] ECR 1999, para 35, and 4 December 1974 in Case 41/74 *van Duyn* [1974] ECR 1337, para 18. Both cases concerned the right of workers according to Article 39 EC, however, an equally narrow interpretation has been applied in the area of establishment and services with respect to Article 46 EC, see, *inter alia*, the decision of 30 April 1986 in Case 96/85 *Commission v France* [1986] ECR 1475, paras 13–14. In the decision of 29 October 1998 in Case C-114/97 *Commission v Spain* [1988] ECR I-6732, the Court declared that Article 46 cannot lead to a general exclusion of an entire business sector.

[32] cf the decision of 24 October 1978, *Koestler* [1978] ECR 1971, at para 5.

come up with an alternative procedure to test the justification of restrictions, a procedure less rigid than the Treaty's provisions on *ordre public*. The decision in *van Binsbergen* not only introduced the notion of direct effect to the area of services but also provided the first example of such an alternative test.[33] This test was a weighing of interests: on the one hand, the interest of the individual to exercise his freedom and, on the other hand, the interest of the Member State to protect what could be euphemistically described as the general good.[34]

The decision in *van Binsbergen* may be the first application of this novel test, but its existence can be traced back to another decision of 1974, that of *Dassonville*.[35] In that decision, the Court expanded the notion of restrictions in the area of the freedom of movement of goods.[36] The expansion was influenced by competition law, especially the wording of the decision in *Grundig*.[37] This was hardly surprising considering that both cases involved the protection of sole distributors. However, where the Treaty's provisions on competition provide for a weighing of interests by way of Article 81(3) EC,[38] the provisions in Article 28 EC on goods only provide an exemption for *ordre public*, cf Article 30 (ex Article 36) EC. To counterbalance its expansion of the notion of restrictions, the Court reserved for itself a possibility to uphold restrictions by a weighing of interests, even though such a procedure was not envisaged by the Treaty. In the area of goods, this test was later applied in *Rewe* and is now, somewhat unfairly, known as the *Cassis de Dijon* formula.[39]

The *van Binsbergen* formula was gradually refined by subsequent decisions, mostly in the area of services. The decision in *van Wesemael* and *Webb* introduced a prohibition against the host state imposing conditions already fulfilled in the home state.[40] The decision in the German insurance case introduced the requirement of proportionality.[41] Eventually the *van Binsbergen* formula took the form of the test referred to in *Gebhard* paragraph 37.

[33] cf para 12 of the decision.

[34] The concept of the general good is examined by Michel Tison, 'What is "General Good" in EU Financial Services Law?' (1997) 2 Legal Issues of European Integration 1.

[35] Decision of 11 July 1974 in Case 8/74, *Dassonville* [1974] ECR 837, cf para 6.

[36] The so-called *Dassonville* formula in para 5.

[37] Decision of 13 July 1966 in Joined Cases 56–58/64, *Grundig*, originally reported [1966] ECR 299.

[38] In US antitrust law this weighing of interests is perhaps better known as *the rule of reason*.

[39] Decision of 20 February 1979 in Case 120/78 *Rewe* [1979] ECR 649.

[40] cf decision of 18 January 1979 in Joined Cases 110–111/78 *van Wesemael* [1979] ECR 35 and the decision of 17 December 1981 in Case 279/80 *Webb* [1981] ECR 3305.

[41] cf decision of 4 December 1986 in Case 205/84 *Commission v Germany* [1986] ECR 3755.

Thus, from *van Binsbergen* and onwards, the Court applied two different tests: one of *ordre public* and one of the general good, the latter being more benevolent towards restrictions than the former. This was recognized with respect to the case law on services but was apparently overlooked in the area of establishment, eventually causing some surprise at the time the *Kraus* and *Gebhard* decisions were handed down. Upon closer inspection the case law on establishment do reveal the application by the Court of the general good test. Beginning with *Thieffry*[42] and upheld as a general principle of Community law in this area in *Vlassopoulou*,[43] the Court would try national regulation of personal qualifications as a weighing of interests: on the one hand, regard would be taken of the individual's right to move freely within the Community and, on the other hand, the Member States were entitled to secure that only the properly qualified could take up certain jobs.[44] The fact that not only the notion of restriction but also the response to these restrictions is shared even though the rights themselves are different, helps explain why certain cases prior to *Gebhard* were handled by the Court in a unified way although concerning different rights.[45]

Apparently, the Court's choice of procedure to test restrictions depends on the form of restriction. If the restriction is insurmountable, ie the restriction has the form of genuine discrimination, it will be submitted to a test of *ordre public*. Otherwise, with respect to restrictions having the form of other discrimination or subjection, the Court will seek to strike a balance between the individual's rights according to the Treaty and the Member State's interest in taking due consideration of the general good.

To prove that the Court does in fact respond to restrictions in this way would in the absence of a clear dictum of the Court require an extensive examination of the decisions in this area. The available space afforded to this chapter does not allow it. Rather, the reasoning behind the obvious differences in the Court's response to various restrictions may be taken as sufficient proof of the said contention. After the expiration of the transition period on 31 December 1969, the Member States were to have achieved full harmonization to provide their nationals with a Common Market free of discrimination except to the extent provided for by the *ordre public* provisions of the Treaty, in the area of establishment and services (Articles 45–46 EC). Having failed this, the Court instead attributed direct effect to various Treaty provisions, *inter alia* Articles 43 and 49 EC. To counter this far-reaching step, the Court at the same time introduced the concept of an

[42] Decision of 28 April 1977 in Case 71/76 *Thieffry* [1977] ECR 765.

[43] Decision of 7 May 1991 in Case C-340/89 *Vlassopoulou* [1991] ECR I-2357.

[44] The decision of 19 January 1988 in Case 292/86 *Gullung* [1988] ECR 111, belongs to this group of cases.

[45] cf *inter alia* the decision of 28 November 1978 in Case 16/78 *Choquet* [1978] ECR 2293, which concerned the Treaty's provisions on workers, establishment and services.

exemption due to considerations of the general good. However, this latter exemption is a dynamic one only available to the Member States insofar as they have not agreed upon harmonization. As more and more activities are covered by harmonization, less and less room is left for arguing that the general good calls for exemptions to the rights originally envisaged by the Treaty Founders. When the intended level of harmonization is reached, should such a day ever occur, there will be no more restrictions in the form of other discrimination or subjection, and hence no need for exemptions other than the *ordre public* clauses in the Treaty itself.

IV. A NEW VIEW

Based on this approach we are offered a new view of the Court's case law.

(1) With regard to intrastate activity, the Member States do not have to fear that they will be called upon by the Court to justify their national regulation as long as that regulation in no way discriminates against foreigners. Discrimination is any form of differential treatment even though it may offer only an inconvenience to the foreigner. This may sound a low threshold of interference from the Court, but it is not. Why, after all, treat foreigners differently? It must be remembered that the actual difference between the regulatory climate among the Member States does not amount to discrimination in itself.[46] As long as national regulations, be it commercial or tax-wise,[47] treat people in the same way within the Member State, no discrimination is present.

(2) With regard to interstate activity, any interference with the activity by the host state or the home state[48] is likely to be considered a restriction and the Member State may be called on to justify it. However, if the restriction has the form of other discrimination or subjection, justification can be sought in a reference to the general good.

(3) Article 12 of the Treaty has been described by the Court in numerous cases as a common denominator, or to paraphrase that, that the freedom of establishment and the freedom to provide services are built upon this provision.[49] Nevertheless, Article 12 is a freedom in its own right. Not only can Article 12 be applied alone without further reference to the provisions on establishment and service,[50] it also has an independent profile different

[46] See, *inter alia*, the decision of 28 June 1978 in Case 1/78 *Kenny* [1978] ECR 1489, with respect to Article 12 (then Article 7 EC).

[47] The decision of 28 January 1992 in Case C 204/90 *Bachman* [1992] ECR I-249, is no exemption. Here, too, the national regulation resulted in a differential treatment.

[48] cf *Alpine Investments* (n 27 above).

[49] cf *inter alia* the decision of 12 December 1974 in Case 36/74 *Walrave* [1974] ECR 1405, para 6.

[50] cf *Boussac* (n 8 above).

from that of the freedoms concerning establishment and services. Article 12 concerns intra- and interstate activities but provides a more narrow scope of protection. The protection is against differential treatment of foreigners where it is explicitly due to their nationality. As such, Article 12 would only protect against the form of restrictions described here as genuine discrimination and resembles the old concept of discrimination with its emphasis on a direct reference to nationality or criteria synonymous with nationality. Article 12 thus overlaps the scope of protection offered by the Treaty's provisions on establishment and service, but they are further reaching.[51]

(4) The freedom to form a secondary establishment concerns interstate activity, and as such restrictions in this area can take the form of discrimination, be it genuine or other, and subjection. This freedom is described in Article 43 EC as a right to establish an agency, a branch or a subsidiary. It is important to note that the Court finds this right to be a right of choice between the three forms of secondary establishment.[52] Even more important is that the foundation of this conclusion is the Court's observation with regard to Article 48 EC that the purpose of a company's seat is to connect the company to the legal regime of that Member State in the same way as nationality is the connection between a person and his State.[53] This is to say that a company has the nationality of the Member State, ie its home state. It is this observation that warrants the conclusion that a company does always have the right to make its secondary establishment in the host state by way of a branch, because only by choosing a branch can the company maintain its nationality.[54] Any national regulation that prevents a foreign company from using a branch[55] or puts it at a disadvantage[56] because of its choice of branch rather than a subsidiary is a restriction of the form of genuine discrimination and can only be justified by *ordre public*. This clear

[51] cf the decision of 7 July 1988 in Case 143/87 *Stanton* [1988] ECR 3877, where the national measure was in violation of Article 43 but not Article 12.

[52] cf the decision of 28 January 1986 in Case 270/83 *Commission v France* [1986] ECR 273, para 22.

[53] cf para 18 of the decision.

[54] A subsidiary would have the nationality of the host state.

[55] cf the decision of 6 June 1996 in Case C-101/94 *Commission v Italy* [1996] ECR I-2691, where a requirement only to organize security trading business as an Italian company (a SIM) was found to be contrary to Articles 43 and 49. It should be noted, however, that the landmark decision of 9 March 1999 in Case C-212/97 *Centros* [1999] ECR I-1459, was not a case of discrimination, but jurisdiction. The Danish authorities refused to recognize the establishment of a branch in Denmark by an English private company because the English company did not conduct business outside Denmark. Thus, the Danish authorities considered the company to be Danish and viewed the prior English establishment as an attempt to circumvent the Danish requirements to pay up a minimum capital in private companies. Thus, the Danish authorities wanted to subject the company to Danish standards, whereas the right of foreign private companies to make a secondary establishment in Denmark *per se* was not disputed. The Court, however, found in favour of the English company.

[56] cf case 270/83 *Commission v France* (n 52 above), and the decision of 13 July 1993 in Case-C 330/91 *Commertzbank* [1993] ECR I-4017.

jurisprudence of the Court seems to be at odds with the 'main-seat theory' (known in Germany as the *Sitztheorie*) according to which a company must conform to the law of the State where it has its principle activity and head of operations.

(5) A complete ban on a certain activity in a given Member State is a truly non-discriminating measure and is thus only challengeable according to the protection afforded interstate activities, eg the provision of services. That was the case in *Schindler*, where Britain at the time had a fairly comprehensive ban on lotteries, which hindered the marketing of a German lottery in the United Kingdom.

One should think that a monopoly would be considered an act of discrimination as it is in favour of a national, ie the monopolist. However, the Court's case law makes it clear that the existence of a monopoly is to be considered a non-discriminating measure.[57] Apparently, the Court applies a distinction similar to that of intellectual property rights, ie a distinction between their existence and their exercise.[58] Monopolies are recognized by the Treaty and regulated by it in Article 86 EC. The exercise of a monopoly may, however, be contrary to competition law or the freedom to provide services.[59]

V. CONCLUSION

Rather than seeing *Gebhard* as the culmination of a trend towards extending the reach of Article 43 to non-discriminating measures, it should be regarded as a consistent application of a practice more than 20 years old. In this chapter, a new approach is offered that is based on a distinction between the content of a right, the notion of a restriction, and the character of the test used by the Court in response to a restriction. It is true that the last two are identical with respect to the freedom of establishment and the freedom to provide services, but the first and most important topic, however, is not.

According to Karl Popper, a theory cannot be proven, only unproven. This would be the case, and as such the end of the theory advanced here, if a national measure that was truly non-discriminating was put aside by the Court applying the Treaty's provisions on the freedom of establishment with respect to an intrastate activity. *Gebhard* was not such a decision, nor have I found any others. It remains to be seen whether they exist or will be made.

[57] cf the Decision of 18 June 1991 in Case C-260/89 *ERT* [1991] ECR I-2925, para 10.

[58] cf *Grundig* (n 37 above) 345.

[59] cf Decision of 26 April 1988 in Case 352/85 *Bond van Adverteerders* [1988] ECR 2085, paras 24–26, where restrictions on advertising favoured nationals. The restriction resulted in genuine discrimination and could consequently only be justified by *ordre public*. That was not possible, cf para 32.

8

Private Parties and the Free Movement of Goods and Services

JUKKA SNELL[1]

I. INTRODUCTION

It is unequivocally clear that the Member States are not allowed to adopt measures restricting trade in goods or services. The main purpose of the Treaty provisions on the free movement of goods and services is to abolish restrictions created by Member States, and the great majority of cases and Community legislation have been aimed at dismantling barriers erected by public authorities. What about measures adopted by private parties? Are they bound by Articles 28 (ex 30) and 49 (ex 59) of the Treaty?

II. FREE MOVEMENT OF GOODS

1. General

The text of the Treaty indicates that Article 28 (ex 30) is aimed at State measures. Although the provision itself does not refer to the author of quantitative restrictions and measures having equivalent effect, prior to the Treaty of Amsterdam other Articles of the same Chapter on Elimination of Quantitative Restrictions (now Prohibition of Quantitative Restrictions) specifically targeted measures adopted by the Member States. Thus, Article 31(1) ECT (repealed) stipulated that 'Member States shall refrain from introducing between themselves any new quantitative restrictions or measures having equivalent effect'. Similarly, Article 32(1) ECT (repealed) stated that '[i]n their trade with one another Member States shall refrain from making more restrictive the quotas and measures having equivalent effect existing at the date of entry into force of this Treaty'. In addition, Articles 33–35 ECT (partly repealed) all showed that Member State measures are the target of these provisions.[2]

[1] The author would like to thank Mads Andenas, Piet Eeckhout, Alison Burton and Kelyn Bacon for many valuable comments.

[2] See P Oliver, *The Free Movement of Goods in the European Community* (3rd edn, London, 1996) 41 and the Opinion of Advocate General Lenz in Case C-265/95 *Commission*

The opinion of the Commission seems to be that Article 28 (ex 30) does not apply to measures adopted by private parties. In the recitals of Directive 70/50[3] it defined 'measures' for the purposes of Article 28 (ex 30) as 'laws, regulations, administrative provisions, administrative practices, and all instruments issuing from a public authority, including recommendations'. In the next recital it made clear that 'administrative practices' referred to standards and procedures followed by public authorities.

A decade later, in reply to Written Question No 909/79[4] by Mr Moreland MEP which concerned industrial action preventing transfer of goods from crossing national borders, such as dock picketing, the Commission stated that:

> The practices . . . do not in themselves constitute a quantitative restriction on trade within the meaning of Article 30 [currently 28] of the EEC Treaty as interpreted by the Court of Justice.
>
> However, the Commission agrees that, although the type of action . . . does not contravene Article 30 [currently 28] of the Treaty, it could in certain circumstances disrupt trade within the Community. The Commission feels that this is a problem which warrants careful investigation.

More recently, in Recital 7 of the proposal for a Regulation creating a mechanism whereby the Commission can intervene in order to remove certain obstacles to trade[5] the Commission commented that a party injured by actions taken by private individuals creating obstacles to the free movement of goods has 'no appropriate instrument to rely on' in defending his rights.

These statements show clearly that, according to the Commission, Article 28 (formerly 30) EC does not bind private parties but is only designed to catch measures adopted by public bodies.

The European Court of Justice has also denied the application of Article 28 EC to private measures. In *Vlaamse Reisbureaus*[6] it had to consider contracts between travel agents and tour operators, contracts between the

v French Republic [1997] ECR I-6959, para 8. Note, however, Case 36/74 *Walrave and Koch v UCI* [1974] ECR 1405, para 20, which will be analysed below. The deletion in the Amsterdam Treaty did not affect 'aquis communautaire'. See Article 10 of the Amsterdam Treaty and Declaration 51 annexed to it.

[3] Commission Directive 70/50/EEC of 22 December 1969 based on the provisions of Article 33(7) EC [repealed], on the abolition of measures which have an effect equivalent to quantitative restrictions on imports and are not covered by other provisions adopted in pursuance of the EEC Treaty OJ Special Edition 1970 I, L 13/29.

[4] OJ 1980 C156/10.

[5] OJ 1998 C10/14.

[6] Case 311/85 *VZW Vereniging van Vlaamse Reisbureaus v VZW Sociale Dienst van de Plaatselijke en Gewestlijke Overheidsdiensten* [1987] ECR 3801. Already in Case 8/74 *Procureur du Roi v Dassonville* [1974] ECR 837, para 5 the Court referred to 'trading rules enacted by the Member States'.

agents themselves and a Belgian Royal Decree reinforcing the system. The agreements purported to oblige the travel agents to observe the prices and tariffs set by tour operators. The agents were prohibited from sharing commissions with or granting rebates to their customers. The Court found that the Belgian system infringed Article 81(1) (formerly 85(1)), and Article 10 (formerly 5) in conjunction with Articles 3(g) and 81 (formerly 85).[7]

The national court had, however, also asked whether the agreements and the Royal Decree were compatible with Articles 28 (ex 30) and 29 (ex 34) EC. The ECJ stated the following:

> [s]ince Articles 30 [currently 28] and 34 [currently 29] of the Treaty concern only public measures and not the conduct of undertakings, it is only the compatibility with those articles of national provisions of the kind at issue in the main proceedings that need be examined.[8]

The Court went on to decide that the sale of travel was provision of services so Articles 28 (ex 30) and 29 (ex 34) EC could not have been breached.[9]

This judgment shows clearly the view of the Court. Articles 28 and 29 EC are not concerned with private measures. Furthermore, the Court has been consistent in its approach. In *Commission v Italy*[10] the Court stated that the subject of the chapter relating to the elimination of quantitative restrictions was State intervention in intra-Community trade.[11] In *Van de Haar*[12] the Court compared Articles 81 (ex 85) and 28 (ex 30) EC stating that the former belongs to rules on competition addressed to undertakings and associations of undertakings while the latter belongs to rules which seek to eliminate measures taken by the Member States which might impede the free movement of goods.[13] In *Bayer v Süllhöfer*[14] the Court pronounced that Article 28 (ex 30) *et seq.* form part of the rules intended to ensure the free movement of goods and to eliminate for that purpose any measures of the Member States forming barriers to inter-State trade, while agreements between undertakings are governed by the rules on competition.[15]

2. Intellectual Property Rights

It has sometimes been argued that in its judgments dealing with intellectual property rights and unfair competition the Court has in fact prohibited

[7] ibid paras 27 and 24. [8] ibid para 30. [9] ibid paras 32–33.

[10] Case 7/68 *Commission v Italy* [1968] ECR 423. [11] ibid at 430.

[12] Joined Cases 177 and 178/82 *Criminal proceedings against Jan van de Haar and Kaveka de Meern BV* [1984] ECR 1797.

[13] ibid paras 11–12.

[14] Case 65/86 *Bayer AG and Maschinenfabrik Hennecke GmbH v Heinz Süllhöfer* [1988] ECR 5249.

[15] ibid para 11.

private measures restricting the free movement of goods.[16] For example, in *Deutsche Grammophon*[17] the Court stated that:

> the essential purpose of the Treaty, which is to unite national markets into a single market . . . could not be attained if, under the various legal systems of the Member States, *nationals of those States were able to partition the market* and bring about arbitrary discrimination or disguised restrictions on trade between Member States.
>
> Consequently, it would be in conflict with the provisions prescribing the free movement of products within the common market for *a manufacturer of sound recordings to exercise the exclusive right* to distribute the protected articles, conferred upon him by the legislation of a Member State, in such a way as to prohibit the sale in that State of products placed on the market by him or with his consent in another Member State solely because such distribution did not occur within the territory of the first Member State.[18]

Similarly, in *Dansk Supermarked*[19] the Court remarked that '. . . it is impossible in any circumstances for agreements between individuals to derogate from the mandatory provisions of the Treaty on the free movement of goods'.[20] In *Merck v Stephar*[21] the Court held that the rules concerning the free movement of goods prevented in certain circumstances the patent owner 'from availing himself of the right conferred by the legislation'.[22] Finally, in *Centrafarm v American Home Products Corporation*[23] the Court applied the Treaty rules on the free movement of goods to the subjective behaviour of a private undertaking in the context of artificial partitioning of the Common Market.[24]

Nevertheless, despite these, and other judgments to the same effect,[25] it can be argued that even in this field the conduct of private parties is not caught.

First, the Court was in these cases not motivated by the desire to widen its interpretation of Article 28 EC. It was not necessarily aiming to extend the application of the free movement of goods provisions to private activi-

[16] See eg N Green, TC Hartley and JA Usher, *The Legal Foundations of the Single European Market* (Oxford, 1991) 53–55 and P Pescatore, 'Public and Private Aspects of European Community Competition Law' (1987) 10 Fordham Int LJ 373, 380–383.

[17] Case 78/70 *Deutsche Grammophon GmbH v Metro-SB Grossmärkte GmbH & Co KG* [1971] ECR 487.

[18] ibid paras 12–13 (emphasis added).

[19] Case 58/80 *Dansk Supermarked A/S v A/S Imerco* [1981] ECR 181.

[20] ibid para 17. See further J Baquero Cruz, 'Free Movement and Private Autonomy' (1999) 24 EL Rev 603 at 607–609.

[21] Case 187/80 *Merck & Co Inc. v Stephar BV and Petrus Stephanus Exler* [1981] ECR 2063.

[22] ibid para 14.

[23] Case 3/78 *Centrafarm B.V. v American Home Products Corporation* [1978] ECR 1823.

[24] See G Marenco and K Banks, 'Intellectual Property and the Community Rules on Free Movement: Discrimination Unearthed' (1990) 15 EL Rev 224, 227 and 253–254.

[25] ibid 224–225.

ties. It was simply still influenced by the doctrine it had developed in the field of competition law in the 1960s.[26]

In *Consten and Grundig*[27] the plaintiffs had argued that the application of Article 81 (ex 85) EC to a use of trademark violated Article 295 (ex 222) EC, which stipulates that the 'Treaty shall in no way prejudice the rules in Member States governing the system of property ownership'. The Court had dealt with the argument by developing a distinction between the existence and the exercise of intellectual property rights.[28] The former was not affected by the Treaty while the latter could be limited to the necessary extent. This distinction, the utility of which has been severely criticized,[29] was then applied in the field of the free movement of goods to the exercise of intellectual property rights by private parties.

Secondly, the judgments dealing with intellectual property can be interpreted in another way as well. It can be said that the Court was attacking national legislation granting private parties the right to exercise their intellectual property in certain situations.[30] The real barriers were created by the national legislation. The only peculiarity was that the law was not enforced by public authorities but by the national courts following an initiative of a private party.[31]

This interpretation is supported by the conflicting language of some of the Court's decisions. For example, in the classic cases *Centrafarm v Sterling*[32] and *Centrafarm v Winthrop*[33] the Court pronounced in the operative parts that the exercise of the intellectual property rights by their owners was incompatible with the rules concerning the free movement of goods. Yet, earlier in the judgments, the Court had stated that an obstacle to the free movement of goods arose from certain provisions of national

[26] See E White, 'In Search of the Limits to Article 30 of the EEC Treaty' (1989) 26 CML Rev 235, 269.

[27] Cases 56/64 and 58/64 *Etablissements Consten SA and Grundig-Verkaufs-GmbH v Commission* [1966] ECR 299.

[28] The Court could have presumably dealt with the argument in another way too. Article 295 (ex 222) EC was intended to protect the right of Member States to determine the private or public ownership of undertakings, not to protect property rights. See Marenco and Banks (n 24 above) 226 and TC Vinje, 'Magill, Its Impact on Information Technology Industry' (1992) 14 EIPR 397, 398.

[29] See eg Korah, *An Introductory Guide to EC Competition Law and Practice* (6th edn, London, 1997) 217–218.

[30] Marenco and Banks (n 24 above) 225–226, Oliver (n 2 above) 59 and White (n 26 above) 268 and 270.

[31] An alternative explanation could be that the measure in the sense of Article 28 (ex 30) EC is the application of legislation by a national court. This interpretation is not convincing as it is not the courts but the legislature that is the real source of the measure: White (n 26 above) 268–269. See also Baquero Cruz (n 20 above) 615.

[32] Case 15/74 *Centrafarm BV v Sterling Drug Inc* [1974] ECR 1147.

[33] Case 16/74 *Centrafarm BV v Winthrop BV* [1974] ECR 1183.

legislation stipulating that the intellectual property right was not exhausted by the marketing of the protected product in another Member State.[34]

In addition, more recent judgments show clearly that even in the field of intellectual property rights Article 28 does not catch private measures. Starting from *Pharmon v Hoechst*[35] the Court has made it clear that it is only State action which is caught. The Court stated in a key paragraph that:

> Articles 30 [currently 28] and 36 [currently 30] of the EEC Treaty *preclude the application of national provisions* which enable a patent proprietor to prevent the importation and marketing of a product which has been lawfully marketed in another Member State by the patent proprietor himself, with his consent, or by a person economically or legally dependent on him.[36]

The ECJ has been consistent in its approach over the recent years. In *Basset*,[37] for example, the referring national court asked whether Articles 28 (ex 30) and 30 (ex 36) EC *prevented a national copyright-management society from charging* users a royalty on public performances. The ECJ answered that the provisions *did not preclude the application of national legislation* that allowed the charging of a royalty. The language of the Court made it clear that the suspect measure originated from the Member State, not from the private party.[38]

The Court has also recently made it clear that the subjective intention of an economic agent is not relevant to the application of Article 28 (ex 30) EC and thus tacitly overruled *Centrafarm v American Home Products*.[39] In *Bristol-Myers Squibb*[40] Paranova had imported drugs produced by plaintiffs from various Member States to Denmark, repackaging them for the purposes of sale. The plaintiffs took action against Paranova for trademark infringements.

The Court held, *inter alia*, that repackaging could not be opposed if certain conditions were fulfilled. One of these conditions was that the reliance upon trademark rights would contribute to the artificial partitioning of the markets between Member States. However, contrary to the argument of the plaintiffs, the importer was not required to establish that the trademark owner deliberately sought to partition the markets.[41]

The case showed that 'artificial partitioning of the markets' was an

[34] See n 32 above para 10 and ibid para 9.

[35] Case 19/84 *Pharmon BV v Hoechst AG* [1985] ECR 2281.

[36] ibid para 22 (emphasis added).

[37] Case 402/85 *G. Basset v SACEM* [1987] ECR 1747.

[38] For a recent example, see eg Case C-316/95 *Generics BV v Smith, Kline & French Laboratories Ltd* [1997] ECR I-3929, para 17 and para 25 of the Opinion of Advocate General Jacobs.

[39] Case 3/78 *Centrafarm B.V. v American Home Products Corporation* [1978] ECR 1823.

[40] Joined Cases C-427/93, C-429/93 and 436/93 *Bristol-Myers Squibb and others v Paranova A/S* [1996] ECR I-3457.

[41] ibid para 57.

objective, not a subjective condition. Thus it offers further support for the proposition that Article 28 EC does not apply to measures adopted by private parties.

Bristol-Myers Squibb was not identical to *Centrafarm v American Home Products*, however. In the latter case the producer had used slightly different trademarks in different countries, so the importer changed the trademark. In the former case the trademark was not changed.[42] As Advocate General Jacobs observed, the altering of a trademark creates more difficult problems than a simple act of repackaging.[43]

Furthermore, in *Bristol-Myers Squibb* the Court was interpreting Article 7(2) of the Trade Mark Directive,[44] not Articles 28 (ex 30) and 30 (ex 36) of the Treaty. It is submitted, however, that this difference was not of significance. The Court observed that the Directive had to be applied in accordance with the Treaty rules on the free movement of goods, and interpreted it in the light of its previous case law.[45] Obversely, in *Loendersloot v Ballantine*[46] the Court used its case law on the Trade Mark Directive to interpret Article 30 (ex 36) on the question of repackaging and the artificial partitioning of the market, arriving at the same conclusion as in *Bristol-Myers Squibb*.[47]

The subjective intention test of *Centrafarm v American Home Products* was finally put to sleep in *Pharmacia & Upjohn v Paranova*.[48] Upjohn Group had marketed an antibiotic, clindamycin, under different trademarks in different Member States. Paranova had purchased Upjohn's clindamycin capsules and injection phials in France and Greece, and sold them in Denmark after replacing the trademarks with the one used there, Dalacin. Upjohn challenged Paranova's actions. It referred to *Centrafarm v American Home Products* and argued that it had the right to oppose the replacement of the trademarks unless it could be shown that it had used the different trademarks with the subjective intention to partition the markets.[49]

[42] The facts were similar as in Case 102/77 *Hoffmann-La Roche & Co AG v Centrafarm Vertriebsgesellschaft Pharmazeutischer Erzeugnisse mbH* [1978] ECR 1139, which was decided a few months prior to *Centrafarm v American Home Products*. In that case it remained unclear whether the test used by the Court was objective or subjective.

[43] See n 40 above para 84 of his Opinion.

[44] First Council Directive 89/104/EEC of 21 December 1988 to Approximate the Laws of the Member States relating to Trade Marks OJ 1989 L40/1.

[45] See n 40 above paras 27, 28, 31, 34, 36 and 41. See also the Opinion of Advocate General Jacobs paras 90, 91 and 98.

[46] Case C-349/95 *Frits Loendersloot, trading as F. Loendersloot Internationale Expeditie v George Ballantine & Son Ltd and others* [1997] ECR I-6227, especially para 36.

[47] See especially ibid para 36 and paras 22–23 and 42 of the Opinion of Advocate General Jacobs.

[48] Case C-379/97 *Pharmacia & Upjohn SA v Paranova A/S* [1999] ECR I-6927.

[49] The use of different marks was explained by an agreement between Upjohn and American Home Products Corporation in 1968.

The Court did not accept Upjohn's argument. It held that the condition of artificial partitioning had to be applied similarly in repackaging and replacing cases, as the effect on intra-Community trade was the same and the parallel importer was in both cases using a trademark not belonging to him. According to the Court, the decisive question is whether the replacement of the trademark is objectively necessary in order that the product can be marketed by the parallel importer, and the intention of the trademark owner was immaterial.[50]

These recent judgments are to be welcomed. Doctrinal clarity requires that the subjective behaviour of an undertaking is not given weight.[51] It is now certain that even in the field of intellectual property rights it is Member State measures, not private actions, that are caught by Article 28 EC.

3. The Concept of Member State

The conclusion that Article 28 EC applies only to State measures does not end the enquiry, however. It has to be determined what meaning is given to the concept of 'Member State' in this context. In general the concept does not have a fixed content in Community law. It must be interpreted in the light of the purpose and the context of the provision in which the concept appears. The concept is given the meaning which best enables the provision to achieve its aim.

Thus, in Article 230 (ex 173) EC the words 'Member State' refer only to the governmental authorities of the country. Regional governments or autonomous municipalities are not covered. This follows from the general system of the Treaty. The institutional balance has to be preserved. Therefore, the number of Member States in this context cannot be higher than the number of parties to the Treaty.[52] Similarly, Article 226 (ex 169) EC actions are rightly taken against the central government even though the fault for a breach of Community obligations may lie with, for example, regional authorities.[53]

In contrast, the duty to implement directives flows from Article 249 (ex 189) (and Article 10 (ex 5)) EC, which stipulates that '[a] directive shall be binding . . . upon each Member State to which it is addressed'. In this context the concept of 'Member State' has been interpreted broadly for the

[50] See n 48 above paras 37–46.

[51] See Marenco and Banks (n 24 above) 253–254. In addition a test based on subjective factors is 'illogical and impracticable'. See the Opinion of Advocate General Jacobs in *Bristol-Myers Squibb* (n 40 above) para 83. The Court admitted that intention is difficult to prove in *Pharmacia & Upjohn v Paranova* (n 48 above) para 41.

[52] Case C-95/97 *Region of Wallonia v Commission* [1997] ECR I-1789, para 6.

[53] See eg Case C-211/91 *Commission v Belgium* [1992] ECR I-6757.

purpose of preventing the State from taking advantage of its own failure.[54] Thus the concept encompasses, unlike in Article 230 (ex 173) EC, local and regional authorities.[55]

In other fields the concept of 'Member State' has been given yet other meanings.[56] Thus Advocate General Van Gerven has stated that 'an interpretation is sought of each measure which is most in keeping with the purpose of the concept of public authority which is used'[57] and that '[there is] a desire to ensure that the concept of "The State" is given full and proper effect, that is to say a meaning which achieves the goals of the measure in question'.[58]

The Court has interpreted the concept of Member State widely when determining which measures fall under Article 28 (ex 30) EC. It is clear, first of all, that the provision applies both to central and regional or local authorities,[59] and not only to the executive, but also to the legislature or the judiciary.[60]

Secondly, the involvement of private bodies does not make Article 28 inapplicable if the State can be seen as the source of the measure. This is the case if the State uses a controlled private body as a medium through which the measure is brought into effect.[61]

Commission v Ireland (*Buy Irish*)[62] concerned a programme promoting Irish products, which was mainly run by the Irish Goods Council, a company limited by guarantee. The Irish Government argued that the activities of the Irish Goods Council could not be attributed to the State. The Court disagreed. Since the Government appointed the members of the Council's Management Committee, granted it subsidies covering the majority of its expenses and defined the aims and the outline of the campaign, the fact that the campaign was conducted by a private company did not remove it from the scope of Article 28 (ex 30).[63]

[54] Case 152/84 *Marshall v Southampton and South-West Hampshire Area Health Authority (Teaching)* [1986] ECR 723, para 49 See also the Opinion of Advocate General Van Gerven in Case C-188/89 *A. Foster and others v British Gas plc* [1990] ECR I-3313 paras 10 and 21.

[55] Case 103/88 *Fratelli Constanzo SpA v Commune di Milano* [1989] ECR 1839.

[56] See analysis of Advocate General Van Gerven in Case C-188/89 *A. Foster and others v British Gas plc* [1990] ECR I-3313 paras 11–16.

[57] ibid para 11.

[58] ibid para 16.

[59] See Case 45/87 *Commission v Ireland* [1988] ECR 4929 and Joined Cases C-1/90 and C-176/90 *Aragonesa de Publicidad Exterior SA and Publivía SAE v Departamento de Sanidad y Seguridad Social de la Generalitat de Cataluña* [1991] ECR I-4151. See also Oliver (n 2 above) 41–42 and S Weatherill and P Beaumont, *EU Law* (3rd edn, London, 1999) 523–524.

[60] See Oliver (n 2 above) 42–43 and Weatherill and Beaumont (n 59 above) 523–524.

[61] It should be noted that additionally Article 86 (ex 90) EC may serve to bring public undertakings and undertakings to which Member States grant special or exclusive rights under the rules on the free movement of goods (and services). On these issues generally, see F Blum and A Logue, *State Monopolies under EC Law* (Chichester, 1998) 99–152.

[62] Case 249/81 *Commission v Ireland* [1982] ECR 4005.

[63] ibid para 15.

Similarly, in *Apple and Pear Development Council*[64] the functions of the Council, which was established by a Ministerial Order, were defined by the State and the members of the Council were appointed by the relevant Minister. The Council's activities were financed by a charge, which the Order enabled it to impose on growers, not by direct subsidies from the government as in *Commission v Ireland* (*Buy Irish*). This final fact was not considered significant as the Court stated that:

> a body . . . which is set up by the government of a Member State and is financed by a charge imposed on growers, cannot under Community law enjoy the same freedom as regards the methods of advertising used as that enjoyed by producers themselves or producer's associations of a voluntary character.[65]

Thus, if a policy is executed through a body established by the State and financed by it, either directly or indirectly, by means of coercive power, it can be caught by Article 28 EC. By contrast, actions of individuals or voluntary associations do not fall within the scope of the provision.

Article 28 also catches measures adopted by bodies which have been granted special powers by the State. The *Royal Pharmaceutical Society*[66] Case concerned a code of ethics adopted by the Society. The first question examined by the Court was whether the code could constitute a 'measure' in the meaning of Article 28.

The Court noted that the Society was incorporated by a Royal Charter and was recognized by the UK legislation. The Society maintained a register in which every pharmacist had to enrol, and adopted rules of ethics applicable to them. It also, most importantly, had a disciplinary committee established by law which could impose sanctions, including removal from the register, for professional misconduct. An appeal could be made to the High Court against a decision of the Committee. The Court, following Advocate General Darmon, stated that 'measures adopted by a professional body on which national legislation has conferred powers of that nature may . . . constitute "measures" within the meaning of Article 28 (formerly 30)'.[67]

The Court reached the same conclusion in *Hünermund*[68] where the relevant measure was again adopted by a pharmacists' professional association. The fact that in this case the association could not revoke a pharmacist's authorization to practise did not change the result, as other disciplinary measures such as fines could be imposed.[69]

[64] Case 222/82 *Apple and Pear Development Council v K.J. Lewis Ltd and others* [1983] ECR 4083.

[65] ibid para 17.

[66] Joined Cases 266 and 267/87 *R v Royal Pharmaceutical Society of Great Britain, ex parte Association of Pharmaceutical Importers and others* [1989] ECR 1295.

[67] ibid para 15.

[68] Case C-292/92 *Hünermund v Landesapothekerkammer Baden-Württemberg* [1993] ECR I-6787.

[69] ibid paras 14–16.

In these situations power was delegated by the State proper to a semi-private body. Instead of regulating a profession itself, the State gave the necessary powers to a professional organization.[70]

It is submitted that the concept of Member State encompasses all bodies through which the State is able to achieve a protectionist effect. The objectives of Article 28 (ex 30) EC, namely the achievement of internal market as stipulated in Articles 3(c) and 14 (ex 7a) EC through the abolition of quantitative restrictions and measures having an equivalent effect, and the uniform scope of Community law, regardless of the different regulatory structures in different Member States, require a wide, flexible concept of Member State, not a formalistic one.

It is interesting to note that the Court in *Dubois*[71] seems to have adopted a widely similar approach[72] for Articles 23 (ex 9) and 25 (ex 12) EC prohibiting customs duties and charges having equivalent effect. The case concerned a contractual charge between Garonor, a private company operating an international road station, and its customers, Dubois and Général Cargo. The charge was to compensate for various services provided by Garonor, including the costs of customs and veterinary services.

The Court found that Articles 23 and 25 EC applied to the charge even though it was not imposed by the State but arose from an agreement concluded by a private undertaking with its customers.[73] A Member State breaches Community law if it charges economic agents the cost of inspections and administrative formalities carried out by customs officers.[74] The nature of the measure requiring the economic agents to bear these costs is immaterial. Even if the charge is imposed as a result of a private contract, it stems from the failure of the Member State to fulfil its financial obligation.[75]

Once again the decisive factor was that the measure (charges) originated from the Member State[76] even though it was implemented through a private undertaking. Payments for truly private services do not fall under Articles 23 and 25[77] but the concept of Member State is interpreted widely and flexibly.

[70] It may be noted that the existence of special powers has assumed some significance in the jurisprudence concerning the extent of direct effect of directives. See Case C-188/89 *A. Foster and others v British Gas plc* [1990] ECR I-3313, paras 18 and 20 and the decision of the English Court of Appeal *Doughty v Rolls Royce* [1992] ICR 538

[71] Case C-16/94 *Édouard Dubois et Fils SA and Général Cargo Services SA v Garonor Exploitation SA* [1995] ECR I-2421.

[72] See G Tesauro, 'The Community Internal Market in the Light of Recent Case-law of the Court of Justice' (1995) 15 YEL 1, 13.

[73] See n 71 above para 21

[74] ibid para 19.

[75] ibid para 20.

[76] In fact, as pointed out by Advocate General La Pergola, the charges were created by the omission of France to bear the cost.

[77] See the Opinion of Advocate General La Pergola ibid para 5.

III. FREE MOVEMENT OF SERVICES

The wording of the Treaty would seem to indicate that Article 49 (ex 59) EC does not cover 'restrictions' created by private parties. Although the provision itself, like Article 28, is silent about the author of prohibited measures, other provisions in the same Chapter on Services show that it is the Member States that are targeted by the rules on the free movement of services. Article 50(3) (ex 60(3)) EC states that '. . . the person providing the service may . . . temporarily pursue his activity in the State where the service is provided, under the same conditions as are imposed by the State on its own nationals'. Prior to the Treaty of Amsterdam, Article 62 ECT (repealed) contained a standstill clause prohibiting the *Member States* from introducing any new restrictions. In Article 53 (ex 64) EC the *Member States* declare their readiness to undertake further liberalization of services. Article 54 (ex 65) EC requires the *Member States* to apply restrictions that have not yet been abolished without distinction on grounds of nationality or residence of the service provider. Finally, Article 46 (ex 56) EC, applicable by virtue of Article 55 (ex 66) EC, allows for the application of 'provisions laid down by law, regulation or administrative action providing for special treatment for foreign nationals on grounds of public policy, public security or public health'. Both the reference to law, regulation and administrative action, and the public nature of the exceptions indicate that the provision is targeted at the Member States.[78]

The text does not necessarily rule out the possibility that Article 49 (ex 59) EC could catch restrictions created by private bodies, however. Article 49 itself does not refer to the Member States as authors of the prohibited restrictions.

Moreover, as organs of the Member States, national courts might be called upon to ensure that private measures breaching the Treaty are not upheld. In the case of *Defrenne v Sabena*[79] the European Court of Justice decided on the scope of Article 141 (ex 119) EC on equal pay between men and women. At that time the Article stipulated that '[e]ach Member State shall during the first stage ensure and subsequently maintain the application of the principle that men and women should receive equal pay for equal work'. The ECJ found that the Article could be applied directly in national courts and, despite the reference to the Member States, covered equally the

[78] Council Directive 64/221/EEC of 25 February 1964 on the Co-ordination of Special Measures Concerning the Movement and Residence of Foreign Nationals which are Justified on Grounds of Public Policy, Public Security or Public Health OJ 1964 Special Edition 850/64 specifies the scope of the exceptions. According to Article 2 the Directive relates only to measures taken by the Member States.

[79] Case 43/75 *Gabrielle Defrenne v Société Anonyme Belge de Navigation Aérienne Sabena* [1976] ECR 455.

actions of public authorities, collective agreements and contracts between individuals, because of its mandatory nature.[80]

The General Programme on Services,[81] adopted unanimously by the Council on the Commission's proposal in 1961, defines as restrictions to be eliminated:

> [a]ny measure which, pursuant to any provision laid down by law, regulation or administrative action in a Member State, or as a result of application of such provision, or of administrative practices, prohibits or hinders . . .[82]

This clearly indicates that the Council was only concerned with Member State measures, not with the actions of private parties. However, as noted by Advocate General Warner in *Walrave and Koch*,[83] the General Programme was not complete. It did not even deal with all restrictions imposed by the Member States.

The Commission was originally of the view that Article 49 (ex 59) EC did not apply to private measures. In its submission in the seminal case *Walrave and Koch*[84] the Commission argued that the freedom to provide services, as well as the freedom of establishment, demanded only the abolition of 'discrimination arising from provision laid down by law, regulation or administrative action of *the Member States* or those "administrative procedures and practices, whether resulting from *national legislation* or from *agreements previously concluded between Member States*"'.[85]

The Court expressed its view in the same case. At issue were the rules of the *Union Cycliste Internationale* (International Cycling Association) requiring that the pacemaker riding a motorcycle had to be of the same nationality as the stayer cycling in the lee of the motorcycle. The *Union Cycliste Internationale* was an association of national bodies concerned with cycling as a sport. It was constituted of International Amateur Cycling Federation comprising over 100 national federations and International Professional Cycling Federation comprising 18 national federations. The private nature of the *Union Cycliste Internationale* was not called into question during the proceedings.

Advocate General Warner was of the opinion that Article 49 (ex 59) was not only binding on the Member States but was also 'apt to relate to restrictions imposed by anyone'. This was due to the general terms and the residual nature of Article 49 (ex 59). As his view was that Article 39 (ex 48) EC, a more specific provision, binds everyone, he thought it would be odd if the residuary provision applied to a narrower category of persons.[86]

[80] ibid paras 37, 39 and 40.

[81] OJ 1974 Special Edition, 2nd Series, IX, p. 3.

[82] ibid Title III A.

[83] Case 36/74 *Walrave and Koch v UCI* [1974] ECR 1405, 1425.

[84] ibid

[85] ibid 1410 (emphasis added).

[86] ibid 1424–1425. It is interesting to contrast this with the opinion of Advocate General Warner in Cases 55 and 57/80 *Musik-Vertrieb Membran v Gema* [1981] ECR 147 where he

The Court followed its Advocate General. It decided that the prohibition of discrimination on the basis of nationality contained in Articles 12 (ex 6), 39 (ex 48) and 49 (ex 59) EC did not only apply to the actions of public authorities but extended 'likewise to rules of any other nature aimed at collectively regulating gainful employment and services'.[87] The Court stated that otherwise organizations not under public law could compromise the achievement of the freedom of movement for persons and services and there could be unequal application of the Treaty freedoms. Moreover, the prohibition contained in Article 49 (ex 59) was expressed in general terms. Furthermore, it had been established that Article 39 (ex 48) EC extended to rules which did not emanate from public authorities and Article 49 (ex 59) had to be interpreted similarly.[88]

It is interesting to note that the Court did not go quite so far as to make Article 49 binding to all private restrictions, although it did not rule this out either. In *Walrave and Koch* only rules aimed at *collectively regulating services* were caught. The scope of Article 49 remained open.

The Court confirmed its approach in its decision in the case of *Donà v Mantero*[89] concerning the rules of the Italian Football Federation. The Court, following Advocate General Trabucchi, cited *Walrave and Koch* and stated that 'rules or a national practice, even adopted by a sporting organisation' could infringe Article 49 (ex 59), as well as Articles 12 (ex 6) and 39 (ex 48) EC, if they limited the participation in professional or semi-professional football to nationals of the State in question.[90] Again, the private nature of the rules was not questioned and again the Court did not extend the prohibition to all private measures but did not exclude them either.

The judgment of the Court in *Van Ameyde*[91] started from the assumption that private parties can infringe Article 49 (ex 59) EC. The facts of the case were somewhat complicated and are therefore only summarized briefly. The defendant, UCI, was the national insurance bureau, recognized in domestic legislation. All or most of national insurers against civil liability in respect of motor vehicles were affiliated with it. Under the so-called green card system based on a network of bilateral agreements between national bureaux and on the domestic law it was responsible for compensation for accidents caused by motor vehicles insured abroad. In this situa-

stated that 'when Article 30 (currently 28) refers to a "measure", it means a measure taken by a Member State; it does not mean a measure taken by a private person'.

87 See n 83 above para 17.

88 ibid paras 18–24.

89 Case 13/76 *Gaetano Donà v Mario Mantero* [1976] ECR 1333.

90 ibid paras 17 and 19.

91 Case 90/76 *Srl Ufficio Henry van Ameyde v Srl Ufficio Centrale Italiano di Assistenza Assicurativa Automobilisti in Circulazione Internazionale* (*UCI*) [1977] ECR 1091.

tion the foreign insurer, against which UCI had a right of regress, had to correspond with a local insurance company nominated by UCI. The nominated company was then the only entity capable of investigating the case. Van Ameyde, a loss adjuster not capable of being nominated, was thus deprived of the possibility to investigate and settle accidents on behalf of foreign insurance companies.

The Court decided, following Advocate General Reischl, that there was no restriction in the meaning of Article 49 as there was no discrimination. However, the Court was of the opinion that in principle the rules or conduct were capable of infringing Article 49. Discrimination resulting from rules of whatever kind seeking collectively to regulate the business could have been condemned. In the Court's view it was irrelevant whether the restriction 'originated in measures of public authority or, on the contrary, in measures attributable to national insurers' bureaux'.[92]

Once again, therefore, the Court confirmed that some private parties could infringe Article 49 but again it stressed the collective nature of the rules.

Haug-Adrion[93] was another case involving motor vehicle insurance. Mr Haug-Adrion, a German national, had purchased a car from Germany and registered it under customs plates as he was planning to export it to Belgium where he resided. The third party liability insurance required was issued by the Frankfurter Versicherungs-AG. The insurance company did not grant him a no-claims bonus despite the fact that Mr Haug-Adrion had driven several years without causing an accident. However, the tariff conditions of the company did not take into account the insured person's driving records when insuring vehicles with customs plates. The conditions had been officially approved by the relevant public authorities. Mr Haug-Adrion claimed, *inter alia*, that there was a restriction on the freedom to provide services.

The Court stated that Article 49 EC was intended to eliminate *all measures* which treat nationals of other Member States more severely or place them at disadvantage when compared with the Member State's own nationals.[94] It then examined the tariff conditions,[95] and found, mostly following Advocate General Lenz, that there was no infringement of Community law in so far as the refusal of no-claims bonus was based on objective actuarial criteria and applied without discrimination.[96] Thus, the Court implicitly accepted that the tariff conditions could, in principle, have fallen foul of Article 49. Yet the conditions were adopted by a single firm,

92 ibid paras 28–30.
93 Case 251/83 *Eberhard Haug-Adrion v Frankfurter Versicherungs-AG* [1984] ECR 4277.
94 ibid para 14 (emphasis added).
95 ibid paras 15–17.
96 ibid para 23.

not an association, and they were simply permitted, not mandated, by the public authorities.[97]

It is submitted, however, that this judgment does not represent a shift in doctrine.[98] First of all, there was a certain element of collectivity, as observed by the Commission.[99] In issue was not a single decision by an independently acting firm but a tariff condition based on governmental regulation and authorization and thus also presumably commonly used by other insurance companies.

Secondly, and in my view more importantly, this was a tersely reasoned judgment by a three-judge Chamber. Attention was not focused on the private character of the rules as they clearly did not infringe Article 49 anyway. If the Court really had wanted to change its doctrine, surely it would have done so in the composition of the Full Court and would have expressed itself more clearly.

Recently in *Deliège*, the Court was once again confronted with rules of sporting organizations. In accordance with settled case law it held that Article 49 (ex 59) EC applies to rules of any nature aimed at regulating the provision of services in a collective manner.[100]

Thus, the Court has not so far applied Article 49 EC to all private measures but has not ruled it out either. The judgments have gone further than in the field of the free movement of goods. Truly private measures have been caught. Crucially, the Court has not even considered it necessary to examine the potential affiliation between the author of the restriction and the State, as it always does in cases concerning the free movement of goods. It is true that the Court has used the words 'rules' and 'regulating', which have a quasi-Statal ring. It is submitted that this is a red herring and should not be given weight, however. The Court will surely condemn a private collective action restricting the free movement of services whether it takes the form of rules regulating services or not, for example actual conduct or practice. The whole system of the free movement law is based on the effect a measure has, not on its form. Despite the docrtrinal disparity, the practical effect of the differences between the free movement of goods and services has not been great. The wide interpretation given to the concept of 'Member State' in the context of goods means that the involvement of private parties does not rule out the possibility of Article 28 (ex 30) EC applying.

97 As pointed out by Advocate General Lenz who expressed doubts as to whether the approval by public authorities could be regarded as equivalent to a governmental measure and thus bring the situation within the scope of Article 29 (ex 34) EC. See ibid para 6 of his Opinion.

98 Doubts were also expressed by W-H Roth, 'Drittwirkung der Grundfreiheiten?' in Due *et al* (eds), *Festschrift für Ulrich Everling* (Baden-Baden, 1995) 1239.

99 See n 93 above 4283–4284.

100 Joined Cases C-51/96 and C-191/97 *Christelle Deliège v Asbl Ligue Francophone de judo et disciplines associées*, judgment of 11 April 2000, para 47.

As regards the free movement of workers, the correct interpretation is even wider. It may be that Article 39 (ex 48) EC applies to all private measures, at least as long as they are discriminatory.

Certainly most parts of Article 39 and the Chapter on Workers are expressed in general terms capable of applying to private measures restricting the free movement of workers. Also, the Community legislator seems to have opted for such a solution in Article 7(4) of Regulation 1612/68,[101] which provides that '[a]ny clause of a collective or *individual* agreement or of any other collective regulation concerning eligibility for employment, remuneration and other conditions of work or dismissal shall be null and void in so far as it lays down or authorises discriminatory conditions'.[102] The regulation was adopted to implement Article 39 (ex 48) EC, and the Court has held that the provision 'merely clarifies and gives effect to rights already conferred by Article 39 (formerly 48) of the Treaty'.[103] Moreover, academic literature seems generally, though by no means universally, to support the view that Article 39 applies to all private measures.[104]

The Court has now ruled explicitly in *Angonese*[105] that Article 39 (ex 48) EC applies to individual as well as collective[106] private restrictions on the free movement of workers, at least if the measure is discriminatory. In this case, a private banking undertaking required that prospective employees provide a certificate of bilinguation issued by the public authorities of the province of Bolzano. The Court held that Article 39 'precludes an employer from requiring persons applying to take part in a recruitment competition to provide evidence of their linguistic knowledge exclusively by means of one particular diploma issued only in one particular province of a Member State'.[107]

[101] Regulation 1612/68/EEC of the Council of 15 October 1968 on Freedom of Movement for Workers within the Community as Amended by Regulation 312/76, OJ 1968 Special Edition L257/2.

[102] Emphasis added.

[103] Case C-15/96 *Kalliope Schöning-Kougebetopoulou v Frei und Hansestadt Hamburg* [1998] ECR I-47 para 12.

[104] See JMF Martin, 'Re-defining Obstacles to the Free Movement of Workers' (1996) 21 EL Rev 313, 323 and S Weatherill, 'Discrimination on Grounds of Nationality in Sport' (1989) 9 YEL 55, 65 and 90 and footnotes contained therein.

[105] Case C-281/98 *Roman Angonese v Casa di Risparnio di Bolzano SpA*, judgment of 6 June 2000.

[106] For a recent discussion on the status of collective agreements see the Opinion of Advocate General Fennelly in Case C-234/97 *Maria Teresa Fernández de Bobadilla v Museo Nacional del Prado and others*, Judgment of 8 July 1999, paras 23–24.

[107] See *Angonese* (n 105 above) para 46.

IV. CRITICISM

The Court's approach to the free movement of goods and services has been doctrinally fundamentally different, for no obvious reason. It seems that no effort has been made to coordinate the jurisprudence, despite the fact that there are arguments for a uniform interpretation of the two freedoms. It is submitted that the Court should adopt a similar interpretation in both fields.[108] It is further submitted that the Court's current approach to Article 49 (ex 59) EC is too wide, as it creates a conflict with competition rules, and that the approach to Article 28 (ex 30) EC is too narrow, as it does not cover obstacles created by private non-undertakings.

The Court should view the issue of private parties from the perspective of the system of the Treaty as a whole. Neither Article 28 nor Article 49 should apply if the measures under investigation were created by one or more private undertakings. Measures adopted by private undertakings or associations of undertakings fall under the competition rules, Articles 81 (ex 85) and 82 (ex 86) EC, which should be regarded as *lex specialis*.[109]

Agreements between undertakings, decisions by associations of undertakings and concerted practices as well as actions by one or more undertakings in a dominant position are caught by Articles 81 (ex 85) and 82 (ex 86) EC if they affect trade and constitute prevention, restriction or distortion of competition, or an abuse. According to the Commission practice and the Court's case law, import and export restrictions do constitute a restriction of competition[110] or an abuse of a dominant position.[111]

Vertical agreements can be used by undertakings to partition the internal market. A supplier can, for example, prohibit a distributor from exporting his products. Both the Commission[112] and the Court[113] have found that these agreements restrict competition.[114] An agreement restricting exports

[108] See Mads Andenas and Jukka Snell, Chapter 4 above.

[109] See, however, the opinion of Advocate General Cosmas in Joined Cases C-51/96 and C-191/97 *Christelle Deliège v Asbl Ligue Francophone de judo et disciplines associées and others*, judgment of 11 April 2000. According to the Advocate General the same restriction could infringe both the provisions on the free movement of services and competition law. The Court found the national court's question concerning competition rules inadmissible, so the reference did not contain sufficient information and the case was decided on the grounds of Article 47 (ex 59) EC.

[110] See generally DG Goyder, *EC Competition Law* (3rd edn, Oxford, 1998) 121–123, Korah (n 29 above) 186–190 and R Whish, *Competition Law* (3rd edn, London, 1993) 203–205.

[111] See generally Goyder (n 110 above) 336–337, Korah (n 29 above) 121 and Whish (n 110 above) 276–277.

[112] See eg Commission decision in *Distillers* OJ 1978 L50/16.

[113] See eg the classic case Cases 56/64 and 58/64 *Etablissements Consten SA and Grundig-Verkaufs-GmbH v Commission* [1966] ECR 299.

[114] See generally Whish (n 110 above) 560–563.

can even be said to have as its object the restriction of competition, in which case it is not necessary to analyse its actual restrictive effects.[115]

Horizontal agreements can restrict trade between the Member States.[116] They can be used to share markets, which is mentioned as an example of an anti-competitive practice in Article 81(1)(c) EC, or a national cartel can act to keep foreign competitors out of the domestic market. Again, these agreements are clearly caught by Article 81 (ex 85)[117] and often the main problem may not be establishing restriction of competition but the detection and proving of the agreement or the concerted practice.

A firm can abuse its dominant position by restricting imports or exports.[118] The Commission and the Court have condemned such actions in many cases[119] and imposed significant fines on the undertakings in question.[120]

Actions by a single non-dominant firm or agreements between firms having only an insignificant effect on the market do not fall under competition rules.[121] These undertakings do not constitute a threat to market integration as they lack the power to create a protectionist effect.[122] If a supermarket, for example, decides to offer inferior or expensive domestic products instead of superior or cheap foreign ones, its customers will simply shop elsewhere.

Application of the free movement rules to acts of private undertakings would in fact amount to inefficient and unnecessary public intervention.[123] The Court with imperfect information could end up striking down private measures which in fact are based on sound business judgment. If the actions

115 See n 113 above Case 19/77 *Miller International Schallplatten GmbH v Commission* [1978] ECR 131, Case T-66/92 *Herlitz AG v Commission* [1994] ECR II-531 and Case T-77/92 *Parker Pen v Commission* [1994] ECR II-549 and Case T-175/95 *BASF AG v Commission*, judgment of 19 May 1999.

116 See generally Whish (n 110 above) 402–403.

117 See eg Case 41/69 *ACF Chemiefarma NV v Commission* [1970] ECR 661 upholding a Commission decision and Case 246/86 *S. C. Belasco and others v Commission* [1989] ECR 2117. Market sharing has been classified as an 'obvious restriction of competition', ie having as its object the restriction of competition, in Joined Cases T-374/94, T-375/94, T-384/94 and T-388/94 *European Night Services Ltd (ENS) and others v Commission* [1998] ECR II-3141, para 136.

118 See generally Whish (n 110 above) 276–277.

119 See eg Cases 40–48, 50, 54–56, 111 and 113–114/73 *Cooperatiëve Vereniging 'Suiker Unie' UA v Commission* [1975] ECR 1663 and the green banana clause in Case 27/76 *United Brands Co. and United Brands Continental BV v Commission* [1978] ECR 207.

120 See eg Case T-30/89 *Hilti AG v Commission* [1991] ECR II-1439, upheld on appeal in Case C-53/92P *Hilti AG v Commission* [1994] ECR I-667.

121 Case 5/69 *Völk v Vervaecke* [1969] ECR 295, para 7. See also Commission Notice on Agreements of Minor Importance which do not Fall Within the Meaning of Article 85(1) [now 81(1)] of the Treaty establishing the European Community OJ 1997 C372/04.

122 G Marenco, 'Competition between National Economies and Competition between Businesses—A Response to Judge Pescatore' (1987) 10 Fordham Int L J 424, 425.

123 ibid.

were based on other considerations, the market forces would punish the undertaking anyway. It would lose market share to competitors offering better value foreign products.

Additionally, it is clear that the use of free movement provisions would be unfeasible. It would be impossible, not to mention ridiculous, to demand a justification for every decision not to buy imported goods or services.[124]

Moreover, the application of Article 28 (ex 30) or 49 (ex 59) EC would be unnecessary as private undertakings with no market power do not normally have any motivation to engage in protectionist activities, and if they do, they do not stay in business for long. For a politician protectionist policies may bring votes and campaign contributions. For an undertaking such policies bring only diminished profits and decreasing market share.[125]

The system of the Treaty indicates that Articles 81 (ex 85) and 82 (ex 86) EC should be given the status of *lex specialis* when it comes to actions of undertakings. Articles 28 and 49 are primarily directed against Member State measures, while the competition rules clearly target the behaviour of private firms. The latter rules were in fact adopted in order to prevent undertakings from re-creating barriers after the Member State restrictions have been abolished.[126] They would be deprived of much of their utility if the free movement rules applied.[127]

The fact that Articles 81 and 82, in conjunction with Article 10 (ex 5) EC, has been applied to State measures,[128] does not mean that the Articles 28 and 49 should apply equally to actions of private undertakings. There is nothing in the Treaty that imposes on private parties an obligation corresponding to the duty of sincere cooperation contained in Article 10 (ex 5) EC.[129]

The system of the Treaty would also be endangered if actions exempted individually or in a group exemption by the Commission under Article 81(3) EC could be challenged under the free movement rules. The power devolved to the Commission would be made illusory and the compromises worked out by it rendered meaningless as they could be opened by litigants using free movement rules to circumvent obstacles to action under Article 81.[130]

Furthermore, the grounds of exemption listed in Article 81(3) are clearly

[124] See L Gormley, *Prohibiting Restrictions on Trade within the EEC* (Amsterdam, 1985) 261 and Oliver (n 2 above) 59.

[125] Marenco (n 122 above) 425.

[126] Roth (n 98 above) 1242.

[127] See M Quinn and N MacGowan, 'Could Article 30 Impose Obligations on Individuals?' (1987) 12 EL Rev 163, 168.

[128] See in general K Bacon, 'State Regulation of the Market and EC Competition Rules: Articles 85 and 86 Compared' (1997) 18 ECLR 283, 284.

[129] See Quinn and MacGowan (n 127 above) 170–171.

[130] See Quinn and MacGowan (n 127 above) 168–169 and Weatherill (n 104 above) 87.

designed with private agreements, decisions and concerted practices in mind. Such actions can be exempted if they improve the production or distribution of goods or promote technical or economic progress, allow consumers a fair share of the benefit, the restrictions imposed are indispensable, and competition is not eliminated.

In contrast, exceptions given in Articles 30 (ex 36) EC and, even more explicitly, in Article 46 (ex 56) EC are just as clearly meant to justify Member State measures.[131] The latter Article spells out that it exempts 'provisions laid down by law, regulation or administrative action'. Private measures are not mentioned. Public morality, public policy and public security, which are found in both provisions, are *public* concerns. This is confirmed by Directive 64/221,[132] which coordinates special measures protecting these interests, and applies by virtue of Article 2 of the Directive only to measures taken by Member States. A truly private party is seldom interested in or suitable for protecting these concerns.

In *Bosman*[133] the Court did rule that individuals could, in principle, justify restrictions to the free movement of workers on grounds of public policy, public security or public health. However, as pointed out by Fernández, this aspect of the judgment is problematic, and can sensibly only be applied when private organizations are entitled 'to regulate conditions of employment in a collective manner . . . and perform therefore a semi-public function'.[134]

Other heads of justification found in Article 30 (ex 36), the protection of health and life of humans, animals or plants, the protection of national artistic, historic or archaeological treasures, and the protections of industrial or commercial property, could in principle be used by private parties, but more naturally by public authorities. Even the two last interests, industrial or commercial property, are protected by the Member States through their laws, to which private parties then have recourse.

Public interest exceptions,[135] developed in the Court's case law,[136] are

[131] See Quinn and MacGowan (n 127 above) 175–176 and Roth (n 98 above) 1241–1242. For a similar interpretation of Article 39(3) EC see Weatherill (n 104 above) 66–67.

[132] Council Directive 64/221/EEC of 25 February 1964 on the Co-ordination of Special Measures Concerning the Movement and Residence of Foreign Nationals which are Justified on the Grounds of Public Policy, Public Security or Public Health OJ 1964 Special Edition 850/64.

[133] Case C-415/93 *Union Royale Belge des Sociétés de Football Association ASBL and others v Jean-Marc Bosman* [1995] ECR I-4921, para 86. See also Case C-350/96 *Clean Car Autoservice GmbH v Landeshauptmann von Wien* [1998] ECR I-2521, para 24.

[134] Fernández 324.

[135] Or 'mandatory requirements'.

[136] Case 33/74 *Van Binsbergen v Bestuur van de Bedrijfsvereniging voor de Metaalnijverheid* [1974] ECR 1299 and Case 120/78 *Rewe Zentrale AG v Bundesmonopolverwaltung für Branntwein* [1979] ECR 649. For a more modern example of the Court examining public interest exceptions to both the free movement of goods and services see Joined Cases C-34/95, C-35/95 and C-36/95 *Konsumentombudsmannen v De Agostini (Svenska) Förlag AB and TV-Shop i Sverige AB* [1997] ECR I-3843.

also public in their nature.[137] Even though a private party could conceivably justify its actions on the ground of, for example, consumer protection, a State can have recourse to all of the exceptions and some of them, such as maintaining the cohesion of national tax system,[138] are clearly available only to public bodies.

It should also be noted that the Commission has been given great powers of enforcement against private undertakings under the competition rules, while under the free movement rules its only enforcement powers are directed against the Member States. Regulation 17[139] grants the Commission *inter alia* the power to require that undertakings stop infringing Article 81 (ex 85) or 82 (ex 86) EC and to reinforce this decision by imposing periodic penalty payments. It even has the power to fine the undertakings concerned. In contrast, to protect the free movement of goods or services, the Commission can take Article 226 (ex 169) EC actions, but only against the Member States, and Article 228 (ex 171) EC allows the Commission to request that the Court impose a lump sum or penalty payment if the *Member State* fails to comply with the judgment. Council Regulation 2679/98 of 7 December 1998 on the Functioning of the Internal Market in relation to the Free Movement of Goods among the Member States[140] does give the Commission additional options in the field of the free movement of goods but again the powers can only be used against the Member States. This discrepancy in the Commission's powers indicates that the free movement rules are primarily directed against the Member States, not against private parties.

All of this makes it abundantly clear that competition rules are much more suitable for dealing with private parties than the free movement provisions. Thus, this aspect of the system of the Treaty strongly supports the argument that Articles 28 (ex 30) and 49 (ex 59) EC should not apply if Articles 81 and 82 EC are available.[141]

In fact, it may be speculated that the relationship between the competition rules and the different free movement rules might have been at least one reason to the dissimilar personal scope given to Articles 28 and 49 EC by the ECJ. For a long time the competition rules were not used very aggressively in the services sector. Very few cases reached the Court and as recently as 1981 in *Züchner*[142] the Counsel for the Bayerische Vereinsbank AG asserted, without much success, that banks were to a large degree

137 See Quinn and MacGowan (n 127 above) 176 and Roth (n 98 above) 1241–1242.
138 Case C-204/90 *Hans-Martin Bachmann v Belgian State* [1992] ECR I-249.
139 Regulation 17, First Regulation Implementing Articles 85 [currently 81] and 86 [currently 82] of the Treaty OJ 1962 Special Edition 204/62.
140 [1998] OJ L337/8.
141 cf, however, Baquero Cruz (n 20 above) 619.
142 Case 172/80 *Gerhard Züchner v Bayerische Vereinsbank AG* [1981] ECR 2021.

exempt from the competition rules. Therefore, it was natural for the Court to use Article 28 solely against the Member States as restrictions on the free movement of goods imposed by private parties were dealt with under competition rules, and correspondingly to extend the personal scope of Article 49 to cover some private parties.[143]

However, in certain circumstances if the private party creating obstacles to the free movement of goods or services is not an undertaking, or an association of undertakings, Articles 28 and 49 should be applicable. Otherwise, a lacuna is formed.

The concept of an undertaking in the meaning of Articles 81 and 82 EC is a wide one. It encompasses any person or entity carrying on a commercial or economic activity, in the meaning of economic trade, regardless of its legal form, even if it does not have a profit motive or an economic purpose.[144] Thus, the Commission and the Court have found that, for example, an opera singer,[145] an inventor exploiting his invention,[146] an agricultural co-operative,[147] a trade association,[148] and a customs agent[149] are undertakings for the purpose of competition rules.

However, there are also purely private entities that do not fall under the competition rules but can seriously threaten market integration. If an entity does not carry out any commercial or economic activity, it is not an undertaking and its actions are not regulated by Articles 81 and 82 EC. Examples of such bodies are an environmental pressure group or a trade union.[150] Yet, such a private non-undertaking may have both the means and the motive to re-create the barriers the Treaty seeks to abolish.

[143] Similarly, the limited impact of competition law on workers may partly explain the finding that Article 39 (ex 48) EC binds even individual employers.

[144] See generally Goyder (n 110 above) 86–87, Korah (n 29 above) 42 and Whish (n 110 above) 187–188.

[145] *RAI v Unitel* OJ 1978 L157/39.

[146] *Reuter/BASF* OJ 1976 L254/40.

[147] Case 61/80 *Coöperative Stremsel-en Kleurselfabriek v Commission* [1981] ECR 851.

[148] Case 71/74 *FRUBO v Commission* [1975] ECR 563.

[149] Case C-35/96 *Commission v Italy* [1998] ECR I-3851, paras 33–38. See also the opinion of Advocate General Cosmas paras 45–55. See also Case T-513/93 *Consiglio Nazionale degli Spedizionieri Doganoli v Commission*, judgment of 30 March 2000.

[150] DW Bellamy and G Child, *Common Market Law of Competition* (4th edn, London, 1993) 40–41 and Whish (n 110 above) 189. For an opposite view see KS Desai, 'EC Competition Law and Trade Unions' (1999) 20 ECLR 175, 176. In Case C-67/96 *Albany*, judgment of 21 September 1999, Advocate General Jacobs pointed out in paras 218–227 of his Opinion that a trade union may run a business, in which non-competition rules would apply, but that in many situations a trade union is not engaged in economic activities and may in any event only be acting as an agent of its members. The Court did not concentrate on this point but decided that collective agreements on conditions at work and employment fall outside the scope of Article 81 (ex 85) EC by virtue of their nature and purpose. See paras 59–60 of the judgment. In Case C-22/98 *Becu*, judgment of 16 September 1999, paras 25–31, the Court decided that dockers performing dock work in the Port of Ghent were not undertakings, but did not rule out the possibility that an organization of dockers could constitute an undertaking.

A private non-undertaking can create obstacles to the free movement of goods and services. For example, industrial action disrupting air traffic or blocking roads, direct action by an environmental pressure group paralysing port facilities, or a general strike aimed to pressure firms or the State to prefer domestic products can certainly severely restrict the movement of products across frontiers.

Obstacles created by these kinds of action can be just as harmful to the internal market as State-imposed restrictions. Well-directed industrial or direct action, or a general strike can have devastating consequences on the movement of products between the Member States.

This is not to say that such actions always constitute restrictions or should be condemned. Rather, it is argued that the Court ought to have a possibility to examine these actions and they should not automatically fall outside the Treaty.

Furthermore, a private non-undertaking may well have a motivation to restrict the free movement of goods or services, unlike private undertakings with no market power, which are usually motivated by profit. Members of a trade union may well calculate that protectionism would help them to achieve higher wages or to avoid lay-offs. A pressure group might place a much higher value on its particular objective than on free trade.

The application of the free movement rules to private non-undertakings would also safeguard the uniform application of Community law, which is an important principle in the Community legal system. The application of the Treaty should not be dependent on whether an individual Member State has placed certain issues into the private or the public sphere. A Member State which leaves many aspects of its socio-economic life for private groups to manage should not be placed in a more favourable position than a State which regulates these issues itself.[151]

Furthermore, in the case of trade unions, pressure groups etc the exceptions found in Articles 30 and 46 EC as well as the public interest exceptions developed in the Court's case law are easier to apply than in the case of private profit-orientated undertakings. It is more conceivable that such an entity is in reality pursuing a goal in the general interest than that a private firm is.

Private individuals acting as ultimate consumers of goods or services should not be caught by the free movement rules, however. First, the idea of the internal market is to allow consumers to choose between products from any Member State and thus allow the free market to work, not to force consumers to buy foreign products. Secondly, it would be ridiculous

[151] See Case 36/74 *Walrave and Koch v UCI* [1974] ECR 1405, para 19 and Roth (n 98 above) 1246–1247. Additionally, the public/private dichotomy is being blurred, *inter alia*, through privatization. See Baquero Cruz (n 20 above) 617.

and impossible in practice to question the justification of individual consumers purchasing decisions, even if they discriminated in favour of domestic goods and services. Finally, it can be argued that an individual consumer's decisions will usually lack the protective effect needed for the application of the free movement rules.[152] They are not capable of hindering trade actually or potentially, directly or indirectly.[153]

The last point is relevant also as regards other private non-undertakings. Some of their actions may fall outside the scope of the free movement rules as they do not have the necessary protective effect. It is important not to stretch this concept too far, however. Even though, for example, a locally arranged campaign against foreign products may have next to no effect on trade in itself, when taken together with similar actions elsewhere the cumulative effect may be substantial.

The fact that the actions of a private non-undertaking may be legal under domestic law is not of importance. National law cannot authorize the private party to infringe the Treaty. A more complicated situation arises if the action amounts to an exercise of fundamental rights. In these cases the court dealing with the case would usually find the action justified.[154]

In fact, it may be noted that in practice the result would not be too dissimilar from the current state of law in the field of the free movement of services. It would not amount to a retrograde step.[155] It would just fill the gaps in the present system, make it more coherent, and unify the approach to goods and services. Restrictions to the free movement of goods created by private non-undertakings would no longer escape the Court's scrutiny. A restriction to the free movement of services created by a private undertaking would no longer fall under both Article 49 (ex 59) EC and the competition provisions.

It must be admitted that the proposed system would not be reconcilable with the Court's interpretation of Article 39 (ex 48) EC. In *Bosman*[156] Advocate General Lenz discussed the relationship between Article 39 on the one hand and Articles 81 (ex 85) and 82 (ex 86) on the other. He came to the conclusion that nothing prevented the application of both rules to the same situation[157] and proceeded to find that both Articles 39 and 81

[152] See Case C-379/92 *Matteo Peralta* [1994] ECR I-3453 and Case C-266/96 *Corsica Ferries France SA v Gruppo Antichi Ormeggiatori del Porto di Genova Coop. arl and Others* [1998] ECR I-3949, especially para 29 of the Opinion of Advocate General Fennelly.

[153] Case 8/74 *Procureur du Roi v Dassonville* [1974] ECR 837.

[154] See on these issues also below.

[155] See also Weatherill (n 104 above) 90 who considers that an interpretation of Article 39 EC depriving it of horizontal direct effect would be an 'unacceptable retrograde step for Community law'.

[156] Case C-415/93 *Union Royale Belge des Sociétés de Football Association ASBL and others v Jean-Marc Bosman* [1995] ECR I-4921.

[157] ibid para 253 of the Opinion.

prohibited the actions of football clubs and sports associations.[158] The Court did not find it necessary to give a ruling on the competition issues as the challenged rules were already contrary to Article 39.[159] Thus *Bosman*,[160] together with the mention of individual agreements in Article 7(4) of Regulation 1612/68,[161] seems to lead to the conclusion that both the provisions on the free movement of workers and the competition rules can apply to the same situation.[162] Here the interpretation of different freedoms may simply have to diverge.[163]

V. MEMBER STATE RESPONSIBILITY FOR PRIVATE RESTRICTIONS

An alternative method of dealing with the problem of obstacles to the free movement of goods and services created by private individuals is to hold a Member State responsible for private conduct in its territory. In the recent case *Commission v France*[164] the Court, following Advocate General Lenz, opted for this solution in the field of the free movement of goods.

At issue in the case were violent acts committed by French farmers, which were directed against agricultural products of other Member States. The actions had been going on for more than a decade and the French authorities had displayed astonishing passivity towards these breaches of law and order.

The Court ruled that Article 28 (ex 30) EC, when read together with Article 10 (ex 5) EC, requires a Member State to take all appropriate measures to ensure that the free movement of goods is respected in its territory.[165] Although the Member States have the exclusive competence as regards the maintenance of public order and the safeguarding of internal

[158] ibid para 287 of the Opinion. See also the Opinion of Advocate General Alber in Case C-176/96 *Jyri Lehtonen and Asbl Castors Canada Dry Namur-Braine v Asbl Fédération royale belge des sociétés de basket-ball und Asbl Basket Liga—Ligue Basket Belgium* of 22 June 1999.

[159] ibid para 138 of the judgment.

[160] The opinion of Advocate General Lenz in *Bosman* demonstrates that even in this field competition rules are a formidable weapon against market partitioning actions of undertakings. I am of the opinion that *Bosman* should have been decided on competition law grounds. See Jukka Snell and Mads Andenas, Chapter 4 above.

[161] Regulation 1612/68 of the Council of 15 October 1968 on Freedom of Movement for Workers within the Community as Amended by Regulation 312/76 OJ 1968 Special Edition L257/2.

[162] On the problems of using both sets of rules see Weatherill (n 104 above) 87–89.

[163] See, however, the opinion of Advocate General Cosmas in Joined Cases C-51/96 and C-191/97 *Christelle Deliège v Asbl Ligue Francophone de judo et disciplines associées and others* of 18 May 1999. The Advocate General uses a similar approach to services examining the alleged restriction against both free movement and competition rules.

[164] Case C-265/95 *Commission v French Republic* [1997] ECR I-6959.

[165] ibid para 30.

security and have a wide discretion in determining the measures needed, it was for the Court to verify whether the appropriate measures had been taken.[166] The acts of violence and threats constituted obstacles, France had failed to take adequate and appropriate measures to deal with these obstacles, and the lack of action by the French authorities was not justified.[167] Thus, France had infringed Community law by failing 'manifestly and persistently' to adopt 'necessary and proportionate' measures to prevent actions by private individuals obstructing the free movement of goods.[168]

One year after the judgment was given Council Regulation 2679/98 of 7 December 1998 on the Functioning of the Internal Market in relation to the Free Movement of Goods among the Member States was adopted.[169] The regulation allows the Commission to take speedy action *inter alia* where a Member State's passivity in the face of activities of private individuals results in obstacles to the free movement of goods.

It is submitted that the reasoning of *Commission v France* applies equally if a Member State fails to take appropriate measures against private individuals creating obstacles to the free movement of services. There is simply no reason to treat the failure of a Member State to take measures against, for example, demonstrators preventing foreign doctors from operating in an abortion clinic any differently from a similar failure affecting the free movement of goods. The fact that the private parties may in some instances be infringing Article 49 (ex 59) EC themselves does not alter the conclusion. If a Member State is under an obligation to take measures to prevent actions committed by private parties which do not violate the Treaty, surely it must also have the duty to take measures to prevent private infringements of the Treaty.

The principle of Member State responsibility for private conduct does not remove the need for the interpretation of the free movement of goods and services that acknowledges their binding force towards private non-undertakings. The principle is useful especially in respect to action by private unorganized groups with no legal personality, but there are still many uncertainties and problems surrounding the principle, and it may not prove to be an adequate remedy in practice.

First, it is logically a rather curious move to place a Member State under an obligation to adopt appropriate measures to ensure that private individuals do not create obstacles to the free movement of goods, when those private individuals do not have any duty not to create those obstacles in the first place. In effect, the Court is creating an indirect obligation to private parties after failing to create the direct obligation in its earlier case law.

[166] ibid paras 33–35. [167] ibid paras 38–64. [168] ibid paras 65–66.

[169] OJ 1998 L337/8. The regulation was based on a more robust Commission Proposal, OJ 1998 C10/14.

Furthermore, it is uncertain what actions of private individuals the Member State should prevent or punish. Advocate General Lenz seems to depart from the very far-reaching assumption that a Member State has to adopt measures to prevent the same acts by private parties that it itself is prohibited from committing.[170] Thus, if the action fell *ratio materiae* under the *Dassonville*[171] and *Keck*[172] formulas and was not justified, a Member State would have to take preventative or punitive measures.

It has, however, been argued that for the Member State to have a duty to take measures, the actions of private individuals would have to have an effect on trade that is not purely local or totally insignificant. The effect and nature of the actions have to be comparable to the effects and nature of a restriction adopted by a Member State.[173] It may be noted that Article 1 of Regulation 2679/98 states that it only applies to:

obstacle . . . which:
- leads to serious disruption of the free movement of goods . . .,
- causes serious loss to the individuals affected,
- requires immediate action in order to prevent any continuation, increase or intensification of the disruption or loss in question.

The conditions given in the Regulation should not be used to limit the general duty of the Member State, however. The Regulation authorizes the Commission to take speedy action to deal with obstacles to the free movement of goods. It is natural that the scope of application of this special system is limited to the most flagrant violations.

It has to also be noted that a test based on comparability with the effects and nature of a Member State measure appears somewhat empty of meaning. A public measure may have a minimal effect on the free movement and still infringe the Treaty.[174] It may take many different forms, fall under public or private law, be legally binding or non-binding, and still fall foul of the free movement rules. There is no agreement within or between the States on the spheres of life that properly fall outside State intervention. Therefore, almost any private measure could be said to be comparable to a State measure as to its effects or nature.[175]

Furthermore, in effect the *Dassonville* formula already requires that the actions must have some protective effect to fall within the scope of the free

[170] The Opinion of Advocate General Lenz (n 164 above) para 12.
[171] Case 8/74 *Procureur du Roi v Dassonville* [1974] ECR 837.
[172] Cases C-267/91 and C-268/91 *Criminal Proceedings against Keck and Mithouard* [1993] ECR I-6097.
[173] A Maunu, 'Jäsenvaltion vastuu yksityisen oikeussubjektin aiheuttamasta sisämarkkinakaupan esteestä' (1998) DL 358, 364.
[174] See eg the arguments and the reply of the Court in Case 249/81 *Commission v Ireland* [1982] ECR 4005.
[175] cf, however, Baquero Cruz (n 20 above) 618.

movement rules. This can be used to weed out absolutely insignificant acts of private individuals. Great care has to be exercised, however, as the individual actions may have a strong cumulative impact.

Moreover, it is important to notice that the factual situation in *Commission v France* was special. First, the acts of the private parties were clearly illegal under French law. It has been argued that the principle of Member State responsibility does not sit well in situations where the actions are perfectly legal under domestic law.[176] In my view, however, the legality under national law is irrelevant. If a Member State is condemned for not applying its criminal law to certain conduct, surely it has to be equally condemned for failing to criminalize the behaviour in the first place. Quite rightly, the Court did not limit its judgment in this respect.

A more problematic situation emerges if the private individuals are exercising their fundamental rights. This would have been the case, for example, if the farmers had used their right to free speech by distributing leaflets advertising domestic products by appealing to the patriotism of consumers or attacking the quality of foreign goods. This kind of advertising campaign would infringe Article 28 (ex 30) EC if adopted by a Member State.[177] It is highly doubtful whether a Member State should have the responsibility to take measures to stop such a campaign conducted by private parties, however. At issue would be the balancing of two rights, the right to free trade and the fundamental right to free speech. Article 2 of the Regulation expressly states that it does not affect in any way the exercise of fundamental rights as recognized in Member States.

More importantly, the remedy created by the principle may not be very useful in practice. An individual who has suffered due to Member State inaction may not be able to gain effective protection.

The situation will always be complicated by the fact that the Member State, against which the legal action will be taken, is not the real source of the problem. Additionally, the Member State may try to justify its inaction by referring to the lack of resources, which may be a difficult argument for a court to deal with.[178] A judicial authority cannot, for example, easily determine that funds should have been transferred from one area of policing to another, or from health services to policing, to deal with obstacles to the free movement of goods created by private individuals.[179] Furthermore, it may be difficult for an aggrieved private party to determine in advance

[176] Maunu (n 173 above) 363–364.

[177] Case 249/81 *Commission v Ireland* (*Buy Irish*) [1982] ECR 4005.

[178] See in this respect the judgment of the House of Lords in *Regina v Chief Constable of Sussex, ex parte International Trader's Ferry Limited* [1999] 1 CMLR 1320.

[179] A court would face an even more difficult problem in a case where it was alleged that a Member State's failure to deal with structural difficulties, such as insufficient port facilities or bad roads, amounted to a violation of Article 28, read together with Article 10 EC.

whether the Member State has infringed Article 28 EC, in conjunction with Article 10 (ex 5) EC, as the Member State has a wide discretion in determining exactly what measures to adopt.[180] This may act as a deterrent for starting proceedings.

Moreover, there may not even be any remedy available as the Member State may have adopted all necessary and appropriate measures. The fact that a private party may have created an obstacle to free trade does not automatically indicate a violation by the Member State. The Member State is after all not under an obligation to guarantee a specific result, only to adopt suitable measures.[181]

An individual affected by private acts creating obstacles to free trade may attack Member State inaction either by complaining to the Commission or by starting proceedings against the Member State in a national court.[182] Both of these options have their weaknesses.

The Commission can start proceedings in the ECJ against a Member State which has failed to take measures against private conduct under Article 226 (ex 169) EC. The Article 226 procedure can be very time-consuming. In 1998 direct action proceedings in the Court alone took on average 21 months.[183] In addition, all Commission activities are constrained by the lack of resources as well as political considerations. Moreover, the judgment of the Court may not have the desired effect. It is just a declaration that a Member State has not fulfilled its Treaty obligations and carries no sanction. It will only have a real 'bite' if the Commission institutes further proceedings under Article 228 (ex 171) EC.[184]

An aggrieved individual can also take legal action in a national court

[180] See n 164 above paras 33–35 of the judgment and para 49 of the Opinion of Advocate General Lenz. See also K Muylle, 'Angry Farmers and Passive Policemen: Private Conduct and the Free Movement of Goods' (1998) 23 EL Rev 467, 471–474, who compares the approach of the ECJ to the approach of the English Court of Appeal in *R v Chief Constable of Sussex, ex parte International Traders' Ferry Ltd* [1997] 2 CMLR 164 and comes to the conclusion that the scrutiny of the ECJ is not as marginal as one might think.

[181] Advocate General Lenz was careful to make a distinction between '*obligation de moyens*' and '*obligation de résultat*'. See para 45 of his Opinion.

[182] In theory another Member State may also challenge the inaction under Article 227 (ex 170) EC.

[183] http://curia.eu.int/en/stat/index.htm. It should be noted, however, that in the context of Regulation 2679/98 the Commission is intending to impose tight deadlines and the Council has invited the Court to consider whether cases can be expedited. See Resolution of the Council and of the representatives of the Governments of the Member States meeting within the Council of 7 December 1998 on the Free Movement of Goods OJ 1998 L337/10, paras 5–7.

[184] See P Craig, 'Once upon a Time in the West: Direct Effect and the Federalization of EEC Law' (1992) 12 OJIL 453, 454–457 generally on problems relating to public enforcement by the Commission.

against the Member State which has failed to fulfil its obligations.[185] This action can be either based on the alleged direct effect of Article 28, in conjunction with Article 10 EC, or regardless of the finding on direct effect the individual can claim damages from the State.[186]

It is unlikely that the obligation of a Member State to take necessary and proportionate measures to prevent free trade from being obstructed by private conduct has direct effect.[187] A Member State is not under a duty to achieve free trade but only under a duty to adopt appropriate measures. It has a wide discretion as to the exact measures it takes, and the Court stated in *Commission v France* that it is

> not for the Community institutions to act in place of the Member States and to prescribe for them measures which they must adopt and effectively apply in order to safeguard the free movement of goods in their territory.[188]

It seems that the obligation imposed by Article 28, in conjunction with Article 10 EC, can hardly be characterized as clear and precise, unconditional and not contingent on any discretionary implementing measures, which are the requirements for a provision of Community law to have direct effect.[189]

An individual who has suffered damages as a result of Member State inaction can claim damages from the State under the principle of Member State liability established in *Francovich*[190] and further specified in *Brasserie du Pêcheur* and *Factortame*.[191] However, for an action for damages to succeed certain conditions have to be fulfilled. In many cases where it is alleged that the Member State has infringed Article 28, in conjunction with Article 10 EC, these conditions make it difficult for the action to succeed.[192]

[185] Weatherill points out that with its judgment the Court supplies the Commission with private allies in policing the internal market; see S Weatherill, 'Free Movement of Goods' (1999) 48 ICLQ 217, 222–223. Member States have agreed to ensure that rapid and effective review procedures are available for any person who has been harmed as a result of a breach of the Treaty caused by an obstacle within the meaning of Regulation 2679/98. See n 180 above para 3.

[186] Joined Cases C-6/90 and C-9/90 *Francovich and Bonifaci* [1991] ECR I-5357, where the Member State liability for a breach of Community law was first established, was a case in which the infringed provision did not have direct effect.

[187] See also the Opinion of Lord Hoffmann in n 175 above.

[188] See n 181 above para 34.

[189] See in general P Craig and G de Búrca, *EU Law, Text, Cases and Materials* (2nd edn, Oxford, 1998) 168–175 and TC Hartley, *The Foundations of European Community Law* (4th edn, Oxford, 1998) 191–196

[190] See n 186 above.

[191] Joined Cases C-46 and C-48/93 *Brasserie du Pêcheur SA v Germany* and *R v Secretary of State for Transport, ex parte Factortame* [1996] ECR I-1029.

[192] For perhaps a more optimistic view see Weatherill (n 185 above) 221–223.

It may not be easy to show that the breach is sufficiently serious.[193] According to *Brasserie du Pêcheur* and *Factortame*[194] the margin of discretion left to the national authorities is a (major) factor that a court has to take into account when deciding on the seriousness of the infringement. Article 28, when read in conjunction with Article 10 EC, leaves the Member State a wide discretion to decide what measures to adopt. A specific act may be more easily found to be a sufficiently serious breach than general inaction.

In addition, it may be difficult to establish a direct causal link between the breach and the damage.[195] The individual will have to show that if the Member State had adopted necessary and proportionate measures, the damage would not have occurred. For example, in the situation of *Commission v France*[196] the plaintiff would have to prove that if the French police had been more active and the French criminal law had been applied more vigorously, the damage caused by the violent farmers would have been prevented, or alternatively the climate of insecurity would have been avoided and trade would have been conducted bringing more profits than were otherwise achieved. This is not a simple task.[197]

Altogether, the principle of Member State responsibility for conduct of private parties in their territory is a useful addition to the Community law but does not remove the need to interpret the free movement rules in such a way that they catch the actions of private non-undertakings in certain circumstances.[198]

VI. CONCLUSION

It has been demonstrated that the scope of application of Articles 28 (ex 30) and 49 (ex 59) EC to the actions of private parties is not the same. The provisions on the free movement of goods only apply to Member State measures while at least some restrictions created by private parties are caught by Article 49. There does not seem to be any sensible grounds for this difference of interpretation. It is submitted that the ECJ ought to adopt

[193] The second condition established in n 191 above paras 51 and 55–64.

[194] See n 191 above para 56.

[195] See n 191 above paras 51 and 65. See also MA Jarvis, 'Case C-265/95, *Commission v French Republic*, Judgment of the Court of Justice of 9 December 1997' (1998) 35 CML Rev 1371, 1382.

[196] Case C-265/95 *Commission v French Republic* [1997] ECR I-6959.

[197] It has also been argued that it may not be easy to establish that Article 28, in conjunction with Article 10 EC, is a rule of law intended to confer rights on individuals. See Jarvis (n 195 above) 1382. This condition was established in n 191 above paras 51 and 54. According to para 54 of the judgment Article 28 in itself does fulfil the condition.

[198] See also Baquero Cruz (n 20 above) 611.

a unified approach to both freedoms. This approach should recognize the *lex specialis* status of competition rules, but apply Articles 28 and 49 to obstacles created by private non-undertakings. The decision of the Court in *Commission v France*[199] helps to alleviate the problem but does not remove the need for this reinterpretation.

The analysis has also demonstrated the inadequacy of the vertical/horizontal direct effect dichotomy in interpreting Treaty provisions. It is not an appropriate tool.[200] The crucial starting point is that the Treaty provisions are *capable* of having both forms of direct effect, unlike for example Directives. After this has been established, the relevant provisions are best constructed by using normal interpretative principles, such as *lex specialis*, found also in domestic legal systems.

[199] Case C-265/95 *Commission v French Republic* [1997] ECR I-6959.
[200] See Baquero Cruz (n 20 above) 604–606.

9

On the Border of Abuse: the Jurisprudence of the European Court of Justice on Circumvention, Fraud and Abuses of Community Law

ANDERS KJELLGREN[1]

It is quite clear that the principle 'Community law cannot be relied on for abusive or fraudulent ends' is a consistent principle in the jurisprudence of the Court . . . To define the principle more precisely is, however, far from easy.

Advocate General La Pergola
16 July 1998[2]

I. INTRODUCTION

Most legislators have probably acknowledged the problematic relationship between the spirit of the law and its practical applications. The ways to prevent 'unintended' usage of legal rights can be diverse—for instance, more detailed rules may be introduced in order to stop circumvention or fill in loopholes detected. In many cases, however, for the legislator to use such practices would, in reality, often amount to the fighting of a losing battle. Circumvention in many cases thrives on detailed rules, making use of the more textual—albeit seldom purpose-oriented—interpretations of applicable legal norms. What, then, can the legislator do? One of the possibilities is to introduce legal norms of more general applicability in order to combat 'abuse' of legal rights. The concept of 'abuse-control' in this sense is therefore, and by necessity, connected with a certain degree of uncertainty. The very *raison d'être* may very well be to introduce a certain measure of discretion for the authorities in situations where rules technically speaking are applied correctly but where the legal outcome nevertheless is considered 'abusive' by society.

[1] The author wishes to thank Pedro Cabral and Carl Fredrik Bergström for valuable comments. The usual disclaimer applies.

[2] See para 20 (my translation) of his Opinion in Case C-212/97 *Centros* [1997] ECR I-1459, discussed further below.

The EC Treaty itself refers to 'misuse of powers' as one of the grounds for judicial review of Community legal acts under Article 169 (ex 173) EC and the European Court of Justice (hereafter referred to as the Court) has also rejected certain references for preliminary references with the motivation that they amounted to misuse of the said procedure. In the former situation, it is clearly for the Court to decide whether misuse of powers has been present but the actual cases where this ground has been applied are quite rare. With regard to the well-known ruling in *Foglio v Novello,*[3] one can observe the criticism directed towards it for essentially disregarding the wording of Article 234 (ex 177) EC, substituting the national court's judgment by its own as to the assessment of the need for a reference,[4] and the apparent lack of further cases confirming the position of the Court.[5] These applications of the notion of abuse will not be further discussed here. This chapter will instead focus on the proposed applications of the principle of abuse, spurred on by the Member States and/or their national courts, to Community rules.

Principles of abuse of rights, or practical equivalents, do exist in several of the Member States[6] but far from all. Hence, the Court has been confronted with two principal questions: are national courts permitted to apply their national rules on abuse to situations where the rights in question stem from Community provisions, and/or does the Community legal system itself contain a principle of abuse which national courts may apply?

This chapter will review a substantial number of cases in which the Court (and a number of Advocates General) have commented on these questions; in themselves reflecting issues related not only to the supremacy of Community law but also to the doctrine of justified Member State derogations from the fundamental principle of free movement.

II. THE MANY FACES OF ABUSE

Abuse of rights can take many forms. In the context of Community law, the practice of so-called U-turn constructions has received special attention.

[3] Case 104/79 *Foglio v Novello* I [1980] ECR 745 and the subsequent Case 244/80, *Foglio v Novello (No 2)* [1981] ECR 3045.

[4] cf eg A Barav, 'Preliminary Censorship? The Judgement of the European Court in Foglio v Novello' (1980) 5 EL Rev 413.

[5] Note, here, especially the judgments in Cases 46/80 *Vinal v Orbat* [1981] ECR 77 and C-150/88 *Eau de Cologne v Provide* [1989] ECR 3891; in particular the latter can be seen as a reversal of the *Foglio* judgment.

[6] See, for a classic survey of the issue, Neville Brown, 'Is there a General Principle of Abuse of Rights in European Community Law?' in Heukel and Curtin (eds), *Institutional Dynamics of European Integration*, vol II (Dordrecht, 1994) 513–515.

Undisputedly, Treaty rules on free movement and a number of other Community provisions that do not totally harmonize the areas concerned normally do not apply to purely internal situations; hence, the legitimate option for a Member State to maintain or introduce more stringent rules for the home population and domestic production than for parties and products from another Member State (the right to reverse discrimination). If persons or goods belonging to a certain Member State would be beneficiaries of Community rights by swiftly crossing the border to another Member State and then immediately return, the first Member State's rights to apply more stringent, internal rules would be seriously threatened and, in at least some cases, probably render the choice of higher standards in relation to implementation of minimum Directives practically meaningless. A similar kind of evasion of national rules, usually involving the provisions relating to the freedom to provide services, is often referred to as *circumvention*. By placing oneself under the jurisdiction of one Member State and then carry out activities directed towards another Member State, the host State's normally applicable rules can be disregarded.

If circumvention often makes use of a cross-border element, there are, however, other possible forms of rights misused. In certain situations, the invocation, although formally correct, of rights contained in harmonized rules may be perceived as producing unwanted outcomes or unfairness, thereby applying to the wielding of the right the label 'abusive'. Admittedly, the dividing line between abuse in the sense of circumvention above and *misuse in general* is not always that clear.

Fraud can be perceived as a special form of abuse, although the claim to rights invoked here generally are based on objectively false premises. Most people would probably not consider it strange to deny Community rights to domestically produced goods which, according to forged documents, have been 'imported'. We would simply conclude that the goods in question actually never did cross the necessary border for the Community rules to apply. Consider, however, a situation where a person has received a residence permit on false grounds and, because of this, is able to stay for a very long time in the host State. Later, when faced with deportation after the fraud has been detected, the person invokes Community rights earned on the basis of the long time now spent in the country: will the initial fraud corrupt all such subsequent, secondary claims?

For the purpose of distinguishing between the different forms of abuse encountered in the case law of the Court, the three catgegories mentioned above—circumvention, misuse and fraud—will be used.

III. THE DOCTRINE ON ABUSE OF COMMUNITY RIGHTS

1. *Van Binsbergen*: The Origins of a Principle?

The first foundation of the Court's doctrine on abuse emerged in the well-known *van Binsbergen* judgment of 1974.[7] The case established the direct effect of Article 49 (ex Article 59) EC and struck down a national requirement on habitation for service providers as being contrary to the very essence of their right to free movement. The Court made clear that, in principle, specific requirements imposed on persons providing services could not—given the particular nature of the service provided (legal advice)—be considered incompatible with the Treaty.[8] That declaration, forming the basis for the *Cassis de Dijon*-like doctrine on mandatory requirements in the areas of free movement of services and establishment, was followed by this statement:

> Likewise, a member state cannot be denied the right to take measures to prevent the exercise by a person providing services whose activity is entirely or principally directed towards its territory of the freedom guaranteed by Article 59 for the purpose of avoiding the professional rules of conduct which would be applicable to him if he were established within that state; such a situation may be subject to judicial control under the provisions of the chapter relating to the right of establishment and not of that on the provision of services.[9]

The *van Binsbergen* statement, persistently cited in the later case law of the Court on the question of abuse, actually seems to be of relatively limited applicability. On the face of it, it only seems to grant a Member State a right to apply its rules of professional conduct not only to established persons but also to service-providers, on the condition that the latter's activities are entirely or principally directed towards the state's territory and this for the purpose of avoiding the professional rules of that state: in other words, an acceptance of host State control in situations where the host State's professional rules otherwise would be circumvented. The circumvention statement contained, however, a number of ambiguous issues. Was it supposed to work as a classifying division-line between being a provider of services and being established? What kind of measures, more exactly, was the host State allowed to adopt? Did the statement only apply to circumvention of professional rules? How much activity would be needed in order to qualify for the criteria 'principally directed towards' a Member State? Was the host State's right to take action against circumventors to be considered as a derogation

[7] Case 33/74 *van Binsbergen v Bestuur van de Bedriffsvereniging voor de Metaalnijverheid* [1974] ECR 1299.
[8] ibid para 12.
[9] ibid para 13.

from the principle of free movement (thereby to be scrutinized accordingly) or rather as a delimitation of the principle itself (thereby not really needing any special justification for its application)?

The first three of these questions have been, at least partly, answered by the Court in subsequent cases.[10] Others remain vital objects for debate.[11] I will briefly return to the last two questions at the end of this chapter.

2. Fraud: The More Obvious Cases

In *van de Bijl*,[12] the validity of a certificate attesting that the Dutch painter van de Bijl had been active in the trade abroad[13] was questioned by the Dutch authorities. One of the reasons for this was that van de Bijl actually had been employed in the Netherlands during the period in which he, according to the certificate, had been pursuing the trade in the United Kingdom. Advocate General Darmon noted that the system introduced by the Directive might be deprived of its efficacy if the host States were recognized as having extensive powers to check the accuracy of the certificates in question beyond 'strictly formal' checks for patent, obvious flaws etc.[14] However, on account of the principle that 'fraud vitiates everything',[15] he considered that the competent national authorities could refuse to take account of fraudulently obtained certificates.

The Court, however, stated that the Community system of certificates would be deprived of its effectiveness if the host Member State were not, in principle, bound by issued certificates. As to the question of manifest inaccuracies, the host State could always approach the Member State that issued the certificate and request further information.[16] After this initial general statement the Court continued in a way that obviously did not endorse the proposed general principle of 'fraud vitiates everything'.

[10] The test is not supposed to differentiate between services and establishment as such, but mainly permits the host State to treat a provider of services as if he had been established in the State; see Cases C-23/93 *TV 10* and Joined Cases C-34–36/95 *DeAgostini*; both discussed below, and C-56/96 *VT4 Ltd v Vlaamse Gemeenschap* [1997] ECR I-3143; the latter commented on in A Türk, 'Recent Case Law in Services and Establishment' (1998) 9 EBLR 193–202, at 194. The exact nature of 'measures' has not been defined, but seems to permit a number of effective national sanctions as long as the cause is justified (see, eg, Case C-148/91 *Veronica* and Case 130/88 *van de Bijl*; both discussed below). By linkage to other areas of Community law, the basic statement in *van Binsbergen* has been extended to cover situations with less obvious links to professional conduct (or, if one prefers to view it in another way, to a very extensive notion of 'professional conduct').

[11] See, for instance, LH Hansen, 'The Development of the Circumvention Principle in the Area of Broadcasting', LIEI 1998/2, 117–120.

[12] Case 130/88 *van de Bijl v Staatssecretaris van Economische Zaken* [1989] ECR 3039.

[13] Thereby being eligible for the rights to perform professionally in another Member State in accordance with Directive 64/427/EEC, OJ 1964 117/1863.

[14] Opinion of the Advocate General, para 14.

[15] ibid para 17; *fraus omnia corrumpit.*

[16] ibid Judgment, paras 22–24.

However, in cases where it is established that a person covered by the Directive has completed a period of insurance or employment in the territory of the host Member State, during the period of professional experience which, according to the certificate, that person has completed in the Member State from which he comes, then the host Member State is not bound by the certificate from the competent authority in the Member State from which that person comes with regard to the duration of the activity pursued in the latter State:

In those circumstances, the host Member State cannot be obliged to overlook matters which occurred within its own territory and which are of direct relevance to the real and genuine character of the period of professional activity completed in the Member State from which the beneficiary comes. Nor may the host Member State be refused the right to take measures in order to prevent the freedom of establishment and the freedom to provide services, which the directive is designed to assure, from being exploited by interested parties with the object of circumventing the rules relating to occupations which that State imposes on its own nationals.[17]

In *Suat Kol*,[18] a Turkish man, Mr Kol, had obtained a permanent residence permit based on false statements concerning his marriage to a German woman. He was later fined for having made the false declaration and an expulsion decision directed towards him was taken. Mr Kol appealed against the decision and claimed that he had a Community-based right to stay in the country because he now had fulfilled a period of legal employment in accordance with specific provision based on the EEC–Turkey Association Agreement.[19] The employment, though, had been carried out during a period under which he had been able to stay in Germany solely because of his purported marital status. Advocate General Elmer concluded that it could scarcely be in accordance with the relevant Community provisions to reward such culpable conduct, which would encourage others to give fraudulent declarations to the immigration authorities of the Member States.[20] The Court was of the same opinion and stated that periods of employment after a residence permit had been obtained only by means of fraudulent conduct, which had lead to a conviction, could not be regarded as legal for the purposes of the relevant Community provision, as the Turkish national did not fulfil the conditions for the grant of such a permit which was, accordingly, liable to be rescinded when the fraud was discovered.[21] The Court also added that employment under a residence permit issued as a result of a fraudulent conduct which had lead, as in the

[17] Opinion of the Advocate General, paras 25–26.
[18] Case C-285/95 *Suat Kol v Land Berlin* [1997] ECR I-3079.
[19] Decision 1/80 of the EEC–Turkey Association Council.
[20] Opinion of the Advocate General, para 19.
[21] Judgment, para 26.

present case, to a conviction, could not give rise to any rights in favour of the Turkish worker, or arouse any legitimate expectation on his part.[22]

3. Fraud: The Dubious Cases

The *Paletta* Case[23] concerned the Community system for migrant workers' sickness benefit. The Paletta family consisted of Italian nationals, all employed by a company in Germany. During the summer leave, the whole family reported sick; something they allegedly had done also during previous years' leaves. They notified the company sickness fund of their incapacity for work and sent a sickness fund certificate issued by a local Italian health unit. The company, however, refused to pay their wages, stating serious doubts as to their alleged incapacity for work, as they once again had fallen sick simultaneously during their holidays. The question referred to the Court was whether the Italian health certificate bound the employer, regardless of the circumstances, being part of the Community social security scheme.[24] The Court had already stated that exclusive evidentiary effect had to be given to the declarations of the doctor in the country where the worker was staying and that a doubtful employer at the most could send a doctor of his choice to the country where the worker was staying, in order to examine him there;[25] the latter a choice not in practice available to the employer of the Paletta family. Advocate General Mischo concluded that the findings of the national institutions might be called into question by a competent authority, if the findings were obtained as a result of fraudulent conduct which misled the institution of the place of residence, and/or they subsequently proved to be manifestly incorrect.[26] Mischo based his conclusion partly by reference to the judgments in *Lair*[27] and *van de Bijl*,[28] in which he considered that the Court had expressly ensured that the interpretation of a provision of Community law was not to be applicable to situations constituting abuse or fraud.[29] He noted[30] that the Court in *van de Bijl* had not expressly based its reasoning on the general principle of *fraus omnia corrupit*, as had been suggested by the Advocate General. Although the Court obviously deemed it sufficient to prevent Community law from being applied in a way 'which went against common sense and ignored obvious and undeniable realities', the fact remained that *van de Bijl* could

[22] ibid para 28.
[23] Case C-45/90 *Paletta and others v Brennet AG* (*Paletta No 1*)[1992] ECR I-3458.
[24] Set up by Regulations 1408/71, OJ 1971 L149/2 and 574/72, OJ 1972 L74/1.
[25] Case 22/86 *Rindone v Allgemeine Ortskrankenkasse Bad Urach-Münsingen* [1987] ECR 1339.
[26] Opinion of the Advocate General, para 30.
[27] Case 39/86 *Lair v Universität Hannover* [1988] ECR 3161, discussed below.
[28] See n 12 above, discussed below.
[29] ibid paras 32–34.
[30] ibid para 34.

be regarded as a precedent in situations where one otherwise would be forced to recognize manifestly incorrect situations and/or possibly fraudulently obtained findings. In view of the importance of the case, the chamber hearing it decided to refer the case to the full court. The oral procedure was re-opened and Advocate General Gulmann issued a new Opinion. The circumstances in *van de Bijl* had been, in his opinion, very specific and he noted that the question of disputed periods in that case made the host State best situated to assess that part of the certificate but not so in this case.[31]

The Court emphasized that the difficulties of checking the accuracy of issued certificates in accordance with the Community provisions could not alter the fact that the host State was bound by an issued certificate. The Court also stated that the reported difficulties present in the case could be resolved by further national or Community-based legislation to improve information exchange and the like.[32]

Despite this ruling, the Court was soon faced with a new reference in *Paletta (No 2)*,[33] this time asked to comment on whether its previous judgment had barred a suspicious employer from adducing evidence, in order to prove that the Community provisions requiring payments to be made had been abused. In Advocate General Cosmas' opinion, in cases where the findings reported in the certificate did not correspond to the truth, a worker would not be entitled to protection under the provisions of Community law: this followed, according to Cosmas, by virtue of the Roman law principle of *fraus omnia corrumpit*, which—although not expressly recognized by the Court—had been suggested by Advocate General Darmon in *van de Bijl* and Advocate General Mischo in *Paletta (No 1)*.[34] He noted that the Court had recognized that host States were not bound by certificates in certain wholly exceptional cases, and, in *Lair*,[35] that abuses established on the basis of 'objective evidence' were not covered by the Community provisions in question. Given the harsh requirement set up by the Court, the Advocate General suggested that employers only would be able to rebut the presumption of the certificates' correctness if their evidence conclusively proved, not only indicated a probability of, abuse.[36]

The Court made a special point of stating that it had not specifically considered the question of abuse or fraudulent use of the relevant Community provision in *Paletta (No 1)*.[37] In comparison to earlier cases, the Court thereafter made a more complex reference to its position regarding these issues:[38]

[31] Opinion, para 12. [32] Judgment, para 27.
[33] Case C-206/94 *Brennet AG v Paletta* (*Paletta* (*No 2*)) [1996] ECR I-2382.
[34] Opinion of Advocate General Cosmas, paras 50–52.
[35] See n 27 above. [36] ibid paras 56–60.
[37] Judgment, para 23. [38] ibid paras 25–26.

As to [whether the national court may, in cases of abuse by the concerned worker, query the certificate of incapacity of work] the Court has consistently held that Community law cannot be relied on for the purposes of abuse and fraud (see, in particular, regarding freedom to provide services, Van Binsbergen and TV 10;[39] regarding the free movement of goods, Leclerc;[40] regarding freedom of movement for workers, Lair; regarding the Common Agricultural Policy, General Milk.[41]

Although the national courts may, therefore, take account, on the basis of objective evidence, of abuse or fraudulent conduct on the part of the worker concerned in order, where appropriate, to deny him the benefit of the provisions of Community law on which he seeks to rely, they must nevertheless assess such conduct in the light of the objectives pursued by those provisions.

After this general statement, the Court added that national requirements under which a worker had to produce additional evidence that the certified incapacity for work was genuine in cases where this was disputed by the employer, were not compatible with the objectives pursued by the relevant Community provision. In fact, the system set up by these provisions sought to eliminate the workers' difficulties in obtaining evidence when the incapacity for work arose in another Member State. This, however, did not preclude employers from adducing evidence to support, where appropriate, a finding by the national court of abuse or fraudulent conduct on the part of the worker concerned, in that, although he might have claimed to have been incapacitated for work and had that condition certified, he was not sick at all.[42]

In *Faik*,[43] the EEC–Turkish Agreement in relation to free movement of persons again appeared before the Court. Mr Faik Günaydin, a Turkish national, had been granted a residence permit in Germany based on an employment arrangement with his German employer. It was envisaged that Mr Günaydin would spend about three years in Germany, after which he would be given a supervisory or managerial post in one of the company's subsidiaries and then be posted to Turkey. However, in the end of the relevant period he instead applied for a permanent residence permit on the ground that, because of the time spent working in Germany, the country had become his real home. The application was supported by his employer, but rejected. The question was whether Mr Günaydin, as possibly belonging to the labour force of a Member State in the meaning of the relevant

[39] C-23/93 *TV 10 SA v Commissariaat voor de Media* [1994] ECR I-4795; discussed further below.

[40] C-229/83 *Association des Centres distributeurs Édouard Leclerc et al v SARL 'Au blé vert' et al* [1995] ECR 1; further discussed below.

[41] C-8/92 *General Milk Products GmbH v Hauptzollamt Hamburg-Jonas* [1993] ECR I-799; discussed further below.

[42] ibid paras 26–28.

[43] Case C-36/96 *Faik Günaydin and others v Freistaat Bayern* [1997] ECR I-5143.

provision, could rely on Community law[44] in order to support his claim for a residence permit. Germany claimed that this could not be the case, as he had obtained the permission to reside on the express condition that he was to leave the country as envisaged from the beginning and that his exercise of such a right in any case would amount to an abuse since he had accepted the initial restriction and had declared his intentions of returning to Turkey after the set period.

Advocate General Elmer, after having interpreted the relevant Community provision and having found that Mr Günaydin did belong to the labour force in the sense of that provision, turned to the question of abuse. In his view, abuse implied an element of deception.[45] He referred to his opinion in *Suat Kol* and concluded that the crucial point was whether the person concerned fraudulently obtained the residence permit, namely by knowingly providing inaccurate information to, or deliberately concealing relevant matters from, the authorities concerned. On the other hand, where at a particular time a Turkish national, acting in good faith, provided information about his personal situation and his intentions, but where the position subsequently changed, without any fault on the part of the person concerned, for example, because of general social developments, that would not constitute deception but rather a failure of general conditions. It seemed unreasonable to Elmers that the Turkish national alone should have to bear the risk for such failures.

The Court went along with the interpretation of the relevant Community provision suggested by the Advocate General. As to the question of abuse, the Court, which by then had stated that this case differed from *Suat Kol* in the sense that Mr Günaydin's right to reside had been undisputed and his situation not insecure, stated that an application of the relevant Community provision could not, in principle, be considered improper because of the worker's previously expressed intention to leave the territory and the fact that he, in the end, instead applied for a permanent residence permit. The Court pointed out that it quite possibly could be that Mr Günaydin really had the intention to return at first, but that new and reasonable considerations had prompted him to change his mind.[46] In such circumstances, it was only if the national court established that the Turkish worker made the statement that he wanted to leave the host State after a specific period with the sole intention of inducing the competent authority to issue requisite permits on false premises, that he could be deprived of the rights flowing from the relevant Community provision in question.[47]

[44] By way of Decision 1/80 of the EEC–Turkey Association Council on the development of the Association.

[45] Opinion of the Advocate General, para 37.

[46] Judgment, paras 58–59.

[47] ibid para 60.

4. Circumvention through U-Turn Constructions

In *Knoors,*[48] the Court had the opportunity to comment on national fears for circumvention in the area of free movement of persons. Knoors, a Dutch plumber, invoked rights under Directive 64/429/EEC[49] in order to continue in the profession on account of qualifications acquired in Belgium. The Netherlands claimed that Knoors, being a Dutch national himself, could not be a beneficiary of the Directive but instead was subject to the relevant Dutch national provisions governing access to the plumbing trade. If nationals of the host State could be subject to the rules of the Directive, this would lead to circumvention of that host State's special provisions regarding the exercise of certain occupations.

Advocate General Reischl found no reason to agree with this fear, as the rules of the Directive itself provided for requirements of foreign practices which in themselves were not so easily fulfilled. It could not be expected that any substantial number of nationals of the host State would use this way to avoid provisions of national law relating to training and examination.[50]

The Court, while confirming that the Treaty provisions relating to establishment and services could not be applied to purely internal situations, basically stated that this was not the case in situations similar to the one at hand. The fact that Knoors was a national of the host State could not exclude him from the benefits of Community law. As to the question of circumvention, the Court added that it was, however:

> not possible to disregard the legitimate interests which Member States may have in preventing certain of its nationals, by means of facilities created under the Treaty, from attempting wrongly to evade the application of their national legislation as regards training for a trade.[51]

After this statement, the Court however noted that the risk of abuse in the present situation effectively was excluded by the precise requirements of the Directive itself. In addition, it remarked that the Council always had the possibility to remove the cause of any abuse of the law by arranging for the harmonization of the trade-training conditions amongst the Member States.[52]

Leclerc 'Au blé vert'[53] concerned, amongst other issues, a U-turn construction in the area of free movement of goods. The French law in question made all books published in France subject to a system of retail

[48] Case 115/78 *J Knoors v Secretary of State for Economic Affairs* [1979] ECR 399.

[49] Concerning the Attainment of Freedom of Establishment and Freedom to Provide Services in respect of Activities of Self-employed Persons, OJ 1964 117/1880.

[50] Opinion of the Advocate General, para 4.

[51] Judgment, para 25.

[52] ibid paras 26–27.

[53] See n 40 above.

price-fixing. The system also applied to books exported from France and subsequently re-imported following exportation to another Member State. The French Government argued that the law was justified and that its inclusion of re-imported books prevented the re-importation from being used as a device for circumventing the law. Advocate General Darmon found that where a retailer exported domestically published books for the sole purpose of re-importation, this was to be classed as an artificial trade flow. He concluded, 'one cannot both avail oneself of the rules of the single market and at the same time take improper advantage of the existence of frontiers. Only *normal* commercial transactions may qualify for Community protection.'[54]

As to the issue of re-importation, the Court found the French requirements on retail prices constituted a measure equivalent in effect to a quantitative restriction on imports and therefore contrary to Article 28 (ex 30) EC.[55] However, it also added the following:

> However, the above finding is not applicable where it is established that the books in question were exported for the sole purpose of re-importation in order to circumvent legislation of the type at issue.[56]

The following year, in 1986, the Court's judgment in the *German Insurance* Case[57] reiterated the anti-circumvention statement from *van Binsbergen*.[58] In 1989, in *van de Bijl* (see under section 2 above), the Court also reaffirmed that Member States were allowed to take measures against interested parties, wishing to exploit Community provisions in order to circumvent national rules applicable to the domestic population and concerning occupations. This point was also made in *Bouchoucha*,[59] where a French national with a British diploma in osteopathy had challenged French rules, requiring practitioners of osteopathy to be doctors of medicine. The Court concluded that the area was not harmonized and that the British diploma did not, at present, enjoy any mutual recognition within the Community (as opposed to the situation in, for instance, *Knoors*). It added, with special reference to *Knoors*, that it was not possible to disregard the legitimate interest which a Member State might have in preventing certain of its nationals, by means of facilities created under the Treaty, from attempting to evade the application of their national legislation as regarded vocational training: that was true in particular where the fact that a national of a Member State had obtained in another Member State a

[54] Opinion of the Advocate General, para 17.
[55] Judgment, paras 25–26.
[56] ibid para 27.
[57] Case 205/84 *Commission v Germany* [1986] ECR 3755.
[58] ibid para 22 of the judgment.
[59] Case C-61/89 *Criminal proceedings against Marc Gaston Bouchoucha* [1990] ECR I-3551.

diploma, whose scope and value was not recognized by any Community provision, might place his Member State of origin under an obligation to allow him to exercise the activities covered by that diploma within its territory even though access there to those activities was restricted to the holders of a higher qualification which enjoyed mutual recognition at Community level and there was nothing to indicate that the restriction was arbitrary. In conclusion, the French rules were considered legitimate.[60]

The well-known case *Surinder Singh*[61] also contained references to the question of abuse in connection with Directive 73/148/EEC.[62] The United Kingdom argued that Mr Singh could not be considered to have any Community law-derived right to remain in the country just because his wife had worked in Germany and then returned to take up professional activity in her home State (as the British rules had as their legitimate objective to prevent foreigners from obtaining a right of residence by way of fictive marriages). The granting of a right of residence to the spouse and other dependent relatives of a British citizen who were not nationals of a Member State would create a real risk of abuse, because that citizen would merely have to travel to another Member State for the purpose of pursuing an economic activity there in order for the nationals of non-member countries to be allowed to enter and reside in the United Kingdom following his or her return. Advocate General Tesauro acknowledged that the concerns for evasion of national rules certainly reflected a real need that merited the greatest attention. He pointed to the Court's jurisprudence within the field of professional training (*Knoors*) but also on the requirements laid down as to the genuine and effective economic nature of occupational activity qualifying someone in accordance with Community law.[63] He also noted that the Directive in question actually allowed Member States to derogate from its provisions on grounds of public policy, public security or public health.[64]

The Court was even shorter.

> As regards the risk of fraud referred to by the United Kingdom, it is sufficient to note that, as the Court has consistently held (see, in particular the judgment in Knoors and Bouchoucha), the facilities created by the Treaty cannot have the effect

[60] Judgment, paras 14–16. The Court's reasoning is interesting, not least in the light of the subsequent year's judgement in *Vlassopolou* (Case C-340/89 *Vlassopoulo v Ministerium für Justiz, Bundes- und Europaangelegenheiten Baden-Würtenberg* [1991] ECR I-2357), where Member States were required by the duty of loyalty to evaluate foreign qualifications and educations even those that had not been subject of any harmonization.

[61] Case C-370/90 *R v Immigration Appeal Tribunal et Surinder Singh, ex parte Secretary of State for Home Department* [1992] ECR I-4265.

[62] On the Abolition of Restrictions on Movement and Residence within the Community for Nationals of Member States with regard to Establishment and the Provision of Services, OJ 1973 L172/14).

[63] cf Case 66/85 *Lawrie Blum v Land Baden Württenberg* [1986] ECR 2121 and Case 139/85 *Kempf v Staatssecretaris van Justitie* [1986] ECR 1741.

[64] Opinion of the Advocate General, para 14.

of allowing the persons who benefit from them to evade the application of national legislation and of prohibiting Member States from taking measures necessary to prevent such abuse.[65]

In 1993 a case concerning the CAP was decided: *General Milk*.[66] One of the principal issues here was the impact of a (possible) U-turn construction, granting Monetary Compensation Amounts (MCAs) on imported and then re-exported Cheddar cheese. Advocate General Darmon discussed the issue but concluded that there seemed to be no evidence in the case at hand which suggested that the release for free circulation had been purely fictitious in order solely to qualify for positive MCAs on re-exportation.[67]

The Court found no reason to prevent MCAs from being applied in the present situation but added that the position would be different if it could be shown that the importation and re-exportation of the cheese were not realized as bona fide commercial transactions but only in order wrongfully to benefit from the grant of MCAs. The bona fide nature of the transactions was a question of fact to be decided by the national court.[68]

5. Circumvention in the Field of Broadcasting

In the 1990s came a number of judgments on circumvention in the field of television transmissions. A special consideration in these cases was the Television Without Frontiers Directive,[69] aiming at the harmonization of the area. Although the exact extent of this harmonization has been debated,[70] the Directive in general aims for a system of home State control. However, the amended Directive expressly recognizes the existence of the Court's jurisprudence on circumvention.[71] The question as to whether the invocation of the circumvention doctrine in each individual case has been justified has merited special attention by the Court.

In *Commission v Belgium*,[72] the latter had tried to invoke the *van Binsbergen* doctrine in order to justify national legislation, barring broadcasters situated in other Member States from access to the domestic cable-TV network, if the programmes were not broadcast in one of the languages of the Member State in which the broadcaster was established. Advocate General Tesauro stated that the judgement in *van Binsbergen* only authorized Member States to adopt specific measures in individual cases of abuse

[65] Judgment, para 24.

[66] See n 41 above.

[67] Opinion of the Advocate General, paras 44–46.

[68] Judgment, para 21.

[69] Council Directive 89/552/EEC, OJ 1989 L298/23, later amended by Council and European Parliament Directive 97/36/EC, OJ 1997 L202/60.

[70] See eg L Woods and J Scholes, 'Broadcasting: the Creation of a European Culture or the Limits of the Internal Market?' in (1997) 17 YBEL, 47–82, and BJ Drijber, 'The Revised Television Without Frontiers Directive: is it fit for the Next Century?' (1999) 36 CML Rev 87–122.

[71] See LH Hansen (n 11 above) 114–115.

[72] Case C-211/91 [1992] ECR I-6773.

and certainly not to exclude an entire category of operators from its market. The national rules were not even designed to prevent any circumvention of national rules on the right of establishment.[73] The Court repeated the statement on circumvention from *van Binsbergen* and added that it did not follow from this that it would be permissible for a Member State to prohibit altogether the provision of certain services by operators established in other Member States, as that would be tantamount to abolishing the freedom to provide services.[74]

In *Veronica*,[75] a Dutch company (Veronica) had been prohibited from helping to set up a commercial station in Luxembourg by the Dutch authorities. The prohibition was based upon the Dutch law on broadcasting (Mediawet), which was aimed to provide for a pluralist, non-commercial domestic broadcasting network.[76] Advocate General Tesauro concluded that the operations of Veronica were liable to undermine the system set up by the Mediawet and, with reference to *van Binsbergen*, the Member State could not be denied the right to take measures to prevent the exercise in circumvention situations like the one at hand.[77] The Court followed the same line of reasoning. It also referred to *van Binsbergen*[78] and added that by prohibiting national broadcasting organizations from helping to set up commercial radio and television companies abroad for the purpose of providing services there directed towards the Netherlands, the legislation 'had the effect of ensuring that such organisations could not improperly evade the obligations deriving from the national legislation concerning the pluralistic and non-commercial content of programmes'.[79] In conclusion, the requirements that national broadcasting organizations did not engage in activities not condoned by the Dutch law and/or authorities could not be regarded as being incompatible with the Treaty provisions on freedom to provide services.[80]

TV 10[81] was a company set up under Luxembourg law and with its seat in that same state. The company had been denied access to the Netherlands cable network, with the motivation that the company could not be regarded as a foreign broadcasting body. It was alleged that TV 10 had established

73 Opinion of the Advocate General, para 4. 74 Judgment, para 12.

75 Case C-148/91 *Vereiniging Veronica Omroep Organisatie v Commissariaat voor de Media* [1993] ECR I-513. See annotation by W Hins in 31 (1994) CML Rev 901–911.

76 The Court had already found that the intrinsic limitations set up by that law constituted, in general, justifiable derogations from the principle of free movement (see Cases C-353/89 *Commission v Netherlands* [1991] ECR I-4069 and Case C-288/89 *Stichting Collectieve Antennevoorziening Gouda v Commissariaat voor de Media* [1991] ECR I-4007).

77 Opinion of the Advocate General, para 9.

78 Judgment, para 12. 79 ibid para 13.

80 Judgment, para 14. Neither was there any infringement of the Treaty provision on free movement of capital (an issue, since Veronica also had supported the Luxembourg station financially).

81 See n 39 above.

itself in Luxembourg manifestly to evade the Mediawet legislation applicable to domestic broadcasting bodies; a fact the referring national court also found confirmed during the national proceedings of the case. Advocate General Lenz first concluded that, contrary to the position of the Netherlands, TV 10 undeniably was to be considered as a service-provider within the meaning of Community law, as the company was duly established in Luxembourg and therefore fulfilled the service provision criteria of cross-border operation.[82] Lenz found that the national court, with binding effect for the ECJ, had determined that circumvention was involved in the present case. Whereas this was a matter of fact to be decided by the national court alone, he still pointed out that it was a different question as to what circumstances such findings could be based on (solely on objective criteria or perhaps also influenced by subjective factors like intention and motive).[83]

He continued to examine the Court's statement on circumvention in *van Binsbergen*, and concluded that the exact interpretation of what legal consequences could be inferred from it was far from clear.[84] Furthermore, he noted that *van Binsbergen* only applied to 'rules of professional conduct'. In conclusion, he found that although the cross-border activity was circumventing the host State's rules, the activity in itself should still be classed as a service within the meaning of Community law. Moving on to the issue of the Court's case law on avoidance of national rules, he basically went on to examine the argument from the Netherlands and Germany, which both had maintained that a principle could be inferred from the Court's case law to the effect that a person could not invoke the fundamental Community freedoms in order to evade legislation applicable to him.[85] Lenz examined the relevant statements in *Leclerc*, *Lair*, *Knoors* and *van de Bijl*, as well as *Veronica*, and reached the conclusion that a Member State was entitled to take measures in order to prevent a provider of services whose activity was entirely or principally directed towards its territory from exercising the freedom to provide services in order to avoid the provisions regulating the relevant occupational activity.[86] Applied to the present case, he noted that the assessment as to whether circumvention in the *van Binsbergen* sense was at hand must be established in the light of objective criteria. Commenting on the findings of the national court in this respect, he added that to determine whether a law has been circumvented or evaded was a legal assessment of facts which could not entirely be withdrawn from the appreciation of the ECJ. In any event, the limits to that legal assessment were subject to legal supervision of the Court. As Lenz found it difficult to determine circumvention by subjective criteria when it came to legal persons, he considered that avoidance of legal provisions by such persons

[82] Opinion, paras 19–20. [83] ibid para 22. [84] ibid paras 25–29.
[85] Opinion, para 21. [86] Opinion, para 53.

must be determined with use of objective criteria, the limits of such assessments still drawn up by Community law. The nationality of shareholders or managers could for instance not be taken into account for the determination, as this would amount to unlawful discrimination on grounds of nationality.[87] He ended, however, by commenting that from the available facts it did seem to be a case of 'true' circumvention in the present case.[88] Under those circumstances, a Member State was empowered to frustrate an attempt by an undertaking to evade the jurisdiction of that State by treating the company in that respect as if it were subject to its jurisdiction.[89]

Under the heading 'The lawfulness of certain restrictions on freedom to provide services', the Court reiterated the well-known formula from *van Binsbergen* and added the following:

> It follows that a Member State may regard as a domestic broadcaster a radio and television organization which establishes itself in another Member State in order to provide services there which are intended for the first State's territory, since the aim of that measure is to prevent organisations which establish themselves in another Member State from being able, by exercising the freedoms guaranteed by the Treaty, wrongfully to avoid obligations under national law, in this case those designed to ensure the pluralist and non-commercial content of programmes.
>
> In those circumstances it cannot be regarded as incompatible with the provisions of Articles 59 and 60 of the Treaty to treat such organisations as domestic organisations.[90]
>
> . . . the Treaty provisions on freedom to provide services are to be interpreted as not precluding a Member State from treating as a domestic broadcaster a broadcasting body constituted under the law of another Member State and established in that State but whose activities are wholly or principally directed towards the territory of the first Member State, if that broadcasting body was established there in order to enable it to avoid the rules which would be applicable to it if it were established within the first State.[91]

In *De Agostini*[92] the questions related to the possible application of the Swedish laws towards, respectively, TV advertising directed to children and the laws on misleading advertising. One of the broadcasting companies (TV 3) was established in the United Kingdom and sent programmes by satellite to Denmark, Sweden and Norway, and it was in this channel the advertising directed towards children had been sent. The allegedly misleading advertising

[87] Opinion, paras 61–63. Here, Lenz made a special reference to the *Factortame* judgment.
[88] Opinion, para 67; the relevant and justified objective criteria were discussed under paras 65–66.
[89] Opinion, para 68.
[90] Judgment, paras 21–22.
[91] Judgment, para 26.
[92] Joined Cases C-34/95, C-35/95 and C-36/95 *Konsumentombudsmannen (KO) v De Agostini (Svenska) Förlag AB and TV-shop i Sverige AB* [1997] ECR I-3875. See, eg, R Greaves, 'Advertising Restrictions and the Free Movement of Goods and Services' (1998) 23 EL Rev 305–319.

concerned not only those products but also skin-care products and detergents. All the commercials had also been shown on a domestic channel (TV 4). The Swedish Consumer Ombudsman argued that TV 3 ought to be treated as a domestic channel, amongst other reasons based upon the Court's circumvention doctrine as stated in *van Binsbergen*, and that the Swedish laws should be applied. Advocate General Jacobs referred to *van Binsbergen* as the first case in which the Court formulated the principle that a Member State is entitled to take measures in order to prevent a provider of services whose activity is entirely or principally directed towards its territory from exercising the freedom to provide services, in order to avoid the legislation applicable in the State of destination.[93] He continued by stating that the Court had applied this principle to the broadcasting sector in its judgments in *Veronica* and *TV 10*.[94] The *van Binsbergen* principle, as he put it, could be seen 'simply as an application of the general principle of abuse of rights, recognized in most systems of law'.[95] As an exception to one of the fundamental freedoms of the internal market, the principle, however, had to be narrowly interpreted as to the scope of intervention conferred on the host Member State. In the present case, he concluded that nothing actually suggested that TV 3 had been established in the United Kingdom in order to avoid the Swedish rules in question: the broadcaster had to act wrongfully or improperly in order for the *van Binsbergen* principle to apply.[96] The burden of proof of such impropriety was on the Member State, seeking to make use of the exception.

The Court did not comment on the purported existence of a 'general principle of abuse of rights', but tried the cases on basis of an interpretation of the TV Directive. By stating that the Directive only partially harmonized the field, and that the Member States thus had a certain margin for application of their own laws, there was never any reason to dwell upon the question of whether the application of the Directive should be disqualified on the basis of the purported circumvention. Instead, the Court stated that it was for the national court to determine whether national provisions, constituting restrictions on the freedom to provide services, were necessary to meet overriding requirements of general public importance or one of the aims laid down in Article 46 (ex 56) EC of the Treaty, as well as to determine whether they were proportionate.

6. Legitimate Circumvention of National Rules

The *Centros* judgment,[97] delivered 9 March 1999, at first glance seemed to concern a typical example of circumvention. A Danish couple had,

[93] Opinion, para 41. [94] ibid paras 40–53. [95] ibid para 45.
[96] Here (para 47), he referred to the wording used in *TV 10* and *Veronica*, respectively.
[97] Case C-212/97 *Centros Ltd v Erhvervs- og Selskabsstyrelsen* [1999] ECR I-1459.

relatively obviously in order to avoid the Danish rules on minimum share capital, founded a private limited company in the United Kingdom in accordance with the there applicable company rules. The company, Centros, was registered in the United Kingdom but carried out no activity there. The two Danish owners instead had applied for the right to register a branch of Centros in Denmark. The registration was, however, refused on the grounds that Centros did not trade in the United Kingdom and that the branch actually was to be the principal establishment, thereby circumventing the Danish rules on, in particular, the paying-up of a minimum capital (which would have exceeded by far what it had cost the couple to start up the company in the United Kingdom). Denmark submitted that it was entitled to take steps to prevent such abuse by refusing to register the branch.

Advocate General La Pergola stated in this respect that there, indeed, was a firm general principle of Community law that it could not be relied on for abusive or fraudulent ends. To define this principle more precisely was, however, far from easy.[98] By referring to the judgment in *Kefalas* and a statement of the French lawyer Planiol ('le droit cesse là où l'abuse commence') La Pergola submitted that the question of abuse in the end had to be solved by interpretation and that the only possible way of concluding, in an actual situation, if a right was being abused was, in fact, to define the content of that right.[99] By referring to the judgement in *Segers,*[100] he submitted that the Danish couple had legitimately exercised the rights of freedom of establishment given to them under the Treaty.

The Court, in respect of the submission of abuse, stated the following:[101]

It is true that according to the case-law of the Court a Member State is entitled to take measures to prevent certain of its nationals from attempting, under cover of the rights created by the Treaty, improperly to circumvent their national legislation or to prevent individuals from improperly or fraudulently taking advantage of provisions of Community law (see, in particular /services—Van Binsbergen, Veronica, TV 10, establishment—Knoors and Bouchoucha, goods—Leclerc, social security—Paletta II, workers—Lair, CAP—General Milk and company law—Kefalas).

However, although in such circumstances, the national courts may, case by case, take account—on the basis of objective evidence—of abuse or fraudulent conduct on the part of the persons concerned in order, where appropriate, to deny them the benefit of the provisions of Community law on which they seek to rely, they must nevertheless assess such conduct in the light of the objectives pursued by those provisions (Paletta II).

[98] Opinion, para 20.

[99] In this last respect, he also referred to C Nizzo, 'L'abuso dei "diritte comunitari": un quesito non risolto', Dir.comm.internaz., 1977, 766.

[100] Case 79/85 *D H M Segers v Bestuur van de Bedrijfsvereniging voor Banken Verzekeringswezen, Groothandel en Vrije Beroepen* [1986] ECR 2375.

[101] Judgment, paras 24–27.

In the present case, the provisions of national law, application of which the parties concerned have sought to avoid, are rules governing the formation of companies and not rules concerning the carrying on of certain trades, professions or businesses. The provisions of the Treaty on freedom of establishment are intended specifically to enable companies formed in accordance with the law of a Member State and having their registered office, central administration or principal place of business within the Community to pursue activities in other Member States through an agency, branch or subsidiary.

That being so, the fact that a national of a Member State who wishes to set up a company chooses to form it in the Member State whose rules of company law seem to him the least restrictive and to set up branches in other Member States cannot, in itself, constitute an abuse of the right of establishment. The right to form a company in accordance with the law of a Member State and to set up branches in other Member States is inherent in the exercise, in a single market, of the freedom of establishment guaranteed by the Treaty.

After having concluded that no acceptable justifications for this obstacle to the freedom of establishment could be found, the Court, however, made this final point:[102]

Lastly, the fact that a Member State may not refuse to register a branch of a company formed in accordance with the law of another Member State in which it has its registered office does not preclude that first State from adopting any appropriate measure for preventing or penalising fraud, either in relation to the company itself, if need be in cooperation with the Member State in which it was formed, or in relation to its members, where it has been established that they are in fact attempting, by means of the formation of the company, to evade their obligations towards private or public creditors established on the territory of a Member State concerned. In any event, combating fraud cannot justify a practice of refusing to register a branch of a company which has its registered office in another Member State.

7. Bending the Rules: Other Ways to Misuse Community Rights

In *Balkan Export*,[103] the Court had an opportunity to comment on the application of a national principle of natural justice in the context of the Common Agricultural Policy (CAP). The question from the referring German court was whether there was any possibility for the national authorities to deal with an application for exemption from charges[104] due to the Community on basis of national law. If the answer was negative, the next question was if there was any legal basis under Community law to

102 Judgment, para 38.

103 Case 118/76 *Balkan-Import-Export GmbH v Hauptzollamt Berlin-Packhof* [1977] ECR 1177.

104 Monetary compensatory amounts (MCAs), as fixed by Regulation 974/71/EEC, OJ 1971 L106/1.

provide relief on grounds of natural justice. Advocate General Reischl took a firm stance against the idea that national principles of law could be permitted to modify Community rules and thus challenge, 'to a certain extent', the application of Community law.[105]

The Commission stated in its submission that the first question related to the problem of distribution of powers between the Community and the Member States. As far as the Community exercised sovereign powers in accordance with the Treaty, it would be impossible for the Member States to exercise their own powers. If 'independent' national rules could be used in order to modify Community law, the scope of the latter would be affected in an undesirable way. If a Member State were to grant an exemption under national law on grounds of natural justice, this would constitute an arbitrary and undesirable intervention by that State within the sphere of Community competence.[106] As regards the existence of a similar principle in Community law, the Court first noted that such an unwritten principle of natural justice allowing exemptions from taxes could not be considered common to the Member States. It added that the practical application of such a principle in the context of Community law would raise virtually insoluble problems. The causes of uncertainty would also be so great that the limits of the Community principle of legal certainty run the risk of being reached or even exceeded. In most cases, the Commission concluded, it would be possible to reach satisfactory solutions by means of interpretation of the aim and spirit of the relevant Community law provisions.

The Court, however, stated that although the distribution of functions between the Community and the Member States could justify the application by a national authority, of a rule of natural justice under national law, such a rule could not be applied in so far as its effect would be to modify the scope of the relevant Community provisions concerning assessment, manner of imposition or amount of the charge in question.[107] As to the second question, the Court stated that there was, in the present state, no legal basis under Community law for exemptions from the charges in question on grounds of natural justice.[108]

In conclusion, the Court did not rule out the application of national rules on situations governed by Community legislation. However, such applications were not be allowed if this would alter the scope and content of such Community provisions; a formula which has been repeated throughout subsequent case law.

In *Neumann*,[109] the Court recalled the conditions for an exercise of

[105] Opinion of the Advocate General, 1195. [106] Judgment, 1184.
[107] Judgement, para 5–6. [108] Judgement, paras 8–10.
[109] Case 299/84 *Neumann v BALM* [1985] ECR 3663. The case concerned the CAP and whether certain of the applicable Community provisions could be held to be inapplicable by the national authorities.

national rules stated in *Balkan Export* and then, in no uncertain terms, made it clear that it would be contrary to the division of authority between the Member States and the Community if a national authority would be entitled not to apply a provision of Community law because of a national principle of objective unfairness.[110] If such a principle was to be recognized, it might prevent the provisions of Community law from having full effect in the Member States and would be prejudicial to the fundamental principle that Community law had to be uniformly applied throughout the Community.[111]

In 1988, in *Lair*,[112] the question was whether Member States could unilaterally make the grant of social advantages (here the benefits of a national student assistance system) granted to workers[113] conditional upon the completion of a given period of occupational activity. The Court answered the question in the negative but added the following remark to the submissions of the Member States taking part in the process:

> In so far as the arguments submitted by the . . . Member States in question are motivated by a desire to prevent certain abuse; for example where it may be established on the basis of objective evidence that a worker has entered a Member State for the sole purpose of enjoying, after a very short period of occupational activity, the benefit of the student assistance system in that State, it should be observed that such abuses are not covered by the Community provisions in question.[114]

8. The Greek Challenge

In 1996 the Court also delivered its judgement in *Pafitis*;[115] the first of a number of Greek references for preliminary rulings of great importance to the doctrine of abuse. The case concerned company law and the possibility for minority shareholders to invoke direct effect of certain parts of Directive 77/91/EEC.[116] An interesting feature here was that the referring Greek court expressly had declared that it would reserve judgment on the merits of an objection of abusive exercise of rights raised in the main proceedings. The objection was based on Article 281 of the Greek Civil Code, stating that the exercise of a right might be prohibited if held to be abusive. The Greek court stated that this provision also could be invoked to prevent the

110 Which provided for such measures in cases where the application of a legal provision would be held to lead to results, which the legislature would have sought to avoid if it had envisaged the eventuality when the provision was enacted.

111 Judgment, para 25.

112 See n 27 above.

113 By way of Regulation 1612/68/EEC, OJ 1968 L257/2.

114 Judgment, para 43.

115 Case C-441/93 *Panagis Pafitis and others v Trapeza Kentrikis Ellados A E and others* [1996] ECR I-1363.

116 The Second Company Law Directive, OJ 1977 L26/1, which relates to the formation of public limited companies and the maintenance and alteration in their capital.

exercise of a right conferred by Community law and that it claimed exclusive jurisdiction to adjudicate on this point. Rightly so, Advocate General Tesauro stressed that the Court ought to rule on the point, since what was at stake actually was the primacy of Community law over domestic law and the effectiveness of the preliminary rulings, as there obviously was a risk that such a ruling in the present case would be negated by the national court by virtue of a principle of national law, conflicting with a Community provision having direct effect.[117] Tesauro found that national courts in nearly all Member States had some possibilities to censure abusive exercises of rights, although by different procedures and in different circumstances.[118] However, where the rights claimed by individuals emanated from Community law, the Court should consider to what extent the judicial protection of that right under national law was adequate. To take the view that the plaintiffs in the present case were abusing their rights appeared, accordingly, to be without foundation. To deny them the protection guaranteed by the Directive in question would be tantamount to censuring not the abusive exercise of the right but rather any exercise of it. The situation would only be different if the actual right not only had been exercised but also exercised in a different, specifically abusive way.[119] He finally called upon the Court to make it clear that national legislation which allowed a national court to prohibit a right conferred by a provision of Community law by describing it as abusive could not be applied merely because the holder of that right sought judicial protection for it, nor, in any case, could it be applied in such a way as to nullify the provision in question entirely.[120]

The Court, hereby following the Advocate General, stated the following:[121]

> Although, since the national court has submitted no question on the matter, it is unnecessary to rule as to whether it is permissible, under the Community legal order, to apply a national rule in determining whether a right conferred by the provisions of Community law at issue is being exercised abusively, the fact remains that, in any event, the application of such a rule must not detract from the full effect and uniform application of Community law in the Member States.
>
> It must be borne in mind in that connection that it is settled case-law that it is for the Court of Justice, in relation to rights relied on by an individual on the basis of Community provisions, to verify whether the judicial protection available under national law is appropriate.

117 Opinion of the Advocate General, paras 27–28.
118 ibid para 28, with special references to *Daily Mail* (n 137 below) and *General Milk* (n 41 above).
119 See n 118 above paras 29–30.
120 ibid para 33.
121 Judgment, paras 68–69.

It continued by stating, in no uncertain terms, that in the present case the uniform application and full effect of Community law would be undermined if a person were to be deemed to be abusing his rights merely because he was acting in the same way as the plaintiffs. To treat the exercise of the right conferred by the Directive as abusive for such reasons would be tantamount to altering the scope of that provision.[122]

The question of the Greek legislation on abusive exercise of rights in relation to Directive 77/91 came up again in *Kefalas*.[123] Certain shareholders sought the annulment of a ministerial decision effecting an increase in capital for a public limited liability company, on the ground that the decision was in conflict with the Directive. The Greek State invoked the objection of abuse of rights. The referring Greek court held that the shareholders had exercised the right abusively in so far as the exercise manifestly exceeded the bounds of good faith, morality and the socio-economic purpose of the right in question; as demonstrated by the evidence. In particular, the court referred to the company's catastrophic financial situation, which made bankruptcy certain, before the ministerial decision remedied this, the evident advantages of the reorganizational measure to the shareholders themselves as well as to the fact that the shareholders had not exercised their pre-emptive rights in respect of the shares issued after the company was reorganized. The Greek court, however, questioned whether its approach was consistent with Community law, as the question on who—and under the rules and/or principles of which legal order—it was to be decided whether or not a right conferred by a rule of Community law had been exercised abusively.[124] Advocate General Tesauro started by examining the question of whether it was permissible under Community law for the application of Community provisions to be subordinated to, and in some cases paralysed by, an abuse of rights. Noting that the Court did not find it necessary to rule on this point in *Pafitis*, but that the present reference made such an approach essential, he stated that to allow a domestic rule on abuse of rights to consolidate a breach of Community law, would go against the fundamental principle that Community law has primacy over national law.[125] With reference to *Neumann*, he continued by establishing that case law showed that provisions of national law could not be applied if it modified thescope of Community rules in question, detracting from its full effect and uniform application and thereby defeated the principle of the primacy of Community law. Therefore, it would not be

[122] Judgment, para 70.

[123] Case C-367/96 *Alexandros Kefalas and others v Elliniko Dimosio* (*Greek State*) *and Organismos Ikonomikis Anasinkrotisis Epikhiriseon AE* (OAE) [1998] ECR I-2843, commented on by D Triantafyllou, 'Abuse of Rights Versus Primacy?' (1999) 36 CML Rev 157–164.

[124] Opinion of Advocate General Tesauro, paras 8–10.

[125] ibid paras 14–15.

permissible under Community law for a national court to apply a domestic rule where that rule would entail a solution inconsistent with Community law.[126]

As to the second question of the national court, namely whether there were principles of Community law capable of sanctioning cases of abuse of rights, he concluded that he had not changed his point of view from the one stated in the *Pafitis* Opinion: no such rule was to be found in Community law, and such a principle would in any case not be a legal concept so well suited for a legal system like the Community's. However, Community law as a system did contain 'self-protective measures' which ensured that rights conferred were not exercised in abusive, excessive or distorted manners. Tesauro referred to the established case law, according to which 'the facilities created by the Treaty cannot have the effect of allowing the persons who benefit from them to evade the application of national legislation and of prohibiting Member States from taking the measures necessary to prevent such abuse'.[127] After recalling the Court's statement in *Paletta* (*No 2*), he concluded that the Court, essentially, recognized that a national court might sanction an excessive or distorted use of Community law only where that would not be prejudicial to the objectives pursued by the relevant provisions. This really meant that the Court reserved to itself the right, as was appropriate, to define the substantive scope of the Community right at issue: to define the 'intrinsic limits of the subjective legal position concerned'.[128] Ultimately, the question of any abuse of rights concerning Community provisions would turn into a question of interpretation of that very provision. Referring to *Faik*, Tesauro finally stated that the Court's case law on the issue essentially allowed each national legal system to apply its own rules of law (whether sanctioning 'fraud' or 'abuse of rights') in order to withdraw the right to rely upon rules of Community law in well-defined cases, in which, in the final analysis, such rules were not meant to apply, and where there therefore could be no adverse effect on the uniform application of Community law.[129]

The Court restated its declaration from *Paletta* (*No 2*), adding now that case (as an example from the area of social security) to the line of supporting judgments, according to which:[130]

> Community law cannot be relied on for abusive or fraudulent ends . . .
>
> Consequently, the application by national courts of domestic rules such as [the Greek legal provision on abuse of rights] for the purposes of assessing whether the

[126] ibid paras 16–17. [127] ibid para 24. [128] ibid para 25.

[129] ibid para 26. Note, along similar but even more explicit lines, Advocate General Saggio's recently delivered Opinion in the not yet decided Case C-373/97 *Dyonisios Diamantis v Greece and others*, delivered 28 October 1999; especially paras 22–25.

[130] Judgment, paras 20–23.

exercise of a right arising from a provision of Community law is abusive cannot be regarded as contrary to the Community legal order.

Although the Court cannot substitute its assessment for that of the national court, which is the only forum competent to establish the facts of the case before it, it must be pointed out that the application of such a national rule must not prejudice the full effect and uniform application of Community law in the Member States. In particular, it is not open to the national courts, when assessing the exercise of a right arising from a provision of Community law, to alter the scope of that provision or to compromise the objectives pursued by it:

In the present case, the uniform application and full effect of Community law would be prejudiced if a shareholder, relying on [the provision of the directive in question] were deemed to be abusing his rights on the ground that the increase in capital contested by him resolved the financial difficulties threatening the existence of the company concerned and clearly enured to his economic benefit.

By means of interpretation of the relevant provision of the Directive, the Court continued by stressing that (although in more general terms) the indications of abuse indicated by the national court would, if used against the shareholders, alter the scope of the Community provision and prejudice the uniform application and full effect of Community law.[131] It did, however, in the end point out that Community law did not preclude a national court, on the basis of sufficient telling evidence, from examining whether a shareholder bringing an action based on the Community provision in question was seeking to derive, to the detriment of the company, an improper advantage, manifestly contrary to the objective of the provision.[132]

In its recently delivered judgment on *Diamantis*,[133] which also dealt with suspected abuse of the provisions of the Second Company Law Directive in Greece, the Court repeated its positions from the preceding cases. In this particular case, however, the Court seemed somewhat more benevolent towards the national court. As to the question of whether Community law precluded the national court from trying to verify if the shareholder had been abusing his rights it stated:[134]

In this case it would not appear that the uniform application and full effect of Community law would be compromised it it were to be held an abuse of rights for a shareholder to rely on Article 25(1) of the Second Directive on the ground that, of the remedies available for a situation that has arisen in breach of that provision, he has chosen a remedy that will cause such serious damage to the legitimate interests of others that it appears manifestly disproportionate. Such a determination would not alter the scope of that provision and would not compromise its objectives.

[131] Judgment, paras 24–27. [132] ibid para 28.
[133] Case C-373/97 *Dyonisios Diamantis v Greece and others* [2000] (ny).
[134] ibid paras 43–44.

The reply to the first question must therefore be that Community law does not preclude national courts from applying a provision of national law which enables them to determine whether a right deriving from a Community law provision is being abused. However, in making that determination, it is not permissible to deem a shareholder relying on Article 25(1) of the Second Directive to be abusing his rights under that provision merely because he is a minority shareholder of a company subject to reorganisation measures, or has benefited from reorganisation of the company, or has not exercised his right of pre-emption, or was among the shareholders who asked for the company to be placed under the scheme applicable to companies in serious difficulties, or has allowed a certain period of time to elapse before bringing his action. In contrast, Community law does not preclude national courts from applying the provision of national law concerned if, of the remedies available for a situation that has arisen in breach of that provision, a shareholder has chosen a remedy that will cause such serious damage to the legitimate interests of others that it appears manifestly disproportionate.

IV. ANALYSIS OF THE CASE LAW

The most striking feature of the case law is that the Court never has recognized the existence of a principle of abuse within the Community legal order. On the contrary, especially in the earlier cases, such an existence has been expressly denied. What we do find, however, is a rather cautiously formulated doctrine on abuse in general which, arguably, does not amount to a full-fledged general principle of law. The doctrine of the Court can be summarized quite easily: Community law cannot be relied on for abusive or fraudulent ends.[135]

The practical implications of this statement, however, are far from clear. One of the Court's more extensive formulations on the matter is also one of its latest: a Member State is entitled to take measures to prevent certain of its nationals from attempting, under cover of the rights created by the Treaty, improperly to circumvent their national legislation or to prevent individuals from improperly or fraudulently taking advantage of provisions of Community law.[136]

One should note that the Court here has merged its former opinions concerning abuse related to circumvention with other situations in which interested parties improperly or fraudulently try to take advantage of Community law. The first part of the statement is basically an extended adoption of the statement in *van Binsbergen*, focusing on the host State's own nationals (improperly) trying to circumvent that State's legislation. The second part relates to other situations where interested parties seek improperly or fraudulently to benefit from Community law. The meaning

[135] See *Kefalas* (n 123 above). [136] *Centros* (n 97 above).

of 'improperly' in the sentence above is certainly not easy to define. However, it seems clear that the Court—when dealing with business transactions over borders, as in the area of free movement of goods or the operations of the CAP—requires genuine transactions to take place. If the evidence is there (an interesting procedural question I will return to below) one can therefore conclude that at least the more obvious U-turns do not bring about any Community rights.

Interestingly, from a constitutional point of view, the Court, while denying the existence of a Community principle, obviously has accepted that national courts may apply nationally existing rules and/or principles on abuse of rights even when the rights stem from Community provisions. In this regard, the Court has also stated that within the realms of the preliminary reference procedure, the national court is the only forum competent to establish the facts of the case before it.

What, with regard to Community law supremacy, first might appear as a principally important concession to national jurisdiction comes bundled with a number of very telling conditions. Before concluding that the behaviour in question really amounts to abuse, the national court must:

(1) assess the conduct in the light of the objectives pursued by the Community-provisions in question (*Paletta No 2*));
(2) make sure that the application of the national rule on abuse of rights does not detract from the full effect and uniform application of Community law in the Member States (*Pafitis*) and
(3) in particular, it is not open to the national courts, when assessing the exercise of a right arising from a provision of Community law, to alter the scope of that provision or to compromise the objectives pursued by it (*Kefalas*).

The alert reader may have noticed that the combined effect of the conditions,[137] very much like the *CILFIT* formula[138] in relation to national courts' application of the *acte clair* doctrine, in most cases would force a conscientious national court to ask for a preliminary reference, before daring to apply a national principle of abuse. Considering the actual cases tried, one may also conclude that the preliminary references given, while often paying lip-service to the division of duties between the court systems, in most cases have left little or no choice for the national court in deter-

[137] That the conditions are to be applied in a combined way is confirmed by the *Diamantis* judgment, paras 34–44 (n 133 above).
[138] See Case 283/81 *CILFIT v Ministero della Sanità* [1982] ECR 3415 and related comments by G Bebr, 'The Reinforcement of the Constitutional Review of Community Acts under Article 177 EEC' (1988) 25 CML Rev 684 and T C Hartley, *The Foundations of European Community Law. An Introduction to the Constitutional and Administrative Law of the EC* (4th edn, Oxford 1998), 284.

mining the question of abuse. As pointed out by Advocate General Tesauro in *Kefalas*, the Court reserves to itself the right to define the substantive scope of the Community right at issue; the question of abuse of those rights therefore, ultimately, turns into a question of interpretation of that very provision. This process obviously may leave very little room for the national court's discretion. One may recall the *Foto-Frost* doctrine,[139] requiring all national courts doubting the validity of Community legislation to apply for a preliminary reference as the determination of such validity is the sole prerogative of the Court. In many aspects, the Court's doctrine on abuse has far more links to the principles of Community law supremacy (and the linked, practical directions given to national courts in *CILFIT* and *Foto-Frost*) than with any real submission to national evaluation of the matter.

The observation that the Court in most cases tries to deal with purported cases of abuse by way of interpretation may seem obvious, given the very purpose of preliminary references. However, it also tells us quite a lot about the Court's approach to abuse. In *Daily Mail*,[140] the Court never commented on whether the proposed transfer of central management amounted to abuse. Instead, the case was resolved by stating that the Treaty did not confer on companies (being creatures of (national) law) any right to 'leave the country but still remain' the way the *Daily Mail* had planned to. Similarly, but with a different outcome, was the ruling in *Centros*. By adhering to its former case law on what constitutes a company's place of establishment (the company's legal seat and, apparently, nothing more), a situation which admittedly seemed like an obvious case of circumvention instead came out as part of the essence of the right to free movement of establishment! The judgment clearly shows that certain evasions of national legislation are sanctioned by Community law, thus adding some extra meaning to the Court's use of formulations like 'wrongful/improper evasion' of national law.[141] The reader may recall that one of the questions related to the statement on circumvention in *van Binsbergen* was whether its application amounted to a derogation from the fundamental freedom of movement (thereby requiring justification of the national rules involved) or whether the circumvention placed the activities outside the Treaty freedom. It is submitted that, given the Court's practice of defining the rights in question, it often becomes unavoidable for the Court to assess the national measures purported to be circumvented, especially if some kind of harmonized rules exists in the

[139] Case 314/85 *Firma Foto-Frost v Hauptzollamt Lübeck* [1987] ECR 4199.

[140] Case 81/87 *R v H M Treasury and Commissioners of Inland Revenue, ex parte Daily Mail and General Trust plc* [1988] ECR 5483.

[141] *Centros* (n 97 above) para 24; see also *Knoors* (n 48 above), para 25, *Veronica* (n 75 above) para 14 and *TV 10* (n 39 above) para 15.

field:[142] if the national measures themselves are incompatible with Community law, clearly there is no need for any application of a possible doctrine of circumvention. In such cases, the evasion of the national rules cannot be considered wrongful or improper, but is perfectly justified.

Returning to *Centros*, it is submitted that if the company had operated in some domestically specifically regulated area, the standard circumvention reasoning applied in, for instance, *Veronica* could have been used here too. One should also note the Court's specific assurance that its findings in *Centros* did not preclude Member States from taking measures to prevent or penalize fraud (in the sense of evading one's obligations in the host State).[143] Perhaps one can conclude that the likelihood of a possible finding of abuse is higher if the abusive behaviour is quite specific and where the consequences of a ruling will be quite limited to similar situations, rather than when the national rules in question are of a more general type, thereby inviting wider applications.[144]

The reluctance to verify national findings of abuse can also be demonstrated by the Court's many alternative suggestions as to how to come to terms with situations that upset the Member States: more cooperation with the relevant authorities in the other Member States concerned,[145] further or refined harmonization[146] or simply by means of the preliminary reference procedure itself.[147]

The Court's cautious approach in letting national courts decide on the question of abuse also shows, in that the three conditions above also applies to the fact-finding in the actual cases.[148] Perhaps the most telling examples can be found in the category of fraud. In the cases where the element of fraud must have been deemed to be obvious,[149] the Court has clearly stated that the Community provisions in question did not apply and that fraudulent conduct which had led to a conviction could not give rise to any

[142] Like in the TV judgements, and, indeed also in the cases dealing with mutual recognition of diplomas and certificates (like *Knoors* and *Paletta*). Compare, though, the discussion of the Court's case law on goods prohibited throughout the whole Community by PJ Wattel in his annotation of the judgment in *TV 10* in (1995) 32 CML Rev 1257–1270, especially 1267–1269.

[143] *Centros* (n 97 above) para 38.

[144] Compare, for instance, the general Greek civil law provision in *Pafitis* (n 115 above), *Kefalas* (n 123 above) and *Diamantis* (n 129 above) and the Mediawet provisions in *Belgium v Commission* (n 72 above) with the specific circumstances in *TV 10* (n 39 above), *Daily Mail* (n 137 above) and the cases concerning fraud.

[145] *Van de Bijl* (n 12 above) paras 22–24, *Paletta (No 1)* (n 23 above) para 27, *Centros* (n 2 above) para 38.

[146] Knoors (n 48 above) para 27.

[147] Neumann (n 109 above) para 33.

[148] As has been pointed out by, for instance, Advocate General Lenz in his Opinion in *Veronica* (n 75 above) 61–63. See also, to the following, CN Kakouris, 'Do the Member States Possess Judicial Procedural "Autonomy"?' (1997) 34 CML Rev 1389–1412.

[149] Suat Kol (n 18 above) and *van de Bijl* (n 12 above).

Community rights or legitimate expectations.[150] The approach in these cases is understandable. Criminal proceedings, for example, can usually be expected to apply demanding rules on evidence in favour of the accused, thus guaranteeing a high degree of procedural safety. The same may not always be true in administrative or civil proceedings, where the rules on evidence may put at least part of the burden of proof on the person accused of abusing his rights. Here, the Court has insisted on minimum procedural safeguards[151] by demanding that judgments be based on objective evidence. Regarding the rather suspicious circumstances in the *Paletta* cases, the Court applied this condition and added that any national requirement that the worker would have to produce additional evidence (other than the disputed certificate) were not permitted.[152] *Faik* points in a similar direction, as well as many statements in the circumvention cases:[153] abuse may only be ascertained if the *sole purpose* of the specific disputed behaviour is wrongfully to circumvent national legislation or fraudulently to obtain certain rights under false premises.[154]

V. FINAL CONCLUSIONS

The Court's doctrine on abuse largely falls back on interpretation of the Community provisions in question themselves: the question of abuse thereby becomes a matter of whether the purported abusive behaviour is inside or outside the scope of the provision. No specific principle of abuse is applied and it is submitted that the Court's early denial of such a principle's existence within the realm of Community law itself still holds true.

The doctrine itself shows an initially surprising acceptance towards the application of national rules on abuse of rights. This acceptance, however, being so conditional that a preliminary ruling in most cases would be essential to fulfil the criteria of assessment set up by the Court. By looking at the cases reviewed in this chapter, it is tempting to conclude that the suggested actual outcomes[155] in most of them suggest that national courts' possibilities

[150] Suat Kol (n 18 above) para 28.

[151] Expressed clearly by the Court in *Pafitis* (n 115 above) para 69, and most probably spurred by the same concerns for the effectiveness of Community law and the protection of the rights given to individuals as found in Case C-213/89 *Factortame* (*No* 2) [1990] ECR I-2433 and Case C-271/91 *Marshall* (*No* 2) [1993] ECR I-4367.

[152] The last statement perhaps not so surprising, but certainly a possible intrusion on national rules on evidence and procedural law.

[153] cf Leclerc (n 40 above) and *General Milk* (n 41 above). See also L Woods and J Scholes, 'Broadcasting: the Creation of a European Culture or the Limits of the Internal Market?', n 75 above, 57 and 76–77.

[154] This observation may be a hint at what will be required for the *van Binsbergen* condition 'Entirely or principally directed towards the host Member State' to apply.

[155] As more or less subtly hinted at by the Court.

to apply their principles of abuse control in actual situations often verge on the theoretical. In much the same way as Member States have the theoretical possibility to justify charges to persons crossing borders, provided that the charges constitute payment for beneficial services actually provided,[156] national courts (or Member States) may try to invoke the notion of abuse. The entry requirements are, however, very narrow. Apart from the most grave and obvious cases, often verging on fraud, the category itself is destined to remain largely empty.

Is this a sad state of affairs? To my mind, it is questionable whether the legal system of the Community really needs a specific principle of abuse. Fair outcomes might in most cases be reached through interpretation of the relevant Community provisions, in much the same way the Court usually resolves the cases today. This opinion is not new and has been raised by, for instance, Advocate General Tesauro.[157]

What, then, can be said about the Court's treatment of national principles of abuse in the context of Community provisions? As has been pointed out by several Advocates General and, indeed, the Court itself, the application of national norms on abuse would principally threaten the supremacy and uniform application of Community law provisions in the Member States. Here, it seems appropriate to state that the Court's present approach makes great sense, in that the position adopted on abuse conforms very well with the doctrines of supremacy and the concern for *effet utile*. Seen from this angle, the case law shows a commendable adherence to the Court's former jurisprudence on the subject. Judgments like *Centros* also seem to confirm that the Court has not given up its ambition to promote further internal market integration and it is possible that future case law will make even more use of the qualifying words 'wrongful / improper' evasion of national laws.

The possible criticism one could make is, however, that the Court's expressed permissive attitude towards the application of national rules on abuse of rights in the end comes out as being quite deceptive. Although it is understandable that the Court may wish to appease Member States and national courts by avoiding a too obvious wielding of the 'Supremacy sledgehammer',[158] one cannot but notice how the Court in the end still takes back most of what it first seemed to grant the national courts. The

[156] See Case 24/68 *Commission v Italy* [1969] ECR 193, Case 63/74 *Cadsky v ICE* [1975] ECR 281 and Case 170/88 *Ford España v Spain* [1989] ECR 2305.

[157] In his opinion in Kefalas (n 123 above).

[158] A tendency noticed by several commentators, for instance D Triantafyllou in his review of the judgment in Kefalas (n 123 above) especially 160. Another possible explanation, when dealing with abuse, may of course be that certain members of the Court, perhaps themselves from national legal systems with principles on abuse of rights, may be unwilling to commit to such statements on the issue.

Dear Dimiter

We are sending the book to you now. You will see, it contains a series of shorter contributions by different people. You should first explain the overall purpose of the book, then deal with each contribution in a sentence or two (x writes about ..., his style is clear as always the the conclusion that ... is at the same time interesting and persuasive). Try to vary the paragraphs a bit that it does not become a treadmill description of the 15 chapters. Then you should add an overall critique of the book, its strengths and weaknesses (such as which topics are missing, is the quality even, how is it edited, printed, etc., what about index and case register etc.) and say something whether you would recommend it and for which target audience.

If you can send the review by the end of the month, it will still go into EJLR Vol. V, No. 1.

1) Overall purpose of the book

More to follow
Kind regards
F.

Prof. Dr. Frank Emmert, LL.M.
Professor of Law and Director
Center for International and Comparative Law
Indiana University School of Law
Indianapolis, IN 46202-3225

femmert@iupui.edu

apparent tension between what seems to be and what really is raises the question as to whether the maintenance of doctrines with stunningly low practical application value is merited, or if a more straightforward attitude better serves the purposes of clearness and predictability.

10

Financial Liberalization and Re-regulation

J H DALHUISEN

I. THE LIBERALIZATION OF CAPITAL FLOWS IN THE EU AND THE REMAINING RESTRICTIONS

If we look back over the last 15 years, the years of internationalization and globalization of the capital markets and of 'Big Bang' in London, it is possible to make a few observations about liberalization and re-regulation and especially on how *uncertain* in its objectives this re-regulation often is.

I think it useful in this connection to distinguish clearly between the liberalization of capital flows on the one hand and the liberalization of financial services on the other, even though the international loan business is an example of both. As far as the financial services are concerned, I limit myself to banking and to investment services and leave insurance to one side.

Regulation was and is quite different in the areas of capital flows and financial services. So was the liberalization, even though the freedom to provide financial services usually follows the free movement of capital as already foreseen in the EC original Treaty 1957. In the EU, that proved indeed to be the case and the liberalization of the capital flows was the catalyst for the development of the European passport for financial services as we now have it. Also the re-regulation of the capital flows following the 1988 Directive and further amendments of the EC Treaty, and that of the financial services following the Second Banking Directive and the Investment Services Directive, were quite different. Maybe one should say that in as far as the capital flows were concerned, the present regulation comprises mainly remnants of the old regime, more in respect of third countries than other Member States. Re-regulation proper took place in particular in the area of financial services, motivated by the need to create some harmonization between Member States to allow subsequently for a broad regime of mutual recognition of brokers' licences and their supervision.

When we talk of the liberalization of capital flows, we think mainly of free capital movements, that is the free export of the own currency and free import of others and full convertibility. We then also think of exchange rates and maybe of interest rates, at least the longer ones, being set by market forces, and of the freedom to raise and invest capital wherever one wants. Another aspect no doubt is the freedom to make and accept payments in any currency one wishes. But that concerns also capital investments, either directly or in investment securities.

Regulating capital movements, investments, exchange rates and payments, and therefore also deregulating them, would largely seem a matter of coordination at international levels, but it is well known that the Bretton Wood Agreements of 1944 setting up the International Monetary Fund (IMF) and the International Bank for Reconstruction and Development (World Bank) left these matters mainly to the domestic authorities of each currency, except for current payments which were freed but only to the extent necessary to support the international sale of goods and services under Article VIII of the IMF Agreement, except for the dwindling number of Members that claimed an exception under the Transitory Arrangements of Article XIV. The EC Treaty essentially proceeded on the same basis (ex Article 106 ECT).

Regulation at first and liberalization later of the capital flows proper was thus mainly handled *unilaterally* by the authorities primarily responsible for each currency. This regulation of the currency was strict in most countries. Only a few such as the USA, Germany, Switzerland, the Netherlands, Australia, Canada and New Zealand had in practice, if not in law, achieved a large measure of liberalization, the United Kingdom only joining in 1979. For other countries, this liberalization ultimately came as a consequence of the intrusion of international market forces. It was therefore largely the result of an *autonomous* market development, preceded by the development of the eurobond and swap markets which eventually found or were allowed to find their way around domestic foreign exchange and other capital movement restrictions in the most advanced economies. It affected economically advanced[1] and less advanced countries alike.[2]

In this way the capital flows (including payments) between the advanced economies were eventually set free. In the EU this development made the Directive of 1988 possible. It was therefore a response rather than a proactive move; many earlier efforts at progress in this field had been made before but always yielded little. The liberalization of the capital flows

[1] Although Member State currencies were left to market forces after the 1988 Directive, this was soon accompanied by exchange rate policies amongst Member States, at the time motivated by the advent of Monetary Union and the new currency, succeeded by a much more tenuous relationship between the ins and outs, as may be seen in the ever rising £. These policies did not of course amount to a form of re-regulation of the capital flows but were aimed at convergence of exchange and interest rates.

[2] We all know that the liberalization of capital flows and capital flight, especially short-term ones, subsequently became a live issue in East Asia and Russia and earlier in Latin America. Not having sufficient reserves has been a severe disadvantage in a liberalized capital flow environment and has sometimes made capital move out faster than it ever came in, hence the corresponding liquidity crises and pressures on exchange rates. Whether re-regulation is useful here and sensible is another matter. It is perhaps rather a question of willingness to accept the internal discipline that goes with external openness.

through market forces is seldom complete, however, and it was also not within the EU. First there are the direct possibilities of restrictions now formulated in Articles 57 and 58. One may here distinguish between capital movements between Member States and with third countries.[3] Secondly, there are the indirect restrictions which resulted mainly from investment limitations.

With regard to third countries, Article 57 EC allows the continued application of restrictions under national and Community law on direct investment, establishment, the provision of financial services or the admission of securities to capital markets from these countries. These restrictions must be narrowly construed, however, and may not give rise to new limitations,[4] but the Council may by qualified majority adopt new measures in these areas. In doing so it must be unanimous if it wants to take a step back in liberalization. In exceptional circumstances the EU (and not individual Member States) may also take safeguard measures in respect of the capital flows for a maximum of six months (Article 59 EC), but only if there are serious difficulties caused or threatened to be caused for the operation of Economic and Monetary Union. It requires a proposal of the Commission, a qualified majority and consultation with the ECB. Finally, under Article 60 EC, capital movement measures may be taken by the EU against third countries in the context of common political measures or economic sanctions under Article 301 EC. It may include the blocking of accounts and other freezing measures.

As between Member States, there are fewer restrictions but they seem still very broad. Article 58 continues to allow tax laws to distinguish between the residence or place of investment of taxpayers. Clearly taxation may take place in the latter which could limit these investments. Member States may further take all measures necessary to uphold national laws in the field of taxation. This clearly guards against capital flight for tax reasons. They may also limit or intervene in the free flows to uphold national laws concerning prudential supervision of financial institutions, and may also enforce the national laws in respect of administrative or statistical information-gathering. They may even take the measures which they deem justified on grounds of public policy or public security. This would seem a very broad power, but no arbitrary discrimination or a disguised restriction on the free movement of capital and payments may result under any of these residual powers.

[3] See also N Horn, 'The Monetary Union and the Internal Market for Banking and Investment Services' (1999) EBLR 150.

[4] See Joined Cases C-163/94, C-165/94 and C-250/94 *Sanz de Lera* [1995] ECR I-4821, 4842 and 4843.

II. INDIRECT LIMITATIONS ON THE FREE FLOW OF CAPITAL IN THE EU

A number of indirect restrictions on investments in other Member States were not considered in Article 58 EC. In practice there may be forms of existing regulation remaining in place or being eased out only gradually. The most important example is in investments of pension funds and life insurance companies, which are often not allowed to mismatch substantially the currency of their assets and liabilities and can therefore not be made in other Member States. This indirect limitation on the freedom to move funds and investments amounts to a most serious limitation on the freedom of capital flows. As we shall see, this remains a problem within the EU even *after* the introduction of the Euro which substantially alleviated the mismatch problem within the EU.

In short, some Member States were and are still afraid that local savings are taken elsewhere even if that could generate a better income or spread of risk elsewhere. Trying to move forward, the preoccupation with savings leaving a Member State claimed as its first victim a proposed Directive of 1991 on the freeing of pension funds. This freedom would seem a basic sequel of the operation of the internal market and the freedom to move capital (Article 56), more so after the new currency, but even a substitute Commission Communication in this area was struck down by the European Court.[5]

There is also the impact of existing national taxation rules concerning foreign investments or the deductibility of life insurance premiums for policies taken out elsewhere. They seem hardly to fit in the scheme of Article 58 EC. Some EU countries have indeed been concerned about the tax-avoidance aspects of foreign investments by individual investors and countries like France and Denmark long supported restrictions on outward capital flows for this more limited reason. In the EU this was all played out after the 1988 Directive, long forgotten, but we see some faithful replay at this moment after the introduction of the euro. In particular, the debate on withholding tax on foreign bonds, initiated by Germany, has again flared up.

It found expression in a new draft Directive of 1 December 1998.[6] Quite apart from the agony it caused in the City of London, it was a muddled proposal that created at least as many problems as it sought to solve and will certainly not be effective. A withholding tax of this nature is usually imposed on issuers of bonds and their coupon payments. As many of these

[5] Case C-57/95 *France v Commission* [1997] ECR I-1627.

[6] Com (1998) 295 final, OJ 1998 C212/09. It followed an Ecofin package of October 1997 and a further Commission Communication of November 1997, see also Fiona Murray, 'EU Package of Measures to Tackle Harmful Tax Competition' (1999) EBLR 237.

issuers are from outside the EU, they cannot be reached. The burden is therefore proposed to be put on paying agents. Most eurobond issues have, however, paying agents in different parts of the world, exactly to avoid an investor being caught in this manner. If squeezed, the paying agents would in any event go elsewhere and take at least the retail eurobond business with them. Capital flight further afield would be the obvious result. The alternative of information-sharing will offend against bank secrecy but even if it were lifted in all of the EU, the moneys would also go outside the EU to countries maintaining such secrecy. The truth is that capital flows themselves should never be burdened by tax collection considerations; they would simply be redirected. This is what freedom of capital movements means. Like markets, flows should be free, only investors should be taxed and intermediaries regulated.

Another practical hindrance of the free flow of capital was that for investors the cost of investments in foreign investment securities remained often high, even for such investments in other Member States. An extra layer of brokerage and settlement cost was frequently involved, at least for the smaller investors who did not have enough clout to face their brokers who under the Investment Services Directive 93/22 have direct access to official and unofficial exchanges everywhere in the EU (the concentration principle having been rejected at the time), but usually prefer local brokers as correspondents. There is here still a lot of abuse, like brokers using sister companies in other countries and still charging extra fees. Maybe the market itself will help out and a merged single European exchange, at least in the major bonds and shares, may help. Off exchange, OTC, telephone or internet markets in them are much more likely to be the way of the future, however, which may cut out the brokers altogether or reduce them to a more modest role only in the clearing and settlement of transactions.

Another point in this connection is that the negotiability of registered shares is still difficult to handle internationally, whilst custody arrangements may still be non-transparent and the status of book-entries uncertain. There remain also major legal problems in the area of proper segregation of client funds and assets in most EU countries. Although, again, these may seem practical rather than regulatory issues, at least in as far as capital flows are concerned, more needs to be done here at the regulatory level in connection with the movement of services and investor protection and I shall come back to it briefly later in the chapter.

A more proper capital movement regulatory issue is that capital raising in the own currency by foreigners may still remain closely controlled too, even in countries with a liberalized capital flows regime. The USA had not wanted this foreign issuing activity in its own currency in the early 1960s and imposed a tax on foreigners issuing bonds in the American capital market (the Interest Equalisation Tax of 1963). It did not apply to dollar issues organized outside the USA. It was at the heart of the development of the eurodollar market from London.

This market subsequently allowed for a facility to issue bonds off-shore in pretty much any currency, but international cooperation between central banks tended to prevent this if the country of the currency did not want it, a form of *informal* regulatory tampering with the capital flows. It applied especially to Swiss franc issues in the eurobond market. Still there is no proper Swiss franc eurobond, but under this arrangement, other countries that allowed in the meantime the free movement of their own currency including the issuing activity in their currency in the eurobond market, were intent to keep at least the issuing activity in their currency in that market at home. Until the advent of the euro, that was the situation in countries like Germany, the Netherlands, France and the United Kingdom, if only to protect the local investment banking community. The liberalization in this area became a matter for the Second Banking and Investment Services Directive, which were on this point often ignored. So the underwiting in German, French, Italian or Dutch eurobonds had still to be conducted from Germany, France, Italy or the Netherlands depending on the currency concerned.

III. FURTHER EU STEPS

It may be clear from this brief review that there remain important direct and indirect national law restrictions on the liberalization of the capital flows, especially in freeing investments and raising capital. These activities may or may not be liberalized at the same time. Even after the freeing of these flows in principle, each country may apparently still limit its own capital seekers in international markets and especially its own investors in their foreign activities. They may also seek to limit capital seekers in their own currency, if only to protect their own underwriting banks although the advent of the euro makes it more difficult to hide behind the currency.

As mentioned above, in the EU, these limitations, whether or not compatible with Articles 56 and 58 EC, remained condoned but the liberalization of pension fund investments in particular reappeared on the Commission's list of activities published in its Communication of 28 October of 1998. It seems to be dropped in its Action Plan published on 11 May 1999, however, although the *Financial Times* tells us that it is still there as a different proposal, but I have been unable to locate it on the Internet.

This recent 1999 EU Action Programme concerning further liberalization and re-regulation including taxation concentrates on the removal of any remaining barriers to raising capital EU-wide and to what extent it is already being informalized or transnationalized. However, it sees this mainly in terms of updating the Directives on the reporting requirements and prospectuses rather than in terms of the issuing activity itself, how and where it may be done. The mutual recognition of listing requirements is here already of some help (although not, perversely, applying to the issuance of government securities which were at the time excluded from these requirements). Mercifully, I do not need to go into the details which have been discussed by others much more competent to do so, but I doubt whether the action is here properly directed.

As far as the access to markets is concerned, the Commission further wants a common legal framework for integrated securities and derivatives markets, but hardly sees this in terms of direct access, costs and settlement and custody risk and conduct of business for retail as it did in 1998, although it talks of a Communication on clarification of the protection rules but no longer on conduct of business as the October 1998 Communication did. It is in any event not a capital movement issue proper and I will return to it below.

The Commission is rightly concerned about market manipulation as a disturbing force and proposes a Directive in this area. It does not refer to updating insider dealing rules in this connection but mentions money-laundering, maybe to bring tax avoidance money under it, who knows? It would destroy much of the credibility of and support for anti-money-laundering measures. Interestingly, the Commission also suggests a Directive on cross-border use of collateral. It must be hoped that in that connection the status of registered shares and book-entries, the position of conditional sales or ownership-based financing especially in repos, bulk assignments in receivable financing, and netting will also be clarified and substantially internationalized.[7] There are here fundamental issues of civil and commercial law and it will be of great interest to see how the EU will deal with them within the limited powers it has to harmonize private law.

IV. THE LIBERALIZATION OF FINANCIAL SERVICES IN THE EU: THE SYSTEM OF HOME AND HOST REGULATION

Let us now turn to the liberalization of the financial services itself. This liberalization has always remained more fundamentally a question of domestic law because of the regulatory aspects connected with these services. Will domestic law allow foreign financial service providers in? Even if it does, it will normally maintain its own regulatory requirements.

[7] See also JH Dalhuisen, 'Security and Ownership Based Funding Techniques' (1998) EBLR 43, 118 and 136.

This may be a severe handicap to liberalization. In economic blocs like the EU, one would expect freedom to provide these services in other Member States as indeed there is in principle, but, as history has shown, the regulatory aspects and domestic regulation of these services, no matter how rudimentary or antiquated, remained a considerable bar. Only the freeing of the capital movements after 1988 provided the impetus for dealing with them. Here again one should distinguish between financial services coming from other Member States or from third countries. The EU is in principle only concerned with the former. The latter may be liberalized further within WTO/GATS. As already mentioned, Article 57 EC exempted these third countries financial services from the area of the free movement of capital.

Even now, after the liberalization Directives, especially the Second Banking Co-ordinaton Directive 89/646 and Investment Services Directive 93/22, we have in the European Union no own regulatory system (in terms of supervisor and prudential rules) or even full harmonization in the domestic supervisory regimes. It proved impossible to achieve. We have in fact only a distribution of powers between home and host regulator operating under their own laws, therefore always between domestic regulatory regimes albeit with some harmonization principles through the EU Directives. This has nevertheless proved decisive progress and allowed the European passport for intermediaries in the financial services industries to emerge largely under their own law and own (home) supervisor (with the regulatory competition connected with it), except for the conduct of consumer business which basically remains under host country supervision.

There are, however, many reasons why this system does not work in practice as well as it might. I have already mentioned that many brokers do not operate for their clients elsewhere, which still leads to double brokerage and settlement cost. There are also the problems with segregation and custody, which may be compounded in cross-border investments. In any event, the notification procedure for rendering direct financial services in other Member States is cumbersome, necessary even if these services are delivered per telephone and has led foreign regulators—only residually involved in the supervision of this activity as host regulators, except for conduct of business concerning consumers—to require these foreign brokers to register with them and pay their fees. The Commission may be minded to propose the abolition of this requirement in view of what it said about it in its 1997 Interpretative Communication concerning the general good, which may be advisable.

In the meantime, the implementation of the Investment Services Directives in the area of a conduct of business rules and segregation of funds remains itself often defective and is by no means uniform. It has much to do with the poor development of the law concerning indirect agency in civil law countries. The 1998 Commission Communication concerning its programme for financial services acknowledged this and asked for much better implementation of the existing Directives. This is not retained in the present 1999 Action Plan.

The disparity in client protection should give a considerable advantage to brokers who are subject to more advanced rules under their home regulation, notably the English broker who may here compete with common law concepts of agency and segregation which are much superior to the civil law equivalents. But as just mentioned, I have the impression that their access to foreign clients—or perhaps more importantly the access of foreign clients to them—still does not work smoothly. It is perhaps also important that English regulators do not like their brokers to go out into foreign retail. That demands too much of a supervision role. An additional problem is of course the interpretation of the general good powers of host regulators elsewhere, rightly a considerable concern for the Commission that issued as a consequence the 1997 Interpretative Communication for banking business and a draft Interpretative Communication for the insurance business. It is not yet planning one for the securities industry, although it would be most welcome.

In the mind of the European Commission, according to its Communication of October 1998 and its recent 1999 Action Plan, a further impetus for the liberalization of the financial services derives from the operation of the euro. Why and how this follows is less clear; this effect must be foremost in the further freeing up of capital raising and investment activity EU-wide as just discussed. The Action Plan states to aim mainly at a single market for wholesale financial services, open and secure retail markets and state-of-the-art prudential rules and supervision (following the guidelines of the Bank of International Settlement (BIS) and the International Organisation of Securities Commissions (IOSCO). The details of the plan do not seem to correspond very closely to these laudable main objectives. It must be said that these Communications and Action Plans of the Commission do not always reflect the clearest thinking. They sound more like advertising pamphlets addressed to an impressionable European Parliament and credulous financial press.

In any event, the Commission does not envisage an own regulatory set up at EU level, therefore not a European SEC operating EU-wide under its own rules. The European passport idea with the divided supervision between home and host regulator remains in place. Whatever its imperfections it is not an illogical system and a similar development in terms of a division between home and host regulator activity will eventually have to occur also within WTO/GATS if worldwide liberalization of financial services is to have a meaning, now that we have within that organization a beginning of liberalization of financial services worldwide, with 70 states having signed up for the financial services agreement which became effective on 1 March (although only with, I believe, 58 ratifications so far). The new negotiation round for the year 2000 or thereafter may shed further light on it.

V. THE OBJECTIVES OF MODERN BANKING REGULATION

Looking now at the impact of the modern liberalization drive on the domestic regulation or re-regulation of financial services, for banking the least seems to have changed. Certainly banking supervision has become tighter and probably somewhat more effective, whilst the BIS Basle Accord of 1989 on capital adequacy and the various subsequent BIS proposals have contributed to what might be considered a somewhat better regulatory banking regime in most modern countries.

What is the true objective of BIS, however? Originally it was of course to provide a better level playing field between banks. The EU Solvency Directive 89/647 in its Preamble still refers to it. Subsequently it was often said to be the avoidance of systemic risk. This seems to be a more recent underlying concern. It was certainly not expressed in the EU liberalization Directives nor in the UK Banking Act 1987. Whether this systemic risk exists or not, it certainly continues to give regulators a brief for involvement. Yet in bad times, bank bankruptcies continue unabated, and it is clear—if it was not always—that modern regulatory requirements like that of adequate capital, can hardly protect against an adverse economic tide or against plain stupidity.

The effect of economic cycles cannot be redressed by capital adequacy requirements which only provide a small buffer. This buffer more properly allows for microeconomic problems and even then hardly for the effects of substantially mismatching assets and liabilities, therefore against ineptitude in asset and liability management or for the effect of pure mismanagement in the loan book.

In the meantime, in the value at risk approach, sophisticated banks are increasingly allowed to set their own minimum capital. It is an unavoidable development but will only reduce the buffer further and bank bankruptcy remains rightly a major worry for banks of last resort and their governments, not only in bad times. New BIS guidance on capital adequacy for banks, as proposed in 1999,[8] will not reverse this trend towards lesser capital at least in better banks. But to operate on 8 per cent risk capital or even less can simply not be prudent and requires indeed the indirect governmental guarantee through bank of last resort arrangements that is effectively in place everywhere.

[8] The Basle Proposals for the reform of the 1988 Accord which is at the heart of the modern capital adequacy requirements for banks, see also JH Dalhuisen, 'Liberalisation and Re-regulation of Cross-Border Financial Services' (1999) EBLR 250.

Rather than to protect the public, the prescribed banking capital appears largely to protect regulators. We spend far too much time on it. To truly avoid systemic risk, that is the risk of bad banking spreading through the inter-bank borrowing network and the payment system, *narrow banking* might be a much better answer. It would lead to much higher capitalization levels, but it is not felt to be the way we traditionally do banking business and the banks' facility to provide random liquidity in good times on the basis of (for the best ones) a mere 8 per cent risk capital and to withdraw it at will in bad times, whilst freely combining lending, deposit and payment activities, seems to remain the way we want banks to operate. Hence the regular banking crises which give us all something to do. Here there seems to be hardly any improvement, whatever the force of modern banking regulation or re-regulation. There may even be acceleration. It was formerly said that banks liked to go broke once in a generation, now it seems to be twice.

Looking at modern banking regulation more closely, it concentrates on authorization, and in that context on the 'fit and proper' test of management, infrastructure and systems, capital and business plan, and on prudential supervision to make sure that subsequently the basic requirements of authorization remain fulfilled. Banking regulation is still less concerned with conduct of business and types of banking products sold to the general public like modern, often insurance-linked, mortgage products or even OTC derivatives.

There is of course the traditional concern for the *depositors*. For the small depositors much of that can be dealt with through deposit guarantee schemes supported by the banking industry itself. Perhaps because of them, it seems that the systemic risk of bank bankruptcies has overtaken the concern for the consequences of bank bankruptcy for depositors. Still the UK Banking Act 1987 concentrates on depositors rather than on the systemic implications of banking activity and sees the licensing and prudential supervision mostly in that context. At least in the United Kingdom, *borrowers*' protection still seems not to be a major focus of banking regulation and there is as a consequence not much concern about conduct of business and the type of banking products offered to the public either.

It is not in the nature of English Statutory Instruments to state objectives clearly. The EU Second Banking Directive does not state clear banking regulation objectives either. This must be seen, however, within the context of its prime objective of dividing the role of home and host regulator. Nevertheless, the note of confusion on the true objective of modern banking regulation remains of considerable interest.

There has never been great regulatory interest in the legal risk inherent in modern banking products either, not for retail but also not for wholesale banking, like the proper characterization and legal status of the modern finance leases, repos and factoring or receivable financing arrangements.

The same is true for the legal status of modern derivative products, securitizations and for the concept of set-off and netting. Only at international level have they obtained some interest through the works of Unidroit and Uncitral and for netting to some extent within the BIS and the Group of 30.

VI. THE OBJECTIVES OF MODERN INVESTMENT SERVICES REGULATION

So much for modern banking regulation. The newer area of regulatory interest and re-regulation concern has been the securities business. Of course it had been substantially regulated in the USA since the 1930s, producing the great model for all. Again we must ask ourselves what the true objectives are and also here it is by no means always fully clear. Systemic risk is, I think, not the real issue, therefore also not bankruptcy of intermediaries as such, even though capital requirements are now imposed, but proper client protection should rather come from compensation schemes and proper segregation of client assets and (on the Continent) proper laws on indirect agency. Reputation of financial centres is important, hence the licensing requirements and prudential supervision, but in this area we have become mainly interested in customer protection especially for retail customers. This would mainly be the conduct of business and products offered but also the need for the efficient, transparent, safe and fair operation of the market-place, free of manipulation and insider-dealing.

The Financial Services Act 1987 in the United Kingdom does not clearly define the regulatory objectives. The EU Investment Services Directive in its Preamble states that investors' protection is one of them but does not clearly specify others. Also here we see a note of uncertainty if not confusion as to the true objectives of modern financial regulation. This uncertainty has of course an effect on how the financial regulation is structured and is probably at the heart of the problems of recasting this regulation in ever more modern ways. It is, I think, behind the protracted discussions on the new Act in the United Kingdom which is bound to give a lead in Europe and should therefore not be seen in isolation. Because of its technical nature, it has not solicited a great deal of public interest, probably also because the modern UK regime since 1987 has been largely successful. The UK cleaning up and streamlining effort is nevertheless important. As far as its objectives are concerned, the Financial Services and Markets Bill now before Parliament (1999) refers in section 2(2) to:

(a) maintaining market confidence which is further defined as confidence in the financial system;
(b) public awareness which is defined as promoting public understanding of the financial system particularly in assessing benefits and risks of investments through appropriate information supply and advice;

(c) the protection of the consumers to secure an appropriate degree of consumer protection taking into account different degrees of risk, different degrees of experience, the need for advice and accurate information but also their responsibility for their own decisions, and
(d) the reduction of financial crime by reducing the likelihood that authorized intermediaries become involved in it or are used by criminals.

According to its title, the new Bill also covers markets (section 3(2)(a)) but not in the sense of regulating them but rather to promote confidence in them. They may apply for recognition (section 256) which exempts them from the general prohibition as respects any regulated activity. This activity is defined in section 20 and Schedule 2 mainly as dealing in investments, managing investments and giving investment advice. Making or organizing markets itself is not such a regulated activity *per se* and as such authorized. As for these markets, the supervisory interest appears to be foremost in proper clearing facilities, not in the distribution of price information.

In the meantime, IOSCO (the International Organisation of Securities Commissions), in its 1998 Principles and Objectives of Securities Regulation states as principle objectives:

(a) the protection of investors;
(b) ensuring that markets are fair and transparent, and
(c) the reduction of systemic risk.

As just mentioned, the latter objective would seem a less obvious regulatory objective in the securities intermediaries business.

Whatever the true objective of modern security regulation, it is clear that we have, at least in the securities area, seen a shift away from regulation of markets and of institutions as such. That is an important liberalization issue. Governments in closed domestic markets, especially in domestic bond markets, might have been able or might have wanted to insulate and manipulate them to facilitate their own funding whilst a small group of insiders around official stock exchanges might have treated that market as their own back-yard, in a club and monopolistic atmosphere subject mainly to self-regulation of them and their members. Much of that has gone.

Institutions as such be they institutionalized markets like stock exchanges or intermediaries like universal banks, are now as such more often left alone in securities regulation. Certainly, in the securities market, we seem to *liberalize institutionally* and *re-regulate functionally*. That is a very important point. In the investment services area, the modern regulatory concern is no longer primarily focused on institutions as such, be they official exchanges or conglomerate banks, but rather on functions or on the types of services provided and sometimes on issuers in primary markets in terms of their financial disclosures through prospectuses and follow-up information supply, at least for listed securities. This does not of course rule out the appearance of one regulator but that should not hide the fact that the regulation of each function is very different.

Thus *universal banks* are, at least for their investment service activity, regulated functionally. *Exchanges*, if they survive in open competition, may become separately regulated for their market, clearing, settlement and custody functions. Indeed, exchanges themselves doing all of this are increasingly becoming antiquated institutions. OTC markets take their place whilst price and other information supply, clearing and settlement, and custody are separated out. They may even be located in other countries. Monopolies are no longer tolerated in any of these functions which can and are often provided by private companies in open competition with a minimum of regulation.

Yet particularly the safety of modern settlement and custody arrangements, access thereto and their cost must be a primary regulatory concern, certainly also the legal side of it. Think of Internet trading in all kind of markets. I do not know whether on this side of the Atlantic it really is safe. At least in the United Kingdom, in these typical market support functions, the emphasis is not in the first place on authorization and supervision. That is also clear elsewhere in the settlement and custody functions—look at Euroclear and Cedel. As for market-makers, the modern emphasis may be rather on disclosure of activity and transparency of operations, although, as for informal market-makers, authorization and supervision may lead to a lesser need of information supply to regulators. Officially recognized markets have in the EU access to other Member States and that may be an important benefit of such recognition. But it remains a matter of choice in the United Kingdom. The SEC in the USA is still much stricter.

Capital is necessary to support all these functions, but like in clearing and settlement, the competitive conditions in the securities business are perhaps automatically expected to guarantee an adequate level of funding (or sufficient other backing) to provide the assurances necessary to be credible and therefore an acceptable player for the public at large. Certainly, the relevant market organizations themselves, in order to survive, will mostly impose the adequate levels of capital on their members, margin requirements on their clients, and supervise them. The members may also (be forced to) accept joint and several liability for each other's commitments. Maybe this is sufficient.

So much for exchanges and their traditional functions. For intermediaries like universal or investment banks, from a regulatory point of view, the functional approach tends to separate out the primary and secondary market functions, brokerage and advisory functions and investment management. The emphasis is here always on investor protection in terms of conduct of business and the types of products offered, again especially in retail. At least for the brokerage and investment management function there is normally also an authorization and supervision requirement, but not necessarily for market-making and underwriting.

VII. CONCLUSION

The conclusion must be that both in the capital flows and the provision of financial services cross-border, there have been substantial autonomous liberalizing forces at work but also attempts at re-regulation, and that this re-regulation is often unfocused. The EU, on the capital flows side, is on the one hand concentrating on greater liberalization especially of pension fund and life insurance investments, on the other hand it is concerned about a uniform system of investment taxation, to be imposed on capital flows. In as far as the capital raising activities are concerned, it sees further action in the strengthening of the listing requirements and regular information supply directives, less in the easy access to ever more informal markets by capital raisers and investors alike.

As far as the financial services are concerned, again what do we truly want to achieve in banking or investment services regulation? Can we focus more clearly than we seem to have done so far? Is the functional approach the answer? If so, can we determine for each of them why we regulate the particular function, what we wish to achieve through it, and how we can efficiently reach the regulatory objective which is likely to differ per function and may also vary in intensity: sometimes authorization and supervision, sometimes conduct of business and product control, sometimes all, sometimes none with instead a mere notification of the activity or information supply on the activities and price formation, or not even that.

Certainly we do no longer want monopolies but competition and alternatives, even in market structures and supporting functions, and never a regulation of capital flows or markets as such in the sense of trying to influence the direction of these flows, the foreign exchange rates, the price formation, or smoothing them out. In an open financial system, such manipulated markets would not survive and others (in the same products) would emerge elsewhere, probably informally. That seems to be the scenario which we see now played and re-played everywhere.

Then there are of course the problems of who should be the regulator, and the sheer organizational problems of proper conglomerate supervision. We must see whether the new English approach of one regulator will work. It makes sense on paper but I am not certain of success and am certainly not an enthusiast. Ever bigger and greater is not in my experience always a clear advantage, certainly not when it comes to the workings of bureaucracies.

The regulatory regimes for the various financial functions remain very different and the distance from a sole regulator to the public and to the relevant central bank might become too large. There may also simply be too much power in such a regulator.

The present debate in the United Kingdom on the Financial Services and Markets Act will give important clues to the resolution for the time being of these issues and show the balance of re-regulation in a liberalized environment. No doubt, it will have a profound effect on the subsequent financial regulatory approaches within the EU, even though, of course, EU law-making and interpretation is conducted at an autonomous level but cannot do without the source from which most of the ideas come, which, at least in as far as investors' protection is concerned, is the United Kingdom and in truth more properly the USA. In the area of the regulation of financial services, we see therefore upon a proper functional comparative law analysis much influence of UK/US concepts at EU level. That is in my view a very good thing, because it comes from where the most experience is. It will also have a unifying effect, amount to better support for investors, and create more confidence in the autonomous globalization through the operation of the international markets themselves.

11

The Home Country Control Principle in the Financial Services Directives and the Case Law

EVA LOMNICKA

None of the parties questions that *the principle of home Member State control* constitutes the guiding principle which has prevailed in the harmonisation of the financial services sector.[1]

I. INTRODUCTION

The cross-border provision of services necessarily entails the potential application of more than one legal system: that of the 'home' State where the undertaking providing the services originates and that of the 'host' State where the provision of services occurs. Traditionally, general principles of private international law operate to allocate the spheres of competence of different legal systems. In some areas of activity, for example in delict and crime, the law of the *host* State plays a dominant role. In commercial activity the position is more complex. Thus under the Rome Convention,[2] absent a choice of law by the parties, the law of the *home* State of the provider of the service is generally given the dominant role unless performance is effected through a branch when the law of the *host* State applies.[3] But in consumer transactions,[4] absent a choice of law, the law of the

[1] From the opinion of Advocate-General Leger in Case C-233/94 *Germany v Parliament and Council* (n 221 below) para 126. He adds '[h]owever, it has not been shown that . . . the Community authorities have adopted that principle with the intention of applying it systematically to [all] measures': para 127.

[2] On the Law Applicable to Contractual Obligations OJ 1980 L226/1. But Article 1(3) excludes from its scope insurance policies covering risks situated in Member States. Article 20 gives precedence to Community Law.

[3] Article 4. The general rule is that the law of the country with which the contract is 'most closely connected' applies, but there is a presumption that this is the law where the service provider ('the party who is to effect the performance which is characteristic of the contract') has his habitual residence or (in the case of an artificial legal person) its central administration or (if performance is to be effected through it) its secondary place of business.

[4] Defined in Article 5(1) of the Rome Convention to mean a supply to a person for a purpose outside his trade or profession.

consumer's habitual residence generally[5] applies. And even if there is a choice of law, it cannot disapply the mandatory rules of the consumer's law.[6]

The establishment of the Common Market by the EC Treaty, with its commitment to facilitate the free movement of, *inter alia*, goods, services and capital, brought with it the possibility of other approaches to the apportionment of legal competencies as well as the theoretical possibility of a completely harmonized, centralized system which would make such allocation of competence between the legal systems of Member States theoretically unnecessary. Detailed harmonization has occurred in various discrete areas where a relatively high level of consensus is possible[7]—the distance marketing of consumer financial services being the latest candidate[8]—but it proved impractical more generally in the financial services field.[9] Therefore (and consistently with the principle of subsidiarity) the focus has been on determining the respective roles of the EC law-making institutions on the one hand and Member States on the other. And once it is conceded that Member States retain significant competence, an equally important issue is to determine the respective roles of the home and host Member States.

The directives in this area attempt to address this issue. As will be discussed below, the 'home country control' principle has been explicitly adopted, with qualifications giving the host State a secondary role. But the directives only go some way towards settling the issue and leave much unresolved; and they hardly begin to tackle the challenges presented by modern electronic methods of attracting and doing business, which require approaches which are not territorially focused. In consequence, general principles of Community law remain pivotal in refining the interface between home and host legal systems.

II. THE HOME COUNTRY CONTROL PRINCIPLE IN GENERAL

As its name suggests, the 'home country control' principle concedes to the

[5] Article 5(3), in the circumstances set out in Article 5(2), ie if the consumer was canvassed and she/he acted in her/his country or if the consumer's order was received there. But note Article 5(4)(b) (exclusion of supply of services exclusively in a country other than her/his habitual residence).

[6] Article 5(2).

[7] See, for example, in the securities trading sphere, the Admissions Directive 79/279, OJ 1979 L66/21, the Listing Particulars Directive 80/390, OJ 1980 L100/1, as amended, the Interim Reports Directive 82/121, OJ 1982 L48/26, the Prospectus Directive 89/298, OJ 1989 L124/8, the Insider Dealing Directive 89/592, OJ 1989 L334/30. See also the Money Laundering Directive 91/308, OJ 1991 L166/77. The 1999 Action Plan of 11 May 1999 promises a Directive on Market Manipulation. Harmonization has also been achieved in the private international law contract field (the Rome Convention, see n 2 above) and in the Jurisdiction and Recognition of Judgements sphere (the Brussels Convention, OJ 1978 L304/36, as amended).

[8] See the Proposal of the Commission, dated 14 October 1998: COM (1998) 468 final; 98/0245 (COD). The Action Plan (n 7 above) calls for its adoption by the end of 1999.

[9] The banking area proved the graveyard for detailed harmonization in the 1970s.

home Member State the primary role of authorizing and supervising an undertaking. Launching the 1992 Internal Market Programme,[10] the principle was famously identified and described by the Commission in its White Paper of 1985:[11]

> [T]he principle of 'home country control' . . . means attributing the primary task of supervising the financial institution to the competent authorities of its Member State of origin . . . The authorities of the Member State which is the destination of the service, whilst not deprived of all power, would have a complementary role.

The programme resulted in three major[12] directives in the financial services sphere—the Second Banking Co-ordination Directive ('2BCD'),[13] the Third Generation Insurance Directives[14] and the Investment Services Directive ('ISD').[15] The Directives do more than merely adopt the concept of 'home country control'. They use it as the basis for elaborate provisions which seek to facilitate[16] the internal market in financial services.[17]

III. THE HOME COUNTRY CONTROL PRINCIPLE IN THE FINANCIAL SERVICES DIRECTIVES[18]

In essence, the strategy adopted in the Directives is as follows.[19] Member

[10] The introduction of QMV (qualified majority voting) by the Single European Act in 1987 was crucial in implementing the programme.

[11] *Completing the Internal Market: White Paper from the Commission to the European Council*, COM (85) 310 final, paras 102–103.

[12] There were many more, see section III below, in relation to each sector.

[13] 89/646, OJ 1986 L386/1, as amended by Directives 92/30, OJ 1992 L110/52 and 95/26, OJ 1995 L168/7.

[14] 92/49, OJ 1992 L228/1 (third non-life insurance directive); 92/96, OJ 1992 L360/1 (third life assurance directive). These were both amended by Directive 95/26, OJ 1995 L168/7.

[15] 93/22 OJ 1993 L141/27, as amended by Directive 95/26, OJ 1995 L168/7.

[16] But in so far as they impose notification conditions before the freedoms of establishment or to provide services may be exercised (see below), they arguably detract from the basic freedoms provided by the EC Treaty and in so far as they introduce uncertainty in application, again they arguably inhibit the operation of the single market (as the Preambles to the Commission's Interpretative Communications in relation to 2BCD and the insurance sector (see n 60 below) admit).

[17] See generally, Fell, 'The Single Passport—An Overview' (1994) 1 EFSL 176 who makes the point that differences in Member States resulting from the implementation of the Directives and the different traditions mean that 'it will be a long time before local implementation leads to a genuine level playing field'. The as yet unharmonized taxation systems of the different Member States could be added to the list of factors inhibiting a true single market. See also, Adams, 'The Single Market in Financial Services—An Orwellian Approach' (1996) 3 EFSL 149.

[18] In the EC context, the term 'financial services' is usually taken to cover three main areas: banking, securities (including investment services) and insurance. This chapter will concentrate on banking and investment services, with incidental reference to insurance.

[19] See the White Paper (n 11 above) paras 102–103, and see 2BCD, Recital (8); ISD, Recital 3 and the Preambles to the Third Generation Insurance Directives (n 14 above).

States are given the task of authorizing and prudentially regulating their 'home' financial services undertakings. Such home authorization must then be recognized throughout the rest of the single market without more, thus conferring a 'single European passport' on the undertaking. And for this approach to be acceptable to all Member States, there obviously has to be a degree of harmonization of national regulatory standards—but only of minimum or 'key' standards.

Each of these three interrelated aspects merit more detailed examination.

1. Home Country Control and its Limits

Sole competency to authorize and prudentially supervise a financial services undertaking is conferred on its 'home' Member State wherever (within the single market) it operates.[20] The 'home' State is essentially the State where the firm's true head office is.[21] The 'host' State is also given a role, although to quote the White Paper,[22] a 'complementary' one.[23] The 'host' State is defined[24] as the State 'in which' a firm establishes a branch or provides services.[25] These 'host State' provisions vary as between the Directives and are rather piecemeal but there is some common ground.[26]

Both 2BCD and ISD confirm that enterprises may advertise their services

[20] For authorization, see ISD, Article 3 and (for banks) the First Banking Directive 77/780, OJ 1977 L322, Article 3 (amended by Directive 95/26, OJ 1995 L168/7) referred to in 2BCD, Article 1 (definition of 'home State'). For prudential supervision, see ISD, Article 8(3); 2BCD, Article 13(1).

[21] If there is a registered office, the head office must be in the same State as the registered office: for banks see the First Banking Directive 77/780, OJ 1977 L322, Article 3.2a (added by Directive 95/26, OJ 1995 L168/7) and for investment firms see ISD, Article 3.2. This definition of 'home State' is explicit in the ISD (see Article 1). The 2BCD is more cryptic, merely defining it (in Article 1) as the State where the bank is authorized in accordance with Directive 77/780 which in turn (see its Preamble, Recitals (3) and (10)) provides for the State of the head office to have primary supervision (reflected in the wording of Articles 4(1), (4), 5, 8(2), (4)) and now (see amendment noted above) requires the head office and registered office to be in the same State. See also 2BCD, Preamble, Recital (8) (and the equivalent in the ISD, Recital (4)).

[22] See n 11 above.

[23] See 2BCD, Article 13(1) and ISD, Article 8(3): home State control is 'without prejudice to those provisions of this Directive which give responsibility to the authorities of the host Member State'.

[24] 2BCD, Article 1; ISD, Article 1.

[25] This immediately raises the problem of deciding where services are provided, considered below.

[26] See especially, the similar provisions in (i) 2BCD, Article 21(11) and ISD, Article 13 (advertising); (ii) 2BCD, Article 19(4) and ISD, Article 17(4) (preparation for supervision of branch—but note the difference between 2BCD, Article 20(2) and ISD, Article 18(2): services); (iii) 2BCD, Article 21 and ISD, Article 19 (considered below); (iv) 2BCD, Article 15; ISD, Article 24 (on-the-spot verification). However, there is no equivalent to 2BCD, Article 14(2) in the ISD itself (but see its Preamble, Recital (15) and Article 19.1, para 2) and no equivalent to ISD, Article 11(2) in the 2BCD.

in host Member States but 'subject to any rules governing the form and content of such advertising adopted in the interest of the general good'.[27] The reference to 'the general good'[28] confirms the effect of Community law that national regulation which restricts the provision of services must be justified in terms of this Community law concept.[29]

In addition, in the context of the establishment of a branch,[30] the host State is to 'prepare for the supervision' of that branch and 'if necessary, indicate the conditions'[31] under which 'in the interest of the general good' the business must be carried on in the host State.[32] This again seems to confirm that host State regulation, if justifiable on the basis of 'the general good',[33] applies to the conduct of business in the host State.

Finally, there are some complex provisions on the relationship between the home and host regulators when transgressions occur of the host State's regulatory regime.[34] Thus the host State regulator, may 'prevent or punish'[35] irregularities within its territory which are contrary to rules[36] 'adopted in the interest of the general good',[37] although it seems that in reacting to breaches of provisions adopted 'pursuant to those provisions of this Directive which confer powers on the host Member State'[38] the host regulators generally[39] need first to ask the undertaking to rectify the

[27] 2BCD, Article 21(11); ISD, Article 13. There are similar provisions in the Third Generation Insurance Directives.

[28] Which also occurs in the Preambles, see especially, 2BCD, Recitals (15), (16); ISD, Recitals (33), (41).

[29] The Commission's 1997 Communications (see n 60 below) seek to summarize the present state of Community law on this concept.

[30] In relation to the provision of cross-border services, ISD (but not 2BCD) also requires the host regulators 'where appropriate' to 'indicate . . . the conditions, including rules of conduct' which 'in the interest of the general good' must be complied with: ISD, Article 18(2), second para. And see ISD, Article18 (3) (changes to business plan).

[31] In the ISD, Article 17(4), the words 'including the rules of conduct' are added. See also ISD, Article 11 requiring these to be drawn up.

[32] 2BCD, Article 18(4); ISD, Article 17(4).

[33] See below, in relation to the ISD, the discussion of whether the conduct of business rules under ISD need to be 'in the general good'.

[34] 2BCD, Article 21; ISD, Article 19. Note also the provisions as to information gathering by the host State in ibid (1)–(2)

[35] 2BCD says 'punish', ISD says 'penalise'.

[36] ISD adds 'rules of conduct introduced pursuant to Article 11 as well as . . . other . . . regulatory provisions'.

[37] 2BCD, Article 21(5); ISD, Article 19(6). The host regulator may also prevent the initiation of further transactions.

[38] 2BCD, Article 21(2); ISD, Article 19(3). 2BCD's wording is slightly different: 'provisions . . . involving powers of the host Member State.' It is not easy to decide which provisions are being referred to. In relation to 2BCD these are probably only Articles 14(2) and 21(1). In relation to ISD, these are probably only Article 19(1), (2).

[39] Except that 'in emergencies' precautionary measures necessary to protect customers may be taken (and the home regulator and the Commission must be informed): 2BCD, Article 21(7); ISD, Article 19(8).

breach[40] and then give the home regulators a chance to react.[41] There are also provisions as to 'on-the-spot verification' of branches by regulators.[42]

Other provisions in the Directives, which are specific to individual Directives, are considered in more detail below.

2. Mutual Recognition: the Operation of the Passport

Once undertakings obtain an authorization (or 'passport') to carry on certain listed activities from their home State regulator, the Directives state that the host State must allow them *either* to establish a branch *or* to provide cross-border services, in relation to the listed activities, without the need for further authorization.[43]

A number of points need to be noted. The undertakings benefiting from the passport are, of course, only those falling within the relevant Directive. Thus, for example, only[44] 'credit institutions' (as defined)[45] may take advantage of the banking passport under 2BCD and only 'investment firms' (as defined)[46] may take advantage of the investment services passport under ISD. And the passport only applies to the listed[47] activities (sometimes termed the 'passported activities') and only if the home authorization extends to the relevant activity.[48]

It is only the establishment of a 'branch'[49] or the provision of services 'within' the host State which is covered by the passport. The passport does not extend to permitting the establishment of *subsidiaries*.[50] These must obtain their own local authorization.[51] However, it seems that once a branch has been established in one host Member State it may provide services, under the passport, 'within' a third Member State.[52] The status of

[40] 2BCD, Article 21(2); ISD, Article 19(3).

[41] 2BCD, Article 21(3); ISD, Article 19(4).

[42] 2BCD, Article 15; ISD, Article 24. Host State regulators must allow home State regulators to perform these in their territory, but without prejudice to the right of host State regulators to verify 'in discharge of their responsibilities under' the Directive.

[43] See 2BCD, Article 18; ISD, Article 14.

[44] And certain of their subsidiaries who are 'financial institutions' as defined, see below.

[45] In Article 1 of the First Banking Directive (see n 20 above): 2BCD, Article 1, but note Article 2.

[46] In ISD, Article 1, but see Article 2.

[47] In the Annex to the Directives. Note the simplified procedure for amending these provided for in 2BCD, Article 22 and ISD, Article 29.

[48] 2BCD, Article 18; ISD, Article 14.

[49] The definition is discussed below.

[50] But see n 114, and accompanying text, below.

[51] This distinction between branches and subsidiaries has been criticized: see, for example, W van Gerven, 'The Second Banking Directive and the Case-law of the Court of Justice' (1990) 10 Yearbook of European Law 59; Usher, 'European Financial Services Law' in Xuereb and Pace (eds), *The State of the European Union 1994* (Malta, 1994) 124, 126.

[52] See 2BCD Communication 13 (n 60 below). It states: 'In such a situation, it is necessary for the branch's home Member State to have sent notification.' See below.

the provision of distance services has caused difficulty. It may be that this is not covered by the ISD passport at all[53] in not being the carrying on of business 'within' a host State.

The exercise of the passport is subject to notification procedures. The undertaking must first notify its home regulator that it intends to exercise its passport and the home regulator must then notify the host regulator.[54] The procedures differ depending on whether the undertaking intends to establish a branch or to provide cross-border services and there are different waiting periods.[55]

These notification procedures have proved controversial. Rather than facilitating establishment and the provision of services in other Member States, they detract from those freedoms enshrined in the EC Treaty in that they place *restrictions* on their exercise. Moreover, they are fraught with practical difficulties.

Given the different procedures in the cases of branches and cross-border services, it is important to be able to distinguish the two situations. The only help given by the Directives themselves is the definition of 'branch' as a 'place of business which forms a legally dependent part of' the enterprise[56] but it is unclear what degree of 'presence' satisfies that test and what other characteristics must be established. A further problem, in relation to the provision of services, is to determine *where* services are being provided for the purposes of deciding if services are provided 'within' another

[53] Although it would be covered by [Article 49 of the EC Treaty]. See 2BCD Communication, 8 (n 60 below), n 74 below (and accompanying text) and the views of Abrams in (1995) 2 EFSL 317; (1997) EFSL 248 who argues that ISD does not apply to the provision of cross-border services where the provider has no physical presence (permanent or temporary) in the client's State.

[54] 2BCD, Article 19 (branch), Article 20 (services); ISD, Article 17 (branch), Article 18 (services). Other information, in particular which activities it wishes to pursue in the host State, must also be provided. There are similar provisions in the Third Generation Insurance Directives. But the UCITS Directive requires the UCITS to notify the *host* regulator: Article 46.

[55] The home State is given the opportunity to refuse to allow the setting up of a branch but not to refuse the provision of services. Additionally, more information needs to be given in the case of a branch: compare 2BCD, Article 19(2) (branch), Article 20(1) (services); ISD, Article 17(2) (branch), Article 18(1) (services). In the case of a branch, the home regulator has *three* months to communicate with the host regulator and the latter has *two* months to prepare for the regulation: see 2BCD, Article 19(3)–(4); ISD, Article 17(3)–(4). In the case of services, under 2BCD the home regulator has *one* month to communicate with the host regulator but (it seems) there is nothing to stop the services being provided immediately on notifying the home regulator (see 2BCD, Article 20, confirmed by *2BCD Communication*, 13 (n 60 below)). Under ISD, the time period is also *one* month but this time the Directive expressly precludes the services being provided until that time has elapsed: ISD, Article 18(2).

[56] 2BCD, Article 1; ISD, Article 1. This is the 2BCD wording. That of ISD is simpler ('a place of business which is part of' the enterprise). All the places of business in the same host Member State are regarded as a single branch: ibid. Thus the detailed notification procedure only applies to the 'first' branch, although the opening of further 'branches' will have to be notified to home and host regulators as a 'change' (see 2BCD, Article 19(6); ISD, Article 17(6)).

Member State.[57] Moreover, the precise effect of failure to notify is unclear. Does it vitiate any consequent transactions and is the firm regarded as unauthorized in the host State for all purposes? Finally, it is also unclear[58] whether an undertaking may both establish a branch and provide cross-border services in the same host State.[59]

Such uncertainties in the context of 2BCD induced the Commission to issue an Interpretative Communication (the 2BCD Communication)[60] which seeks to clarify some of these difficulties. The Communication is not binding on the European Court of Justice,[61] but nevertheless is clearly of significant persuasive impact,[62] especially in view of the lengthy consultation period which preceded it.[63]

The 2BCD Communication discusses at some length, in particular in relation to independent intermediaries and electronic banking machines such as ATMs,[64] the difference between the exercise of the right of establishment and the freedom to provide services. Drawing on ECJ case law in the context both of the EC Treaty[65] and the Brussels Convention,[66] it concludes that an *independent* intermediary might provide services but, being independent (and thus not 'part' in the sense of an extension of, the enterprise) is unlikely to be regarded as a 'branch'. It has some difficulty

[57] And see n 53 above (Abrams).

[58] Statements in Case C-205/84 *Commission v Germany* [1986] ECR 3755 appear ambiguous on the point: see W van Gerven (n 51 above) 63–64.

[59] For arguments that it can, see Dassesse, Isaacs, Penn, *EC Banking Law* (2nd edn, London, 1993) ch 4; Clarotti, 'Revue Banque (France)', *Supplement Revue Banque et Droit*, 1988, 140; Edward, 'Establishment and Services: an Analysis of the Insurance Cases' (1987) 12 EL Rev 231. For a more cautious view (this is possible, but perhaps only in relation to different types of activity), see W Van Gerven (n 51 above) 63–64.

[60] *Freedom to provide services and the interest of the general good in the Second Banking Directive*, OJ 1997 C209/6 ('2BCD Communication'). See also the draft Communication on the insurance sector, OJ 1997 C365/7 (the 'Draft Insurance Communication').

[61] As the Preambles to both 2BCD and the Draft Insurance Communication make clear: '[They] do not prejudice the interpretation that the Court of Justice . . . might place on the matters at issue.' In Case C-57/95 *France v Commission* [1997] ECR I-1627, the Court annulled the Commission Communication on pension funds (OJ 1994 C360/7), issued in the wake of the failure of its proposal for a Directive on Pension Funds (OJ 1991 C312/3) and containing the provisions in the proposal.

[62] For other possible effects, see Andenas, 'The Financial Market and the Commission as Legislator' (1998) Co Lawyer 98, 102–104; Andenas, 'Financial Market Regulation and the Case Law' [1998] EBLR 203, 205–206.

[63] A draft was issued: OJ 1995 C291/7. For a discussion on the Communications, see Andenas (n 62 above).

[64] But not 'mobile, data processing equipment . . . provid[ing] . . . distance banking services e.g. through the Internet': 2BCD Communication, 12, n 14.

[65] Article 49 (services) and Article 43 (establishment), especially Case C-205/84 *Commission v Germany* [1986] ECR 3755, see above; Case C-55/94 Gebhard [1995] ECR I-4165.

[66] Interpreting the concept of 'branch, agency or other establishment' in Article 5(5): Case C-14/76 *De Bloos* [1976] ECR 1497; Case C-139/80 *Blanckaert & Willems* [1981] ECR 819; Case C-33/78 *Somafer* [1978] ECR 2183.

accommodating electronic machines within the wording of the Directive[67] but again suggests they might result in the provision of services but not the establishment of a 'branch'.[68] This discussion hardly solves the many other difficulties of demarcation and, more fundamentally, it fails to question whether the distinction makes any sense.[69]

For the purposes of whether notification is required for the provision of banking services,[70] it puts forward a test which significantly narrows the scope of those requirements. Thus it suggests the concept of 'the place of provision of . . . the characteristic performance of the [banking] service'[71] as determinant of *where* a service is provided.[72] Thus no notification is required in relation to preliminary activities such as advertising, offering services or seeking customers.[73] Moreover, it suggests that 'the provision of distance banking services, for example through the Internet' does not require notification.[74]

As to the effect of lack of notification, the 2BCD Communication suggests that this should not affect the validity of consequent transactions,[75] but is more cryptic about its precise effect on the right to provide the services.[76]

The interpretative doubts surrounding the notification procedure and its unpopularity in relation to the provision of services have led to hints in the 2BCD Communication that it may in the future be abolished.[77] In any event, on the basis of the Communication's narrow view of when notification is required, in particular its suggestion that it is not required for distance banking services, its application is likely to diminish.

[67] 'The present legal framework in fact rests on mechanism[s] which are still based on a "human" concept of "branch" ': 2BCD Communication, 12.

[68] Unless the machine was attached to a branch or agency in which case that branch would be subject to the relevant provisions.

[69] Although there is the cryptic hint, at 7: '[t]he growth of distance services, particularly those using electronic means (Internet, home banking, etc) will undoubtedly soon result in excessively strict criteria on location becoming obsolete.'

[70] The 2BCD Communication is at pains to stress that this is the only issue addressed: 'The fact that certain types of supplies of services do not . . . [need notification] does not mean that such activities are not the subject of mutual recognition and home-country control': ibid 8 and see 7.

[71] A concept apparently borrowed from the Rome Convention, Article 4 (n 2 above).

[72] 2BCD Communication, 7.

[73] ibid 8–9. See also 11 (intermediaries and freedom to provide services, second para).

[74] 'Since the supplier cannot be deemed to be pursuing its activities in the customer's territory', ie (it seems) he is not carrying on business 'within' the territory, as required by 2BCD, Article 20 and ISD, Article 18. But this does not address the issue of whether the client's State is a State 'in which' services are provided for the purposes of the definition of 'host' State (Article 1) and conduct of business rules (ISD, Article 11(2)). The proposals for the Distance Marketing Directive (see n 8 above) will affect distance service provision.

[75] 2BCD Communication, 9.

[76] It is at pains to downplay the notification requirement as 'procedural' (8, 9) and as 'pursu[ing] a simple objective of exchange of information between supervisory authorities' (9) and stresses that it is Article 18 (not Article 20) which establishes 'mutual recognition'.

[77] ibid 9.

Finally, the 2BCD Communication comes down in favour of the view that the simultaneous exercise in a host State of the freedom to provide services and the right of establishment is possible, even in relation to the same activity, but cautions that the activity must be 'connected'[78] with one or the other for regulatory and tax purposes.

3. Minimum Standards

The Directives require Member States to establish a regulatory regime complying with certain (harmonized) minimum or 'key' standards, the application of which (both initially on authorization and subsequently through supervision and monitoring), they agree are the province of the 'home' State. It should be noted that Member States must require *all* home undertakings to be authorized and regulated whether or not those undertakings wish to exercise the passport.

Thus the Directives harmonize, for example, capital adequacy requirements,[79] require fitness of controllers, provide for vetting of controlling interests and[80] require a degree of transparency in the case of a group of undertakings. The Directives are 'minimum standards' Directives[81] which allow Member States to impose more onerous regulatory requirements on their home undertakings, although there may be difficulties in doing this under either Community law[82] or national law.[83] However, as that Member State will have to permit firms established and authorized in other Member States complying with those minimum standards, to operate within its territory, the disincentives to apply higher standards to its home enterprises are obvious. In so far as regulation inevitably imposes costs and restraints, those home enterprises will be placed at a competitive disadvantage and this suggests that such minimum standards harmonization may result in a 'rush to the bottom' of regulatory standards.[84] On the other hand, there may be

[78] This 'connection' must not be 'artificial' so as to evade otherwise applicable legal provision: ibid 12–13.

[79] For banking see nn 125–127 below. In relation to investment services, see CAD (n 162 below). A 'level playing field' is achieved by applying CAD to the trading book activities of banks.

[80] After the amendments made by Directive 95/26, OJ 1995 L168/7 (the so-called BCCI Directive).

[81] The UCITS Directive (n 88 below) (see Article 1(7)) and the Deposit-Guarantee and Investor-Compensation Schemes Directives (n 170 below) (see Article 7(3) and Article 4(3), respectively) are the most explicit. 2BCD and ISD have a Recital to that effect in their Preambles, see 2BCD, Preamble, Recital (9) and ISD, Preamble, Recital (27).

[82] See the challenge under Community law to more onerous regulation in the *Alpine Investments* Case (n 211 below).

[83] See Dassesse, Isaacs, Penn, *EC Banking Law* (2nd edn, London, 1993), ch 4: it seems some Member States (for example, France) consider such 'reverse discrimination' contrary to the principle of equality before the law enshrined in the National Constitution.

[84] See Bradley, 'Competitive Deregulation of Financial Services Activity in Europe after 1992' (1991) 11 OJLS 545, 554–555.

competitive advantages in stricter regulation.[85] Moreover, the responsibility for compensation imposed on home States[86] is a further incentive to apply high standards of regulation.

To avoid 'regulatory arbitrage', an undertaking may only obtain authorisation from its 'home' regulator. It cannot obtain authorization elsewhere in the single market.[87]

IV. THE DIRECTIVES

1. The UCITS Directive

The first financial services directive to adopt the 'home country control' approach was the UCITS Directive[88] concerning 'undertakings for collective investment in transferable securities'. The relative ease with which this measure was agreed on illustrates that in a narrow area on which there is general consensus on regulatory standards, such an approach is very workable. As stated in the Preamble,[89] the UCITS Directive harmonizes the 'rules as to the authorisation, supervision, structure and activities of [certain] collective investment undertakings situated in the Member States and the information they must publish' with a view to furthering the single market[90] and ensuring a minimum standard of investor protection.

The Directive only applies to certain types of collective investment undertakings. The relevant characteristics of those undertakings are that (a) their sole object is the collective investment in 'transferable securities',[91] (b) of capital raised from the public, (c) which operate on the principle of risk-spreading and (d) whose units are redeemable out of the undertaking's

[85] In creating the reputation of a sound and safe financial environment, see the *Alpine Investment* Case (n 211 below).

[86] See the Deposit-Guarantee and Investor-Compensation Directives, discussed below.

[87] See n 21 above and 2BCD, Preamble, Recital (8); ISD, Preamble, Recital (4).

[88] Directive 85/611, OJ 1985 L375/3 (amended by Directive 88/220, OJ 1988 L100/31 and 95/26, OJ 1995 L168/7) on the co-ordination of laws, regulations and administrative provisions relating to undertakings for collective investment in transferable securities.

[89] Recital (4).

[90] But it remains the case that investors usually prefer their domestic funds or offshore funds controlled by domestic institutions: see Little, 'Marketing Investment Funds in some Major European Markets' (1994) EFSL 170, 199. UK unit trusts have had particular problems penetrating Continental Europe (due to the unfamiliarity of the trust device) and therefore the United Kingdom has introduced the more familiar open-ended investment companies (OEICs) (see the Open-Ended Investment Companies (Investment Companies with Variable Capital) Regulations 1996, SI 1996/2827).

[91] The Commission proposed in July 1998 to extend it to cover collective investment in bank deposits, money market instruments, standardized option and futures contracts dealt on regulated exchanges and units in other UCITS. The *Action Plan* (n 7 above) calls for the adoption of this proposal by the end of 1999.

assets.[92] However, the Directive accommodates various types of UCITS, whether constituted under the law of contract (eg common funds), trust law (eg unit trusts) or statute (eg open-ended investment companies).[93]

Member States are obliged to apply the common regulatory standards to UCITSs situated[94] within their borders[95] and then, in accordance with the home country control principle, they must allow UCITS from other Member States to market within their borders without applying their own authorization provisions.[96] The UCITS Directive is expressly stated[97] to be a minimum standards Directive and so Member States may impose stricter regulatory standards on their own UCITSs if they wish.[98] It also precludes 'regulatory arbitrage' in obliging Member States to require the head office of the UCITS to be situated in the same Member State as the registered office.[99]

The passport under the UCITS Directive enabling the UCITS to market its units in other Member States is subject to restrictions. First, before doing so, the UCITS must notify the host regulators[100] and then wait two months. Secondly, the Directive expressly requires the UCITS to comply with host State regulation in so far as it has not been harmonized by the Directive.[101] Essentially, this means that the UCITS must comply with the marketing rules of the host State.

Although the UCITS itself obtains a passport under the UCITS Directive, its managers and depositories do not. Moreover, as noted below, both 'collective investment undertakings' themselves and their depositories and managers are expressly ineligible for the passport available under the Investment Services Directive.[102] Thus depositories and managers must obtain individual authorization in each Member State in which they wish to operate.[103]

[92] UCITS Directive, Article 1(2). Intervention by UCITS in stock exchange trading to ensure that the price of the units 'does not significantly vary from their net asset value' satisfies (d): ibid.

[93] UCITS Directive, Article 1(3). But note Article 2, which excludes certain undertakings, including closed-ended undertakings (such as the UK 'investment trust').

[94] A UCITS is situated where the investment company or management company of a unit trust is situated: UCITS Directive, Article 3.

[95] UCITS Directive, Article 1(1).

[96] But note Article 44, considered below, which enables the host State to control the marketing of the units.

[97] Article 1(7).

[98] Subject to the difficulties noted above, see nn 82 and 83 above.

[99] ie of the investment company or management company of a unit trust: Article 3.

[100] UCITS Directive, Article 46. The host authorities are entitled to certain detailed information. This is in contrast to the position under the 2BCD and the ISD where the exercise of the passport is subject to notification of the *home* regulators only (the home regulators being obliged to pass on the notification to the *host* regulators), see above.

[101] UCITS Directive, Article 44(1). Article 44(2) expressly states that a UCITS must comply with the host State's advertising provisions.

[102] ISD, Article 2(2)(h), see below.

[103] However, 'units in collective investment undertakings' (generally) are 'instruments'

2. The Banking Directives

The home country control approach then became the basis of the Second Banking Co-ordination Directive (2BCD).[104] As a degree of harmonization of banking regulatory standards had already been achieved by the First Banking Directive,[105] it was not surprising that 2BCD was again adopted with relative speed and ease. Indeed, it was the only 'single European passport' Directive in the financial services area to meet the '1992' deadline.[106]

2BCD applies to 'credit institutions' which are defined[107] as undertakings whose business is to receive deposits (or other repayable funds) from the public and to grant credits for their own account. It requires credit institutions to obtain authorization in their home State[108] and this authorization confers a passport on them to operate throughout the single market, whether by establishing branches or providing cross-border services, without the need for further authorization.[109] The 'passported activities' are listed in the Annex to the Directive. They are not limited to the 'core' activities, which characterize banking ie the taking of deposits, the granting of loans and money transmission services. The Directive is based on the German model of the so-called 'universal bank' and therefore the passported activities extend[110] to certain activities in relation to securities ie trading in certain securities and similar instruments, participation in securities issues, advice as to mergers and acquisitions, portfolio management and advice, safekeeping and administration of securities. However, as will be noted below in relation to ISD, when banks undertake those 'securities' activities which are also 'passported' under ISD,[111] ISD applies certain aspects of its prudential regime to them.[112]

within ISD, see ISD, Annex, Section B 1(b), so any passport obtained under the ISD by an eligible enterprise extends to the relevant activities in relation to such units (eg dealing in them).

[104] See n 13 above. For some commentaries see Strivens, 'The Liberalisation of Banking Services in the Community' [1992] CML Rev 283; Zavvos, 'Banking Integration and 1992: Legal Issues and Policy Implications' (1990) Harvard Int LJ 463; Dassesse, Isaacs, Penn (n 83 above); van Gerven (n 51 above).

[105] See n 20 above.

[106] In theory. The United Kingdom implemented it in some haste on 31 December 1992 but only eight of the (then) 12 Member States actually met the deadline. The deadline for the relevant Insurance Directives was 1 July 1994 and that for ISD was 31 December 1995.

[107] By the First Banking Directive (n 20 above) Article 1.

[108] See n 21 above.

[109] 2BCD, Article 18.

[110] Also included are: financial leasing (para 3), issuing and administering means of payment (para 5), guarantees and commitments (para 6), credit reference services (para 13) and safe custody services (para 14).

[111] ie are listed in the Annex to ISD, Section A. But Section A of the ISD Annex is by no means co-terminous with the relevant parts of the Annex to 2BCD.

[112] See ISD, Article 2(1). However, in so far as an activity falls within the Annex to 2BCD but not within Section A of the Annex to ISD (for example, advice as to mergers and acquisitions or safe custody services—which are both in Section C of the Annex to ISD), then the 2BCD prudential regime continues to apply.

To accommodate those Member States where banks cannot undertake certain non-core banking activities except through subsidiaries, the Directive also extends the passport to certain such subsidiaries.[113] The subsidiaries which qualify are so-called 'financial institutions' (defined[114] as undertakings other than credit institutions whose principal activity is either to acquire holdings or to carry on any of the activities other than deposit-taking listed in the Annex to 2BCD)[115] if they are 90 pe cent owned by one or more credit institutions authorized in the State under whose law the subsidiary is formed, are covered by the consolidated supervision of their parents and comply with other stringent conditions including the need for a guarantee from the parent(s).[116] Most aspects of 2BCD's provisions as to supervision of banks are applied, *mutatis mutandis*, to such subsidiaries.[117]

Once a bank has obtained from its home State regulator authorization for any of these activities, the host State cannot preclude the pursuit of such activities by that bank in its territory even if its own local banks are not permitted to pursue them. This had important consequences for non-credit institutions (such as insurance and investment subsidiaries of UK banks) in Member States (such as the United Kingdom) where the 'universal bank' model is not adopted. They could not acquire a passport under 2BCD as they were not 'credit institutions' nor subsidiaries thereof qualifying for the passport,[118] yet they were in competition, in relation to those investment activities, with universal banks and their subsidiaries which could. These non-credit institutions now acquire their passport under ISD (for investment firms)[119] and the Third Insurance Directives (for insurance firms).[120] But during the hiatus between the implementation of 2BCD and these other Directives, the universal banks had a competitive advantage: their passport under 2BCD. Thus the adoption and implementation of 2BCD provided a further incentive for progress towards the adoption of the Investment Services and Life Insurance Directives.

The issue of the demarcation of the regulatory role between the home and host States has been discussed generally above[121] but there is an additional provision peculiar to 2BCD. Thus the host State retains responsibility for supervising the liquidity of bank branches[122] and implementing its own monetary policy.[123]

113 2BCD, Article 18(2).

114 2BCD, Article 1.

115 And other than credit reference and safe custody services.

116 See 2BCD, Article 18(2).

117 See 2BCD, Article 18(2).

118 Under 2BCD, Article 12(2), see above.

119 See below.

120 See below.

121 See Section III (i), above.

122 In co-operation with the home State regulators.

123 2BCD, Article 14(2), although such measures are 'without prejudice to the measures necessary for the reinforcement of the EMS' and may not (of course) provide for discriminatory or more restrictive treatment for non-domestic banks. Only ISD has a recital dealing with monetary policy, see Preamble, Recital (15).

2BCD is complemented by a number of other directives,[124] in particular,[125] the Own Funds Directive[126] and the Solvency Ratio Directive[127] which implement international capital adequacy standards in the banking sector.[128] The Own Funds Directive defines the term 'own funds' (ie defines what is meant by 'capital' in the banking context) and this term is then used as the basis for the harmonization of solvency ratios (ie how much capital banks must have) in the Solvency Ratio Directive.

3. Insurance[129]

Insurance was the next area where, again because of previous harmonization activity,[130] the 'home country control' approach was adopted with relative ease in the so-called Third Generation Insurance Directives covering both life[131] and non-life[132] insurance business. However, they missed the 1992 deadline and had to be implemented by 1 July 1994.

4. Investment Services

The investment services sector proved more contentious and the relevant measures missed the 1992 deadline by three years.[133] There are marked

[124] A consolidation to replace 19 banking directives was proposed by the Commission in December 1997.

[125] See also the Large Exposure Directive 92/121, OJ 1992 L29/1 (which had to be implemented by 31 December 1993) and the Second Consolidated Supervision Directive 92/30, OJ 1992 L110/52. The latter and the Own Funds and Solvency Ratio Directives had the same implementation date as 2BCD (1 January 1993).

[126] Directive 89/299 OJ 1989 L124/16.

[127] Directive 89/647 OJ 1989 L386/14 (as amended by Directives 91/31, OJ 1991 L17/20; 98/32, OJ 1998 L204/26 and 98/33, OJ 1998 L204/29).

[128] Seven Member States were (and eight now are) members of the Basel Committee—hence the convergence of standards. In June 1999 the Basel Committee began a review of its 1988 Capital Accord and in November 1999 the EU also embarked on a parallel (but wider) consultation process (see the European Commission Services' Consultation Document, *A Review of Regulatory Capital Requirements for EU Credit Institutions and Investment Firms* (23 November 1999).

[129] See generally, MacNeil, 'The Legal Framework in the UK for Insurance Policies sold by EC Insurers under Freedom of Services' (1995) 44 ICLQ 19.

[130] The First Generation Directives enabled the establishment of a branch or agency (but subject to local rules including those requiring the establishment of such a presence before conducting business and those controlling policy terms): 73/239, OJ 1973 L228/3 (First Non-Life) and 79/267, OJ 1979 L63/1 (First Life)—both amended by Directive 95/26 OJ 1995 L168/7. The Second Generation Directives enabled the provision of cross-border services: 88/357, OJ 1989 L172/1 (Second Non-Life) and 90/619, OJ 1990 L330/50 (Second Life).

[131] Directive 92/96, OJ 1992 L360/1 (amending the First and Second Life Assurance Directives and itself amended by Directive 95/26, OJ 1995 L168/7).

[132] Directive 92/49, OJ 1992 L228/1 (amending the First and Second Non-Life Insurance Directives and itself amended by Directive 95/26, OJ 1995 L168/7).

[133] Both ISD and CAD were due for implementation by 31 December 1995. They were only

similarities[134] in approach (and drafting) between 2BCD and ISD, similarities which have been carried through into the Deposit-Guarantee and Investor-Compensation Schemes Directives considered below.

ISD applies to 'investment firms'. These are defined as persons[135] whose regular occupation or business is the provision of 'investment services' for third parties on a professional basis.[136] An 'investment service' is defined[137] as any of the services listed in Section A of the Annex to ISD relating to certain 'instruments'.[138] ISD requires investment firms to obtain authorization in their home State[139] and provides that this authorization confers a passport on the investment firm to operate throughout the single market, whether by establishing branches or providing cross-border services, without the need for further authorizations.[140] The activities which may be covered by the ISD passport (the 'passported activities') are listed in the Annex to the Directive. The activities are divided into two categories: those in Section A[141] and those in Section C ('non-core services').[142] The latter are only covered by the passport if carried on additionally to Section A activities.[143] In consequence, authorization may cover (and thus a passport may be acquired for) one or more of the services in Section A and may extend to one or more of those in Section C. However, under ISD, authorization cannot be granted (and so a passport cannot be acquired) solely to carry on those activities in Section C.[144] This dual categorization of investment services was a

adopted in 1993. For commentaries, see Ferrarini, 'Towards a European Law of Investment Services and Institutions' (1994) 31 CML Rev 1283; Cremona, 'A European Passport for Investment Services' [1994] JBL 195.

[134] Pointed out below, but there are also considerable differences in detail, see for example, nn 26, 30, 55 above.

[135] Generally, only 'legal persons' are covered but special provision is made for 'natural persons' in Article 1.

[136] ISD, Article 1. Article 2(1) generally excludes credit institutions from the ISD although it then applies certain ISD provisions to them. Article 2(2) contains wide-ranging exclusions including insurance undertakings (but see the insurance harmonization programme noted above), central banks and other bodies managing the public debt, collective investment undertakings and depositories and managers thereof (but see the UCITS Directive (n 88 above)).

[137] ISD, Article 1.

[138] Listed in Section B of the Annex to ISD to cover (1) transferable securities and units in collective investment undertakings (both defined in Article 1), (2) money-market instruments, (3) financial futures contracts, (4) forward interest-rate agreements (FRAs), (5) swaps and (6) options in the above (including options on currency and on interest rates). Commodity-based investments and life assurance are not included.

[139] ISD, Article 3(1).

[140] ISD, Article 14.

[141] These cover (1) broking in, (2) dealing in, (3) managing of portfolios containing and (4) underwriting of 'instruments' (as listed in Section B, see n 138 above).

[142] These cover (1) safekeeping and administration in relation to instruments within Section B, (2) safe custody services, (3) lending to facilitate a transaction in such instruments, (4) corporate finance advice, (5) services related to underwriting, (6) investment advice in relation to instruments within Section B and (6) certain foreign-exchange services.

[143] ISD, Article 3(1).

[144] ibid.

response to the problem of defining the scope of the Directive. All Member States must regulate activities within Section A. However, they do not have to (but may) regulate Section C activities and if they do, then the passport they confer may extend to them.

The list of activities in the ISD Annex, although similar to, is by no means coterminous with the 'securities' activities listed in the Annex to 2BCD,[145] although neither covers commodities activities,[146] life assurance selling[147] or establishing and operating collective investment schemes.[148]

A word again needs to be said about the demarcation of regulatory role between the home and host States in addition to the general discussion above.[149] Special provision is made as to conduct of business rules. Member States are required to draw up such rules[150] and, pending any harmonization of such rules, the implementation and supervision of compliance with them is stated to 'remain' with the host State.[151] There is no reference to 'the general good' here but it seems[152] that nevertheless, this is implicit[153] and that the host State will only be able to apply those conduct

145 The mis-match was examined by the UK's Securities Investment Board (the SIB) in its Discussion Paper on *Implementing the ISD and CAD* (1993).

146 ISD, Article 2(1)(i) excludes persons whose main business is trading in commodities from the definition of 'investment firms'. There are no concrete plans, although there is talk of, another Directive covering these.

147 But see above. ISD, Article 2(1)(a) excludes insurance undertakings from the definition of 'investment firm'.

148 See above. But as units in collective investment undertakings are 'instruments' (Section B 1(b)) certain activities in relation to them such as dealing in them (Section A 2) or advising on them (Section C 6) are covered.

149 See section III.1 above. Note also ISD, Recitals (8) (doorstep selling) and (15) (monetary policy).

150 ISD, Article 11(1), which lays down the principles these rules must comply with. These are not dissimilar to the United Kingdom's General Principles presently issued under the Financial Services Act 1986, s 47A which apply to all authorized firms. They also reflect some in the Commission's European Code of Conduct Recommendation of 1977 (Recommendation 77/534 of 25 July 1977, OJ 1977 L212/37) and in IOSCO's Principles (December 1990). For a discussion of whether the conduct of business rules drawn up in the United Kingdom (by the (then) SIB under the Financial Services Act 1986, s 48) comply with the ISD, see Thorkildsen, 'Conduct of Business Rules; What We Have and What We Can Expect' (1995) 16 Co Lawyer 300.

151 ISD, Article 11(2). The term 'host State' is not used, but Article 11(2) talks of the State 'in which a service is provided' and 'host State' is defined in Article 1 as the State 'in which [a firm] . . . provides services'. It seems that Article 11(2) applies to *any* firm providing services 'in' another State, even to firms relying on Article 59 of the EC Treaty to whom the ISD passport does not apply.

152 Despite the reference in ISD, Article 19(6) (which concerns the enforcement of the host State's regulatory regime, see above) to 'rules of conduct introduced pursuant to Art 11 *as well as* to the other legal or regulatory provisions adopted in the interest of the general good' (emphasis added).

153 On the basis of general principles of Community Law, see Wouters, 'Rules of Conduct, Foreign Investment Firms and the EC's case law on Services' (1993) Co Lawyer 194. For a more hesitant view, on the basis of the *Keck and Mithouard* Case ([1993] ECR I-6097) see Andenas, 'Rules of Conduct and the Principle of Subsidiarity' (1994) 14 Co Lawyer 61. See

of business rules that are justifiable on that basis. The other host State provisions in ISD, like those in 2BCD, are qualified by reference to the 'general good'.[154] Once more, drawing the line between 'prudential rules'[155] (which are the province of the home State) and 'rules of conduct'[156] (which are the province of the host State) is not easy. For example, rules concerning conflicts of interest appear, at least in the case of a branch, to be the province of both.[157]

For completeness, mention should be made of the ISD provisions concerning 'regulated markets',[158] that is, certain securities exchanges in Member States. In essence, ISD[159] provides for access to these markets for investment firms with the ISD passport[160] and imposes certain transparency requirements.[161]

ISD is complemented by a capital adequacy measure, the Capital Adequacy Directive (CAD).[162] CAD, as its name suggests, imposes[163] capital adequacy requirements for investment activities both for credit institutions (within 2BCD) and for non-credit institutions (within ISD) undertaking them. Recent amendments[164] have brought the requirements in line with the Recommendations of the Basle Committee on capital requirements for securities activities of banks and investment firms.[165]

5. Deposit-Guarantee and Investor-Compensation Schemes Directives

Ensuring that consumers are covered by a deposit-guarantee scheme (in banking) or investor-compensation scheme (in the investment services area)

also, Thorkildsen, 'Power to Draw up Conduct of Business Rules after the Investment Services Directive' (1995) 15 Co Lawyer 102.

[154] ISD, Article 13 (advertising), Article 17(4) (notification of branches), Article 18(2) (notification in relation to services).

[155] Made under ISD, Article 10.

[156] Made under ISD, Article 11.

[157] See ISD, Article 10, the prudential rules article, (indent 5) and Article 11(1), the conduct of business rules article, (indent 6).

[158] Defined in ISD, Article 1

[159] It was the inclusion of these matters (and the problems of achieving agreement on them) that was partly responsible for some of the difficulties in negotiating the ISD.

[160] ISD, Articles 15, 16. There are transitional provisions for countries with restricted access.

[161] ISD, Articles 20–21.

[162] Directive 93/6, OJ 1993 L141/1, amended by Directives 98/31, OJ 1998 L204/13 and 98/33, OJ 1998 L204/29.

[163] And lays down rules as to the calculation of the same.

[164] See n 162 above. Most Member States delayed the implementation of CAD, pending the amendments.

[165] See the Amendment to the Basle Capital Accord to incorporate Market Risks (January 1996, amended September 1997). For a discussion of the amendments, see Nielsen, 'The Recent Updating of EU Financial Market Legislation' (1998) EBLR 307. In the wake of the review of the Basel 1988 Capital Accord, the EU has embarked on a wider review of its capital adequacy policy, covering both banks and investment firms, see n 128 above.

has always been Community policy. Despite arguments against such schemes,[166] they are justified on the basis of consumer protection and the maintenance of market confidence.[167] Even before 2BCD, proposals for deposit-guarantee schemes were emerging[168] and when work began on ISD, again it was envisaged that a compensation schemes would eventually be part of that regulatory structure.[169] So as not to delay the main Directives themselves, separate and subsequent provision has been made for such schemes by the Deposit-Guarantee Scheme (DGS) Directive[170] in the sphere of banking and the Investment-Compensation Scheme (ICS) Directive[171] in the investment services area.

Before the adoption of the home country control principle, it was envisaged that the *host* State would be responsible for providing deposit-guarantees in the banking sphere.[172] But once the home State approach was adopted for authorization and prudential supervision, it followed that it should also apply to the provision of deposit-guarantees. The State responsible for the former, in being in the best position to assess the risks, should also be responsible for the latter.[173] This reasoning breaks down in relation to risks arising from market conduct which are primarily[174] within the supervisory province of the *host* State, but it would clearly be unworkable to divide up responsibility for compensation between regulators to reflect their respective regulatory role so the home State scheme is given primary responsibility.[175] However, only a modified version of the principle of home

[166] That (i) they distort competition in requiring the successful (and scrupulous) enterprises to contribute to the failings of the less successful (or less scrupulous) and (ii) they create 'moral hazard' (consumers lacking incentive to take care in their selection of services providers). See Cartwright and Campbell, 'Deposit Insurance: Consumer Protection, Banks Safety and Moral Hazard' [1999] EBLR 96.

[167] See the ICS Directive, Preamble, Recital (4); the DGS Directive, Preamble, Recital (1).

[168] See n 172 below.

[169] See ISD, Article 12 (repealed by the ICS Directive, Article 16). Para 1 required information about applicable schemes to be given to investors and para 2 noted the steps that were being taken to harmonize schemes.

[170] Directive 94/19/EC, OJ 1994 L135/5 (adopted May 1994 for implementation by 1 July 1995). For commentaries (in the light of *Germany v Parliament and Council*) see n 221 below.

[171] Directive 97/9/EEC, OJ 1997 L84/22 (adopted March 1977 for implementation by 26 September 1998). See Wessel-Aas, 'The Directive on Investor Compensation Schemes', [1999] EBLR 103 and, on the earlier Commission's proposal COM (93) 381 final, OJ 1993 C321/15, see Lomnicka, 'EC Harmonisation of Investor Compensation Schemes', (1994) 1 EFSL 17.

[172] See the Commission Proposal for a Directive on the re-organisation and winding up of credit institutions, OJ 1985 C356/55 (COM (85) 788 final), Article 16 and Commission Recommendation 87/63/EEC, OJ 1987 L33/16.

[173] See DGS Directive, Preamble, Recital (7).

[174] But the home State may also regulate how its firms behave throughout the internal market: see the *Alpine Investment* Case (n 211 below).

[175] Advocate-General Leger, in *Germany v Parliament and Council* (n 221 below) said (at para 130) that the DGS Directive was 'chiefly based' on the home country control principle, citing Recital (7).

country control is in fact adopted by the Directives, which adopt a similar approach.[176]

The Directives require[177] Member States to have[178] a minimum standards deposit-guarantee scheme (in the case of banking) and investor-compensation scheme (in the case of investment firms), covering at least 90 per cent[179] of any claim a consumer has, up to 20,000 ECUs,[180] against a firm which cannot meet its commitments. In accordance with the home country control principle, this cover is provided by a firm's home State regulator and applies to firms wherever within the single market they establish branches.[181] Information about applicable cover must be given to depositors and investors but Member States are required to limit the use in advertising of such information.[182]

Special provision is made for cases where there is disparity between home and host State schemes and this special provision detracts from the home country control principle. First, rather than allowing firms to take advantage of more generous schemes in their home State[183] when operating in a host State, the Directives provide[184] that, at least for a probationary period,[185] the host State's compensation scheme should be the *maximum* a consumer is entitled to. This is the so-called 'levelling-down' or 'export prohibition' provision. Thus the host State, in effect, can determine the maximum cover in relation to its consumers. Secondly, should the host State's scheme be *more* generous than that of the home State, the host State must ensure that non-host State regulated firms are given the

[176] There are provisions to deal with overlap, see ICS Directive, Article 2.3 (and Preamble, Recital (9)). Banks may comply with both Directives by belonging to a single scheme.

[177] DGS Directive, Article 3; ICS Directive, Article 2.

[178] The means whereby compensation is to be delivered is left to each Member State: DGS Directive, Preamble, Recital (23); ICS Directive, Preamble, Recitals (23) and (25).

[179] DGS Directive, Article 7.4 (but full cover is possible to some extent: Article 7.3); ICS Directive, Article 4.4. Requiring the consumer to bear some of the loss is intended to meet the 'moral hazard' objection to compensation schemes (see DGS Directive, Preamble, Recital (19); ICS Directive, Preamble, Recital (13)): see n 166, above.

[180] DGS Directive, Article 7; ICS Directive, Article 4.1

[181] DGS Directive, Article 4.1, para 1; ICS Directive, Article 7.1, para 1. When a firm establishes a branch in another Member State and the home regulator notifies the host State accordingly, details of the scheme must also be notified (2BCD, Article 19(3); ISD, Article 17(3)).

[182] DGS Directive, Article 9; ICS Directive, Article 10. The Preambles state that the 'unregulated use in advertising of references to . . . scheme[s] could affect the stability of the banking/financial system or depositor/investor confidence': ibid. Recital (21) *bis*.

[183] The Preambles to the Directives explicitly reject the idea that 'the level of cover offered by . . . schemes should become an instrument of competition': DGS Directive, Recital (14); ICS Directive, Recital (16). There is similar nervousness at the advertising of schemes, see n 182 above.

[184] DGS Directive, Article 4(1), para 2; ICS Directive, Article 7, para 2.

[185] ibid until 31 December 1999, pending further consideration by the Commission whether to continue the provision.

opportunity[186] to 'top-up' their home cover:[187] the so-called 'topping-up' or 'supplementary guarantee' provision.[188] This cuts across at least the rationale underlying the home country control principle in that the host State providing the 'top-up' is not in such a good position as the home State in assessing the firm's prudential risks and in seeking to minimize them,[189] although it is in a better position to assess the market conduct risks. Such a sharing of responsibility for compensation inevitably means complex mechanisms for allocating liability between home and (top-up) host schemes. Thus provisions are included in the Directives to facilitate co-operation between home and host schemes,[190] amplifying the underlying obligations of co-operation in the EC Treaty.[191]

These two provisions were understandably controversial. Germany, with its generous compensation scheme for customers of its universal banks,[192] not only voted against them[193] but also (unsuccessfully) challenged the DGS Directive in the ECJ, *inter alia* on the grounds that, in relation to the 'supplementary guarantee' provision, the 'home State control' principle was breached.[194] The provisions are subject to reassessment by the Commission.[195]

V. THE COMMUNITY LAW BACKGROUND

1. The EC Treaty

Despite being very detailed, the provisions of the Directives are in no way exhaustive of Community law applying to the provision of financial

186 A *requirement* to 'top-up' would be a restriction on the freedom of establishment and perhaps not justifiable as it would be disproportionate (given the obligation to inform consumers of the level of protection, see n 182 above). However, ISD, Preamble, Recital (38) provided that host States *could* impose their compensation requirements, pending harmonization.

187 DGS Directive, Article 4(2); ICS Directive, Article 7(1), para 3.

188 But 'the possibility that home Member States' schemes should themselves offer such supplementary cover . . . is not ruled out': DGS Directive, Preamble, Recital (15); ICS Directive, Preamble, Recital (15).

189 Indeed, the 'top-up' provision was challenged on this basis, see below.

190 DGS Directive, Article 4.3 and Annex II; ICS Directive, Article 7, para 5 and Annex II.

191 Article 10, para 1 as interpreted in Case C-251/89 *Athanasopoulos* [1991] ECR I-2797, para 57; Case 235/87 *Matteucci* [1988] ECR 5589, para 19.

192 Advocate-General Leger, in *Germany v Parliament and Council* (n 221 below) said it was the most generous in the Community. The UK ICS Scheme, presently operating under the Financial Services Act 1986, is also considerably more generous (both in relation to coverage and amount payable) than the ICS Directive minimum.

193 The Directives were made under Article 250 (ex 189a) EC and utilized the conciliation procedure.

194 See below.

195 See DGS Directive, Article 4.1, para 3, 4.5 and ICS Directive, Article 7.1 para 2.

services throughout the single market. As the Preambles to the Directives themselves acknowledge,[196] they operate against the background of the EC Treaty. Indeed, even in decisions concerning Directives, the ECJ generally starts from first principles, giving priority to the relevant Treaty provisions and its own case law rather than those of Directives.[197]

Thus it is important to recall that early case law established that Article 43EC[198] in relation to the freedom of establishment[199] and Article 49 EC[200] in relation to the freedom to provide services,[201] were directly applicable[202] and that they could be used to further the single market in the insurance context.[203] That those Articles still have a significant role to play in the financial service area is demonstrated by more recent case law. Thus in *Commission v Italy*,[204] Italy's Securities Act of 1991, which required firms (other than banks) dealing in securities to have their registered office in Italy, was held in breach of those Articles. And in *Parodi*[205] the ECJ considered that French requirements as to the authorization of mortgage lenders, which existed before the implementation of 2BCD, fell with Article 49 EC[206] and needed to be justified. More generally, Article 49[207] is the basis of the freedom to provide services in cases to which the passports provided by the Directives do not apply.[208]

[196] The following Recitals confirm that activities *not* within the Directives enjoy the right of establishment and the freedom to provide services under the general provisions of the Treaty: 2BCD, Preamble, Recital (13) and ISD, Preamble, Recital (28). See, also, 2BCD, Preamble, Recitals (15), (16) and ISD, Preamble, Recitals (23), (41) (references to the 'general good').

[197] See, for example, Joined Cases C-34/95, C-36/95 *KO v De Agostini and TV-Shop* [1997] ECR I-3843; [1998] 1 CMLR 32 and *Germany v European Parliament and Council* (n 221 below).

[198] Ex Article 52.

[199] Case C-2/74 *Reyners v Belgian State* [1974] ECR 631; [1974] 2 CMLR 305.

[200] Ex Article 49.

[201] Case C-33/74 *Van Binsbergen v Bestuur van de Bedrijfsvereniging voor de Metaalnijverheid* [1974] 1 ECR 1229; [1975] 2 CMLR 298.

[202] But not the original freedom of capital provision in Article 67 of the EC Treaty: *Casati* ECR I-2595, hence the Freedom of Movement of Capital Directive (Directive 88/361, OJ 1988 L178/5). See also Case C-484/93 *Svensson and Gustavsson v Ministre du Logement et de l'Urbanisme* [1995] ECR I-3955. See now Article 56 (ex 73b) EC and Joined Cases C-163, 165, 250/95 *Sanz de Lera* [1997] ECR I-4821 (Article 73b ECT directly effective).

[203] See Case C-205/84 *Commission v Germany* [1986] ECR 3755; [1987] 2 CMLR 69; *Commission v France* [1986] ECR 3663. These 1986 insurance cases held that national laws requiring insurers to be established in that state could be in breach of Article 49 (ex 59) EC.

[204] Case C-101/94 [1996] ECR I-2691, noted, Andenas, 'Italian Nationality Requirement and Community Law', (1996) 17 Co Lawyer 219.

[205] Case C-222/95 *Societe Civil Immoboliere Parodi v Banque H. Albert de Bary et Cie* [1997] ECR I-3899; [1998] 1 CMLR 115.

[206] See n 200 above.

[207] Ibid.

[208] For example, if the distance provision of services is not covered by the passport, it is covered by Article 49 (ex 59) EC, see n 53 above.

2. The Case Law

The origins of the principle of home country control can be traced to the jurisprudence of ECJ. It emerged, as the well-known *Cassis de Dijon* doctrine,[209] in the case law on free movement of goods.[210] Despite its explicit adoption by the Financial Services Directives, subsequent case law in that area has not found either the Directives or the principle itself particularly helpful in drawing the line between home and host responsibilities.

Alpine Investment BV v Minister van Financien[211] concerned a challenge to the Dutch law regulating 'cold-calling' in relation to commodities futures. There was no applicable Directive: ISD does not extend to commodities futures[212] and, in any event, was not in force at the relevant time. Moreover, it is unclear whether and how the ISD applies to cold calling. First, it is unclear if ISD passport applies at all.[213] Secondly, the effect of the Article expressly giving the host State the power to implement and supervise compliance with its conduct of business rules[214] is also unclear. It is arguable that this precludes the home State imposing conduct of business rules, but it is more probable that it[215] merely confirms, in the context of a Directive applying the home country control principle, that the host State's rules apply, without necessarily excluding the home State's. The home State may both have an interest in ensuring its firms have a reputation for acting in accordance with high standards and be in a better position in some cases (for example, distance selling) to regulate its firms' conduct.[216] ISD was nevertheless referred to by the Advocate General for guidance[217] but, unsurprisingly, he found it 'not entirely clear . . . how responsibility is

[209] Case 120/78 *Rewe-Zentral AG v Bundesmonopolverwaltung fur Branntwein* [1979] ECR 649. The '*Cassis*' doctrine has been re-appraised in Joined Cases C-267/91 and C-268/91 *Keck and Mithouard* [1993] ECR 1-6097. A similar approach emerged in the context of movement of *services* as illustrated by Case 262/81 *Coditel and others v Cine-Vog Films and others* [1982] ECR 3381. See, more recently, Case 76/90 *Sager v Dennemeyer* [1991] ECR I-4221.

[210] The White Paper (n 11 above) characterized financial services as giving rise to 'financial products' (para 102) and hence was able to draw analogies with the *Cassis de Dijon* doctrine.

[211] Case C-384/93, [1995] ECR 1–1141. See also the opinion of Advocate-General Jacobs. For comments, see Hatzopoulos, (1995) CML Rev 1427; Andenas, 'Cross Border Cold-Calling and the Right to Provide Services', (1995) 16 Co Lawyer 249; Andenas, 'Current Developments: EC Law, IV. Insurance and Banking', (1996) 45 ICLQ 230.

[212] See n 138 above.

[213] See the discussion above that the provision of distance services is not provided 'within' the customer's territory for the purposes of ISD, Articles 14 and 18.

[214] ISD, Article 11(2), see the discussion above.

[215] Article 11 read together with Article 13.

[216] This is supported by the *Alpine Investments* Case itself where it was accepted that the *home* State could impose conduct of business rules.

[217] Paras 13–19, citing Articles 11 and 13. He also referred to the Doorstep Selling Directive 85/577/EEC, OJ 1985 L372/31 and the (then) Proposal of the Distance Selling Directive, COM (93) 396, OJ 1993 C308/18.

divided between the authorities of the home and the authorities of the host State'. He therefore went back to the principles of the Treaty and ECJ's jurisprudence.

The challenge to the Dutch law was made on the basis that, in so far as it precluded Dutch firms from cold-calling in other Member States, it contravened Article 59[218] of the EC Treaty in restricting cross-border market access.[219] Whilst agreeing that Article 59 ECT did apply where the 'exporting' (rather than the 'importing') Member State imposed the restriction and that the Dutch law, although non-discriminatory, did indeed impose a restriction on the freedom to provide services within the meaning of the Article, the Court took the view that the restriction was justified in the public interest of safeguarding the reputation of the Dutch securities markets.[220]

The home country control principle was also considered briefly by the ECJ in *Germany v European Parliament and the Council of the European Union*,[221] the challenge by Germany to the DGS Directive. One of the many arguments advanced for the annulment of the 'supplementary guarantee' provision was that it infringed the home country control principle in that responsibility (by the host State) for top-up compensation did not go hand-in-hand with responsibility (by the home State) for prudential supervision. The Court rejected that argument rather peremptorily. First, it denied that the Community legislature had 'laid down the principle of home State supervision in the sphere of banking law with the intention of systematically subordinating all other rules in that sphere' to it. Secondly, as this principle is not in the Treaty itself, the legislature could, in any event, depart from it provided legitimate expectations were not infringed (which they were not). The Advocate-General's Opinion contains a more detailed examination of the home State control principle, which he characterized as 'the guiding principle' in the harmonization of the financial sector. But he ultimately took the view, accepted by the ECJ, that departure from it was justified in moving towards the single market.

[218] See n 200 above.

[219] Thus an analogy with *Keck* (n 153 above) was rejected.

[220] Whilst Advocate General Jacobs stressed the *twin* rationales: protecting the consumer *and* protecting the integrity of the markets, the Court relied only on the latter, stating that the protection of consumers outside the national market was not a matter for that market's regulators except to the extent that it affected the reputation of that market.

[221] C-233/94, [1997] ECR I-2405; see Andenas, 'Directive on Deposit Guarantee Schemes Challenged', (1995) 16 Co Lawyer 18; Andenas, 'Deposit Guarantee Schemes and Home Country Control', in Cranston (ed), *The Single Market and the Law of Banking* (1995) 105, 109. See also, Landsmeer and Van Empel, 'The Directive on Deposit-Guarantee Schemes and the Directive on Investor Compensation in View of Case C-233/94' [1998] EFSL 143; Roth, 'Case C-233/94, Federal Republic of Germany v European Parliament and Council of the European Union' (1998) 35 CML Rev 459.

VI. CONCLUSION

The home state control principle evolved primarily from the *Cassis de Dijon* jurisprudence of the ECJ on free movement of goods, although there is an early reference to it (although not in name) in the First Banking Directive.[222] It was transplanted into the financial services area as a useful concept in allocating prudential regulation[223] over financial services undertakings to one State—the State where they primarily operate from. The concentration of regulatory competence in one primary regulator is sensible in that it avoids both regulatory gaps on the one hand and, importantly from the point of view of establishing a single market, regulatory duplication with its unnecessary burdens on enterprise on the other.

But the limits of the concept are obvious in that the host State clearly must have some role in regulating the operations of enterprises within its territory. This is accepted both in the *Cassis de Dijon* case law—where host State regulation justified in the 'general good' is recognized—and explicitly in those provisions of the Directives, which address the respective roles of home and host State. Yet the very general wording of those Directive provisions do little to clarify the extent of the host State's regulatory responsibility. At best they merely confirm that the host State retains some responsibility but at worst they compound the problem by creating confusion—as illustrated by the Commission's attempt in its 2BCD Communication to dispel it. That the Directives do not really contribute to the difficult process of drawing the line of demarcation between responsibilities of the home and host State is also illustrated by the ECJ case law. Thus, in a masterly understatement,[224] ISD was found 'not entirely clear' on this point.

Lest it be thought that the home country control principle itself is a useful doctrine which can be used as an analytical tool in determining competence, the case law reminds us of its limitations: it is not a Treaty principle and can be departed from.

The conclusion must be that, however descriptively useful the home country control principle is in indicating that the home State has responsibilities for prudential supervision, it does no more than that.

[222] See n 20 above, Recital (10).
[223] And later, responsibility for compensating consumers.
[224] See n 217 above and accompanying text.

12

Unravelling the General Good Exception: The Case of Financial Services

MICHEL TISON*

I. INTRODUCTION

The ever-widening interpretation of the Treaty freedoms given by the European Court of Justice in its jurisprudence over the last decade raises new questions as to the scope and limits of these freedoms. As the case law at present seems to promulgate the prohibition of all restrictions to free movement, whether discriminatory or not, as a general principle of Community law common to all Treaty freedoms, the discussions shift to another level: on the one hand, questions arise as how to circumscribe the notion of 'restriction' to free movement. The step backwards taken by the Court in *Keck* illustrates the complexities of the issue, and the consequences of an uncontrolled extension of the Court's scrutiny of national law in the past. On the other hand, the more national law is caught by the general 'restriction-based' prohibitions to free movement, the more interpretation problems will arise with respect to the possibilities for Member States to uphold restrictive rules under the heading of the 'general good'.

In reality, the 'general good' has evolved over the past decade as a central, but yet very vague, notion in the balance of interests between Treaty freedoms and legitimate regulatory interests of the EU Member States. Furthermore, the 'general good' clause continues to play an important role in the operation of many directives enacted by the Community institutions within the framework of the 1992 Internal Market Programme. Notably, the legal uncertainty surrounding the interpretation of the general good clause in the Banking and Financial Services Directives has emerged as one of the most controversial interpretation issues in the operation of the Directives, both among legal scholars, and at institutional level (supervisory authorities, Member States and the European Commission). The European Commission for its part has provoked a public discussion on the issue and published a communication ('the Interpretative Communication'),[1] which

* This chapter builds on a paper previously published in (1997) 24 Legal Issues of European Integration No 2, 1–46.

[1] See Commission of the European Communities, Commission Interpretative Communication: *Freedom to provide services and the interest of the general good in the Second Banking Directive* OJ 1997 C-209/6. See also URL: http://europa.eu.int/comm/internal-market/en/finances/banks/bank1en.pdf.

provides its (non-binding) view on the interpretation of the general good clauses in the Banking Directives.[2] A similar Communication has been published in the field of insurance,[3] while a draft communication is said to be being prepared in the area of investment services.

The present chapter will try to provide some elements in circumscribing the notion of general good within the context of financial services in general and of the EU Directives on Banking and Investment services in particular. This will enable us to take a position on the Commission's Interpretative Communication with respect to this issue. As the general good doctrine originates in the case law of the ECJ with respect to the Treaty freedoms, we shall first briefly recall the Court's view on the scope of these freedoms (section II). Section III will focus on the notion of general good, both in the overall context of freedom to provide services and in the case of financial services in particular. Section IV will proceed with an analysis of the general good provisions in the Second Banking Directive and the Investment Services Directive, from the angle of both the material scope of these clauses and their procedural aspects, in particular the question of the notification of general good provisions by the host states' competent authorities. Finally, in section V we will try to shed some light on an issue which is highly relevant for the provision of cross-border (financial) services, namely the relationship between the general good, rules of contract law and private international law rules in the Member States.

II. THE ROOTS OF THE GENERAL GOOD: THE ECJ'S CASE LAW ON THE TREATY FREEDOMS

1. Overview of the Relevant Case Law[4]

The general good, as is well known, is a concept which finds no explicit legal basis in the EC Treaty, but which has been created by the ECJ. The

[2] It would seem that the Commission has waited to launch its Interpretative Communication until the ECJ delivered its judgment in the so-called *Pension Funds* Case, concerning the action for annulment introduced by the French Republic against a Communication by the Commission to the Member States on the investment rules for pension funds (Case C-57/95 *France v Commission*, 20 March 1997 (nyp)). The outcome of this case had a direct bearing on the question whether the Commission would be further allowed to use the communication as a useful means to provide its point of view on questions of interpretation of the EC Treaty and other binding legal instruments (directives etc). Although the Court quashed the Communication, it may be submitted that the motives underlying the Court's ruling do not create a specific risk as to the validity of the Commission's Interpretative Communication.

[3] Commission Interpretative Communication, *Freedom to provide services and the general good in the insurance sector*, OJ 2000 C43/5.

[4] As part of its continuous efforts to inform citizens and business operators, the European Commission has recently drafted an extensive guide to the Court's case law on freedom to

general good doctrine must be seen as the necessary counterweight for the Court's judicial activism in widening the scope of the Treaty freedoms from mere non-discrimination principles to general prohibitions on all measures, whether discriminatory or not, which constitute a *restriction* to free movement across borders. More specifically, the general good exception mitigates the effects of the restriction-based approach to the Treaty freedoms, thus striking a balance between the interests of free movement as a precondition for market unification on the one hand, and the preservation of other social values by the Member States on the other.

This tendency was first clearly identified in the area of free movement of goods: in *Dassonville*,[5] the Court considered as contrary to free movement of goods all measures which directly or indirectly, actually or potentially hindered transborder trade, unless they could be reasonably justified. This latter 'rule of reason' was further refined in the landmark *Cassis de Dijon* Case: a Member State may uphold its restrictive regulation as far as it finds a reasonable justification in imperative reasons relating to the general good.[6] In a positive sense, the Court's position came down to formulating a principle of mutual recognition: a product legally manufactured and marketed in its Member State of origin, should in principle be allowed to be offered on the market of other Member States under the same conditions as in its Member State of origin. The host Member States are entitled to apply their own laws only under two circumstances: (1) either they do not qualify as restriction to the free movement of the imported product, or (2) when they do constitute a restriction on cross-border free movement, they should be properly justified by an imperative reason relating to the general good.[7] It is well known that this mutual recognition principle later served as the regulatory model for the Commission's single market programme.

The ECJ gradually extended its broad interpretation of the free movement principle and the general good exception as mitigation of the rule, to the other Treaty freedoms. The *German Insurance* Case[8] witnessed the Court's firm determination to transpose the *Cassis de Dijon* model to services.[9] However, it was not until the *French Tourist*[10] and the *Säger*

provide services: see European Commission, *Guide to the Case Law of the European Court of Justice on Articles 59 et seq. EC Treaty. Freedom to Provide Services* (1999) 190.

[5] Case 11/74 *Dassonville* [1974] ECR 837.

[6] Case 120/78 *Rewe v Bundesmonopolverwaltung für Branntwein* [1979] ECR 649 ('*Cassis de Dijon*').

[7] Compare the Commission's viewpoint in a Communication issued shortly after the *Cassis de Dijon* Case: OJ 1980 C256, 2–3.

[8] Case 205/84 *Commission v Germany* [1986] ECR 3755.

[9] One should note, however, that even before *Cassis de Dijon*, the *van Binsbergen* Case already contained some elements pointing in the direction of an interpretation of the Treaty Free movement of services extending beyond the non-discrimination principle.

[10] Case C-154/89 *Commission v France* [1991] ECR I-659.

Cases[11] that the Court unequivocally prohibited all, even non-discriminatory, restrictions on free movement of services, unless they were duly justified by an exception provided for in the Treaty (public order, Article 46 EC) or by the general good.

More recently, the Court extended the same restriction-based interpretation to the freedom of establishment: although the Court initially showed some reluctance in fully transposing the principles (*Vlassopoulou*[12] and *Kraus*[13] Cases), the judgment in *Gebhard* left no doubts as to the willingness of the Court to read into Article 43 EC a general ban on all restrictions to the freedom of establishment. Finally, the Court seems inclined to adopt the same restriction-based approach in the area of capital movements, although the case law—in particular the *Veronica*[14] and *Svensson*[15] Cases—initially appeared less pronounced in this sense.[16] The Court's judgment in *Trummer*[17] however seems to adhere to the broader interpretation.

The evolution of the Court's case law over the last few years thus clearly indicates a movement of convergence in the interpretation of all Treaty freedoms. This was amply demonstrated in the *Gebhard* judgment,[18] where the Court affirmed the restriction-based concept of free movement as a general principle common to all Treaty freedoms. Hence, after *Gebhard* the general good will serve as a common standard for the justification of restrictions on the free movement in the context of all Treaty freedoms (goods, services, persons—both workers and self-employed—and capital).

Taking *Cassis de Dijon* as a model, the extension of the restriction-based concept of free movement may be positively translated into a principle of mutual recognition: in the area of services, this means that a service legally

[11] Case C-76/90 *Säger* [1991] ECR I-4239.

[12] Case C-340/89 *Vlassopoulou* [1991] ECR I-2357; more recently confirmed in Case C-104/91 *Aguirre Borrell and others* [1992] ECR I-3003; Case C-319/92 *Salomone Haim* [1994] ECR I-425.

[13] Case C-19/92 *Dieter Kraus* [1993] ECR I-1663.

[14] Case C-148/91 *Vereniging Veronica Omroep Organisatie* [1993] ECR I-487.

[15] Case C-484/93 *Svensson and Gustavsson* [1995] ECR I-3955.

[16] The restriction-based interpretation of the free movement of capital is, however, widely accepted in legal writing: see, *inter alia*, J-M Hauptmann, 'Article 73 B', in Constantinesco, Kovar and Simon (eds), *Traité sur l'Union européenne* (Economica, Paris, 1995) 176–177; C Ohler, 'Die Kapitalverkehrsfreiheit und ihre Schranken', WM, 1996, 1806; W Pfeil, 'Freier Kapitalverkehr und §110 I Nr. 2 BewG', *RIW*, 1996, 790; JA Usher, *The Law of Money and Financial Services in the European Community* (Clarendon Press, Oxford, 1994) 38–39 and 73; H-K Ress, JZ, 1995, 1010; S Weber, 'Kapitalverkehr und Kapitalmärkte im Vertrag über die Europäische Union', *EuZW*, 1992 (562), 562–563; R Zäch, UM Weber, 'Die Entwicklung des freien Kapitalverkehrs im Recht der Europäischen Gemeinschaft', in Walder, Jaag and Zobl (eds), *Aspekte des Wirtschaftsrecht. Festgabe zum Schweizerischen Juristentag 1994* (Schulthess, Zürich, 1994), 417–418. See on the contrary P. Pertsch, 'Libre circulation des capitaux: jurisprudence récente et perspectives', *JTDE*, 1996, 101, No 15, who regards this interpretation as premature.

[17] Case C-222/97 *Trummer* [1999] ECR I-1661, *Euredia*, 1999/3, 399, note J Usher.

[18] Case C-55/94 *Gebhard* [1995] ECR I-4165.

provided in one Member State may be offered under the same conditions in the other Member States, thus prohibiting the host Member State from imposing additional—by assumption restrictive—requirements on the foreign service provider. As an exception to the mutual recognition principle, the host Member State may continue to apply to the imported service those provisions of its laws which are justified by the general good. The same principle applies with respect to establishment: a EU national may not be subjected to additional—and by assumption restrictive—conditions by the host Member State when setting up an establishment in the State, except when the general good provides a reasonable justification for the application of the host State's laws.

The mutual recognition principle is thus based on the assumption that disparities amongst Member States' laws may by themselves be tantamount to a restriction on free movement, although this is not necessarily the case.[19]

2. Material Scope of the Treaty Freedoms

A second question with respect to the interpretation of the Treaty freedoms concerns its material scope: which rules in the host States should qualify as a restriction on cross-border free movement? The issue was for long considered of minor importance in both the Court's case law and in legal writing. It is only with the judgment in *Keck* and in subsequent cases that the discussion appeared at the forefront. Indeed, the definition of a 'restriction' to free movement has a direct bearing on the scope of the general good exception: host State rules which by their nature are considered not to have a restrictive effect on free movement, can be applied in cross-border situations without the need to satisfy the general good test. Only the general non-discrimination principle would then apply for these rules.

(a) General principles

In general, the Court's approach to the interpretation of the Treaty freedoms has been characterized by a functional approach to the notion of 'restriction': the restrictive character of a Member State's measure is determined not by its nature, but by its *effects* on the cross-border free movement. This implies that in principle, and irrespective of the freedom at stake, rules of both public and private law may run contrary to the Treaty freedoms, provided they are likely to produce a restrictive effect on cross-border free movement. This conclusion is supported by the Court's judgment in

[19] See *inter alia* Case C-379/92 [1994] *Peralta* ECR I-3453. On the definition of a 'restriction', see below.

Hubbard, involving the application of the *cautio iudicatum solvi* in a national court to a foreign service provider. The Court stated that 'the effectiveness of Community law cannot vary according to the various branches of national law which it may affect'.[20] The European Commission takes the same view, in particular with respect to the private law relating to financial services.[21]

It should be noted that the Court until now never explicitly applied the general prohibition of non-discriminatory restrictions to regulations in the private law area. Neither did it however at any time reject such application. It is true that in the *Koestler* Case, involving the prohibition under German law to recover debts incurred in speculative securities transactions, the Court only applied a non-discrimination test, and concluded that the German law did not infringe the principle of free movement of services.[22] The Court's approach to the case should however be situated within its proper context, as it was decided in 1978, even before the *Cassis de Dijon* Case. Other cases in which the Court had to decide on the compatibility of private law rules with the free movement of goods or services all concerned alleged discriminatory provisions.[23] Therefore, the Court was not given the opportunity to give a ruling on the general prohibition of non-discriminatory restrictions.[24]

In summary, one could consider that, in order to determine the material scope of the Treaty freedoms on the Member States' laws, three main areas of law may be distinguished in which the free movement of services or goods and the freedom of establishment are likely to interfere.

(1) Rules relating to market access for offerors of goods and services: mainly originating in public law, these rules concern the conditions under which the manufacturers and distributors of goods and services obtain access to the market (rules on the legal form and the internal organization of the enterprise, including requirements originating in general company law, own funds requirements, professional rules) and the instruments through which these rules are enforced (registration with a public body, licensing, supervision by an administrative body).

[20] Case C-20/92 *Hubbard* [1993] ECR I-3777; see with respect to rules of criminal law: Case 82/71 *SAIL* [1972] ECR 119.

[21] Interpretative Communication (n 3 above) 23.

[22] Case 15/78 *Koestler* [1978] ECR 1971.

[23] See eg Case C-339/89 *Alsthom Atlantique* [1991] ECR I-107; Case C-93/92 *Motorradcenter* [1993] ECR I-5009. With respect to rules of private procedure: Case 22/80 *BoussacSaint-Frères* [1980] ECR 3427; Case C-20/92 *Hubbard* [1993] ECR I-3777; Case C-398/92 *Mund and Fester* [1994] ECR I-467; Case C-43/95 *Forsberg* [1996] ECR I-4661.

[24] See, however, Case C-177/94 *Perfili* [1996] ECR I-161, where the Court refused to decide whether the non-discriminatory procedural rule (*in casu* the rule in Italian law according to which a victim of a criminal offence who wishes to bring suit as a civil party in criminal proceedings should grant his representative a special power of attorney) could constitute a non-discriminatory restriction to free movement, with the argument that it did not have the necessary elements to make a judgment.

(2) Rules on market behaviour by the goods and services offerors: these rules of both public and private law relate to the way in which goods and services are offered on the market, with respect to *inter alia* advertising, joint or tied offers and, in general, the rules on unfair competition. In some Member States, the enforcement of these rules is entrusted to a public law body, while in others only private enforcement mechanisms are provided.

(3) Private law rules purporting to the contents or substance of the goods or services offered on the market: these 'product rules' relate to the proper characteristics of the material good (weight, composition, presentation, labelling) or of the service.[25] With respect to the latter, a service being immaterial by its very nature, the contractual relationship between service provider and receiver will play a central role (object of the contract, mutual rights and obligations of parties, liability rules, unfair or mandatory contract terms).

(b) Material scope and proper function of the Treaty freedoms

In theory, the general prohibition of non-discriminatory restrictions may affect the Member States' regulatory powers in all the aforementioned areas of law, on the sole condition that the obligation for the market participant to comply with the said rule qualifies as a 'restriction' to cross-border free movement. Surprisingly the Court, except in the context of free movement of goods, never clearly defined the notion of 'restriction' itself. It may be submitted that the Court implicitly relied on the broad *Dassonville*-formula when extending its jurisprudence to the other Treaty freedoms. Consequently, all measures which directly or indirectly, actually or potentially affect the cross-border free movement will be caught by the prohibition. The Court will examine whether the rules under scrutiny in one way or another make the exercise of the freedom either impossible,[26] more costly[27] or less attractive.[28]

Should one conclude from the *Gebhard* judgment that all Treaty freedoms today enjoy a convergent or even identical interpretation, implying

[25] See in this respect the distinction drawn by the ECJ in *Keck* between 'product rules' and 'selling arrangements' as the basis for the more lenient regime applying to the latter.

[26] See the Court's approach in Case C-76/90 *Säger* [1991] ECR I-4221, para 12.

[27] See Case 205/84 *Commission v Germany* [1986] ECR 3755, para 28, where the Court found in the requirement for a foreign insurance undertaking to have a permanent presence in the host country a restriction on free provision of services inasmuch as it increases the cost of insurance services in the State in which they are provided.

[28] See Case C-55/94 *Gebhard* [1995] ECR I-4188, para 37, which refers to the general prohibition of all national measures which 'hinder or make less attractive' the exercise of fundamental freedoms. The general wording of the cases now refer to all measures which 'prohibit, impede or render less advantageous' the exercise of the freedom: see *inter alia* Joined Cases C-369/96 and 376/96 (nyp) *Arblade and Leloup*, 23 November 1999 para 33.

that the law of a Member State which qualifies as a restriction to the freedom to provide services automatically constitutes a restriction on the freedom of establishment? The answer is negative, in so far as this conclusion omits to take account of the proper functions and objectives of the different Treaty freedoms. Indeed, a teleological approach to the interpretation of the Treaty freedoms may lead to varying results as to the material scope of the different freedoms considered separately. As a matter of fact, different objectives may be attributed to each Treaty freedom: it is clear that the free movement of goods is mainly concerned with mobility of material products across borders. In the same line, the free movement of services essentially involves the cross-border mobility of the immaterial product (the service), and, ancillary to the product mobility, the (temporary) cross-border mobility of the person providing or receiving the service.[29] On the other hand, the freedom of establishment and the free movement of workers are essentially concerned with the mobility of 'natural and legal' persons across borders, and remain largely unrelated to the mobility of the goods or services manufactured or distributed by these persons: establishment supposes the setting up of an entity integrated in the economy of the host Member State,[30] from where it will develop its activities. The free movement of capital finally relates to the free flow of all capital substance in any form.

Bearing in mind the specific objectives of each Treaty freedom, further refinements could be made as to which constitutes a 'restriction' to free movement. Thus, the freedom of establishment being related essentially to the movement of persons, only the Member States' measures which are related to the mobility of the person, ie influencing the decision to set up or to maintain an establishment, or with respect to the internal organization and functioning of the enterprise as such, will qualify as a restriction to cross-border establishment (so called 'enterprise-related' rules). Hence, it is difficult to see how non-discriminatory product-related rules (eg mandatory contractual clauses, rules on advertising for a given product) could be regarded as restricting the freedom of establishment, as these rules do not interfere with the proper function of that freedom. On the contrary, the same non-discriminatory product-related rules may amount to a restriction on the free movement of services, in the situation where the service provider does not maintain an establishment in the host Member State: the host State's rules oblige the foreign service provider to modify the substance of the service or the way in which it is offered when extending his activities to the host State's market, and therefore directly affect the proper function of

[29] See with respect to the latter Article 50(2) EC.

[30] Compare on the notion of establishment Case C-221/89 *Factortame* (*No* 2) [1991] ECR I-3905; Case C-55/94 *Kraus* [1995] ECR I-1663, para 25; Case C-56/96 *VT4* [1997] ECR I-3143, para 17 (in the context of Article 49 EC).

the free movement of services, ie the cross-border mobility of the service as an immaterial product. A restriction to free movement of services will therefore not necessarily amount to a restriction on the freedom of establishment, when the same activity would be taken up through an establishment in another Member State. Measures which do not, by their very nature, influence the movement of the enterprise itself, but merely the way in which the activity is exercised, can therefore be considered to remain outside the material scope of the freedom of establishment.[31]

An example will illustrate the former. According to Belgian law, enterprises offering mortgage credit have to register with the Office de Contrôle des Assurances, by whom they are supervised, in order to grant mortgage credit to consumers with habitual residence in Belgium.[32] The Law on Mortgage Credit further contains, for the sake of consumer protection, specific rules on contractual clauses, *inter alia* with respect to interest rate variability: parties must relate the interest rate of the credit to the rates for Belgian treasury bills when the credit is denominated in Belgian francs or in euros; moreover, the interest rate may not vary to the consumer's detriment during the first three years of the credit (Article 9). Finally, the Law imposes specific requirements on advertising for mortgage credit and the availability of all useful information on the credit under the form of a prospectus (Article 47).

For a financial institution established and properly supervised in another EU Member State, the obligation to register with and submit specific documents to the supervisory authorities in Belgium when offering mortgage credit contracts on the Belgian market, will undoubtedly constitute a restriction on free movement, irrespective of whether the activity is undertaken through a Belgian branch or directly under the freedom to provide services.[33] Indeed, the regulatory cost involved with the supervisory requirements directly influences the foreign institution's decision to set up an establishment in the host Member State. It also clearly affects the freedom to provide services, as it imposes an additional burden on the financial institution wishing to offer its services without establishment.

[31] Compare the distinction operated by P Troberg between 'institutional' and 'functional' regulation: P Troberg, 'Artikel 59' in H von der Groeben, J Thiesing, C-D Ehlermann, *Kommentar zum EWG-Vertrag* (4th edn, Nomos, Baden-Baden, 1991) 1064. See for a more extensive analysis of this proposition, and its possible applications to financial regulation: M Tison, *De interne markt voor bank- en beleggingsdiensten* (Intersentia, Antwerp, 1999) paras 86–94, 167–184 and 284–309.

[32] Law of 4 August 1992 on mortgage credit, *Mon*, 19 August 1992.

[33] Compare the French cases which gave rise to the Court's judgment in Case C-222/95 *Parodi* [1997] ECR I-3899 and its aftermath, in particular the outcome of the case in the judgment of the French Cour de Cassation of 20 October 1998. (On this case and subsequent judgments of French courts in similar cases, see M Tison, 'Rebondissements de l'affaire *Parodi* en France: entre nationalisme juridique et libertés communautaires', *Euredia*, 1999/4, 574.)

However, the requirements with respect to interest variability and advertising by the mortgage credit enterprise are unrelated to the transborder mobility of the financial institution as corporate entity, but solely concern the way the enterprise offers its products in the host Member State. Hence, these non-discriminatory requirements under Belgian law may amount to a restriction to the free movement of services, because they prevent the financial institution from offering its services in the host State under the same conditions as in its home State. However, they do not constitute a restriction to the freedom of establishment, as they do not affect the setting up, the internal organization or the functioning of the enterprise itself.

The further refinement operated above with respect to the varying significance of the 'restriction' according to the specific objectives of each Treaty freedom has not until now been corroborated by the case law of the ECJ. Neither did the case law provide any argument against this approach. Indeed, the cases which formulated the restriction-based concept of the freedom of establishment all, *Gebhard* included, concerned 'enterprise-related' professional rules in national law. However, the recent *Centros* judgment indicates the willingness of the ECJ to consider the proper scope of the Treaty freedoms as foundation for their interpretation: with respect to the freedom of establishment, the Court held that Member States should, in combating fraud by foreign companies, take account of the objectives of the Treaty freedoms. The Court further emphasised that the proper objective of the freedom of establishment consisted in guaranteeing the possibility for companies established in a Member State to take up activities in other Member States through a subsidiary, branch or agency. In view of this objective, the Court operated a distinction between rules relating to the creation of companies on the one hand, and rules on the exercise of professional activities on the other, to support its conclusion that the former category belonged to the very essence of establishment, and therefore could by no means be restricted by the host Member State. Although the Court did not conclude that rules on the exercise of a professional activity remained outside the restriction-based interpretation of freedom of establishment, the Court nevertheless cleared the path for a 'variable geometry' approach in interpreting the Treaty freedoms: in identifying the rules of the Member States which constitute a restriction to one or another Treaty freedom, the objective of the freedom at stake will serve as primary reference. As a consequence, some rules will, by their very nature, more than others impair the essence of the freedom and hence qualify as a restriction.[34] In *Centros*, this was the case with rules which interfere with the possibility of setting up an

[34] The opposite is also true: as appears from *Keck and Mithouard* (n 40 below), 'selling arrangements' which only have a limited effect on intra-Community trade because they intervene only in a late stage of distribution of goods, will not qualify as restriction to free movement.

establishment: the likelihood of a reasonable justification for such restrictions will be far less than for restrictions relating to the exercise of an activity in the host State through an establishment. In conclusion, *Centros* illustrates the move by the Court to identify the essence of the Treaty freedoms, in view of their objectives in the Treaty system, as a method of interpreting and assessing their impact on national regulation.

In the context of freedom of establishment, the issue of delimiting the scope of the freedom as a basis for its interpretation is not new. Several authors have made attempts to formulate criteria to delimit the material scope of non-discriminatory 'restrictions' with respect to freedom of establishment: distinction between rules on access to and exercise of a profession;[35] distinction between objective and subjective regulation;[36] criterion of market access as proper function of establishment.[37] None of these proposals lead to fully satisfactory results: the first is artificial and has been clearly rejected by the Court in *Gebhard*, the others are based on rather vague concepts which find no clear justifications in the Treaty itself. Although the *Centros* judgment could be invoked in support of a distinction between rules on market access and exercise of an activity in the host State through an establishment, it should be noted that this distinction served a specific purpose in the context of the facts of the case and the solution envisaged by the Court: the distinction made by the Court was intended to stress the 'untouchable' nature of rules on market access—and the setting up of a corporate entity in particular—in the light of the host State's competencies to counter alleged abuse of Treaty freedoms or fraud by the use of a pseudo-establishment.[38]

The distinction operated above between 'enterprise related' and 'product-related' rules necessarily determines the scope of the general good as exception to the prohibition of non-discriminatory restrictions to free movement: the measures in the law of a Member State which are unrelated to the proper function of a Treaty freedom and therefore escape the restriction-based prohibition, will not need any justification on grounds of general

[35] See eg U Everling, 'Das Niederlassungsrecht in der Europäische Gemeinschaft', *Der Betrieb*, 1990, 1858; L Roeges, 'L'exercise de l'activité bancaire par la voie d'une succursale après la deuxième directive bancaire', *Revue de droit bancaire et de la bourse*, 1994, 19 and 115.

[36] W-H Roth, 'Niederlassungs- und Dienstleistungsfeiheit—Grundregeln', in Dauses (ed), *Handbuch des EG Wirtschaftsrecht* (Beck, Munich, looseleaf, 1993), E.1, 22; Roth, 'The Freedom of Establishment and the Free Provision of Services in the Financial Services Sector', in Stuyck and Looijestijn-Clearie (eds), *The European Economic Area EC-EFTA. Institutional Aspects and Financial Services* (Kluwer, Deventer, 1994) 86.

[37] See J Wouters, 'Conflicts of Laws and the Single Market for Financial Services' (1997) Maastricht Journal of European and Comparative Law 201–203.

[38] cf EM Kieninger, 'Niederlassungsfreiheit und Rechtswahlfreiheit', ZGR, 1999, 743; H De Wulf, 'Brievenbusvennootschappen, vrij vestigingsrecht en werkelijke zetelleer', *Vennootschapsrecht & Fiscaliteit*, 1999/1, 10, para 37.

good: it is sufficient for these measures to satisfy the non-discrimination test, which forms part of the general principle of equal treatment in Community law.[39]

(c) Effects of the Keck *jurisprudence*

An additional difficulty in delimiting the material scope of the prohibition of non-discriminatory restrictions on free movement stems from *Keck and Mithouard*[40] and subsequent cases, in which the Court held that the regulation of selling arrangements which does not imply any unequal treatment in law or in fact to the detriment of imported goods, could no longer be considered to unduly restrict free movement. Apparently, the Court thus excluded a specific category of laws ('selling arrangements') from the prohibition of non-discriminatory restrictions. Other cases illustrate that 'selling arrangements' also include rules on advertising for goods.[41]

It is not possible to enter in the present contribution into further details on the interpretation of *Keck*.[42] With respect to financial services, however, two specific questions arise: is *Keck* likely to be applied to the other Treaty freedoms; and if so, under which conditions should it apply?

As to the first question, the movement of convergence witnessed in the interpretation of the Treaty freedoms suggests that the development in the field of goods could equally be mirrored in the other Treaty freedoms. As demonstrated in *Alpine Investments*, the Court does not exclude a transposition of *Keck* to the area of (financial) services.[43]

However, it may be doubted whether *Keck* could receive a useful application in the area of freedom of establishment. Given the proper function of freedom of establishment—promoting the mobility of persons and enterprises—the present case law already seems to exclude product-related regulation from the scope of the freedom of establishment: 'selling arrangements', which relate to the way a product is offered on the market, will

[39] This is confirmed by the Court's case law which analyses the Treaty freedoms primarily as a specification of the general non-discrimination principle, as laid down in Article 2 EC.

[40] Case C-267–268/91 *Keck and Mithouard* [1993] ECR I-6097.

[41] See, *inter alia*, Case C-292/92 *Hünermund* [1993] ECR I-6787; Case C-412/93 *Leclerc-Siplec v TFI and M6* [1995] ECR I-179.

[42] See S Weatherill, 'After *Keck*: Some Thoughts on How to Classify the Clarification' [1996] CMLR 885. For an extensive analysis of the *Keck* ruling and its possible consequences for cross-border activities of financial institutions, see M Tison (n 31 above), paras 488–520.

[43] Case C-384/93 *Alpine Investments* [1995] ECR I-1141. The rejection of the *Keck* rule by the Court in *Alpine Investments* may be attributed to the specific facts of the case, which concerned an export restriction—the prohibition of cold calling for financial products towards customers in other Member States—directly affecting the *access* of the service provider to the market of another Member State. The Court did not exclude the application of the *Keck* rule in cases where the host Member State would impose a similar non-discriminatory prohibition on services provided in its territory by an enterprise established abroad.

therefore only infringe the freedom of establishment when containing an overt or disguised discrimination on grounds of nationality. The interpretation of the freedom of establishment suggested above is therefore already in line with the *Keck* jurisprudence.[44]

The second question—under which conditions could *Keck* apply in the area of services—is more difficult to answer. In our opinion, the rule in *Keck* was not intended to overrule all previous jurisprudence on the application of *Dassonville* in the field of 'selling arrangements', but merely wanted to return to the basics of the restriction-based interpretation of the free movement of goods, ie prohibiting the measures in the Member States which, without operating any formal or material discrimination, nevertheless result in an unequal treatment of imported goods due to their submission, in their Member State of origin, to equivalent rules. The factual context in *Keck* and similar cases specifically concerned selling modalities which intervened in an advanced stage of distribution within the host Member State, and therefore could be largely assimilated to internal situations. On the contrary, the regulation of selling arrangements which more directly affect the cross-border movement of goods, remains in our view subjected to the prohibition of all restrictions (eg the prohibition of direct advertising by the foreign distributor for his goods in the host country).[45]

This interpretation of *Keck* has important consequences for its transposition to services. The cross-border element in transborder services usually relates to the service provider and receiver being established or resident in different Member States. Moreover, unlike goods, the distribution of services usually does not take place through extensive distribution channels, but most of the time directly between the 'manufacturer' (provider) and the receiver (consumer) of the service. Consequently, the regulation in a Member State with respect to 'selling arrangements' of a service will usually directly affect the cross-border flow of services, and therefore continue to be subjected to the general prohibition of non-discriminatory restrictions. Only in the hypothesis that the service is offered in the host State through the intervention of intermediaries, could *Keck* be applied by analogy to the regulation restricting the use of 'selling arrangements' by the intermediary.[46]

[44] See, however, Wouters (n 37 above) 207–208.

[45] cf in this respect *GB-Inno-BM* Case C-362/88 [1990] ECR I-667 (prohibition under Luxemburg law for a Belgian supermarket to announce in its publicity leaflets, distributed in Luxembourg, price reductions which also mentioned the old prices).

[46] However, even in that case the service, unlike the distribution of goods, will create a contractual relationship between service provider and receiver. This specificity could argue against the transposition of *Keck* to the sphere of transborder services.

3. Conclusions on the ECJ's Case Law with respect to the Treaty Freedoms

The analysis of the Court's case law on the Treaty freedoms shows a clear movement of convergence in the interpretation of all freedoms as prohibiting not only overt or disguised discrimination on grounds of nationality, but also all other non-discriminatory measures which restrict cross-border free movement. However, the general prohibition on all restrictions needs further refinement in the light of each freedom's proper objectives, which in turn will affect the extent to which the general good exception applies. On the other hand, the *Keck* jurisprudence does not seem to produce a significant effect in the fields of establishment and services in general, and financial services in particular.

III. THE 'GENERAL GOOD' EXCEPTION AND ITS APPLICATION IN THE AREA OF FINANCIAL SERVICES

1. General Principles

Although some attempts have been made to provide a definition of the concept of general good,[47] it should be stressed from the outset that the Court has always refrained from building upon an abstract approach to the concept of 'general good' in its jurisprudence. Indeed, given its evolutionary nature, a definition of general good could at most point to the *functions* it fulfils within the system of the Treaty. The general good may then be described as an open-ended concept, embracing the possibility for Member States to maintain, in the absence of Community legislation, their regulation which ensures the protection of specific social values which are not incompatible with the objectives of the Treaty. The general good thus operates an arbitrage between the fundamental Treaty freedoms and the Member States' interests in the regulation of other, non-economic values.[48] The general good thus primarily proceeds from the Member States' regula-

[47] J Pardon, 'Liberté d'établissement et libre prestation dans le domaine bancaire', *Revue de Droit Bancaire et de la Bourse*, 1991, at 220.

[48] U Everling, 'Sur la jurisprudence de la Cour de Justice en matière de libre prestation de services rendus dans d'autres Etats-membres', Cah dr eur, 1984, 14; B Dubuisson, 'Unité ou diversité des notion d'intérêt général, d'ordre public et de normes impératives dans les directives communautaires relatives aux assurances', in *L'Europe de l'assurance. Les directives de la troisième génération* (Maklu, Antwerp, 1992) 244, No 70; B Dubuisson, 'L'intérêt général en droit communautaire de l'assurance. La réaction thermidorienne', *RGAT*, 1995, 815, No 4; C van Schoubroeck, 'The Concept of the General Good', in McGee and Heusel (eds), *The Law and Practice of Insurance in the Single European Market* (Bundesanzeiger, Köln, 1995) 151.

tory policies, but is to be balanced against the need to ensure free movement of products (goods and services) and of production factors (human and other capital).[49] This balancing of possibly conflicting interests implies that, due to the precedence of Community law, the Member States' autonomy in defining and implementing the general good will find its limits in Community law. These limits are incorporated in the conditions formulated by the Court in order for the general good exception to prevail over the free movement principle. This approach also implies that the ECJ will be the final judge in deciding on the compatibility of Member States' regulation with the general good exception, thus achieving more uniformity in the application of Community law.

This peculiar relationship between general good and free movement may be compared to the 'public order' exception to the Treaty freedoms: the question which measures qualify as 'public order' is a matter of national law, but its application is limited by the need to ensure a proper balancing of interests with the free movement principle.[50] The main difference between the 'public order' and 'general good' interests lies in the possibility for the former to justify discriminatory restrictions on free movement: the availability of the 'public order' exception is restricted to those social values, the disruption of which would affect one of the fundamental interests of society.[51] Therefore, it may be submitted that interests such as consumer protection are not so fundamental to the social order as to justify discriminatory restrictions to free movement of (financial) services.

2. Conditions Attached to the General Good

The conditions under which a Member State is allowed to invoke the general good as a barrier to free movement are well established in the Court's case law, and may be summarized as follows:

[49] Some have, however, expressed their support for a qualification of the general good concept under Community law, instead of under national law: see Conclusions of Advocate General Verloren van Themaat in Case 286/81 *Oosthoek* [1982] ECR 4575, at 4598.

[50] See also the Court's decision in Case 147/86 *Commission v Greece* [1988] ECR 1637; for an overview of the case law with respect to the 'public order', see W van Gerven and J Wouters, 'Free Movement of Financial Services and the European Contracts Convention', in Andenas and Kenyon-Slade (eds), *EC Financial Market Regulation and Company Law* (Sweet & Maxwell, London, 1993), 51–55. Inversely, the circumstance that a Member State considers a law to belong to its (internal) public order, does not automatically imply that it is exempted from the application of Community law. As correctly held by the ECJ in *Arblade and Leloup*, the precedence and uniformity of Community law require that the application of 'public order' laws which impose a restriction on free movement be justified by an overriding ground of public interest under Community law ('public order' or general good): see Joined Cases C-369, C-376/96 *Arblade and Leloup*, 23 November 1999 (nyp).

[51] See in particular the Court's decision in Case 30/77 *Bouchereau* [1977] ECR 1999.

- justification by a general good motive;
- absence of harmonization;
- absence of discrimination on grounds of nationality;
- absence of duplication of home State rules;
- objective necessity (adequacy and proportionality).

(a) General good motive

First, the Member State has to justify the restriction on free movement with reference to a general good motive which is not incompatible with the objectives of the EC Treaty. In general, the Court refuses, as within the context of the 'public order' exception, the recourse by the Member States to motives of an economic nature, such as a protection against foreign competitors, the reduction of inflation or of unemployment. These motives will, in view of their protectionist nature, automatically interfere with the aims of the Treaty in creating a single market and eliminating all distortions of competition.[52]

The Court's scrutiny of the compatibility of Member States' general good motives with the Treaty objectives is effected on a case-by-case basis. In general, the Court will investigate whether the invoked motive is in line with the Treaty objectives, and whether the Member State's measure effectively pursues that motive. Hence, the Court is entitled to 'pierce the Member State's veil' when it appears that the measures in reality pursue other, protectionist, goals.[53]

The motives of general good may relate to matters falling both within or outside the Community's competencies, in the former hypothesis on condition that the Community has not yet adopted harmonization measures in the same field. Furthermore, the Court's scrutiny in this case would appear to be more severe: the Court will not limit itself to checking the conformity of objectives, but will also make sure that the Member States' measures do not run against possible future harmonization actions to be undertaken by the Community legislator.[54]

[52] See, respectively, Article 3(a) and (f) EC.

[53] See for an application the Court's decision of 16 December 1992 in Case C-211/91 *Commission v Belgium* [1992] ECR I-6757, where the Court rejected the defendant's justification on grounds of cultural policy with the argument that the measure at stake in reality aimed at protecting the own market against foreign competitors; more recently: Case C-67/98 *Zenatti*, 21 October 1999 (nyp), where the Court verified whether the limits on the organization of commercial betting activities in Italy effectively pursued the aim of protecting consumers and the social order. See also C Gavalda and G Parleani, *Traité de droit communautaire des affaires* (2nd edn, Litec, Paris, 1992) 73, No. 52-11.

[54] For instance, the Court relied in *GB-Inno-BM* on the Council's consumer protection action programme to illustrate the Community's adherence to issues of consumer protection with respect to advertising: see Case C-362/88 *GB-Inno-BM* [1990] ECR I-667; see also

(b) Absence of harmonization

In order for a Member State to justify a restriction on free movement by the general good, the matter—by hypothesis falling within the Community's regulatory competencies—may not have been the subject of harmonization measures at Community level. The underlying idea is that the exercise by the Community of its regulatory powers will be regarded as the codification at Community level of the Member States' powers under the general good.

However, the Court should in every case verify whether the Community harmonization is sufficient to produce a complete substitution of the Member States' powers on grounds of general good. This is well illustrated in the *German Insurance* Case: notwithstanding the harmonization of supervisory standards for insurance companies by the First Non-Life Insurance Directive, the Court recognized that several supervisory issues were not covered by this Directive, thus leaving room for the Member State to regulate foreign insurers in the interest of the general good.[55]

The extinction of Member States' powers in the interest of the general good as a consequence of sufficient Community harmonization, is one of the cornerstones of the 'new approach' to harmonization set forth in the 1985 Commission White Paper on the Completion of the Internal Market, and put in practice in the Internal Market Directives on, *inter alia*, financial services: the Directives aim at reaching a minimum, but sufficient level of harmonization, which corresponds to the codification of the general good, in order to produce full mutual recognition of regulatory standards. This 'perfect' mutual recognition means that the Member States are no longer entitled to invoke the general good as a justification for the application of more restrictive rules in cross-border situations.

The 'sufficient' minimum harmonization as mentioned above is to be distinguished from the 'partial' minimum harmonization effected by other Directives adopted or elaborated in the first half of the 1980s, *inter alia* in the field of misleading advertising or consumer credit. These directives do not aim at exhaustively harmonizing what otherwise would fall under the general good powers of the Member States, but clearly only intended to achieve a partial harmonization of specific issues, leaving room for the Member States to introduce or maintain more restrictive standards.[56] However, in view of the jurisprudential developments in the field of free movement, Member States should, where it produces restrictive effects on

German Insurance Case 205/84 [1986] ECR 3755, where the Court paid attention to the draft Second Non-Life Insurance Directive in deciding whether the defendant could maintain a licensing requirement for foreign insurers.

[55] Case 205/84 *Commission v Germany* [1986] ECR 3755.

[56] See in particular Directive 84/450/EEC on Misleading Advertising, Article 7; Directive 87/102/EEC on Consumer Credit, Article 15.

cross-border free movement, use this clause in accordance with the general good exception.

The recent decision of the ECJ in *Ambry*[57] illustrates the difficulties of ascertaining whether harmonization is to be considered as 'sufficient' or only 'partial'. The Court was asked whether the French law which obliged travel agencies to dispose of sufficient financial resources under the form of, for instance, a bank guarantee, could require that, when the guarantee was provided by a credit institution established in another EU Member State, an additional agreement be concluded between that credit institution and a French bank or insurance undertaking in order to ensure the immediate availability of the payment under the guarantee. The ECJ ruled that the French law was contrary to both the Treaty freedom to provide services (Article 49 EC) and to the right to provide services under the Second Banking Directive. It then went on to verify whether the restriction could be maintained under the general good clause, but held the French law to create a disproportional restriction on free movement.

Without challenging the outcome of the case, it may be questioned whether the Court's reasoning was fully coherent in on the one hand acknowledging that the French law was contrary to the single passport provided in the Second Banking Directive, which is based on 'sufficient' harmonization of prudential standards, and on the other hand proceeding to the general good test notwithstanding the existence of harmonization. It is true that the Second Banking Directive did not specifically harmonize the conditions under which a credit institution is allowed to provide financial guarantees for travel agents.[58] It may, however, be submitted that the French law constituted a direct *access* barrier for foreign credit institutions to the extent that the latter were obstructed in the possibility of providing bank guarantees which would be recognized as equivalent to a guarantee offered by a domestic credit institution.

(c) Non-discrimination

The prohibition on a general good rule containing any discrimination on grounds of nationality distinguishes, as already stated, the judge-made concept of the general good from the 'public order' exceptions contained in the Treaty with respect to the different freedoms. The non-discrimination

[57] Case C-410/96 *Ambry* [1998] ECR I-7875, *Euredia*, 1999/1, 55, note M Vereecken.

[58] In the absence of harmonization of this specific issue—the recognition of a financially sound guarantee for the sake of protection of clients of travel agencies—the general good clause would consequently fully apply: compare M Vereecken, 'Can a Member State Require an Additional Guarantee Agreement in the Interest of the General Good?' *Euredia*, 1999/1, 62; see also W-H Roth, 'Bancassurfinance and the European Passport for Financial Institutions', in *Bancassurfinance* (Cahiers AEDBF-Belgium, Brussels, Bruylant, 2000), para 2.1.5.

principle should be understood in a broad sense: it includes both overt and disguised discriminations, the latter pointing to situations where the measure at stake makes use of a distinctive criterion not relating to nationality, but producing in practice, due to factual circumstances, the same effects as a distinction based on nationality.

It should be noted that the Court does not always seem to follow this principle with the same rigour: especially in tax matters, the Court envisages the possibility of justifying a restrictive measure, notwithstanding its discriminatory character, by the general good, ie the coherence of the fiscal system.[59] However, as recent case law seems to have limited to a great extent the possibility of relying on the coherence of the fiscal system as general good justification (see below), this should not be of major concern.

(d) Absence of duplication of home State rules and controls

The non-duplication principle perfectly illustrates the background of the restriction-based interpretation of the Treaty freedoms: a measure in national law will be regarded as impeding free movement because, although operating no discrimination towards foreign products or persons, the duplication with the home State rules results in additional costs for the foreign product or person when entering the host State market. The non-duplication requirement underlines, together with the proportionality rule, the need for the Member States to have regard, within a unified economic area, to each other's laws before applying their own laws in cross-border situations.[60]

An analysis of the case law on free movement of services and the general good shows that the Court's attention to the non-duplication principle varies considerably: very often, the general good test is effected without having regard to the rules or controls to which the service provider is subjected in its home State. In matters where the cost of double regulation appears overtly, the Court would however more strongly emphasize the non-duplication principle. This was made most clear in the cases where the Court has had to decide on the application of various host State's laws and regulations on the temporary posting of workers by EU-based employers in the context of cross-border service contracts. In *Vanderelst*[61] and more

[59] See in particular the decisions of 28 January 1992 in Case C-204/90 *Bachmann* [1992] ECR I-249 and in Case C-300/90 *Commission v Belgium* [1992] ECR I-305, which concerned the tax deductibility of life insurance premiums by Belgian residents, granting the benefit only when the insurance company had an establishment in Belgium. It has been rightly stressed that this rule in reality discriminated against companies established in other Member States: cf J Wouters, 'The Case-Law of the European Court of Justice on Direct Taxes: Variations upon a Theme' (1994) Maastricht Journal of European and Comparative Law 179, 189–190; D Fosselard, 'L'obstacle fiscal à la réalisation du marché intérieur', *Cah dr eur*, 1993, 492–493.

[60] See also van Schoubroeck (n 48 above) 155, No 2.

[61] Case C-43/93 *Vander Elst* [1994] ECR I-3803.

recently in *Arblade and Leloup*,[62] the Court strongly objected to the imposition by the host State of social security contributions upon the workers or their employer which are aimed at covering interventions which are equally guaranteed by the home State and for which similar contributions are already paid in the home State. The duplication of financial burdens is clearly tantamount to a restriction which will place the employer at a competitive disadvantage compared to its host State equivalent.[63]

The comparison with the rules of the Member State of origin of the product or the person in assessing the non-duplication requirement, implies that the general good test may produce different results depending on the law applicable in the Member State of origin of the product or person, the one disposing of equivalent rules while the other does not. Theoretically therefore, a Member State should, when drawing up lists of general good rules applying to a foreign service provider,[64] make a different list for each Member State of origin separately.

(e) Objective necessity (appropriateness and proportionality)

The proportionality or necessity requirement has emerged in the Court's case law as the cornerstone in the general good test, as it is the condition through which the arbitrage between the Community interest and the Member States' regulatory interests is effected. The test in reality involves a double requirement: first, the Member State's measure must be useful and appropriate to reach the general good objective, ie it must be possible for the public interest to be effectively achieved through the measures invoked (*appropriateness*); secondly, the measure must be *necessary* for achieving the general good objective. This necessity requirement itself contains both a positive and a negative element: in a positive sense, the restriction, provoked by the general good measure must be in proportion to the benefits resulting from the measure of the attainment of the general good objective (*proportionality*); in a negative sense, there should be no equivalent alternative available which is less restrictive to cross-border free movement.

The latter requirement leaves ample room for jurisprudential activism in the application of the general good test, as it allows the judges to decide on the equivalence of different policy alternatives against the background of the free movement. As an example, the *GB-Inno-BM* Case illustrates a clear policy choice with respect to consumer protection: by expressing its preference for sufficient information to consumers as equivalent alternative for prohibitive regulation, the Court rejected the traditional 'paternalistic'

[62] Joined Cases C-369/96 and 376/96 *Arblade and Leloup*, 23 November 1999 (nyp).
[63] See *Arblade and Leloup*, at para 50.
[64] See on this issue section IV.5 below.

approach to consumer protection as a necessary precondition for market integration.

The division of powers between the ECJ and the national judge in preliminary procedures in the context of the general good test has been summarized by Advocate General van Gerven as follows:

- the national judge must provide the ECJ with all factual elements which are important for the interpretation of the Treaty;
- it is up to the ECJ to lay down the general contents of the proportionality requirement, and the criteria according to which the proportionality of the Member State's measure should be measured;
- the actual decision on the proportionality lies with the national courts, as it concerns an application of the abstract criteria to the factual elements of the case.

In reality, the ECJ very often rules itself on the proportionality issue, provided the case discloses all necessary elements of fact to give guidance to the national judges. This approach further strengthens the Court's activism, and is likely to promote unity in the application of Community law. However, the Court seems more reluctant in applying the proportionality test when the case appears more sensitive. This was demonstrated in the *Parodi* Case, involving the compatibility with Article 49 EC of the French banking law which required EC credit institutions offering banking services in France prior to the entry into force of the Second Banking Directive to obtain a licence from the French banking authorities, and even to have an establishment in France. The impact of the question was considerable as several dozens of cases had been brought before the French courts by borrowers who invoked the infringement of the banking law as ground for the annulment of the credit agreements and security interest. The Court stated that the case did not disclose sufficient elements as to the objectives of the French banking law to proceed to the proportionality and necessity test. The result was that the French Cour de Cassation ruled the French law to satisfy the general good test, and declared void all transactions entered into by the foreign bank in contravention to the licensing requirement.[65] Interestingly, some lower French courts in very recent decisions have openly deviated from the ruling of the Cour de Cassation and come to opposite conclusions on basis of another interpretation of the judgment of the ECJ in *Parodi*.[66]

[65] Cass. fr., 20 October 1998, *Euredia*, 1999/1, 65, note B Sousi-Roubi, *Recueil Dalloz*, 1999, jurispr., 10, note B Sousi-Roubi, *Dalloz Affaires*, 1999, 69, note XD, *RTDCom.*, 1999, 166.

[66] For a comment on these cases, see Tison (n 33 above).

(f) Burden of proof

As an exception to the basic freedoms of the Treaty, the burden of proof with respect to the general good justification lies with the person who invokes it.[67] For example, when a financial services provider claims the benefit of the free movement of services against the application by the host State of its supervisory regulations, the service provider will be entitled to claim the benefit of free movement simply by demonstrating that he falls within its ambit: existence of a cross-border service, and existence of a restriction on the free movement of services (eg submission to equivalent rules in the home member State). It will then be up to the host State's supervisory authorities to prove that the application of its regulations satisfies the general good test.

The same principles apply when the issue is raised in a direct procedure of the Commission against a Member State. The latter will have to demonstrate that its laws, the restrictive effect of which has been demonstrated by the Commission, can be maintained on grounds of general good.

3. The General Good Exception in the Field of Financial Services

As mentioned above, the 'general good' by its very essence is an open-ended concept, which implies that over time new legitimate motives might emerge in the case law of the ECJ. With the relative growth of cases in the field of free movement of services in recent years, the potential for further refinements and innovations in the general good doctrine has increased. This is also illustrated in the case law on financial services, which, though still limited, gives some useful guidance on the importance of the general good clause. These cases bear specific importance in further clarifying the general good clauses contained in the internal market Directives on Financial Services.

Within the inventory of general good motives currently accepted by the ECJ,[68] five motives deserve specific attention in the area of financial services:

- consumer protection;
- the fairness of commercial transactions;
- the integrity of the financial system;

[67] Compare with respect to the banking directives: M Tison, 'Europese bankintegratie en het algemeen belang', *Revue de la Banque*, 1993, 211, at 227–228, No. 51; U Bernitz, S Mohamed, 'National Prudential Rules Override Capital Freedom', *JIBL*, 1996, 236. This seemed not always to have been the leading opinion: see conclusions of Advocate General Slynn in Case 279-80 *Webb* [1981] ECR 3305, 3335, putting the burden of proof on the service provider; see also BFH 19 July 1994, *RIW*, 1994/11, 984, 986 sub ee.

[68] See for an overview of the current situation the Interpretative Communication (n 3 above) 17.

- the coherence of the fiscal system;
- the effectiveness of fiscal supervision.

(a) Consumer protection

The protection of the consumer of financial services has received special attention in the Court's jurisprudence since the *German Insurance* Case.[69] The case showed the Court's consideration for the protection of the weak party in complex financial services, such as insurance products, as a justification for the submission of foreign insurers to a licensing requirement under German law.

In the view of the Court, the necessity and extent of consumer protection is not a monolithic concept in the context of financial services, but will vary according to the type, risk level and complexity of the financial service on the one hand, and of the degree of sophistication of the recipient of the service on the other. With respect to insurance products, these criteria led to a further distinction between coverage of commercial risks and of private risks, where only the latter could reasonably justify specific protective measures in the absence of sufficient community harmonization.

In *Parodi*, the Court confirmed this approach with respect to banking services.[70] In considering the necessity of the host State's law imposing an additional banking licence for a credit institution duly licensed in its home State and providing banking services in the host State, the Court indicated to the national judge that a further refinement should be made according to the type of banking activity and the type of customer. The Court further suggested that the requirement of a banking licence apparently was more inspired by the protection of the depositors with banks, who should be confident in dealing with a solvent and reliable institution, than with the protection of borrowers.

In its Interpretative Communication, the Commission also relies on the degree of vulnerability of the recipients of banking services in deciding whether the host State acts in the interest of the general good when applying its own rules to foreign financial institutions on grounds of consumer protection. In general, the Commission finds in the Deposit Guarantee Directive[71] an appropriate criterion to assess whether a recipient is to be regarded as circumspect: financial institutions, institutional investors and larger enterprises which can be excluded form coverage by a deposit protection scheme, should in general be expected not to need any protection with respect to banking services, as they are in a position to assess properly the

[69] Case 205/84 *Commission v Germany* [1986] ECR 3755.
[70] Case C-222/95 *Parodi* [1997] ECR I-3899.
[71] Directive 94/19/EC, OJ 1994 L135/5.

risks they are running when acquiring banking and investment products. It might be doubted whether this proposition holds true for all banking services: several recent examples illustrate that even larger enterprises are often unaware of the risks inherent to sophisticated (derivative) financial products. This could lead to the conclusion that the financial intermediary might have limited professional duties towards 'professional clients' for highly sophisticated products.[72] Moreover, the rationale for prudential supervision is partly to be found in the prevention of systemic risk, ie maintaining the overall confidence in the banking system (see below), and cannot therefore be reduced to the sole protection of the 'weak' consumer.

(b) Fairness of the commercial transactions

The need to ensure fairness in commercial transactions as a general good motive will to a large extent be related to the protection of the financial consumer: the risks involved with and complexity of many financial products may justify restrictive rules on advertising, selling methods, transparency of prices etc for financial services. As for consumer protection in the narrow sense, the extent to which such protective measures may result in restrictions on cross-border free movement will primarily depend on the nature of the financial product and the type of customer.

(c) Financial market integrity

Although the need to ensure financial market integrity only recently received explicit backing as a general good motive by the Court, it goes without saying that this motive underpins much of the legislative efforts at Community level in the fields of banking and investment services.

The relevant case law shows that the integrity motive in reality has a double dimension. At the micro-level, it refers to the vulnerability of financial markets to the confidence of consumers in the quality of the products offered on the market and of the intermediaries active in it. This will usually call for rules with respect to specific market practices by financial intermediaries towards financial consumers, such as a prohibition on 'cold calling' for highly speculative products. In this sense, financial market integrity is closely related to consumer protection as a general good motive. This was clearly illustrated in *Alpine Investments*, where the Court in part justified the ban on 'cold calling' with reference to the complexity and high risk level of the financial products involved. The scope of the protective measures

[72] Compare the duty on the Member States to elaborate conduct of business rules for investment firms, which should take account of the professional nature of the person for whom the service is provided: Investment Services Directive 93/22, Article 11.

allowed under the integrity motive nevertheless seems broader than under the classical consumer protection motive: first, as the protected interest is related to the market itself, the Member State of the market may also assume the protection of the financial consumer in other Member States, although this protection would normally be best ensured by their countries of residence. Furthermore, it is not excluded that market participants other than 'consumers' in its traditional understanding[73] could enjoy protection under the banner of financial market integrity.

At macro-level, the integrity of the financial markets refers to the particular functions of financial intermediaries in the economic process. Excessive risk-taking by credit institutions may provoke a confidence crisis on the part of depositors resulting in a run on deposits, and a contagion effect on the financial soundness of other banks. Equally, the capital markets may suffer high damage from investment firm failures, due to the loss of client money and the loss of open positions on the failed firm by other investment firms. The confidence risks involved at the macro-level therefore mainly call for prudential rules preventing excessive risk-taking by the financial intermediaries and guaranteeing their financial strength.

The macro-dimension of financial market integrity, referring to overall financial stability, in part underpinned the decision in *Alpine Investments*, where the Court referred to the importance of financial markets in the financing of economic subjects. Equally important in this respect is the view of the Court in *Panagis Pafitis*.[74] Although unrelated to the freedom to provide services as such—the questions raised before the Court concerned a Greek law which had allowed the raising of capital in ailing banks without intervention of the general meeting of shareholders—the Court in general held that prudential requirements could constitute a valid general good motive. It is surprising that the Court did not seize the opportunity to confirm the prudential dimension of financial regulation as an autonomous general good motive in subsequent cases: neither in the *SIM* case,[75] involving the requirement under Italian law for foreign securities brokers to have an establishment in Italy, nor in *Parodi* did the Court at any time refer to the systemic dimension of prudential regulation. Reducing the rationale of banking regulation to a matter of consumer protection, as the Court did in *Parodi*, might however impair on the outcome of such cases: it could be difficult to demonstrate the objective necessity of prudential regulations to the extent that the *individual* banking customer, as recipient of services, is protected through the application of its domestic consumer laws.

[73] See Case C-269/95 *Benincasa* [1997] ECR I-3767, where the Court adopted a fairly restrictive approach to the notion of 'consumer' for the application of the Brussels Convention 1968.

[74] Case C-441/93 *Panagis Pafitis* [1996] ECR I-1347.

[75] Case C-101/94 *Commission v Italy* [1996] ECR I-2691.

In conclusion, some of the Court's recent case law demonstrates that the integrity and stability of the financial system constitute autonomous justification grounds for measures restricting free movement. Given the present state of Community harmonization with respect to prudential standards for financial institutions, the practical importance of this general good motive will however be limited to those financial institutions not covered by the internal market Directives (eg financial institutions attracting deposits from the public without granting credit[76] or *vice versa*).

(d) *Coherence of the fiscal system*

The Court's case law accepting the coherence of the fiscal system as a general good motive to justify trade-restrictive measures is to be regarded in the perspective of the difficult relationship between the Member States' regulatory powers in the field of direct taxation on the one hand, and the overall scope of the free movement principles on the other.[77] The only case in which the Court accepted the tax coherence motive, is precisely to be found in the area of financial services: in *Bachmann* and *Commission v Belgium*[78] the Court upheld the Belgian tax regime for deduction of life insurance premiums, which was granted only for contracts offered by insurers established in Belgium: the deductibility of the premiums paid by the insured being closely linked with the taxation as income of the capital paid at the end of the contract, the tax deduction could logically be refused in cases where no taxes could be levied on the capital, *in casu* when the insurer has no fiscal establishment in Belgium.

The Court's positive attitude towards the possibility of maintaining discriminatory tax provisions has been highly criticized by many authors, as it had potentially far-reaching effects for the liberalization of cross-border financial services in a non-unified tax environment: Member States could, by maintaining fiscal provisions of the kind, raise barriers to the free provision of services which the internal market Directives precisely intended to eliminate.[79] However, in subsequent cases the Court seems to have significantly

[76] See in this respect Article 3 of the Second Banking Directive: in the cases expressly covered by national legislation the deposit-taking business by non-banks is still permitted, provided that these activities are subject to regulation and controls intended to protect depositors and investors.

[77] The Court's practice over the last few years amply demonstrates this difficult symbiosis, and the Court's determination, in particular in the area of establishment, to reject all discriminatory regimes in direct taxation. See for an overview of the issues: J Wouters, 'Fiscal Barriers to Companies' Cross-Border Establishment in the Case-Law of the EC Court of Justice', YEL, vol 14, 1994, 73–109.

[78] Both cited in n 59 above.

[79] See, *inter alia*, M Dassesse, 'Tax Obstacles to the Free Provision of Financial Services: The New Fronter?', JIBFL, 1993, 12–16.

narrowed the concept of fiscal coherence: in *Wielockx*,[80] the Court clarified that the coherence between direct benefits and future costs should exist with respect to the situation of one and the same person. Furthermore, the coherence should, when applied in an international tax context, take account of its potential neutralization by double taxation treaties,[81] an aspect of the problem apparently left open by the Court in *Bachmann*.[82]

The Court's judgment in *Svensson*[83] further narrows the fiscal coherence movement: the case concerned interest rate subsidies granted under Luxembourg law for the financing of the acquisition of housing by Luxembourg residents. For this regime to apply, the mortgage loan had to be concluded with a credit institution licensed in Luxembourg. The applicants claimed the benefit of the subsidy for a loan obtained with a Belgian credit institution, and invoked the incompatibility of the Luxembourg regime with the free movement of capital and services. The Court rejected the argument based on the coherence of the fiscal system for the justification of the restriction put forward by the Luxembourg Government, as there was no direct relationship between the cost of the subsidy regime for the public authorities and the expected benefits stemming from the general income taxes raised solely on the income of Luxembourg credit institutions. The need to demonstrate a direct and necessary interrelationship between fiscal costs and benefits for the same person was further more recently stressed in *Asscher*.[84]

In view of the recent developments in the Court's case law, one may therefore conclude that the Court reduced the coherence motive to more or less reasonable proportions. Even if it can be deplored that the Court ever went down that road in *Bachmann*, there seems at present to remain little scope for a multitude of applications of the *Bachmann* jurisprudence with respect to taxation of financial products by the Member States.

(e) The effectiveness of fiscal supervision

In *Cassis de Dijon*, the Court included among the non-exhaustive list of general good motives the 'effectiveness of fiscal supervision'. Even if this

[80] Case C-80/94, [1995] ECR I-2493.

[81] Compare J de Weerdt, 'EG-Recht und Direkte Steuern', RIW, 1995, 928, at 930.

[82] See also M Dassesse, 'Examen de jurisprudence. Les services financiers: banques et assurances', *Journal des Tribunaux Droit européen*, 1996, 15, 19. Others have indicated that the double taxation treaty between Belgium and Germany did not apply to insurance premiums, so that the Court in *Bachmann* did not have to rule on the impact of double taxation treaties on assessing fiscal coherence as a general good motive: W Devroe, 'Samenhang van nationale fiscale stelsels en algemeen belang: de rechtspraak na Bachmann', *Tijdschrift voor Rechtspersoon en Vennootschappen* 1996, 310, at 316, No. 15.

[83] Case C-484/93 *Svensson and Gustavsson* [1995] ECR I-3955.

[84] Case C-107/94 *Asscher* [1996] ECR I-3089; see on this case also J-M Binon, 'Avantages fiscaux en assurance de personnes et droit européen', *Revue du Marché Unique européen*, 1996/2, 129, at 138, No 14.

motive has not given rise to extensive case law from the ECJ,[85] one might wonder whether it could be used in the area of (direct) taxation of financial services. The combination of capital movement liberalization and the absence of common European rules with respect to direct taxation of income on financial products (withdrawal tax) creates a large potential of fiscal evasion through the use of the Treaty freedoms.

As a rule, Member States should, in the exercise of their fiscal competencies, comply with the fundamental freedoms of the EC Treaty,[86] which implies the obligation to maintain only those fiscal supervision measures which, if they produce restrictive effects on free movement, are objectively necessary to ensure the effectiveness of fiscal supervision.[87] However, the Court's attitude in *Bachmann* does not seem to leave much room for the Member States in restricting the free movement of financial services for the sake of effective fiscal supervision: in the Court's view, Directive 77/799/EEC on the mutual assistance between Member States in the field of direct taxation[88] provides an adequate framework for co-operation between Member States. Moreover, Member States are not automatically entitled to impose restrictions on free movement for tax supervisory reasons outside the (limited) scope of the mutual assistance imposed by the Directive when other alternatives are available which do not restrict free movement to the same extent: in *Bachmann* it was held that the tax authorities had a valuable alternative for the restriction by asking the insured person to give proof of the payment of insurance premiums to the foreign insurance company as a condition for obtaining the tax benefit, without having recourse to measures restricting the free provision of services by foreign insurance companies.

However, it may be doubted whether this line of reasoning can be extrapolated to the taxation of financial services in general. It should be borne in mind that in *Bachmann* the information provided by the individual could be considered as a satisfactory alternative for the co-operation between tax authorities: the insured had a proper interest in providing the information, as it led to a tax benefit (deductibility of premium payments). The same motives underpinned the judgment in *Futura Participations*,[89] where the Court held that the requirement for a EU-based undertaking to hold separate accounts for its Luxembourg branch in compliance with the Luxembourg accounting rules in order to be allowed tax deduction of losses incurred by the branch under the Luxembourg corporate tax law, was not

[85] See for an overview P Oliver, *Free Movement of Goods in the E.E.C.* (European Law Centre, London, 1988) 205–208.

[86] Case C-127/86 *Ledoux* [1988] ECR 3741.

[87] Case C-250/95, *Futura Participations and Singer* [1997] ECR I-2471, para 31.

[88] OJ 1977 L336, 15.

[89] *Futura Participations and Singer* (n 87 above) paras 38–40.

necessary to ensure the effectiveness of fiscal supervision. As the undertaking had a specific interest in proving the losses for obtaining the tax benefit, a valuable alternative could consist of allowing the undertaking to use other reliable means.

However, a voluntarist alternative allowing the taxpayer to prove his fiscal situation may not be sufficient when it comes to raising taxes on the income of a resident with respect to financial services obtained with a bank licensed in another Member State, and active under the regime of free movement of services. The customer will have no interest at all in declaring his income in his state of (fiscal) residence, especially when the income is not taxed abroad, while on the other hand, the collection of information in the home State of the credit institution via the mutual assistance procedure may be obstructed by banking secrecy laws.

It appears therefore that the need to ensure the effectiveness of fiscal supervision might lead to specific measures by a Member State towards foreign credit institutions, with a view to supervising properly the tax obligations of resident bank customers. The proportionality requirement will however act as an important filter on the Member States' discretion. This would in the first instance rule out measures which generally impede the free provision of services through measures barring the access to the domestic market. For instance, it seems to be excluded for the host Member State to subject the right to provide services by foreign credit institutions in general to the obligation for the latter to provide the tax authorities with all data on the income received by all its customers resident in the host Member State. Moreover, the tax authorities should in any case have regard to the right to passive freedom of services: a Member State may not unduly restrict the right as its residents to have services provided on their own initiative by financial institutions in other Member States. Therefore, imposing tax supervisory obligations on these credit institutions by the residents' Member State could easily constitute a disproportionate restriction on the free flow of services.[90]

(f) Conclusions on the general good motives in the context of financial services

The analysis of the Court's case law on the general good as applied in the area of financial services, shows that the concept intrinsically is surrounded

[90] In this respect, it should be noted that in Belgium a draft bill was submitted a few years ago for advice to the Conseil d'Etat, which would impose specific tax obligations on foreign financial institutions as regards their Belgian resident customers, *inter alia* the obligation to freeze all accounts upon decease of the client until the Belgian tax administration has been informed on the existence and the state of the account. The bill was, however, never introduced in Parliament.

by uncertainties: first, the general good in its very essence is an evolutionary concept, and hence new motives might in the future be validated by the ECJ as legitimate restrictions to free movement. Furthermore, although the conditions attached to the general good exception might at present be firmly established in the Court's case law, they nevertheless are often difficult to apply in specific situations. It goes without saying that the legal uncertainty thus created imposes important impediments on the financial institutions which want to enjoy the benefit of the freedoms of movement. It is therefore essential to find effective means to reduce the cost of this legal uncertainty. An important step in this direction appeared to be made in the context of the Financial Market Directives, by requiring the Member States to notify to foreign financial institutions wishing to enter the market, which rules apply in the general good. However, Member States have managed largely to reduce the practical importance of the relevant provisions in the Financial Services Directives to the extent that they do not impose any obligation upon the Member States (see below).

IV. THE GENERAL GOOD IN THE DIRECTIVES ON BANKING AND INVESTMENT SERVICES

1. The Function of the General Good in the 'New Approach' to Harmonization

It cannot be denied that the 'new approach' to harmonization which the Commission proposed in its 1985 White Paper on the Completion of the Internal Market gave a significant boost to the market unification efforts, at least as concerns its legal framework: harmonization was to be limited to those elements which were necessary but sufficient to ensure Member States' mutual confidence in each other's regulatory and supervisory standards, and hence to come to a mandatory application of the mutual recognition principle. In effect, this approach could be considered as an application of the subsidiarity principle *avant la lettre*: Community legislation is only required to the strict extent necessary for enabling the unification of the national markets in a single market.[91]

A comparison between the mutual recognition as deriving from primary EC law, ie the Treaty freedoms, and the same principle in the internal market Directives, reveals the complementary nature of the latter to the former. Under the Treaty freedoms, the mutual recognition could be quali-

[91] Compare Padoa-Schioppa *et al*, *Efficacité, stabilité, equité* (Economica, Paris, 1987) 14; C Boye Jacobson, 'Rapport communautaire', in *Rapports au XV° congrès de la FIDE*, vol. I: *Les prestations de services au sein de la CEE et avec les pays tiers* (Lisbonn, 1992), 30–31.

fied as 'imperfect': the host Member State is entitled to put aside the mutual recognition principle when the application of its own laws to the cross-border situation, which by assumption produces a restrictive effect on free movement, is justified by the general good. By contrast, the mutual recognition principle as formulated by the internal market Directives is absolute or 'perfect': the minimum harmonization Directives having introduced equivalent regulatory standards in all Member States, the host Member State is no longer entitled to invoke the general good to justify the application of its own laws to the foreign service provider. In other words, the minimum harmonization constitutes, in the view of the Community legislator, the codification of what in the absence of harmonization would fall under the general good exception.

However, the 'new approach' based on minimum harmonization does not entirely paralyse the Member States' regulatory powers. In the field covered by the 'minimum' harmonization, Member States are enabled to maintain or introduce stricter standards than the minimum level imposed by Community law, provided the stricter standards apply solely to the domestic enterprises.[92] The risk of reverse discriminations and competitive disadvantages for the domestic industry are likely to highly reduce the use of these powers. In effect, one can observe a *de facto* convergence of prudential standards to the 'minimum' imposed by the Directives.[93]

Outside the fields covered by the minimum harmonization and 'perfect' mutual recognition, Member States also retain full regulatory powers. The use of these powers will, however, in line with the case law on the Treaty freedoms, have to conform to the general good exception when it leads to restrictions on free movement.

2. References to the General Good in the Banking and Investment Services Directives

It is well known that several provisions in both the Second Banking Co-ordination Directive 89/646 (2BCD) and the Investment Services Directive 93/22 (ISD) refer to the general good. These may be summarized as follows:

[92] To the extent that the use by a Member State of these powers restricts the 'outward' free provision of services by a credit institution, the restriction should also satisfy the general good test: compare in the context of cross-border television broadcasting Case C-6/98 *ARD and PRO Sieben*, 28 October 1999 (nyp) paras 49–52.

[93] It should be noted, however, that the Banking and Investment Services Directives in general led to higher prudential standards than those previously contained in the law of the Member States. This conclusion should to a certain extent mitigate the classical argument against the 'new approach' as provoking excessive regulatory competition between Member States to the detriment of sufficiently high regulatory standards.

- in general, the Preamble to both 2BCD and ISD impose upon the Member States the duty to ensure that there are no obstacles to carrying on banking and investment activities receiving mutual recognition in the same manner as in the home Member State, as long as the latter do not conflict with legal provisions protecting the general good in the host Member State;[94]
- host Member States are entitled to take appropriate measures to prevent or to punish irregularities committed within their territories which are contrary to the legal rules they have adopted in the interest of the general good;[95]
- credit institutions and investment firms can advertise their services in other Member States through all available means of communication in the host Member State, subject to any rules governing the form and the content of such advertising adopted in the interest of the general good;[96]
- at a procedural level, the host State's competent authority will 'if necessary' notify to the credit institution or investment firm wishing to open a branch in the host Member State the conditions under which, in the interest of the general good, those activities must be carried on in the host Member State;[97] for investment firms, the procedure also applies in the context of the first cross-border provision of services.[98]

The community legislator has deliberately refrained from giving a general definition of the 'general good' in the Directives on Banking and Investment Services. It is commonly accepted that the general good in these provisions has to be understood as referring to the same concept in the Court's case law on the justification of restrictions to free movement, and the conditions attached to the use of the general good exception.[99] However, it has been indicated above that the general good exception no longer applies in the fields where the Directives constitute the 'perfect' mutual recognition principle. In order to assess the practical meaning of the general good clauses in the Banking and Investment Services Directives, it is

[94] Recital (16) of the Preamble to 2BCD; Recital (33) of the Preamble to ISD.
[95] 2BCD, Article 21(5); ISD, Article 19(6).
[96] 2BCD, Article 21(11); ISD, Article 13.
[97] 2BCD, Article 18(4); ISD, Article 17(4).
[98] ISD, Article 18(2).
[99] See the answer by Sir Leon Brittan on behalf of the Commission to written question No 916/89, OJ 1990 C139, 14; W van Gerven, 'La deuxième directive bancaire et la jurisprudence de la Cour de Justice', *Revue de la Banque*, 1992, 39, at 43 (also published as 'The Second Banking Directive and the Case-law of the Court of Justice', YEL, 1990, 57; S Katz, 'The Second Banking Directive', YEL, 1993, 249, at 261; M Dassesse, S Isaacs, G Penn, *EC Banking Law* (2nd edn, LLP, London, 1994) para 4.39, 43; W-H Roth, 'General Introduction to the Second Banking Directive and the Proposal for a Directive on Investment Services', in Stuyck (ed), *Financial and Monetary Integration in the European Community* (Kluwer, Deventer, 1993) 77; B Sousi-Roubi, *Droit bancaire européen* (Dalloz, Paris, 1995) No. 285, 145.

therefore important carefully to delimit the proper scope of the 'perfect' mutual recognition principle, in contrast to the situations in which the Member States still are entitled to apply their laws which satisfy the general good test.

3. Material Scope of the General Good in the Banking and Investment Services Directives

In determining the material scope of the general good as an exception to the mutual recognition in the context of the Banking and Investment Services Directives, a further distinction can be drawn between (1) rules on market access and prudential regulation; (2) rules on market behaviour, including advertising, and (3) private law regulation of financial products. In section II, we demonstrated that the 'imperfect' mutual recognition as formulated by the Treaty freedoms is likely to apply, with varying intensity, in all of these areas.

(a) Market access and prudential regulation

(i) Overview of the Directives

Both the Second Banking Co-ordination Directive and the Investment Services Directive introduce a single European passport and the principle of home country prudential supervision for the financial institutions to which they apply. On the basis of the minimum harmonization of prudential standards, the Directives thus attribute, unless otherwise provided, exclusive regulatory and supervisory competence in prudential matters to the home country of the banking and investment firms. The other Member States in which these institutions wish to set up a branch or to be active under the free provision of services, can no longer exercise any competence in these fields: any recourse to the general good doctrine has been eliminated by the 'minimum' harmonization at Community level, except where the Directives allow for such exceptions.

The exceptions to the home State principle in the *prudential* area are limited. In the context of the 2BCD, the residual powers of the host State prudential authorities are restricted to the liquidity supervision of branches.[100] This competence should, moreover, be exercised in co-operation with the home State authority, which is competent for the overall liquidity supervision of the credit institution as a whole (head offices and branches altogether). 2BCD also contains a particular division of supervisory competencies with respect to open market positions resulting from the credit institutions' transactions carried out on the financial markets of other

[100] 2BCD, Article 14(2).

Member States.[101] In view of the harmonization effected by the Capital Adequacy Directive,[102] it may be submitted that at present the supervision of these risks falls under the exclusive competence of the home country supervisor.

Outside the area of prudential supervision, 2BCD, pending further Community initiatives, attributed to the host country full competence with respect to monetary supervision.[103] With the transfer of monetary supervision to the European System of Central Banks (ESCB) since 1 January 1999 (Stage 3 EMU), this provision may be considered to have become obsolete, at least for the Member States of the euro-zone. This implies that a Member State of the euro-system is no longer entitled to invoke monetary reasons to justify the application of a restriction on the free provision of services by an EU credit institution,[104] unless the restriction would flow from a decision taken in accordance with the division of powers within the ESCB.[105]

In the context of the Investment Services Directive, the home country principle with respect to prudential supervision has an absolute character: no exception applies with respect to liquidity supervision of branches, nor does the ISD provide for any explicit host State residual power for monetary reasons. However, it may be submitted that the host State could exercise competencies in this field under the overall general good clause contained in ISD, Article 19(6), as far as compatible with the transfer of monetary powers to the ESCB.[106]

(ii) Implications of 'perfect' mutual recognition for the general good exception

The main implication of the 'perfect' mutual recognition principle with respect to market access and prudential supervision is the impossibility for

[101] 2BCD, Article 14(3).

[102] Directive 93/6/EC, OJ [1993] L141/1.

[103] 2BCD, Article 14(2).

[104] In recent months, a peculiar problem has arisen with the so called 'ni-ni' principle in French law, according to which it is prohibited to offer interest-bearing current accounts in France denominated in French francs. The prohibition, which used to be motivated on grounds of monetary policy, has since the introduction of the euro been extended to accounts denominated in euro and in all other currencies of the euro-zone. Surprisingly, the French authorities no longer refer to monetary motives as a justification—which would no longer be valid in view of the transfer of monetary powers to the ESCB—but now invoke the general good clause as a justification, and consumer protection in particular (see also J Ferry, 'Le "ni-ni" à l'épreuve de Maastricht', *Banque & Droit*, 1999, No 65, 17–21.

[105] See in this respect the general overview by Ch Zilioli and M Semayr, 'The European Central Bank, its System and its Law', *Euredia* 1999/2, 187–230 and 1999/3, 307–364.

[106] Compare ISD, Article 19(1), which empowers the host State, in the discharge of its responsibilities in the conduct of monetary policy, to require from branches of foreign investment firms the same information as from domestic firms. The provision, which implicitly confirmed a proper competence of the host State in the field of monetary policy, must at present be read in conjunction with the Treaty provisions on the powers of the ESCB.

the host State to interfere in any way in the home State's exclusive competence, not even on basis of the residual general good clause of 2BCD, Article 21(5) ISD, or Article 19(6). This principle does not only apply in the specific areas of prudential regulation which were the subject of minimum harmonization, but extends to prudential regulation in general.[107] For instance, host States may not impose any additional prudential obligation upon the credit institution or investment firm duly authorized in another Member State (eg own funds requirements of any kind,[108] fit and proper-test for managers).[109] The Interpretative Communication on the contrary suggests that the elimination of host country competence would only apply to the fields of prudential regulation which were effectively harmonized.[110] Finally, as was made clear by the Court's decision in *Ambry*,[111] the extent to which the host State is empowered to take measures which impair the access to the market by an EU-based credit institution, may still give rise to interpretation problems: does the access to the market solely relate to the possibility for a credit institution to take up a banking activity in the home Member State without obtaining a new authorization, or should it be considered to include all rules of the host Member State which impose additional requirements upon EU credit institutions in order to have their banking products recognized as fully equivalent to the products offered by a domestic credit institution? In view of the objectives of the 2BCD, it may be submitted that the latter broader interpretation should prevail.

More delicate is the question whether the host State may impose upon the foreign financial institution a prior control on the compatibility of financial products with its mandatory contract law before taking up a banking activity in the host State with use of the single banking licence. This is for instance the case in Belgian law as concerns the granting of consumer or mortgage credit: the foreign financial institution wishing to offer such credits in Belgium under the single passport regime should first notify its model contracts to the competent supervisory authority. The latter may

107 Indeed, the attribution of general regulatory and supervisory competence to the home State with respect to prudential supervision forms the corollary of 'minimum' but 'sufficient' harmonization of prudential standards: see 2BCD Recital (4), Preamble; ISD, Recital (3), Preamble.

108 ISD, Article 15(2) contains however a limited exception to this rule: a Member State could formulate additional own funds requirements as a condition for obtaining access to the regulated markets by investment firms. These requirements may also be applied to investment firms authorized in another Member State, provided they relate to risks not covered by ISD.

109 See for instance the point of view of the Belgian Banking and Finance Commission (BFC) with respect to the fit and proper test for managers of Belgian branches of foreign credit institutions: the BFC is of the opinion that it may, under the general good, revoke a manager who has previously been convicted for certain criminal offences, mainly in the financial area (see Annex to circular letter of 19 March 1993). In view of the home country principle, however, only the home country supervisor will be competent for exercising this competence.

110 Interpretative Communication (n 3 above) 19.

111 Case C-410/96 *Ambry* (n 57 above).

prohibit the financial institution from offering these contracts when they are contrary to the provisions of Belgian law justified by the general good.[112] It is true that this kind of—non-prudential—supervision may be related to the residual host State's powers under the general good exception, which can also include powers to *prevent* irregularities on the host State's territory. However, it is doubtful whether the exercise of these competencies could interfere with the right to market access guaranteed by the Directives: the host State's procedure may not result in a disguised authorization procedure frustrating the *effet utile* of the single passport. Therefore, it may be submitted that the contract supervision should be effected on an *ex post* basis, and cannot be incorporated in the procedures for obtaining market access in the host State.[113] This is also the solution adopted within the context of the Insurance Directives.[114]

The elimination of general good competencies for the host Member State in the area of market access and prudential supervision will of course only apply to those financial institutions to which 2BCD or ISD apply, and for the banking and investment services defined in the Directives for which these institutions obtained an authorization in their home State. For other services of other financial institutions, the general Treaty principles apply: the host State will be entitled to apply its domestic laws, which, if they amount to a restriction to cross-border free movement, must satisfy the conditions attached to the general good exception.[115] This will under certain circumstances require that the host Member State duly takes account of guarantees which the service provider already satisfies on the basis of the rules applicable in its home State.

Two examples will illustrate the above principles. First, when a credit institution wishes to act as insurance intermediary in another Member State—an activity which is not included in the list of banking activities enjoying mutual recognition—the host Member State could impose its own requirements justified by the general good (eg rules on specific professional skills and experience with respect to insurance products). Host State rules could also include an authorization procedure applying specifically to the activity as insurance intermediary. However, it will be up to the home State

[112] See Law of 12 June 1991 on Consumer Credit, Article 75 bis and Law of 4 August 1992 on Mortgage Credit, Article 43 bis (both introduced by Law of 11 February 1994, *Mon*, 16 March 1994.

[113] It should be noted that in the Netherlands, the implementation of 2BCD has led to a modification in the Law on Consumer Credit. The prior control on contracts has been substituted by an *ex post* control: immediately after having obtained market access, the foreign credit institution should notify its model contracts to the competent supervisor, which can prohibit the further use of these models when contrary to the general good.

[114] See in particular the Third Non-Life Insurance Directive 92/49/EEC, Article 29; the Third Life Insurance Directive 92/96/EEC, Article 29(1).

[115] Compare 2BCD Recitals (13), (15), Preamble; ISD, Recital (28), Preamble.

banking supervisory authority to decide whether the activity as insurance intermediary is compatible with the banking activity, and whether it does not imply prudential risks for the latter.

Secondly, the home country principle will generally[116] not apply to specialized financial institutions which do not qualify as 'credit institution' (eg enterprise for consumer or mortgage credit) or 'investment firm' (eg specialized investment adviser). Their cross-border activities will be subjected to the regulations protecting the general good in the host State, which may possibly include the submission to prudential regulations and a separate authorization in the host State. The latter should, however, in view of the Court's case law on the Treaty freedoms, take due account of the guarantees which these financial institutions already offer by virtue of the supervision regime in their home State. If for instance the financial institution is submitted in its home State to similar prudential obligations as credit institutions which satisfy 2BCD,[117] it is doubtful whether the host State still could apply its own prudential regulations, and impose a separate authorization: the prudential standards contained in 2BCD are supposed to codify the general good, and will therefore also influence the application of the general good clause to financial institutions offering banking services without qualifying as credit institution.

(b) Regulation of market behaviour

(i) General principles

Contrary to the areas of market access and prudential regulation, the regulation of market practices to a large extent is left untouched by 2BCD and ISD: except with respect to conduct of business rules (see below), substantial harmonization in this field has not at present been realized.[118]

In this context, proper consideration should be given to the already cited Recitals in the Preambles to both Directives, which formulate a principle of mutual recognition with respect to the way the banking and investment business is carried on in the host Member State, without prejudice to the application of the host State's rules which are justified in the general

[116] Except when they are 80 per cent subsidiaries of a credit institution and satisfy specific requirements imposed by 2BCD, Article 18.2.

[117] This will in particular be the case for financial institutions in Germany and France which qualify as credit institutions under their home laws, but not under 2BCD, and therefore, do not enjoy the benefit of the single passport provided by 2BCD.

[118] See, however, the amended draft Directive on distance selling of financial services (COM(1999)385 def. of 23 July 1999), which, contrary to the initial Commission proposal, is not based on the paradigm of minimum harmonization and mutual recognition, but instead would apply the principle of maximum harmonization: the Preamble considers that allowing Member States to enact or maintain divergent or stricter rules would produce adverse effects on the functioning of the internal market and on competition.

good.[119] The reference to the way the business is carried on could be interpreted as including the rules on commercial practices and unfair competition, including the regulation of advertising. In the same way, both Directives explicitly allow a financial institution to advertise its services in the host Member State, without prejudice to the latter's right to impose its general good rules with regard to the form and content of the advertisement.

The practical significance of the cited Recitals and provisions on advertising should not be overestimated. Both the wording of the Recitals and its evolution in the drafting process of 2BCD[120] suggest that the Directive did not intend to formulate mutual recognition in the same absolute sense as with respect to market access and prudential supervision. These Recitals should merely be regarded as declaratory in comparison with the Court's case law on the free movement of services: this freedom entitles a credit institution to rely on the market behaviour rules of its home State as being equivalent to those in the host State with respect to the offer of its financial products; the host State may apply its rules which constitute a restriction to this freedom only in so far as justified by the general good. The mutual recognition of the home State rules, and the general good as correction to the rule, are therefore directly rooted in the EC Treaty, and cannot be restricted in any way by the internal market Directives. In this approach, the mutual recognition principle as enshrined in the Recitals to the Directive is to be considered 'imperfect', and merely refers to the present state of the Court's case law on the free provision of services (Article 49 EC).

(ii) Extension of the mutual recognition principle to branches?

An additional difficulty in the interpretation of the mutual recognition principle for market behaviour rules, as written down in the Preamble to both 2BCD and ISD, stems from its general wording, which operates no distinction between the activities undertaken through free provision of services or through a branch located in the host Member State. This would imply that the out-of-state branch of a credit institution may invoke in the host State the mutual recognition of the home State rules on eg distance selling or tied product offers, against the application of the host State's rules, unless the latter satisfy the general good test. In this respect, the Directive would in our view[121] be an effective innovation compared to the current

[119] See n 94 above.

[120] It should be remembered that the initial draft of 2BCD laid down a principle of mutual recognition of 'financial techniques', a notion which subsequently disappeared, due to fierce criticism on the part of some Member States. See, for an overview of the drafting process in this respect, Dassesse, Isaacs, Penn (n 99 above) 37–40.

[121] See section II.1(b) above with respect to the material scope of the restriction-based concept of the freedom of establishment and the distinction between 'enterprise-related' and 'product-related' rules.

interpretation of the Treaty provisions on freedom of establishment: it has been advocated above that the general prohibition on non-discriminatory restrictions in the freedom of establishment did not apply to those rules in the host Member State which are unrelated to the cross-border mobility of enterprises, in particular the product-related rules on market behaviour. Consequently, under Article 43 EC the host State could apply these rules to the branch on the sole condition of being non-discriminatory.

This point of view, previously expressed by former Advocate General van Gerven,[122] was initially backed by the Commission in its Draft Interpretative Communication.[123] Others have rejected this point of view, arguing that the—quite vaguely formulated—mutual recognition principle in the Preamble to the Directives could not express the intention to add new elements to the interpretation of the Treaty freedoms by the ECJ.[124] However, it should be noted that the extension of the mutual recognition principle to the activities of branches can not only be deduced from the Preamble to the Directive, which in any case may act as element in the interpretation of the provisions of a directive.[125] This interpretation is also corroborated by the substantive provisions of the Directive: indeed, the principle of notification of general good provisions by the host State's authorities to the branch of a foreign credit institution or investment firms,[126] cannot be given a reasonable significance, unless one accepts this extension of the mutual recognition principle to the activities of branches. If not, the application of host State's rules to branches outside the fields of market access and prudential regulation, which are covered by the 'perfect' mutual recognition, would be limited by the non-discrimination principle only, and there would be no reason for notifying any 'general good' provisions.

In its final Interpretative Communication, the European Commission defends a more advanced interpretation of the Treaty freedom of establishment: the mutual recognition of home State rules relating to the way banking and investment services are conducted in the host country through a branch, would now be directly rooted in Article 43 EC, as would appear from the Court's ruling in *Gebhard*.[127] Host States could consequently apply their own restrictive rules to a branch only when the general good test is satisfied. Hence, the Preamble to 2BCD and ISD would even in the

[122] See van Gerven (n 99 above) 42; Roth (n 99 above) 78; Tison (n 67 above) 219, No. 24.

[123] Draft Communication, OJ 1995 C-291, 17.

[124] In this sense L Roeges, 'L'exercice de l'activité bancaire par la voie d'une succursale après la deuxième directive bancaire', *Revue de Droit bancaire et de la Bourse*, 1994, 115.

[125] See for a recent example in which the Court extensively relied on the Preamble of a Directive in interpreting its substantive provisions: Case C-222/94 *Commission and France v United Kingdom* [1996] ECR I-4025.

[126] See 2BCD, Article 19(4); ISD, Articles 17(4), 18(2).

[127] Interpretative Communication (n 3 above) 16.

context of establishment be merely declaratory compared to the interpretation of the EC Treaty.

We may conclude from above that the Preambles to 2BCD and ISD, in conjunction with specific provisions of the Directives, effectively have a significance compared to the situation under primary EC law, by extending the paradigm of mutual recognition/general good to 'product-related' rules in the context of cross-border branching by credit institutions and investment firms.

Although clear in principle, the practical implementation of this extension raises new questions as how to apply the general good test. In the Commission's view, the assessment of the proportionality requirement might give different results depending on the mode of operation—free provision of services or branch—of the foreign financial institution: a restriction in the host State's law could more easily be regarded as proportionate towards a branch, which is permanently integrated within the economy of the host Member State, than towards a non-established service provider. Consequently, a single host State measure could constitute a restriction on the free provision of services, but at the same time be justified towards the branch.[128]

The Commission's point of view cannot be shared. It is true that the Court's case law in the past often stressed the objective difference between services and establishment, in order to demonstrate that a service provider should not be submitted to the same rules as the person established in the host country and integrated in its social order. However, this case law precisely developed in the context of the evolution of the freedom to provide services from a discrimination to a restriction-based freedom, at a time when the freedom of establishment still was interpreted as prohibiting only discriminatory measures. Since the beginning of the 1990s, the dichotomy services establishment, at least with respect to enterprise-related rules, has been largely abolished in the Court's case law. Furthermore, it should be stressed that 2BCD and ISD precisely aim at placing the activity through direct provision of services and establishment of a branch on an equal footing. It might therefore be argued that reintroducing a distinction between services and branch activities *via* the proportionality requirement would counter the objective of both Directives. Finally, it is totally unclear using which criteria a distinction should be drawn between the provision of services and the establishment of a branch when addressing the proportionality of a restriction to free movement. It is difficult to understand the relevance of the more or less permanent integration in the host State's economy as a valid distinctive criterion in the context of market behaviour rules.

128 Interpretative Communication (n 3 above) 22–23; see also Draft Interpretative Communication, 22–23.

In its final Interpretative Communication, the Commission partially reviewed its position: in the field of consumer protection rules, the proportionality test should now give identical results independently from the mode of operation of the foreign financial institution: it would indeed be unacceptable for a consumer to be less protected when receiving the service from a non-established undertaking, than from a branch in the host country.[129]

We can conclude that, by extending the mutual recognition principle applicable within the area of services to the activities of branches, the Community legislator aimed at extending the general good test to branches in an identical way as it applies to the provision of services. Consequently, there is no reason to further differentiate in the assessment of the proportionality requirement when applying the general good test. It is nevertheless debatable whether this extension should be welcomed. On the one hand, this would substantially enhance the intensity of regulatory competition between Member States: the risk of reverse discrimination not only exists in the field of prudential standards, but also in the areas of market behaviour and private law rules, where the branch could evade the application of restrictive rules in the host Member State. It is also true that the risk of excessive regulatory competition to the detriment of consumer protection would be limited by the continuing validity of the general good clause as an exception to the mutual recognition in the fields of market behaviour and financial contract regulation. On the other hand, the above analysis has shown that the concept of general good itself is surrounded by many uncertainties. Extending the mutual recognition/general good paradigm to the activities of branches, which are fully integrated in the economy of the host Member State, would only enhance this uncertainty, as consumers generally will not make the distinction between domestic institutions and branches of foreign institutions. In the absence of minimum harmonization of market behaviour and production-related rules at Community level, as is the case with prudential rules, it may be feared that the cost of legal uncertainty for all market participants—both financial institutions and consumers—will outweigh the potential benefits stemming from the extended mutual recognition. The extension of the mutual recognition/general good paradigm to the activities undertaken through a branch in another Member State therefore only seems feasible when two additional conditions are met: (a) a sufficient flow of information between Member States and the market participants on the actual use and implementation of the general good clause in each Member State; and (b) a strict monitoring by the Commission of the use by the Member States of the general good clause.

[129] Interpretative Communication (n 3 above) 23.

(iii) Conduct of business rules

Within the context of the Investment Services Directive, the interaction between the conduct of business rules and the general good exception raises specific difficulties. It is well known that Article 11(1) of ISD lays down a number of general principles with which the Member States should at least comply in the elaboration of conduct of business rules to be satisfied by investment firms and credit institutions in the exercise of their activities. The main problem stems from the fact that Article 11(2) of ISD attributes the competence to lay down and supervise the conduct of business rules to the Member State in which the service is provided, without further specifying how to determine the competent Member State. In reality, several Member States could simultaneously claim competence as the Member State in which the service is provided. For instance, when an investment firm, authorized in Member State A, receives an order from a customer resident in Member State B, and executes it on a regulated market in Member State C, it is unclear which Member State should apply its conduct of business rules: Member State A could claim application as state of reception of the order; Member State B could assert that the service has been provided in the Member State of the customer; Member State C could apply its conduct rules as law of execution of the service. Consequently, the attribution of powers in ISD, Article 11(2) may be considered non-exclusive, which could lead to burdensome, and sometimes conflicting obligations to be met by the investment firm in conducting its cross-border business.

The general obligation to interpret national and Community law in conformity with the Treaty, ie the free movement principle, leads to the introduction of the general good test in the application of the conduct of business rules: an investment firm which in one Member State is subjected to conduct of business rules, will have to comply with the conduct rules of other Member States in which he offers investment products only as far as the application of these rules, assuming that they lead to a restriction to free movement, satisfies the general good test.[130]

[130] In the same sense Ch Cruickshank, 'The Investment Services Directive', in Wymeersch (ed), *Further Perspectives in Financial Integration in Europe* (De Gruyter, Berlin, 1994) 73; J Wouters, 'Rules of Conduct, Foreign Investment Firms and the ECJ's Case-Law on Services' (1993) 14 Comp Lawy 194, 195; P Lastenouse, 'Les règles de conduite et la reconnaissance mutuelle dans la directive sur les services d'investissement', *Revue du Marché Unique européen*, 1995/4, 79, 101–102; LR Theil, 'The EC Investment Services Directive: A Critical Time for Investment Firms', JIBFL, 1994, 61, 64; A Alcock, 'UK Implementation of European Investment Services Directives' (1994) 15 Comp Lawy 291, 299; E Wymeersch, 'Les règles de conduite relatives aux opérations sur instruments financiers', *Revue de la Banque*, 1995/10, 574, 591; N O'Neill, 'The Investment Services Directive', in *The Single Market and the Law of Banking* (2nd edn, LLP, London, 1995), 201–202; D Dax, 'L'impact de la communication interprétative pour le secteur des services d'investissement', *Bulletin Droit & Banque*, 1999, No 28, 11, para 36.

How should the general good test in practice be applied within the context of the conduct of business rules?

First, it goes without saying that the conduct of business rules may be related to a general good motive, either the protection of financial market integrity, or more generally consumer protection.

The requirement of non-harmonization could be more problematic, as ISD, Article 11(1) already contains a harmonized catalogue of conduct of business rules, although limited to the formulation of general principles. It could be argued that the Member States' conduct of business rules which aim at achieving the objectives of Article 11(1) are to be considered as equivalent. Consequently, the host State's conduct of business rules could never satisfy the general good test as these have made the object of harmonization. In reality, this would come down to considering that the catalogue of conduct of business rules in Article 11(1) constitutes a 'minimum' but sufficient harmonization excluding the application of host State rules.[131] However, neither the legislative history of the ISD nor its provisions can support this conclusion. In reality, Article 11(1) intended to give Member States actual autonomy in elaborating their conduct of business rules, taking account of the proper characteristics of their markets and the policy choices in the protection of the consumers of investment services. Hence, the catalogue of objectives in Article 11(1) cannot be considered to constitute a 'sufficient' harmonization of conduct of business rules excluding all recourse to the general good. The only useful function of Article 11(1) in the general good test may be to create a refutable presumption of equivalence between the Member States' conduct of business rules worked out within these objectives.[132] This equivalence will mainly appear in the context of the conduct rules relating to market integrity, while Member States usually will enjoy greater discretion in the elaboration of the conduct of business rules related to the protection of the consumer.[133]

Finally, as the catalogue of objectives in Article 11(1) only constitutes a minimum, Member States are free to set other general principles with corresponding conduct of business rules. When these rules are to be regarded as restricting cross-border investment business, they should also satisfy the general good test.

The European Commission's Interpretative Communication on the

[131] See SM Carbone and F Munari, 'The Enforcement of the European Regime for Investment Services in the Member States and Its Impact on National Conflict of Laws', in Ferrarini (ed), *European Securities Markets. The Investment Services Directive and Beyond* (Kluwer, London, 1998) 342–343.

[132] Compare Wymeersch (n 130 above) 592, No. 45.

[133] See G Hertig, 'Imperfect Mutual Recognition for EU Financial Services', in Buxbaum, Hertig, Hirsch, Hopt (eds), *European Economic and Business Law* (Walter de Gruyter, Berlin, 1996) 225.

Second Banking Co-ordination Directive does not give any guidance on the relationship between the conduct of business rules and the general good. Although credit institutions should also observe these rules when supplying investment services, the Commission formally restricted the scope of its interpretation to the 2BCD.[134]

(c) Private law regulation of financial products

As for the rules on market behaviour, the private law regulation with respect to the financial products offered by credit institutions and investment firms is not covered by the 'absolute' mutual recognition applicable to market access and prudential rules. However, the Preambles to 2BCD and ISD may also be regarded as laying down a principle of mutual recognition in the area of private law regulation, and thus mainly confirming the current state of the Court's case law with respect to the free provision of services: a financial institution may offer its financial products in the host Member State under the same conditions as in its home Member State. The financial institution will have to satisfy the mandatory contract rules of the host Member State which constitute a restriction to free movement only as far as these rules also satisfy the general good test.

Equally, Recital (16) of the Preamble to 2BCD and the corresponding Recital (33) to ISD may be interpreted as extending the mutual recognition/general good paradigm to the financial products offered through a branch in the host Member State. The principles developed with respect to market behaviour regulation will apply by analogy.

4. Elaboration of Host State Powers in the Interest of the General Good

The powers of the host States to impose their general good rules within the general good exception are further, and in identical terms, clarified in 2BCD and ISD: the Directives enable the host Member State to take appropriate measures to prevent or to punish irregularities which are contrary to the general good rules. This competence includes the possibility of preventing institutions from initiating any further transaction within their territories.[135]

The aforementioned provision calls for several remarks. First, it is clear that the general good clause of 2BCD, Article 21.5 and ISD, Article 19.6 should take account of the material scope of 'perfect' mutual recognition under both Directives, as analysed above. This means that the clause cannot possibly be invoked in the fields of market access and prudential supervision

134 Interpretative Communication (n 3 above) 3.
135 2BCD, Article 21(5); ISD, Article 19(6).

by an EU financial institution, which have made the object of sufficient harmonization.[136]

Secondly, the host State general good competence is not attributed specifically to the prudential authority, but to the Member State in general. It is up to the Member State to decide which authorities are competent to control or enforce the general good rules. This might be an administrative body (eg the authority competent for supervision of mortgage contracts) or a judicial entity (eg an injunction imposed by a court in a matter of unfair competition). However, host Member States may not use this provision to declare the host State prudential authority competent for supervising compliance by an EU financial institution with the—non-prudential—general good rules.[137] Such attribution could only be valid under condition of non-discrimination, the domestic financial institutions in the host State being subjected to the same kind of supervision.

Finally, the host State intervention for reasons of general good may be both repressive and preventive, although in the latter case the intervention may not interfere with the very principle of the single passport and restrict the right to market access for financial institutions in general. The host State power should furthermore be limited to taking 'appropriate' action, ie the nature and gravity of the sanction should be proportionate to the gravity of the violation of the general good rules.[138] The general non-discrimination principle finally will fully apply to the nature of sanctions to be applied in case of non-compliance with host State general good rules:

[136] The exercise by the host State prudential authority of its residual powers with respect to liquidity supervision of foreign credit institutions is covered by the procedure of 2BCD, Article 21(2) to (4) and (7). In summary, the host State must first ask for intervention by the home State; only when this leads to unsatisfactory results will the host State have authority to intervene itself; however, in case of emergency, the host State authority is entitled to take the necessary precautionary measures without prior consultation of the home State authority. It should be stressed that the latter host State powers apply exclusively within the scope of the competencies attributed to it by the Directive, ie essentially the liquidity supervision over branches. It may not be used to intervene in matters which fall under the exclusive prudential competence of the home State supervisor, for instance in order to remedy alleged deficient prudential supervision by the home State authorities.

[137] See, however, E Balate, 'L'intérêt général en droit communautaire: observations critiques au regard de la loi du 22 mars 1993 relative au statut et au contrôle des établissements de crédit', in *Liber amicorum Paul De Vroede* (Kluwer, Antwerp, 1994) 56 and 62–63; Dassesse, Isaacs, Penn (n 99 above) § 13.11, 124–125. See also in Belgian law article 11 of the Royal Decree of 20 December 1995 on foreign investment firms, which initially attributed competence to the Belgian Banking and Finance Commission (BFC) for the supervision of compliance by foreign investment firms with the (non-prudential) general good rules which apply to them. The provision was subsequently redrafted in order to limit its scope to power for the BFC to take appropriate sanctions at the request of other authorities in charge of the supervision of general good provisions in the host State (art 1, RD of 27 January 1997, *Mon*, 15 February 1997).

[138] Compare the Court's judgment in *Skanavi*, applying the proportionality criterion to the sanctions imposed under German law for the failure by a non-national to exchange a driving permit obtained abroad: Case C-193/94 *Skanavi* [1996] ECR I-1307.

foreign credit institutions may not suffer more severe sanctions than domestic institutions.

By way of conclusion, it can be stated that the provisions in 2BCD and ISD on host State's powers under the general good are mainly of declaratory nature: the provisions should be read as a mere confirmation of normal host State powers under the EC Treaty. The nature of the intervention by the host Member State should however be in accordance with the proportionality requirement, and may in no case frustrate the *effet utile* of the single passport.

5. Procedural Aspects of the General Good Powers: Notification of General Good Rules by the Host State Authorities

With a view to facilitating the use of the single passport by financial institutions and reducing information costs related to the identification of the rules in the host State with which the financial institution should comply, 2BCD and ISD both introduced a notification procedure with respect to general good rules: prior to the granting of the single passport to a foreign financial institution, the host State authority should notify 'if necessary' the rules under which, in the interest of the general good, the activities enjoying mutual recognition must be exercised in the host State. Both Directives apply the notification procedure for the setting up of a branch in the host Member State; ISD also extends the notification to the first cross-border provision of services.

The legal significance of the notification of general good rules is controversial with respect to both its nature (mandatory or optional) and the legal consequences of non-notification. The Commission seems to have been sensitive to the arguments advanced by several Member States, as the Interpretative Communication favours the approach of a non-mandatory notification.

(a) Mandatory or optional notification?

At the time of adoption of the Second Banking Co-ordination Directive, there seemed to be no controversy as to the nature of the notification: most authors, including Commission officials, and several Member States considered the general good notification by host State authorities as mandatory,[139] and some Member States indeed prescribed the notification of

[139] van Gerven (n 99 above) 46; Balate (n 137 above) 45; M Dassesse, '1992: An EEC Update', JIBFL, 1991, 384, 385; R Smits, 'Freedom of Establishment and Freedom to Provide Services under the Second Banking Directive', in *Banking and EC Law Commentary* (Amsterdam Financial Series, Kluwer, looseleaf, 1992), 34; sub 6.3.4; Tison (n 67 above) 225, para 42; W Wilms, *De Europese regelgeving inzake banktoezicht* (Mys & Breesch, Ghent, 1996) Nos 194–195, 130–131; compare with respect to insurance: van Schoubroeck (n 48 above) 154.

general good as an obligation into their national implementation laws.[140] However, only a few Member States went on to draft lists of general good rules.[141] The existing lists moreover witnessed a very extensive view on the general good rules to be complied with by foreign financial institutions. Meanwhile, several Member States lobbied in favour of interpreting the relevant provisions as constituting no obligation on the host State authorities. This viewpoint has been supported by several authors[142] and, perhaps surprisingly, by the European Commission.[143] The Commission nevertheless deplored the state of affairs and announced that it would 'make every attempt to remedy this situation', however without further specifying possible action.[144] More recently, the Commission even seems to favour the complete abolition of the notification procedure prior to first cross-border provision of services—which would imply the abolition of the notification of general good rules by the host State.[145]

The main interpretation issue concerned the words 'if necessary' in the relevant provisions on notification: those who support the optional nature of the notification consider that it is up to the Member States to decide whether there is a need for notifying these general good rules; the proponents of a mandatory notification on the contrary consider that the necessity does not

[140] The Belgian law considers the notification as mandatory, however without any liability for the Banking and Finance Commission with respect to the content of the notification: see article 70 Law of 22 March 1993 (credit institutions) and article 8 Royal Decree of 20 December 1995 (investment firms). Likewise, notification of the general good rules is mandatory for the French authorities in relation to incoming financial institutions: see *La libre prestation de services en matière de services d'investissement. Rapport au CECEI* (Paris, 1998) 33 (document available at URL: http://www.banque-france.fr/fr/telechar/lps2.pdf).

[141] In Belgium, the Banking and Finance Commission issued a circular letter enumerating which provisions were to be considered, in its view, as falling under the general good; in France, a list of general good rules has been adopted by way of *règlement* issued by the *Comité de la Réglementation bancaire et financière*; in Germany, the banking law itself contains a limited catalogue of general good rules to be complied with by foreign credit institutions.

[142] See B Sousi-Roubi, *Droit bancaire européen* (Dalloz, Paris, 1994) No. 284, 145; J Stuyck and G Straetmans, *Financiële diensten en de consument* (Kluwer, Antwerp, 1993) No 673, 218. Implicitly: Usher (n 16 above) 78; M Egan, J Rushbrooke, and N Lockett, *EC Financial Services Regulation* (London, 1994), No. 3.20, 3–9; compare with respect to the Insurance Directives: B Dubuisson, 'L'intérêt général en droit communautaire de l'assurance', *RGAT*, 1995/4, 809, 815, para 6. The same opinion is now defended by the Commission officials: P Clarotti, 'The Implementation of the Second Banking Directive and its Aftermath', in Wymeersch (ed), *Further Perspectives in Financial Integration in Europe* (De Gruyter, Berlin, 1994) 55.

[143] Interpretative Communication (n 3 above) 15.

[144] ibid. In an interim report drafted after consultations on the Draft Communication (document XV/1104/96 of 16 July 1996), the Commission considered proposing amendments to 2BCD, which would make the notification of general good rules mandatory towards credit institutions passporting in through either a branch or free provision of services. Moreover, all Member States would be required to communicate these lists, and draft legislation purporting to the general good to the European Commission.

[145] See the viewpoint of the European Commission in the context of the SLIM working party on the simplification of European banking legislation: see European Commission (DG XV), *Single Market News*, No 10, December 1997, 4–5.

refer to an option for the Member States, but to the very existence of general good rules: as soon as such rules exist there will be a necessity for Member States to notify them to the incoming financial institution.[146]

Even if the wording of the relevant provisions cannot lead to a conclusive interpretation, it does nevertheless appear more in line with the proper aims of the Directives to interpret them as imposing an obligation upon the host State authorities. It is true that, as the Commission states,[147] the principle that anybody should know the law equally applies to financial institutions wishing to deploy activities in another Member State. However, it should be borne in mind that the general good concept is uncertain by its very nature. Consequently, it seems inappropriate to shift the information costs with respect to the application of the general good test in the Member States' laws from the host State to the financial institutions. It would be advisable to create a more balanced situation between the principle that the financial institution should know the law, and the information duty upon the host State with respect to the general good. Thus, without prejudice to the obligation for the financial institution to enquire about the application of the host State's laws, the primary task of informing the financial institution would rest on the host State. This is also more in line with the general obligation of Member States to co-operate in order to achieve the *effet utile* of Community law (Article 10 EC). Finally, it should be stressed that a mandatory notification of general good rules is likely to create a more dynamic application of the general good clause: the publication of a general good list could provoke discussions at Community level on the application of the general good test by the Member States. The Commission could exercise its moral authority (and, possibly, the threat to bring cases before the Court), to discipline Member States in the use of the general good clause. Bearing in mind the risk of a 'nationalistic' approach towards the own general good by Member States, as was recently illustrated by the *Parodi* case and its aftermath in the French courts, it is imperative to strengthen the monitoring by the Community institutions of the use by the Member States of the general good clauses.

(b) Consequences of deficient notification of general good rules by the host State

The interpretation of the notification of general good rules as optional or mandatory also bears consequences on the legal effects to be attached to deficient notification by the host Member State, ie notification of a rule as

[146] See also the opinion of the Economic and Social Committee on the Draft Commission Communication, OJ 1996 C-204, 72.
[147] Draft Interpretative Communication, 14.

falling under the general good while it does not, or *vice versa*, non-notification of a host State rule while it does qualify as falling under the general good.

It seems normal to accept that, if notification is optional, the host Member State should not suffer any liability from errors in the notification. However, the Commission is of the opinion that, if the host State voluntarily agrees to notify the general good rules on a financial institution's request, it will be bound by an obligation as to means.[148] Implicitly, the Commission therefore does not totally exclude the possible liability of the host State authority under national law for shortcomings in the notification.

The issue becomes more delicate when the notification is to be regarded as mandatory. Should the negligence of the host Member State in notifying a rule lead to non-applicability of this rule towards the foreign credit institution? In other words, would the applicability of a host State's rule in the interest of the general good depend upon its notification to the foreign financial institution? This sanction would seriously disrupt the balance between the financial institution's obligation to enquire about the application of the host State law, and the duty of the host State authorities properly to inform the financial institution. The question as to the application of host State law in the interest of the general good should better primarily depend on a substantive compatibility test, and not on a purely formalistic element.

Therefore, it may be submitted that the non-notification of a general good rule will usually not prevent the host State from effectively applying it to the foreign financial institution.[149] A more appropriate sanction probably is to be found in liability rules: the host State authority may be held liable for the damages suffered by the financial institution due to the latter's reasonable expectation that the non-notified rule would not apply. This liability could find a legal basis not only in national law, but possibly also directly in Community law, on basis of the *Francovich* jurisprudence: the notification being imposed by the internal market Directives, the negligence of the host State authority in assessing which rules could fall under the general good, could constitute a breach of the obligations under the Directives which engages the Member State's liability.[150]

148 Interpretative Communication (n 3 above) 15.

149 See in the same sense van Gerven (n 99 above) 46; A Bruyneel and M Fyon, 'La loi du 2 mars 1993 relative au statut et au contrôle des établissements de crédit', *Journal des Tribunaux*, 1993, 565, 569, No. 22 and n 84; Dassesse (n 139 above) 385; Smits (n 139 above) 39, sub 6.3.4; Wilms (n 139 above) No 194, 131. Compare in the field of insurance: van Schoubroeck (n 48 above) 154.

150 See on the conditions of Member State's liability for breach of Community law: Joined Cases C-46, 48/93, *Brasserie du Pêcheur/Factortame (No 3)* [1996] ECR I-1023.

V. THE GENERAL GOOD AND CONFLICT OF LAWS IN PRIVATE LAW

1. Mutual Recognition and Conflict of Laws

The ever widening scope of the principles of free movement in the Court's case law, in particular in the private law area, increasingly raises questions with respect to the relationship between the Treaty freedoms and the Member States' conflict rules in private international law. More specifically, how do the principles of mutual recognition as resulting from the Treaty freedoms, and the general good as exception to the principle, affect or influence the traditional techniques for the solution of conflicts of law in the private law area? This issue will be the more important in the area of cross-border services, the substance of which are determined mainly by contract law.

In general, one can consider that the free movement principle and the conflict of law rules are closely related to each other. Both the principle of free movement and the conflict of law rules apply in a legal situation with a transnational dimension. With respect to services, the cross-border element needed for the application of Article 49 EC will usually also contain an element of internationality involving a possible conflict of laws.[151] Moreover, both sets of rules proceed to a kind of arbitrage between several legal provisions which may come into play as applying to the cross-border situation. A traditional conflict of laws rule will incidate which law should govern the cross-border situation, on the basis of objective connecting factors to the one or the other Member State. On the other hand, the principle of free movement of services will result in the non-application of the rules of the home State—or, as the case may be, of the host State—which are regarded as unduly restricting cross-border trade. This example also points to a fundamental difference between both sets of rules: while the conflict of law rule will lead to indication of a law applicable to the transaction, the free movement principle merely produces a negative effect, by disapplying those rules which are considered restrictive to free movement.

2. Does the Free Movement Principle Result in a Conflict Rule?

In legal writing,[152] several authors have echoed the point of view that the mutual recognition principle resulting from the free movement under

[151] The most common example will be the cross-border service relationship, where provider and customer are established in different Member States.

[152] See for a general overview of the doctrinal debate in general and with respect to financial services: Tison (n 31 above) paras 777–803; J Wouters, 'Europees en nationaal conflictenrecht en de interne markt voor financiële diensten', Metro Working Paper (Maastricht, 1996) 54–61.

primary EC law results in formulating a conflict of law rule: with respect to cross-border transactions in goods or services, this would usually result in the application of the home State law.[153] As an exception to this 'home State rule' (*Herkunftlandsprinzip*), the application of host State rules could prevail on grounds of general good. In conflict of law terms, the general good exception would thus qualify as *ordre public* rules.[154] More recently, another author further refined this approach: the free movement principle would result in a conflict rule opting for the law which is most favourable for the service provider (*Gunstigkeitsprinzip*): home State law when host State rules are more restrictive and *vice versa*.[155]

The conception of the free movement as formulating a conflict of law rule must be rejected, as it does not reflect the actual effects of the Treaty freedoms on national law. As already indicated, the Treaty freedoms have a purely negative impact on national law: when a measure in the law of a host Member State is considered contrary to the free movement of services, it will be disapplied by virtue of the precedence of EC law. The measure thus ruled out is, however, not substituted by the law of the Member State of origin of the service or the service provider. The host State Measure continues to apply in internal situations, but is merely declared non-applicable in cross-border situations.

In reality, the free movement does not interfere in the process of *formulating* the conflict of law rules in cross-border transactions.[156] The free movement principle only intervenes at a later stage, namely in the *actual application* of the substantive law declared applicable by the conflict of law rules. This view is corroborated by the Court's case law: in all cases where it has to decide on the compatibility of national law with the free movement of goods or services, the Court assumes that the said rules apply to the

[153] M Wolf, 'Privates Bankvertragsrecht im EG-Binnenmarkt', *Wertpapier-Mitteilungen*, 1990, 1945; E Jayme and Ch Kohler, 'Das Internationale Privat- und Verfahrensrecht der EG 1991 . . .', *IP Rax*, 1991, 369; compare KF Kreuzer, 'Die Europäisierung des Internationalen Privatrechts—Vorgaben des Gemeinschaftsrechts', in Müller-Graff, *Gemeinsames Privatrecht in der Europäischen Gemeinschaft* (Nomos, Baden-Baden, 1993) 420–421.

[154] This was also the position of the European Commission in its Draft Interpretative Communication: 'the principle of mutual recognition . . . tends towards application of the substantive law of the service provider.'

[155] See in particular J Basedow, 'Der Kollisionsrechtliche Gehalt der Produktfreiheiten im europäischen Binnenmarkt: favor offerentis', *RabelsZ*, 1995, (1), 12.

[156] In the same sense H Duintjer Tebbens, 'Les conflits de lois en matière de publicité déloyale à l'épreuve du droit communautaire', *RCDIP*, 1994, 451, 474–478; M Gebauer, 'Internationales Privatrecht und Warenverkehrsfreiheit in Europa', *IP Rax*, 1995, 152, 154–155; Ch Kohler, 'La Cour de Justice des Communautés européennes et le droit international privé', *Trav. du Comité français de droit international privé*, 1993–94, 71, 75–77; W-H Roth, 'Der Einfluß des Europäisches Gemeinschaftsrechts auf das Internationale Privatrecht', *RabelsZ*, 1991, 623, 668–669. The same point of view was already defended in the early 1980s in reaction to the Court's decision in *Koestler*: J Samtleben, 'Das Internationale Privatrecht der Börsentermingeschäfte und der EWG-Vertrag', *RabelsZ*, 1981, 240, 243.

cross-border transaction at stake by virtue of the normal conflict of law rules in national law.[157] The Court will then analyse whether the substantive law thus declared applicable constitutes a restriction, and, if so, preclude the Member State from applying it in the cross-border situation.

This is not to say that the home State rules will be irrelevant in the context of the free movement principle. In particular, the circumstance that the service complies with the rules of its home Member State will be important in assessing whether the host State rules constitute a restriction to free movement. This 'conformity' of the service with home State rules as precondition for the existence of a restriction to the free movement explains why the free movement principle may be translated into a principle of (imperfect) mutual recognition: a service which complies with the home State rules cannot be submitted to the host State rules (negative effect), as both laws are assumed to achieve the same interests. However, should the service not comply with its home State rules, then neither would the application of the host State rules, then neither would the application of the host State rules be considered a restriction to the free movement of services: the service is not already subjected in its home State to rules which are deemed equivalent to those in the host State.

The above principles can be fully applied to the regulation of financial services: the Treaty freedoms and the mutual recognition principle resulting from it do not affect the normal conflict of law rules for cross-border financial services. In the field of contract law, the Rome Convention of 19 June 1980 constitutes the common framework for most Member States with respect of conflict rules.[158] As a rule, parties to the financial service will enjoy freedom of choice as to the applicable law. The main exceptions to party autonomy in the Rome Convention with relevance for financial services concern contracts concluded with consumers (Article 5), or in general the application of mandatory rules (*lois de police*) of either the forum, or another State (Article 7). With respect to rules of market behaviour (unfair competition, advertising etc), the applicable law will usually be determined by a conflict rule referring to the 'market principle': the law of the market on which the behaviour produces significant effects, ie where the

[157] The most illustrative example in this respect is the *GB-Inno-BM* Case, which concerned the application of the Luxembourg law to publicity leaflets distributed in Luxembourg by a Belgian supermarket. The Court was asked whether the provisions of Luxembourg substantive law, which were applicable by virtue of the Luxembourg conflict of law rules, constituted an undue restriction to free movement of goods.

[158] It should be noted that the Rome Convention does not *stricto sensu* form part of the Community legal order, as it is not based on Article 293 EC. However, the Convention is regarded as so closely related to the objectives of the Treaty that the accession treaties for new Member States systematically prescribe signature of the Rome Convention as a condition for accession to the European Union. Moreover, in the post-Amsterdam era, the Rome Convention is considered to fall within the scope of Title IV EC (on judicial co-operation in civil matters), in particular Article 65(b) EC.

interests of competitors or consumers may be affected, will apply.[159] Only when the law thus declared applicable qualifies as a restriction to cross-border free movement—a question which should be considered having regard to the proper contents of the applicable substantive law—will the primacy of the free movement principle come into play.

3. Can Conflict of Law Rules Constitute a Restriction to Free Movement?

Once it is established that the free movement principle does not interfere with the technique of determining the applicable law by a conflict rule, the next question arising is to what extent the conflict rule itself could be regarded as a restriction to free movement, and consequently would be subjected to the general good test.

In this context, one should first have regard to the specificity of conflict rules in assessing whether a rule of substantive law should be regarded as constituting a restriction to free movement. In the field of contract law, it has been mentioned that the determination of the *lex contractus* in first instance is a matter of party autonomy. For the service provider, the free choice of applicable law implies that he will be able to stipulate application of its home State law with respect to the community-wide provision of services, thus in effect realizing the 'mutual recognition' which is also achieved by the free movement principle.[160] Consequently, it may be submitted that, as far as parties to the contract enjoy freedom of choice with respect to the applicable law, a substantive law provision cannot be regarded as constituting a restriction to free movement, as parties are able to rule out the possibly restrictive rules through the choice of another law for the service contract. This view seems also to be supported by the Court's jurisprudence.[161]

Not only when parties to the contract have made an express choice of applicable law, will the possible 'restrictive' effect of national law be neutralized. The same principles should reasonably prevail when, in absence of choice of law clause in the contract, the applicable law is determined by reference to the country with which the contrast is most closely

[159] See for a comparative overview of the conflict rules in different European countries: H Duintjer Tebbens, 'Les conflits de lois en matière de publicité déloyale à l'épreuve du droit communautaire', *Rev Crit dip*, 1994, 451, 455.

[160] Compare, *inter alia*, UH Schneider, 'Europäische und internationale Harmonisierung des Bankvertragsrechts', *Neue Juristische Wochenschrift*, 1991, 1985, 1992; B Smulders and P Glazener, 'Harmonization in the Field of Insurance Law Through the Introduction of Community Rules of Conflict' [1992] CMLR 775, 777, n 4.

[161] See in particular the Decision of 24 January 1991 in Case C-339/89 *Alsthom Atlantique* [1991] ECR I-107.

connected.[162] Indeed, in this case the applicable law may be presumed to result from an *implicit* choice of law: parties to the contract had the opportunity to disapply an alleged provision in national law through their choice of law clause, and cannot therefore invoke the 'restrictive' effect of this provision for their freedom to provide services.

It follows from the foregoing that, with respect to rules of contract law, a restriction to cross-border free movement can only be identified where the alleged provisions in national law are imposed through mandatory conflict rules which they cannot rule out. Within the context of the Rome Convention, these relate mainly to consumer contracts (Article 5), mandatory provisions of the *lex fori* or of another law (Article 7) and the public order of the competent judge (Article 16).

The European Commission's position on these issues is far from clear: on the one hand, the Interpretative Communication suggests, in line with the principles set out above, that provisions in national law could only qualify as a restriction when applied pursuant to mandatory conflict rules.[163] However, when the Commission comes to exemplifying this principle on banking contracts concluded by the branch of a foreign credit institution in the host State, the Commission adopts different standards: it seems to accept that, even in the absence of a mandatory conflict rule, the application of host State law when no express choice of law was made by the parties, could be overruled by the free movement principle, and consequently only be maintained under the general good exception.[164]

The next question is whether the conflict rule itself could be regarded as constituting a restriction to free movement. In this respect, one should have regard to the very nature of a conflict of law rule: in most cases, the sole function of the conflict rule is to determine, on the basis of objective

[162] Article 4 of the Rome Convention contains a (refutable) presumption that a contract is most closely connected with the country where the party who is to effect the most characteristic performance of the contract has its habitual residence or central administration.

[163] Interpretative Communication (n 3 above) 25: 'Thus, . . . the provisions of substantive law applicable to a banking service pursuant to the choice-of-law rules laid down in the Rome Convention (*it being possible for freedom of choice to be overriden by mandatory rules, mandatory requirements and public policy*) may, if they constitute a restriction, be examined in the light of the general good' (emphasis added).

[164] Interpretative Communication (n 3 above) 25: 'The Convention . . . implies that, where a service is supplied by a bank branch, the law of the country where the branch is situated is presumed to prevail *in the absence of a choice by the parties concerned*. In accordance with the principle of the precedence of Community law, the Commission considers that, where the legal provisions of the country of the branch constitute a restriction, they may be put to the general good test and, if necessary, overruled' (emphasis added).

The Interpretative Communication provides a second example with respect to banking contracts concluded with consumers, to which Article 5 of the Rome Convention applies. Here, the Commission only mentions the possible restrictive character of the mandatory provisions of consumer protection in the country of residence of the consumer, which results from a mandatory conflict rule.

connecting factors, which law will be applicable to a transnational situation, without anticipating the result of the application of the substantive rules thus designated. For instance, when the conflict rules of a Member State indicate the market law as being applicable to cross-border advertising, they do not contain any indication as to the possible restrictive nature of the substantive law declared applicable. Consequently, these purely indicative conflict laws cannot by their nature contain any restriction to the free movement of goods or services.

Some conflict rules might however contain elements which refer to the contents or the purpose of substantive law in order to determine which law should apply. A typical example in the context of the Rome Convention is to be found in Article 5 with respect to contracts concluded with consumers: the principle of party autonomy in the determination of the law applicable to the contract does not prejudice the application of the law of the consumer's place of residence when it offers the consumer a more extensive protection than under the *lex contractus*: the possible application of provisions of the consumer's law thus depends on a comparison of its substantive provisions with the *lex causae*. In the same way, the possible mandatory application of *lois de police* to the contract will depend upon the purposes achieved by these provisions of substantive law, and which justify their unilateral application to the contract notwithstanding the *lex contractus*.

The circumstance that conflict rules take into account elements of substantive law in determining which law should apply, does not in our view modify the essentially indicative nature of the conflict rule: the restriction imposed by national law on freedom of movement is the sole consequence of the effect of the rules of substantive law applied pursuant to the conflict rule. Consequently, it may be submitted that even the conflict rules which cannot be considered as 'neutral' as to the substantive content of the conflicting laws cannot by themselves be considered contrary to EC law.

Nevertheless, it cannot be denied that some conflict rules will be 'suspect' in view of the free movement principle, and their application should therefore be watched with particular vigilance. In the field of financial services, this will in particular hold true for contracts with consumers: the prevalence of the more protective law of the consumer's residence, ie the host State law, over the law of the financial institution (the home State) pursuant to Article 5 of the Rome Convention, could for the latter constitute a restriction to free movement of services, as it impedes the possibility of the financial institution distributing the same service community-wide. However, its restrictive nature does not in itself invalidate the conflict rule as such, but only intervenes at the level of the application of the rule of the substantive law provisions. Moreover, it should be borne in mind that consumer protection is accepted as legitimate general good motive in the field of financial services.

4. Conflict of Law Rules and the General Good

It follows from the above analysis that the principle of free movement basically does not interfere with the determination of the applicable law to cross-border services by virtue of the normal conflict of law rules. Their interference is to be situated at the level of the application of the substantive law provision applied pursuant to these conflict rules. If the substantive law provisions are considered a restriction to the free movement, the Member State will not be allowed to apply them in the cross-border service relationship, unless they could be justified by the public order exception of Article 49 EC, or under the general good exception.

It has therefore been rightly pointed out that the relationship between free movement, conflict of law rules and the general good could be regarded as a 'mariage à trois':[165] the freedom of choice with regard to the determination of the *lex contractus* to a cross-border (financial) service may be ruled out in whole or in part by a mandatory conflict rule; the application of the substantive law provisions pursuant to this mandatory conflict rule should in its turn, when constituting a restriction to free movement, satisfy the general good test. If this test fails, the substantive provisions may not be applied to the cross-border service, which in practice comes down in the continuing application of the normal *lex contractus*. Thus, the general good test must be incorporated in the application of the conflict rules, in order for these conflict rules to produce their plain effects.

The former may be illustrated by an example: a French credit institution wishes to grant mortgage credit to Belgian residents under the regime of free provisions of services. The contracts stipulate application of French law. However, by virtue of Article 5 of the Rome Convention,[166] this choice may not prejudice to the application of the provisions of Belgian law which protect consumers more than the *lex contractus*. Therefore, the French credit institution will have to comply with the Belgian law concerning *inter alia* the variability of interest rates, which is more favourable for the

[165] W van Gerven, 'Convention de Rome, Traité de Rome et prestations de services dans le secteur financier', in *La Convention de Rome, Banque & Droit*, 1993, special issue, 23, 30, No 32; see also J Biancarelli, 'L'intérêt général et le droit applicable aux contrats financiers', *Banque*, 1992, 1090, 1098; D Carreau, 'Banques', in *Juris-Classeurs Traité de Droit européen*, fasc 1023 (9, 1994), No 79, 16; B Sousi-Roubi, 'La Convention de Rome et la loi applicable aux contrats bancaires', *Recueil Dalloz*, 1993, Chron, 183, 189.

[166] It is assumed here that the specific conflict rule of Article 5 of the Rome Convention does apply to mortgage credits granted to consumers. The issue is, however, the subject of debate among scholars (see, for instance, W Devroe and E Bodson, 'Tweespraak. Internationaal privaatrechtelijke aspecten van de nieuwe wet op het hypothecair krediet', *Tijdschrift voor rechtspersoon en vennootschap*, 1993, 320–323), and for a general overview of the controversy: Tison (n 31 above) paras 707–711. In the hypothesis that the law of the consumer's residence would not apply by virtue of Article 5 of the Convention, the protective rules of the *lex fori* could nevertheless come into play.

consumer than French law. For the French credit institution, this obligation may be regarded as a restriction of his freedom to provide services: the credit institution has to tailor its product to the Belgian market, which implies additional costs and might possibly influence its financing techniques. Consequently, the rules of Belgian law can only be maintained under the general good exception, in particular the need to protect the consumer. It is in this respect not sufficient for the Belgian law to be justified by the need to protect the consumer. The restriction imposed by the Belgian law should under the general good test also satisfy the proportionality requirement, which is absent in the context of Article 5 of the Rome Convention. If the general good test fails, the more protective provision of Belgian law will be inapplicable, and consequently the *lex contractus* will again produce its full effects.

A similar additional general good test should be applied when the application of restrictive substantive law results from other mandatory conflict rules. Thus, the *loi de police* applied to the contract must be disapplied when it does not satisfy the general good test. Equally, the judge of the forum must, in applying its *ordre public* to reject the result of the application of the *lex contractus* (Article 16 of the Rome Convention), check whether this intervention may be related to a justification in the general good or the community public order (Article 46 EC). In the context of regulation of advertising, the mandatory application of the host State rules by virtue of the 'market' principle should also be submitted to the general good test when a restriction to free movement results from it.

VI. CONCLUDING REMARKS: MONITORING MUTUAL RECOGNITION AND THE USE OF THE GENERAL GOOD CLAUSE

The analysis of the general good in the Court's case law and in the Directives on Banking and Investment Services reveals that there is much scope for the application of the general good exception in the context of financial services. However, although the concept itself does not give rise to difficulties, many uncertainties surround the actual application of it to the Member States' laws. The implementation of the Banking and Investment Services Directives in the Member States also demonstrates the risks of abuse of the general good clause by the Member States. Not only have different Member States used the general good clauses as an alibi for attributing specific residual powers to their prudential authorities towards foreign financial institutions; but the lists of general good rules established by some Member States are moreover illustrative of the sometimes very extensive conception of the general good by the host countries.

The initiative of the Commission to clarify the issue of the general good in the context of the Second Banking Co-ordination Directive—and in the future for the Investment Services Directive—should be welcomed. However, the Interpretative Communication does not always bring the clarification which market participants need: the Communication does not modify in any respect the fundamental problem underlying the general good concept: in the absence of Community harmonization of financial product regulation, financial institutions cannot be expected to rely on a vague and exclusively case law built construction. It goes without saying that the uncertainties surrounding the general good present a major impediment for financial institutions effectively to make use of the single passport. In practice, it would seem that the financial institutions do not take the risk of clashing with host State authorities, and simply obey the rules of the host State. As a consequence, one can hardly speak of the existence of an actual 'internal' market without frontiers. Indeed, one should admit that, apart from supervisory aspects, the market remains largely fragmented along national borders. The competition between financial institutions does not take place at the product level, but is mainly limited to price competition.

Which alternatives are available for improving the use of the single passport at the level of financial products? A first step could be to improve the flow of information and discussion about the use by the Member States of the general good clause. In this respect, it seems essential that the notification of the general good rules by host Member States be made clearly mandatory, thus provoking a more dynamic interaction between the financial institutions and the host States even before the start of the activity in the host State. In this respect, it may be deplored that the final Interpretative Communication did not contain the suggestions made by the Commission during the consultation process on the draft Communication[167] to amend the Second Banking Co-ordination Directive in order to take away its current ambiguity and to consider the notification requirement as mandatory.

A further step could be to improve the communication between the European Commission and the Member States on the general good issue, in order for the former to exercise effectively its monitoring function under Article 211 EC. A recent Communication by the European Commission to the European Parliament and the Council on the problems surrounding the application of the mutual recognition principle in the internal market provides some interesting indications on the Commission's policy intentions with respect to the effective monitoring of the principle of mutual recognition in the area of both products and (financial) services.[168] While stressing

[167] Document XV/1104/96 of 16 July 1996.

[168] European Commission, *Mutual Recognition in the Context of the Follow-up to the Action Plan for the Single Market* sl, sd (URL:http://europa.eu.int/comm/dg15/en/update/general/mutualen.pdf).

the landmark importance of the mutual recognition principle in the operation of the internal market, as it provides a pragmatic and powerful tool for economic integration, the Commission acknowledges the difficulties arising from the use by the Member States of the general good exception.[169] Specifically in the field of financial services, the Commission intends to improve transparency as to the legitimate motives of consumer protection which might justify an exception to (imperfect) mutual recognition of home State rules in the cross-border provision of financial services. To this end, the Commission will draw up, in co-operation with the Member States, an inventory of obstacles to cross-border transactions, and analyse the conditions under which the host State rules should apply their rules of consumer protection in the interest of the general good.[170] It goes without saying that this exercise should not be limited to repeating the abstract criteria of the general good test, as was done in the Interpretative Communication, but should effectively apply the test to the concrete rules under scrutiny. Of course, the viewpoints thus expressed by the Commission and the Member States will not prejudice the point of view of the European Court of Justice, which might subsequently be asked to rule on a similar issue in a preliminary proceeding.

In addition, the Commission is considering the creation of a Community network for dealing with complaints by consumers in retail financial services, in order to promote co-operation between the national bodies (ombudsmen etc) entrusted with the amicable settlement of disputes between consumers and financial institutions.[171] Such a network could also produce valuable information on the way the Member States apply and impose on financial institutions the general good clause. It could therefore constitute, together with the other information means described above, an additional tool to monitor the mutual recognition in cross-border financial services.

[169] ibid 4 and 6.

[170] In its Financial Services Action Plan, the European Commission indicated that work could be undertaken to establish possible equivalence between clearly similar rules in different Member States, hence ruling out the possibility for the Member States to invoke the general good clause (see European Commission, *Financial Services: Implementing the Framework for Financial Markets: Action Plan*, COM(1999) 232 of 11 May 1999, 11). It is, however, debatable whether such a 'negative' approach towards the general good clause will produce significant results. Given the diversity of regulation in many Member States in the area of retail financial services, it may be submitted that the cases where clearly equivalent rules of different Member States can be identified, will be of marginal importance. Apparently, the European Commission is not considering any concrete initiative in this respect in the near future. As a matter of fact, the first Progress Report on the Financial Services Action Plan does not mention this initiative as a possible policy priority (see European Commission, *Financial Services Action Plan. Progress Report*, sd; see URL: http://europa.eu.int/comm/dg15/en/finances/actionplan/progress1en.pdf).

[171] See European Commission (n 168 above) 10–11; see also European Commission (n 170 above) 10–11.

Another important recent evolution can be found in the judgment of the ECJ in the so-called *Foie Gras* Case: the European Commission brought an action before the ECJ against the French Republic, which had adopted a decree which imposed minimum quality standards for *foie gras* products. The effect of the decree was to prohibit the distribution in France of *foie gras* products under certain denominations which did not satisfy the French product standards. Interestingly, the ECJ followed the argument of the European Commission, which considered the French decree to be contrary to Article 28 EC to the extent that it did not contain a mutual recognition clause which allowed the distribution in France of imported *foie gras* products, which were legally manufactured and distributed in their Member State of origin.[172] The Court's judgment could have far-reaching implications, as there is no reason not to transpose it to the other Treaty freedoms, in particular the free provision of (financial) services. It would imply that a Member State, when enacting national rules on financial products (eg mandatory contract clauses) the effect of which is to prohibit the offering of financial services by EU-based financial institutions which are legally offered in their home countries, should include in its legislation a mutual recognition clause. Such a clause would not eliminate the possibility that the host State rules prevail under the general good clause. It would nevertheless provide an important signal to foreign service providers that cross-border distribution of financial services is allowed under a mutual recognition regime.

In connection with the former consideration, it should be examined whether inspiration for future action could for instance be found in Directive 98/34/EC of 22 June 1998[173] which, in the field of free movement of goods, imposes upon Member States the obligation to notify its technical rules to the Commission as a precondition to their application. As was illustrated by the *Foie Gras* Case, such a notification requirement could, even before adoption of new legislation in a Member State, provoke an exchange of views with the European Commission, and pos-sibly with other Member States, on the international application of the draft rules and the possibility of invoking the general good in this context. Introducing a similar notification requirement for, for instance, all national regulation relating specifically to banking and financial services, would constitute an important step in that direction. Not only could the dialogue provoked by the notification requirement in the end lead to more clarification for the

172 Case C-184/96 *Commission v France* [1998] ECR I-6197, para 28.

173 Directive 98/37/EC of the European Parliament and the Council of 22 June 1998, laying down a procedure for provision of information in the field of technical standards and regulations, OJ 1998 L204, 37, which repealed Directive 83/198/EEC.

participants in the markets; it could moreover constitute the point of departure for new harmonization initiatives in the field of financial product regulation, which eventually would foster the cross-border mobility of financial products in a genuine internal market.

13

Localization of Financial Services: Regulatory and Tax Implications

MARC DASSESSE

I. WHERE IS THE FINANCIAL SERVICE LOCATED? REGULATORY IMPLICATIONS

1. Introduction

A fundamental difference between the international trade in goods and the international trade in financial services is that no one has ever seen a financial service cross a border.

By its very nature, a financial service is immaterial. Since no one can come up with concrete evidence of where a financial service is physically delivered (or consumed), both regulators and tax authorities have to answer the question of localization (or consumption) by applying a set of abstract rules.

Three issues (at least) arise in this respect:

(a) the rules applied for the localization of financial services (which term includes hereafter banking services, investment services and life insurance services) at a European Union level are different in nature and in scope from the rules applicable in a World Trade Organization context;

(b) the localization rules applicable to banking services (which term refers hereafter to services provided by credit institutions and investment services firms) differ in several respects from the regulatory and tax rules applying for the localization of insurance services;

(c) the rules applied by financial regulators to determine where a financial service is provided (and hence the extent to which it comes within their prudential jurisdiction) are not (always) the same as the rules applied by the tax authorities.

Before addressing these issues below, a reminder may be appropriate: the freedom of services is two-sided. It encompasses obviously the right of the provider of the service to provide a service to a (prospective) purchaser resident in another country (either by entering that country temporarily, or at a distance). It also encompasses, however, the right of a person resident in one country to purchase a service from a provider established in another country (either by entering that country temporarily, or at a distance).

2. The Localization Rules Applicable to Financial Services at EU level

(a) Scope of the EU rules: applicable only to EC incorporated financial services providers

It should be stressed at the outset that the EU localization rules for financial services briefly examined below only apply for financial services provided by a financial services provider which is incorporated in one of the EU Member States and has been granted a so-called 'single passport' by the supervisory authorities of said Member State, giving it the right to provide its services throughout the European Union, subject only, as a rule, to the supervision of its 'home country' supervisor.

Indeed, these rules have been enacted, pursuant to a number of so-called Financial Services Directives for the purpose of facilitating the exercise of the freedom of services granted by the EC Treaty to nationals of the EU Member States, including the legal persons incorporated under the laws of the Member States.

As a result, EU localization rules do not apply:

(a) in the case of services provided by a company established outside the European Union to a purchaser established within the European Union; nor

(b) in the case of services provided by a so-called 'third country branch'. These terms refer to a branch established in the European Union of a company incorporated outside the European Union (that is, in a so-called 'third country').

As a matter of EU Law, third country branches, including third country branches of a financial services provider incorporated outside the European Union, are not entitled to avail themselves of the freedom of services provided for by the EC Treaty—since such freedom is only provided for the benefit of nationals of, and companies incorporated under the laws of, a Member State.

True, Article 49 (ex 59) EC provides that the Council (made up of representatives of the EU Member States) may, by a qualified majority, acting upon a proposal from the European Commission, extend the benefit of the freedom of services 'to nationals of a third country [which term includes a legal person] who provide services *and* who are established within the Community'.

However, to date, neither the Council nor the Commission have made use of this option for any third country. Indeed, it is understood that the request to do so for the benefit of branches within the Community of Swiss insurance companies (a request made after Switzerland voted in a referendum, a few years ago, against joining the EU) met with a polite refusal.

It is also worth noting that all EU Member States which submitted observations to the European Court of Justice in connection with the request put to the Court to clarify the respective jurisdictions of the Member States and of the Community in terms of the commitments made at the WTO (GATS) level were anxious to stress the fact that third country branches of financial services providers established within their respective territory cannot avail themselves of the freedom of services provided for by the Treaty (and, as a result, stay firmly, in this respect, within the exclusive jurisdiction of the Member State on whose territory they are located, to the exclusion of the Community).

(b) *A growing divide in terms of prudential localization rules between banking/investment services and insurance services*

All 'single passport' Financial Services Directives (banks, insurance, investment services) have a principle in common: a financial services provider which has been incorporated in accordance with the laws of a Member State (and has its head office therein) is entitled to a so-called 'single passport' which gives it the right to sell its services in all other Member States (and, conversely, would-be purchasers established in all other Member States have the right freely to purchase these services). As a rule, this cross-border provision of financial services is subject to the exclusive jurisdiction of the supervisors of the Member State of incorporation, since it is the authorities of this latter Member State which have exclusive jurisdiction to issue the 'single passport' in the first place.

Identical procedures also apply when it comes to the effective use of the 'single passport': if the financial services provider wishes to provide its services 'on the territory' of another Member State (that is, the Member State where the would-be purchasers are established) it must notify beforehand its intention to do so to its own supervisory authorities (that is, the authorities which have issued its 'single passport'). The supervisory authorities of the home country will, in turn, inform the supervisory authorities of the Member State on whose territory it is proposed to provide services. Thus, if a financial services provider having its head office in France wishes to provide services 'on the territory' of Belgium, it must inform beforehand the French supervisory authorities of the same and, in turn, the French supervisory authorities will inform the Belgian supervisory authorities.

A contrario, this 'notification procedure' is not applicable when the service is not provided (in the above example) by the French financial services provider 'on the territory' of Belgium.

It is therefore of crucial importance for the purpose of the notification procedure (but also for other purposes examined below) to determine when a service is provided by a financial services provider 'on the territory' of another Member State.

(i) When is a financial service provided 'on the territory' of the would-be purchaser?

With regard to banking services this question has had to be addressed very early.

The reason for the Commission's speedy efforts to address it lay, among others, in a number of French court cases involving mortgage credits provided to French borrowers by a number of Belgian banks and Dutch banks: when the bottom fell out of the French real estate market at the beginning of the 1990s (concomitantly with the coming into force of the Second Banking Co-ordination Directive), a number of borrowers (or their sureties) were quick to develop a keen interest for European law issues—and to invoke the nullity of said loans on the ground that the Dutch or Belgian mortgage providers had not complied with the notification procedure.

One should recall, in this respect that, in a number of countries (Belgium being one), mortgage credit may be granted not only by banks but also by insurance companies. Indeed, in Belgium, it is the Belgian insurance commissioners and not the Belgian banking supervisor which is the supervisory authority for mortgage credits, even when they are granted by credit institutions.

It is also worth recalling that certain so-called 'capitalization products' are, in some Member States, viewed as banking services (and hence may only be provided by credit institutions) whereas in other Member States, they are viewed as insurance services (and hence may only be provided by insurance companies).

The Commission's Interpretative Communication, *Freedom of Services and the General Good under the Second Banking Directive* was adopted in 1997 for the purpose, among others, of clarifying the answer to the question 'when is a banking service provided on the territory of another Member State and hence give rise to the notification procedure?'. The Commission has, after much deliberation, opted for the so-called 'characteristic performance test'. As a rule, application of this test leads to the result that the banking service is localized 'on the territory' of the Member State where the credit institution is established. The characteristic performance test thus strongly reduces the number of cases in which the notification procedure must be implemented.[1]

As noted by the Commission's Communication, the characteristic performance test leads to the conclusion that the provision of banking

[1] The Commission's Communication has also indicated that, in the Commission's view, failure to observe the notification procedure, in those cases where it remains applicable, may not result in the nullity of the contract between the bank and the client: European Commission, *GATS 2000—Opening Markets for Services* (2000) 66.

services via the Internet does not, as such, result in the provision of services by the credit institution 'on the territory' of the Member State of residence of the client. In other words, a credit institution having its head office, for example, in Luxembourg may put in place an interactive website, which can be accessed by residents of all other Member States, without, as a result, providing services 'on the territory' of those Member States.

The Commission's Communication has been, on this point, hotly disputed by the supervisory authorities of a number of Member States, among which one may count Belgium, France and Italy.

However, one clearly sees today the strategic importance of the Commission's Communication for the future development of banking services. The position taken in 1997 in the Commission's Communication regarding the provision of banking services via the Internet resulted in 2000 in the inclusion of banking services—at least as a matter of principle—in the scope of application of the so-called Electronic Commerce Directive 2000/31/EC. It will be recalled that the objective of this Directive is to make it possible for a provider of services established in Member State A to sell its services via the Internet to customers established in all other Member States while having only to comply, as a rule, with the binding rules applicable in the Member State on the territory of which he is established.

(ii) A missed opportunity for life insurance services

After lengthy consultations with insurers and insurance intermediaries, the Commission has published on 2 February 2000 its Interpretative communication, *Freedom to Provide Services and the General Good in the Insurance Sector.*

The so-called 'Insurance Communication' takes a totally different view from the Banking Communication when it comes to the scope of application to the notification procedure.

The Insurance Communication rests on the assumption—enthusiastically supported of course by insurance supervisors of all Member States—that whenever a life insurer having its head office in Member State A accepts to sell a policy to an individual resident in Member State B, there is automatically a provision of service by said insurer 'on the territory' of the Member State of residence of the client (being the Member State where the risk is located), and this even though the insurer may have never set foot on the territory of Member State B and has no wish whatsoever to do so.

In other words, according to the Insurance Communication, there is no need to distinguish between provision of service 'on the territory' of the Member State of residence of the client, and purchase of insurance services by the client 'on the territory' of the Member State of residence of the insurer.

The consequences of this approach are far-reaching: indeed, the

Insurance Communication takes the view that an insurance company wishing to provide insurance services via the Internet to cover a risk localized on the territory of other Member States must comply with the notification procedure with respect to all such Member States on the ground that it is deemed to be providing insurance services 'on their territory'.

It is worth recalling, in this respect, that the implementation of the notification procedure in the case of insurance companies very often goes hand-in-hand with the obligation for the insurer to appoint a tax representative in the Member State of residence of the client (as well as the need to amend its standard contract to make it compatible with the laws justified by the general good of the Member State of residence of the client).

It is to be regretted that the insurance companies—and the insurance intermediaries—have not made use of the hearings organized two years ago by the European Commission with regard to what was then the draft Insurance Communication to attack this reasoning, which appears incompatible with the basic principles of the Treaty, which principles may not of course be restricted by the Insurance Directives, the purpose of which may only be to facilitate the exercise of the basic freedoms, and not to restrict them: freedom of services is not only the right of the provider of the service to go 'on the territory' of residence of the client. It is also the right of the client to go 'on the territory' of the provider of the service. It is also the right of the consumer who 'surfs' the Internet to contact the website of a foreign insurer with a view to purchase, on his own initiative, a life insurance product or a capitalization product from such foreign insurer.

Indeed, as noted by the Insurance Communication itself, in the vast majority of cases the conclusion of insurance contracts via the Internet is the result of the initiative taken by the purchaser, who decides to contact or solicit, with its own equipment, an insurance company which is willing to conclude insurance contracts by way of electronic means.

The net result of the restrictive approach taken by the Insurance Communication is that insurance services are excluded from the E-Commerce Directive. Thus, the difference in treatment which already existed, in terms of localization, between insurance services and banking services at the supervisory level is now transposed at the e-commerce level. The next step, unless insurance companies and insurance intermediaries get their act together quickly, will be differentiation in treatment at the distribution level. At the time of writing, the Commission is finalizing a draft directive dealing with insurance intermediaries to the exclusion of intermediaries involved in the distribution of other financial products.

3. The Localization Rules Applicable to Financial Services in a WTO Context

The General Agreement on Trade in Services (GATS) makes a distinction, when it comes to financial services, between 'cross-border services' on the one hand, and 'consumption abroad', on the other.

However, with respect to the major players in the financial services field, much more far-reaching commitments have been entered into by those countries (mostly OECD countries) which are signatories of the so-called 'memorandum of understanding'.

Indeed, the 'memorandum of understanding' replaces the concept of 'consumption abroad' by that of 'purchase abroad' as a mode of delivery of financial services. Countries bound by the 'memorandum of understanding' 'shall allow the purchase abroad of a number of financial services, regardless of where the financial service is actually supplied or consumed, and without requiring any movement of a physical person into the territory of another country'.[2]

'Purchase abroad' includes for example the right of a resident of, say, France to purchase in, say, Switzerland or the USA a financial product if the same has been liberalized under the 'memorandum of understanding'.

In terms of cross-frontier services, liberalization commitments are minimal for banking services, even under the 'memorandum of understanding'.[3] However, the position is totally different when it comes to the purchase abroad of banking services. In effect, the 'memorandum of understanding' liberalizes the purchase abroad of most banking services.

The 'generosity' of this liberalization commitment is probably to be explained by the fact that it was negotiated at a time when e-based banking services were essentially limited to professionals.

However, there is a potential restriction to this liberalization, which also applies for the 'purchase abroad' of banking services. This is the so-called 'prudential carve-out'. This gives in effect the right to the country of residence of the client to take restrictive measures justified (in sum) by its general good requirements, including, of course, the protection of investors.

A country bound by the 'memorandum of understanding' may obviously be tempted to restrict the ability of its residents to purchase abroad certain banking services by relying on the 'prudential carve-out' exception. Whether it uses the 'prudential carve-out' beyond what is allowed by the true scope thereof will of course be, in case of disagreement with the country where the

[2] We will not address here the position with regard to insurance services which is even more restricted.

[3] Any decision in the value added tax field must, at least for the time being, have the unanimous approval of all Member States.

provider of the service is established, a matter to be eventually decided by the Dispute Settlement Body.

4. Difficult Cohabitation within the European Union of EU localization Rules and GATS Rules

The present situation rests on the assumption, clearly contrary to reality, especially since the advent of the mass use of the Internet and rapid means of communication, that the European Union territory is an island and, in addition, that third country branches established on the territory of a Member State of the European Union do not provide services to residents of other Member States than the Member State in which they are established.

This point may be illustrated by the following example. True, it is caricatural, but not that far removed from everyday reality.

Let us assume that Mr Dupont, a resident of Northern France, boards the Eurostar high-speed train to London. He disembarks at Waterloo Station and, across the street, he sees two life insurance offices: the offices of UK Life Insurance Co Ltd and the offices of the London branch of Japan Life Insurance Co (incorporated in Japan with head office in Tokyo).

Let us assume that both insurance offices sell identical products. Both are regulated by the UK authorities.

Scenario No 1

Mr Dupont enters the offices of UK Life Insurance Co Ltd to buy, say, a single premium life insurance product, for which he is willing to pay £10,000.

If UK Life Insurance Co Ltd agrees to do business with Mr Dupont, the following situation will obtain (on the assumption that it has not done business before with any customer resident in France):

- UK Life Insurance Co Ltd must notify beforehand the UK insurance authorities of its intention to provide services 'on the territory' of France (even though it has no intention whatsoever of ever sending a representative there to visit Mr Dupont);
- the UK insurance supervisors must, in turn, inform the French insurance supervisors;
- the French insurance supervisors will, in turn, 'invite' UK Life Insurance Co Ltd to appoint a tax representative in France with a view to the payment of local taxes on insurance premiums;
- UK Life Insurance Co Ltd will also need to seek legal advice so as to amend its standard insurance contract (governed by English law) to

make it comply with the French laws governing life insurance products, which laws are of course justified (in the view of the French authorities) by French general good;
- Finally, to top it all, the £10.000 single insurance premium paid by Mr Dupont must be reported (on a 'no name' basis) by UK Life Insurance Co Ltd to the UK insurance supervisor as being a premium collected as a result of providing life insurance services 'on the territory' of France.

If UK Life Insurance Co Ltd is not prepared to go through all this, its only alternative is to say to Mr Dupont: 'Sorry, we are not willing to do business with you because you are French and we do not wish to provide services "on the territory" of France.'

Scenario No 2

Mr Dupont decides to enter the offices of the London branch of Japan Life Insurance Co.

As far as the local Japanese insurer is concerned, this is a domestic sale, that is, a sale made on the domestic UK market. Thus:

- no notification procedure is required with respect to the provision of services 'on the territory' of France;
- there is no need to appoint a tax representative in France;
- there is no need to amend its standard contract governed by English law to make it conform to the laws of France justified by the general good, since it is not providing services 'on the territory' of France anyway.

It takes a very convinced European to feel that, in such circumstances, one should pity the London branch of Japan Life Insurance Co because it cannot avail itself of the benefits of the freedom to provide services under EU law, and because it cannot apply for a single passport.

A very delicate question, which we leave unanswered here, is the following: may the French authorities, by invoking the 'prudential carve-out', forbid their residents to buy financial products from third country branches established in other Member States (a difficult proposition to accept on the face of it, since those third country branches are supervised by the same supervisor who issues a 'single passport' to locally incorporated institutions having the right to operate throughout the European Community, including France).

Even more delicate is the answer to the question whether the UK authorities may (should?) forbid the third country branch, the operations of which they have authorized in the United Kingdom, from selling its services *in London* to residents of other Member States.

II. TAX IMPLICATIONS OF THE LOCALIZATION OF FINANCIAL SERVICES

Since the purpose of this book is not, generally, to address the issue of taxation, we will be very brief on this subject.

The tax treatment of financial services is of course inextricably linked to the question where the financial service is localized or rather, for taxation purposes, consumed.

Indeed, as a general rule, the jurisdiction of national tax authorities does not extend beyond their national boundaries.

In the example given in the preceding section, French taxes on insurance premiums will be applicable if the insurance service is deemed to be provided (or consumed) in France. If, on the other hand, the service is deemed to be consumed in the United Kingdom, French taxes will not apply but—possibly—corresponding UK taxes.

The danger of double taxation is obvious: to revert to the example of Mr Dupont purchasing a single premium life insurance product from the London branch of Japan Life Insurance Co, taxes could be payable in France (because, in the view of the French authorities, the service is being consumed by a French resident), and could be payable in the United Kingdom (on the ground that the service is being sold on the London market).

The same situation may arise for investment products: if I buy some international blue-chips from my local broker, he will charge me local stamp duty tax. If I call a broker in New York to buy those shares, he may end up having to charge me New York stamp duty tax. Query whether my country of residence will not take the view that taxes must also be paid locally because the service is 'consumed' in my jurisdiction?

The attention of the reader of this chapter is drawn to two moves which are afoot in this field at the time of writing.

First, the European Commission has formally adopted its proposal for a directive on the taxation of e-commerce services. In a nutshell, the purpose of this directive is to change the general rule on localization of services for value added tax purposes. Presently, as a general rule, services are deemed to be located in the country of residence of the provider. As a result, if the end-user who cannot recoup VAT (such as an individual, or a pension fund) buys a service from a service provider based outside the European Union, he does not have to pay VAT, whereas he must do so if he buys an identical service from a provider established within the European Union.

The Commission proposes to amend this localization rule in a general way. With the unanimous support of all Member States, it amended the rule of localization for telecommunication services (to combat the massive use of telecommunication services based outside the European Union by end-users based within the European Union). Henceforth, all e-commerce services would be similarly deemed, for VAT purposes, to be provided within the European Union and, hence, subject to VAT.

As such, this proposal for a directive has no impact for financial services. Indeed, at present, financial services are, in most cases, outside the scope of application of VAT.

However, for reasons which we will not go into here, the Commission may shortly propose to extend the scope of application of VAT to all financial services (insurance services; investment services; banking services). It has already conducted, with the assistance of outside consultants, a number of studies in this respect and the project (known as the Tax Calculation Account, TCA) is now very advanced.

It seems to be gathering increased speed as a result of the growing use of e-based financial services by users at large (one reason being that third country financial institutions have a competitive advantage over EU-based financial institutions because the latter have to pay VAT on their input yet cannot recoup it, so that it increases their cost base).

The net result of the TCA project would be to apply VAT, as aforesaid, to all financial services.

However, in order to avoid putting EU-based financial institutions at an increased handicap vis-à-vis financial services providers based outside the European Union, one must then also provide that all financial services provided to an EU resident are deemed to be provided within the European Union, and hence, are subject to VAT.

The question which arises in this context is whether the European Union (and its constituent Member States)[4] may, without breaching the commitments made at the GATS 'memorandum of understanding' level, provide that a financial service 'purchased abroad' by an EU resident from a financial services provider based outside the European Union is deemed to be provided 'within the European Union', that is, to be purchased locally, in the place of residence of the purchaser, and not 'abroad', that is, in the place of residence of the provider of the service.

Indeed, if the tax authorities of the country of residence of the service provider take the view that the service is provided locally (in the above example, in New York), and tax it accordingly, a new risk of double taxation arises.

This issue looks all the more sensitive since the net result of the TCA project would be that financial services purchased by an EU resident from, say, a New York bank would be subject to VAT (with an obligation for the New York bank to appoint a VAT representative in the European Union), whereas purchase by a New York resident of a financial service from an EU-based financial service provider would be exempted from VAT.

Here again, all the ingredients for a potentially damaging trade dispute at the WTO level would appear to be present.

[4] Any decision in the value-added tax field must—at least for the time being—have the unanimous approval of all Member States.

14

Financial Services, Taxation and Monetary Movements

JOHN A USHER

I. INTRODUCTION

In the context of a discussion of a unified freedom jurisprudence, the aim of this chapter is to look at the linkages between freedom to provide financial services, freedom to make monetary movements, and the issue of taxation. In brief, there cannot be freedom to provide financial services without freedom to make monetary movements, and for the private citizen the freedom to purchase financial services or to make investments in another Member State only becomes a reality where there is no exchange risk and no risk of government-inspired differences in interest rates between those States, a situation which now exists for the euro-12. However, if advantage is taken of such opportunities by private citizens, governments become all too well aware of the consequences for their exchequers of a lack of tax co-ordination—hence the current proposals *inter alia* for a withholding tax. Conversely, even if there is no exchange risk and no interest-rate risk, a failure to grant the same tax concessions to those purchasing eg a pension abroad, will make that purchase unattractive. The situation is compounded in Community law by the fact that at first sight, there is a conflict between the taxation provisions of the current capital movement rules[1] and other Treaty freedoms, yet at the same time the capital movement rules are broader in their scope than the other Treaty freedoms, in that they apply outside as well as inside the Community.[2]

This chapter will look in particular at the relationship between the free movement of capital and freedom to provide services, investigating the potential for overlap and the different legal consequences associated with categorization as a capital movement rather than as a service, and also investigating the extent to which the tax provisions relating to capital movements may limit the freedom to provide services.

As is well known, the legal need to distinguish services from other Treaty freedoms arises from the fact that under Article 50 EC, in order to be considered as services, activities must not be governed by the provisions

[1] Article 58(1)(a) EC. [2] Article 56 EC.

relating to the free movement of goods, capital and persons. In other words, provision of services is treated as a residual category to be applied only if the situation does not fall under one of the other Treaty freedoms; implicit in this appears to be the idea that the other freedoms and provision of services are mutually exclusive. It may however be wondered whether this concept remains appropriate in the modern single internal market, and some of the modern case law is difficult to reconcile with the wording of the Treaty. In Case C-484/93 *Svensson and Gustavsson v Ministre du Logement*,[3] it was held that loans from a bank in another Member State to buy a house fell within the scope of Directive 88/361 on Capital Movements,[4] but that such transactions also[5] constituted services within the meaning of what is now Article 49 EC. This approach was subsequently criticized by Advocate General Tesauro in his Opinion in Case C-118/96 *Safir v Skattemyndigheten i Dalarnas Län*,[6] where he suggested that the concepts should be kept separate and that a narrower concept of capital movements should be adopted. However, in its judgment in that case,[7] the Court held it to be a breach of Article 49 EC for Sweden to impose a different tax regime for insurance policies purchased from providers outside Sweden which would have the effect of deterring Swedish residents from taking out such policies, even though it was intended to achieve tax neutrality between policies purchased inside and outside Sweden. The Court then, however, added that the decision on this point made it unnecessary to determine whether the legislation was also incompatible with Articles 56 and 58 EC on capital movements—even though under the express terms of Article 50 EC, services are only services within the meaning of the Treaty to the extent that they do not fall under one of the other Treaty freedoms, and it might therefore have been expected that the first question should be whether the matter fell under the capital movement rules. Indeed, the Court confirmed that a mortgage fell within the scope of a capital movement as defined in the Directive in Case C-222/97 *Trummer and Mayer*,[8] and further held that this interpretation should continue to apply to the free movement of capital under Article 56 EC. However, in Case C-410/96 *Ambry*[9] it was held that for France to require the compulsory financial security provided by a travel agent to be guaranteed by a credit institution or insurance company situated in France breached the Treaty rules on freedom to provide services, although it may be observed that the list in the Annex to the 1988 Capital Movements Directive expressly includes guarantees granted by non-residents to residents.[10]

Against this background of conflicting case law, the first section of this

[3] [1995] ECR I-3955.
[4] OJ 1988 L178/5.
[5] [1995] ECR I-3955 para 11.
[6] [1998] ECR I-1897, 1905–1907.
[7] [1998] ECR I-1897.
[8] [1999] ECR I-1661.
[9] [1998] ECR I-7875.
[10] Annex I, heading IX A.

chapter will examine the broad concept of capital movements exemplified in *Trummer and Mayer*.[11]

II. THE BROAD INTERPRETATION OF CAPITAL MOVEMENTS

It is not often that a reference to the European Court of Justice from a national court, in which neither the parties to the main action nor the national government concerned submit any observations, is deemed worthy of a judgment delivered by a Full Court of all 15 judges, but that is what occurred in *Trummer and Mayer*. In its judgment, the Court clarified the relationship between the concept of capital movements in Articles 56 to 60 of the EC Treaty, which were introduced by the Maastricht Treaty, and the definitions of capital movements set out in the earlier Directives. However, in so doing it raised further questions as to the relationship between the free movement of capital and the freedom to provide services, and indirectly it raised questions as to the scope of the taxation provisions set out in Article 58.

The facts were quite simple and undisputed. In 1995 Mr Mayer, a German resident, sold a share in a property situated in Austria to Mr Trummer, an Austrian resident. It was agreed that Mr Trummer could have until the end of 2000 to settle the purchase price, which was fixed in German marks, and that payment should be secured by way of a mortgage over his share of the property. The problems arose when they tried to register the transaction in the local land register: registration of the mortgage was refused on the ground that the sum involved was not denominated in Austrian schillings. This view was upheld in the regional appeal court (Landesgericht Graz); in the Oberster Gerichtshof (which eventually made the reference) it was said that registration of a security right in respect of a foreign-currency debt was valid only where it was denominated in Austrian schillings in a sum corresponding to the foreign-currency debt as at the date of application for registration. The Oberster Gerichtshof therefore considered that the claim could only be allowed if the refusal of registration constituted a restriction on the movement of capital and payments prohibited by Article 56 of the EC Treaty, and it referred to the European Court the question of the compatibility of the Austrian rule with Article 56 (ex 73b) of the EC Treaty.

The Court observed that it was necessary first of all to consider whether the creation of a mortgage to secure the payment of a debt payable in the currency of another Member State was covered by Article 56 EC. Article 56 requires in its first paragraph that, within the framework of the Chapter

[11] [1999] ECR I-1661.

in which it appears, all restrictions on the movement of capital between Member States and between Member States and third countries shall be prohibited, and paragraph 2 states that within the same framework, all restrictions on payments between Member States and between Member States and third countries shall be prohibited. Unfortunately, as the Court noted, the EC Treaty does not define the terms 'movements of capital' or 'current payments'. However, the basic pattern established by the early Directives issued under the original Treaty rules on capital movements was to divide capital movements into four lists (eventually three), with different degrees of liberalization.[12]

A new approach was followed by Council Directive 88/361,[13] which finally established the basic principle of free movement of capital as a matter of Community law with effect, for most Member States, from 1 July 1990. Subject to its other provisions, Article 1(1) of the 1988 Directive provided that 'Member States shall abolish restrictions on movements of capital taking place between persons resident in Member States', and although there was still a nomenclature of capital movements annexed to the Directive, it was stated to be to facilitate its application, rather than to introduce distinctions in treatment. Annex I itself stated that the nomenclature was not intended to be an exhaustive list of the notion of capital movements, and it should not be interpreted as restricting the scope of the principle of full liberalization of capital movements in Article 1. However, in the absence of a Treaty definition, the headings of the nomenclature (which in reality owe much to the previous lists) indicate the concept of capital underlying the Directive: direct investments, investments in real estate, operations in securities normally dealt in on the capital market, operations in units of collective investment undertakings, operations in securities and other instruments normally dealt in on the money market, operations in current and deposit accounts with financial institutions, credits related to commercial transactions or to the provision of services in which a resident is participating, financial loans and credits, sureties, other guarantees and rights of pledge, transfers in performance of insurance contracts, personal capital movements, physical import and export of financial assets, and 'other capital movements' (defined so as to include transfers of the money required for the provision of services).

The introduction to the Annex further states that the capital movements mentioned are taken to cover all the operations necessary for the purposes of capital movements, ie the conclusion and performance of the transaction and related transfers, and should also include access for the economic oper-

[12] See Usher *The Law of Money and Financial Services in the EC* (2nd edn, Oxford University Press, Oxford, 2000) 17–19.

[13] OJ 1988 L178/5.

ator to all the financial techniques available on the market approached for the purpose of carrying out the operation in question.

The present author suggested in 1994[14] that in the continued silence of the Treaty the Annex to the Directive remained a useful source of illustration of the principle of the free movement of capital even after the entry into force of Articles 56 to 60 EC under the Maastricht Treaty. Such a view had in fact been accepted by the Landesgericht in *Trummer and Mayer*, but the Landesgericht interpreted the Annex so as not to cover the transaction in question. For its part, the European Court took the view that Article 56 'substantially reproduces the contents of Article 1 of Directive 88/361' and held that 'the nomenclature in respect of movements of capital annexed to Directive 88/361 still has the same indicative value, for the purposes of defining the notion of capital movements, as it did before the entry into force of Article [56] et seq., subject to the qualification, contained in the introduction to the nomenclature, that the list set out therein is not exhaustive'.

The Court had in fact already held that borrowing money from a bank in another Member State to buy a house fell within the scope of the Directive, in Case C-484/93 *Svensson and Gustavsson v. Ministre du Logement*.[15] Though, as noted at the outset of this chapter, it had subsequently been suggested by Advocate General Tesauro in his Opinion in Case C-118/96 *Safir v Skattemyndigheten i Dalarnas Län*[16] that a narrower concept of capital movements should be adopted, the Court confirmed in *Trummer and Mayer* that a mortgage fell within the scope of a capital movement as defined in the Directive. More specifically, it was held both that the mortgage in this case was inextricably linked to a capital movement—the liquidation of an investment in real property[17]—and that the mortgage as such was a capital movement under Point IX of the nomenclature as an 'other guarantee' under the heading 'sureties, other guarantees and rights of pledge'. In those circumstances, the Court held that an obligation to have recourse to the national currency for the purposes of creating a mortgage must be regarded, in principle, as a restriction on the free movement of capital within the meaning of Article 56 of the EC Treaty.

While *Trummer and Mayer* may have involved a private transaction, in the commercial world such a broad definition of capital movements raises problems with regard to the status and scope of the freedom to provide services. In that case, the Court confirmed that a mortgage falls within the scope of a capital movement as defined in the Directive, and further held

14 Usher, 'The Law of Money and Financial Services in the European Community' (Oxford UP 1994) 19.

15 [1995] ECR I-3955.

16 Opinion delivered 23 September 1997, [1998] ECR I-1899.

17 Point II of Annex I to the 1988 Directive.

that this interpretation should continue to apply to the free movement of capital under Article 56. However, a few months earlier in Case C-410/96 *Ambry*[18] it had been held that for France to require the compulsory financial security provided by a travel agent to be guaranteed by a credit institution or insurance company situated in France breached the Treaty rules on freedom to provide services—although it may be observed that the list in the Annex to the 1988 Capital Movements Directive expressly includes guarantees granted by non-residents to residents.[19] It may be submitted that this is an area in urgent need of clarification. Be that as it may, given the scope of the capital movement provisions, serious legal issues arise from the classification as a capital movement of an economic activity which might otherwise be regarded as a service.

III. THE SCOPE OF THE CAPITAL MOVEMENT PROVISIONS

As has already been indicated, the Maastricht Treaty on European Union introduced new provisions on 'capital and payments' with effect from 1 January 1994, the date set for the start of the second stage of Economic and Monetary Union. The fundamental rules are set out in Article 56, paragraph 1 of which states that within the framework of the provisions set out in that Chapter, all restrictions on the movement of capital between Member States and between Member States and third countries shall be prohibited, and paragraph 2 of which states that within the same framework, all restrictions on payments between Member States and between Member States and third countries shall be prohibited.

A fundamental distinction between these provisions and the original provisions—and indeed from the situation reached under the 1988 Directive—is that it appears that movements to and from third countries are to be treated the same way as movements between Member States. With hindsight, this can be seen as anticipating the need to ensure the external movement and availability of the euro. There are nevertheless apparent differences which remain. Under Article 57 EC, the provisions of Article 56 EC are stated to be without prejudice to the application to third countries of any restrictions which exist on 31 December 1993 under national or Community law adopted in respect of the movement of capital to or from third countries involving direct investment (including investment in real estate), establishment, the provision of financial services or the admission of securities to capital markets; in other words, they do not require existing lawful restrictions to be abolished in these (admittedly limited) areas. Furthermore, the second paragraph of Article 57, empowering the Council

[18] [1998] ECR I-7875. [19] Annex I, heading IX A.

to legislate on those capital movements, makes reference to 'endeavouring' to achieve the objective of free movement of capital between Member States and third countries to the 'greatest extent possible', language redolent of the original capital movement provisions in relation to movements between Member States. Under Article 59, where, in exceptional circumstances, movements of capital to or from third countries cause, or threaten to cause, serious difficulties for the operation of Economic and Monetary Union, the Council, acting by a qualified majority on a proposal from the Commission and after consulting the European Central Bank, may take safeguard measures with regard to third countries for a period not exceeding six months if such measures are strictly necessary. Finally, by virtue of Article 60 EC, the Council may take urgent measures under Article 301 EC, where Community action to interrupt or reduce economic relations with one or more third countries is required by a common position or in a joint action adopted under the European Union provisions on a common foreign and security policy, in relation to the movement of capital and on payments as regard the third countries concerned; indeed, pending such measures, Member States themselves may, under the second paragraph of Article 60, take unilateral measures against a third country with regard to capital movements and payments 'for serious political reasons'. The freedom is therefore not absolute. However, these provisions have been narrowly construed as exceptions to the basic rule of freedom of capital movements both inside and outside the Community, and to the extent that a payment or capital movement is not specifically excluded, Article 56 has been held to be directly effective even with regard to capital movements to third countries such as Switzerland and Turkey.[20]

This in itself is an interesting development given the Court's reluctance in earlier case law automatically to extend concepts developed in the context of the internal market to situations governed by similar language in relations with third countries. So, for example, in Case 270/80 *Polydor v Harlequin*[21] in the context of the free movement of goods, it was held that even where a free trade agreement does expressly prohibit not only quantitative restrictions but also measures having effects equivalent to quantitative restrictions, the same interpretation of that phrase need not be given in the context of trade with a non-Member State as will be given in the context of trade between States, since there is no intention to create a single market under free trade agreements.

A synthesis of the approach to the direct effect of provisions of international agreements was given in the context of an agreement between the

[20] Joined Cases C-163, 165 and 250/94 *Sanz de Lera* [1995] ECR I-4821.
[21] [1982] ECR 379.

Community and Portugal in the *Kupferberg* Case.[22] The Court started from the principle that it is open to the Community and the third country to agree what effect the provisions of the agreement are to have in the internal legal order of the contracting parties, and that the matter fell to be decided by the court only in the absence of express agreement on the point, emphasizing, however, that it was open to the courts of one contracting party to consider that certain provisions were directly effective even if that view was not shared by courts of the other contracting party. It then went on to consider whether the provision at issue could be regarded as unconditional and sufficiently precise to have direct effect in the light of the object and purpose of the agreement, concluding that the provision at issue imposed an unconditional rule against discrimination in matters of taxation, dependent only on a finding that the products affected were of like nature, so that it could be applied by a court and produce direct effects throughout the Community. The Court did, however, emphasize that, despite the fact that the provision at issue had the same object as Article 90 of the EC Treaty, each of these provisions should be interpreted in its own context, and that the interpretation given to Article 90 could not be applied by way of simple analogy to the corresponding provision of an agreement on free trade. However, in *Sanz de Lera* the judgment does not discuss these issues, and simply holds Article 56 to be directly effective in itself and on its own terms.

It does not take much imagination to envisage the possible consequences of this approach to the capital movement provisions if, as in Case C-222/97 *Trummer and Mayer*,[23] they are interpreted broadly so as to include activities which might economically be regarded as the provision of services, such as the provision of mortgage credit. Does it mean that a borrower resident in the Community has an enforceable Community law right to take out a mortgage with a provider in a third country, and does it mean that a lender in a third country has an enforceable Community law right to offer a mortgage to a borrower in a Member State? Conversely, does it mean that a lender in the Community has an enforceable Community law right to offer a mortgage to a borrower in a third country, and that a borrower in a third country has an enforceable Community law right to take out a mortgage with a provider in the Community (and therefore presumably the right to enter the Community for that purpose)?

Their broader geographical scope is not the only way in which the broad interpretation of the capital movement provisions may give rise to problems with regard to the provision of services: tax discrimination is also an issue.

[22] Case 104/81 *Hauptzollamt Mainz v C. A. Kupferberg & Cie KG* [1982] ECR 3641, [1983] 1 CMLR 1.

[23] [1999] ECR I-1661.

IV. CONSEQUENTIAL QUESTIONS: THE PROBLEM OF TAX DISCRIMINATION

While questions of taxation did not arise directly in the *Trummer and Mayer* Case, the broad interpretation of the concept of capital movements does raise an issue as to the scope of Article 58 EC. Article 58(1)(a) states that the provisions of Article 56 (ie the liberalization of capital movements and payments inside and outside the Community):

> shall be without prejudice to the right of Member States:
>
> (a) to apply the relevant provision of their tax law which distinguish between tax-payers who are not in the same situation with regard to their place of residence or with regard to the place where their capital is invested; . . .

At first sight this might be taken as a clear authorization to discriminate in the tax system between residents and non-residents. Most of the discussion has centred on the question whether this provision allows discrimination *against* non-residents, which could clearly conflict with the fundamental Treaty freedoms relating to establishment, provision of services, and movement of workers. On the other hand, it has been suggested that the aim of Article 58(1)(a) was to permit discrimination *in favour of* non-residents, which could conflict with the State Aids rules, and which also raises the question of tax competition.

The provision must however be taken in its context: in effect it is drafted as a permission to take measures which might interfere with the free movement of capital and payments, rather than *carte blanche* to discriminate. In other words, the fact that a measure may be justifiable as a restriction on the movement of capital and payments does not necessarily make it acceptable as a State aid. However, this is a matter on which there has not been any litigation, and arguments could be made for a broad interpretation. In any event, Article 58(1)(a) is subject both to the caveat that such measures 'shall not constitute a means of arbitrary discrimination or a disguised restriction on the free movement of capital and payments as defined in Article 56', and to a Declaration made by the Member States when the Maastricht Treaty was signed stating that:

> The Conference affirms that the right of Member States to apply the relevant provisions of their tax law as referred to in [Article 73d(1)(a)] of this Treaty will apply only with respect to the relevant provisions which exist at the end of 1993. However, this Declaration shall apply only to capital movements between Member States and to payments effected between Member States.

It may be suggested that this at the least amounts to a political commitment not to introduce any new measures of the type at issue in the context of monetary movements between Member States.

In so far as Article 58(1)(a) does provide that in the context of free movement of capital and payments, the prohibition of restrictions on capital movements and payments is without prejudice to the right of Member States to apply provisions of their tax law which distinguish between taxpayers who are not in the same situation with regard to their place of residence or with regard to the place where their capital is invested, it may be wondered how this provision may be reconciled with the concept of a single market for financial services, and more particularly how it may be reconciled with the principle of non-discrimination underlying the Treaty provisions on free movement of persons and provision of services. The most straightforward approach would be to argue that it is only concerned with monetary movements as such[24] and that it does not apply to situations governed by the other Treaty freedoms. While the thesis pursued in this chapter may lead to a similar result, it may be submitted that this straightforward approach does not appear to take account of Article 43 EC (second paragraph) or Article 51(2) EC. These provisions were not altered by the Single European Act or by the Maastricht or Amsterdam Treaties. The second paragraph of Article 43 defines freedom of establishment as including the right to take up and pursue activities as self-employed persons, and to set up and manage undertakings, 'subject to the provisions of the Chapter relating to capital', and Article 51(2) states that the liberalization of banking and insurance services connected with movements of capital shall be effected in step with the progressive liberalization of the movement of capital. This link between the Treaty rules on establishment and the provision of services and the rules relating to the movement of money was noted in the recitals to the Second Banking Co-ordination Directive, which recognized that capital safeguard measures under the 1988 Capital Movements Directive[25] may lead to restrictions on the provision of banking services. The provision of banking and insurance services therefore appears expressly to be subordinated to the rules on monetary movements, though it may be observed that in Case C-118/96 *Safir v Skattemyndigheten i Dalarnas Län*[26] the European Court held that the Swedish tax regime for insurance policies taken out in other Member States concerned the provision of services, so that there was no need to consider the capital movement provisions. Such an approach is difficult to reconcile with the wording of the Treaty, though it may be suggested that the wording of the Treaty is hardly appropriate in the context of the 11 States sharing a single currency.

More generally, the provisions of Article 56, and therefore the exception in Article 58(1)(a), relate not only to capital movements as such but also to

[24] See Vanistendael, 'The consequences of *Schumacker* and *Wielockx*: Two Steps Forward in the Tax Procession of Echternach' (1996) 33 CMLR 255, and Wattel, 'The EC Court's Attempts to Reconcile the Treaty Freedoms with International Tax Law' (1996) 33 CMLR 223.

[25] Council Directive 88/361, OJ 1988 L178/5.

[26] [1998] ECR I-1897.

payments, which, as 'current payments' under ex Article 106(1) ECT were defined in terms of payments or transfers relating to the exercise of the other Treaty freedoms. Indeed, it may be wondered how far payments and transfers can be separated from the substantive Treaty freedom: in Case 95/81 *Commission v Italy*[27] an import deposit scheme imposed in the context of exchange control legislation was classified as a measure equivalent to a quantitative restriction on the import of goods.

In the context of the Treaty rules on the provision of services there is, as has been mentioned above, an express link with the provisions governing free movement of capital in Article 51(2) which states that the liberalization of banking and insurance services connected with movements of capital shall be effected in step with the progressive liberalization of the movement of capital. This link was applied in a restrictive way by the European Court in Case 267/86 *Van Eycke v ASPA*[28] where it was held that since the opening of a savings account in another Member State was not at that time liberated under the Capital Movements Directive, it was not a breach of the Treaty provisions on freedom to provide services for Belgium to limit tax exemptions on such accounts to deposits in local currency at credit institutions having their head office (*siège social*) in Belgium. It might have been thought that such rules would have to be changed when a Community law right to set up savings accounts in other Member States came into operation under the 1988 Capital Movements Directive.[29] However, the Court did actually accept a requirement of local establishment in Case C-204/90 *Bachmann v Belgium*.[30] There, the Court held that tax deductions on life and sickness insurance premiums could be limited to payments made to insurers established in Belgium, on the basis that there was no other way of preserving the integrity of the tax system (which required tax to be paid on the ultimate benefits). It might be observed that if a requirement that a provider of a financial service should be established within the jurisdiction of the Member State concerned is the only way of ensuring that a Member State's tax legislation is observed, it indicates a need for a considerably greater degree of co-operation between the tax authorities of the Member States. It also has the effect of making provision of services in the Treaty sense impossible.

However, it is not the end of the story. The European Court returned to the matter in Case C-80/94 *Wielockx v Inspecteur der Directe Belastingen*.[31] This involved a Belgian national resident in Belgium who was a partner in a business established in the Netherlands and whose entire income was earned in the Netherlands. He paid money into a pension

[27] [1982] ECR 2187. [28] [1988] ECR 4769.
[29] Council Directive 88/361, OJ 1988 L178/5.
[30] [1992] ECR I-249. [31] [1995] ECR I-2493.

reserve in the Netherlands, and claimed tax relief on that part of his income. This was refused on the basis that relief was only given to Dutch residents, and the Netherlands Government invoked the *Bachmann* Case to argue that in the case of a Belgian resident, the Netherlands authorities would grant the tax relief on the pension contributions but the Belgian authorities would collect the tax on the pension when it was received. However, the Court, while accepting that in principle the situations of residents and non-residents are not generally comparable, held that a non-resident taxpayer who receives all or almost all his income in the State where he works is objectively in the same situation as concerns income tax as a resident of that State. Furthermore, on the question of tax cohesion, the Court followed Advocate General Léger in noting that the arrangements between the Netherlands and Belgium resulted from a double taxation convention following the OECD model under which a State taxes all pensions, irrespective of their source, received by residents, but waives the right to tax pensions received abroad, irrespective of their source. It therefore held that tax cohesion was to be established not at the level of one individual taxpayer but in the reciprocity of the rules applicable in the Contracting States. The Netherlands could not therefore justify a discriminatory refusal of tax relief in this case.

While there may be some debate as to the Court's analysis of the double taxation agreements[32] (though they are hardly a matter of Community legislation falling within the Court's jurisdiction), it may indeed be wondered whether this effectively overrules the *Bachmann* judgment. Indeed, in Case C-118/96 *Safir v Skattemyndigheten i Dalarnas Län*,[33] it was held that for Sweden to impose a different tax regime for insurance policies purchased from providers outside Sweden which would have the effect of deterring Swedish residents from taking out such policies, even though it was intended to achieve tax neutrality between policies purchased inside and outside Sweden, was a breach of Article 49 EC.

Similar issues also arise in the context of the free movement of persons.

V. TAX DISCRIMINATION AND THE FREE MOVEMENT OF PERSONS

While the second paragraph of Article 43 EC defines freedom of establishment as including the right to take up and pursue activities as self-employed persons, and to set up and manage undertakings, 'subject to the provisions of the Chapter relating to capital', there is a long line of case law indicating that those falling within its scope may not be subjected to tax discrimination.

[32] See Vanistendael (n 24 above), and Wattel (n 24 above).
[33] [1998] ECR I-1897.

In the context of freedom of establishment, if an undertaking does establish a permanent presence in another Member State, then whatever form that establishment takes, it has been clear since Case 270/83 *Commission v France*,[34] that Member States may not treat companies differently for tax purposes depending on the type of establishment present within their jurisdiction. It was there held, in the context of French legislation granting shareholders' tax credits to French insurance companies but not to branches or agencies in France of foreign insurance companies, that France could not treat the branches of foreign insurance companies whose main offices were in other Member States differently from those insurance companies which took the form of French-based companies which were subsidiaries of those foreign insurance companies. In other words, branches (which are a part of the foreign undertaking in another Member State) and subsidiaries (which are formed under local law but controlled by the foreign undertaking) had to be treated the same way, both being forms of establishment recognized in what is now Article 43. Furthermore, it was made clear in that case that there was no way that restrictions could be imposed on the freedom of establishment in order to prevent tax evasion, even though it might be legitimate outside that context to operate differential tax treatment on the basis of residence, as was subsequently held in Case C-112/91 *Werner v FZA Aachen-Innenstadt*.[35]

However, when the question of residence did arise in the context of freedom of establishment in Case C-330/91 *R v Inland Revenue Commissioners, ex parte Commerzbank*,[36] it was held that a German company which traded in the United Kingdom through a branch established there but which was fiscally non-resident in the United Kingdom, was entitled to receive interest on the repayment of tax which should not have been charged to it, if an undertaking resident in the United Kingdom would have received interest on such a repayment—and it made no difference that the only reason for the repayment of the tax was the fact that the German company was not resident in the United Kingdom. A similar approach has been taken in Case C-264/96 *ICI v Colmer*,[37] where tax relief for a holding company depended on the residence of its subsidiaries.

With regard to free movement of workers, in Case C-279/93 *Schumacker*[38] and Case C-151/94 *Commission v Luxembourg*[39] it was made clear that discrimination cannot be justified where the taxpayer benefits from the rules on free movement of workers, and in Case C-107/94 *Asscher*,[40] it was made clear that discrimination cannot be justified where

[34] [1986] ECR 273; [1987] 1 CMLR 401.
[35] [1992] ECR I-249. This case nevertheless distinguished and reaffirmed the judgment in the French tax case.
[36] [1993] ECR I-4017.
[37] [1998] ECR I-4695.
[38] [1995] ECR I-225.
[39] [1995] ECR I-3685.
[40] [1996] ECR I-3089.

the taxpayer benefits from the rules on freedom of establishment. In the *Schumacker* Case it was held that where the State of residence could not take account of the taxpayer's personal and family circumstances because the tax payable there was insufficient to enable it to do so, the Community principle of equal treatment required that in the State of employment the personal and family circumstances of a foreign non-resident be taken into account in the same way as those of resident nationals, and the same tax benefits should be granted. In the *Luxembourg* Case it was held that it was a breach of the rules on the free movement of workers for Luxembourg to retain and not repay excess amounts of tax deducted from the earnings of Community nationals who resided or worked in Luxembourg for less than the whole tax year, and in the third case, the Netherlands could not impose a higher income tax liability on a non-resident to compensate for the fact that he paid social security contributions in another Member State. On the other hand, it was accepted by the European Court in Case C-336/96 *Gilly v Directeur des Services Fiscaux du Bas-Rhin*[41] that a frontier worker may have to accept less than perfect equality of treatment under a double taxation agreement.

VI. CAN ARTICLE 58(1)(A) EC BE RECONCILED WITH THE TREATY FREEDOMS?

While at an earlier stage the present author may have been among those who suggested that Article 58(1)(a) represented a continuation of the *Van Eycke* and *Bachmann* case law, it is now clear that there is a conflict between the Treaty rights of freedom of establishment and free movement of workers as interpreted in *Commerzbank*, *Wielockx*, *Schumacker*, *Luxembourg* and *Asscher*, and the discriminatory tax treatment apparently authorized by Article 58(1)(a). As indicated above, one simple explanation would be to say that a situation governed by another Treaty freedom does not fall within Article 58(1)(a), but that is hardly compatible with the express terms of Article 51(2), subjecting freedom to provide services in the financial sector to the liberalization of capital movements, or with the fact that current payments will normally relate to another Treaty freedom. However, in the more recent decision in Case C-118/96 *Safir v Skattemyndigheten i Dalarnas Län*,[42] where it was held to be a breach of Article 49 EC for Sweden to impose a different tax regime for insurance policies purchased from providers outside Sweden which would have the effect of deterring Swedish residents from taking out such policies, even though it was intended to achieve tax neutrality between policies purchased inside and outside Sweden, it was stated that the decision on this point made it unnecessary to determine

[41] [1998] ECR I-2793. [42] [1998] ECR I-1897.

whether the legislation was also incompatible with Articles 56 and 58 EC—even though under the express terms of Article 50, services are only services within the meaning of the Treaty to the extent that they do not fall under one of the other Treaty freedoms.

Be that as it may, Article 58(1)(a) EC only entered into force on 1 January 1994, and as has been noted earlier, there is attached to the Maastricht Treaty a Declaration in the following terms:

> The Conference affirms that the right of Member States to apply the relevant provisions of their tax law as referred to in [Article 73d(1)(a)]of this Treaty will apply only with respect to the relevant provisions which exist at the end of 1993. However, this Declaration shall apply only to capital movements between Member States and to payments effected between Member States.

While a mere Declaration may not amend the terms of the Treaty, it has long been established in other areas of Community law that it may be binding upon its author.[43] If the Member States are bound by their Declaration, it may be submitted that its effect is that with regard to monetary movements between Member States, the only discriminatory measures which may be maintained under Article 58(1)(a) are those which were lawfully in force at the end of 1993. Since the *Commerzbank*, *Wielockx*, *Schumacker* and *Asscher* cases all relate to situations arising before the end of 1993, it may be suggested that the discrimination on the basis of residence found unlawful in those cases cannot be revived under Article 58(1)(a). However, this approach will not work if situations which at first sight might appear to involve the provision of services, such as the creation of a mortgage, are categorized as movements of capital—unless, as in *Safir*, the wording of the Treaty is ignored, and it is held that the free movement of capital rules do not have to be considered if a situation can be categorized as provision of services.

Be that as it may, in those situations where it does apply (presumably where the taxpayer does not fall within a substantive Treaty provision prohibiting discrimination, and where monetary movements outside the Community are involved), it may be observed that Article 58(1)(a) is drafted in very broad terms. It allows Member States to apply the relevant provision of their tax law which distinguish between taxpayers (with no mention of nationality) who are not in the same situation with regard to their place of residence or with regard to the place where their capital is invested. However, it is still subject to the general requirement in Article 58(3) that the measures in question should not constitute a means of arbitrary discrimination or a disguised restriction on the free movement of capital and payments.

[43] In the context of declarations under Regulation 1408/71 on social security, see Case 35/77 *Beerens* [1977] ECR 2249, 2254.

The particular question arises here as to how to reconcile a provision which expressly allows differences in treatment on the basis of residence or place of investment with a provision which prohibits arbitrary discrimination.

It may be submitted that to avoid being characterized as 'arbitrary', the discriminatory tax treatment must be shown to be objectively justified, and that in this context the criteria laid down by the Court in Case C-204/90 *Bachmann v Belgium*[44] continue to be relevant: the measures must be intended to protect the coherence of the national tax system, and must be shown to be necessary for the achievement of that objective.[45] Applying the principles developed in the context of Article 30 of the EC Treaty on restrictions on the free movement of goods by analogy to Article 58(1)(a), it may be suggested that in order to justify differential tax treatment under that provision, not only must the measure be justified to protect the coherence of the tax system but it must also be shown that effective measures are taken at the domestic level in the national tax system to deal with the perceived problem.[46]

VII. CONCLUSION

The present author does not disagree with the notion of using the list attached to the 1988 Directive to illustrate the meaning of a capital movement as a matter of legislative interpretation. However, with hindsight, it can be seen that the list was very broadly drawn. While a broad concept of capital movements may benefit traders in some respects—Article 56 is after all the only Treaty freedom to apply to movements outside the Community as well as within it—it clearly raises problems in relation to the tax discrimination apparently allowed under Article 58. It may more generally be wondered whether the wording of the Treaty putting the freedom to provide services in a residual position is appropriate in the context of the modern single internal market, particularly for the 12 States sharing a single currency.

On the other hand, the approach adopted in Case C-118/96 *Safir v Skattemyndigheten i Dalarnas Län*,[47] under which the free movement of capital rules do not have to be considered if a situation can be categorized as provision of services, can hardly be reconciled with the wording of the Treaty providing that services is a residual concept. Nevertheless it avoids

[44] [1992] ECR I-249.

[45] This approach was followed by the Court in Case C-35/98 *Verkooijen*, judgment of 6 June 2000 (nyp).

[46] Case 4/75 *Rewe-Zentralfinanz v Landwirtschaftskammer Bonn* [1975] ECR 843 and Case 121/85 *Conegate v H.M. Customs and Excise* [1986] ECR 1007.

[47] [1998] ECR I-1897.

the problems with regard to the scope of the freedom and with regard to tax discrimination which arise from a broad interpretation of the concept of capital movements, and it may be suggested that it is a more appropriate approach in the current state of development of Community law. It is perhaps therefore unfortunate that the 2000 Inter-governmental Conference was to be concerned only with institutional issues.

15

The Liberalization of Interstate Legal Practice in the European Union: Lessons for the United States?

ROGER J GOEBEL*

Since the mid-1970s, the European Union (EU)[1] or, more precisely, its core element, the European Community (EC),[2] has recognized and protected more liberal rights for lawyers to engage in interstate practice than does the USA. In the last 25 years, a combination of legislation and case law of the European Court of Justice[3] has steadily expanded the recognized level of interstate legal practice rights.[4] Multi-state legal practice is now a reality

* This chapter was initially published in (2000) 34 International Lawyer 307 (Spring) and is reprinted with slight stylistic changes with the consent of the International Lawyer editors. The author would like to express his appreciation for the assistance of his research assistant, Eric Siddall.

[1] The European Union is a regional intergovernmental political system comprised of 15 European countries (customarily called Member States), ie Austria, Belgium, Denmark, Finland, France, Germany, Greece, Ireland, Italy, Luxembourg, the Netherlands, Portugal, Spain, Sweden and the United Kingdom. The European Union was created by the Treaty on European Union (TEU), often called the Treaty of Maastricht after the city in which it was signed on 7 February 1992. The TEU entered into force on 1 November 1993. Its text is in the OJ 1992 C224/1, [1992] 1 CMLR 719.

[2] The European Community (EC) is a regional intergovernment political and legal system comprised of the Member States listed in n 1 above. The EC is at the core of the European Union and comprises virtually all of EU activities. The EC has its own institutional structure—the Commission, Council, European Parliament, ECJ and European Central Bank—with binding legislative and judicial powers in a wide variety of fields. Although not a state, the European Community is an internationally recognized legal entity created by a partial transfer of sovereignty from the Member States. The European Community's initial name was the European Economic Community when it was created by the EC Treaty on 25 March 1957, 298 UNTS 11. The EC Treaty has been substantially amended, notably by the Treaty on European Union (n 1 above), and the Treaty of Amsterdam, signed on 2 October 1997, and effective 1 May 1999, OJ 1999 C340/1. The Treaty of Amsterdam renumbered the articles of the EC Treaty as of 1 May 1999. Both the new and the initial numbering of Treaty articles will be indicated in this chapter.

[3] The ECJ has appellate and other types of jurisdiction set out in the EC Treaty (n 2 above), in Articles 226–245 (ex 169–188). Its judgments interpreting the EC Treaty and legislative or other legal acts are legally binding on all Member State governments and courts. The ECJ thus effectively has the status of a supreme court in EC legal matters.

[4] My prior article, R Goebel, 'Lawyers in the European Community: Progress Towards Community-Wide Rights of Practice' (1991–92) 15 Fordham Int'l LJ 556 (hereinafter referred to as 'Lawyers in the European Community'), provides a detailed analysis of EC legal rules on interstate legal practice prior to 1992. The article was reprinted in M Daly and R Goebel (eds),

within the European Union. Lawyers and law firms from any EU state are able to represent clients on a continuous basis throughout the European Union, practice in almost all commercial law fields in any EU country, and form multi-national law firms with offices as desired in any EU commercial centre—in short, are able to carry on freely modern international legal practice throughout most of Europe.[5]

This picture is in sharp contrast with the much more limited legal rules governing interstate law practice within the USA. The rules of admission to the bar and rights of practice, including any tolerance of interstate practice, are set by the states. These state rules have traditionally been founded upon a double concern for effective representation of clients, a type of consumer protection interest, and for the efficient administration of court litigation, a civil and criminal justice interest. Arguably, however, rules ostensibly set and enforced with these concerns in some instances mask a desire to protect the local legal profession against interstate competition. Although the Supreme Court has to some degree limited state rules in order to protect lawyers' rights under the Privileges and Immunities Clause of the Constitution, the Court has in large measure accorded great discretion to the states in setting professional qualification standards and delineating the right of legal practice.

The purpose of this chapter is, first of all, information in character. In section I, the chapter will describe the rules in the European Union that govern lawyers' rights to practise on a temporary or occasional basis in countries other than their home State, notably the 1977 Directive on Lawyers' Freedom to Provide Services[6] and related case law. These rules are based upon the EC Treaty articulation of the basic right to carry out cross-border professional services.[7] In section II, the chapter will again fulfil an informational role in describing the much more limited character of temporary interstate legal practice rights within the USA. Initially, the chapter

Rights, Liability and Ethics in International Legal Practice (1994) 239, a volume which contains 35 articles contrasting professional responsibility and legal ethics rules in Europe with those in the USA. A recent authoritative description of EC rules governing interstate legal practice is contained in ch 8 of Sydney Cone III, *International Trade in Legal Services* (1996).

[5] Besides the Member States listed in n 1 above, the legislation and Court doctrines described in this chapter will become binding in Bulgaria, Cyprus, the Czech Republic, Estonia, Hungary, Latvia, Lithuania, Malta, Poland, the Slovak Republic and Slovenia when, as presently expected, they join the European Community around 2003. The legislation will probably also be adopted by Iceland, and Norway, pursuant to obligations under their treaties with the EC.

[6] Council Directive 77/249 to facilitate the effective exercise by lawyers of freedom to provided services, OJ 1977 L78/17 (hereinafter called the Lawyers' Services Directive).

[7] The EC Treaty (n 2 above) initially described the freedom to provide services in Articles 59–66 (now Articles 49–55). See the text at nn 12–16 below. Incidentally, the custom in the EC is to refer to cross-border legal services, while in the USA we tend to refer to interstate legal practice.

will describe the limited degree to which state regulation of the practice of law has been governed by federal constitutional principles. Then, the chapter will discuss the limitations which state courts place upon out-of-state lawyers who attempt to appear in court proceedings or engage in temporary interstate transactional practice, criticizing some of the leading precedents. Section III will attempt to provide an analytic comparison of the US and EU rules, commencing with consideration of the interests of clients, courts and society. The chapter will conclude by suggesting that the time has come for a re-examination of present state rules by state authorities and courts to permit greater liberalization, to some degree along the lines of the European Union model.

It should be noted at the outset that the legislation and case law in the European Union not only recognizes the right of lawyers to carry out interstate legal practice on a temporary basis, but also the right of EU lawyers and law firms to set up permanent offices in Member States other than those in which their initial legal practice capacity has been recognized. This type of legal practice right is categorized under the EC Treaty provisions on freedom of professional establishment.[8] The ECJ has greatly facilitated this development through its liberal case law, most recently in the famous 1995 *Gebhard* judgment.[9] The recent 1998 Directive on Lawyers' right to conduct legal practice on a permanent basis in any Member State[10] has radically expanded legal practice rights in this regard. The earlier 1989 Directive on recognition of higher education diplomas[11] also facilitated the ability of lawyers and law students to become fully admitted to practice rights in any EU state.

These liberal EU rules sharply contrast with the USA's far more restrictive state rules governing admission to the bar, together with some states' limited recognition of prior admission in other states, and some states' rules permitting limited practice rights for foreign legal consultants. Space considerations prevent any discussion of the topic of permanent interstate legal practice rights, which must be deferred to a later article. The liberality of the EU's recognition of rights of permanent interstate legal practice does however definitely enhance the strength of the argument that this chapter will make in favour of more liberal treatment of temporary interstate legal practice in the USA.

[8] The EC Treaty (n 2 above) initially described the right of establishment in Articles 52–58 (now Articles 43–48).

[9] Case C-55/94 *Gebhard v Consiglio dell'Ordine degli Avvocati di Milano* [*Milan Bar Council*] [1995] ECR I-4165. See the text at nn 45–48 below.

[10] European Parliament and Council Directive 98/5 to facilitate practice of the profession of lawyers on a permanent basis in a Member State other than that in which the qualification was obtained, OJ 1998 L77/36.

[11] Council Directive 89/48 on a general system for the recognition of higher-education diplomas awarded on completion of professional education and training of at least three years duration, OJ 1989 L19/16.

I. PROVIDING TEMPORARY INTERSTATE LEGAL SERVICES IN THE EUROPEAN UNION

1. The Treaty Basis for the Right to Provide Temporary Interstate Legal Services within the European Union

The starting point in any presentation of EC law is the text of the relevant EC Treaty Articles. Fortunately for lawyers and other professionals, the EC Treaty contains a chapter dealing with the right to provide both commercial and professional services throughout the European Union.

The basic Article 49 EC[12] provides for the abolition of 'restrictions on freedom to provide services within the Community' whenever the provider of the service is established in a Member State different from the State of the recipient of the service. Article 50 EC supplements this by specifying that professional services are covered as well as commercial and industrial services.[13] Article 50 further states that persons providing services cannot be discriminated against on the basis of their nationality whenever the service provider is 'temporarily' pursuing activities in a host State.[14] Article 52 enables Community legislation to achieve the goal of freedom to provide services throughout the Community.[15] Article 55 authorizes Member States to restrict the providing of cross-border services on the grounds of 'public policy, public security or public health',[16] but this exception has rarely been used by the Member States. This detailed coverage of the right to provide interstate services set forth in the EC Treaty is in contrast to the absence of any specific mention of the topic in the US Constitution, as we shall see in section II.1 below.

Prior to 1974, the prevailing view at the EC Commission[17] and the Council of Ministers[18] was that the EC Treaty provisions according the freedom to provide professional services and the related right of professional establishment required legislative action before they could be effective. In 1974, the ECJ rejected this view and instead held that individuals

[12] Article 49 (ex 59) EC. [13] Article 50 (ex 60) EC. [14] ibid at second para.
[15] Article 52 (ex 63) EC. [16] Article 55 (ex 66) EC.

[17] The Commission, comprised of 20 members or Commissioners designated for five-year terms by the Member States, is the central administrative body of the European Community. The Commission's role is described in Articles 211–219 (ex 155–163) EC. Among its other powers, the Commission has the right of legislative initiative, ie, essentially the sole power to initiate Community legislation with a first draft. See, eg, Article 251 (ex 189b) EC.

[18] Although commonly called the Council of Ministers, this body's official title since 1 November 1993 has been the Council of the European Union. The Council consists of representatives of Member States at the level of cabinet ministers and meets most often as the so-called General Council in the composition of Ministers of Foreign Affairs. The Council's present role is described in Articles 202–210 (ex 145–154) EC. Until 1 July 1987, the Council had the sole power to enact Community legislation; since then, it shares legislative power with the European Parliament.

could immediately rely on these Treaty-based rights in national court proceedings.[19]

A landmark judgment, *Van Binsbergen*,[20] involved the question whether a Dutch lawyer authorized to handle matters before a Dutch social security administrative body could continue to do so after moving to Belgium. The Dutch authorities maintained that only a Dutch resident should be permitted to conduct this type of legal representation. A Dutch administration tribunal asked the ECJ[21] whether Articles 49 and 50 (ex 59 and 60) EC could have direct legal effect in a national court proceeding, providing immediate rights to individuals.[22]

The ECJ's response enunciated the doctrine that Articles 49 and 50 EC do have direct legal effect, so that nationals of any Member State can rely upon them to carry out professional (in this case legal) services across the frontiers in any other Member State.[23] Recognition of this Treaty-based right in a national court proceeding did not have to await any Community legislation, although such legislation could facilitate the exercise of the right.[24] Moreover, the Court established the principle that a Member State must not only not discriminate against nationals of another State, but also that a State cannot apply its own non-discriminatory rules regulating a profession unless the rules are 'justified by the general good'.[25] Finally, the Court concluded that no 'general good' interest justified barring a non-resident lawyer from providing legal representation in an administrative proceeding, although Dutch rules on 'professional ethics, supervision and liability' might govern the non-resident lawyer's conduct in the proceeding.[26] (American lawyers will immediately see the analogy to our Supreme Court's conclusion in the 1985 *Piper* Case that New Hampshire could not bar an otherwise qualified Vermont lawyer from interstate practice in New

[19] The first judgment to this effect was Case 2/74 *Reyners v Belgium* [1974] ECR 631, which held that a Member State could not require its lawyers to be citizens, because this would violate the EC Treaty's guarantee of a right of professional establishment.

[20] Case 33/74 *Van Binsbergen* [1974] ECR 1299.

[21] Under Article 234 (ex 177) EC, any Member State court or tribunal may refer questions concerning the Treaty or Community legislative or legal acts to the ECJ whenever an answer is relevant in a national court proceeding. The ECJ reply is not only binding on the court referring the question, it is also an authoritative interpretation of Community law for all other courts or tribunals.

[22] The doctrine of direct legal effect of EC Treaty articles is of fundamental importance in making Community law effective. The doctrine essentially states that certain Treaty Articles, or sections thereof, are sufficiently precise, absolute and unconditional in their articulation of rights that these rights can be given immediate effect by Member State courts. There is no need to wait for Community legislation to give legal effect to the Treaty-based rights. The direct legal effect doctrine was first enunciated in a landmark judgment, Case 26/62 *Van Gend en Loos v Nederlandse Administratie Der Belastingen* [1963] ECR 1.

[23] *Van Binsbergen* (n 20 above) at 1311–1312.

[24] ibid. [25] ibid at 1309. [26] ibid.

Hampshire solely because she was a non-resident, but that New Hampshire could require her to follow its legal ethics rules.)[27]

Van Binsbergen is a leading precedent. The Court doctrine that freedom to provide services under the Treaty not only prevents discrimination based on nationality, but also bars the application of state rules unless they are objectively 'justified by the general good', has been applied in many subsequent judgments, not only for professional services, but also commercial and financial services,[28] and has greatly influenced the text of Community legislation in the services field.[29]

2. The Impact of the 1977 Lawyers' Services Directive

For our purposes, the most important impact of *Van Binsbergen* came through its influence upon the Council Directive on lawyers' freedom to provide services (hereinafter referred to as the Lawyers' Services Directive), adopted on 22 March 1977.[30] This Directive constitutes the legal framework which governs the rights of lawyers to provide interstate services on a temporary or occasional basis throughout all the Member States of the European Union, and merits careful examination.

The Lawyers' Services Directive first defines the class of legal professionals entitled to perform services throughout the Community. In Article 1, the Directive lists, country by country, the regulated legal profession that customarily provides courtroom services, such as the *avocat* in France, the *Rechtsanwalt* in Germany, and the *avvocato* in Italy. For the United Kingdom and Ireland, the list includes not only barristers, who plead before higher courts, but also solicitors, who can plead before some lower courts, but who chiefly provide general corporate and commercial services.

[27] *New Hampshire v Piper*, 420 U.S. 274 (1985). See the text at nn 68–75 below.

[28] Probably the two most important recent cases applying the Court's doctrine that national laws and regulations can limit the interstate providing of commercial and financial services, or the right of establishment in commercial and financial sectors, only if the national rules are objectively 'justified by the general good' are Case C-384/93 *Alpine Investments BV v Minister van Financien* [1995] ECR I-1141 (Dutch rule prohibiting unsolicited interstate telephone marketing of commodities futures is justified by 'an imperative reason of public interest') and Case C-101/94 *Commission v Italy* [1996] ECR I-2691 (Italian stock exchange rule requiring brokers to be Italian residents or corporations not 'justified by the general interest').

[29] Probably the most important single Community legislative act limiting national rules in the financial services sector to those 'justified by the general good' is Council Directive 89/646 on the co-ordination of laws relating to the business of credit institutions, OJ 1989 L386/1 (commonly known as the Second Banking Directive). For an overview, see G Zavvros, 'Banking Integration and 1992: Legal Issues and Policy Implications' (1990) 31 Harv Int'l LJ 463. See also the Commission Interpretative Communication, *Freedom to Provide Services and the Interest of the General Good in the Second Banking Directive*, SEC (97) 1193 final (20 June 1997).

[30] See n 5 above. The Directive is described in Serge-Pierre Laguette, *Lawyers in the European Community* (1987) 241–248, and Linda S Spedding, *Transnational Legal Practice in the EEC and the United States* (1987) 185–200. My own analysis is in R Goebel, 'Lawyers in the European Community' (n 4 above) 576–580.

It is noteworthy that the Directive does not define the nature of the legal services that a lawyer may perform in a host State. Article 1(1) does expressly permit host States to 'reserve to prescribed categories of lawyers the preparation of formal documents' in the administration of decedents' estates or the transfer of real estate interests. By implication, this would indicate that lawyers from the listed classes may perform any other legal services in the host State, whether courtroom or administrative agency practice, or corporate or commercial counselling, or the negotiation or drafting of agreements and other legal transactions. Presumably, Article 1(1) permits Member States to reserve estate administration and real estate title transfers to 'prescribed categories of lawyers' because in most civil law States these activities are the monopoly of a separate legal profession, known as notaries (in France, the *notaire*, in Germany, the *Notar*, etc). Note that Article 1(2) does not include notaries in the list of lawyers entitled to provide cross-border services.[31]

Article 3 of the Lawyers' Services Directive states an important rule: in performing the cross-border services, the lawyer must use his or her home title. This Article was clearly intended both to prevent inadvertent confusion with a host State professional, as well as any foreign lawyer's attempt to deceive clients by passing himself or herself off as a local lawyer.

Article 5 sets a limit on cross-border practice in 'legal proceedings' (this is not a defined term, but it presumably refers to civil and criminal litigation before courts). The host State may require the foreign lawyer to be formally introduced to the presiding judge and the president of the local bar and 'to work in conjunction with a lawyer who practices before the judicial authority in question and who would, where necessary, be answerable to that authority'. By implication from Article 5, a lawyer providing any other form of cross-border services, such as assistance in negotiation, drafting of commercial, financial or other documents, counselling on legal or tax matters, or representation before an administrative agency or in a private arbitration proceeding, does not need to be associated with a host State lawyer.

Under Article 6, if the host State does not permit its domestic house counsel to engage in 'activities relating to . . . legal proceedings', the host State can likewise exclude foreign house counsel from such litigation activities. Practice within the European Union varies with regard to the status of house counsel. For example, in the United Kingdom, house counsel may be solicitors and in Germany they may be *Rechtsanwalts*, entitled to appear in court on behalf of their employers, but in France they cannot be *avocats* and hence cannot appear in court.

[31] The Directive's list of types of lawyers also does not include the former French legal professional, the *conseil juridique*, the German *Rechtsberater* or *Rechtsbeistand*, and some other groups of legal professionals in other countries. See R Goebel, 'Lawyers in the European Community (n 4 above) 577.

Article 4 of the Directive sets out a complicated formula to determine the rules of conduct applicable to the lawyer providing services. Article 4(2) states that if the services involve legal proceedings or proceedings before public authorities, the rules of professional conduct of the host State are to be observed, but 'without prejudice' to those of the home State of the foreign lawyer. For all other legal services (eg, standard commercial or corporate practice), the rules of the home State are to apply, albeit 'without prejudice' to the application of several important host State rules, notably those on 'professional secrecy, relations with other lawyers, the prohibition on the same lawyer acting for parties with mutually conflicting interests, and publicity'. However, these latter home State rules only apply if they meet an objective necessity standard: 'their observance [must be] objectively justified to ensure, in that [host] state, the proper exercise of a lawyer's activities, the standing of the profession and respect for the rules concerning incompatibility.'[32]

Manifestly, it is not always clear when the home State or the host State rules (or perhaps both states' Rules) govern a lawyer's interstate legal practice. Accordingly, it is quite desirable that the Directive's provisions on applicable professional rules have been supplemented by a private initiative of the Council of the Bars and Law Societies of the European Community (CCBE), a co-ordinating group for all the national bar associations. The CCBE adopted, on 28 October 1988, the Code of Conduct for Lawyers in the European Community,[33] which has since been enacted into the rules of each national bar association. Professor Laurel Terry has provided an excellent analysis of the Code of Conduct for Lawyers, contrasting its provisions with the professional rules in the USA.[34] This Code of Conduct for lawyers has recently been amended on 28 November 1998 to provide somewhat more comprehensive and detailed rules,[35] which are currently being adopted by each national bar association.

The CCBE Code of Conduct for Lawyers is too complicated for any detailed description here, but essentially it provides a series of harmonized rules of professional conduct in some areas, and a choice between conflicting rules of ethics in other areas, thus eliminating many potential areas of

[32] For a discussion of the complexity and uncertainty of the text in Article 4, see Spedding (n 30 above) 187–190.

[33] The 1988 Code of Conduct was published as a brochure by the CCBE. Its text is annexed to J Toulmin, 'A Worldwide Common Code of Professional Ethics?' (1991–92) 15 Fordham Int'l LJ 673, reprinted in M Daly and RJ Goebel (eds), *Rights, Liability and Ethics in International Legal Practice* (1994) 207.

[34] L Terry, 'Introduction to the EC's Legal Ethics Code' (1993) 7 Geo J Legal Ethics 1 and (1993) 7 Geo J Legal Ethics 345.

[35] Code of Conduct for Lawyers in the European Union, CCBE (adopted at Lyons, 28 November 1998). The Code of Conduct will also apply to lawyers in Iceland, Liechtenstein and Norway, countries linked to the European Union in the European Economic Area.

conflict between home and host State rules in interstate legal practice. The starting point of the Code is that lawyers owe 'legal and moral obligations' to the client, the courts, the legal profession and fellow lawyers, and to the public at large. Specifying its field of application, the Code states in Article 1.5 that its rules are intended to cover all cross-border activities of lawyers, whether or not the lawyer is physically present in the host State.

The Code of Conduct of Lawyers sets forth a number of minimum harmonized rules of conduct, for example, concerning the independence of the lawyer, the protection of client confidentiality, the segregation of and proper accounting for client funds, and the avoidance of conflicts of interest. Of particular interest in interstate legal practice is the Code's section 3.1.3 on lawyers' competence, which forbids the handling of a matter for which the lawyer is not competent. Obviously, this means that a lawyer should not attempt to provide advice or assist in transactions in a host State without the requisite knowledge of the host State law that governs, or is relevant to, the advice or transactions. Of considerable practical importance in interstate practice is the obligation in the Code's section 3.9 to carry adequate professional indemnity insurance, which is normally supposed to be home State insurance that also covers any interstate legal practice, or, if that is not available, supplement insurance in the host State. Following the traditional approach in Europe, the Code's section 3.3 generally prohibits contingent fees.

In some instances the Code of Conduct for Lawyers sets rules for a choice of professional ethics rules. In accord with the Lawyers' Services Directive, the host State rules govern a lawyer's appearance before a court or tribunal, but the Code adds to this any appearance before arbitral bodies. The Code's section 2.6 states that a lawyer is bound by any host State rules on advertising and publicity, and Code section 2.5 declares that a lawyer permanently established in a host State must abide by the latter's rules on incompatible occupations (eg, not being able to serve as a member of a corporation's board of directors). In contrast, by virtue of Code section 3.4, normally the home State rules on fees should govern.

3. Recent ECJ Case Law

The 1977 Lawyers' Services Directive has been the subject of several ECJ judgments. In the first important judgment, the Commission brought an action against Germany for violation of its obligations under the EC Treaty,[36] on the grounds that the German rules did not properly follow the

[36] Under Article 226 (ex 169) EC, the Commission may sue a Member State before the ECJ for an alleged infringement of its obligations under the EC Treaty or under any Community legislative act or decision.

language of the Directive.[37] When Germany introduced its national rules to apply the terms of the Directive, Germany required the foreign lawyer to collaborate with a German lawyer when providing services in litigation or in certain administrative proceedings. The German rules then gave the German lawyer the primary role of the authorized representative of the client and the defending counsel in the proceeding. Moreover, the local German lawyer had to be present at all times during the court or administrative proceedings.

The ECJ ruled that the above-described German requirements were excessive and were not necessary when a foreign lawyer seeks to act in legal proceedings 'in conjunction with' a host State lawyer, as required by the Directive. The Court specifically held that Article 5 of the 1977 Directive, which refers to the local lawyer as being 'answerable' to the host State court, did not imply that the local lawyer had to be the primary authorized representative of the client or the defending counsel, or that he or she must take the leading role in drafting pleadings or in oral argument, or even necessarily be continuously present during the court proceedings.[38] The foreign lawyer providing interstate legal services and the local lawyer should decide upon their respective roles in a 'form of co-operation appropriate to their client's instructions'.[39]

The ECJ also rejected the German contention that foreign lawyers acting without the full co-operation of host State counsel might have an insufficient knowledge of the rules of substantive and procedural law. The Court referred to the need to have an adequate knowledge of German law as 'part of the responsibility of the lawyer providing services vis-à-vis his client, who is free to entrust his interests to a lawyer of his choice'.[40] This is a particularly interesting point, as it appears to imply that a host State may not compel a foreign lawyer engaged in standard commercial practice to be associated with a home State lawyer when the foreign lawyer provides an opinion on host State law, or drafts a document governed by the host State law, even when, as in Germany, the national law grants a monopoly on counselling on domestic law to local lawyers.[41]

[37] Case 427/85 *Commission v Germany* [1988] ECR 1123, noted by Professor Julian Lonbay in (1989) 13 Eur L Rev 347 and by Valerie Pease in (1988) 22 Int'l Law 543. My own analysis of the judgment is in R Goebel, 'Lawyers in the European Community' (n 4 above), at 580–582.

[38] Commission v Germany (n 37 above) [1988] ECR at 1160–1163.

[39] ibid at 1161.

[40] ibid at 1162.

[41] See R Waegenbaur, 'Free Movement in the Professions' (1986) 23 Common Mkt L Rev 91, at 96 (contending that the Lawyers' Services Directive enables a foreign lawyer to advise clients on the host State law as well as home State law or Community law). Philippa Watson in a note on Klopp, (1985) 22 Common Mkt L Rev 736, 750, came to the same conclusion. Foreign lawyers who provide advice on complex issues of host State law without consulting an expert host State lawyer may, of course, run a risk of malpractice liability in case of error.

Thus, in *Commission v Germany*, the ECJ facilitated interstate legal practice by its liberal interpretation of the application of the Lawyers' Services Directive in the context of courtroom litigation, and, by implication, in the context of interstate corporate and commercial practice as well.

On two occasions the ECJ has interpreted the scope of a state's definition of what falls in a Member State's defined legal monopoly, ie, the acts properly reserved to lawyers. Both judgments involved German rules. In *Reiseburo Brode*,[42] the Court held that the German rules restricting to lawyers the collection of debts in court proceedings could be deemed to serve an objective 'general good' interest because the rules 'protect creditors or safeguard the sound administration of justice'.[43] Accordingly, a French debt-collection enterprise was blocked from carrying on its activities in Germany. The judgment is rather deferential to the German point of view—most EU States do not restrict debt collection to lawyers, and the Commission considered the German rule to be unjustified. This judgment may be contrasted with *Sager v Dennemeyer*,[44] where the Court held that a German law requiring that only German lawyers or patent agents could handle routine patent renewals was disproportionate to the general good interest served. The judgment held that a UK patent agent company could properly provide these services in Germany.

The most important recent judgment applying the Lawyers' Services Directive is *Gebhard v Milan Bar Council*,[45] a December 1995 decision. Gebhard, a qualified German *Rechtsanwalt* with a part-time practice and office in Stuttgart, took up residence in Milan in 1978, living with his family and paying taxes there. Gebhard initially collaborated with an Italian *avvocato* firm, but in 1989 he opened his own office in Milan. Gebhard's practice chiefly consisted in the representation of German and Austrian clients in Italy, with the aid of Italian *avvacatos*, although he retained his status as 'collaborator' in a Stuttgart firm and about a third of his practice consisted in the representation of Italian clients in Germany and Austria.

In 1989 the Milan Bar Association began disciplinary proceedings against Gebhard because of his permanent practice in Italy using the title '*avvocato*', without being qualified as an Italian lawyer. When in 1992 the Milan Bar Council imposed upon him the sanction of a total prohibition of practice for six months, Gebhard appealed to the National Bar Council, claiming in particular that his practice in Italy was justified under the 1977 Lawyers' Services Directive. In order to resolve this issue, the National Bar

[42] Case C-3/95 *Reiseburo Broede* [1996] ECR I-6511.
[43] ibid at 6539.
[44] Case C-7/90 *Sager v Dennemeyer* [1991] ECR I-4221.
[45] See n 9 above. See notes by M Jarvis (1996) Eur L Rev 247 and by Professor Julian Lonbay (1996) 33 Common Mkt L Rev 1076.

Council asked the ECJ whether a 1982 Italian law had properly implemented the Lawyers' Services Directive, and how to assess the criteria to be used in determining to what extent a foreign lawyer could practise in Italy under the terms of the Directive.

Not surprisingly, the Court concluded that Gebhard's permanent residence in Italy and his legal practice 'on a stable and continuous basis' in Milan took him out of the category of temporary interstate cross-border service providing, and dictated that his rights be appraised under the Treaty's establishment provisions (which, incidentally, the Court also interpreted in a very liberal manner).[46]

The ECJ did, however, provide useful guidance in the determination of the dividing line between service-providing and establishment, helping future courts to determine how far lawyers can go in providing interstate services on a temporary or occasional basis without being deemed to be established in a host State. Largely following the analysis of Advocate General Leger,[47] the Court held that the temporary nature of the activities in question has to be determined in the light, not only of the duration of the provision of the service, but also of its 'regularity, periodicity or continuity'. The fact that Article 50 (ex 60) EC refers to the 'temporary' providing of services does not mean that the provider of services may not equip himself with some form of infrastructure in the host Member State (including an office, chambers or consulting rooms) in so far as such infrastructure is necessary for the purposes of performing the temporary services in question.[48]

In an earlier commercial services case, *Rush Portuguesa*,[49] the Court held that a Portuguese construction firm, working on railroad construction in France, should be considered as carrying out interstate cross-border services 'temporarily' even though the railroad construction project might take many months to complete. The Portuguese construction firm accordingly did not have to comply with French labour law as it would be obliged to do if the firm were deemed to be established in France.

[46] Although the Court naturally declared that the host State could regulate the activities of a permanently established lawyer, the Court applied the *Van Binsbergen* doctrine that the host State rules must be justified in the general interest and not go beyond what is necessary to achieve the interest: *Gebhard* (n 9 above) at ¶ 37. The Court's opinion has influenced the text of the recent 1998 Directive facilitating the practice of law on a permanent basis in a host State (n 10 above).

[47] Advocate General Philippe Leger's opinion is in [1995] ECR I-4165, at 4168. In the ECJ, an Advocate General has equal status to a Judge, with the role of providing a thorough legal analysis of the issues in a case before the Court deliberates to reach its own judgment. For an excellent description of the important role of Advocates General and their influence on Court judgments, see Nial Fennelly, 'Reflections of an Irish Advocate General' (1996) 5 Irish J Eur L 5.

[48] *Gebhard* (n 9 above) 4195.

[49] Case C-113/89 *Rush Portuguesa Lda v Office National d'immigration* [1990] ECR I-1417.

Consequently, an analysis of the Court's doctrinal conclusions in *Gebhard* and *Rush Portuguesa* indicates that lawyers and law firms will have considerable leeway in carrying out temporary and occasional law practice on an interstate basis within the European Union. Thus, a lawyer should normally be considered to provide cross-border services, and not be permanently established, even if occupied in another EU Member State for a number of weeks, perhaps even months, on a specific project (eg, a complex acquisition, real estate financing or arbitration). A law firm is presumably engaged in temporary interstate services even if it frequently sends lawyers to another EU state to engage in legal practice for short or even moderately long periods of time (eg, frequent appearance in arbitrations in London or Paris, or in banking transactions in Frankfurt, or in dealings with EU officials in Brussels). A law firm might even maintain a permanent office with non-legal staff (eg, administrators, secretaries, lobbyists) to serve as support in carrying out frequently offered interstate legal services.

Gebhard thus expands the perimeters of the liberal extent of the right to provide temporary interstate legal services set out in the Lawyers' Services Directive. Essentially, based upon the rules set out in the Directive and the Court's doctrinal development of the right to provide interstate services under Articles 49 and 50 EC, lawyers and law firms from any EU state can provide occasional (but not continuous) cross-border interstate commercial and corporate legal services easily and freely throughout the territory of the European Union. They can also occasionally represent clients in host State litigation, subject to the Directive's obligations that they be associated with qualified host State lawyers and that they satisfy objectively justified host State professional rules of conduct.

II. US RULES REGULATING TEMPORARY INTERSTATE LEGAL SERVICES

1. State Regulation of the Practice of Law within the Federal Constitutional System

In contrast to the explicit provisions in the EC Treaty setting forth the freedom to provide interstate professional services and the related right of establishment, the US Constitution contains no express statement of such rights. Curiously, Article IV of the Articles of Confederation did have a rather precise statement of these rights: 'The people of each state shall have free ingress and regress to and from any other state, and shall enjoy therein all the privileges of trade and commerce, subject to the same duties, impositions and restrictions as the inhabitants thereof . . .'

The US Constitution did not carry over the Articles of Confederation text, although the Privileges and Immunities Clause is believed to have been intended to cover the rights described in Article IV of the Articles. Article IV Section 2 of the Constitution declares: 'The Citizens of each State shall be entitled to all Privileges and Immunities of Citizens in the several States.' This has, of course, been supplemented by the Fourteenth Amendment, Section 1: 'No State shall make or enforce any law which shall abridge the privileges or immunities of citizens of the United States . . .'

Whether interstate legal (or other professional) practice rights have a constitutional basis has usually been determined by an application of the two Privileges and Immunities Clauses, or occasionally (or alternatively) through application of the Dormant Interstate Commerce Clause. Obviously, lawyers' interstate practice rights in the US constitutional system are less precise and more difficult to substantiate than those in the European Union.

In the USA, rules governing the practice of law are almost entirely state measures, sometimes legislative, more often in the form of court rules.[50] In *Leis v Flynt*[51] (discussed below in section II.2), a *per curiam* Supreme Court opinion declared that 'the licensing and regulation of lawyers has been left exclusively to the States'.[52] Professor Geoffrey Hazard, a leading expert on professional ethics, has accurately described this as 'a simple result of our nation's history . . . Regulation of the legal profession [remains] with the states as a matter of tradition and by default [of federal regulation].'[53] Professor Charles Wolfram's treatise on professional ethics pithily describes the American legal profession as being 'balkanized by the geographical limits of state lines'.[54] Although the Congress may have the power to regulate interstate aspects of the practice of law on a nationwide basis under the Interstate Commerce Clause of the Constitution, it has never attempted to do so. Some commentators have recently urged the creation of a national bar under some system of federal minimum rules,[55] but this is presently quite unlikely. The American Bar Association does not even have the subject under active review, and state Bar associations would almost certainly vigorously oppose any form of a national bar.

[50] E Moeser, 'The Future of Bar Admissions and the State Judiciary' (1997) 72 Notre Dame L Rev. 1169. In 1997 Ms Moeser was the President of the National Conference of Bar Examiners.

[51] 439 U.S. 438 (1979).

[52] ibid at 442.

[53] G Hazard, Jr, 'State Supreme Court Regulatory Authority over the Legal Profession' (1997) 72 Notre Dame L Rev 1177. Professor Hazard has recently retired from his post as Executive Director of the American Law Institute (ALI).

[54] C Wolfram, *Modern Legal Ethics* (1986) 865.

[55] See M Comisky and P Patterson, 'The Case for a Federally Created National Bar by Rule or by Legislation' (1982) 55 Temp L Q 945; E Williams, 'A National Bar—Carpe Diem' (1996) 5 Kansas J L & Pub Pol'y 201; F Zacharias, 'Federalizing Legal Ethics' (1994) 73 Texas L Rev. 335.

State regulation of legal practice is however subject to constitutionally imposed limits. In a leading nineteenth-century case, *Dent v West Virginia*,[56] the Supreme Court upheld a state law requiring a licence to practise medicine against a challenge under the Due Process Clause of the Fourteenth Amendment, because the professional licence system was necessary 'for the protection of society',[57] but the Court noted that the licence should be based upon reasonable educational qualifications and an examination, applied in a non-arbitrary manner. These principles undoubtedly also govern the state regulation of law practice. In *Shware v Board of Bar Examiners*,[58] the Supreme Court declared that, pursuant to the Due Process and Equal Protection Clauses, 'officers of a State cannot exclude an applicant when there is no basis for their finding that he fails to meet [the bar] standards, or when their action is invidiously discriminatory'.[59]

The use of the Article IV Privileges and Immunities of Citizens Clause to protect the interstate providing of business and commercial services became well-established in the nineteenth century. In the famous 1823 case, *Corfield v Coryell*,[60] Justice Washington on Circuit proclaimed that the Clause covered a variety of fundamental rights, including '[t]he right of a citizen of one state to pass through, or to reside in any other state, for purposes of trade, agriculture, professional pursuits or otherwise'.[61]

In its 1870 judgment, *Ward v Maryland*,[62] the Supreme Court unanimously relied upon the Privileges and Immunities Clause in striking down a state statute imposing a heavy licence fee on out-of-state persons selling goods within the state. Justice Clifford held that the Clause 'plainly and unmistakably secures and protects the right of a citizen of one state to pass into any other state for the purpose of engaging in lawful commerce, trade or business'.[63] More recently, in the 1948 judgment, *Toomer v Witsell*,[64]

[56] 129 U.S. 114 (1889).
[57] ibid at 122.
[58] 353 U.S. 232 (1957). Justice Black held that the New Mexico bar could not exclude an applicant with well-attested current moral fitness credentials merely because he had been a member of the Communist party and arrested prior to the Second World War.
[59] ibid at 239.
[60] 6 F. Cas. 546 (Cir, E.D. Pa. 1823).
[61] ibid at 551. Note the inclusion of 'professional pursuits'. Justice Washington's seminal views are not diminished by his ultimate holding that oyster beds in New Jersey waters were the common property of New Jersey residents, so that out-of-state fisherman could be barred from oyster fishing there.
[62] 79 U.S. 418 (1870). Accord, *Blake v McClung*, 172 U.S. 239 (1898) (the Privileges and Immunities Clause prevents Tennessee from giving its residents a preference over non-residents in liquidation of a Tennessee corporation).
[63] ibid at 430. Justice Bradley concurred in order to argue that Maryland also violated the Dormant Commerce Clause. In *Welton v Missouri*, 91 U.S. 275 (1875), a state law requiring a licence for peddlers of goods produced outside the state was held to violate the Dormant Commerce Clause.
[64] 334 U.S. 385 (1948). Justices Frankfurter, Jackson and Rutledge concurred, contending that the state law violated the Dormant Commerce Clause.

the Supreme Court followed *Ward* in holding that non-resident fishermen could not be charged a $2,500 shrimp boat fee when residents were charged only $25. Chief Justice Vinson specifically declared that 'one of the privileges which the Clause guarantees to citizens of State A is that of doing business in State B on terms of substantial equality with the citizens of that State'.[65] The Court did however expressly hold that the application of the Privileges and Immunities Clause was not absolute—a state may treat non-residents disparately from residents when there is a valid reason for doing so.[66] Likewise, in 1978 in *Hicklin v Orbeck*,[67] the Supreme Court unanimously held that an Alaskan statute giving a hiring preference to residents for employment connected with development of Alaskan oil and gas resources violated the Privileges and Immunities Clause. Justice Brennan held that Alaska's legitimate concern for unemployed Eskimo and Indian residents could not justify the sweeping preference for Alaskan residents.

The first modern important interstate legal services case is the 1985 landmark judgment, *New Hampshire v Piper*.[68] In *Piper*, the Supreme Court held, 8–1 through Justice Powell, that the Privileges and Immunities of Citizens Clause in Article IV of the Constitution was 'intended to create a national economic union',[69] and was also intended to grant the rights described in the Articles of Confederation language quoted previously.[70] Justice Powell then held that the Privileges and Immunities Clause covered lawyers as well as businessmen, both because 'the practice of law is important to the national economy' and because lawyers provide an important 'noncommercial role' in the 'vindication of federal rights'.[71]

Applying these principles, Justice Powell concluded that New Hampshire could not require a lawyer to be resident within the state, observing that 'the opportunity to practice law should be considered a "fundamental right" ',[72] and that state rules must not constitute 'economic protectionism'.[73] Although he accepted *Toomer's* exception permitting state discrimination against non-residents if justified by an independent substantial

[65] ibid at 395.

[66] ibid. The Court found no valid reason for the discriminatory licence fee, specifically rejecting any claim that non-residents did any greater harm to shrimp conservation than did residents.

[67] 437 U.S. 518 (1978). Justice Brennan suggested the Alaskan law might also violate the Dormant Commerce Clause, noting the 'mutually reinforcing relationship' between the two clauses and 'their shared vision of federalism': ibid at 531–532.

[68] 470 U.S. 274 (1985).

[69] ibid at 280.

[70] ibid at 279. Justice Powell noted that Charles Pinckney, who drafted the Priviliges and Immunities Clause, had affirmed that it originated in Article IV of the Articles of Confederation: ibid at 279 n 7.

[71] ibid at 281.

[72] ibid.

[73] ibid at 285 n 18. Justice Powell cited a former American Bar Association President's expressed concern that some state barriers to out-of-state lawyers existed 'primarily to protect [the state's] own lawyers from professional competition': C Smith, 'Time for a National Practice of Law Act' (1978) 64 ABAJ 557.

reason, Justice Powell concluded that no independent substantial reason existed in this case, specifically rejecting New Hampshire's arguments that a non-resident lawyer would be less familiar with local rules and procedures or more apt to behave unethically. The Court did however recognize that a non-resident lawyer must comply with the state's ethical rules and be subject to the state Supreme Court's disciplinary rules.[74] The sole dissenter, Justice Rehnquist, contended that a state had a substantial interest in requiring its lawyers to be residents, because they would then be more conversant with local concerns in adjudicating cases.[75]

In a later case, *Virginia v Friedman*,[76] the Supreme Court struck down a residence requirement imposed on out-of-state lawyers seeking admission to the Virginia bar on motion based on prior practice, without taking a bar examination. Justice Kennedy devoted most attention to Virginia's claim of a substantial state interest, notably that only attorneys admitted on motion who were residents would have a sufficient interest in obtaining and maintaining familiarity with Virginia law. As in *Piper*, the Court rejected that argument as unpersuasive, suggesting that Virginia had the less burdensome alternative of requiring continuing legal education courses.[77] However, Justice Kennedy noted the Virginia rule obliging lawyers admitted on motion to engage in full-time legal practice within the state without making any suggestion that such a full-time practice obligation was invalid.[78] Chief Justice Rehnquist and Justice Scalia dissented, believing that Virginia's independent state interest arguments were persuasive.[79]

Finally, in *Barnard v Thorsten*,[80] the Court held, 6–3, that the Federal District Court for the Virgin Islands could not impose a one-year residence requirement before admission to its bar. While the relative geographic isolation of the Virgin Islands, accessible for non-resident lawyers only by airline, clearly presented a stronger justification for a residence requirement, Justice Kennedy's majority opinion stressed that non-resident lawyers could not be assumed to fail to familiarize themselves with local law and could make arrangements with local lawyers to handle urgent court hearings.[81] Chief Justice Rehnquist's dissent argued that the Virgin Islands' unusual situation could justify a residence requirement.[82]

It is important to note that practice before federal courts is regulated independently of any state rules. The federal district and circuit courts set their own standards for attorneys' appearance in litigation in their courtrooms, usually admitting lawyers who are already authorized in any state

[74] ibid at 286. [75] ibid at 292–293. [76] 487 U.S. 59 (1988).
[77] ibid at 68–69. Justice Kennedy noted that Friedman worked full-time as a house counsel in Virginia, even though she resided in Maryland.
[78] ibid at 69–70. [79] ibid at 70–71. [80] 489 U.S. 546 (1989).
[81] ibid at 553-556. [82] ibid at 559–560.

court. Thus, in *Murphy v Egan*,[83] a federal district court in Pennsylvania admitted to practice before the district court a lawyer who was qualified in California, but whom Pennsylvania had refused to admit to its bar. There also exists a *de facto* bar of lawyers specializing in specific areas of federal law—patents, trademarks, copyright, tax, social security, securities regulation, banking, etc. Federal agencies set their own standards for lawyers appearing in administrative proceedings before them.[84] In general, a lawyer may engage in the practice of these federal law specialities before administrative agencies or before federal courts without being admitted to the bar of the state in which the agency or federal court is located.[85] However, a lawyer who is only admitted to practice before a federal district court, but not in the state in which the district court is located, cannot practise state law, even if some federal issues are mixed with state law issues.[86]

In summary, the Supreme Court has solidly established the principle that lawyers can claim the benefit of the Privileges and Immunities Clause in some circumstances when engaging in interstate legal practice. To date, the cases in the Supreme Court have all involved the right of non-resident lawyers to be admitted to a state bar. Although in *Piper* and *Friedman*, the non-resident lawyer intended to practise principally or exclusively within the state where admitted, it appears in *Barnard* that non-resident lawyers would have the right to be admitted to a bar (if otherwise qualified) even if not principally practising there. As yet, the Supreme Court has not had occasion to consider whether the Privileges and Immunities Clause grants any right to non-resident lawyers to provide occasional legal services of a transactional character in a state where they are not admitted to the bar, the topic to which we now turn.

2. Temporary Interstate Legal Practice in the USA

Lawyers sometimes seek to appear in courtroom litigation in a state other than that in which they are admitted. In that event, they usually are permitted to do

[83] 498 F. Supp. 240 (E.D. Penn. 1980). Lawyers admitted to practise in a federal court are not automatically disbarred when a state has disbarred them from practice in the state: *Theard v United States*, 354 U.S. 278 (1957).

[84] See C Wolfram, 'Sneaking Around in the Legal Profession: Interjurisdictional Unauthorized Practice by Transnational Lawyers' (1995) 38 S Tex L Rev 666, at 674–676.

[85] See, eg, *Sperry v Florida*, 373 U.S. 379 (1963) (Florida cannot prevent a patent agent from practising patent law out of a Florida office; patent law practice does not constitute the unauthorized practice of Florida law). Accord, *Spanos v Skouras Theatres Corp.*, 364 F.2d 161 (2d Cir. *en banc* 1966) (California lawyer may provide legal services in antitrust proceeding in federal district court in New York). See the analysis of *Spanos* in the text at nn 148–152 below.

[86] *Ginsburg v Kovrak*, 139 A.2d 889 (Pa. 1958, leave to appeal denied, 358 U.S. 52 (1958). Although enjoined from practising state law, a lawyer admitted to practise before a federal court has a right to continue to practise before that court: *Kennedy v Bar Association*, 561 A.2d 200 (Md. 1989).

so by the local court in a procedure called *pro hac vice* admission. This procedure dates to colonial times and exists in all states.[87] Although the decision whether or not to permit the out-of-state lawyer to appear in litigation is discretionary, courts will usually grant admission if the client so desires and the lawyer is in good standing, and appellate courts will, on occasion, strike down unnecessary or unreasonable limits placed by trial courts on *pro hac vice* appears.[88] *Pro hac vice* counsel are particularly desirable when the client has a long-standing relationship with the out-of-state lawyer, or when the latter is a renowned trial lawyer with particular expertise in the subject-matter of the trial (eg, securities rules, criminal conspiracy, mass torts).

The principal operational restraint upon *pro hac vice* appearances stems from the requirement in many states that the out-of-state counsel be associated with a local lawyer.[89] The purpose of requiring local counsel to be involved is to ensure knowledge of, and compliance with local court procedure, which is certainly a valid concern for competent legal representation of the client,[90] but difficulties may arise in allocating responsibilities between the associated counsel. In any event, this approach significantly increases the cost to the client. In such a case, if the client is unable to afford the out-of-state counsel, the client's right to counsel is not deemed to be violated.[91]

The only significant constitutional examination of the status of *pro hac vice* admission came in *Leis v Flynt*.[92] *Hustler* magazine and its publisher, Larry Flynt, were prosecuted in Ohio for the dissemination of material harmful to minors. When they sought to be represented by two New York attorneys, specialists in criminal defence and obscenity law, the Ohio trial court denied the attorneys *pro hac vice* status. Because their out-of-state attorneys appeared to have been denied *pro hac vice* admission without good reason, Flynt and *Hustler* obtained an injunction in a federal district court against their prosecution. However, on appeal the Supreme Court in

[87] For a detailed analysis of *pro hac vice* proceedings, see S Brakel and W Loh, 'Regulating the Multistate Practice of Law' (1975) 50 Wash L Rev 699, and T Canfield, Note, 'The Criminal Defendant's Right to Retain Counsel Pro Hace Vice' (1989) 57 Fordham L Rev 785.

[88] See, eg, *Sanders v Russell*, 401 F.2d 241 (5th Cir. 1968); *Enquire Printing & Publishing Co. v O'Reilly*, 477 A.2d 648 (Conn. 1984); *Hahn v The Boeing Co.*, 621 P.2d 1263 (Wash. 1980), *State v Von Bulow*, 475 A.2d 995 (R.I. 1984).

[89] eg *Duncan v St. Romain*, 569 So. 2d 687 (Miss. 1990); *In re Smith*, 272 S.E.2d 834 (N.C. 1981).

[90] Competent legal representation covers not only knowledge of local laws and procedures, but also 'local conditions, personalities, customs and prejudices': Brakel and Loh (n 87 above) 705.

[91] In *Ford v Israel*, 701 F.2d 689 (7th cir.), cert. denied, 464 U.S. 832 (1983), the court held that the client's right to counsel was not violated because the client was still represented by a Wisconsin public defence lawyer.

[92] See n 51 above.

a *per curiam* opinion held that federal courts had no power to review any alleged deficiency in a state court's failure to permit a *pro hac vice* appearance, because *pro hac vice* appearances were strictly within a state's discretion and were not subject to any constitutional standards. The opinion observed that 'no right of federal origin . . . permits [out-of-state] lawyers to appear in state courts without meeting that State's bar admission requirements'.[93]

Justice Stevens dissented, joined by Justices Brennan and Marshall, contending that lawyers enjoyed a Fourteenth Amendment Due Process right to appear *pro hac vice*.[94] Justice Stevens stressed the high mobility and interstate character of modern legal practice and the value provided to clients when they can use the services *pro hac vice* of out-of state expert litigators, often in specialized fields of practice.[95]

Far more important in temporary interstate legal practice than occasional *pro hac vice* court appearances is the involvement of lawyers in out-of-state contracts, transactions or arbitrations. Commentators have frequently observed that modern commercial operations and the increased mobility both of clients and lawyers make temporary interstate legal practice of a transactional nature both functionally desirable and also increasingly commonplace.[96] They have also stressed the increased involvement of lawyers in federal regulatory practice and in dealing with federal issues, as well as the trend toward uniform or parallel rules in state law, due to uniform acts and the influence of the Restatements of fields of law.

Interstate transactional legal practice may occur in a variety of modes. At one extreme, a lawyer may draft contracts or other instruments for use in another state, or provide opinions based on the law of another state, without ever leaving the state in which he or she is admitted to practice. At the other extreme, lawyers may attempt to engage in transactional practice in a state where they are not admitted while residing there, perhaps serving on an in-house counsel staff, or while working in some form of association

[93] ibid at 443.

[94] ibid at 445.

[95] ibid at 448–451. Justice Stevens cited Daniel Webster, Clarence Darrow, Charles Evans Hughes, John Davis and Thurgood Marshall as examples of great litigators who frequently appeared *pro hac vice*.

[96] The leading prior articles analyzing temporary interstate legal practice and state restraints upon it are Brakel and Loh (n 87 above); C Needham, 'Splitting Bar Admission into Federal and State Components: National Admission for Advice on Federal Law' (1997) 45 Kan L Rev 453; O Reynolds, Jr, 'Practice and Performance by the Out-of-State Attorney—The Jealous Mistress Becomes an Interstate Traveler' (1974) 6 Toledo L Rev 63; and Wolfram (n 84 above). D Babb, Note, 'Take Caution When Representing Clients Across State Lines: The Services Provided May Constitute the Unauthorized Practice of Law' (1999) 50 Ala L Rev 535 is a useful current survey of the case law. For a thoughtful review of the reasons for the growth of multijurisdictional practice, see M Daly, 'Resolving Ethical Conflicts in Multijurisdictional Practice' (1995) 36 S Tex L Rev 715, at 723–742. See also excellent symposium on Ethics and the Multijurisdictional Practice of Law (1995) 36 S Texas L Rev 657.

with a local law firm. In between are the instances in which a lawyer travels occasionally, for relatively short periods of time, to other states in order to assist in negotiations, draft contracts or other instruments, or provide legal advice. Sometimes, of course, the lawyer may spend a substantial period of time in another state, even several weeks or months in a protracted matter.

All US states forbid the unauthorized practice of law.[97] Even in recent years in a modern legal practice context, there have been a number of state Supreme Court judgments holding that non-resident lawyers who engage in temporary or occasional interstate legal practice of a transactional character are engaging in the unauthorized practice of law. These judgments have resulted in injunctive relief against any further such practice within the state in which the practice occurred,[98] or in a court order prohibiting the collection of fees from the client in the matter.[99]

The American Bar Association's 1983 Model Rules of Professional Conduct (MRPC), adopted by the large majority of states, declares in Rule 5.5(a) that '[a] lawyer shall not . . . practice law in a jurisdiction where doing so violates the regulation of the legal profession in that jurisdiction'. The ABA's earlier 1969 Model Code of Professional Responsibility (CPR), still in effect in New York and a minority of states, contains essentially the same rule in Disciplinary Rule 3–101(B). However, the CPR added a comment concerning 'the demands of business and the mobility of our society' in Ethical Consideration 3–9, declaring that 'the legal profession should discourage regulation that unreasonably imposes territorial limitations upon the right of a lawyer to handle the legal affairs of his client or upon the opportunity of a client to obtain the services of a lawyer of his choice'. Although the MRPC Comment to Rule 5.5 contains no similar language, it does assert that the purpose of the rule is to protect 'the public against rendition of legal services by unqualified persons', which would appear to leave room for consideration whether an out-of-state attorney should, or should not, be considered an 'unqualified person' in various contexts.

Professor Charles Wolfram, a leading authority on professional ethics, has vigorously argued in a valuable analytical article that, on the whole, 'professional discipline for out-of-state unauthorized practice is minimal'[100] and that there has been 'a fair amount of pointless rigor in applying the

[97] For a review of the nature of unauthorized practice of law restrictions which sometimes include contempt of court or criminal penalties, see Needham (n 96 above) 458–462; Reynolds (n 96 above) 70–72.

[98] eg *Ginsburg v Kovrak* (n 86 above).

[99] The most recent prominent example is *Birbrower, Montalbono, Condon & Frank v Superior Court*, 949 P.2d 1 (Cal. 1998). Earlier instances are *McRae v Sawyer*, 473 So. 2d 1006 (Ala. 1985), and *Spivak v Sachs*, 211 N.E.2d 329 (N.Y. 1965).

[100] Wolfram (n 96 above).

prohibition against unlicenced local law practice'.[101] He urges courts to be more sympathetic 'to the needs of the national economy and its inevitable interstate implications',[102] permitting interstate transactional practice on a much more liberal basis.

The American Law Institute's recently approved Restatement of the Law Governing Lawyers (upon which Professor Wolfram served as Reporter) takes the position that a lawyer may engage in such out-of-state transactional practice so long as '[t]he lawyer's activities in the matter arise out of or are otherwise reasonably related to the lawyer's practice'.[103] Although there is no clearly prevailing legislative or case law support for this relatively new standard, its policy rationale is that 'the need to provide effective and efficient legal services to persons and businesses with interstate legal concerns requires that jurisdictions not erect unnecessary barriers to interstate legal practice'.[104] The ALI view certainly does in large measure reflect the realities of modern commercial life and the consequent need for liberalization of rules governing temporary interstate transactional practice. Nonetheless, there are a number of significant precedents that suggest that temporary interstate legal practice is presently subject to very substantial risks and restraints.

The Restatement does appear to be both pragmatically sensible and on reasonably solid ground in adopting the view that all interstate transactional legal practice conducted from a lawyer's home State office, through the use of the telephone, correspondence, or electronic communication, is 'clearly permissible'.[105] In support of this view is *El Gemayel v Seaman*,[106] in which the New York Court of Appeals held that a Lebanese lawyer assisting New York residents in a child custody proceeding who provided most of his services in Lebanon, but did telephone the clients in New York to report on progress, could not be considered to be engaged in the unauthorized practice of law. In *Condon v McHenry*,[107] a California Court of Appeal held that a Colorado attorney, representing a Colorado resident who was co-executor in a California probate proceeding, was not engaged in the unauthorized practice of law when he drafted documents in Colorado and provided advice by telephone. The court also considered that the out-of-state attorney could properly advise on California law (subject to the

101 Wolfram (n 96 above) at 693.
102 ibid at 707.
103 ALI, Restatement (Third) of the Law Governing Lawyers, Proposed Final Draft No. 2, at section 3(3) (1998). The Restatement's complete text was approved by the ALI at its May 1998 meeting. A final edited text is scheduled for publication in 2000. Proposed Final Draft No 1 (1996), Proposed Final Draft No 2 (1998) and Tentative Draft No 8 (1997) contain the current text.
104 ibid at Comment b.
105 ibid at Comment e.
106 533 N.E.2d 245 (N.Y. 1988).
107 64 Cal. Rptr. 2d 789 (Cal. Ct. App. 1997).

risks of malpractice).[108] This view has been endorsed by the Restatement of the Law Governing Lawyers, which declares that '[t]here is no per se ban against [an out-of-state] lawyer giving a formal opinion based in whole or part on the law of another jurisdiction'.[109] Unfortunately, some doubt has been cast on the Restatement view, as well as some aspects of the *Condon* judgment, by the recent California Supreme Court decision in *Birbrower, Montalbano*,[110] discussed below.

At the other extreme from interstate services provided by telephone or correspondence is any attempt by an out-of-state attorney who has become resident in a state to practise the law of that state without being admitted to its bar. This is usually considered the unauthorized practice of law. In *Perlah v SEI Corp*,[111] a New York attorney, resident in Connecticut, provided corporate transactional assistance to a client for several weeks prior to his admission to the Connecticut bar. The court held that the attorney could not recover fees for these services, which constituted the unauthorized practice of law. Similarly, in *Chandris v Yanakadis*,[112] the Florida Supreme Court concluded that a retired Massachusetts attorney and professor of maritime law, resident in Florida, could not provide services to an injured sailor in tort litigation against his employer under the federal Jones Act, because such pre-litigation advice constituted the unauthorized practice of law in Florida. The majority opinion refused to accept that the lawyer's advice on a federal maritime law issue could be treated as a so-called federal law practice exception to the unauthorized practice of law.

Moreover, in a recent 1998 Ohio Supreme Court *per curiam* judgment, *Cleveland Bar Association v Misch*,[113] the court held that an Illinois attorney resident in Ohio engaged in unauthorized legal practice, and was not merely a business consultant, when he acted as consultant to a local law firm, providing legal assistance directly to clients. The Illinois attorney had drafted buy–sell agreements and financing arrangements, negotiated with creditors and labour unions and provided assistance in Ohio tax law.

[108] ibid at 793. The court suggested that this was desirable to avoid unnecessary expense to clients.

[109] ALI, Restatement (Third) of the Law Governing Lawyers (n 103 above) at Comment e.

[110] See n 99 above. In the appeal of the *Condon* judgment (n 107 above), the California Supreme Court ordered a re-hearing in the light of its *Birbrower* opinion. The Court of Appeal still permitted the Colorado attorney to recover his fees, but emphasized that his services were considered to be provided to the Colorado co-executor: *Estate of Condon v McHenry*, 76 Cal. Rptr. 2d 922 (Cal. Ct. App. 1998). See the text at nn 132–135 below.

[111] 612 A.2d 806 (Conn. App. 1992); accord, *Ginsburg v Kovrak* (n 86 above). See also *Ranta v McCarney*, 391 N.W. 2d 161 (N.D. 1986) (a Minnesota attorney's tax services provided from a branch office in North Dakota constituted unauthorized practice of law).

[112] 668 So.2d 180 (Fla. 1995). The dissenting judges argued that the retired Massachusetts attorney, clearly expert in maritime law, should have been permitted to give pre-litigation advice, noting that the attorney had never claimed to be admitted in Florida.

[113] 695 N.E.2d 244 (Ohio 1998).

Similarly, a New York federal district court held that a Maryland lawyer, also licensed to appear before the US Court of Federal Claims and the Court of Appeals for the Federal Circuit, could not recover fees for his services in a federal contract action, including appearances before both those courts, because the lawyer's sole law office was one conducted in New York in association with a New York lawyer.[114]

In contrast to these rather stringent judgments, there are some cases where residents have been permitted to practice law even though not admitted within the state of practice. Thus, the ALI Restatement of the Law Governing Lawyers urges that lawyers working as house counsel should usually be allowed to engage in transactional practice for their employer, even it not admitted to the bar in the state where they are employed and resident, and some state rules or practices clearly tolerate such legal practice by house counsel.[115] Also, the Tenth Circuit has held that a law professor (Ted Fiflis, an expert in legal accounting), resident in Colorado but only admitted in Illinois, could provide counsel to local attorneys in a bankruptcy litigation without being deemed to be engaged in the unauthorized practice of law in Colorado.[116] Similarly, the Maryland Court of Appeals held that a North Carolina attorney acting 'of counsel' to a Maryland law firm for a three year period should not be considered to be engaged in the unauthorized practice of law, even though he drafted pleadings and briefs and supervised associates and paralegals, because he never directly advised the Maryland firm's clients.[117] The court noted that the lawyer 'of counsel' gave advice only to the firm, in a manner analogous to the role of a house counsel providing services only to the employing corporation.

Unfortunately, the extent to which a lawyer may travel occasionally and

[114] *Servidone Construction Corp. v St. Paul Fire & Marine Insurance Co.*, 911 F. Supp. 560 (N.D.N.Y. 1995). While the court accepted that a non-resident out-of-state lawyer could provide advice on a federal claim if the advice is given in conjunction with a New York lawyer, the court concluded that a Maryland lawyer's permanent practice within an office in New York constituted unauthorized practice and made his retainer fee agreement void on public policy grounds, citing *Spivak* (n 99 above) as the controlling precedent.

[115] ALI, Restatement (Third) of the Law Governing Lawyers (n 103 above), at Comment f. The Reporter's Note indicates that Florida, Idaho and Missouri expressly follow this approach. Professor Carol Needham (n 96 above) 485, lists nine states which do so. Professor Mary Daly (n 96 above) cites empirical evidence that suggests that house counsel are rarely limited by unauthorized practice of law rules, noting that '[d]isciplinary proceedings are virtually nonexistent; inhospitable opinions by state bar associations' ethics are few and far between': ibid at 729–730.

[116] *The Dietrich Corp. v King Resources Co.*, 596 F.2d 422 (10th Cir. 1979). Accord, *Spanos v Skouras Theatres Corp.* (n 85 above).

[117] *In re R.G.S.*, 541 A.2d (Md. 1988). A peculiarity of the case was that the lawyer, a former law professor, was applying for admission in Maryland on motion, so that he had to satisfy Maryland's requirement of legal practice for five of the prior seven years. The Court of Appeals majority felt that his 'of counsel' work constituted legal practice, but not unauthorized legal practice, while the dissent considered his failure to advise clients directly meant that his activities were not legal practice at all.

even for short periods to other states to provide legal services of a transactional character, eg, to assist in negotiations, draft contracts or legal instruments, provide legal counsel, assist in arbitrations, review corporate documents, assist in an acquisition or merger, etc, has to be considered very much in a grey area of doubt. That such interstate legal transactional practice is common and usually tolerated is evident.[118] There exists, however, a risk that it may be the subject of sanctions by the bar or the courts of the state where the practice physically occurs. Three prominent cases demonstrate the risk.

In *Spivak v Sachs*,[119] the New York Court of Appeal held that a California attorney who spent two weeks in New York, providing counsel to a New York resident upon a Connecticut divorce proceeding, was engaged in the unauthorized practice of law and could not recover legal fees or travel expenses from the client. The legal services included review of a draft settlement, consideration of New York as a preferable divorce venue, and advice on selection of a New York lawyer for the litigation. The client had specifically requested the California attorney to come to New York and agreed to pay his fees and expenses, and the California attorney clearly disclaimed any ability to provide anything other than advice in conjunction with the client's current counsel. Although three dissenting judges felt that this conduct constituted an 'isolated situation' which did not rise to the level of practice of New York law,[120] Chief Judge Desmond held that it represented unauthorized practice of law. His opinion stressed that the New York policy protected 'citizens against the dangers of legal representation and advice given by persons not trained, examined and licensed for such work [even if they are] lawyers from other jurisdictions'.[121] *Spival v Sachs* is presumably still good law in New York.[122]

Several courts in other jurisdictions have come to similar conclusions.[123] For example, in *Ranta v McCarney*,[124] a Minnesota attorney, specialized in tax advice, could not recover fees for assistance to a North Dakota resident

[118] See Wolfram (n 84 above) 668–671; Daly (n 96 above) 725–731.

[119] See n 99 above.

[120] The dissenting judges adopted the majority opinion in the Appellate Division which took this view: *Spivak v Sachs*, 21 N.Y. App. Div. 2d 348 (1st Dept. 1964).

[121] 211 N.E.2d 329, at 333 (N.Y. 1965).

[122] The 1988 Court of Appeals opinion in *El Gemayel v Seaman* (n 106 above) cited *Spivak* with approval, although distinguishing it on the facts. *Servidone* (n 114 above) expressly followed *Spivak*.

[123] See, eg, *Lazoff v Shore Heights*, 362 N.E.2d 1047 (Ill. 1977) (Wisconsin lawyer expert in real estate transactions could not recover fees for aid in negotiations for the sale of real estate in Illinois); *McRae v Sawyer* (n 99 above) (Mississippi lawyer cannot recover fees for legal service to Alabama residents rendered in a personal injury litigation in Alabama); *Taft v Amsel*, 180 A.2d 756 (Conn. 1962) (New York attorney specialized in transportation law could not recover fees for legal services in the creation of a national transportation company in Connecticut).

[124] See n 111 above.

in the sale of the latter's business in North Dakota. The North Dakota Supreme Court held that the concept of legal practice encompassed legal advice and drafting of instruments as much as it did court appearances, and declined to recognize any exception for advice on federal tax matters.[125] A sharp dissent argued for recognition of a federal tax advice exception, and bluntly stated that '[t]he only protection effected by the holding in this case is the protection of the economic interests of the attorneys of this state'.[126]

The most recent major judgment restricting interstate transactional legal practice is *Birbrower, Montalbano*,[127] a 1998 decision of the California Supreme Court. In 1992–93, Birbrower, Montalbano, a New York law firm, performed legal services for a California corporation, ESQ Business Services. This corporation was owned by the Sandhu family, Birbrower clients since 1986, largely for New York matters. ESQ had a software development and marketing contract dispute with Tandem, another California corporation. The contract, which apparently, had been drafted by Birbrower, was governed by California law. Two Birbrower attorneys travelled several times to California to perform legal services, notably negotiating with Tandem representatives and preparing and filing a complaint for arbitration in San Francisco. After the ESQ–Tandem dispute was settled, Birbrower sued for over one million dollars in legal fees.

On this record, Judge Chin's opinion for six judges of the California Supreme Court held that the Birbrower firm's services in California constituted the unauthorized practice of law and consequently barred the collection of legal fees (except for such portion of fees as represented compensation for corporate case research performed in New York). Ruling out '[m]ere fortuitous or attenuated contacts', the court's test was 'whether the unlicenced lawyer engaged in sufficient activities in the state, or created a continuing relationship with the California client that included legal duties and obligations'.[128] The court declined to recognize an exception for legal services incidental to private arbitration[129] (although that aspect of the holding has been effectively nullified by the California state legislation's adoption of a law on 1 July 1999 specifically authorizing the appearance of out-of-state attorneys in private arbitrations).[130] The court also refused to accept an estoppel rationale that would permit recovery of fees when a client engages a lawyer with full knowledge that the lawyer is not admitted

[125] See n 111 above at 163–164.
[126] ibid at 166.
[127] See n 99 above.
[128] ibid at 5.
[129] ibid at 7. Justice Kennard's dissent essentially argues for excepting services in a private arbitration from the unauthorized practice of law.
[130] California Rules of Court, Rule 983.4 Out-of-state Attorney Arbitration Counsel (West 1999). The out-of-state attorney must be in good standing and admitted to practice before the bar in any US court and approved by the arbitrator(s) or the arbitral forum.

in the state where the services are to be rendered.[131] Although recognizing the need to 'accommodate the multistate nature of law practice'. Judge Chin ruled Birbrower's activities to be too extensive to escape treatment as unauthorized practice.[132]

The California Supreme Court also observed that a lawyer 'not physically present' can still engage in unauthorized practice 'by advising a California client on California law in connection with a California legal dispute by telephone, fax, computer or other modern technological means', although it added that such practice using technological communications did not automatically constitute unauthorized practice—a fact review would be necessary.[133] When *Condon v McHenry*, discussed above,[134] was appealed, the California Supreme Court ordered its reconsideration in the light of *Birbrower*. In its reconsidered *Condon* opinion, the Court of Appeals emphasized that the Colorado co-executor's choice of the Colorado law firm to provide services in a California probate proceeding was reasonable, since the Colorado firm had drafted the will and prepared the estate planning documents for the decedent.[135] The Court of Appeals considered that the fact that the Colorado law firm's services for the Colorado co-executor were almost entirely performed in Colorado distinguished the case from *Birbrower* and concluded that 'California has no interest in disciplining an out-of-state lawyer practicing law on behalf of a client residing in the lawyer's home state'.[136] Moreover, the Court of Appeals repeated its view that the Colorado law firm's communications by telephone, fax or mail with California beneficiaries did not represent the practice of law in California.[137]

Although the Restatement of the Law Governing Lawyers characterizes *Spivak* and *Birbrower* as 'unduly restrictive' and does not follow their policy view,[138] the two decisions, together with *Ranta* and a number of others reaching the same result, demonstrate that there can be a serious risk in providing temporary interstate legal services.

[131] ibid at 11; accord, *Ranta v McCarney* (n 111 above) 164. Adopting the contrary view is *Freeling v Tucker*, 289 Pac. 85 (Id. 1935), where an Oklahoma attorney was permitted to recover fees for services in an Idaho probate proceeding because he fully disclosed his lack of a local licence.

[132] ibid at 10.

[133] ibid at 6. This aspect of the judgment, probably technically dicta, was sharply criticized by Professor Wolfram as setting 'the legal field back a quarter of a century'. He was quoted in D Baker, 'Lawyer Go Home', ABA Journal 22 (May 1998).

[134] See text at nn 107–108 above.

[135] *Estate of Condon v McHenry* (n 110 above) 925.

[136] ibid at 927. The court observed that only 10 of the firm's 316 billable hours represented the time spent by one of its lawyers while physically providing services in California.

[137] ibid at 928. Moreover, the court also maintained its view that out-of-state attorneys could advise their clients on California law when in their home jurisdiction: ibid.

[138] ALI, Restatement (Third) of the Law Governing Lawyers (n 103 above) at Reporter's Note to Comment e.

Fortunately, there are some judgments that take a more liberal view. In *Appel v Reiner*,[139] a New Jersey Supreme Court decision held that a New York attorney who provided services to a New Jersey resident in the extension of credit and compromise of claims held by New York and New Jersey creditors was not engaged in the unauthorized practice of New Jersey law. The court noted the difficulty in disentangling the New York and New Jersey elements, and the fact that a New York creditor was owed more than half of the debt involved. The New Jersey Supreme Court has also authorized the award of fees to a New York lawyer selected by an executor to handle most of the legal work for the estate of a New Jersey decedent. In re *Waring's Estate*,[140] the court emphasized that the New York firm had previously served as the decedent's legal counsel and prepared the will, that the work largely involved federal tax issues and that New Jersey issues were handled by consultation with a New Jersey lawyer. The court declared notably:

> Multistate relationships are a common part of today's society and are to be dealt with in common sense fashion. While the members of the general public are entitled to full protection against unlawful practitioners, their freedom of choice in the selection of their own counsel is to be highly regarded and not burdened by 'technical restrictions which have no reasonable justification'.[141]

A 1998 judgment of the Hawaii Supreme Court, *Fought & Co. v Steel Engineering*,[142] also took a more liberal view in authorizing the payment of fees to an Oregon law firm, general counsel to a client involved in litigation against the state of Hawaii arising out of the construction of an airport in Hawaii. Hawaii lawyers directly handled the litigation, but the Oregon firm assisted them with legal research and in the preparation of briefs. The Oregon firm did not make a *pro hac vice* appearance but it essentially supervised the conduct of the litigation on behalf of the client. Noting 'the transformation of our economy from a local to a global one', the Hawaii Supreme Court specifically rejected the approach of *Birbrower* in this context.[143] The court emphasized the necessity for co-operation between local firms and out-of-state firms which customarily handled a client's affairs, stating notably: 'a commercial entity that serves interstate and/or international markets is likely to receive more effective and efficient representation when its general counsel, who . . . is familiar with the details of its operations, supervises the work of local counsel in each of the various jurisdictions in which it does business.'[144]

There is some support for excluding certain fields of practice from state unauthorized practice prohibitions. Thus, in *Williams v John B. Quinn*

[139] 204 A.2d 146 (N.J. 1964).
[140] 221 A.2d 193 (N.J. 1966).
[141] ibid at 197.
[142] 951 P.2d 487 (Haw. 1998).
[143] ibid at 497.
[144] ibid.

Construction Corp., a New York federal district court held that a New Jersey law firm could properly provide legal assistance in a private arbitration proceeding, essentially on the rationale that services provided in an arbitration in New York are not to be considered the practice of New York law.[145] In 1964 a California court held that an Illinois attorney could properly assist a California client in a federal bankruptcy proceeding, since federal bankruptcy rules are not to be considered as part of California state law.[146] Somewhat in contrast, a bankruptcy court in Connecticut held that a New York lawyer could not claim a federal law exception for his services concerning bankruptcy law in Connecticut because he provided the services from a permanent Connecticut office, instead of occasionally providing services in specific bankruptcy court appearances.[147]

The only attempt to use the Privileges and Immunities Clause in the context of temporary interstate legal services came in *Spanos v Skouras Theaters*,[148] a Second Circuit *en banc* opinion written by Judge Friendly, one of the leading jurists of his generation. Spanos, a prominent California lawyer specializing in the antitrust rules governing the motion picture industry, was invited by Skouras Theaters to come to New York to assist in a major motion picture antitrust action in federal court. During 1953–58, he assisted New York counsel in the proceedings, residing for long periods in New York, without being admitted *pro hac vice*. Spanos' suit for fees was dismissed by a Second Circuit panel in an opinion by Chief Judge Lumbard, who applied the *Spivak v Sachs* broad interpretation of what constituted practice in New York, and concluded that Spanos' services represented unauthorized practice of law in New York.[149]

In the 7–2 *en banc* reversal of the panel, Judge Friendly's legal analysis was founded on the Privileges and Immunities Clause, but focused on clients' rights rather than lawyers' rights: 'under the privileges and immunities clause of the Constitution no state can prohibit a citizen with a federal claim or defense from engaging an out-of-state lawyer to collaborate with an in-state lawyer and give legal advice concerning it within the state.'[150] He stressed that in 'an age of increased specialization and high mobility of the bar' a client should be able to obtain the services of 'a lawyer licensed [in any] state who is thought best fitted for the task'.[151] Judge Friendly did however limit this perceived client right to the assistance of out-of-state attorneys who 'work in association with a local lawyer on a federal claim or defense', rejecting the New York City Bar Association's *amicus* view that

[145] 537 F. Supp. 613 (S.D.N.Y. 1982).

[146] *Cowen v Calabrese*, 41 Cal. Rptr. 441 (Cal. Dist. Ct. App. 1964).

[147] *In re Peterson*, 163 B.R. 665 (Bkrtcy. D. Conn. 1994); accord., *Attorney Grievance Com'n of Maryland v Harris-Smith*, 737 A.2d 567 (Md. 1999).

[148] See n 85 above.

[149] ibid at 164–165.

[150] ibid at 170.

[151] ibid.

the out-of-state lawyer could represent the client independently in connection with a federal action.[152] The holding in *Spanos* has however been undercut by *Norfolk* and *Western Railway*, where the Supreme Court summarily affirmed a district court ruling that Missouri lawyers specialized in Federal Employers' Liability Act matters could nonetheless be denied admission *pro hac vice* in proceedings related to the federal act in Illinois state courts.[153]

Finally, an unusual application of the Dormant Commerce Clause occurred in *National Revenue Corp. v Violet*.[154] The First Circuit, in an opinion by Judge Aldridge, concluded that the Rhode Island statute that defined debt collection as the practice of law, thus limiting it to Rhode Island lawyers, constituted an excessive and unjustified burden on interstate commerce. The court noted that no other state restricted debt collection to members of its bar. (The opinion contrasts with the ECJ's conclusion that Germany could restrict debt collection to German lawyers in *Reiseburo Brode*,[155] discussed above.) The court's analysis raises the interesting possibility that states' reservation of certain types of legal services to their attorneys might be challenged on Dormant Commerce Clause grounds.

As previously observed, the recently approved ALI Restatement of the Law Governing Lawyers attempts to provide a broader rule justifying temporary interstate legal practice which would permit out-of-state lawyers to act whenever 'the lawyer's activities in the matter arise out of or are otherwise reasonably related to the lawyer's practice' in his or her home state.[156] With regard to transactional matters, the Restatement advances the view that an out-of-state lawyer should be able to provide legal assistance when physically present in a state where he or she is not admitted if one or more of several factors justify this.

The Restatement considers that one such factor justifying such interstate transactional practice by an out-of-state lawyer relates to the status of the client, namely, if the client 'is a regular client, or, if a new client, is from the lawyer's home state . . . or contacted the lawyer there'.[157] Other factors relate to the nature of the services: if 'significant aspects of the lawyer's activities are conducted in the lawyer's home state' or involve the home

[152] ibid at 171. Note that in *Servidone* (n 114 above) the district court emphasized that the out-of-state lawyer must provide legal advice or assistance in association with a licensed local lawyer.

[153] *Norfolk & Western Ry. Co. v Beatty*, 400 F. Supp. 234 (S.D. Ill. 1975), aff'd without opinion, 423 U.S. 1009 (1975). The *per curiam* opinion in *Leis v Flynt* (n 51 above) at 442 n 4, declares that *Spanos* was 'limited, if not rejected entirely', by *Norfolk & Western*, but that seems to be a rather sweeping appraisal of the implications of *Norfolk & Western* without any analysis of the merits of Judge Friendly's reasoning.

[154] 807 F.2d 285 (1st Cir. 1986).

[155] See the text at n 42 above.

[156] ALI, Restatement (Third) of the Law Governing Lawyers (n 103 above) at Comment e.

[157] ibid.

state law, or if a 'multistate transaction has other significant connections with the home state', or if 'the legal issues involved are primarily either multistate or federal in nature'.[158] The Restatement also considers that, although sometimes desirable, association with an in-state lawyer should not be required, essentially because this may cause substantial added expense and burdens for a client.[159]

The Restatement's fact-oriented approach has great pragmatic appeal and represents a common sense approach. By emphasizing several substantive contact tests—the level of closeness in the link between the client and the out-of-state lawyer, the extent of the value provided by the out-of-state lawyer in view of the nature of the legal activity concerned, the differing degree to which home State or host State legal issues are involved—the Restatement enables courts to focus on several different factors that might, or might not, justify the temporary interstate practice by out-of-state lawyers. The Restatement would also seem to be supported by sound policy considerations in suggesting that out-of-state lawyers may justifiably provide occasional interstate legal services when federal law, or multistate law, issues either predominate or are substantial in character. Given the high regard courts traditionally accord to Restatements, the approach of the Restatement of the Law Governing Lawyers may be expected to influence quite significantly future case law.

Nonetheless, the picture of present court doctrine is not a bright one for temporary interstate legal practice. So far as appearance by out-of-state lawyers in courtroom litigation is concerned, *pro hac vice* appearance is totally within the discretion of the local courts. Although *pro hac vice* appearance is certainly common, the Supreme Court in *Leis v Flynt* rejected any effort to impose constitutional standards on state court discretion, despite Justice Stevens' strong dissent. Although the more recent *Piper* line of Supreme Court judgments has forcefully introduced the Privileges and Immunities Clause as a protection of out-of-state lawyers' right to admission to a state bar when they are non-resident, it would be hazardous to infer from the constitutional rule governing in that different context that the vitality of *Leis* as a precedent has been significantly undermined.

The status of temporary interstate transactional practice outside of a courtroom is more complicated. The summary of the case law presented above tends to show that interstate legal practice conducted by modern means of communication, eg, mail, telephone, fax, computer, would seem to be fairly well justified and permitted, despite the unfavourable dicta in *Birbrower*. Less clear-cut is the right of the lawyer to provide opinions or give advice upon, or draft documents or contracts governed by the law of a state in which he or she is not admitted—certainly this is a common practice, but

[158] ibid. [159] ibid.

the right to do so is not free from doubt. There is some support for permitting out-of-state lawyers' activities on an occasional basis when federal law issues are predominately concerned, but other precedents reject any so-called federal exception, or narrowly limit it to specific services relating to appearances before a federal court.

The ability of lawyers to provide legal assistance to clients, even at the latters' request, while physically present in a state where they are not admitted to practice must be considered to be subject to considerable risk. Leading precedents, *Birbrower*, *Spivak* and *Ranta*, quite decisively characterize this as unauthorized practice of law, whenever the physical presence of the out-of-state lawyer is more than extremely brief and minimal. The application of constitutional standards, notably the principles of the Privilege and Immunities Clause and the Dormant Commerce Clause, has thus far only occurred in *Spanos* (whose precedential value is uncertain), and *Violet*, whose impact is limited.

One bright spot in this rather sombre picture is the possibility of action by the state legislature or Supreme Court to modify the rules governing the practice of law. Thus, Michigan amended its rules in 1996 to permit temporary interstate transactional legal practice. The Michigan Judicature Code section on Unauthorized Practice of Law provides: 'This section does not apply to a person who is duly licensed and authorized to practice law in another state while temporarily in this state and engaged in a particular matter.'[160] Reaching the same result in a different manner, the District of Columbia Rules of Court were recently amended to define the jurisdictional scope of its Unauthorized Practice of Law Rule to be 'conduct in, or conduct from an office or location within, the District of Columbia, where the person's presence in the District of Columbia is not of incidental or occasional duration'.[161] In 1997 the Supreme Court of Virginia amended its rules to permit legal services by out-of-state lawyers, provided that the out-of-state lawyer is 'admitted to practice and in good standing in any state', the client is informed that the attorney is not admitted in Virginia, and the legal services are rendered 'on an occasional basis only and incidental to representation of a client whom the attorney represents elsewhere'.[162] Bar committee reports strongly influenced the modifications in the rules in all three jurisdictions.

The influence of the modern fact-oriented approach of the Restatement of the Law Governing Lawyers or the adoption of the Michigan, Virginia or District of Columbia Court Rules as models in other states may liberalize the

160 Mich. Compiled Laws Annotated, Revised Judicature Act of 1961, § 600.916 Unauthorized Practice of Law (West 1999).

161 District of Columbia Rules of Court, Rule 49(b)(3) (West 1999).

162 Virgina Rules of Court, Part 6 (I) Unauthorized Practice Rules and Considerations, § C (West 1999).

rules to be applied to temporary interstate legal practice, but that remains to be seen. The present US scene thus contrasts sharply with that in the European Union presented in section I above.

III. COMPARATIVE COMMENTS AND REFLECTIONS ON THE US RULES

1. Consideration of the Relevant Interests

At the outset, before commencing any comparisons, it is helpful to try to identify the legal and societal interests that ought to be considered in determining the appropriate limits of interstate legal practice. The two most salient are manifestly the effective representation of clients, a type of consumer protection interest, and the efficient conduct of court litigation, a civil and criminal justice interest, but there are other interests that should also be considered. In their current casebook on legal ethics, Professors Hazard, Koniak and Cramton describe the interests usually cited to justify local legal practice rules in the USA as: 'the harmful effects on local consumers of the provision of allegedly incompetent or unethical services by out-of-state practitioners; the relative ignorance of local substantive law and procedure on the part of out-of-state practitioners; and the difficulty of applying local disciplinary machinery to out-of-state lawyers.'[163]

To take the consumer interest first, clients need to be served competently, efficiently, vigorously and ethically by their lawyers. All of these factors should be considered when clients are served by lawyers outside of the lawyers' state of qualification. In addition, the client's freedom of choice of his or her preferred counsel is also a value of great weight. In the previously cited view of the New Jersey Supreme Court: 'While the members of the general public are entitled to full protection against unlawful practitioners, their freedom of choice in the selection of their own counsel is to be highly regarded and not burdened by "technical restrictions which have no reasonable justification" '.[164] It can plausibly be posited that if an out-of-state lawyer is fully capable of meeting all of the client service criteria mentioned above, a *prima facie* case is made for permitting the out-of-state lawyer to serve the client. On the other hand, if the out-of-state lawyer can only partially fulfil these criteria, then local lawyers should at least be associated in representing the client and, in some instances, may be justified in sole representation of the client. Professor Needham has rightly observed that

[163] G Hazard, Jr, S Koniak and R Cramton, *The Law and Ethics of Lawyering* (1999) 1060.
[164] *In re Waring's Estate* (n 140 above) 197. Moreover, as Professor Needham has well said: 'A client's preference of counsel can be especially strong when an out-of-state lawyer has been representing the client in other matters and they have developed a strong working relationship': Needham (n 96 above) 476.

the collaboration of a local lawyer often provides the client with 'an extra person thinking through the issues and an extra source for recovery if malpractice occurs'.[165] However, the greater economic cost resulting from the need to remunerate a local lawyer for time devoted to gaining familiarity with a client's affairs, and the lowered efficiency in representation due to that unfamiliarity, are both factors pointing in the direction of permitting the out-of-state lawyer to assist the client.[166]

When considering the out-of-state lawyer's ability to represent a client competently and efficiently in any state, the nature of the substantive legal issues involved in the representation is manifestly critical. If the out-of-state lawyer is expert in one or more specialized fields covering the legal services concerned (eg, acquisitions, antitrust, entertainment law, securities, taxation, to name but a few), a strong case is made for permitting the out-of-state lawyer to act for the client, solely or in conjunction with a local counsel. Commentators frequently observe that legal practice has increasingly become specialized throughout the USA[167] (and obviously also throughout the European Union). Professor Mary Daly has well observed that the increased specialization in legal matters 'drives [clients] to hire national experts whose offices may be far from the clients' actual place of business or headquarters'.[168]

The case for contending that out-of-state lawyers are usually able to represent a client competently in any state is reinforced when the area of law is substantially federal in character in the USA[169] (or the law of the EC in the European Union). If the legal issues involved in the interstate legal service are essentially federal in nature, then there is no need to employ an in-state lawyer in order to achieve competence in the service to the client. When relatively uniform laws or rules exist in several states (eg, in a Uniform Commercial Code or uniform law context in the USA,[170] or where legislation has harmonized a field of substantive law in the European Union), there is also frequently little or no need to employ an in-state lawyer, because out-of-state lawyers are usually equally capable of providing competent legal

165 C Needham, 'Negotiating Multi-state Transactions: Reflections on Prohibiting the Unauthorized Practice of Law' (1993) 12 St. Louis U Pub L Rev 113, at 132. She also rightly warns against using the local lawyer as 'mere window-dressing', ibid at 124.

166 Professor Wolfram warns that a policy of always requiring the hiring of 'in-state practitioners would be costly for clients and disruptive both for law firms and for commerce in general': Wolfram (n 84 above) 677.

167 See Brakel and Loh (n 87 above) 699–700; Reynolds, Jr (n 96 above) 64–65.

168 Daly (n 96 above) 725.

169 The enormous increase in federal regulation in the USA in the last 40 years is incontestable and has incited the argument for either a national bar or special federal rules of ethics. See Zacharias (n 55 above) 341–355.

170 Twenty-five years ago Brakel and Loh (n 87 above) 699, noted the 'increasing degree of uniformity of [state] law [through] model codes, uniform state acts . . . and similar substantive and procedural developments'.

services in an interstate matter involving the uniform rules. If, in contrast, relatively idiosyncratic local substantive rules are concerned (eg, in domestic relations law, or trusts and estates, or state tax law), then a strong case is made for restricting the practice to local lawyers, or at least for requiring collaboration between local and out-of-state lawyers.

When considering the out-of-state lawyer's ability to represent a client ethically, one concern is obviously the lawyer's past ethical record in his or her state of admission. More often, however, the chief concern is with regard to the lawyer's knowledge of, and likely capacity to follow, the ethical rules of the jurisdiction where the legal services are rendered. This latter concern is substantially alleviated whenever there exists a close similarity in ethical rules between the relevant jurisdictions, as is definitely the case in the USA, where all states follow either the Model Rules of Professional Conduct or the Code of Professional Responsibility (in its original or amended form). This concern is somewhat reduced in the European Union, where the CCBE's Code of Conduct for Lawyers has introduced a system of partial harmonization of key ethical standards and a choice of rule approach for others. Nonetheless, both in the USA and the EU, there remains a certain level of legitimate concern that out-of-state counsel properly follow any relevant ethical rules of the host jurisdiction (presuming that they are objectively justified, which has not always been the case either in the USA or the EU), especially in courtroom litigation. Linked to this is a legitimate interest in being certain that a delinquent lawyer will be subject to an effective disciplinary control. Moreover, it should not be forgotten that adversaries of clients, both in a litigation or a transaction context, are also intended to be the beneficiaries of proper ethical behaviour of an out-of-state lawyer.

In the context of courtroom litigation, host state interests are decidedly stronger than in transactional practice. The host state courts are the guardians of the proper administration of justice in a litigation, whether criminal or civil. Not only is the adequate knowledge of court procedural law a critical factor in competent representation of a client, an awareness of the customs prevailing in any local trial practice may also be essential to enable the adequate representation of a client.[171] The concern for proper compliance with ethical rules and for effective disciplinary sanctions is also heightened in a litigation context. All of these factors suggest a strong case for requiring at least the participation of local lawyers in courtroom practice. On the other hand, the efficient representation of the client may point in the direction of permitting out-of-state lawyers to litigate when they are well acquainted with the client's business affairs or the contract or transaction which is the subject of the litigation, or when they are experts in the

[171] See Brakel and Loh (n 87 above) 705.

subject matter involved in the litigation (eg, in antitrust, securities, mass torts or acquisition-related litigation). Highly skilled out-of-state trial lawyers will often have the capacity to provide a client with more effective and vigorous service than local lawyers are able to provide.[172]

Societal concerns also come into play. On the one hand, it is apparent that the demands of a modern integrated economy within the USA and within the EU strongly press in favour of greater legal integration and the more efficient providing of legal services throughout the entire market area. Concerns for the economic interests of a local bar should not lead to disguised protectionism. Professor Wolfram has well observed that there is a 'distinct possibility that [local practice] rules are motivated by the local bar's desire to be protected against out-of-state competition'.[173] Moreover, a chauvinist regard for traditional ways of conducting local legal practice must not seriously limit the modern need for effective legal practice across the entire market area. Enhancing the ability of lawyers and law firms to conduct interstate legal practice may better serve the needs of modern enterprises and reduce efficiency costs in the legal market.

On the other hand, there are legitimate societal concerns for the protection of public interests in sensitive sectors or for the protection of the unsophisticated or those in economically disadvantaged positions. Thus, states have a legitimate interest in preserving a legal framework for healthy domestic relationships and family units, in protecting title to real estate, and in ensuring the safe and efficient regulation and transmission of property in the field of trusts and wills. Adequately safeguarding these interests may dictate the restriction of some areas of legal practice to local lawyers. Also, the state has a special interest in protecting weaker members of society from over-reaching and sometimes unethical practices of lawyers. For example, minority language communities may need particular protection from out-of-state lawyers who speak their language but are neither fully competent nor ethical in providing legal services.

Finally, there is also a societal interest, particularly felt by courts and bar associations, in maintaining public confidence in lawyers and in protecting their professional reputation for competence, honesty and ethical behaviour. There is certainly the risk that this interest may degenerate into a persistent adherence to traditional modes of practice, whether or not suited to modern social conditions, or may serve as a cloak for economic protectionism of the

[172] Justice Stevens' dissenting argument to this effect in *Leis v Flynt* (n 51 above) is extremely persuasive, even if one does not agree that it justifies the application of the Privileges and Immunities Clause in the context of *pro hac vice* appearances.

[173] C Wolfram, *Modern Legal Ethics* (1986) 865. Professor Gillers has stated more bluntly: 'If you doubt whether economic protectionism influences professional regulation, I've got a courthouse to sell you': S Gillers, 'Protecting Their Own', The American Lawyer 118 (November 1998).

local bar. Nonetheless, there exists a proper core to the interest, which may legitimately come into play in regulating interstate legal services.

Having reflected a bit on the interests that are at stake, let us turn first to the subject of interstate courtroom litigation before finally considering interstate transactional practice.

2. Comparative Comments Concerning Interstate Practice in Litigation

As set forth in section I above, the European Community rules start from an express Treaty right to provide interstate or transborder services, enunciated in Articles 49 and 50 EC and liberally interpreted by the ECJ in *Van Binsbergen*, *Gebhard* and other judgments. The 1977 Lawyers' Services Directive sets out in detail the rules governing the right of lawyers qualified in one Member State to engage in courtroom or administrative litigation in any other State.

This very liberal starting point is limited to some degree. The Lawyers' Services Directive places two substantive conditions on the exercise of the right: (1) Article 5 of the Directive permits a host State to require the out-of-state lawyer 'to work in conjunction' with a local lawyer, who is answerable to the local court or tribunal; and Article 4(2) requires the out-of-state lawyer to abide by the rules of professional conduct of the host State. In *Commission v Germany*, the ECJ construed the first condition narrowly, enabling the out-of-state lawyer to take the leading role in the litigation and recognizing the client's right to determine the respective roles played by the out-of-state and local lawyer. The Directive's requirement that the out-of-State lawyer follow the host State professional rules is also nuanced by the Court's insistence since *Van Binsbergen* that the State ethical rules be objectively justified.

Case law has provided two further principles. With regard to any host State concern that the out-of-state lawyer might have an insufficient knowledge of local substantive or procedural law, the ECJ in *Commission v Germany* stated that the client's right to choose his or her counsel meant that the client should decide whether the out-of-state lawyer has sufficient competence in the local law. Further, in *Gebhard*, the Court rather liberally interpreted the nature of 'temporary' service providing, even permitting the out-of-state lawyer or law firm to make use of an office or other infrastructure in the host State, so long as the interstate services are occasional rather than permanent.

In contrast, US states have a long-standing custom permitting out-of-state lawyers to appear in court litigation *pro hac vice*, but the courts have total discretion in deciding when the out-of-state lawyer may appear—there exists no recognized right of an out-of-state lawyer to litigate or of a client to choose counsel freely from outside the state. Although higher state courts do police the discretion of trial courts, the Supreme Court in *Leis v Flynt* adopted the view that no constitutional review of state court discretion was possible.

Whether the European Union or the US approach is preferable represents a value judgment that obviously depends on an analysis of the essential interests involved. Looking first at the interests of the client, the EU position is clearly superior. It recognizes the client's right freely to choose his or her counsel, a matter of particular importance for large enterprises that are apt to be involved in litigation in many States.[174] The determination whether or not the out-of-state lawyer is competent seems better left to the client, who can appraise the value brought by out-of-state experts in a particular type of litigation as opposed to the value provided by local lawyers familiar with local court practices. Justice Stevens' dissent in *Leis v Flynt* well notes that '[a] client may want a particular lawyer for a particular kind of case, and a lawyer may want to take the case because of the skill required'.[175] The legitimate concern that out-of-state lawyers must behave ethically is satisfied by subjecting them to the host state rules, as is clearly stated both in Article 4 of the Lawyers' Services Directive and in Rule 8.5 of the Model Rules of Professional Conduct.

As noted before, the interest of courts in the sound and efficient administration of justice in litigation is certainly a strong one. Here, the European Union rules permit States to require that local lawyers collaborate in the litigation as a means of reassuring the local court that its rules and procedures will be properly followed. The principle of client choice enables the client to decide which lawyer takes the lead in the litigation. The EU approach appears to satisfy the natural concern for the sound and efficient handling of litigation. The US *pro hac vice* approach obviously protects the courts' interest in assuring that litigators know local court procedures, but may nonetheless still be criticized for its failure to respect a client's right to choose counsel freely.

If, then, there appear to be valid reasons for considering that the USA should recognize *pro hac vice* appearances as a right which clients and/or out-of-state counsel should enjoy, rather than a privilege subject to a court's discretion, what can be done to bring this about? Unfortunately, unless and until *Leis v Flynt* is overturned or substantially narrowed, not much. Congressional legislation is out of the question—the Congress' legislative power under the Commerce Clause to deal with a subject so closely related to state courts is quite dubious,[176] and political realities rule any such law out. A state uniform act would also appear to be unlikely.

[174] See Needham (n 96 above) 476.
[175] *Leis v Flynt* (n 51 above) 451.
[176] cf Wolfram (n 84 above) 704 n 125.

The only possible amelioration would come from the reversal of *Leis v Flynt* and the application of the Privileges and Immunities Clause to the field of *pro hac vice* appearances, making analogous use of the doctrines expressed in the *Piper* line of cases. In particular, in analysing whether or not state rules limiting *pro hac vice* appearances serve an independent substantial interest, one might draw on Justice Kennedy's analysis in *Barnard v Thorsten* to the effect that non-resident lawyers could be expected to familiarize themselves with local laws and to associate themselves with local lawyers as needed. Judge Friendly's analysis in *Spanos* merits serious consideration, for he laid stress on the client's right to choose counsel under the Privileges and Immunities Clause, rather than analysing the out-of-state lawyer's right to practice in terms of the Clause. This might be a more fruitful starting point. Finally, in terms of legal policy, Justice Stevens' dissent in *Leis*, emphasizing the high value provided to clients by out-of-state experts in complex or specialized fields of practice, would seem to have gained in force in the last 20 years.

3. Comparisons and Reflections Concerning Temporary Interstate Transactional Practice

Starting with the right to perform interstate professional services specified in Articles 49 and 50 EC, liberally interpreted by the ECJ in *Van Binsbergen* and *Gebhard*, the European Union permits lawyers to carry out interstate transactional legal practice with only few limitations.

The 1977 Lawyer' Services Directive provides the essential framework. All lawyers fully qualified in their home State may provide any form of legal services of a contractual or transactional character throughout the EU, with the sole exception being practice involving 'the preparation of formal documents' in the transfer of real estate interests or the administration of decedents' estates. The out-of-State lawyer must use his or her home State title, and is usually only subject to his or her home State ethical rules, although the Directive provides that some important host State rules may also apply, if objectively justified, eg, rules concerning the safeguard of professional secrecy, the avoidance of conflicts of interest, and rules governing lawyers' publicity. The priority given to the home State ethical rules probably reflects the view that the home State disciplinary authorities are better suited to handle ethical issues arising out of interstate transactional practice, and perhaps also the view that the host State's interest in having its ethical rules apply in transactional practice (other than the more important ones listed) is much less substantial than in a courtroom setting. In any event, the CCBE Code of Conduct for Lawyers has harmonized some essential ethical rules and provides a choice between conflicting rules in other areas.

An important point is that the Directive does not require any collaboration with local lawyers in transactional practice, in contrast with the enunciation of such a collaboration obligation for courtroom and administrative litigation. Moreover, the prevailing view since the ECJ's review of German rules in *Commission v Germany* is that the out-of-state lawyer may freely advise on local law, if the client chooses to have the lawyer do so.

Finally, the temporal extent of interstate service providing has been quite liberally construed by the ECJ in *Gebhard* and *Rush Portuguesa*. It is clear that out-of-state lawyers may be physically present in the host State for significant periods of time, presumably weeks or months, when engaged in a particular legal transaction that requires such a lengthy presence (eg, a commercial arbitration, an acquisition, complex financing arrangements, or joint venture negotiations). The out-of-state lawyers may even maintain an office or infrastructure staffed by administrative or secretarial personnel, if necessary to facilitate occasional cross-border legal practice. Examples of this might be the use of an office in Brussels when out-of-state lawyers must often visit to deal with European Union officials, or in Paris if the out-of-State lawyers are engaged in a lengthy ICC arbitration.

In contrast, in the USA, despite the fact that modern interstate transactional practice is increasingly important and common, there exists no solid doctrinal view permitting such practice. Although interstate legal practice of a transactional character is relatively unlikely to be considered the unauthorized practice of law when conducted by modern modes of communication (mail, telephone, fax or computer), whenever out-of-state lawyers are physically present in a state to engage in transactional practice there exists a significant risk that they may be considered to be engaged in the unauthorized practice of law in that state.

The modern fact-oriented approach of the Restatement of the Law Governing Lawyers, based in part on some precedents, may liberalize the current rules, but this remains to be seen. There has also been to date little effort to apply the constitutional principles of the Privileges and Immunities Clause and the Dormant Commerce Clause to this field.

Given this sharp contrast between the USA and the EU, how should the two different approaches be evaluated? Certainly from the point of view of the societal interest in economic efficiency in the marketplace, the liberalization of interstate legal services in the European Union is vastly to be preferred to the fragmentation produced by much of the US case law. The EU approach obviously facilitates the operations of commercial enterprises, both large and small, which can utilize their customary counsel throughout their markets, whenever the lawyers are deemed by the client to be competent. The ability to use the same qualified counsel, particularly when parallel transactions are undertaken in a number of States, undoubtedly represents a considerable cost-saving and a substantial enhancement of efficiency for modern clients. As Professor Wolfram has observed, 'the driving notion is client need . . . the client would be better served by legal services provided by familiar, regular counsel or counsel particularly skilled in dealing with a particular specialty'.[177] Manifestly, this approach also favours the development of large multi-city and interstate law firms capable of providing a wider range of expertise to even the largest multinational clients. Although such a development does pose a certain risk that local firms may not be able to compete in trying to service large multinational enterprises, the legal field is far more fragmented than the accounting field—we are certainly some distance from a time when large law firms become so dominant in any market that the societal interest in pluralistic legal service providing is jeopardized.

However, the societal interest in economic efficiency in legal services is certainly not the principal interest courts consider. That is apparent in many US cases, where the dissent often cites this interest, while the majority emphasizes the protection of clients or the assurance of state ethical standards.

Turning then to the interests of the client, the client's need for competent services is presumably the paramount concern. Yet here, on examination, the leading US precedents restricting interstate legal practice appear extremely dubious. This is particularly so when the added factor of permitting a client free choice in selecting his or her attorney is considered. Thus, in *Spivak*, the client not only chose the out-of-state counsel because of her respect for his expertise, she urged him to come to New York to provide her with his services (rather than, one supposes, herself incurring the necessary expense to consult the attorney in California). In *Birbrower*, although the immediate client was a California corporation, the ultimate client was the New York-based family that owned the corporation and had used the Birbrower firm for years. Moreover, the firm was expert in the contractual field involved and apparently well-qualified to carry out an arbitration. The California Supreme Court's emphasis on the need to reserve legal practice within California to California lawyers seems decidedly misplaced when the substantive issues involve software licensing and arbitration, neither of which represent peculiarly Californian fields. Indeed, it is noteworthy that the California legislature has now opened the field of private arbitrations to out-of-state lawyers, thus effectively nullifying that aspect of *Birbrower*. In *Ranta*, the principal legal services apparently concerned federal tax issues, not at all a matter of local substantive law, and the out-of-state lawyer specialized in federal tax practice (although admittedly part of the North Dakota Court's judgment rested on the out-of-state lawyer's regular practice from an office in North Dakota).

With regard to the client concern for ethical representation by out-of-

[177] Wolfram (n 84 above) at 712.

state legal counsel, none of the leading precedents restricting interstate legal services cite any ethical lapse in the out-of-state lawyer's activities. Moreover, in no leading precedent does the out-of-state lawyer appear to have made a false representation to the client that he or she was admitted in the local jurisdiction. The Supreme Court's holding in *Piper* that there is no reason to believe that a non-resident lawyer would engage in unethical behaviour any more than a local lawyer would do so would appear to apply in the circumstances of temporary interstate transactional practice as well. Finally, Rule 8.5 of the Model Rules of Professional Conduct unequivocally places the responsibility for disciplinary review of possible unethical conduct upon the home State of the lawyer engaged in interstate transactional practice.[178] The Comment to Rule 8.5 contends that it is desirable to make a lawyer's conduct subject to only one set of rules, those of the home State.

What the precedents restricting interstate transactional practice appear to come down to is a concern that the out-of-state lawyer's lack of training or knowledge in the local substantive law might harm the client at some point, even if there is no evidence that it did so in the particular case. This concern is decidedly speculative.[179] Moreover, the risk of malpractice litigation, which is certainly increasingly common, would appear adequately to police any lack of competence of the out-of-state lawyer with regard to local substantive law. A court's justifiable pride in the competence of its local bar should not lead it to conclude that out-of-state lawyers cannot have a sufficient competence in most modern corporate or commercial practice to provide professionally adequate legal services on an occasional basis within the state.

On reflection, the European Union's liberal approach in freely permitting cross-border transactional legal services, except in real estate title transfers of decedent estate administration, appears better to satisfy the interests of clients and society at large. What, then, might be done to move the US rules in that direction?

Since the current US limitations on interstate transactional legal practice are almost entirely based on leading precedents, the most obvious effort should be to modify the doctrinal rules prevailing in some states. Here the

[178] Although Rule 8.5, a 1993 amendment to the Model Rules, has thus far been only adopted in a few jurisdictions, home State disciplinary proceedings for out-of-state legal practice occurred prior to Rule 8.5. See, eg, *In re Washington*, 489 A.2d 452 (D.C. 1985) (District of Columbia bar discipline of one of its lawyers for practising law in Maryland without a licence); *Matter of Stults*, 433 N.Y.S.2d 22 (App. Div. 1980), appeal denied, 423 N.E.2d 58 (N.Y. 1981) (New York lawyer properly disbarred in New York for misappropriation of client funds while practising in London).

[179] Professor Needham has sensibly observed that at least 'the assumption that an out-of-state lawyer is not qualified should be recast as a rebuttable presumption': Needham (n 96 above) 468.

impact of the pragmatic fact-oriented tests advanced by the recent ALI Restatement of the Law Governing Lawyers can be most beneficial. Academic commentary urging courts to take a more liberal approach may also help.

Probably the greatest impact upon both courts and local bar groups could be attained through an American Bar Association initiative for greater recognition of lawyers' right to practise on an interstate basis, and for greater acceptance of a client's right to choose freely out-of-state lawyers when they can better serve the client's interests. An ABA study on the subject, reviewing both the case law and the Restatement view, and analysing the policy interests at stake in our modern society, would already be helpful. Its influence would be substantially increased if the ABA annual meeting would ultimately adopt a statement in favour of enhanced interstate transactional legal practice.

The adoption of one or more of several approaches recognizing specified exceptions to rules on the unauthorized practice of law could usefully liberalize temporary interstate legal practice. First, the right of out-of-state lawyers to litigate before federal courts and administrative agencies, which presently is generally accepted by state courts as an exception to the unauthorized practice of law, could be expanded to encompass a broader right to engage in transactional practice when federal issues are solely concerned, or when they predominate. Thus, a right to provide legal advice, issue opinions, prepare documents and contracts, negotiate transactions, etc might be recognized in the fields of federal antitrust, copyright, patents and trademarks, federal securities and federal taxation, or other practice areas which are largely controlled by federal rules. While it is true that sometimes clients' activities in these fields also raise issues under state law, the lawyers specializing in the federal law field are often likewise competent (or can readily gain competence) in the related substantive state law fields, so that clients can be safely and efficiently served by the same lawyers. Often, in fact, lawyers specializing in the federal field are more likely to be competent in the related state field (eg, antitrust or securities) than resident state lawyers who do not work in these fields. Even when that is not the case, an out-of-state lawyer might be permitted to work on federal law issues in cooperation with local lawyers who deal with the related state issues.

Secondly, an exception permitting out-of-state house counsel to work for their employer in all transactional and contractual matters throughout the USA would seem easily justifiable. The operational efficiency of this approach is obvious. Often when the employer engages frequently in a specific type of legal transaction (eg, acquisitions, distribution arrangements, franchises, leases, loans, sales), the house counsel is far more expert in that type of transaction than local lawyers would be. House counsel can and usually do obtain advice or assistance from local lawyers when local substantive law issues are significant and not easily resolved. The management personnel of the house counsel's employer are well placed to ensure that the house counsel will have the necessary competence or obtain it.

Thirdly, an exception might be recognized when out-of-state lawyers come into a state to engage in a private arbitration proceeding. The leading arbitration bodies set their own procedures, with which arbitration law specialists are quite familiar. The arbitration clause in a contract frequently has a choice of law for a substantive law other than the state which is the site of arbitration. Even when the substantive law of the state which is the site of the arbitration governs in the arbitration, there are solid policy reasons for permitting clients freely to choose their customary counsel, who often represented the client in the transaction which gave rise to the arbitration, or to choose a law firm specializing in arbitration practice. In-state counsel can always provide advice or be associated with the out-of-state lawyers if the substantive state law issues warrant this.

In a variety of contexts, it would be helpful to recognize a client's freedom of choice of his or her preferred lawyer. If a client desires to be represented both by out-of-state lawyers and local counsel in a particular transaction, and determines which should take the leading role, it is hard to see any state interest that would objectively justify the conclusion that the out-of-state lawyer is engaged in the unauthorized practice of law. The Hawaii Supreme Court has rightly observed that such co-operation between a client's customary out-of-state counsel and the in-state counsel is functionally efficient and desirable.[180] Even if a client desires to be represented only by an out-of-state lawyer in a transaction, are not the client's interests in competent, effective and ethical service sufficiently protected by malpractice litigation or ethics procedures rather than the use of the unauthorized practice of law doctrine? Despite the rejection of this view in *Birbrower* and *Ranta*, it would appear both more sensible and more equitable to follow earlier case law which obliged clients who deliberately selected out-of-state lawyers to pay reasonable fees for their services,[181] instead of giving the clients a windfall through use of the unauthorized practice of law doctrine.

Furthermore, renewed analysis under the Privileges and Immunities Clause and the Dormant Commerce Clause would be helpful. In particular, it would be useful to start from the analysis of the client's right as a citizen to secure the legal service that he or she prefers, as was ably done by Judge Friendly in *Spanos*. A part of the Supreme Court analysis of the justification for the right of non-resident lawyers to practise as members of a state bar as set out in Justice Powell's opinion in *Piper* and Justice Kennedy's opinion in *Barnard* might well carry over to the context of occasional inter-

[180] *Fought & Co. v Steel Engineering* (n 142 above) 497.
[181] *Freeling v Tucker* (n 131 above).

state transactional practice. One might argue, for example, that there is no reason *a priori* to assume that otherwise competent and ethical out-of-state counsel will fail to familiarize themselves with local substantive law where relevant, or will fail to obtain the aid of local counsel where necessary, especially when malpractice rules protect the client. One might likewise contend that a state's total prohibition of occasional transactional practice by out-of-state lawyers, especially when the use of local counsel would create substantial added costs to the client, represents economic protectionism of the local bar. Dormant Commerce Clause principles might also be invoked to weigh the added value provided to the interstate conduct of business by competent lawyers engaged in modern interstate legal practice.

Finally, efforts might be undertaken on the legislative front. The American Bar Association and other organized bar groups might urge the states to adopt legislation, or state Supreme Courts to adopt rules, permitting out-of-state lawyers to provide occasional services in transactional practice, on the model of the Michigan statute or the District of Columbia or Virginia Court Rules. They might even press for the adoption of a uniform law. Although perhaps less likely to meet with success, since legislative agendas are always crowded, and lobbying to protect local bar interests is always apt to represent a strong disincentive to legislation or a change in Supreme Court rules, still the effort to adopt legislation enabling out-of-state lawyers to provide occasional interstate legal services may prove successful in some states.

IV. CONCLUSION

This chapter has initially described the liberalization within the last 25 years of the rules governing interstate legal practice on a temporary or occasional basis in the European Union. Qualified lawyers from any Member States are now able to provide all legal services of a transactional nature in any other European Union State (except if the host State restricts practice in the transfer of real estate interests or the administration of decedents' estates), while subject to the home State ethical rules in the execution of the transactional services. Qualified lawyers from any Member State may also litigate in courts in any other State, subject to the host State ethical rules, and in association with a local lawyer if the host State so requires. It is important to note that this high degree of liberalization has occurred without any evidence of significant functional problems or risks to clients and without any serious opposition from national bar associations—and this despite the fact that the differences in substantive laws and procedural rules are far greater among the Member States than they are among the states of the USA.

The chapter has also served an informational purpose in presenting a detailed, up-to-date picture of the limitations placed upon interstate legal practice in the USA. While the *pro hac vice* appearance of out-of-state lawyers in litigation is common, the state courts retain total discretion in deciding when an out-of-state lawyer may so appear. With regard to transactional practice, the stringent application of unauthorized practice of law rules in many states, including the prominent jurisdictions of California and New York, places out-of-state lawyers at the risk of disciplinary sanctions or the inability to collect fees from clients. Despite some precedents favourable to interstate transactional practice, and the more pragmatic approach to interstate legal practice rules advocated by the recently approved Restatement of the Law Governing Lawyers, the overall picture is one in which, in the words of Professor Wolfram, 'by and large local lawyers have been able to take advantage of the opportunity presented by federalism to place high walls around their own preserve'.[182]

The final part of the chapter attempted to review the interest of clients in obtaining competent and ethical legal representation, the interest of courts in the effective conduct of courtroom proceedings, and the interest of society in promoting modern, efficient interstate commerce. The chapter contends that the liberal approach to interstate legal practice in the European Union better promotes all three interests than the more restrictive rules in the USA.

The chapter accordingly concludes by urging that state courts be influenced by the pragmatic views of the Restatement of the Law Governing Lawyers, whose acceptance would significantly enhance the amount of authorized interstate legal practice, and that state legislatures and Supreme Courts adopt new rules permitting occasional interstate legal practice on the model of those recently approved in Michigan, Virginia and the district of Columbia. The chapter further argues that state courts should recognize a number of specific fields of exception to the unauthorized practice of law rules, and that both *Leis v Flynt* and precedents limiting transactional interstate practice should be re-examined and perhaps reversed through a modern application of the Privileges and Immunity and the Dormant Interstate Commerce Clause.

As we move into a new century, it would seem high time to breach some of the walls protecting state legal practice in the USA and to adopt more liberal rules more in consonance with modern commercial and legal realities, perhaps along the lines of those now prevailing in the European Union.

[182] Wolfram (n 173 above) 865.

Index